New Horizons In Buddhist Psychology

Relational Buddhism
For Collaborative Practitioners

Edited by
Maurits G.T. Kwee

Editorial Consultants
Ruth T. Naylor & Asanga Tilakaratne

Series Editor
Kenneth J. Gergen

Taos Institute Publications
Chagrin Falls, Ohio

NEW HORIZONS IN BUDDHIST PSYCHOLOGY

In Dedication to Dr. Yutaka Haruki
Emeritus Professor of Psychology, Waseda University, Tokyo, Japan
&
In Memory of Padmal de Silva (1944-2007)
Inspirational Clinical Psychologist and Endearing Dharma Friend

COVER IMAGE: Jack Thewlis
COVER DESIGN: Kris Harmat

"Aren't we all embarked on a boat with one certainty that it will sink one day?
So, while sailing let's cheer and celebrate life!"

– Maurits G.T. Kwee

FIRST EDITION
Copyright © 2010 Taos Institute

Library of Congress Catalog Card Number: 2010929367

Taos Institute Publications
A Division of the Taos Institute
Chagrin Falls, Ohio
USA

ISBN 0-9819076-6-0
ISBN-13: 978-0-9819076-6-6

Printed in the USA and in the UK

Taos Institute Publications

The Taos Institute is a nonprofit organization dedicated to the development of social constructionist theory and practice for purposes of world benefit. Constructionist theory and practice locate the source of meaning, value, and action in communicative relations among people. Our major investment is in fostering relational processes that can enhance the welfare of people and the world in which they live. Taos Institute Publications offers contributions to cutting-edge theory and practice in social construction. Our books are designed for scholars, practitioners, students, and the openly curious public. The **Focus Book Series** provides brief introductions and overviews that illuminate theories, concepts, and useful practices. The **Tempo Book Series** is especially dedicated to the general public and to practitioners. The **Books for Professionals Series** provides in-depth works, that focus on recent developments in theory and practice. Our books are particularly relevant to social scientists and to practitioners concerned with individual, family, organizational, community, and societal change.

Kenneth J. Gergen
President, Board of Directors
The Taos Institute

For information about the Taos Institute and social constructionism
visit: www.taosinstitute.net

Taos Institute Publications

Taos Tempo Series:
Collaborative Practices for Changing Times

Riding the Current: How to Deal with the Daily Deluge of Data, (2010) by Madelyn Blair

Ordinary Life Therapy: Experiences from a Collaborative Systemic Practice, (2009) by Carina Håkansson

Mapping Dialogue: Essential Tools for Social Change, (2008) by Marianne "Mille" Bojer, Heiko Roehl, Mariane Knuth-Hollesen, and Colleen Magner

Positive Family Dynamics: Appreciative Inquiry Questions to Bring Out the Best in Families, (2008) by Dawn Cooperrider Dole, Jen Hetzel Silbert, Ada Jo Mann, and Diana Whitney

Focus Book Series

The Appreciative Organization, Revised Edition (2008) by Harlene Anderson, David Cooperrider, Ken Gergen, Mary Gergen, Sheila McNamee, Jane Watkins, and Diana Whitney

Appreciative Inquiry: A Positive Approach to Building Cooperative Capacity, (2005) by Frank Barrett and Ronald Fry

Dynamic Relationships: Unleashing the Power of Appreciative Inquiry in Daily Living, (2005) by Jacqueline Stavros and Cheri B. Torres

Appreciative Sharing of Knowledge: Leveraging Knowledge Management for Strategic Change, (2004) by Tojo Thatchekery

Social Construction: Entering the Dialogue, (2004) by Kenneth J. Gergen, and Mary Gergen

Appreciative Leaders: In the Eye of the Beholder, (2001) edited by Marge Schiller, Bea Mah Holland, and Deanna Riley

Experience AI: A Practitioner's Guide to Integrating Appreciative Inquiry and Experiential Learning, (2001) by Miriam Ricketts and Jim Willis

Books for Professionals Series

Positive Approaches to Peacebuilding: A Resource for Innovators, (2010) edited by Cynthia Sampson, Mohammed Abu-Nimer, Claudia Liebler, and Diana Whitney

Social Construction on the Edge: 'Withness'-Thinking & Embodiment, (2010) by John Shotter

Joined Imagination: Writing and Language in Therapy, (2009) by Peggy Penn

Celebrating the Other: A Dialogic Account of Human Nature, (reprint 2008) by Edward Sampson

Conversational Realities Revisited: Life, Language, Body and World, (2008) by John Shotter

Horizons in Buddhist Psychology: Practice, Research and Theory, (2006) edited by Maurits G.T. Kwee, Kenneth J. Gergen, and Fusako Koshikawa

Therapeutic Realities: Collaboration, Oppression and Relational Flow, (2005) by Kenneth J. Gergen

SocioDynamic Counselling: A Practical Guide to Meaning Making, (2004) by R. Vance Peavy

Experiential Exercises in Social Construction – A Fieldbook for Creating Change, (2004) by Robert Cottor, Alan Asher, Judith Levin, and Cindy Weiser

Dialogues About a New Psychology, (2004) by Jan Smedslund

Table of Contents

About this Book

The Buddha's pivotal insight is that the human predicament of suffering is relational and rooted in these *3-Poisons*: greed, hatred, and ignorance, particularly ignorance regarding the illusion of self or soul and the delusion of the existence of god(s). This social vision is as valid today as it was 2600 years ago, since it is undeniable that greed is the root cause of global financial crises and hatred is the root cause of terrorism in the world. The end result is Duhkha (fear, anger, sadness, depression, and premature death) unless we know how to modify these interactive relational performances with savvy and wisdom. Arising from relationships, Karma defined as intentional action concurs with "meaningful-thought-and-relational-performance" whose malfeasance is transformable by collaborative action and interpersonal practice. During his time the Buddha called himself a *Kammavadin*, someone who deals with Karma and its transformation through discourse and dialogue. Dealing with meaningful scenarios by detecting and changing its cognitive, behavioural, volitional, and motivational causes in co-action, "Buddhist appreciative inquiry" mobilizes people to eradicate unwholesome anti-social affect by exercising wholesomeness through embodying pro-social Sukha (bliss) in equanimity via the social meditations of loving kindness, empathic compassion, and shared joy. The collaborative practice of "Karma Transformation" systematically integrates the Buddha's teachings (Dharma), the co-arrangement of evidence-based interventions, and the meta-psychology of Social Construction from a "new" Buddhist Psychology perspective.

The Buddha summoned those who travel in his footsteps not to follow him blindly, but to be "a light onto oneself". Firmly embedded in the path is the Buddha's gift that he offered humanity: a family of *12-Meditations* wherein mindfulness constitutes the groundwork for "awakening" and which is viewed here as a process of de-construction toward "not-self". A non-foundational "empty self" is not a goal in itself but a reset point for the social re-construction of *Relational Interbeing* (which we already are). In the past three decades a form of mindfulness which has been de-contextualized from the Dharma has become fashionable amongst health professionals, corporate coaches, and mentors/teachers in the West. Mindfulness-based interventions cleverly foster attention, awareness, and concentration, but conspicuously disregard the cultivation of judgmental insights in the karmic interpersonal virtues within the framework of the *4-Ennobling Realities*. These social realities inhere in the Buddha's causality hypothesis of interconnectedness (Dependent Origination) whose heartfelt understanding might lead to liberating emptiness. Entwined in the *8-Fold Balanced Practice*, mindfulness is more than bare attention to what arises in the here-now, clarity, and focus. It also requires an insightful introspection of Karma's relational impact and an interactional balancing whilst expanding the social meditations. Advocating a wholistic mindfulness, Asian Buddhist psychologists do not belittle the mindfulness-based outcome research but rebut the somehow Dharma-alienated, reductionist, and fragmented "Buddhist-Lite" approaches (grossly neglecting the Dharma's heart-core: Dependent Origination and Karma) as a western expropriation of some kind. Notwithstanding, as Padmasiri de Silva, a doyen of Buddhist Psychology, observed: "Converting mindfulness to the status of a pill to get rid of a headache is harmless, but building a psychological system around Buddhist practice is a serious mission."

Indeed, it is the latter which is aimed at by this edition, a testimony of collaborative practice, encompassing 24 essays by 20 seasoned authors who are *au courant* and *au fait* in their area of expertise. The contributors to this sumptuous volume are clinicians, coaches, and teachers who are well-versed in the Buddhist literature and are of the highest caliber. This volume's golden thread and cohering element can be found in each of the chapter's deepening of Buddhist Psychology by highlighting the scriptures relevant for psychology and by using concepts grounded in the rudimentary psychology of the *Abhidharma*. Upholding the Dharma as a pro-social way of life, all authors endorse a pan-Buddhist Psychology characterized by a secular form and demythologizing content. This Buddhist Psychology refutes craving projections which view the pristine Buddha as an omniscient saviour who performs magic miracles or who promises Nirvana as a palpable paradise or a heaven in a beyond to transmigrate to *postmortem*. Spanning 2600 years of history, Buddhist Psychology is classified into four periods: archaic, classic, modern, and post-modern. After delving into the "old" Buddhist Psychology, a New Buddhist Psychology is formulated and defined as an integrated social-clinical-neuropsychology of Body/Speech/Mind which embraces Social Construction, a meta-vision discarding "Transcendental Truths". This marks a major move away from religion and highlights an ongoing paradigm shift towards involving psychology as an efficient vehicle to disseminate the Dharma in the 21st century. By blending commonalities, pinpointing parallels, and confirming differences, this work is a critical appraisal of current trends in Buddhist Psychology. It also accommodates a comprehensive roadmap to deal with the existential suffering of everyday life by a relational *modus vivendi* in line with what the Buddha had taught. This book culminates in a postmodern rendition called *Relational Buddhism* which also provides the framework of this anthology.

Acknowledgements

This anthology came about with the help of many colleagues and friends from different parts of the globe. Each of them is an author or co-author of a chapter in this book. Many others, non-authors, stood at the basis of the social construction of the here presented work. I shall mention a few, first of all my teachers, colleagues, and friends: the late Albert Ellis, the late Michael Mahoney, Arnold Lazarus, Kenneth Gergen, and Yutaka Haruki. In the spirit of integration, I owe them many thanks for enabling me to trail-blaze some of their intellectual inheritance. I combined it with the timeless teachings of Gautama the Buddha (5th century BCE), Nagarjuna (2nd century), Vasubandhu (4th century), and of several others. I deeply appreciate the co-operation of the many fine authors from Sri Lanka who have contributed with a chapter to this book. It was the late Padmal de Silva who facilitated my contacting many outstanding scholars united in the Sri Lanka Association for Buddhist Studies.

While compiling and editing this volume, Padmal, my gentle comrade in psychology and loyal companion in the Dhamma, passed away suddenly. Just a few weeks before he deceased, Padmal sent me his final corrections in handwriting. His passing away left a void. An exemplary Buddhist, a pioneer in Buddhist Psychology, and a wise teacher in Cognitive-Behavior Therapy is no more. I have vivid memories of Padmal, fellow traveler on the Buddhist path. We enjoyed each other's company in Amsterdam, Tokyo, Beijing, and Montreal, and had a plan to attend a convention at the University of the West in California together. Since 1990, we belonged to a Japanese-lead group, the Transnational Network for the Study of Physical, Psychological & Spiritual Wellbeing, which was transformed in 2000 into the Transcultural Society for Clinical Meditation (TSCM). Padmal served on TSCM's board < http://transcultural.meditation.googlepages.com >. He might have had, I surmise, hundreds of publications on a variety of subjects. Buddhist Psychology is but one of them, although one that is dear to his heart < www.inst.at/trans/15Nr/03_8/kwee_intro15.htm >. I had the privilege to incorporate six of his chapters, including the present one, in previous edited books. His contributions were widely read by insiders and so influential that he became an Honorary Professor at the University of Flores, Buenos Aires, Argentina. While writing these words thoughts wander to Dona Vasantha, Padmal's wife, and their children for whom the grief and the void that is left must be greater than ours...

Let me close these acknowledgements by mentioning that this anthology is TSCM's sixth book and the second volume socially constructing a New Buddhist Psychology, a Buddhist Psychology from a social constructionist perspective culminating in Relational Buddhism. The present volume is a sequel and a further deepening of the previous *Horizons in Buddhist Psychology: Practice, Research & Theory* (2006; Taos Institute Publications). I thank everyone involved in realizing this work, particularly the authors, my consultant editors Ruth Naylor and Asanga Tilakaratne, Aat de Bruijn for his cogent comments while reading along, my love Marja Kwee-Taams for her continuing support. Last but not least, I wish to thank "Stichting Psychotherapie en Boeddhisme", Paul van der Velde, and Ad van Lieshout for their sponsoring. Thank you all in *metta* from the bottom of my heart.

Maurits G.T. Kwee, project manager

Preface

Yutaka Haruki, Ph.D.
Fellow of The World Academy of Art and Science
Founder of the Transcultural Society for Clinical Meditation
Em. Professor of Psychology, Waseda University, Tokyo, Japan

People say the world has entered into a borderless age. To be sure, information gets around across the borders of countries and any country's economy moves on an international scale. No country can expect to have a viable economy unless it follows the policy of interdependence. It is under these circumstances that the idea that the world is one seems to be gaining wide acceptance and it seems certain that this oneness will gain further ground in the future. Does "the world is one" mean that the world is homogeneous? One might get a clear idea if one thinks about this in terms of the language one speaks. There is little doubt that the English language is going to stay as the world's common language. This is quite significant because by using a common language we will be well able to communicate with one another and to share our knowledge. The world seems to be moving in that direction. However, does that mean that it would be wonderful if there is only one common language to the detriment and extinction of all other languages? Language is tightly interwoven with country and culture. For example, there is this Japanese word "shibui". When we in Japan praise a stage actor for his excellent performance, we say "Her/his performance is shibui" (sober, quiet, and refined). Originally shibui means a bitter taste (so bitter that it numbs the mouth). This is the experience when eating an astringent Japanese persimmon. We use such an expression for a quiet, refined, and skillful performance, and not for a showy or flashy one. There does not seem to be an English equivalent for this word. Loosing various languages through the adoption of a single language could mean the loss of the unique cultural spirit of each country's. In bygone history many forms of spiritual culture may have disappeared like that.

Just like diversification contributed to the advancement of forms of life, spiritual richness could be attained through diversification, not unification. The disappearance of borders between countries in the world might mean the invigoration of mutual interchange and the creation of new cultures of diversification. In other words, this does not necessarily mean that one single culture will take control over other cultures and create a unified and monotone culture. That would result in digression and the destruction of cultures. Cultural diversity ideally nurture respect for difference rather than overemphasizing disparity and discontinuing interchange. The interchange of different cultures will bring in different cultures and enrichment of one's own culture. Furthermore, it will breed new cultures and create further diversification. This is a process with an underlying commonness and it seems utmost important and worthwhile to seek and find this commonness. Without some joy of finding commonness, there can be no interchange. Such commonness is not simply a cultural similarity (analogy) but a cultural homogeneity (homology) somewhere deep down under the surface. Conceptually, commonness is situated on an ultra high level of abstraction as a part of a meta-theory. Any other kind of theory would be monotonous and destructive for diversity. If we then would, for instance, discover the simple fact that we are all human beings, the meaning of "transcultural" would gain tremendous impact.

Different things have already been pointed out with respect to the differences between western and eastern culture. Here I would like to address a couple of issues regarding meditation by taking up the example of Buddhist meditation, particularly meditation as practiced in the Zen denomination. The essential aspect of Zen meditation is the requirement for strict control of body posture. Particularly one is required to sit with the back straight without using any physical strength. "Why is that?" you may ask. The results of our somatic-psychological studies showed that if you hunch up your back and stoop, you will end up in a depressive mood or worsen it and that if you straighten your back, you will invite a positive mood. Such was also pointed out earlier by William James. Evidently, physical responses are closely related to mood. For this reason it is important to keep the back straight. Furthermore, breathing is emphasized as an important point in Zen practice because breathing, needless to say, is essential to life. At the same time it is assumed that the breath is deeply related to one's mind. Zen is based on this assumption because, according to eastern thought, "body-mind" are inseparable and interrelated to each other; besides, all living human beings function on the basis of breathing. The mind is necessarily related to the body and the body is necessarily related to the mind. In western spirituality one is not required to be aware of one's posture or way of breathing. This is just one example how western and eastern thinking differ. With all respect to this difference, what could be the commonness lurking behind this difference? Again, a meta-theoretical purview would be helpful for an in-depth understanding of meditation.

Then, there is the issue of the self often pointed out as a big difference between western and Buddhist culture. While westerners contend that the self is hard to crack and persists to exist, Buddhists maintain that self does not exist and that, for instance, Zen aims at attaining a state of not-self. Discussing the difference between the two approaches using body and mind as an example, I could feel a pain in my body after being hit. The pain is mine and no one else's. This is a secure sign that my body exists. But, where does my body come from? I did not create it and neither did it engender itself. My body was conceived by my parents and further sustained by the intake of nutrients like milk, meat, and vegetables, etc. I did not create my own body. Through drinking milk, the life of cows is transferred into my body, by eating meat, poultry is part of my body; and by eating vegetables, plants are incorporated in my body. This is why I cannot claim any part of my body as purely "mine". There is a distinctive difference between a self existing as something like a "god-given" element which is hard to crack and as "self-existing" like an indivisible atom. As one's sense of self may differ from anyone else's, the difference discussed here refers to the "cause" of self's existence. Cultural differences originating in this difference of self conceptualization may be deeply rooted and the very cause of cultural diversity. Tracing commonness to the abstruse meta-theory is also important to see the Buddhist self. Imagine the self as a swirl formed in a river. Standing on a bank and watching the surface of a river, one can clearly tell the difference between a big and a small swirl and between a strong and a weak swirl. Different selves as swirls exist. However, what is the true nature of a swirl? A swirl comes about by the dynamic force of a river, thus its nature is none other than the flow of a river. A swirl cannot be detached from the flow of the river flow. The self exists and its true nature is being inseparable from the world's dynamics. A self separated from the communal world only exists artificially. Swirls disappear and re-appear along with the flow.

It would be wonderful if viewers of different cultural backgrounds could sit together and enjoy watching a performance called "Clinical Meditation" by stage performers in different national costumes on the stage called *New Horizons in Buddhist Psychology* and discover that they have something in common and share the joy of such a discovery.

Preface

Maurits G.T. Kwee
Taos Institute Associate
Em. Hon. Professor, University of Flores, Buenos Aires, Argentina
Director "Institute for Buddhist Psychology &
Relational Buddhism", France

Although the historicity of the Buddha is universally accepted, there is no unanimity on the exact date. For instance, in Sri Lanka 483 BCE is believed to be the date of his passing away while in Burma 543 BCE is surmised. In Tibet it is conjectured to be 835 BC, while in China, 11th century BCE is an accepted date. The Indian tradition holds on to 1793 or 1807 BCE. Leaving these vagaries aside, for all 400 million Buddhists around the world, the Buddha's quest finds its origin and beginnings with the story of Siddhartha (someone-who-has-all-his-worldly-wishes-fulfilled). His circumstances bear resemblance with those of many third millennium working citizens who dwell comfortably in relative material luxury. The person referred to here, Gautama, who lived in utmost refinement roughly 100 generations ago in the iron age, when the globe was considered flat, is also someone who might be considered as the most victorious (*tama*) on earth (*gau*). His family name Shakya (kindness) hints at another sublime quality which the historical "awakened one" (the Buddha) must have had. The subject of this book is not per se the person of Shakyamuni – a moniker pointing at kindness in charitable stillness (*muni*) – but the psychological content of his teachings, referred to as the Dharma (Sanskrit) or the Dhamma (Pali). While Sanskrit is the high-brow language of the upper classes in Jambudvipa (ancient India), Pali is a language that is close to Magadhi, a dialect the Buddha had most probably spoken. This exemplifies that the Dharma can be taught in any language as long as the message of Siddhartha Gautama the Buddha reaches the people's hearts. The language proposed here is that of social constructionist psychology.

The Dhamma refers to the Buddha's "Middle Way", a way that not only keeps the middle ground between self-mortification and self-indulgence, but also denotes the middle ground between eternalism and nihilism. The Buddha proposed instead the negation of the existence of an eternal god (theism) as well as the negation of the non-existence of a god (atheism), thus leaving one in a meditative "emptiness" of non-theism to be filled with kindness, compassion, joy, and equanimity, relational qualities to be practiced daily. The Buddha did not claim to be a prophet or assign people to worship. Despite promoting emptiness instead of dogma, he is often classified on the same list with Abrahamic figures like Moses, Jesus, and Mohammed. In my humble opinion the Buddha does not belong to this illustrious company of believers. At bottom the Dharma, a reaction to polytheistic Brahmanism, considers any god concept – even if upgraded to "the-one-and-only" – as a delusion. Phenotypical similarities mask genotypical differences. Vodka and water look the same, until you taste them. The Dharma is not a sky-god religion but a social construction on the move, ever changing going forward.

To be a traveler on the Buddhist path without a god to talk to is lonely indeed. Unlike a loneliness of the desert where sun-strokes and *fata morganas* are rampant and a consequent flight into god delusions is likely, the Buddha did not take refuge in the fantasy of heavenly holy cows. On the contrary, he totally faced and radically stayed in the self-imposed utmost adverse and devastating lonely condition until he found the key to end existential suffering (Duhkha) in order to benefit all fellow human beings. This key, which is of a nondual nature, is ineffable much like the concept of zero (empty) was for the ancient Greek mathematicians who hence allocated the "missing nothing" to the realm of the sacrosanct. We unfortunately lack a linguistic foundation for understanding this key, therefore the many words for the psychological reset point of null in this book and the overall emphasis on meditation practice. Thus, for the Buddha's students it was/is a lonely journey too, if admonished – like in the case of radical fellow travelers of the Chan/Zen denomination – to kill the Buddha (nothing but a mere image or proverbial concept since he is already dead) whenever one meets him on the road. Other masters advised to urinate on Buddha statues or to clean one's arse with Buddhist scriptures to emphasize that the Dharma is not about abstractions and concepts but about daily experiential practice to improve oneself and mankind. What does such iconoclastic advice imply? How can the Buddha's causality hypothesis of Dependent Origination (the non-independent arising, peaking, subsiding, and ceasing of all that is perceivable) make the refuge and clinging to some god redundant and unnecessary? Does the Dharma as a contemporary psychology exclude the Dharma as a religion or philosophy? What is the meaning of life? Where do we come from and go to? Is there life after death? What is the difference between rebirth and reincarnation? These and other tantalizing questions necessitate a grand quest. This book explores the Buddhist radical deconstruction toward a "non-foundational emptiness" and invites practitioners to collaborate in the Buddhist reconstruction of the world in terms of the postmodern psychology of Social Construction. Whether we have succeeded in this challenging task is up to you, the reader, to judge.

Before starting, here is a guideline to read this book. It is recommended to begin reading the first chapter which functions as a torch. This chapter lays the foundations for a New Buddhist Psychology with cross references to all other chapters of this anthology. Each of the chapters is a deepening of the various topics raised in the leading chapter. To make this work accessible for a large audience from various disciplines of scholarship, the use of Sanskrit and Pali is kept to a minimum. But several terms are advertently kept in Pali or Sanskrit to avoid ambiguity and to augment authenticity. Sanskrit terms refer to Mahayana scriptures, while Pali terms refer to Theravada scriptures. Please note that the Sanskrit term Dharma is applied throughout to denote the entire body of the Buddhist teachings, including the Theravada, Vajrayana, and Tantrayana teachings. The context will leave no doubt to which meaning the term Dharma refers. However, the Pali term Dhamma will solely denote the Theravada scriptures. With regards to the various discourses of the Buddha (*Nikayas*) as the source of *suttas* (Pali) and *sutras* (Sanskrit), each chapter makes use of its own abbreviations. All abbreviations are used only if previously written in full once. The specific way to refer to a particular discourse by each author is left untouched in the editing. Respecting each author's scholarly background, referencing habits are left intact. Thus, some refer to a list of titles (gathered at the end of the book), others use notes to refer, and still others apply a combination of notes and references. Finally, while the British spelling is given priority, the American authors' spelling is left intact.

On behalf of my fellow travelers who embarked with me on this "New Horizons" endeavor – the late Padmal de Silva, Ruth Naylor, Asanga Tilakaratne, Ven. Soorakkulame

Pemarathana, Marja Kwee-Taams, Ven. Guang Xing, Paul van der Velde, David Kalupahana, Pahalawattage Premasiri, Tilak Kariyawasam, Yakupiyage Karunadasa, Zhihua Yao, Bill Mikulas, Paul Fleischman, Padmasiri de Silva, Ven. Sik Hin Hung, Aung Myint, Lobsang Rapgay, James Austin, Yutaka Haruki, and Kenneth Gergen – I wish the reader an illuminating reading venture in *kalyana mittata* (ennobling friendship). Maurits G.T. Kwee, editor

Foreword

Kenneth J. Gergen
President of the Taos Institute
Senior Research Professor, Swarthmore College, USA

Social scientists are fond of characterizing the major difference between Eastern and Western cultures in terms of collectivism and individualism. While Eastern cultures are said to place a high value on the groups to which one belongs, Western cultures prize individual freedom. To be sure, cultural differences are always more complex than our characterizations, but most would agree that there is more than a grain of truth in such views. It is precisely this grain of truth that is magnified in the ways in which Buddhist practices have been absorbed by practitioners and devotees in the West. For example, in the mental health arena, there has been a longstanding assumption that one's problems are essentially psychological nature. Thus, therapy is variously oriented toward removing repression, enhancing self-acceptance, reshaping individual cognition, and so on. Buddhist practices could congenially be folded into this tradition, as they could be viewed as bringing about mental transformation. Thus, where Zen Buddhists saw meditation as entering a state of "no mind," Western therapists and researchers focus on the individual's state of "mindfulness." In the popular realm, the Western public has long embraced practices of self-improvement. The popular press provides daily doses of advice on self-help, boosting self-esteem, developing a winning personality, and so on. Buddhist practices can again be folded into this tradition, as they seem to provide means of improving self-control, reducing anxiety, and inviting tranquility. Yet, in the Eastern tradition, it is precisely this preoccupation with the self that such practices are designed to discourage. Seldom do we find in the Western literature on Buddhist practices an emphasis on inter-being, inter-dependent arising, or Indra's net of infinite connection. Nor is there pervasive interest in the relational outcomes of Buddhist practices, namely a tolerant, nurturing, and compassionate orientation toward others.

It is precisely this door to a more relational conception of Buddhist practice that the present volume begins to open. This relational emphasis takes several forms. For some contributors to this volume it is a concern with the way in which Buddhist practices contribute to the social good. Pressing beyond self-improvement, the interest is in the ramifications of Buddhist traditions and practices for communal life. One essentially practices "for others." For other authors, the interest is in the ways in which Buddhist practices grow out of cultural traditions. Thus, rather than "a pill to be swallowed" for self-benefit, entering such practices is more promisingly viewed as participation in a tradition of relationships. Still others focus on the relationships between teacher and student or clinician and client, and the dialogic participation required to bring about effective practice. One may appear to practice meditation alone, but such practice always carries with it the traces of those from whom one has learned. One is never alone.

Finally, we find various authors emphasizing the more cosmological implications of

Buddhist practices. Especially important is the sense of an ultimate interdependence of all beings. This sensitivity is expressed in many ways. On a small scale it is there in the various chapters that speak of the unity of mind/emotion/body/action. Segmenting these elements off, and treating them as causally related (as often done in the Western tradition) is viewed as misleading and possibly harmful to a fully engaged practice. There are also chapters exploring the ways in which engaging in Buddhist practices is an immersion in relations and preparing an entry into relations, and thus gives expression to an overarching sense of connectivity. Or as Dr. Haruki expresses it in his Preface, "The self... is inseparable from the world's dynamics."

We must also be grateful for the wisdom and talents of Maurits G.T. Kwee, the master orchestrator of this work. Above all, he is acutely aware of these dynamics and what this might mean for the future of Buddhism. Any body of theory or practice that becomes solidified – completed in itself – is endangered. It cuts itself away from the continuous, emergent process of relationship that sustains vitality and engagement. And so it is that Dr. Kwee has presciently created links between this ancient tradition and cutting edge ideas in the contemporary intellectual world. Slowly the world's peoples are becoming conscious of the massive anguish spawned by competing claims to superiority – whether in matters of spirit, morality, rationality, or objectivity. And there is a simultaneous realization of the potentials inherent in newly emerging conceptions of multiple truths, dialogue, and collaborative practice. By exploring the strands of Buddhism that resonate with these developments, not only is the Buddhist tradition revitalized, but the wisdom and insights contribute more fully to contemporary debates and developments on human well-being. We owe to Dr. Kwee an appreciation for his fostering this precious synergy.

It is my personal hope that through this blending of pursuits we move at least one small step toward a world in which all traditions may share these joys of mutual exploration. This would indeed be a world in which tolerance, nurturance and compassion would prevail, and thus, cherished goals of Buddhism would be realized.

For on-line ordering of books from Taos Institute Publications visit
www.taosinstitutepublications.net

For further information, call: 1-888-999-TAOS, 1-440-338-6733
Email: info@taosoinstitute.net

General Introduction

The unadulterated message of the Buddhist teachings (the Dharma) has most likely survived the ravages of time because of its multidimensional and multidisciplinary nature and its ability to flexibly adjust and adapt to the changing needs and demands of various peoples, times, and environments. This notion suggests that the Dharma, which may look to some like a religion, a philosophy, or a science, is actually an open, living, relational system that is ever learning and changing through feedback/feedforward processes. Qualities like these are likely to be those which warranted the Dharma being integrated into and taking root in the various cultures where it happened to dwell, and to be taken up with conservation of the peculiar and undiluted characteristics of its teachings. While on the surface its form of expression appears to be totally different and to vary from culture to culture, its core message does not seem to have been altered in principle: emptiness and interconnectedness.

In seeking for a transcultural Dharma, a Dharma as a contemporary psychology of Social Construction is an excellent candidate for being taken up by 21st century secular societies. Dharma as psychology is complementary to Dharma as religion or philosophy and may serve as a rational alternative for people who are allergic to metaphysics or who view metaphysics as poetry. Having gone through ups and downs in the past 2600 years, the Dharma which was disseminated as a religion and a philosophy successfully survived and grew worldwide. However, at this juncture in history, which is an era dominated by the language games of science, religion and metaphysics may lack relevance. For this reason the old stream Dharma may appear to outlive its usefulness. If the *raison d'être* of the Dharma is to cease Duhkha, existential emotional suffering, through awakening and through an insight in the processes how Duhkha comes about and can be extinguished, it seems to me that this Dharma is a psychology. Dharma as a psychology, which on the meta-level conceives mental life as relational, to help people unchain themselves from being stuck in unwholesome mental states is the main theme of this compilation. As this editor wishes to engage a broad audience of readers, scholars, students, clinicians, coaches, teachers, psychologists and non-psychologists alike, the hope is to bridge the "between-group" problem. Most psychologists know little about the Dharma and look at the Dharma with some mistrust particularly when Buddhist scholars apply religious language with which they are unfamiliar. In order to reach as many readers as possible, this introduction aims to clarify the scope, breadth, and depth of the present overarching framework: psychology. The quest centres round the question: What is a "new" Buddhist Psychology?

Both the "old" Buddhist Psychology of the *Abhidhamma* (the 3rd "canonical" book of the Theravada denomination) and a "new" Buddhist Psychology adhere to the Buddhist construction of Body/Speech/Mind which corresponds to a mainstream health care paradigm: the Bio/Psycho/Social systemic model (Kwee & Holdstock, 1996). On the basis of this wholistic tripartition, the "New Buddhist Psychology" implies a social constructivist social-clinical-neuro-psychology that integrates the third (Body/Bio), second (Speech/Social) and first person (Mind/Psyche) research methods in a complementary way. Leaving plenty of room for individual interpretation of the reader and not acknowledging any absolute authority, New Buddhist Psychology is a social construction that moves away from religion and philosophy. By doing so, this book breaks away from the tradition of Louis de Vallée Poussin (1869-1939), who contended that the Dharma is a religion, and of Fyodor Stcherbatsky (1866-1942), who insisted that the Dharma is a philosophical system. While both scholars were specialists in the Mahayana sutras, the tradition followed here is that of Caroline Foley Rhys Davids (1857-1942). She worked with Theravada texts of Sri Lanka and was the first scholar who recognized the psychological content in Early Buddhism, and was the first to subsume the Dharma under the rubric of psychology. The latter is reflected in her landmark book *Buddhist psychology – An inquiry into the analysis and theory of mind in Pali literature* (1914). It is a privilege to stand on her giant shoulders as well as on those of Padmasiri de Silva, David Kalupahana, and Padmal de Silva. Academic psychologists whose mainstay is in logical-positivism contend that psychology is largely about the study of the mind and behaviour. Traditionally, the psychologist's project is to understand behaviour as a function of emotion, motivation, perception, attention, cognition, learning, and the like. This "old-stream" psychology seeks to account for behaviour as a function of an individual agency's isolated mind. This editor, however, embraces a relational perspective that views the human mind as socially constructed. Individual mind and all that we consider to be true, real, and rational emerge out of relationships in "Dependent Origination" (*pratityasamutpada*), hence "Relational Buddhism".

The basic idea of this book concurs with the Buddhist understanding that mind is not self-contained but operates in-between people in Dependent Origination: to be is to inter-be and to act is to inter-act. This idea has ramifications for practice; if not for practice Buddhist Psychology has no reason to exist. The Buddhist caring for relationships is focused on cultivating the social meditations of kindness, compassion, and joy. These are attitudes considered relevant as communicative performances to create rationality which comes about by collaborative effort through conversational exchange. Buddhist practices aim to extinguish the relational poisons (greed, hatred, and ignorance) hampering human interconnectedness. The Buddha's pivotal insight is that psychological suffering is rooted in the irrational relational stances of greed and hatred due to ignorance on human interconnectedness. This understanding is more valid than ever today as it is undeniable that greed is the root-cause of the credit crisis the world is facing today and hatred is the root cause of terrorism threatening everyone on the planet. The end result is fear, anger, sadness, and depression or premature death, unless we know how to appropriate the cultural scenarios of emotional relating with savvy and wisdom. The Buddha practised wisdom by dealing with Karma, i.e. intentional action which implies relational meaning and interpersonal activity. Karma is expressed through Body/Speech/Mind (*Kamma Sutta*). The Buddha's causality hypothesis of Dependent Origination necessitates a communal view of human life that considers the self not as self-contained but as constituted in multiple relationships from the cradle to the grave. The Buddhist vision concurs with collaborative practice and reflective negotiation as reflected by "Interbeing" (*Heart Sutra*), "Relational Being" (Gergen), and the confluence of the two: "Relational Interbeing". The Gergenian adage "I am linked therefore I am" endorses the view that psychological processes are not so much in-between the ears as in-between people.

Focussing within in meditation we see the relational everywhere and the self encountered inside is a social construction which is at bottom "empty". Mindfulness is not a matter of experimental control and empirical data, but is rather a qualitative clinical N=1 study that allows repeated measuring to gain a generalized reliability and which might generate a theory grounded in relational experience. Buddhist Psychology is not so much focussed on collecting data on what reality is (ontology), but is rather about how to gather reliable knowledge from what is perceived and expressed about life as lived (epistemology). In other words, Buddhist

Psychology is about perceptual knowledge that is experiential and not easily transmittable verbally but can be socially constructed and negotiated. Everything recognizable must have been learned and is necessarily a social construction. The other person and the self that we talk and think about are provisional linguistic creations. Both are dialogical-narrative constructions existing only in conversational construction, deconstruction, and reconstruction through continuous interacting in multiple relationships. Such I-me-mine/self is always performing; I am as many potential selves as are embedded within and constructed through conversation. Identity and continuity, or what I think of as selfhood, become maintaining coherence and continuity in the stories I tell about myself. This self or rather self-narrative does not represent a single voice but is a multi-authored polyphony self, a "multibeing" (Gergen, 2009). Since I-me-mine/self does not exist outside of language and discourse, there is no inner-core self and no fixed self. Lacking a substantial/inherent self, the self is empty. At this point the Dharma and the psychology of Social Construction merge. Does this view absolve the individual from responsibility? As non-solitary Relational Interbeing, we are confronted more not less with issues of social responsibility in striving toward emptiness, here-now.

Thus, New Buddhist Psychology emphasizes a spirit of collaborative practice for the clinician, coach, and teacher. Rooted in a relational orientation (Anderson, 2008; < www.taosinstitute.net >) it endorses:

(1) Skepticism. The Buddha was a non-theistic skeptical free thinker who ran against the institutionalized belief system of his time. He questioned ingrained traditions, transcendental knowledge, and universal truths, none of which were to be taken for granted. Instead of blindly buying into the assumption and pre-understandings of a teacher, prejudiced theories, or societal criteria, one examines for oneself what is wholesome or unwholesome in each particular situation. While thus remaining humble about one's own knowledge, one stays open to self-critique and challenges one's own understandings in a changing world. Realizing that one can never have absolute knowledge about anything, one is receptive to learning about the uniqueness and novelty of life through dialogue.

(2) Particularism-relativism. Avoiding overgeneralization, the Buddha espoused Upaya allowing the Dharma to be reinvented time and again by disseminating it in tune with the particular people, local culture, specific language, and special circumstances which require unique interpersonal skills relative to time and place. The practitioner prevents a limiting of others people's possibilities. By engaging in a dialogue, listening, and responding, one openly encounters other descriptions, meanings, and understandings of lived experiences. Privileging local/home-grown knowledge of the particular community is important for acquiring relational expertise which is relevant, pragmatic, and sustainable. Each one contributes to the conversation and designs meaning, activity, and its outcome.

(3) Interactionism. Understanding and insight are relational processes. The relational poisons are engendered in an interpersonal context. Existential

suffering emerges out of lacking psychological insight and results in illusions and delusions like seeing the devil and the divine outside ourselves. Generated through language in social discourse, the Dharma became embedded in various cultures and histories. The construction of "Buddhist realities" is an interactive process of interpretation by community members who constantly create, sustain, and change form and content, and which are therefore fluid, not fixed, or definitive. The Dharma is not to be foisted upon another; it occurs in the "space" between people, not transmitted from one head to another.

(4) Connectivism. As to be is to be related (Korzybski) and we are because we are linked (Gergen), we are interconnected through verbal and non-verbal speech. "Balanced Speech" is a noteworthy part of the *8-Fold Balanced Practice* and is considered to be relevant in connecting Body/Mind. Language is the product of social interaction, a complex process through which we communicate with ourselves by self-dialogue and with others in conversation. As a medium within which we create knowledge, insight, and understanding, words become meaningful as we speak and in the way we speak. Clients or students exchange views with their clinician, coach, or teacher, who is the catalyst in a mutual transformational partnership. These dynamics likely generate a change of meaning and action through construction and reconstruction in the space of Relational Interbeing.

This book is the fruit of Relational Interbeing. Symbolising the merger of Buddhist Psychology and Social Construction, this term also refers to a meta-psychological framework that transcends traditional views of the self. The self as a "common intersection of multiple relationships" (multibeing) necessitates an empty self, because this "being" is considered to be located in-between interacting people. To luxuriate in a metaphor, as a function of the relational, this anthology is the harmonious sound of a choir singing in many tones from a Buddhist and a social constructivist hymn sheet. New Buddhist Psychology is not a clear-cut product but a work in progress: a process that is constantly under construction. According to Wittgenstein, terms derive their meanings from the members of a particular language. In turn, meaning is determined by its place in the context of a family of words according to cohering rules of grammar and syntax. Thus, linguistic meaning is not a product of a single mind but comes into existence through communal action from inter-being. Through Speech people narrate the wordless, express and communicate what is mindfully conceptualized and what is sensory/emotionally bodily felt in interpersonal relationships. Buddhists are intrigued by the wholistic notion of Body/Mind and its bridge, Speech (verbal and non-verbal), used to story-tell the basically inexpressible and "wordless" emotions. Speech seems to be the near equivalent of emotion, a concept that does not exist in the Buddhist idiom and if alluded to like in greed, hatred or kindness, compassion, and joy, it is something relational, not a solipsistic entity of an independent agency. Thus, in Buddhist Psychology emotions as "inner feelings" are viewed in relationship, in relationship to others as well as in relationship to oneself. In the latter case one might consider emotions to bridge and connect Body/Mind. From a New Buddhist Psychology integrative stance, modifying "intrapersonal stories" through self-speech/self-talk and walking this talk on the affective/emotional level is a healing step. This step is often engendered through a dialogue or conversation in co-action on meaningful views of reality leading to a wholesome change of meaningful action which is relational (to be found out).

According to the Buddha helping takes place in a conversation of "ennobling friendship" which seems to point at a "talking cure" complementing meditation. Notably, guidance by a role model refers to dealing with and overcoming self-talk on "hindrances", stumbling blocks on the path like doubtfulness and lack of confidence in progress. The Buddha admonished in the "greater discourse on emptiness" (*Mahasunnata Sutta*) to be mindfully aware that:

Talk which is... leading [not] to... freedom from passion, not to cessation, not to tranquillity, not to higher knowledge, not to awakening, not to Nibbana, namely, talk about kings, robbers and ministers, talk about armies, dangers and war, about food and drink, clothes, couches, garlands, perfumes, relatives, cars, villages, towns, cities, and provinces, about women and wine, gossip of the street and of the well, talk about the ancestors, about various trifles, tales about the origin of the world and the ocean, talk about what happened and what did not happen, such and similar talk I shall not entertain... But... talk which is conducive to... Nibbana, namely, talk about a life of frugality, about contentedness, solitude, aloofness from society, about arousing one's energy, talk about virtue, concentration, wisdom, deliverance, about the vision and knowledge of deliverance, such talk I shall entertain.

The above concurs with Gergen's (2009) "deficit discourse" which, centred round problem thinking, is suppression rather than construction or appreciation of positive possibilities. A "transformative dialogue" dissolves the barriers of meaning separating parties and promotes a conversation that nurtures and elevates relationships.

New Buddhist Psychology is about transforming Karma based on an analysis of feeling-thinking-doing-and-emotions which all come about in interrelationship. Karmic causality is hypothesized by the Buddha as Dependent Origination, an arising-peaking-subsiding-ceasing of human experience in non-independence, interdependence or codependence. Negative emotions are to be eradicated by not clinging-grasping-craving to I-me-mine/self and by experiencing emptiness which is not a goal in itself but is a set-point to start the promotion of "positive" emotions. Evidently, "psychology" and "psychologist" did not exist as a science or as a title in the Buddha's time. During his time the Buddha was known as a "Karmavadin" which is a self-proclaimed role as a teacher of Karma: one who uncovers its unwholesome root causes (*hetu*): greed, hatred, and ignorance. The "awakened one" revealed the conditional relations, causes/functions, or reasons/motives of experiential events in interpersonal contexts. He was a teacher of effective action (*kiriya*) devoted to summoning up in others the strength (*viriya*) needed for action resulting in increasing wholesomeness (Swaris, 1997). The heavy valorisation of karmic intentional/meaningful feeling-thinking-doing-in-relationship by the Buddha combined with the present clinical practice of evidence-based interventions in co-action lead to coining the terms Karma Transformation and Relational Buddhism.

In effect, this anthology is a testimony of collaborative practice and social construction presented in 23 intertwined chapters organized in seven themes: *The Buddha's Pursuit:*

Alleviating Existential Suffering, The Dharma As An Upaya Of Communal Construction, The Buddha's No-Nonsense Empty-Self Psychology, Digging Into The Mind The Buddhist Way, Buddhist Psychology Expanding From Within the West, Mindfulness Issues In Psychotherapy Along Buddhist Lines, and *Towards Karma Transformation By Selfless Dialogue.* The volume opens with an introductory chapter on *The Social Construction Of A New Buddhist Psychology* and closes with a chapter on *Relational Buddhism.*

Chapter 1

The Social Construction Of A New Buddhist Psychology

Maurits G.T. Kwee

Introduction

This chapter offers a social constructionist view of the Dharma and gives a comprehensive account of Buddhist Psychology as a contemporary applied psychology. Founded on pan-Buddhist unadulterated principles and core teachings, a "new" Buddhist Psychology goes beyond the "old" Buddhist psychology of the *Abhidhamma*. This implies a "social-clinical-neuro-psychology" which concurs with the Buddha's Body/Speech/Mind paradigm. By emphasizing the void nature of "Transcendental Truth" and expounding "Relational Being" that corroborates "not-self" and "emptiness", the metapsychology of Social Construction bears a striking resemblance with much that is exhibited in the *Avatamsaka Sutra*. A social constructivist approach underpins a de-colonised view revisioning the traditional provisions of the Dharma as a sky-god religion and a metaphysical philosophy regarding "selfness" as empty. In Buddhist Psychology emptiness is not a goal in itself but a reset-point for meaningful action derived from compassion and care (through kindness and joy) for harmonious relationships. While deeply respecting the Buddhist denominations of the past, the cosmology of Mahayana/Vajrayana-Tantrayana is qualified as an exotic atavism that has outlived its usefulness for those who prefer a down-to-earth approach. In order to divest the Dharma of its non-secular attributes and to present it as a social constructivist psychology, a reinterpretation of a dozen Buddhist keywords is recast into everyday speech in a Wittgensteinian new language game. This game goes along with a new idiom and a vocabulary which is in accord with the relational spirit of the scriptures. The postulated New Buddhist Psychology seems for the time being adequately equipped to serve secular societies of the 21st century. Transforming the Dharma from a religion and metaphysics into a psychology of Relational Buddhism requires a thorough elaboration which is ventured in this anthology.

The Dharma as a psychology

The psychological content of the Buddhist teachings (Dharma) is contained in the Buddha's discourses. According to the *Kevatta Sutta* the Buddha did not expound an other-worldliness, he expounded a this-worldliness, did not satisfy seekers of an eternalistic "all" or an annihilistic "nothing"; instead he kept a Middle Way – a "neither all, nor nothing". He refused to formulate a final truth as this would lead neither to an understanding how the mind works, nor to liberation from existential suffering (Duhkha), the psychological agony due to the emotional ramifications of birth, aging, illness, and death. The Buddha is renowned for his "classical unanswered questions", like: "Is the world (this universe) eternal or finite, or both, or neither?", "Are the self and the body identical or different, or both, or neither?", and "Will a Buddha exist or not exist after death, or both, or neither?" According to the Buddha, entertaining these metaphysical questions leads to speculation and generating religious and metaphysical debates which are not conducive to liberation from Duhkha (*Avyakata Sutta*). Along this line of reasoning, dogma, creed, belief, and miracles (Kalupahana, see Ch.9) are anathema as are the soul, transmigration, and reincarnation, since all of these can neither be confirmed nor denied. The *Kalama Sutta* conveys a charter of free inquiry (Byrom, 2001):

> Do not believe on rumours or hearsay, because it is reported to be good, ancient or practiced by tradition... because it is in the scriptures or because of logic, inference or metaphysics... because the speaker appears believable or you are shown the testimony of an old sage. Do not believe in what is fancied, because it is extraordinary, it must have been inspired by a god or other fancy being... because presumption or custom of many years inclines you to take it as true... just because of someone's reputation and authority or because he is a guru.

Thus, the Dharma is a discipline of free inquiry, a set of practices, which takes nothing on blind faith and does not confess a personal holy figure or some godhead. If the Buddha's words are taken as hypotheses, the Dharma suggests an evidence-based-research-as-action method. The Buddhist community is studious, not religious in a western sense.

Let us call to mind the historical datum that the Dharma was a non-theistic reaction to Brahmanism (better known by its colonial name: Hinduism), a dialectical anti-thesis countering polytheism. Being non-theistic, the Dharma had no involvement in religious practices in the usual sense: god is simply not an issue at all. Non-theistic means: neither theistic, nor atheistic, and not even something in the middle. Instead, the Dharma brings the liberating experience of emptiness to the fore. Thus, the Dharma is neither gnostic (god can be known), nor agnostic (god cannot be proven): god is "none of our business". The undiluted Buddhist teachings acknowledge that the Buddha did not establish a religion, did not declare himself to be a godly/omniscient manifestation (messiah, saviour, or prophet), and did not derive inspiration from any deity or other external power. In his criticism of Brahmanism the Buddha was quite humorous. In the *Tevijja Sutta* a Brahman (Vasettha) debated about the union with Brahma, the creator, with the Buddha. The Buddha asked him whether he, or his teacher, or his teacher's teacher up to the seventh generation had ever seen Brahma. Vasettha's denial sparked the Buddha's comment on the opponent's logic by comparing his behaviour with that of a person who decides to seek out and love the most beautiful girl without knowing her name, looks, complexion, height, dwelling, or descent. Furthermore, the Buddha discouraged religious rituals. Never did he teach his students to pray, nor did he ever wish to be worshipped, nor did he claim to be anything else than an awakened but fallible human being. The most probable conjecture is that he lived with human uncertainties, not knowing that his teaching would ever become "Buddhism" and extant in the 21st century *(Guang, see Ch.2)*.

In spite of the metaphysical flirtations of later Buddhists, the Buddha was not concerned with the cosmological order of the universe. He was almost exclusively involved with the impermanence of the human condition and with the quest to know how to come to grips with the existential troubles of imperfection. The Buddha's discourses breathe a this-worldly spirit as in the following quote: "In this fathom-long living body – with perceptions and thoughts –

lies the world, the arising and cessation of the world" (AN4, MN1, SN2). Obviously, by the world is not meant the world out there (in the Buddha's era of the iron age conceived as flat) or a world somewhere in the beyond, but the world within the psyche, with all its data entering through the sense doors and which minutiae are observable in meditation. The Buddha's rejection of metaphysics, cosmology, and ontology is clear in the following quote:

> The eyes and forms, the ears and sounds, the nose and smells, the tongue and tastes, the body and tangible things, the mind and mental objects... If someone should set this "All" aside and proclaim another "All", it would be just talk... beyond the limits of his abilities. (SN 28)

In the *Brahmajala Sutta* the Buddha straightened out a Vedic myth on the origin of the world by re-contextualizing the Vedic account. "Brahma as the origin of all existence" showed ignorance regarding the Dependent Origination of "the divine". Contesting the Brahmins, he renounced their god delusions.

As illustrated in the above examples, the psychological content of the Dharma as registered in the Nikayas (collections of suttas, the Buddha's discourses) is included in the pan-Buddhist unadulterated secular core concepts, terms, and themes. These examples are unequivocally acknowledged by all denominations and go beyond the particular and local tenets of Theravada ("teaching of the elders", practiced in Kampuchea, Laos, Myanmar, Sri Lanka, Thailand) and Mahayana ("great vehicle", practised in China, Japan, Korea, Vietnam) which includes the Vajrayana ("adamantine vehicle", practiced in Bhutan, Mongolia, Sikkim, Siberia, Tibet). The Nikayas comprise commonly shared, pan-Buddhist core insights – acknowledged by all denominations – insights which anyone can acquire through the study and practice of meditation. These include the topics listed in Table 1, some of which will be elaborated in the paragraph on "languaging" below.

Table 1.
Pan-Buddhist Secular Core Concepts and Themes of Buddhist Psychology

(1) The Four Noble Truths, here called the *4-Ennobling Realities* (as social constructions)

(2) The Eightfold Path, here called the *8-Fold Balanced Practice* (of collaboration)

(3) The *Skandhas* (psychological modalities of mind or self: feeling-thought-action)

(4) The "ultimate not-self" of "emptiness" and the "provisional self" for everyday life

(5) The notion of Karma: intentional/meaningful thought-feeling and concomitant action

(6) The *"dharmas"*: the smallest "units of experience" ("perceivables" and "knowables")

(7) The "sixth sense": the mind's eye that perceives dharmas during mindful awareness

(8) The experience of Nirvana: a state/trait of extinguished unwholesome thought-affect

(9) The *3-Poisons*: greed, hatred, and ignorance on self illusions and god delusions

(10) The Immeasurables: social meditations to augment kindness, compassion, and joy

(11) The three "Empirical Marks of Existence": suffering, impermanence, and not-self

(12) The Dependent Origination of modalities: a psychological causality hypothesis

(13) The 12-Meditations with mindfulness (observe and watch) as the general factor

(14) The foundations of mindfulness: the fluctuations of body/feelings and mind/thoughts

(15) The *"patthanas"*: 24 functional conditions and relations linking feeling-thought-action

~~The Buddhist tradition allows a cultural interpretation of its teachings on emptiness. That~~ is how metaphysical atavisms, e.g. the soul, its transmigration and reincarnation, and other non-Buddhist notions could have entered and contaminated the Dharma via a back door in the Mahayana and Vajrayana, and even in the Theravada denominations (Conze, 1980). Thus, a teaching of emptiness is able to cater the illiterate masses, superstitious people who are used to believe in magic, miracles, metaphysics, rituals, and omniscience (Kariyawasam, see Ch.8). The informed reader is aware of *Upayakaushalya* (or Upaya), skilful means of educating and disseminating the Dharma, which helped the Dharma to blossom in numerous eras and across cultures by accommodating and adapting it to local customs of various audiences (Van der Velde, see Ch.5). These skills to methodically present the Dharma as an adequate means to arrive at emptiness, adjusted to culture and era, made it possible that from their first encounters, western scholars saw an Abrahamic type of religion in the Vajrayana, a philosophy in the Mahayana, and a psychology in the Theravada. Ironically, none of these cases of *hineininterpretieren* are per se wrong. It seems to me that they need to continually exist alongside each other to cater for different strokes for different folks. This holds in the West where religious sentiments even after decades of secularization still loom large and are even regaining ground in post-secular societies as observed by Habermas < www.signandsight.com/features/1714.html >. Nevertheless, I submit from a non-theistic stance that religion and philosophy as a paradigm for the Dharma have outlived their usefulness and contend that psychology is the most apt Upaya for 21st century people who consider themselves "secular". This assertion does not mean that psychology is truer than other disciplines: practical outcome is what matters.

Toward a "new" Buddhist Psychology

Since encountering western civilization, the Dharma has been moulded into categories to which they do not exactly belong: a religion and a philosophy. The Dharma has subsequently evolved further amongst others as a system of ethics, a way-of-life philosophy (Premasiri, see Ch.7), and a cognitive behavioural clinical psychology (P. de Silva, see Ch.4; Kwee & Kwee-Taams, see Ch.20 and Ch.21). To view the Dharma as a *modus vivendi* based on psychological insights is not a matter of course. Adopting this viewpoint requires a paradigm shift from conceptualizing the Dharma as a religion or metaphysics to a cutting-edge psychology of Social Construction (Kwee & Taams, 2006).

Buddhist Psychology has a long past but a short history. Roughly four periods can be discerned: an archaic, classical, modern, and postmodern period. The *archaic* period is a stage of philosophical psychology during which the term psychology was unknown. This period starts with the discourses of the Buddha and continues in the philosophical reflections as written down post the Buddha in the *Abhidhamma* which became one of the three canonical books in the early Buddhist literature. These "deeper" teachings were written by anonymous scholars until the 4th century and seemingly left with an open end to be updated by their successors. The *classical* period is landmarked by William James (1842-1910) and Caroline Rhys Davids (1857-1942). The founding father of American psychology, James (1890), was one of the first who recognized that the Dharma inheres in a psychology and who agreed on the notion of Karma as the interplay of cognitive-affective intentions and manifest behavioural (inter)action.

He broke new ground for psychology by inviting Dharmapala, a later Bhikkhu from Sri Lanka, to guest-lecture in 1903 at Harvard and by declaring that that lecture on the Skandhas (psychological modalities) would be the psychology everybody would be studying 25 years hence (Guruge, 1965). Drawing on the Dharma, James wrote about the "stream of consciousness", "pure" experience (called "nondual" in the Dharma), and the functional value of meditation to be fully "awake" and "*compos sui*" (master of oneself) if one is able to bring back attention over and over again. In *A Buddhist manual of psychological ethics of the fourth century B.C., being a translation, now made for the first time from the original Pali, of the first book in the Abhidhamma Pitaka, entitled, Dhammasangani (compendium of states or phenomena) with introductory essay and notes* (1900), Caroline Rhys Davids referred to the psychological content of the *Abhidhamma*. She particularly referred to the enumerations of *dharmas,* the smallest units of experience, which she qualified as a "dry valley of bones". She coined the term "Buddhist Psychology" in her 1914 book. The paradigm shift Buddhist Psychology made at that time, from an archaic psychology to a scientific discipline, parallels western psychology's development in the 19th century, when it moved away from religious and philosophical approaches. This move was marked by the formal start of scientific psychology: the opening of Wilhelm Wundt's psychological laboratory in 1879.

The next step, moving from a classical (1st generation Buddhist psychologists) or "old" Buddhist Psychology to a *modern* Buddhist Psychology (2nd generation Buddhist psychologists) is covered by numerous articles in psychology journals, book chapters, and two books: *An Introduction to Buddhist Psychology* by M.W.P. de Silva (1979, updated in 2005; see Ch.13) and *The Principles of Buddhist Psychology* by Kalupahana (1987; see Ch.3). While the aforementioned works refer to the Theravada Dhamma or "Pali teachings of the elders", after WWII other authors stemming from the Mahayana tradition played a significant role as well. This current is championed by Daisetz Teitaru Suzuki (1870–1966; Zen perspective) and Chögyam Trungpa Rinpoche (1939-1987; Tibetan Buddhist [Vajrayana] perspective). Reaching out from a psychotherapy point of view were Carl Jung (1875-1961), Abraham Maslow (1908-1970), Alan Watts (1915-1973), and Erich Fromm (1900-1980). Although Maslow (in the 1950s) valued the Dharma's positive psychology, Freud (1865-1939) viewed Buddhist meditation as pathological: a regression to "narcissistic primitivism" and "infantile helplessness"; it was even referred to as a "self-induced catatonia" (Alexander, 1931). These views are now overturned. The present *Zeitgeist* is in favour of connecting the Dharma and psychotherapy (e.g., Wallace & Shapiro, 2006; Sugamura, Haruki, & Koshikawa, 2007; Naylor, see Ch.15; Sik, see Ch.19).

The cognitive neuroscientist, Francisco Varela (1946-2001), belonged to a large group of scientists, including but not limited to psychologists, spearheaded by the 14th Dalai Lama < www.mindandlife.org > who indefatigably promotes: "The creation of a contemplative, compassionate, and rigorous experimental and experiential science of the mind which could guide and inform medicine, neuroscience, psychology, education and human development." His "Mind & Life Institute", convening every two years since 1987, is currently engaged in a "Cultivating Emotional Balance" research program (P. Ekman, et al.). Its board of directors includes R. Davidson, D. Goleman, and J. Kabat-Zinn. Kabat-Zinn (2003a) devised an 8-week outpatient training "Mindfulness-Based Stress Reduction" which from 1979 on had been applied in thousands of patients with various chronic and debilitating maladies. Subsequently, adherents developed "Mindfulness-Based Cognitive Therapy", "Mindfulness-Based Relapse

Prevention", "Mindfulness-Based Eating Awareness Training", to mention a few programs. Others have also included Buddhist mindfulness meditation in their approaches, like M. Linehan (Dialectical Behavior Therapy) and S. Hayes (Acceptance and Commitment Therapy). Still others (e.g. psychoanalyst M. Epstein and neurologist J. Austin, see Ch.22) and less well-known groups are committed to further Buddhist Psychology, e.g., the Transcultural Society for Clinical Meditation,[1] founding president: Prof. Emeritus Y. Haruki < http://transcultural.meditation.googlepages.com >.

The latter group promotes a *postmodern* or a "new" Buddhist Psychology by venturing an integration of all evidence-based data connecting the Dharma and psychology (Kwee, Gergen, & Koshikawa, 2006); this chapter is written from this stance of a 3rd generation of Buddhist psychologists. In essence we aim to "translate" the Dharma to become a social constructivist psychology, a clinical psychology, and a neuropsychology according to the Buddhist tradition of Upaya. As a *neuropsychology*, on a 3rd person "objective" level of inquiry, we are on the lookout for neuroscientific correlates of Buddhist concepts and practices. In a framework of "erklaeren" (explaining) we attempt to meaningfully connect scattered neuroscientific knowledge in Buddhist psychological terms as initiated by Japanese neurophysiologists, e.g., A. Kasamatsu, T. Hirai, and Y. Akishige in the 1950s, and currently vigorously pursued by scientists affiliated with the Dalai Lama's "Mind & Life Institute" and others (e.g., Kelly, 2008; Hanson, 2009). Notably, Austin (2006) reviewed neuroscientific studies from a Zen Buddhist perspective. Neuropsychology from a Buddhist perspective is interested in topics like these: EEG study of "free won't" rather than "free will" in habitual responding (Libet, 2004); neuroprosthetics (via implanted brain-computer interfaces) showing that conation of the mind is able to manipulate a cursor to command action (e.g., drawing or operating a TV remote control) (Donoghue in *Nature, 442*, 2006, pp.109-222); search for the Buddha's 6th sense in terms of neuroplasticity and dynamic brain circuitries (e.g., Varela, Lachaux, Rodriguez, & Martinerie, 2001); neuroimaging of "me-definers", self and "not-self" (perceiving without perceiver; Malach, Harel, Chalamish, & Fish, 2006); neurological correlates of awakening, supposedly the left prefrontal area connected to the left amygdala, specialized in positive affect (Davidson, Kabat-Zinn, Schumacher, Rosenkranz, Muller, et al., 2003); offsetting age-related cortical thinning (Lazar, Kerr, Wasserman, Gray, et al., 2005). Studies have also been done on the neuropsychology of compassion (DeLuca, 2005; < http://fearlessheart.com >). For an overview on meditation and the neuroscience of consciousness, see: Lutz, Dunne, and Davidson (2007). Notwithstanding the interesting findings, the present social constructivist Buddhist purview cautions for any claims of truth based on "objective science". It is at least doubtful whether the cortical data accrued by techniques of brain scanning of reason and emotion will exceed the usual speculative guesswork and could open up human mind to inspection. This caveat, however, is not to demoralize researchers to study the rewiring of the brain for the good.

As a 1st person "subjective" level of inquiry, *clinical psychology,* necessitates an evidence-

---

1. "Clinical" refers to the person-tailored approach to alleviate emotional suffering and to further health and wellbeing in the context of collaborative practice and transformational dialogue wherein the skill of "double listening" in communication, which discerns "content" meaning and "relational" meaning, is practised.

based approach, that is, empirical proof as best as can be found in outcome studies for the methods applied. To date, cognitive-behavioural interventions practiced by mental health clinicians and corporate wellbeing coaches belong to the most effective and efficient group of therapies (Butler, Chapman, Forman, & Beck, 2006). Their methods of assessment and intervention use concepts whose rationale is grounded in the Dharma and whose *modus operandi* of meditation coincide with cognitive-behaviour principles. The latter notion, increasingly becoming commonplace, has been pioneered by Mikulas (1978), De Silva (1984), and Kwee (1990). Despite the mushrooming of publications, a systematic and parsimonious account of the Dharma as a cognitive-behavioural psychology has only been presented recently (Kwee & Taams, 2006; De Silva, see Ch.4; Mikulas, see Ch.14; Rapgay, see Ch.18) sparked by research done on "Mindfulness-Based Cognitive Therapy" (Segal, Williams, & Teasdale, 2001; Ma & Teasdale, 2004; Kenny & Williams, 2007; Kuyken, Byford, Taylor, Watkins, Holden, et al., 2008). While in the West the leap from philosophy to psychology formally took place when Wundt opened his laboratory, the Dharma seems to have made a similar symbolical step only in 2005 when in Sweden A.T. Beck (founding "grandfather" of Cognitive Therapy) had a historical dialogue with the 14th Dalai Lama at the 5th International Congress of Cognitive Psychotherapy and the simultaneously held IX World Congress on Constructivism (for a transcript, see Taams & Kwee, 2006). At this groundbreaking summit a paradigmatic confluence of the two disciplines took place in an extensive series of symposia on Buddhist Psychology which was fully embraced by mainstream psychologists and cognitive-behavioural clinicians. This landslide event took place 101 years later than James had predicted. It may, however, not be left unnoticed that a decade earlier another "grandfather of Cognitive-Behaviour Therapy", the late legendary Albert Ellis already declared Rational Emotive Behaviour Therapy's allegiance with the Dharma (Kwee & Ellis, 1998; Christopher, 2003; Whitfield, 2006). The interface of the Dharma and cognitive-behavioural psychology will be elaborated by Kwee & Kwee-Taams, see Ch.20 and Ch.21. A new current called "Positive Psychology" is beginning to produce a number of studies on the outcome of interventions of Buddhist practices, e.g., loving kindness (Fredrickson, Cohn, Coffey, Pek, & Finkel, 2008; Hutcherson, Seppala, & Gross, 2008), compassion (Gilbert & Procter, 2006), happiness and joy (Lyubomirsky, 2008).

As a *social psychology*, on a 2nd person "inter-subjective" level of inquiry, we adopt a Social Construction viewpoint which contends that there are no "Transcendental Truths" and that reality and facts, as well as much of existential suffering, are man-made in interpersonal contexts. From a postmodern attitude we view reality as a community consensus of a local culture: science and all varieties of authority are considered to be relative. In this framework of "verstehen" (understanding), there is a need to eradicate the outdated linguistics of western cultural dominance shaping the Dharma into a sky-god religion and to re-conceptualize some key terms now applied in the Dharma. As proclaimed by Gergen (1999), Social Construction contends: "I am networked, therefore I am." In full, humans are "biochemical-sensing-moving-thinking-emoting-relational-constructs" whose minds usually function at the pre-rational (child-like), irrational (foolish) and rational (scientific) levels, but seldom at the post-rational/wisdom level. It is on this wisdom level that we are able to see and understand that to be means to "inter-be" and that to act is to inter-act. Wisdom enables us to understand the ubiquitous and pervasive interconnectedness of humanity. Thrown from birth onwards into a social web, we cannot be self-contained. There is nothing that we can conceive of that is not injected by interpersonal meaning. Even "private worlds" are encapsulated in inextricable relational networks. We are embedded in interrelatedness from the cradle to the grave. Such a metavision is depicted in the Dharma by "Indra's Jewel Net" (*Avatamsaka Sutra*; Cleary, 1993) which is a matrix which at each crossing has mirrors/beings reflecting and interpenetrating each other infinitely. In this vision truth is always provisional, linguistically co-constructed by a group and negotiated in a dance of meanings. In the same vein reality, even if and as unveiled by science, is considered to be a culture-bound narrative to be replaced by "better" constructions, going forward. In the end it is not about discovering the truth/reality as revealed but the truth/reality as constructed (as imbued with meaning): the Buddhist liberation is a relational event.

Kuhnian paradigm shifts

The magnificent move from religion and metaphysics to psychology as from William James is a major switch that warrants its framing as a paradigm shift. To Kuhn (1962) a paradigm shift occurs when a previous view is transformed into a new one. Before Kuhn, scholars saw the history of scientific thought as a slow, progressive, evolutionary accumulation of knowledge across generations. Kuhn contends that the history of science is not a development of natural progression, but reflects a long series of conflicts between competing methods of processing data and explaining results without revealing the Truth. Thus, Darwin's theories grew out of Lamarck's theories and Einstein's relativistic physics were an extension of Newton's classical physics. In psychology, there were conflicting stances in the 1950s-60s between those who viewed observable behaviour as central to studying psyche as opposed to the non-behavioural view of those who placed cognition in the centre of study. The present social constructional meta-vision views the cognitive and behavioural approaches as "atomistic", not as the ultimate vantage point. To date, neither rocket science nor religious beliefs have brought us closer to Truth

In the same vein – through conflicting ways to attain emptiness – several paradigm shifts have taken place in the Dharma during its 2600 years of history. By transforming form and adopting habits from alien cultures it had survived the ravages of time. As mentioned earlier, its survival was sanctioned by Upaya, the intelligent use of teaching methods to skilfully expedite transfer of the Dharma relative to circumstances. Specific periods, cultures, audiences, and individuals with specific capacities and levels of understanding, each require specific teachings. To cater to a variety of peoples the Dharma needed to adjust to changing times and peoples by assimilating and adapting to the environment without being disloyal to its core teaching of emptiness. In the 6th century BCE the Buddha started a meditative life of meaningful action to end Duhkha, the raison d'être of his Dharma. From the 4th century BCE until the 5th century CE, the Dharma developed into a philosophy of life expounded in the *Abhidhamma* by the Theravada school, the only extant tradition out of 18 early Buddhist schools with a canon, the *Tipitaka* (three baskets), which is ten times as big as the Bible, written down in the 1st century BCE after being transmitted orally. Partly overlapping this development, from the 1st century BCE on through the 7th century, the Dharma also became a metaphysical teaching with "religious" characteristics. Its adherents, the Mahayanists – who have practiced in more than 12 schools continuously, until today – denigrated the adherents of the early Buddhist schools as being "primitive" and called them Hinayanists, "small vehicle" disciples. Two great Mahayana sub-traditions, the Vajrayana which includes Tantrayana (vehicle of sacred texts, practiced in 4 schools), developed from the 4th until the 13th century. These emphasize god-like figures, magical/devotional rituals, and presumed supernatural phenomena. Each of these two transformational steps within the Dharma is a colossal paradigm shift à la Kuhn. Underlying these shifts, even within one school of thought, are competing intellectual ideas and disagreements about how to interpret the Dharma and attain emptiness.

Within the Mahayana movement a titanic intellectual conflict was sustained between Nagarjuna (2nd century), also known as the 2nd Buddha, and Vasubandhu (4th century), also called the 3rd Buddha, and their proponents. They peacefully battled over their ideas for centuries but have never settled the conflict until today. Nagarjuna and his Madhyamaka school, which finds itself in-between the *Abhidhamma* and Vasubandhu's Yogacara school, is based on the "Perfection of Wisdom" sutras, written by numerous anonymous Buddhist scholars in the 1st century BCE to the 4th century. These sutras expound a thundering "emptiness-only" rational teaching of negation to arrive at point zero of total emptiness. The Yogacara school expounds that the "emptiness-only" doctrine leaves the student in too much of a void and teaches a "mind-only" doctrine based on the so-called "Buddha Womb" sutras, also written by anonymous scholars between the 1st century BCE and the 4th century.[2] Yogacara is a positive and metaphoric/poetic approach to emptiness which elaborates on the Buddha-womb out of which emanates Buddha-nature, Buddha-bodies, and celestial Buddhas in a cosmological pantheon. However the Yogacarins, who also emphasize meditation (*yoga*) practice (*cara*), never abandoned the pan-Buddhist basic emptiness. This approach is evident in the Chan/Zen denomination which belongs to the Yogacara tradition. The number of sutras of the Mahayana is immense and equals 50 times the size of the Bible. According to the Buddhist traditional wisdom of the "Dharmachakra", there are three turnings of the wheel which starts with the Buddha's Middle Way balancing all extremes, followed by a *via negativa* of "non-selfness", i.e. Nagarjuna's systematization of the "Perfection of Wisdom" sutras eradicating all poisons. This may leave the student in a *horror vacuum* and a self-contained empty Nirvana, and backed by the "Buddha Womb" sutras the Yogacara asserts a *via positiva* by a cosmology wherein revered qualities like kindness, compassion, and joy became deities. In particular, Vasubandhu's half brother Asanga (of the Yogacara Cittamatra/Mind school) was a proponent of deifying rituals. Allowing people to believe in transcendence and metaphysics in order to lure the meek amongst potential followers has likely contributed as well – due to a lack of differentiation with the prevailing Brahmanism – to the decline of the Dharma in the India of the 13th century.

Thus not only Kuhnian paradigm shifts can be discerned in the history of the Dharma, but Hegelian dialectical dynamics as well. If Nagarjuna's *via negativa* is the thesis and Vasubandhu's *via positiva* is the anti-thesis, what then is the synthesis? Vasubandhu – through his Yogacara Vijnavada/consciousness school, to which belonged Dignaga (6th century) and

---

2. All Theravada Pali suttas and Mahayana Sanskrit sutras were written by anonymous authors living in communes of brotherhoods as from the 1st century BCE until the 4th-5th century. Suttas and sutras narrate the Buddha's discourses. However, considering their date of appearance and the absence of prior oral transmission, the sutras, although written in a discourse format, cannot possibly be a recording of the Buddha's spoken words. The suttas were passed down through four centuries by oral tradition.

Dhamakirti (7th century), who also dealt with inferential knowledge, logic, and valid/invalid conclusions adumbrated psychology. They also presented an epistemological synthesis of non-duality regarding the *subject* (the perceiver/conceiver) and the *object* (the perceived/conceived); see Table 2 (and Table 2 of Ch.21). From a social constructivist and the present Buddhist perspective this dichotomy is at bottom indefensible: the interrelationships of things in the world are too much intertwined to be perceived as such. There is a merit in a deconstruction process.

Madhyamaka Yogacara	Functional/provisiory reality (verbal space)	Ultimate/deathless reality (nonverbal space)
Subject: perceiver/conceiver of outer world thru 6 senses	1. Samatha meditation *Tranquillity*	3. Vipassana meditation *Dependent Origination*
Object: perceived/conceived, inner world thru the 6th sense	2. Samadhi experience *Nirvana*	4. Sunyata experience *Emptiness*

Table 2. Quadrant of Madhyamaka and Yogacara Synthesis

If Vasubandhu's perceptual epistemology and theory about the eight consciousnesses are taken into account – the six defiled sensorial, a 7th I-me-mine/self (dualistic), and an 8th mirror (non-dual) consciousness (Yao, see Ch.12) – and are combined with Nagarjuna's elaboration on the Buddha's *provisional-functional/conditioned* reality and the *ultimate-deathless/unconditioned* reality, a synthesis is made possible. The functional reality of the householder comprises having a name, a passport/I.D.-card, or a self which contribute to making our lives comfortable, the shadow sides of which like craving, grasping, and clinging, can be extinguished by the tranquilizing meditation of Samatha leading to equanimity, not disinterest, with incoming stimuli and which via the flow of Samadhi experience eventually resulting in the Nirvana of silence. The ultimate reality of a Buddha or an Arahant, someone who has eradicated her/his inner enemies in the non-verbal space, is attained by insight meditation (Vipassana) allowing "Seeing Things As They *Become*", which is in Dependent Origination, and of the simultaneous and subsequent arising and subsiding of feeling-acting-thinking, a process conducive to arriving at deconstruction toward emptiness (Sunyata) (Fleischman, see Ch.16). This empty experience is not a goal in itself, but a reset-point to reconstruction by a balanced practice of kindness, compassion, and joy.

While Vasubandhu's epistemological psychology failed to integrate the middle, negative, and positive ways of the Dharma, this effort invites postmodern Social Construction to give a helping hand to arrive at a social epistemology of deconstruction and reconstruction. A Buddhist Psychology resting on social constructivist tenets might provide a synthesis:

(1) A *re-definition* of "empirical" such that the human *sensorium* is expanded to include a 6th sense (the mind's eye), which is the brain's capacity to be aware of awareness as consciousness of *dharmas* (the smallest units of experiencing) in non-duality (Karunadasa, see Ch.11). This capac-

ity of perceiving the brain's projections and the capacity of "meta-perception" – to perceive each of the six senses' empirical data separately and in their interrelatedness – suggests a "social brain", brain circuitries, and a cortical integration that might constitute the neurophysiological correlates of the "mind's eye".

(2) A *re-visioning* of *dharmas* (here defined as "perceivables", "imaginables", "knowables", "memorables", dreams, and illusions/delusions) as social constructions. They are "real" only if agreed upon by the community involved (e.g., the perception of an airy Kwan Yin by Chinese Buddhists). While the Buddha emphasized *dharmas'* impermanence, Nagarjuna (2ⁿᵈ century) pointed at their "non-selfness", Asanga (4th century) at their "transcendence", and Vasubandhu (4th century) at their "nonduality", Gergen (21ˢᵗ century) stresses the socially constructed (non-abiding) nature of *dharmas* corroborating the Buddhist ubiquitous-pervasive emptiness.

(3) A *re-generation* of the Dharma by reformulating the Buddhist scriptures as a social-clinical-neuro-psychology of Social Construction. Based on more than a century of exchange between the Dharma and academic psychology, this movement deserves a new name: *Neoyana*, meaning "new vehicle". This new Buddhayana carries with it a moving away from religion and metaphysics by using the Upaya of an applied evidence-based psychology as a way of life for secular audiences. Neoyana requires a social re-construction of several key concepts, terms, and themes derived from religious and metaphysical languaging.

Whether an integrative science of psychology will synthesize the thesis of subtraction and annulment versus the anti-thesis of addition and aggrandizement and revamp the Dharma as a Middle Way remains to be seen. The fact that a Buddhist cultural-scientific revolution and a paradigm shift have already begun cannot be denied, but will be argued and debated. Much of this recent shift is to be credited to the 14th Dalai Lama. The spirit of his immense efforts can be read in his poignant assertion: "If the words of the Buddha and the findings of modern science contradict each other, then the former have to go." (The Boston Globe, 9/14/03). From a postmodern perspective the Dalai Lama expresses a modern view of reality which helps humanity to view inside the brain but which is just another map of reality, not the "be all and end all". As M.W.P. de Silva (pers. comm., 2008) cogently remarked: "science may enhance the credibility and relevance of Buddhist concepts, but awakening may be achieved without science." A social constructivist position asserts that knowledge of the world is not acquired in a passive way, but through collaborative engaging with the world and ascribing meaning to perceptions of the world. Meaning is thus to be made by us.

Dharma and Social Construction

Social Construction is compatible with the Dharma (Gergen & Hosking, 2006) by asserting that on an interpersonal meta-level of "speech" the locus of study is not the individual, but people's interacting networks. As reality is not a solipsistic matter, but a narrative construction between communicating people, it may thus be "real" in one community, but "unreal" in another community. For instance, the scientific accounts of psychoanalysis or humanistic psychology differ from those within the parochial boundaries of Cognitive-Behaviour Therapy. A social constructionist perspective as a theory in use has given birth to "Relational Being" (Gergen, 2000, 2009). This notion was already known in the Buddhist lore of the Heart Sutra as "Interbeing" (Thich, 1998) and is here called "Relational Interbeing" to denote the amalgamation of the two traditions. The terms refer to a non-foundational "social self". The self's emptiness is the Buddha's psychological proposition *par excellence*. To date there is no evidence whatsoever to corroborate the existence of a "homunculus self" residing in the brain. Apparently, there is a perceiving without a perceiver, feeling without a feeler, doing without a doer, and thinking without a thinker: "no ghost in the machine". Although Social Construction stems from the discipline of social psychology and did not start as a postmodern Buddhist teaching, it can be viewed as such due to its account on self and discarding Transcendental Truth. In addition, by expounding that "being pro-social is spiritual enough" (sic), a "this-worldly" stance refutes an "other-worldly" spirituality implying the existence of the spirit, the soul, and the self, all anathema in the Dharma.

For those who are resilient and seek new practices, the horizons to embark on the social constructional venture, which views Transcendental Truth and absolute reality as cultural-historical narratives, are exciting (Kwee, Gergen, & Koshikawa, 2006). A social constructivist meta-psychological stance:

(1) challenges Cartesian types of knowledge that separate body-mind; not "I think", but "I am linked", therefore I am" (Gergen);

(2) is sceptical about accounts of "reality" based on rationality, testability, and objectivity as absolutely true (including those of Social Construction);

(3) questions the permanence of "reality" and the immutability of Transcendental Truth (of science, ethics, and religious beliefs);

(4) submits that communal meta-processes bring about co-constructions intelligible in the particular community, not "eternal/timeless truths";

(5) takes empirical data as socially constructed, fabricated, and based on local agreements that lack everlasting foundations as assumed by empiricists;

(6) does not seek "permanent truths" *about* subjects, but emphasizes qualitative research *with* people as immediate social action;

(7) does not discard findings of quantitative research, it views positivistic science as a relevant narrative about "reality", not as "absolute truth"; and,

(8) endorses evidence-based outcome like that of cognitive-behaviour interventions as entwined meaning and action generated in concurrence.

Both Social Construction and Buddhist Psychology practice de-construct and reconstruct.

They de-construct by dis-identifying and by making transparent the taken-for-granted illusions (like permanence or a solitary self) that are habitually taken as an "abiding truth", but which are in fact socially constructed. This non-permanence applies even to "scientific facts" about which Giambattista Vico (1668-1744) said: "they are man-made" (*verum ipsum factum*). In order to deconstruct illusions the illusionary character of language itself has to be critically examined. Language creates a picture of provisional reality, but cannot ever fully represent or express the unspeakable ultimate emptiness that can only be experienced. Language is to be understood as a social construction, as a means, or a map that serves an interpersonal purpose. Although deconstruction has a liberating effect – it frees from the automatisms of conditioning and literalization – reconstructive practices are still needed. It may be clear by now that reconstruction requires a keeping on seeing how daily realities owe their existence to relationship and to people's interacting networks. From this and the insights in the processes and potentials of "Relational Interbeing" come forth the social constructionist practice of appreciating and accepting the other. The latter does not mean approving "bad" behaviours. Both disciplines consider care for relationships as the most worthy value. The Buddhist caring is operationalized in the social contemplations, a meditation practice existing for 100 generations since the Buddha. It aims to immeasurably multiply the core affects of loving kindness, empathic compassion, and shared joy by radically applying these values in daily life in equanimity until there is enough love to go round in the world.

By incorporating Social Construction, the present Buddhist Psychology emphasizes the *Avatamsaka Sutra* (Flower Garland Sutra, a "Buddha Womb" sutra from the 1st-3rd century). Reverence for this sutra began in China and continues today. It is known in Japan as *Kegon*. Named after the sutra, the *Hua-yen* or "Flower Garland" School, which was innovated by Fatsang in the 7th century, embraces notions which are compatible with Social Construction and are therefore highlighted here. This sutra conveys that the metaphysical realm is empty through a kind of "Lucy in the sky with diamonds" account of prince Sudhana's search for wisdom and illumination.[3] The prince undertook a developmental journey to become a Buddha; he was helped by 53 teachers-friends symbolizing phases, principles, and virtues to be adhered. He discovered that life is a teaching and learned from everyone he met, from a Brahmin, to king, slave, merchant, fool, boatman, doctor, prostitute, child, and animal. What he learned varied from mindful awareness to compassion, kindness, joy, equanimity, purity of mind, and so on. Finally, he had no more strivings either toward attaining or not attaining Buddhahood. He ended up with a teacher who pointed at a "Jewel Tower" high upon a steep mountain. He reached the tower after a dangerous journey. There he found a room full of generosity. And while his body radiated bliss, a vision of the interdependence of beings and events dawned. He experienced the interpenetration of all things in the universe and saw "Indra's Jewel Net". This is a net wherein each crossing of the net is interpenetrated by a jewel, whose reflecting surface reciprocally mirrors appearing images in the jewel at every crossing of the net, causing one's

---

3.   The story can be found in the 39th and last book of the *Avatamsaka Sutra*. It is also depicted on most of the panels of the Borobudur on the island of Java where this author was born.

light to be part of the others' and accepting their light as part of one's own. Thus Indra's net symbolizes the interconnectedness of all things *ad infinitum*. This non-obstruction-of-all-phenomena was the entrance of "one into all and all into one" to the highest room in the tower, where he finally found the ultimate wisdom that turned out to be: an empty room. The universe is an empty bubble! Sudhana ended his journey and devoted the rest of his life to compassionate service of his fellow human beings (Cleary, 1993). For obvious reasons the metaphor of "Indra's Jewel Net" as a "universal matrix" is appealing to social constructionists.

The interdependence of existence was the Buddha's extraordinary vision when he awakened under the bodhi-tree in 528 BCE. It was based on this deep insight that he formulated as a causality hypothesis (*pratityasammutpada*) known as Dependent Origination and which refers to the non-independent, co-dependent, or interdependent origination-arising-peaking-subsiding-and-cessation of *dharmas*, the smallest discrete experiences of feeling-acting-thinking, and Relational Interbeing. Buddhists and social constructionists view the discernment of the psyche in modalities as "atomistic" and "elemental" if these vicissitudes of human functioning are not embedded in interpersonal relationships. By its nature of co-dependency or interdependency, human action originates and arises by necessity in interaction: to act is to interact. Like in the Buddhist vision, Gergen (1999) replaced the binary "inner-outer"/"I-other" by a socially "co-constructed" self that necessarily repudiates the individual self under the skin as an explanatory entity. Because of unobstructed mutual identity penetration, each individual is interconnected in Dependent Origination with other individuals. A change in one individual results in a relative change in all her/his interrelations. Looking outside ourselves in the social realm, we see mirrors of our inner worlds; looking inside ourselves in the private realm (like in wall gazing meditation), we see the social everywhere. And although we are dancing all alone in the room, the social dimension is still omnipresent. Because we are intricately related to each other, it is safe to conclude that even the private is a social construction. In such a vision, we are all subsumed under a meta-order of the interpersonal. This meta-vision necessitates a view of reality as a joint venture and as mutual responsibility.

The love affair with Social Construction is centred round Relational Interbeing that does not simply exist behind the eyeballs but also exists in-between people. Focusing on interactions, the binary "you-me" collapses and crumbles in emptiness. Relational Interbeing necessitates the emptiness of solitary selves which is at the heart of the Buddha's psychology. Endorsing the view that individuals are manifestations of relationships, not independent agents, the present "new" Buddhist Psychology of "Relational Buddhism" sees that persons are empty of the pure private. Even private thoughts cannot be solipsistic as they emerge from a history of language and long lasting relations. The relational perspective does not discard psychobiology, but completes the picture of the human being as a Bio-Psycho-Social system or as a Body/Speech/Mind being as the Buddha contended. Relational Interbeing and its speech is neither within the body, nor within the mind, but in its members' encounters and dialogues (Gergen & Gergen, 2004). For Relational Interbeing to become, the members must necessarily move together, as in a dance. Thus, not only Relational Interbeing comes to be, but reality as well; both are defined by what the social group thinks it is. In other words: reality is not a solipsistic matter. It is not located within the body or the mind, it exists in the social experience: $2 + 2 = 4$ or can equal 5, if we agree it is so. Thus, reality is constructed between communicating people and may be considered "real" in one community, but "unreal" in another community. Beyond community there is thundering silence. Reality is provisional, linguistically co-constructed by people, and negotiated in a dance of meanings. Even if revealed by science, data remain generated in agreement, and are thus man-made, inter-subjective, and relative. Even science and its artifacts are inextricably space-time-and-culture bound. Conceived by scientists, they are narratives to be amended and replaced by better constructions going forward. Actually, such is happening with the Dharma in its present transition from religion and metaphysics into psychology.

"Languaging" and Buddhist Psychology

"If you call this a stick, you affirm, if you call it not a stick, you negate: beyond affirmation and negation what would you call it?" (Ta-hui, 12th century). This is a famous Chan *kung-an*, a case of "jurisprudence" that has proven its utility to awaken, better known by its Zen name Koan, a paradoxical riddle that cannot be solved by reason or language. Language and speech are tools of provisionally mapping the world and a form of life within relationship. Theories are not telling how the world "really" is; they are a springboard for participation in relationships. It is important, therefore, to be aware of the social constructional, interpersonal, and gaming character of language, including the language of Buddhist Psychology (Gergen & Hosking, 2006). Because we cannot escape the local culture we live in, all that we systematically conceive is a polyvocal narrative. This is also the case with the Dharma as a religion, as metaphysics, or as psychology.

Wittgenstein (1953) – on whose work Social Construction draws heavily – claimed that words derive meaning from their use in language games. Words by themselves have no intrinsic meaning. Meanings are socially – not privately – constructed through their interactive use by members of a community who develop ways of speaking to serve their needs as a group. Thus, from a language game perspective there are no absolute meanings. Consequently, science itself is as much scientific as linguistic and social. Dharma qua religion applies the language game of religion to a family of terms from which each word derives its meaning and out of which corresponding beliefs and attitudes emanate. In the same vein, a Dharma qua philosophy uses philosophical terminology and adheres to the rules of the language game of philosophy including the fabric of emotion and action into which it is woven. The present proposition – to view the Dharma as a psychology – applies the rules, affect, and behaviours of a language game of psychology. These words are tools helping to structure reality conceptualisations in a psychological way. Dharma as psychology tries to be the top game in town.

What is the practical implication of this exposition? If we agree on the proposition that a language game of psychology is the most apt to serve 21st century secular people, then it is imperative that we transform the religious and metaphysical idioms of the Dharma which hamper its development as a psychology. However, *this is not to silence religious or metaphysical interpretations or to declare that psychology or Relational Buddhism is superior but to celebrate the creative construction of a new Upaya of the Dharma.* It is arduous to unlearn the religious and metaphysical meanings of the Buddhist vocabulary, to adopt instead psychological meanings, and to learn a new stock of terms. Conforming to to a set of rules in a Wittgensteinian language game, Buddhist psychologists might want to acquire fresh interpretations of at least 13 key words and concepts (the list is not exhaustive): (1) Dharma, (2) *4-Ennobling Realities*, (3) *8-Fold Balancing Practice*, (4) Duhkha, (5) Nirvana, (6) Karma, (7) *5-Skandhas*, (8) Mara, (9) Sati, (10) Bodhi, (11) Arahant, (12) Bhikkhu, and (13) Ethics. In line with the Buddha's admonition not to cling to concepts and views (Soorakkulame, see Ch.6), the following is like a raft to be set aside when arrived at the other shore.

(1) The Dharma is a term for which there is no western equivalent. It is not a religion of worshipping rituals or a faith referring to the supernatural or the sacrosanct. Nor is it exactly a philosophy, a belief system theorizing about metaphysics, ontology, epistemology, logic, ethics, politics, or aesthetics. The 19th century western fabrication Buddh-*ism* has no Pali or Sanskrit equivalents. When curious colonial scholars tried to catch the meaning of the Dharma, they looked for a convenient category within their own language game for the alien soteriology. Moulding the Dharma in the unfortunate Eurocentric container term Buddhism, to the detriment of emptiness and of a life rooted in meditation, the implied referent of this -ism carries religious and metaphysical overtones. Thus, a continued use of this word, unless as a container term, like in Relational Buddhism, would lead to misguided western semantics. Furthermore, Dharma with a capital D must be differentiated from *dharma* with a lower case *d*, typed in italics to denote the smallest unit of experience: "perceivables" and "knowables", including memories, dreams, illusions, and delusions. These *dharmas* are social constructions manifesting in a protean versatility, changeable in form and content.

(2) The *4-Ennobling Realities*, instead of the Four Noble Truths. Truth is a word which carries with it the smell of blind faith while the Dharma breathes the spirit of free inquiry. The Pali word *sacca* from which the noun is derived might indeed mean reality. Depending on context, other alternatives for Truths are also possible: inquiries, examinations, quests, hypotheses, postulates, propositions, experiences, data, or facts. Furthermore, in place of the usual adjective noble, the gerund ennobling is preferred. One will not become a duke or count by practicing the Dharma. Rather, one might become liberated by daring to traverse an inner process of courageously facing adversities by walking the Dharma talk to cease the discontentment and suffering of life. The Dharma as a psychology might correctly refer to verifiable or falsifiable experiencing and more satisfying new practices centred round these four issues: Is there existential suffering? Which are the causal factors? Is there a way out? Is the *8-Fold Balancing Practice* effective?

(3) The *8-Fold Balancing Practice* is a Middle Way referring to a balancing act in the process to end suffering. Thus, the qualifier "balanced" to denote the entwined eight practices of the path (views, intentions, speech, action, livelihood, effort, awareness, and attention), is preferred above the qualifier "right". A psychological perspective of the Dharma refers to guiding and counseling people toward awakening to emptiness while journeying the path. Obviously, right means correct, not wrong. Because this is a dualistic and lopsided term, "balanced" is the preferred mentality while travelling the Middle Way as the Dharma was called by the Buddha. Balanced reflects a relativistic spirit of equanimity. Sin is anathema in Buddhist Psychology, because there is no absolute wrong or a hell to go to in the beyond and because morality is from a Gergenian social constructional perspective a "non-foundational morality of collaborative practice", a process taking place not so much in the head but in relationships. Neither Buddhist Psychology nor Social Construction is a-moral or nihilistic. Both credit moral activism (Kwee, see Ch.23) and both question claims to transcendental moral foundation.

(4) Duhkha has been translated as suffering which is a loose but not per se an incorrect translation. Arising from non-satisfaction or discontentment particularly in interpersonal relationships, Duhkha is omnipresent, inherent in existence itself, and is not a religious punishment

or sacrifice. It is caused by the impermanence of life – human beings' given condition of death, birth, aging, illness, and of not getting that which one craves mostly from others. Life is imperfect, full of gnawing imbalances to be endured, and is therefore a "dis-ease" process. Imperfection gives rise to unsteadiness, uneasiness, and disquietude regarding what the next moment will bring. While the agony of human fate is unavoidable, inner freedom, that is liberation from suffering due to gnawing mental imbalances, is possible. The result of not being liberated is being stuck in a state of affliction, anger, angst, anguish, anxiety, aversion, discomfort, despair, fear, frustration, grief, lamentation, misery, pain, sadness, sorrow, or stress. Duhkha is likely to perpetuate and augment itself and become cyclical (Samsara), with the recurrence or "rebirths" of such affective episodes. Daily life does not spin around smoothly when adversity is met. Even if joyous and happy, there remains an uncertainty as regards to what the next moment will bring.

(5) Nirvana (from *nir* [un] and *vana* [binding]) is not a paradise in the beyond, but is a state or trait of mental coolness breaking the cycle of Samsara. Nirvana is a temporary state when hot arousal states re-arise and a trait if it is long lasting and relatively enduring. Nirvana is the logical result of the extinction of the *3-Poisons*: *ignorance*-craving and its cognitive/affective/emotive-behavioural-interpersonal ramifications of *greed*-grasping, and *hatred*-clinging. While greed inheres in anxiety (fear of shortage) and sadness (grief of loss), hatred inheres in anger (other-blame) and depression (self-blame). Nirvana may also refer to smiling contentment and silent emptiness as unwholesome affect extinguishes. Happiness is an epiphenomenon while on the path and is necessarily *chaironic*, i.e. occurring amidst adversity (Kwee, 2010a). Nirvana is not a paradise in the afterlife like paradise is in the Abrahamic religions of the early translators (Tilakaratne, see Ch.10).

(6) Karma is meaningful intention, manifest in conjunction with imagery, cognition, affect/emotion, generated in interaction and expressed in relational performance. There is confusion with the Brahmanistic Karma as an account of good and bad deeds, and the Abrahamic interpretations as fate, punishment, and reward. A didactic anecdote clarifies the Buddhist view. In 521 Bodhidharma visited the emperor Wu, a great patron of the Dharma. Having built many priories, he asked what merit his generosity had earned. "No merit," was the answer. Astonished, he asked what the Dharma's supreme essence is. "Vast emptiness, nothing holy", was the reply. Finally, he asked, "Who are you?" "Don't know" said Bodhidharma referring to not-self. However, emptiness is not the end. We live in a "multiverse" of meaning emerging from shared culture and personal histories, and are able to abandon dysfunctional lives by creating alternatives together. Our understanding of the world is intricately related to interaction and we act as a function of what we regard to be true, real, savvy, and wise. These valuations are engendered in relationship, a *conditio sine qua non* for meaning without which Buddhists would have little worth doing in the world. Paraphrasing Gergen (2009), worlds of meaning may be different and conflicting but when they intersect creative possibilities may occur, new ways of relating and new outcomes. By caring for relationships the alienating, aggressive, and destructive potentials of conflict can be reduced or transformed. The Buddhist proposition to care for relationships is a down-to-earth understanding of Karma and does not constitute beliefs: thus, it is neither true nor false but a liberating life approach. New meaning requires Karma-transforming collaborative practitioners.

(7) The *5-Skandhas* usually translated as aggregates or heaps refer to the BASIC modalities. These are: Behaviour (*rupa*, bodily), Affect (*samskara*, motivational), Sensation (*vedana*,

perceptual), Imagery/Cognition (*samjna*, conceptual) and consciousness/awareness (*vijnana*, mindful). These psychological modalities move in a flux of Dependent Origination in conjunction with biological processes and in interpersonal contexts. They constitute the provisional self and are subject to habits of clinging and attachment. On the ultimate level, this I-me-mine/self is empty which is obvious when its nature as a reified abstraction is understood. The BASIC emptiness implies that there is no ghost in the machine and no soul to identify with implying no reincarnation leaving only daily cyclical rebirths of emotional episodes. The Skandhas are known as the Buddhist "all and everything" which is a testimony of the fact that the Dharma is a down-to-earth psychology of not-self. In the West, only the socially constructed dialogical-narrative self is compatible with the Buddhist non-foundational self. This self is a linguistically constructed concept merely existing in dialogical relationships and is thus empty. Based on the key premise that knowledge and language are communal-relational and generative-transformative, emptiness is ubiquitous.

(8) Discarding literal exegesis, the demon Mara and the various realms are viewed as mental projections of inner states and relational stances. Mara stands for four inner foes of awakening (the fear of death, the illusions of self/soul, the delusions of god and celestial beings, and the "Six Realms") which the Buddha has overcome. From a psychological perspective, not only is Mara not interpreted as a tempting demon seducing the Buddha, the realms are not interpreted as other-worldly beings or tangible places either. Thus, "gods" is a metaphor for bliss-pride, "demi-gods" for envy-struggle, "animals" for greed-ignorance, "hell" for hate-anger, "hungry ghosts" for craving-grasping, and "humans" for doubting-clinging on the one hand and awakening-Nirvana on the other hand.

(9) *Sati* or mindfulness takes on both a narrow meaning – to be attentive, concentrative, and alert – and a generic meaning including a combination of attention (*sati*), awareness (*sampajanna*)[4], concentration (*jhana*), and vigilance (*appamada*) (*Appamada Sutta*). In keeping with the Pali canon, the latter concept is also to be found in the Buddha's very last words *appamadena sampadetha* meaning strive on with mindfulness or rather with mindful discernment for what is wholesome (not defiled by the *3Poisons*, i.e. the Brahmaviharas). Western interpretations of mindfulness emphasize a non-judgmental attitude producing a lopsided/non-Buddhist explanation by explicitly and purposefully excluding an inherent aspect of vigilant introspection of the un/wholesomeness of meaningful intentional action (Karma) and its ramifications (*vipaka*). Non-Buddhist practices of mindfulness are not meant nor designed to lead to the quintessential insight of Dependent Origination which is at the heart of the Dharma. For the Buddhist practitioner this insight is a *conditio sine qua non* holding the remedy for Duhkha (Myint, see Ch.17).

(10) The term *bodhi* means awakening, i.e. not being asleep. However, it is usually translated as "enlightenment" which is a Eurocentric term laden with misunderstandings relating to the 18th century western "Age of Enlightenment" marking the start of a modernism, character-

---

4. *Sampajanna* might mean the awareness, comprehension, understanding, knowing, or discrimination of impermanence.

ized by an adamant belief in the light of reason and in timeless truths. Modernism upholds the Cartesian idea of supremacy of positivist science. In contrast, *bodhi* stems from the root *budh* meaning "to be wakeful and aware of" and consequently to be neither illusioned by the concept of self, nor deluded by the concept of god. The Dharma may illuminate, elucidate, or indeed "enlighten" with knowledge and heartfelt understanding. The potential for *bodhi* inheres in everyone and simply needs to be uncovered like in a smelting process separating gold from ore.

(11) An Arahant is someone who has overcome her/his "inner enemies" and thus awakened to understand the in-depth meaning of the Dharma. Having fathomed the why and how of non-selfness s/he is able and capable to compassionately help others ceasing Duhkha. The Arahant is sometimes erroneously equalled to a saint resembling someone who has been called to holiness.

(12) A Bhikshu or Bhikshuni is not like a Christian monk or nun. They "earn" a living by begging so that they can spend their life memorizing sutras, studying, and meditating. By making a lifetime effort to read scriptures and to disseminate the Dharma to the next generation, they are self-appointed students or self-proclaimed experts. Fostering a spirit of free inquiry, Buddhist adherents do not acknowledge the absolute authority of anyone; they rely on their own experience while in a process of liberation.

(13) We need to be skeptical about the term *Buddhist ethics* as ethics is a term derived from western philosophy, referring to a system of moral principles and rules. Not rule-bound, the Buddhist morality is without ethics (Keown, 2005). This concurs with the social constructivist "non-foundational morality of collaborative practice". Buddhist and social constructivist practices re-conceptualize ethics as based in differing interpersonal values and motivation, and variegated communal conduct. There is no morality without relationship; therefore the focus is on the relational process itself in reflective negotiation and transformational dialogue. This notion is exemplified in allegories of the *Jataka stories* where the Buddha allegedly lied and killed in his "previous lives". Obviously, Robin Hood's morality is different from the sheriff's. However, not evading karmic responsibility, Buddhists avoid the relational non-virtues of Body (killing, stealing, misconduct), Speech (lying, divisive/harsh/idle talk), and Mind (envy, harmful intent, erroneous views) while embracing the interpersonal performances of generosity, virtue, renunciation, insight, effort, forbearance, honesty, resolution, kindness, and equanimity. Going beyond absolutism/relativism, this understanding offers a morality continuum ranging from a rigid to a tolerant sense of right. Even within one community there are multiple voices of what is acceptable; various relationships generate different moralities. The Buddhist moral stand is pragmatic and practical by submitting that a morality claiming to be Transcendental Truth is inimical to human well-being. Thus, Buddhist Psychology is not a set of rules. Contrary to an absolutist system of "dos and don'ts", the Buddha prioritized free inquiry above all else.

A non-religious/non-metaphysical Dharma

In trying to grasp the Dharma, the European interpreters of two centuries ago forced it into western and Abrahamic conceptual casts and moulds. Their colonial assumptions produced interpretations that rest on infirm foundations and meanings twisted or lost in translation. Lingering on in written texts, these inferences, inconsistencies, and falsehoods persist to this day. Most strikingly, and mentioned earlier, despite the fact – and perhaps because of the fact – that "Buddhism" knows no equivalent, the Dharma is still viewed as an "-*ism*" with all its ramifications. The preconception to view the Dharma as a kind of sky-god devotional religion of self-surrender seems to be a common prejudice causing cognitive dissonance in people who have heard that the Dharma is about inner growth. However, due to Upaya the Dharma is remarkably resilient. It can, as a teaching of emptiness, be a kind of religion without a god, a non-theistic religion as some call it, but can also be a philosophy of self-development and a psychological quest of self-discovery. The Dharma can indeed be all of these co-existing practices of inner freedom.

The confusing suggestion that the "down-to-earth" Buddha is a being hovering in the sky was imposed by Mahayanists, revered by the present author as this is the tradition he stems from. For more than two millennia Mahayana Buddhism taught that about Buddhas as celestial beings, an unfortunate development that led many to believe that the Dharma is a worshipping religion. Flirtation with religion to lure the masses was a great Upaya trick which was at one point in time functional for reanimating an anaemic Dharma. To be tricky was sanctioned if warranted by the person's karmic intentions and wholesome motivations. For instance, just like a father who lures his kids out of a burning house with toys and sweets in order to rescue them, the *Lotus Sutra* allows the lie in order to liberate people. Thus, a vehicle sustaining an inflated cosmology and an airy pantheon as a glimpse of the beyond in order to seduce and attract the devout, the meek, and the illiterate into a basically empty Dharma was sanctioned by Mahayana, Vajrayana, and Tantrayana. By incorporating atavistic beliefs in oracles, magic, and reincarnation, the Dharma – while contending a ubiquitous and pervasive emptiness – finds itself in the treacherous situation of being trapped as a religious-metaphysical-cosmological doctrine, a doctrine which may have outlived its usefulness in secular milieus of the 21st century. Although this cosmology might satisfy some westerners' curiosity for exoticism, there is no compelling reason to believe in any medieval superstitious system other than for its poetic beauty. I am referring to the cosmic language game wherein the universe is played as a fivefold mnemonic; a sample of topics and themes is depicted in Table 3.

Endorsed in the Mahayana-Yogacara and Vajrayana/Tantrayana, these traditions revere five heavenly Buddhas (Buddhanatures) surrounded by five heavenly Bodhisattvas (Buddhas-to-be), metaphors for psychological traits strived at. To speak of a Buddhawomb giving birth to Buddhanature, pervading all sentient beings, and of Buddha-bodies, ubiquitous in the universe, and so on, is no doubt mythology. As an explaining vehicle it contains meaningful stories with an infinite beauty not to be literally believed. As long as one is able to unveil the cosmological myth as an empty fiction, dare to discard a divine house of cards, and dissolve it back into Sunyata, there is hope to only use it as a raft to put away when on the other shore. The concern is that people will not see the forest for the trees and impute delusive inherent existences to it and get lost in the thicket. Such airy and insubstantial ideas have gone far beyond the notion of the Buddha as a refuge and as an ordinary and fallible mortal man who taught about a down-to-earth awakening attainable by everyone and unambiguously rejected metaphysics. In the Buddhist lore it is said that it is impossible to say whether a Buddha does exist or does not exist after death, both does and does not exist after death, or neither exists nor does not exist after death. Religion and metaphysics are incompatible with a Dharma as a psychology of emptiness.

Table 3.
Mahayana Cosmology of Divinity against a Backdrop of Emptiness

Buddhanature Meaning:	Vairocana Illuminating	Akshobhya Imperturbable	Ratnasambhava Jewel-born	Amitabha Infinite Light	Amoghasiddhi Invincible
Family name:	Dharma	Vajra	Ratna	Padma	Karma
Colour:	White	Blue	Yellow	Red	Green
Location:	Centre	East	South	West	North
Element:	Void	Water	Earth	Fire	Wind
Mantra:	Om	Hum	Tram	Hrih	Aah
Posture:	Teaching	Grounding	Giving	Meditating	Fearing not
Symbol:	Chakra	Thunderbolt	Gem	Lotus	Action
Aggregate:	Vijnana	Rupa	Vedana	Samjna	Samskara
Modality:	Cs-Awareness	Body/Form	Sense feeling	Imagery/ Cognition	Affect/Behaviour
Consciousness:	Buddha Cs	Memory Cs	Self Cs	6th Sense Cs	5 Senses Cs
Awareness:	Emptying	Mirroring	Harmonising	Discriminating	Accomplishing
Affliction:	Ignorance	Hatred	Pride	Greed	Envy
Realm:	Animals	Hell-beings	Gods	Hungry ghosts	Demi-gods
Bodhisattva:	Samantabhadra	Vajrapani	Ratnapani	Avalokiteshvara	Visvapani
Interbeing:	Loving Kindness	Joy	Equanimity	Compassion	Friendliness
Transportation:	Lion	Elephant	Horse	Peacock	Garuda
Spouse:	Vajradhatvisvari	Locana	Mamaki	Pandara	Syamatara

Fostering a trend separating people rather than connecting them, religions seem to be a pre-modern remnant of tribalism foisted upon a postmodern global village. Granted, Buddhist psychology is – like religion and metaphysics – a pigeon hole as well, but it is one that is more palatable to the West. It is also, in my humble opinion, a psychology that has the intrinsic capacity to be a transcultural bridge to eventually connect people through kindness, compassion, and joy, when practiced experientially as meditation in daily action. Reinventing the Dharma as a psychology frees it from many sky-god images and cultural rituals which function as mystifying impediments. Respecting traditions but moving beyond them, a call is made for a Neoyana of Relational Buddhism – a new vehicle for the Dharma in a new era – defined as a social constructivist social-clinical-neuro-psychology of Body/Speech/Mind which could be called an applied, evidence-based, and integrated New Buddhist Psychology. Much work is still to be done to equip Buddhist Psychology to adequately serve secular people in the 21st century. The hope is that many societies across various cultures may profit from this revamp which is not to be absolutely believed in as *the* Truth, but to be looked at as another provisional stage in the continuing quest to end Duhkha.

Part I

The Buddha's Pursuit: Alleviating Existential Suffering

Chapter 2 by Guang Xing presents a psychological portrait of the Buddha, not as a godhead, but as a fallible human being whose primary pursuit was to alleviate experiential suffering in daily life. His account covers the Buddha's attitudes (relational stances) which dismiss personal divinity, cult, dogma, magic, blind faith, and the Buddha's personality traits (habitual relational proclivities) of practicality, confidence, tolerance, indignation, and humour. It seems that the Buddha has a genius for identifying the essence of postmodern Social Construction by pointing at the Dharma as linguistically constructed (by supporting its dissemination in local languages which might include the language of psychology), as community developed (by adjusting the rules of the commune life in the Sangha), and as a practice that appreciates free inquiry, deconstructs "Transcendental Truth", and reconstructs relationships (by kindness, compassion, and joy). Although the Buddha urged us to look inside individual heads behind the eyeballs and in-between the ears, he enlightened us at the same time that the world can only become a better place if we focus on our often unnoticed karmic interactive and joint-action with others. By inspiring us to learn for ourselves that the mind comes about in Dependent Origination, the Buddha conceptualized the mind as a social construct rather than as a solipsistic entity.

In Chapter 3 Kalupahana lays the foundations for a Buddhist philosophical psychology by examining three most relevant Buddhist psychological concepts: thought, mind, and consciousness. Regretfully, these concepts have been misinterpreted in the past as synonyms by some Buddhist scholars who are not psychologists by education. A psychological interpretation of the Buddha's discourses indicates that these words in fact have three different meanings. The reader is reminded that one of the sources of confusion is the vocabulary meaning attributed to "mind". Whereas in the western psychology the mind equals psyche, in the Dharma, i.e. Buddhist Psychology, the mind not only refers to people's "hearts" but might also mean a sixth sense. This is not something mysterious, but refers to an organic function with the subtle capacity to sense and perceive the palpable phenomena of one's idiosyncratic internal-Body/Speech/Mind-world. Like the other sense organs and their functions (eyes/seeing, ears/hearing, nose/smelling, mouth/tasting, and skin/touching), the Buddhist sixth sense is most probably also a "tangible" sense organ, i.e. brain circuitries, and this sense organ is able to internally see, view, notice, attend, observe, watch, and witness, and could therefore be called the "mind's eye".

In Chapter 4, Padmal de Silva - to whose memory this anthology is warmly dedicated – builds further on these foundations by pioneering the connection between the early Buddhist teachings of the Theravada and Cognitive-Behaviour Therapy (CBT). In a selective account, the author explores the potential value and some major aspects of the "old" Buddhist Psychology derived from the Theravada teachings of the elders for the practice and theory of cognitive-behavioural therapy. Particularly, he discusses some additional key psychological concepts of the Buddhist teachings in the areas of motivation (i.e., human cravings), perception, and cognition, and focuses on some Buddhist meditative practices as well as on other strategies that are relevant to behaviour change, prevention, and positive mental health

Chapter 2

The Historical Buddha: A Psychological Analysis

Guang Xing

Introduction

Generally speaking, ancient Indian people were a mystic people insofar as they sought by contemplation and self-surrender to obtain unity or identity with the Deity Mahabrahma (Great Brahma) or the absolute or the ultimate reality beyond human intellect and understanding. But Gautama Siddhartha, the historical Buddha, was quite different from them. He was more practical and was concerned only with the things that were conducive to the elimination of human suffering. He did not believe in the very existence of a supreme god. In this way he was quite similar to Confucius, who replied when Chi Lu, his student, asked him about death: "While you do not know life, how can you know about death?" As Smith pointed out, the Buddha probably did not belong to the Aryan but belonged instead to the Mongolian race.[1] He argues that pre-Brahmanic Nepal was inhabited by hill-men, like by the Gurka nowadays, who are of the Mongolian race by birth and presented a rough race-map of the area around the Buddha's birth place, Lumbini. There were discussions about this topic at the dawn of Buddhist Studies, but definite conclusions were never reached. It has been stated that there are some points in the Buddhist canonical texts which support the idea that the Buddha was non-Aryan. Further research is warranted to determine distinct proofs of the accuracy of this hypothesis.

Many scholars express their admiration and reverence towards Gautama the Buddha in their writings, agreeing that he was one of the greatest personages in the whole of human history. The intuitive wisdom in his message to mankind stands the test of time. Just as Foucher said,

> …nearly twenty five hundred years after his death his memory is still very much alive. Apparently as long as world suffering is to last – and it will last as long as the world – the memory of the great doctor of the soul whose life was spent in trying to find its cure will persist as a shining light on the horizon.[2]

---

1.   V.A. Smith, 1958, 47.
2.   A Foucher, 1964, 243.

Rhys Davids also rightly observed that the Early Dhamma is so original that they are far beyond the capacity of the early Buddhists, and it is very probable that before the end of his long career Gautama himself had completely worked out and enunciated them.[3] When one reads the Buddhist scripture one will not fail to notice that "the suttas are full of his inventiveness."[4] In this chapter, I will analyse the personality of the historical Buddha by using the Pali Nikayas and Vinaya as well as the Chinese translation of the Agamas and Vinayas of different schools as Buddhist scholars all over the world agree that these are the earliest Buddhist literature and probably contain the real words of the its founder.

The Buddha's attitude of mind

(1) The Buddha rejected all forms of divine power and claimed no divinity whatsoever.
As the well-known Buddhist scholar Rahula points out, all the founders of religions claimed some kind of divinity either as a god or his incarnations in different forms, or inspired by him, or his messengers.[5] The Buddha was the only teacher who claimed no inspiration in any form from any outside power or agent. By attributing all his achievements to human endeavour and intelligence, he is rather a founder of a psychology of not-self rather than of a religion. Therefore, he did not promise anybody salvation by simply believing in him. On the contrary, he advised his disciples to work out their emancipation through their own effort because he recognised the will power of the individual. Furthermore, the Buddha rejected all forms of divine power and declared that purity and impurity depend on oneself, and no one can purify another.[6] In addition, he even did not claim that he knew everything.

Concerning the Buddha's attainments and achievements, there are two suttas in the canon: Ariyapariyesana and Mahasaccaka, which relate the Buddha's exertion in the search for awakening.[7] In the description of his searching for the truth, Gautama Buddha first learned and practised meditation under the guidance of two teachers, Alarakarama and Uddaka Ramaputta. However, he could not find the solution to existential problems in their teachings and meditation. Then he practised extreme austerities to such an extent that he was on the verge of death. But he still could not achieve his aim. He then recalled an experience of meditation which he had during his childhood. After abandoning austerities, he went his own way and practised meditation under the bodhi-tree and finally attained Buddhahood through his *own* effort. In this description there is no mention of any supreme being such as god or a holy spirit who helped or revealed or even inspired him to reach his Dharma on human life, when he resolutely sat at the foot of the bodhi tree. But by his personal effort and intuition, Gautama Buddha attained realization.

---

3. T.W. Rhys Davids, 1881, 150.
4. R.F. Gombrich, 1996, 65.
5. W. Rahula, 1990, 1.
6. Dhammapada, verse No. 165.
7. No. 26, *Ariyapariyesana Sutta* and No. 36, *Mahasaccaka Sutta* of the Majjhima Nikaya. The counterpart of the *Ariyapariyesana Sutta* is also found in the Chinese translation of the Madhyamagama, No. 204 sutra, CBETA, T01, No. 26, 775c4-778c8.

Some people may argue that the Buddha won his awakening only after the fight of Mara, the demon, which might relate to some kind of mystic. However, Mara in the early Buddhist literature represents the defilements which include the worldly attractions and the evil thoughts in human mind such as discontent, hunger, thirst and craving, and so on. There is nothing mysterious in this. The *Padhana Sutta* of the Suttanipata relates the striving of the Buddha for awakening under a bodhi tree and his fighting with Mara.[8] The sutta state,

> Sensual pleasures are your first army; discontent is called your second; your third is hunger and thirst; the fourth is called craving. Sloth and torpor are your fifth; the sixth is called fear; your seventh is doubt; hypocrisy and obstinacy are your eighth.

Thus, what the Buddha fought against are the human weaknesses and nothing mysterious. In this description of his fight no external supernatural power is involved.

With reference to a passage in the Anguttara Nikaya, some scholars argue that Gautama Buddha denied even being a human.[9] But in the same passage we find that it is because he destroyed all defilements (*asava*), the cause and root for rebirth as a human being, a Deva (god), a Gandharva (celestial being), and a Yaksa (demon), that he declared he was not a human but a Buddha. He proclaimed that he was born in the world, grew up in the world, having overcome the world, he abided in the world unsoiled by it. So spiritually, he transcended the world in which the five kinds of beings are found. This transcendence is purely a mental state, not a physical state of being, and it is precisely due to such spiritual experience and attainments that Gautama Buddha was greater than and above the ordinary worldly human beings. But this does not mean that he was away from and above this empirical world. On the contrary, he was born, grew up, lived and taught in the world as all other human beings do, but he was not afflicted by the worldly passions.

Since Gautama Buddha attained awakening through human effort, he did not promise salvation from suffering and sorrow as a reward of simply believing in him. Hence he rejected all forms of a divine power and recognized only the will power of individuals. Therefore, the Buddhist literature argues against the creation of the world and human by a god. The Jataka says, "If god designs the life of the entire world – the glory and the misery, the good and the evil acts – man is but an instrument of his will and god (alone is responsible)."[10] Another argument is based on the existence of evil, "If Brahma is the lord of the whole world and creator of the multitude of beings, then why has he ordained misfortune in the world without making the whole world happy, for what purpose has he made the world full of injustice,

---

8.   K.R. Norman, 2001, 51-53.
9.   A ii, 36-38. A Brahmin asked the Buddha whether he was a *Deva*, a *Gandhabba*, a *Yakkha*, or a human being, the Buddha denied all and said because he destroyed, uprooted the *asavas* which is the cause for the birth as those beings, therefore he said, "As a lotus, fair and lovely, by the water is not soiled, by the world am I not soiled; therefore, Brahmin, I am a Buddha."
10. Jataka, V. 238.

deceit, falsehood, and conceit, or the lord of beings is evil in that he ordained injustice when there could have been justice."[11] As the Buddha totally rejected almighty power, he often compared himself to a physician and his teaching to medicine.[12] Even taking refuge in the Buddha is only to declare that one becomes his student, it does not guarantee salvation or spiritual attainment. So when Ganaka Moggallana asked the Buddha whether all those who had been instructed by him attained their goal, the Buddha replied that among his students those who practised diligently would attain Nirvana, the ultimate goal, while those who did not follow the instruction would not, because Tathagatas only shows the way.[13] Therefore even lying on his deathbed, the Buddha admonished his students to rely on the Dharma and to rely on themselves not anyone else. They should make their own effort and work out their own emancipation.[14] The path to liberation prescribed by Gautama Buddha is the eight-fold path, a path which is simple and practical, is acceptable in every civilized society as a description of good life.[15] Nothing mysterious or ceremonious is involved in it. On the contrary, will power and activity of the individual are emphasized. The individual is the captain of his own destiny, responsible for all he has done. The Buddha is only a torch bearer to humanity.

Unlike the other teachers of his day such as Nigantha Nataputta, the founder of Jainism, who claimed omniscience, the Buddha did not make such claim at all. In the *Tevijjavacchagotta Sutta*, the *sramana* (ascetic) Vacchagotta approached the Buddha and wished to clarify the report of his omniscience. The Buddha categorically said,

> Vaccha, those who say thus do not say what has been said by me, but misrepresent me with what is untrue and contrary to fact.[16]

The teaching is based on his own experience. This point will be resumed later.

(2) The Buddha, led by virtue and example, did not foster a personality cult.

Although the Buddha was considered a leader by the Sangha, the community of Bhikkhus, full-time Dharma scholars, and all other students came to him for solutions whenever they met any kind of problem in their life and practice, he did not encourage them to build a kind of personal cult whatsoever around him. According to the *Mahaparinibbana Sutta*, Ananda asked the Buddha to give his final instructions moments before his death. The Buddha said,

> Whosoever may think that it is he who should lead the community of

---

11. Jataka, VI. 208.
12. M ii, 260. T2, 105a-b. Here Gautama Buddha compared himself to a physician and the first noble truth of suffering as sickness, second noble truth as the cause of the sickness, the third noble truth as the release from suffering and the fourth noble truth as the prescription.
13. M iii, 6; T1, 652c; Dhammapada, verse No. 276, "You yourself should make the effort; the Awakened Ones are only teachers. Those who enter this Path and who are meditative, are delivered from the bonds of Mara."
14. D ii, 100-101.
15. Sir Charles Eliot, *Hinduism and Buddhism*, part I, 145.
16. Bhikkhu Nanamoli, 587-8.

Bhikkhus, or that the community depends upon him, it is such a one that would have to give last instructions respecting them. But, Ananda, the Tathagata has no such idea as that it is he who should lead the community of Bhikkhus, or that the community depends upon him. So what instructions should he have to give respecting the community of Bhikkhus?[17]

Then the Buddha advised Ananda,

Therefore, Ananda, be islands unto yourselves, refuges unto yourselves, seeking no external refuge; with the Dhamma as your island, the Dhamma as your refuge, seeking no other refuge.[18]

At another occasion, the Buddha gave similar advice to Bhikkhus when they thought that they were going to loose their teacher.

Ananda, the Dhamma and Vinaya that have been expounded by me will be your teacher after my death.[19]

Thus, before his death, the Buddha did not appoint any successor to take his role because he never even considered himself to be the leader of the Sangha. This is also reflected from the *Gopaka Moggalana Sutta* of the Majjhima Nikaya when Vassakara asked Ananda whether the Buddha appointed a successor and the latter answered in negative.[20] The Buddha was just like any of his students and other *sramanas* leading a simple life with only three robes and a bowl, nothing else while he was alive. Therefore, those who were never introduced to the Buddha could not recognize him when they met for the first time. Pukkusati was just such a person. When he met the Buddha for the first time, he recognized him only after a long conversation.[21] The park keeper for Anuruddha and other two students of the Buddha also could not recognize him and asked him not to enter the park.[22] All these incidents suggest that the Buddha enjoyed no privileges in any form at all, but was a simple person living a simple life.[23]

---

17. D ii, 100. This passage is also found in the three Chinese translations of the *Mahaparinirvana Sutra*: T1, No. 1, 15a; No. 5, 164c9-13; No. 6, 180a18-b2. So it must have come down from a common tradition shared all early Buddhist schools in India.

18. Ibid.

19. D ii. 154. This passage is found in four Chinese translations of the *Mahaparinirvana Sutra*: T1, No. 1, 26a; No. 5, 172b; No. 6, 188a; No. 7, 204b-c. So it also must have come down from a common tradition shared by all schools.

20. M iii. 9. The counterpart of this sutta is also found in the Chinese translation of the Madhyamagama and the same question and answer are also there. CBETA, T01, No. 26, p. 654, a19-25.

21. M iii. 238-247.

22. M i. 205-6.

23. Although sometimes some suttas say that the Buddha travelled with a large multitude, this would be strange because it was quite difficult to get alms food for all. Most probably, the Buddha travelled with only a few students.

Next, the Buddha considered neither himself as the leader of the Sangha, nor his teaching as the only "truth". That is why the Buddhist scripture has grown more and more since the Buddha's death. The Buddha considered that attachment to any view is a kind of bondage, an obstacle to right understanding. So when the Buddha explained the teaching of cause and effect to his students, they said that they saw it and understood it clearly. The Buddha advised them,

> O Bhikkhus, purified and bright as this view is, you should not adhere to it, cherish it, treasure it, and treat it as a possession, then you understand Dhamma that has been taught [by me] as similar to a raft, being for purpose of crossing over, not for the purpose of grasping.[24]

The same idea concerning his teaching is also expressed in another sutta,

> You, Bhikkhus, who understand that the teaching is similar to a raft, should give up even the [virtuous] things [dhamma]; how much more then should you give up [vicious] things [adhamma].[25]

This very idea is taken up by the Mahayanists as the emptiness of Dharma, one of the important teachings taught in the Mahayana sutras such as the Diamond and Lotus, etc.

This attitude towards the teaching of the Buddha is also reflected in Vasumitra's treatise on the origin and doctrine of early Indian Buddhist schools. The Sarvastivada school proclaimed, "Not all the speeches of the Tathagata can be regarded as the preaching of the righteous law... The World-Honoured One also utters words which are not in conformity with the truth... The sutras delivered by the Buddha are not all perfect in themselves. The Buddha himself said that there were certain imperfect scriptures."[26] Although here the ideas are not exactly the same as above, but the analytical attitude is the same. So in a word, the Buddha did not give any room for his students and followers to think that he was either a god or some kind of supreme leader to be worshipped. The Buddha foresaw the danger of the transmission of leadership and therefore established a democratic institution so that the Buddhist community could choose their head by vote as described in the Vinaya.

(3) The Buddha had no dogmatic attitude, but was open-minded.

Most religions have some kind of rigid rules and regulations. In the Judeo-Christian tradition, the Ten Commandments are claimed to be of divine origin, as God gave them to Moses on Mount Sinai.[27] Thus, violation of these commandments results in punishment from the godhead. Similarly, the rules of the ancient law-codes of the Hindus such as those of Vasista and those in the *Acaranga Sutra* of the Jains, were imposed one after another in conjunction with

---

24. M i, 260. The translation with a few changes is adapted from Bhikkhu Nanamoli (1995) 352-3.
25. M i, 134-5.
26. Vasumitra, 52.
27. *The Bible*: Ex 20.

religious discourses. These religious laws are designed to express the divine will. However, the Buddhist Vinaya rules reveal no divine origin at all as the law maker, the Buddha himself, was not a god. The following example of the rule concerning one meal a day shows how Vinaya rules were laid down.

> Bhikkhus, I eat at a single session. By so doing, I am free from illness and affliction, and I enjoy health, strength, and comfortable abiding. Come, Bhikkhus, eat at a single session. By so doing, you too will be free from illness and affliction and you will enjoy health, strength, and a comfortable abiding.[28]

All the Vinaya rules were laid down gradually in such a way as occasions demanded. But the Buddha was open for suggestions and always considered any request regarding rules from members of the Sangha, and never hesitated to revise or amend the existing rules to comply with the needs, changes in time, circumstances and environment. The liberal and practical attitude of the Buddha towards the Vinaya rules as well as other matters can be seen from the following examples.

First and probably the most important is the Buddha's advice to Ananda just before he died. He told Ananda, "If it is desired, Ananda, the Sangha may, when I am gone, abolish the lesser and minor rules." This advise is quite important as it is found in both the Theravada *Mahaparinibbana Sutta* and Vinaya, the Chinese translations of the *Mahaparinirvana Sutra* of the Dirghagama, and the Vinayas of different schools such as the Mahisasaka, the Mahasanghika, the Dharmagupta, the Sarvastivada, the Mulasarvastivada Samyutavastu and even the *Vinaya Matrtka Sutra*.[29] It shows the Buddha's liberal attitude towards Vinaya and other matters, which is one of the crucial reasons that Dhamma can successfully spread from India to other parts of Asia and to the rest of the world today. Jainism also rose in India at the sixth century BCE together with the Dhamma, but the former still virtually confines itself in India. One of the main reasons is that the Jains went to the extreme in their practice of non-violence. The Buddha not only gave this advice about lesser and minor rules at his deathbed, but he was liberal on the minor rules even during his life-time. He said to the Bhikkhus,

> A Bhikkhu keeps the laws of morality in full, he is moderately given to mental concentration, moderately given to striving for insight. Whatever minor, trifling observances he may transgress, he is cleared of them. Why so? I do not declare him to be rendered unfit because of them, for he strict-

---

28. M i, 437-440. The translation is adapted from Nanamoli's translation: *The Middle Length Discourse of the Buddha.*

29. D ii, 154; Pali Vinaya Cullavagga, xi, 286. Book of Discipline, v. 398. The Chinese translations of the *Mahaparinirvana Sutra*, T1, 26a28-9 and Mahisasaka Vinaya, T22, 191b3-4; Mahasanghika Vinaya, T22, 492b4-5, c7; Dharmaguptaka Vinaya, T22, 967b11-13; Sarvastivada Vinaya, T23, 449b13-4; Mulasarvastivada Vinaya Samyutavastu, T24, 405b3-5 and *Vinaya Matrika Sutra*, T24, 818b3-4.

ly observes the rudiments of the awakened life, the constituents of the awakened life: he is established in morality, he is trained himself in the rules of training by undertaking them. Such a one, by destroying three fetters is a stream-winner, one not doomed to the down-fall, one assured, one bound for awakening.[30]

However, Devadatta, one of the Buddha's students, was not happy about his liberal attitude and asked him to make the following five propositions to be obligatory for all his Bhikkhus, the latter did not do so, but allowed those who felt so inclined to follow these rules - except that of sleeping under a tree during the rainy season. Devadatta's five propositions are that Bhikkhus, for as long as life lasts, should be forest dwellers, beg for alms, wear ragged robes, reside at the foot of a tree, and refrain from eating fish or meat.[31] As Dutt pointed out Devadatta was an advocate of a more austere discipline and these five propositions are rigid ascetic practices just like that of the Jains.[32] The Buddha was not against the five propositions as optional practices for all his students as they were common practices among the recluses at that time, but he would not make them obligatory for all Bhikkhus, and certainly not for life.[33] In other words, the Buddha rejected Devadatta's inflexible attitude to these practices, as this attitude might impose limits to the development of the Dharma and Sangha. The Buddha criticised austerities as paying too much attention to the body rather than to the mind, which really mattered, as he knew through his own experience that these ascetic practices do not lead one to liberation. Indeed such asceticism was not associated for the most part with the quest for understanding or insight as the solution to existential problems. Instead, asceticism, as Gombrich pointed out, has been more closely associated with another strand in Indian thought, the tradition that the root of all evil is too much passion, and that salvation lies in eradicating these passions and no longer having any likes and dislikes.[34]

Devadatta's followers survived at least until the late seventh century and the Chinese traveller Yijing recorded their life thus:

[The followers of Devadatta] do not have large monasteries, but dwell in villages solitarily, beg alms food and practice pure conduct. [They] use bottle gourds as bowls, have only two robes, the colour of which is similar to the dried mulberry tree leaves [brown yellow] and they do not eat curd.[35]

But there is no mention of them in any literature after Yijing. This suggests that the love of ascetic practices of Indian people provided the soil for them and hence the Buddha allowed

---

30. A I, 231. The translation is adapted from Woodward: *The Book of the Gradual Sayings,* Vol. I, 211.
31. Pali Vinaya, iii, 171; ii, 196-197; Sarvastivada Vinaya, T23, 265a13-4.
32. S. Dutt, 1945, 6-7.
33. What Devadatta proposed were common practices amongst the Sramana groups as reported in the *Mahasaccaka Sutta* of the Majjhima Nikaya. M I, 238.
34. R.F. Gombrich, (1994) 44.
35. T24, 495c. Mulasarvastivada Vinaya.

such practices as options for his students, but they were not compulsory. However, Devadatta's followers have not survived to the present day and this probably can be attributed to their dogmatic attitude to Vinaya practices.

The Buddha's liberal and open attitude to Vinaya practices can also be seen from the following example. A Bhikkhu from the Vajjiputtas came to the Buddha saying he was unable to endure to recite 250 rules fortnightly. Then the Buddha said to him, "Well Bhikkhu, can you stand the training in three particulars: That in the higher values, in the higher thought, in the higher insight?"[36] The Bhikkhu then answered affirmatively and the Buddha told him,

> Then Bhikkhu when you are proficient in the higher morality, thought and insight, then lust, malice and delusion will be abandoned by you. When you have abandoned these you will not perform any wrong deed, you will not follow any wicked way.

Second, the Buddha's language policy also reflects his liberal and open attitude. According to the *Cullavagga*, there were two Brahmin brothers who became the Buddha's students. They had a good voice and were experts in conversation and told the Buddha that Bhikkhus of various names, clans and social strata had gone forth from various families and corrupted the speeches of the Buddha by not using the Buddha's own idioms and vernaculars. They wished to translate the words of the Buddha into Sanskrit.[37] Then the Buddha rebuked them and said, "I allow you, Bhikkhus, to learn the word of the Buddha each in his own language."[38] Here "his own language" can be interpreted in two ways: in the Buddha's language or in his students' own language. But when we look at the Chinese translation of the Vinaya from different schools, it is clear that the students learn the word of the Buddha in their own dialects and languages not in the Buddha's language.[39]

Here it is quite clear that the Buddha did not want to make any language into the only sacred one and require all his students to learn it. Otherwise, this would limit the teaching of the Buddha from spreading. Just as the Vinaya Matrika Sutra says, "The Buddha told the Bhikkhus saying, 'In my teachings emphasis is not laid on rhetoric. What I mean is that the doctrines should not be misunderstood. They should be taught in any language which is understood by the people, according to their suitability.'"[40] Thus, the emphasis is not on the language but on the understanding of the teaching of the Buddha. This also reflects the practical attitude of the Buddha. Instead of a dogmatic attitude, the Buddha was quite open and accepted whatever good suggestions arose. For instance, some lay devotees suggested that Bhikkhus should

---

36. A I, 230.
37. Some scholars think that they wished to translate the words of the Buddha into Sanskrit while others think about metrical form only. This story is found in the Vinaya texts of different schools: the *Vinaya Matrika Sutra*, T24, p.822; the Dharmaguptaka Vinaya, T24, p.955; the Mahisasaka Vinaya, T22, p.174; the Sarvastivada Vinaya, T23, p.274; the Mulasarvastivada-Nikaya-Vinaya-Samyuktavastu, T24, p. 232.
38. Cullavagga, V. 33.1.
39. The *Vinaya Matrika Sutra*, T24, 822a; the Dharmagupta Vinaya, T22, 955c; the Mahisasaka Vinaya, T22, 174b; the Sarvastivada Vinaya, T23, 274a; the Mulasarvastivada Vinaya Samyutavastu, T24, 232b-c.
40. The *Vinaya Matrika Sutra*, T24, 822a15-23.

also settle down at some places for raining retreat without travelling since groups of other disciplines did so in order not to tread on insects and accidentally kill them. So the Buddha laid down a rule that Bhikkhus should settle down for retreat during raining season. Many Vinaya rules were laid down in a way as just described and had even been changed or modified several times, either due to changes in circumstances or suggestions from Bhikkhus or even from lay people.

Another example, the Buddha prohibited Bhikkhus accepting alms with their hands, departing their quarters without wearing their robes properly, spending the rainy retreat in the hollow of trees, storing unnecessary goods in their Viharas (residents), enjoying secular pleasures, and eating the flesh of elephants.[41] Similarly, the Buddha prohibited the ordination of criminals, debtors and slaves. Other amendments were made on the acceptance of silk robes, the prohibition of admitting anyone to the Sangha who suffered from one of five diseases, as requested by Jivaka Komarabhacca,[42] and the acceptance of invitations to meals as requested by Mendaka. Rules about forbidding of, Bhikkhunis', female Bhikkhus', naked bathing or bathing in the same place as courtesans were loosened at the request of Visakha Migaramata; the sanction against accepting a personal benefactor was loosened at the request of Anathapindaka. The Buddha also made rules at the request of King Bimbisara in order to comply with some of the requirements of the state; for example, warriors were not allowed to be ordained. Many rules developed on the suggestions of Bhikkhus or Bhikkhunis, such as the admission of women at Ananda's intervention, and the formation of most of the rules concerning bathing, at the request of Gotami.

The open-mindedness of the Buddha is also reflected in the way he taught his students without any reservation.[43] There is no rigidity in the Buddha's teaching and he taught all that is necessary for liberation. Therefore, whenever his students, not only those great ones like Sariputta and Moggallana, but also Bhikkhunis, delivered a good sermon he would approve it with a loving heart. Thus, when Pasenadi told the Buddha of a talk the Bhikkhuni Khema had given to the King of Kosala, the Buddha, hearing of this, said, "Even if you asked me, I would give you the same answer."[44] The Buddha's open attitude is also seen in his teaching to lay people on how to spend their wealth. He advised them to spend their wealth on making offerings to local gods and deities in addition to supporting their family, friends and making merits.[45] It is due to this open

---

41. Cited from Jing Yin's unpublished PhD dissertation *The Vinaya in India and China — Spirit and Transformation*, 2002, p.84. For a detailed discussion, please read "The Buddha and the Vinaya" in section two: The ethos of the Vinaya in Chapter two: "The Spirit of the Vinaya".

42. The five diseases are leprosy, boils/eczema, ringworm, tuberculosis, and epilepsy. The Dharmagupta Vinaya, T22, 808c2-809a8; the Sarvastivada Vinaya, T23, 152b9-c12; the Theravada Vinaya, I:72-73.

43. A i, 283. D ii, 100.

44. S iv, 374.

45. Both the *Pattakamma Sutta* (A, ii, 67-8) and the *Pancakaripada Sutta* (A, iii, 45) of the Anguttara Nikaya mention that the Buddha advised lay people to spend their wealth on the following five things: (1) support of oneself, one's family and dependents, (2) sharing with one's friends and associates, (3) investment against future misfortune, (4) making five-fold offering: a. to relatives, b. to guests (in reception), c. to the departed (by dedicating merits), d. to the government (i.e., taxes etc.), e. to the deities (according to one's faith); (5) support of spiritual teachers and virtuous Bhikkhus.

attitude that the Dharma has accepted local deities as their guardian gods wherever it is spread. For instance, the local deities in Sri Lanka, in Thailand and in China all have been accepted as important guardian gods and have been given an important place in the life of the devotee.

(4) The Buddha used educational instructions and eschewed magic and miracles.

Just as Rahula has said, many miraculous powers were attributed to the Buddha, and according to the suttas he performed a number of miracles during his ministry.[46] However, most of these miracles took place in his early life after his awakening, such as the miracle of hiding Yasa so that his father could not see him, and the series of miracles to convert the three Kasyapa brothers.[47] But the Buddha changed his attitude to miracles as he grew older and did not consider magical powers to be of primary importance. His attitude to miracles and magic can be seen from the following suttas.

First, in the *Kevaddha Sutta*, a lay student of the Buddha named Kevaddha asked him to perform miracles in order to attract people but he refused to do so. Instead, the Buddha said that there are three kinds of miracles: the mystic wonder, the wonder of thought reading and the wonder of education. Amongst the three, the Buddha liked the wonder of education most, because without resorting to any other means, education directly appeals to the listeners' mind so that the listeners are convinced through understanding not by faith. Concerning the first two kinds of wonders, the Buddha said that he did not like them,

> ...because I perceive danger in the practice of mystic wonders and the wonder of thought reading, so I loathe, and abhor, and am ashamed thereof.[48]

In order to illustrate the uselessness of mystic wonder, the Buddha told a story of one of his students who had the physical power to perform miracles. The Bhikkhu, in order to find out the answer to a question, used his magic powers by flying to different heavens and asked the heavenly beings but they could not answer his question. At last, he flew to the highest heaven and asked the Mahabrahma who took him by hand to a corner and said that the Buddha was the best person to answer such a question. So what the Buddha wanted to convey is that magic power cannot solve any problem. The Kevaddha Sutta is also found in the Chinese translation of Dirghagama with the same description of the three miracles.[49]

This attitude is also reflected in the Sangarava Sutta in which the Buddha explained the three wonders to Sangarava, a Brahmin. The Buddha tells Sangarava that the first two kinds of miracle were of the nature of illusion and the last one was more wonderful and excellent after listening to the teacher.[50] So we can see that the Buddha did not allow his students to perform

---

46. *Encyclopedia Britannica*, Gotama Buddha.
47. Vinaya Mahavagga, i, 15-34. The Book of Discipline, iv, 24-46.
48. D i, 213-4. The translation with a few changes is adapted from Rhys David, *Dialogues of the Buddha*, I, 278-9. Italics mine.
49. Sutra No. 24 of the Dirghagama.
50. A iii, 169-71.

physical miracles in order to win over followers and further that he laid down a monastic rule concerning this.

> Bhikkhus... a wonder of psychic power is not to be exhibited to household-ers. Whoever should exhibit them, there is an offence of wrong-doing.[51]

The Buddha did not equivocate on this point. He compared the display of miracles in front of the laity to a respectable woman showing her loin-cloth in the public.[52]

The *Patika Sutta* and its Chinese translation in the Dirghagama have the same description of Sunakkhatta's talk with the Buddha, and this is another text in which the miracles are discussed. It is said that Sunakkhatta, a student of the Buddha, left the Order because the Buddha did not perform miracles for him.[53] The Buddha told him that whether miracles are performed or not, the purpose of teaching the Dhamma is to lead whoever practices it to the total destruction of suffering. In other words, the performance of miracles is not relevant to the destruction of suffering. So, the Buddha did not like to do it. The Patika Sutta is also found.[54]

The *Samannaphala Sutta* identifies six modes of higher knowledge.[55] They are (1) super-natural power, (2) the divine ear, (3) penetration of the minds of others, (4) memory of former existences, (5) the divine eye, and (6) extinction of all cankers. These six modes of knowledge are in an ascending order and the knowledge of the extinction of all cankers is the highest which can be attained only by three persons: a Buddha, a Pratyekabuddha and an Arhat. The first five are mundane and the last is supramundane, thus it is only through acquiring the sixth knowledge that one becomes emancipated. The first two kinds of miracles, that of mystic wonders and that of thought reading are mentioned in the *Kevaddha Sutta*. The others belong to the first and third kinds of higher knowledge. So in other words, they are lower kinds of knowledge and can be achieved by anyone who has some kind of concentration. But it must be emphasized that one obtains liberation only by attaining the sixth knowledge. Thus, the Buddha did not like to perform miracles because first they are the nature of illusion and not relevant to liberation and second they are mundane matters. Because of his deep understanding of the nature of knowledge the Buddha used the "miracle" of education in his entire life and went from villages to towns and told the Dharma.

(5) The Buddha emphasised understanding and freedom of thought, not faith.
Rahula discussed this point so well in the first chapter of his book *What the Buddha Taught* that I will just summarize it here for the purpose of discussion. Like psychology, but unlike most religions, including some Mahayana schools, the Dharma is not built on faith. According to the early Buddhist literature, the Buddha's emphasis is laid on "seeing", knowing, and understanding. It is

---

51. Cullavagga, V. 8. The translation is adopted from The Book of Discipline, V. 152.
52. Cullavagga, V. 8; The Book of Discipline, V. 151.
53. D iii, 2-4.
54. Sutra No. 15 of the Dirghagama.
55. Sutta No. 2 of the Digha Nikaya and the sutra No. 27 of the Dirghagama.

not on faith or belief. Although in Buddhist texts there is a word *saddha* which is usually translated as faith or belief, it is not faith as such, but rather confidence born out of conviction. Therefore, in the *Vimamsaka Sutta*, the Buddha even asked his students to investigate themselves so that they might be fully convinced of the true value of the teacher and his teaching that they followed.[56] So faith or belief as understood by religions has little to do with the Dhamma.

According to the Buddha's teaching, faith, particularly blind faith, does not help one to get release from suffering and attain the highest goal, Nirvana. As the Buddha said:

> Bhikkhus, I say that the destruction of defilement and impurities is [meant] for a person who knows and who sees, and not for a person who does not know and does not see.[57]

In fact, ignorance together with craving and hatred are considered in the Dharma as the very roots of suffering. So when a student of the Buddha named Musila attained Arhatship he told another Bhikkhu:

> Friend Savittha, without devotion, faith or belief, without liking or inclination, without hearsay or tradition, without considering apparent reasons, without delight in the speculations of opinions, I know and see that the cessation of becoming is Nibbana.[58]

So the Venerable Rahula said,

> It is always a question of knowing and seeing, and not that of believing. The teaching of the Buddha is qualified as *ehi-passika*, inviting you to come and see, but not to come and believe.

The expressions used everywhere in Buddhist texts referring to persons who realized awakening are:

> The dustless and stainless Eye of Dharma has arisen... He has seen [the] Dharma, has attained [the] Dharma, has known [the] Dharma, has penetrated into [the] Dharma, has crossed over doubt, is without wavering... Thus with right wisdom he sees it as it is.[59]

The Buddha used to criticize blind faith and superstitions as they do not lead one to liberation

---

56. M i, 319-20. There is a Chinese translation of this sutta in the Madhyamagama with the same contents, but slightly different wording.
57. S iii, 152.
58. S ii, 117.
59. S v, 423; iii, 103; M iii, 19.

and to the end of suffering. When a group of Brahmins came to the Buddha and discussed the ways leading to union with Brahma, as told in the Vedas, the Buddha asked them whether their teacher or teacher's teacher back to the seventh generation versed in the three Vedas had seen the Brahma. They replied negatively. So the Buddha said that "It is just like a string of blind men clinging one to the other, the first does not see, the middle does not see and the last also does not see."[60] This metaphor clearly illustrates the Buddha's insight that blind faith leads one nowhere. And so with reference to his own awakening when he told his five students at the Deer Park, the Buddha said: "The eye was born, knowledge was born, wisdom was born, science was born, and light was born."[61] Even the Dharma taught by the Buddha is based on his experience and intuitive wisdom. As discussed in the *Brahmajala Sutta* in reference to other teachers and their philosophies based on either faith or tradition or logical inference, and so on, he said:

> These, Bhikkhus, are those other things, profound, difficult to realise, hard to understand, tranquillising, sweet, not to be grasped by mere logic, subtle, comprehensible only by the wise, which the Tathagata, having himself realised and seen face to face, has set forth; and it is concerning these that they who would rightly praise the Tathagata in accordance with the truth, should speak.[62]

Therefore, when Sunakkhata, a student who left the Buddha, was reported to have said that the latter taught a doctrine based on his power of reasoning, but not on supernatural power, the Buddha seemed quite irritated, for he used to insist on the point that his teaching was based on his own (heartfelt) experience (not just pure intellect).[63]

As Rahula pointed out, according to the Buddha, man's emancipation depends on his own realization of the Dharma and not on the benevolent grace of a god or any external power as a reward for his obedient good behaviour, so the freedom of thought and enquiry is essential.[64] Thus, the freedom of enquiry allowed by the Buddha as explained in the well known *Kalama Sutta* is unheard elsewhere in the history of meaning and values, including religious history.

> Yes Kalamas, it is proper that you have doubt, that you have perplexity, for a doubt has arisen in a matter which is doubtful. Now, look you Kalamas, do not be led by reports, or tradition, or hearsay. Be not led by the authority of religious texts, nor by mere logic or inference, nor by con-

---

60. D i, No.13 *Tevijja Sutta.*
61. S v, 422.
62. D i, 12ff. The same paragraph is repeated eight times in the sutta after the discussion of the teachings and philosophies of each group. The translation is adopted from Rhys Davids, *Dialogues of the Buddha,* i, 26.
63. M i, 68. *Mahasihanada Sutta.*
64. W. Rahula, 1990, 2.

sidering appearances, nor by the delight in speculative opinions, nor by seeming possibilities, nor by the idea: 'this is our teacher'. But, O Kalamas, when you know for yourselves that certain things are unwholesome, and wrong, and bad, then give them up... And when you know for yourselves that certain things are wholesome and good, then accept them and follow them.[65]

The Buddha advocated this principle of free enquiry throughout his life and encouraged his students to search for awakening. So in the *Canki Sutta*, the Buddha told the Brahmins how to find out bodhi.

Here, Bharadvaja, a Bhikkhu may be living in dependence on some village or town. A householder or a householder's son goes to him and investigates him in regard to three kinds of states: in regard to states based on greed, in regard to states based on hate, and in regard to states based on delusion.[66]

Even just a few minutes before his death, he requested his students several times to ask him if they had any doubts about his teaching, and not to feel sorry later that they could not clear those doubts.

The Buddha's personality

(1) The Buddha was a practical teacher
The most prominent characteristic of the Buddha is his pragmatism and it is because of this that he taught only those things useful for the elimination of human suffering and avoided addressing metaphysical issues. He did not like to discuss metaphysical questions or speculative views, as they are purely for the purpose of debate or intellectual curiosity. He in fact disregarded all forms of dogmas and did not even hold, cling or became attached to any view as reported in the *Sallekha Sutta* as the Buddha says,

...we shall not adhere to our views or hold on to them tenuously, but shall relinquish them easily. Effacement should be practiced thus.[67]

During the Buddha's life time, India experienced political stability for the first time. Before this freedom of thought and expression were unheard of. In this open political climate various philosophers and teachers appeared and disseminated their thoughts and theories regarding life and the world around them and the kings supported them in various ways like giving food, arranging debates and putting up convocation halls, and sometimes seek advice from them.

---

65. Cited from W. Rahula, 1990, 2.
66. M ii, 171-2.
67. M i, 43.

The ten well-known classical unanswered questions such as whether the universe is finite or infinite are typical examples of the content of their debate and discussion.[68] These debates usually erupted into disputes and quarrels. In the Suttanipata, one of the oldest collections of discourses, we come across many passages:

> The doctrine which some people call the highest, others call the lowest. Which of these is the true statement? For all these [people] indeed call themselves experts. They say that their own doctrine indeed is superior, but they say another's doctrine is inferior. Thus contending they dispute. They each say their own opinion is true.[69]

These metaphysical questions cannot be solved by speculation. Each teacher remained attached to her/his own opinion and view. "So having thus got into arguments, they dispute (among themselves). They say 'the other person is a fool not an expert.'"[70]

Gautama Buddha, realising the danger and vanity of such debate, did not join their discussion, because in his view, this kind of discussions does not lead one to freedom and liberation from problems of living. Therefore, the Buddha kept his council, he did not give any definite answer, and just kept silent when the wanderer Malunkyaputta put these ten classical questions to him. He answered by saying that these questions have nothing to do with the awakened life. Whatever opinion one may have regarding to these questions, there is still suffering. Then the Buddha said, "...the cessation of suffering (Nibbana) I declare is in this very life."[71] The Buddha expressed the same view when the mendicant Vacchagotta asked whether he held any speculative views.[72] The Buddha said that a speculative view was something that he had put away for he had seen this: the five aggregates, their origin and disappearance. Thus he was liberated through not clinging to any of them, because the goal of the Dhamma is not achieved by universalizing oneself, but by completely giving up the notion of self. It is just as Lamotte has pointed out: it is not because the Buddha did not know the solution, but because he considered any discussion regarding these metaphysical questions to be useless for the deliverance, dangerous to good understanding and likely to perturb minds.[73]

---

68. The ten classical questions which the Buddha never answered are (1) is the universe eternal or (2) is it not eternal, (3) is the universe finite or (4) is it infinite, (5) is soul the same as body or (6) is soul one thing and body another thing, (7) does the Tathagata exist after death, or (8) does he not exist after death, or (9) does he both (at the same time) exist and not exist, or (10) does he both (at the same time) not exist and not not-exist. D i, 187-8; M i, 157, 426, 282; S iii, 213 sq., 258; iv, 286, 391; v, 418. But in Madhyamakakarika, 22, 2., Nagarjuna gave the number as fourteen. They are as follows: (1) Whether the world is (a) eternal, (b) or not, (c) or both, (d) or neither. (2) Whether the world is (a) finite, (b) or infinite, (c) or both, (d) or neither. (3) Whether the Tathagata (a) exists after death, (b) or does not, (c) or both, (d) or neither. (4) Whether the soul is identical with the body or different from it.
69. Sn. Verse Nos. 903, 904. The translation is adopted from Norman, *The Group of Discourses*, 118.
70. Sn. Verse No. 879.
71. *Culamalunkyaputta Sutta* in M i, 426-430; T1, 804a; 917b.
72. *Aggivacchagotta Sutta*, M i, 485.
73. Lamotte, 1988, 48.

The Buddha was equally pragmatic about presenting his own teachings, confining himself to the revelation of those ideas which were relevant to the goal only. He declared that just like the ocean has one taste, the taste of salt, his teaching also has one flavour, the flavour of deliverance.[74] During the 45 years of his career as a teacher, the Buddha taught only teaching concerned with liberation, leading to Nirvana, and he often spoke with concrete examples from the life around him to elucidate his teachings. Once when the Buddha was residing in the Simsapa forest in Kosambi, he explained to his students that what he taught is like the leaves in his hand and what he had not taught is like the leaves in the forest: "And why have I not told you (all I know)? Because that is not useful... not leading to Nibbana. That is why I have not told you those things."[75]

When the Buddha was falsely accused of teaching the annihilation, the destruction, the extermination of an existing being, he explicitly stated: "Bhikkhus, both formerly and now, what I teach is suffering and the cessation of suffering."[76] So what concerned the Buddha was very practical: human suffering and its elimination, nothing more, nothing less. Again when Subhadda, the last student of the Buddha, came and asked him who among the six *sramana* teachers understood things as they claimed, the Buddha said, "Enough, Subhadda! Let this matter rest whether they, according to their own assertion, have thoroughly understood things, or whether they have not... The Dhamma, Subhadda, will I teach you. Listen well."[77] Then the Buddha went on to explain the "Eight-Fold Path" and its fruit. He did not waste time on explaining who among the six teachers were true to their assertion and who were not. This same pragmatic spirit is again showed in the *Culasakuludayi Sutta* when the wanderer Udayin asked the Buddha about the claim of omniscience made by other teachers. The Buddha told him:

> Let us put aside questions of the Beginning and the End. I will teach you
> the Dhamma: That being thus, this comes to be. From the coming to be of
> that, this arises. That being absent, this does not happen. From the cessation
> of that, this ceases.[78]

So here the Buddha was interested only in how things operate, how they work, not how things begin or the ultimate beginning of things which is obviously impossible to know.

In the early fundamental teaching of the Buddha, the "Four Noble Truths" which are concerned with the existence of human suffering, the third noble proposition, which is technically called Nirvana, is about the elimination of craving, hatred and ignorance (illusion/delusion). In other words, from the experiential point of view, Nirvana is the highest happiness and thus it can be attained in this life itself. So even if there were no "rebirths", Nirvana is still mean-

---

74. A iv, 201; tr. F.L. Woodward, vol. IV. 139.
75. S v, 437.
76. M i, 140.
77. D ii, 150-1.
78. M ii, 32. Also at A iv, 428, when a Brahmin asked the Buddha regarding omniscience, the Buddha said, "Enough, Brahmans! ... who speaks the truth, who lies? Let it be! I will teach you Dhamma, Brahman; listen, pay heed, I will speak."

ingful. During the Buddha's life time, many of his students attained Nirvana, Arhathood. Since the Buddha mainly concerned himself with the elimination of human suffering, he did not like people talking nonsense to waste their valuable time and he used to advise his students either to discuss the Dharma or to work diligently day and night. In the early scriptures, we often come across the description that the ascetics and wanderers gathered together discussing various worldly topics.[79] But Gautama Buddha advised his students to do two things when they gathered together: either hold discussions on Dharma or maintain "noble silence".[80] On a certain occasion when a number of Bhikkhus staying at the house of Migara's mother talked frivolously and were empty headed, the Buddha asked Moggallana to perform a magic trick to calm them down.[81] Right speech, one of the practices of the "Eight-Fold Path", is about avoiding the four kinds of speech: falsehood, malicious talk, harsh words, and frivolous talk.[82] The Buddha especially did not like people speaking ill of others even regarding Devadatta. Once being informed by his attendant that Devadatta had an evil wish of taking over the Sangha, Moggallana told the Buddha about it. Then the Buddha said, "Ward your words, Moggallana, ward your words, for even now the foolish fellow will betray himself."[83] The Buddha even did not like people to praise him without a basis and without good reason. In the scripture, Sariputra is reported to have praised him by saying that Gautama Buddha was wonderful and marvellous surpassing the past and future Buddhas. Then the Buddha reproached him saying

> How dear you are, you even do not understand the present Buddha fully
> while the Tathagata is still living, how can you talk about Tathagata in the
> past and future?[84]

So Gautama Buddha, transcending all speculative views and theories, did not enter into useless dispute in the world. He was a pragmatist. So he even did not purposefully formulate any philosophy to counter the existing views. Buddhist philosophy is an "unexpected consequence" of the Buddha's pragmatic nature. He said, "Seeing all these views, but not grasping them and searching for the end of suffering, I found inward peace."[85]

(2) The Buddha was confident, determined, and tolerant
Early Buddhist literature shows the Buddha to be a man of great confidence and tolerance, dis-

---

79. M i, 513-514. The stock passage is "talk of kings, robbers, ministers, armies, dangers, battles, food, drinks, clothing, beds, garlands, perfumes, relatives, vehicles, villages, towns, cities, countries, women, heroes, streets, well, the dead, trifles, the origin of the world, the origin of the sea, etc." also M ii, 1-2; 23; 29-30; iii, 113; D iii, 36.
80. M i, 161. T1, 775c-776a. MA points out that the second *jhana* and one's basic meditation subject are both called "noble silence". Those who cannot attain the second *jhana* are advised to maintain noble silence by attending to their basic meditation subject.
81. S v, 270.
82. M i, 288; 179-180; 345; iii, 49.
83. A iii, 122.
84. S v, 159-160.
85. Sn. verse no. 837.

playing calmness and self-control in whatever difficult situations he found himself. The Buddha was confident because he acted and did according to what he said and what he taught. He even asked his students to examine him so that they could establish a firm conviction within them. Therefore, when many distinguished young Magadha noblemen led an awakened life under the direction of the Blessed One, a rumour spread in Magadha saying that the Buddha made fathers childless, women widows and families broken, and asking whom he was going to convert the next time. The Buddha taught his students that they should reply to the revilers in the following way: "Verily, great heroes, Truthfinders, lead by what is true Dhamma. Who would be jealous of the wise, leading by Dhamma?"[86] Thus what the Buddha taught, the Dhamma, is the psychological reality which he experienced and upon which he acted accordingly. So some of his students asked him to leave Magadha, but the Buddha told them that the rumour would be over within seven days and it died out as he predicted.

The confidence of the Buddha is explicitly shown in the suttas. For instance, the Buddha practised austerities for six long years with the hope of finding the solution to problems of living, but found it futile so at last he gave up the practice. At this time, his five companions left him. He was deserted and left alone, but was not disappointed. In such a desperate situation, the Buddha persisted with strong will and determination and achieved his goal at last. When Devadatta premeditated his assassination, the Buddha is said to have told his students, who were worried and tried to protect him, that they should not feel uneasy because it was physically impossible to kill a Buddha. So when Devadatta tried to kill him three times, the Buddha faced it – as described – calmly and turned every situation from tragedy into peace.

The Buddha never started a debate with others or made a challenge in the first place. It was only when they came and challenged him that he then began to talk to them with confidence and good intention. The Buddha was pragmatic and regarded these debates as pointless, but when they challenged him, he used to engage in such discussions. He usually gradually diverted the debate into a discourse on his teaching with patience, effort and sincerity. He faced challenges from his opponents in debates and conversations with confidence. His answers to their planned and thoughtful questions were tactful and he rarely fell into the pit of his opponents and defeated as showed in the scripture. On the contrary, he gradually led the opponent party to his own line of reasoning and the consequence was often that the opposition was converted and sometimes even went forth into homelessness under him. Sometimes he even told the opposing party about his own life and experience. Such was the case with Saccaka, the wanderer who was "a debater and a clever speaker regarded by many as a saint".[87] He challenged the Buddha boasting that he could shake the Buddha up and down and thump him about. But when he finally met the Buddha and their discussion took some unexpected turns, Saccaka was defeated. At the end, he admitted that the Buddha remained calm without showing any anger, hate or bitterness even when he was spoken to offensively and assailed by dis-

---

86. Mahavagga, I. 24. I. B. Horner, *The Book of Discipline*, part 4, 56-7.
87. M i, 237. There are two suttas in the Majjhima Nikaya, No. 35 and 36 about the debates and discussions between the Buddha and Saccaka, the wanderer. Saccaka was defeated but did not become a member of the Sangha. He still regarded himself to be a "saint".

courteous courses of speech. Nigantha Nataputta, the Jain leader, sent his disciples several times to debate with the Buddha with different dilemmas in order to defeat the latter. He sent outstanding disciples like Upali, Prince Abhaya and Asibandhakaputta, but they all were defeated and became students of the teaching of the Buddha at the end of their discussion with him.[88]

The Buddha was reported to be tolerant, because he regarded the world not as evil, but rather thought that people do bad things due to their ignorance. He, therefore, never scolded people as sinners but simply as fools, and he used to converse with his opponents or even persecutors with good intention and tried to help them. He rarely showed any anger or was displeased when people abused him, but was usually in a state of calm and tranquillity. Among the lay followers of Nigantha Nataputta, Upali, as mentioned above, was a wealthy householder and after he was defeated in debate, he asked the Buddha to accept him as his lay student. The Buddha advised him to think twice before making that decision for he was a well-known person. This made Upali more convinced of the Buddha's tolerance so he made a request for the third time and was finally accepted. Then the Buddha asked him to continue to support and honour his former teacher as before.[89] The same spirit of tolerance is also expressed in the Anguttara Nikaya when Siha, the general, also a lay disciple of the Jain Order, became a student of the Buddha.[90]

In the early suttas there are many instances showing that the Buddha faced abuse and persecution with confidence and tolerance and even convinced the persecutors, who became his students in the end. When the Bharadvaja brothers abused him with all kinds of rude and harsh words the Buddha remained silent and undisturbed.[91] After they had finished their curse, the Buddha calmly talked to them and turned them into his students. When a Brahmin shouted at the Buddha who was approaching him: "Stop there, shaveling, stop there, ascetic, stop there, outcaste", he quietly conversed with him and told him what constituted an outcaste.[92] The Brahmin was pleased with his talk and the new interpretation of outcaste and gave him abundance of choice food. The Buddha was a tolerant teacher, with a tolerance unheard of in the history of thought. His unconditional patience appears clearly in three stanzas of the Dhammapada, numbers three, four and five, in which he described non-resistance as the means of bringing enmity and hatred to cessation. He taught his students that even in the mind, one should not harbour evil thoughts and bad intentions. He not only taught tolerance, he practised tolerance himself.[93]

There are two incidents concerning the Buddha being slandered by his opponents in the

---

88. Upali's debate is found in the *Upali Sutta*, No. 56 of the Majjhima Nikaya. Prince Abhaya's debate is found in M i, 392-396. While Asibandhakaputta's debate is found in S iv, 322ff. According to the Chinese translations, Nataputta, the Jaina teacher sent Asibandhakaputta twice to debate with Gautama Buddha when the latter came to Nalanda. T2, 230b-232b.

89. M i. 372-387.

90. A iv, 179-188. The same sutta is also found in Mahavagga, IV. 31.

91. S i, 161-3.

92. Sn. *Vasala Sutta*, 1. 7.

93. Dhammapada, No. 3. "He abused me, he beat me, he defeated me, he robbed me", in those who harbour such thoughts hatred is not appeased. No.4. "He abused me, he beat me, he defeated me, he robbed me", in those who do not harbour such thoughts hatred is appeased. No. 5. Hatred never ceases through hatred in this world; through love alone it ceases. This is an eternal law.

early Buddhist literature and they are referred to in the Pubbakammapiloti of the *Apadana* as the remaining effects of the Buddha's past Karma.[94] First, Cincamanavika, a beautiful female ascetic from another Order, was persuaded by her fellow ascetics to discredit the Buddha because they found that their gains diminished due to the popularity of the Buddha. She pretended to have become pregnant by the Buddha by tying a wooden disc around her body and came to where the latter was addressing a large congregation. Her accusation was soon discovered to be false and she was chased out by the audience.[95] The second story is recorded in the Udana about Sundari, also a female ascetic from another Order, who was persuaded by her fellow ascetics to insult the Buddha and his students. She visited Jetavana where the Buddha was residing and pretended to have stayed in the evenings and left in the mornings. After some days, the heretic ascetics hired some villains to kill Sundari and hide her body under a heap of rubbish near Jetavana. When this was reported to the king, a search was carried out and her body was found. Her fellow ascetics then went about the streets of the city crying: "Behold the deeds of the Sakya Bhikkhus."[96] In these two incidents, both reported in the suttas, the Buddha also remained calm and self-controlled without any sign of anger.

Even on his deathbed, the Buddha was not worried and discouraged but faced death bravely. He consoled Ananda who was weeping and much troubled by the fact that his teacher was going to die. The Buddha said to him:

> How, then, Ananda, can this [that I should not die] be possible – whereas anything whatever born, brought into being, and organized, contains within itself the inherent necessity of dissolution – how, then, can this be possible, that such a being should not be dissolved? No such condition can exist![97]

At the moment the Buddha was dying, he was not troubled by his own death, and was concerned to console others. This really highlights the Buddha's courage and compassion.

(3) The emotions and indignations of the Buddha.

Although he was quite patient with his opponents and even persecutors, the Buddha would not tolerate misunderstandings and misrepresentations of his principles and major teachings. A few cases in the Tipitaka (the Theravada canon) suggest that the Buddha felt uneasy and even reproached his students when they misunderstood and wrongly interpreted his teachings. As the Dharma was his great discovery, his lifetime work and message to the suffering world, he would not tolerate his own Bhikkhus who misrepresented the Dhamma through carelessness

---

94. Apadana, i, 299-301.
95. Apadana, i, 299-301, verse: 7-9; Jataka, iv, 187f.; Dhammapada commentary, iii, 178f.; Itivuttaka commentary, 69.
96. The Udana, iv, 8; the Udana commentary, 256ff.; the Dhammapada commentary, iii, 474f.; the Samyutta commentary, ii, 528f.; the Jataka, ii, 415f.; and the Apadana, i, 299-301, verse: 4-6. According to the commentary of the Majjhima Nikaya, this is also referred to in the Bahitika Sutta of the Majjhima Nikaya about which King Pasenadi aked Ananda some questions.
97. D ii, 144. The English translation is adopted from the *Dialogues of the Buddha*, ii, 159.

or ill-will. This was the case particularly when their task was to pass this message down to future generations. Sati, a fisherman's son, is a good example. He wrongly understood the master's teaching (on the aggregates), believing that consciousness survived the body and took another form in the new life. Upon hearing this, the Buddha cried out:

> Foolish man, to whom have you ever known me to teach the Dhamma in
> that way? Foolish man, in many discourses have I not stated consciousness
> to be dependently arisen, since without a condition there is no origination
> of consciousness? But you, foolish man, have misrepresented us by your
> wrong grasp and injured yourself and stored up much demerit.[98]

Arittha, a former vulture-trainer, was another Bhikkhu who was reproached by the Buddha in a similar manner for his misunderstanding of the Dhamma. The Buddha blamed him for being a foolish and misguided man.[99] The commentary explains that while reflecting in seclusion, Arittha came to the conclusion that there would be no harm for Bhikkhus to engage in sexual relations with women, and he therefore maintained that this should not be prohibited by the monastic rules.[100] In both cases the Bhikkhus were of humble origins and probably did not have any education at all, so they had difficulty in understanding the Buddha's teaching in its philosophical dimensions. But the two topics concerning a fundamental teaching and a fundamental practice are crucial in the understanding of the Dhamma. It therefore appears that the Buddha reproached them with a personal feeling.

In these two cases, it may perhaps be argued that the Buddha was annoyed, but what he said concerning Devadatta suggests that he was perhaps compassionately "angry" (for want of a better word) at least in the literal sense of the word. Devadatta wanted to intrigue to take over the leadership of the Sangha and asked the Buddha, during his lifetime, to hand it over to him. The Buddha said: "Not even to Sariputta and Moggallana would I hand over the Order, and would I pass it to thee, vile one, to be vomited like spittle?"[101] In the Anguttara Nikaya, we find the following saying of the Buddha when Ananda made enquiries about Devadatta:

> And so long as, Ananda, I saw a bright spot in Devadatta, even the prick-
> end of a horse-hair in size, I declared not: 'Devadatta is wayward gone,
> hell-bound for a kalpa, unpardonable' – but it was when I saw none, that I
> declared thus…[102]

---

98. M i, 258.
99. M i, 132.
100. This is referred to in The Middle Length Discourse of the Buddha, end note 249.
101. Vinaya, ii, 188. It is also found in T22, 592b; the Dasabhanavara Vinaya (T23, 258b), the Mulasarvastivada Vinaya (T23, 701c), the Mulasarvastivada Vinaya Samghabhedavastu (T24, 169b). This incident is also referred to in the *Abhayarajakumara Sutta* (M i, 393). The sense and meaning of the quotation are basically the same in the Vinaya of all these schools and traditions although the wording and expression are slightly different. This suggests that it is probably historical in nature.
102. A iii, 401. The translation is adapted from *The Book of the Gradual Sayings,* III, 287.

The same comment is also found in the Chinese counterpart, the Ekottaragama.[103] This statement is not unlike a curse, arguably motivated by anger. The Devadatta incident was a bitter experience in the life of the Buddha because as a Bhikkhu and student in his own community, Devadatta had tried with a certain success to split the Sangha the Buddha had established with much effort. Therefore, whenever Devadatta was mentioned, the Buddha would speak of him as a bad person of vicious intention.

The Sangha was the vehicle for disseminating the Buddha's message to the world. Gautama Buddha was very concerned about the split of the Sangha for he had seen what had happened to Jain monks in the last few years of his life.[104] The *Mahavibhasa Sastra*, with reference to Devadatta, mentions that the bad Karma entailed by the destruction of the Sangha is graver or heavier than that of shedding the blood of the Buddha. The split of the Sangha was explained as the destruction of the Dharmakaya (the metaphorical body of the teachings) while shedding the blood of the Buddha harms the Rupakaya (the biological body of the Buddha).[105]

Apart from these, there are at least two cases in the *Mahaparinibbana Sutta* that illustrate the Buddha displaying an emotion of feeling appreciation towards beautiful places and things. The first incident was when the Licchavis of Vesali (or Vaisali, Skt), wearing clothes of different colours and adorned with various kinds of ornaments, approached the Buddha in carriages. Gautama said to his students:

> O brethren, let those of the brethren who have never seen the Tavatimsa gods, gaze upon this company of the Licchavis, behold this company of the Licchavis, compare this company of the Licchavis, for they are even as a company of Tavatimsa gods.[106]

The second incident occurred after the Buddha and Ananda had returned from a begging tour in Vesali. The Buddha addressed Ananda: "How delightful a spot, Ananda, is Vesali, and how charming the Udena Shrine, and the Gotamaka Shrine..."[107] These two incidents are also mentioned in the Chinese translations of the *Mahaparinirvana Sutra*.[108] These pieces of literature suggest that the Buddha had emotions which he manifested in different ways. If a sense of appreciation shows the compassion of Gautama Buddha, then anger definitely shows the human side of him because a Buddha, at least by definition, is a person who has eliminated the 3-poisons: greed, hatred, and ignorance. These incidents reveal an emotional human aspect of the Buddha.

---

103. T2, 567a-c.
104. According to the *Samagama Sutta* (M ii, 243-244), in his last few years, the Buddha observed that Jain Bhikkhus split after the death of their master because of different views and understandings on the master's teachings.
105. T27, 601c-602a.
106. D ii, 96. The translation is adapted from *The Dialogues of the Buddha*, II, 103.
107. D ii, 102. The translation is adapted from *The Dialogues of the Buddha*, II, 110. It is also mentioned in the Samyutta Nikaya, v, 258.
108. The praise of the Licchavis is mentioned in all the four Chinese versions: T1, 13c, 164a, 179b, 194b, but the praise of the city of Vesali is only found in two: T1, 165a, 180b.

(4) The Buddha was humorous

The Buddha was quite humorous in his speech, like in his debates and conversations. Thus, in the *Tevijja Sutta*, as mentioned above, a Brahman named Vasettha discussed the teachings in the Vedas concerning the union with Brahma, the Creator, with the Buddha. The Buddha asked him whether he, or his teacher, or his teacher's teacher even back to seventh generation had seen Brahma. Vasettha answered in the negative. Then the Buddha humorously point out that this is just like a person who loves a lady on sight but knows neither her name, nor where she dwells, nor her complexion, nor whether she is tall or short, nor whether she is of Brahman or sudra descent, and so on.[109]

The *Kevaddha Sutta* tells us another humorous story narrated by the Buddha. A student of the Buddha who had psychic powers wished to find out the answer to a question so he flew to different heavens in order to find out the answer. But all the gods there said to him that they did not know the answer to his question. So at last he decided to go to the Great Brahma since he was the Creator, the All-seeing. But for the first two times when the Bhikkhu asked the Mahabrahma the same question, he said,

> I, brother, am the Great Brahma, the Supreme, the Mighty, the All-seeing, the Ruler, the Lord of all, the Controller, the Creator, the Chief of all, appointing to each his place, the Ancient of days, the Father of all that are and are to be![110]

When the Bhikkhu asked him for the third time, the Great Brahma took him by his arm, led him aside, and said,

> These gods, the retinue of Brahma, hold me, brother, to be such that there is nothing I cannot see, nothing I have not understood, nothing I have not realised. Therefore I gave no answer in their presence. I do not know, brother, where those four great elements – earth, water, fire, and wind – cease, leaving no trace behind. Therefore you, brother, have done wrong, have acted ill, in that, ignoring the Exalted One. You have undertaken this long search, among others, for an answer to this question. Go you now, return to the Exalted One, ask him the question, and accept the answer according as he shall make reply.[111]

In this story, the Buddha illustrated two things. First, the psychic power is useless in solving problems so that the Buddha did not like to use it as pointed out above. Second, according to the Vedas, the Great Brahma is "the Supreme, the Mighty, the All-seeing, the Ruler, the Lord

---

109. D i, No. 13 *Tevijja Sutta*. This sutta is also found in the Chinese translation of the Dirghagama, no.26. The same story is found at T1, 105c04.
110. D i, 221-2. The translation is adopted from the *Dialogues of the Buddha*, I, 282.
111. Ibid.

of all, the Controller, the Creator, the Chief of all, the Father of all that are and are to be." But he did not know the question asked by the Bhikkhu and therefore, he took him away and told the "truth". The Anumana Sutta teaches that a Bhikkhu should always be self-reflective, should review within himself whether he has vicious thoughts, defiled ideas, or unwholesome states of mind. If he has, he should make an effort to abandon them all and then he can abide happy and glad. This the Buddha compared with a woman who looks at herself in a clear and bright mirror. If she finds a smudge or blemish on her face, she makes an effort to remove it and then she becomes happy when she sees no smudge on her face.[112]

In the Anguttara Nikaya, the Buddha told the Bhikkhus that mother and father should be worshipped and venerated as Brahma.[113] This is quite humorous when we look at it against its background: the creation of Brahmanism, being that the world with its sentient beings is created by Mahabrahma. What the Buddha most probably wanted to say is that instead of worshipping and venerating Brahma, it is better to worship your parents, because it is not Brahma but your parents who have created you.

In closing

From the above treatise, I come to the following provisional concluding remarks on Gautama Buddha. Unlike the other Indian teachers of his time, the Buddha not only rejected all forms of divinity as other ascetic teachers, but also loathed magic and tricks when he disseminated his teachings and conversed with different people. The Buddha used to emphasize education and understanding, not blind faith. His sole objective was to get rid of the suffering inherent in life by means of persuasion. This practical, open, rational but heartfelt and no-nonsense attitude of the mind of the Buddha, anchored in the psychology of his personality, influenced his students and later generations of Bhikkhus and other devotees. Once the Buddha said to his Bhikkhus:

> Go forth, [Bhikkhus], for the good of the many, for the happiness of the many, out of compassion for the world, for the good, benefit, and happiness of gods and men. Let not two go by one way: Preach, [Bhikkhus], the Dhamma, excellent in the beginning, excellent in the middle, excellent in the end, both in the spirit and in the letter.[114]

The attitude of the Buddha's mind and his personality eventually contributed much to the success of spreading his message in the world. By his resilience and adaptive character, the Buddha created teachings that have the ability to assimilate with the cultures and modes of the local traditions and various countries over time. Now after more than 2500 years, one might say that the Dharma has proven to be capable of surviving the ravages of time. It is even reviv-

---

112. M i, 99.
113. A. I. 131. This passage is also found in the Itivuttaka, No. 106; *Samyuktagama, T2, 404a.
114. Mahavagga 19-20.

ing in the present postmodern era outside Asia, thanks to the genius of Gautama Buddha and his students down the ages up until today.

For the meaning of the abbreviations referring to the Buddhist original sources, see the References at the end of this book. Abbreviations of the used primary resources:
PTS Pali Text Society
T   Taisho Tripitaka
tr   Translation
*   Indication of a reconstructed Sanskrit title from an ancient Chinese translation of Buddhist text whenever the original Sanskrit is lost.

Primary resources with English and Chinese translations:
Anguttaranikaya, Vol. I-V, Oxford: PTS. English translation: *The Book of the Gradual Sayings,* Vol. I, II, V, by F.L. Woodward, Vol. III & IV by E.M. Hare.
*Dharmaguptaka Vinaya, T22, No.1428, tr. by Buddhayasas in 405.
Dighanikaya, Vol.I-III, Oxford: PTS. English translation: T.W. Rhys David, *Dialogues of the Buddha*, Vol.I-III.
*Dirghagama, T1, No.1, tr. Buddhayasas and (Chu) Fo-nien in 413.
*Ekottarsgama, T2, No.125, tr. Gautama Sanghadeva in 397.
Itivuttaka, Oxford: PTS. English translation: *The Itivuttaka The Buddha's Sayings*, by J.D. Ireland. Sri Lanka: Buddhist Publication Society, 1991.
*Madhyamagama, T1, No.26, tr. Gautama Sanghadeva between 397-398.
*Mahaparinirvana Sutra. There are four Chinese translations of the Hinayana version: T1, No.1, tr. Buddhayasas, 19a-b; T1, No.5, tr. Baifazhu, 168a-b; T1, No.6, translator lost, 183c-184a; and T1, No.7, tr. Faxian, 198a-b.
*Mahasanghika Vinaya, T22, No.1425, tr. by Buddhabhadra and Faxian in 416.
*Mahisasaka Vinaya, T22, No.1421, tr. Buddhajiva and (Zhu) Daosheng in 423 or 424.
Majjhimanikaya, Vol.I_III, Oxford: PTS. English translation: *The Middle Length Discourse of the Buddha*, by B. Nanamoli, Boston: Wisdom Publication 1995.
*Mulasarvastivada Vinayavibhanga, T23, No.1442, tr. Yijing in 703.
Mulasarvastivada-vinaya-bhaisajyavastu, T23, No.1448, tr. by Yijing in 700-711.
*Samyuktagama, T2, No.99, tr. Gunabhadra between 435-443. There is another shorter version of the text: T2, No.100, translated into Chinese by an unknown translator in 352-431.
Samyuttanikaya, Vol.I-V, Oxford: PTS. English translation: *The Book of the Kindred Sayings*, Vol.I-II, C.A.F. Rhys Davids, Vol.III-V, F.L. Woodward.
*Sarvastivada Vinaya, T23, No.1435, tr. Punyatara and Kumarajiva in 399-413.
Suttanipata, Oxford: PTS. English translation: V. Fausboll, *The Sutta-nipata, A collection of discourses*, Vol. X Part II of *The Sacred Books of the East*, 1881. K. R. Norman, *The Group of Discourses (Sutta-nipata)*, Oxford: Pali Text Society, 2001. Reprint.
Vinaya, Oxford: PTS. English tr.: I.B. Horner, *Book of the Discipline*, Oxford: PTS, Vol. I-VI.

Chapter 3

The Foundations Of Buddhist Psychology

David J. Kalupahana

Introduction[1]

Three terms used in the early discourses can explain the fundamental aspects of the psychological speculations of the Buddha. They are called fundamental aspects because hundreds of other psychological concepts in the early discourses can be brought under one or the other of these three terms, which explain the entirety of original Buddhist Psychology: thought (*citta*), mind (*nama*) and consciousness (*vijnana*). The SN (2.94-97) contains two short discourses that outline the nature of these three psychological phenomena and the manner in which they should be treated in order to be free from the suffering associated with human life. As they are also wrongly interpreted in order to justify some form of metaphysical idealism, and considering the enormous significance of these two discourses, I propose to begin this discussion with a complete translation of the first of them.

> (1) Thus has been heard by me. Once the Fortunate One was living in Savatthi, at Jeta's garden... Then the Fortunate One addressed the [Bhikkhus]: "[Bhikkhus]!" "Yes, Fortunate One," responded the [Bhikkhus]. The Fortunate One said thus:
>
> (2) "[Bhikkhus], an individualist without learning should be disgusted with, dispassionate toward and released from this body made of the four great elements.
>
> (3) What is the reason for this? [Bhikkhus], seen is the accumulation, also the dissipation, also the grasping and also the abandoning of this body made of the four great elements. Therefore, therein an individualist without learning should be disgusted with, dispassionate toward and released from this body made of the four great elements.
>
> (4) Whatever, [Bhikkhus], is called 'thought', and also 'mind' and also 'consciousness,' therein it is not easy for an individualist without learning to be disgusted, to be dispassionate, to be released.

---

1.   References to Pali texts are to the editions of the Pali Text Society, London.

(5) What is the reason for this? For a long time, [Bhikkhus], it has been clung to, appropriated and grasped on to as 'This is mine; he is me; this is my self.'

(6) It is better, [Bhikkhus], an individualist without learning should approach this body made of the four great elements as the self, but not 'thought.'

(7) What is the reason for this? [Bhikkhus], this body made of the four great elements is seen to be remaining for even one year, remaining for even two years, remaining for even three years, remaining for even for four years, remaining for even for five years, remaining for even for ten years, remaining for even twenty years, remaining for even for thirty years, remaining for even for forty years, remaining for even for fifty years, remaining for even for hundred years, remaining for even more. Whatever, [Bhikkhus], is called 'thought,' also 'mind,' also 'consciousness,' that, during day and night, arises as one and ceases as another.

(8) Just as, [Bhikkhus], a monkey, moving along in a forest, a thicket, takes hold of one branch, having released it takes another, even so, [Bhikkhus], whatever is called 'thought,' and also called 'mind,' and also called 'consciousness,' that, during day and night, arises as one and ceases as another.

(9) Therein, [Bhikkhus], the Worthy One's disciple with learning reflects well according to genesis on dependent arising (*pratityasamutpada*): 'When that exists, this comes to be; on the arising of that, this arises. When that does not exist, this does not come to be; on the ceasing of that, this ceases.' For example, dependent upon ignorance are dispositions; dependent upon dispositions is consciousness,... thus is the arising of this entire mass of suffering.

(10) On the residueless ceasing of ignorance is the ceasing of dispositions; dependent upon the ceasing of dispositions is the ceasing of this consciousness,... thus is the ceasing of this entire mass of suffering.

(11) Seeing thus, [Bhikkhus], the Worthy One's disciple with learning is disgusted with material form, is disgusted with feeling, is disgusted with perception, is disgusted with dispositions, is disgusted with consciousness. Being disgusted, is dispassionate; being dispassionate, is released. In the one who is released, there is the knowledge of release 'I have been released,' and that 'Spewed out is birth; done is what ought to be done; there is no more of thisness for me.'[2]

---

2. This is a very literal translation. The reason for making it literal is that an important aspect of the discourse is lost if we attempt to render it into idiomatic English. Thus, it was necessary to highlight the manner in which the terms thought, mind and consciousness are described. They are placed within quotes. Therefore, they can be understood as references to separate concepts, not synonyms. This will be discussed in detail later on.

The Buddha seems to have been quite aware of the fact that whenever a name is used to refer to some phenomenon, it tends to be metaphysically conceived as a real existing entity. Such an entity is more often perceived as existing beyond experience and/or description. The same can be said of the three terms under consideration. To avoid any such perspective, the Buddha used the verbal forms, "thinks" (SN 5.418, also: 3.151), "minds" (MN 1.1 ff) and, very specifically in the case of "consciousness" where, in order to highlight the idea that it is no more than the function of being conscious, it is said: "Is conscious, is conscious, therefore, friends, it is called 'consciousness'." (MN 1.292)

Thought

According to the *Brahmajala-suttanta*, one of the most important aspects of thought is its instrumentality in the formulation of many of the metaphysical views prevalent in India before the Buddha (DN 1.28-38). Let us leave aside the theories that are the result of logic and investigation (MN 1.29), because they are directly based upon thought. What is more interesting is that some of these metaphysicians depended on extraordinary powers or higher forms of knowledge to justify their metaphysical speculations. Following is a typical passage:

> Herein, some ascetics and Brahmans, following exertion, striving, contemplation and proper reflection, achieves such concentration of thought, and when the thought is thus concentrated, remembers the variously established previous abodes, as for example, one birth, two births, three births, four births, five births, ten births, twenty births, thirty births, forty births, fifty births,, hundred births, hundred thousand births, a manifold thousands of births, a manifold hundreds of thousand births. "There in, I was of such name, such clan, such caste, [eating] such food, experiencing such happiness and suffering and of such span of life. He having passed away from there, I was born here." And so does he remember, with form and content, the previous abodes established in a manifold way. He said thus: 'The self and the world are eternal, barren, standing erect, stable like a pillar, and these living beings run around, roam around, and indeed exist like the eternal.' (MN 1.13-14)

Compare the above statement which is supposed to have been presented by the traditional pre-Buddhist contemplatives regarding retrocognition and their explanations, with the following statement presented by the Buddha.

> He, when his thought is thus concentrated, purified, cleansed, free from blemish, with defilements gone, become soft, pliable, stable and attained stability, directs and bends his thought toward the knowledge of the memory of previous abodes. He remembers variously established previous abodes, as for example, one birth, two births, three births, four births, five births, ten births, twenty births, thirty births, forty births, fifty births, hundred births, hundred thousand births, numerous aeons of destruction,

numerous aeons of evolution, numerous aeons of destruction and evolution. "There, I was of such name, such clan, such caste, [eating] such food, experiencing such happiness and suffering and of such span of life. He, having passed away from there, was born here. There too, I was of such name, such clan, such caste, [eating] such food, experiencing such happiness and suffering and of such span of life. He having passed away from there, I was born here." And so does he remember, with form and content, the previous abodes established in a manifold way. (MN 1.81)

The two passages are very similar in the description of retrocognition except in regard to the conclusion in the first one which assumes that retrocognition finally leads to the conception of the permanent and eternal self and the world, a theory put forward by the traditional Indian philosophers. However, the description of the memory itself does not allow room for such a conclusion. The Buddha's description of retrocognition seems to have been carefully worded in order to avoid any notion of absolute identity. Here again he comes up with a rather unusual linguistic construction mixing up the subjects within one sentence. Thus we have the statement: "He, having departed from there, I was born here."[3] In so describing the memory, the Buddha was presenting a non-identity theory of survival.

Another important aspect of the second paragraph is that it says that the contemplative directs and bends his thought toward the development of retrocognition. While it is thought that is normally carried too far to assume metaphysical positions relating to the origin and duration of human life as well as the universe, another passage in the early discourses giving the same description of retrocognition maintains: "There and there indeed he arrives at the appropriateness of an eyewitness whenever there exists a faculty." (MN 1.494-496; AN 3.17-19)[4] This rather enigmatic statement could be understood as indicating the suitability of having a faculty as an eyewitness. This means that the thought, if it had no reins in the form of faculties, can move beyond experience to assume the existence of unverifiable entities. These faculties are referred to in the chart included in the section on the "mind".

Reflection and investigation are considered to be the activities associated with thought. Reflection is the process of examining the past, and investigation is intended to expand the horizon of inquiry. The Buddha, who was quite aware of the functioning of the thought process, admonished the contemplatives to restrain from the pursuit of these processes. He probably felt that these two processes were those that led to speculation about the origin and extent of the universe. Thus, after collecting whatever information one could through these means, a contemplative temporarily suspends these two pursuits during the third preliminary stage of contemplation. Together with the achievement of the moral standing during the first stage and the restraint of the emotive commitment to an object of experience, a contemplative

---

3.   The editor of the text seems to have difficulty in understanding the subject in the first part of the sentence, which is in the third person singular, and the verb in the second part of the sentence being in the first person singular.

4.   Note my translation "whenever."

is able to achieve the stage of "consideration", literally "taking a close look". It is only after reaching such a state that the contemplative can bend his thought toward the development of the higher forms of knowledge.

Even though the restraining of thought is important in epistemological matters, surprisingly the non-restraining of thought is considered essential in the area of some forms of moral practice. Thus the limits set on thought should be abandoned when one is extending friendliness and compassion to all (SN 2.173; 3.31). In general it was felt that the world is led by thought, thereby highlighting its power either for "good" or for "bad" (SN 1.39).

One more rather pervasive misunderstanding about the conception of thought needs to be clarified. This is the view that thought is originally luminous, but that it becomes defiled by adventitious elements. The statement in the discourses runs thus:

> [Bhikkhus], this thought is luminous, but that is indeed defiled by adventitious defilements. That an individualist without learning does not know as it has come to be. Therefore I say that for an individualist without learning there is no development of thought. [Bhikkhus], this thought is released from adventitious defilements. That a disciple of the Worthy One with learning knows as it has come to be. Therefore I say that for a disciple of the Worthy One who is with learning there is the development of thought."
> (SN 1.10)

Possessing thought that is originally luminous and making thought luminous as a result of proper cultivation and development are two different things. The first represents the belief of a transcendental idealist who assumes that thought is naturally pure. Yet, the original text indicates simply luminous, not *originally* luminous. The second is the view of a pragmatist who considers that thought can be made to be pure and luminous through human effort. It is precisely this latter perspective that the Buddha adopted. In fact, he compared thought to gold-ore, literally (AN 3.16) "the form in which [something is] born." Gold-ore is not gold but something mixed with lot of other elements, hence not luminous. It needs to be smelted and washed and made to be pure gold before one can make valuable gold ornaments with it. Similarly, thought needs to be cleaned up of at least the five defilements in order it to be flexible, luminous and pliable, and be utilized in the achievement of awakening and freedom.

Mind

Unlike thought, mind was always included under the category of faculties of sensory perception. As mentioned earlier, the faculties are very important as a means of keeping a check on thought which sometimes tends to move far away from the verifiable objects of experience. They include the six internal faculties, namely, eye, ear, nose, tongue, body (or skin) and mind (or brain) as well as the six external faculties to wit material forms, sounds, smells, tastes, tangibles, and ideas (MN 1.111-112). The editors of the Pali Text Society's *Pali-English Dictionary* had difficulty finding one English term to express the idea in which both the senses and the objects are included under the faculties. The best English term is "gateway" or "sense door. I will continue to use the familiar translation, namely, faculty to refer to a sensory/perceptual function.

While the five physical faculties have their own particular objects, they all depend on the (brain's) mind, while the mind has its own object when experiencing the objects of all other faculties (1.295). This relationship of the faculties to the objects should apply also to the objects of extraordinary perceptions, because it is the faculties that seem to provide a valid foundation for them as well. We may present them in the form of a diagram (see below Chart of faculties and objects). According to the Buddha faculties function in terms of the principle of dependent arising, and this is the central explanation of the functioning of all experienced phenomena. The oft-quoted statement of the MN (1.111-112) describes the ordinary unrestrained process of sense experience involving internal and external faculties as follows:

> Depending upon the eye and the material form, friends, arises visual consciousness; the meeting of the three is contact; depending upon contact is feeling; what one feels, one perceives; what one perceives, one reflects upon; what one reflects upon, that causes obsession; what causes obsession, the obsessions of perception and conception resulting from that overwhelm a man in regard to material forms to be known by the eye during the past, future and the present.

The same statement is repeated in regard to the other five faculties. In these statements, we find the principle of dependent arising applied to explain the process until the arising of feeling. It is at this stage that the emotive aspect overwhelms the life of a human being. In order to express this in the description, the passive language of dependence is replaced by the active form of the language, and which facilitates a notion of oneself, harmless in itself. However, as the process of perception continues that notion of self grows into a metaphysical entity that is thought to be permanent and eternal. In this manner, the illusory belief in an ego-centric self – as well as all the obsessions associated with it – are generated.

The restraint of the faculties is meant to eliminate the generation of such obsessions. In the course of a discussion with King Bimbisara of Magadha, the Buddha explains this restraining in the following manner:

> O, Great King, how does one become restrained in the faculties? Herein, Great King, a [Bhikkhu], having seen a material form with the eye, is not one grasping on to a mysterious cause [= substance], is not one grasping on to a quality. Because of living without restraining the visual organ, there will be the influx of evil and bad tendencies [such as] excessive greed and melancholy, one takes the initiative for restraining it, protects the visual organ, attains the restraint of the visual organ.

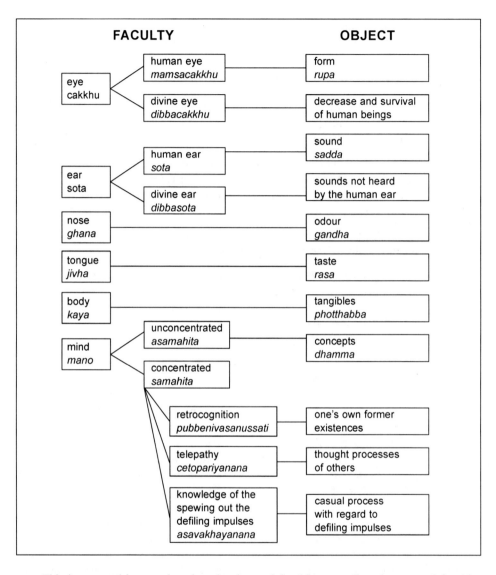

This is repeated in regard to the other internal faculties as well as the external faculties (DN 1.70). I have already referred to the elimination of the intellectual preoccupations and emotional commitment achieved during the state of contemplation called "consideration". Elsewhere I have presented detailed descriptions of these different stages of contemplation.[5] It

---

5.   See my *History of Buddhist philosophy*. Honolulu: The University of Hawaii Press, 1992, pp.36-43.

is because of the development of one's thought to such a level that one can bend thought toward achieving the extraordinary forms of knowledge. As such, there is no reason to brand them as mystical and distinguish them totally from the restrained forms of sense experience. The extraordinary perceptions recognized in the Pali teachings are as follows:

(1) Psychokinesis, which is not a form of knowledge but a capacity. It consists of various manifestations of the "power of will" during the contemplations (*Visuddhimagga* 405).

(2) Clairaudience, the faculty of perceiving sounds even at a distance, far beyond the reach of ordinary auditory faculty. This extension of the auditory perception both in extent and in depth enables a person to directly perceive certain correlated phenomena that are otherwise only inferred.

(3) Telepathy, which enables one to comprehend the general state as well as the functioning of the mind of another person.

(4) Retrocognition, the ability to perceive one's own past history. This ability is dependent on memory and brings out the information, not only of the past in this life, but also some rather strong impressions in human evolutionary development.

(5) Clairvoyance, the knowledge of the decease and survival of other beings who wander along in the life-process conditioned, among other factors, by one's own behaviour. What is interesting to note about this form of knowledge is that, unlike in the case of retrocognition that is based upon one's own memory, the information that can be gathered is of the being at the moment of its decease and survival. Hence the Buddha's description utilizing the present participles as "sees beings who are passing away, are being born and moving according to their deeds." This, together with retrocognition, enables one to confirm the survival of oneself, as well as of other beings, as a species.

Thus, after presenting a critique of the epistemological theories of his day, the Buddha accepted a form of empiricism, one which was not strictly confined to sensory experience, as it is in the western world, but one which also included the information by observation gathered through extraordinary mind perceptions. This is succinctly stated in a short but extremely important discourse called *Sabba Sutta* (SN 4.15). Considering the importance of this discourse especially in determining the nature of the Buddhist theory of empiricism, here is a full quote.

Thus has been heard by me. Once the Fortunate One was living in Savatthi, at Jeta's garden... Then the Fortunate One addressed the [Bhikkhus]: "O, [Bhikkhus]!" The [Bhikkhus] responded: "Yes, Sir." The Fortunate One said thus: "[Bhikkhus], I will preach to you *everything*. Listen to it. What, [Bhikkhus], is *everything*? Eye and material form, ear and sound, nose and odour, tongue and taste, body and tangibles, mind and concepts. These are called *everything*. [Bhikkhus], he who would say: 'I will reject this *every-thing* and proclaim another *everything*', he may have a theory [of his own]. But when questioned, he will not be able to answer and would, moreover, be subject to vexation. What is the reason for this? Because it is not within the range of experience."[6]

This discourse undoubtedly is the best proof one can adduce in favour of the utmost significance of the faculties in the Buddha's teaching. In addition to the epistemological significance of mind (or rather cortex) as the sixth sense, it is also one that plays a prominent role in corroborating the Buddhist teachings as a psychology. I have already presented sufficient evidence, on the basis of the structure of the *Dhammapada*,[7] that it was compiled by the later Buddhists as a response to the *Bhagavadgita* (ca. 200 BCE). However, the verses were taken from the early discourses and were arranged to fit into the structure of the argument. Therefore, the propositions are themselves traceable to the Buddha himself. The prominence given to the mind by the compilers of the *Dhammapada* is evident from the first two verses of the text.

> (1) Experience has mind as its pre-condition, is dominated by the mind and is mind-made. If one were to speak or act with a polluted mind, as a result, suffering follows him, like the wheel that follows the foot of the beast of draught.

> (2) Experience has mind as its pre-condition, is dominated by the mind and is mind-made. If one were to speak or act with a cleansed mind, as a result, happiness follows him like the shadow that does not depart.

This means that the life conducive to happiness or unhappiness is based primarily on the nature and state of the human mind. The mind, being at the centre of all the faculties, demonstrates its relevance to the Buddha's psychological theory of mind.

Consciousness

Consciousness is an integral part of the human personality. In the discourses we find the human personality analyzed into five factors (psychological modalities). They are material form (the behaviours of the body) (*rupa*), feeling (motivating affects) (*vedana*), perception (the six senses) (*sanna*), dispositions (cognitions and images) (*sankhara*) and consciousness (awareness) (*vinnana*). It is an analysis that is very popular in the discourses. The reason for its popularity is that it was intended to demonstrate the absence of a substantial, permanent, or eternal self

---

6. The Chinese version introduces a Brahman named Janussoni (misunderstood and mistranslated as Sheng Wen) as the interlocutor. See Takakusu, J., & Wanatabe, K. (Eds.).(1924-1929). *Taisho shinshu daizokyo.* Tokyo: Taisho Shinshu Daizokyo Kanko Kai, 1924-1929, 2. 91a-b. In fact, according to other discourses in Pali, Janussoni is one who comes to the Buddha inquiring about all kinds of metaphysical questions.
7. See *Dhammapada*. Lanham: University Press of America, 1986.

(*atman*). Taking each one of the factors, it is said: "It is not mine. He is not I. He is not my self." (AN 1.284-285; 2.171, 202, etc.[8]) A person who perceives the factors as they have come to be is compared to a warrior who shoots (an arrow) to the longest distance. The five factors represent the longest distance a person can shoot, hence having a limited, though extensive, reach. Yet it is not unlimited, as it is the case with one who believes in a self that is permanent and eternal. On the contrary, a personality consisting of the five factors is limited, hence impermanent (*anatman*). To avoid any conception of annihilation that could be associated with the notion of impermanence, it is very often qualified as something that is of the nature of transforming, thereby highlighting its continuity (SN 2. 274; 3. 8, 107-108; 4. 7 ff., 25, 34, 40, 67 ff.).

The five factors are not separate and distinct elements but integrated. They are connected and function together in concert. Otherwise there would be no complete human person. Material form (*rupa*) is the physical basis of the human personality (psychologically manifested in behaviours). A person who assumes that there can be a psychic personality without a physical basis is mistaken (SN 3.53, 55, 58). Feeling accounts for the affective component and emotive content of personality, especially in its threefold qualities: happiness (*sukha*), suffering (*dukkha*) and neutrality. In contemporary psychological terms, this modality is about the basic emotions like fear, anger, sadness, joy, love, the affective disorder of depression, and the serene state of relaxation and silence. Perception represents the sensory modality of the personality that is mostly intricately connected with cognition. The term expresses the pragmatic character of perception, since it means something that "has been put together and is known." In other words, it is neither what is independent of knowing nor a pure mental fabrication. It is, on the contrary, something that has been put together by the person on the basis of the information presented and that has entered through one gateway or through a combination of the six sense doors.

To train the mind to purely perceive is one of the aims in meditative awareness. The dispositions stand for the conative aspect of human behaviour. They replace the conception of a "will" posited by the metaphysicians. They are themselves conditioned by the interests of the human person. Conation usually refers to intention, a relevant concept for Karma (as intentional behaviour), or indeed to volition, a concept that refers to a commitment to act to attain a goal of choice. Finally, there is consciousness, which is not merely a cognitive activity, but also what accounts for the continuity of the human being as a living personality. This is because consciousness functions in the wake of memory (DN 1.134), and is able to bring back impressions and filtered information from one's previous experiences. The significance of consciousness is further exemplified by the Buddha's assertions that material form depends upon the four great elements (water, earth, wind, and fire), that affective feeling, sensory perception, and thinking disposition depend upon contact, but that consciousness depends upon the awareness of one's entire personality as a psychophysical entity (*nama-rupa*) (SN 1. 101-102).

Two of the functions of consciousness briefly mentioned earlier need further elaboration.

---

8.   Note the use of the neuter singular in the first statement which refers to each one of the five factors, while the second and third statements are in given in the masculine pronoun since they refer to the "I" and the "self".

The first is its relevance to human knowledge and the second is its relationship to survival of the human personality after death. It may be noted that unless the activities of the sense faculties and their objects do not lead their respective forms of consciousness, there would not be any knowledge or understanding (SN 2. 72-75). Thus, corresponding to the six sense organs and the six sense objects, we find the six forms of consciousness one can be aware of, namely: visual, auditory, olfactory, gustatory, tactile, and mental consciousness. The epistemological value of consciousness is further exemplified by a statement of Sariputta, the leader among the students of the Buddha in regard to the possession of great wisdom (AN 1. 23). Questioned by a Bhikkhu, Sariputta maintained that there is no difference between consciousness and wisdom. The only difference between them is that wisdom should be developed and consciousness should be thoroughly examined (MN 1. 293). This means that if someone can understand the nature of consciousness and act according to that knowledge one becomes an awakened person. What makes it difficult for a person to understand consciousness?

This leads us to the second function of consciousness as the factor that determines the continuity of the human personality. Whenever that continuity is felt, not only during one experiential term, but also from some of the previous experiences to the present, it is very easy for an unawakened person to come to the conclusion that it is one and the same consciousness that runs from the past to the present. As mentioned earlier, even a contemplative can come to such a wrong conclusion. This is why some of the contemplatives of the pre-Buddhist tradition reached the conclusion that there is a self, permanent and immutable. Thus we come across the famous heresy of Bhikkhu Sati, the son of a fisherman (MN 1. 256-271). Sati held the view that, according to the Buddha, it is this very same consciousness that runs and moves along, not another (MN 1. 256-257). When this was reported to the Buddha by some of the Bhikkhus, the Buddha summoned Sati, and in his usual fashion, questioned him about what he meant by this consciousness. Sati responded that it is the person who speaks and who experiences in such and such places the consequences of the good and bad actions. The Buddha rebuked Sati for attributing such a view to him and insisted that he has spoken in various ways of consciousness being dependently arisen, and that there will not be the arising of consciousness apart from causal conditions of the moment. The Buddha made it an occasion to give a lengthy discourse on how consciousness is conditioned and how it conditions persons from moment to moment.

As I have mentioned elsewhere,[9] it was only to induce human beings to adopt a life conducive to happiness that the Buddha utilized the possibility of rebirth in the four lower destinies, which include the animal-like emotions and attitudes. Nothing had been said regarding the actual occurrences of being literally reborn as an animal. Indeed, he never claimed that animals possessed consciousness, even though he admitted that some of the larger animals could have something like a thought process that enables them to put together certain events. Could this account for what is sometimes called the animal instinct? This brings us to the most important feature of consciousness, namely, how the correct understanding of it can lead to awaken-

---

9.   See my *Karma and rebirth*. Dehiwela, Sri Lanka: Buddhist Cultural Centre, 2006, pp.70-83.

ing and freedom. If a person, through the proper understanding of consciousness, can eliminate the emotive commitments to the world of experience, that person will, at the same time,
spew out attraction, revulsion and confusion/ignorance. This is awakening and liberation one
achieves while living in the present, which is called: "the element of freedom with residual
substrata" (*Ittivutaka* 38). If the realization – that consciousness is dependently arisen – elim-
inates the conditions that contribute to its establishment in a future life and if these conditions
are also eliminated, then that person is said to pass away, at death, with consciousness that is
non-established (SN 1.120-122; 3.119-124). This is "the element of freedom without a residual substrate" (*Ittivutaka* 38). Such is the manner in which consciousness contributes, either to
bondage and suffering, or to freedom and happiness, the Buddhist ultimate goal.

Closing remarks

The above explanation of thought, mind and consciousness was not acceptable to some of the
later Buddhist or to some of the non-Buddhist metaphysicians. They were interested in formulating the Buddha's Middle Way as metaphysical idealism (that emphasizes the supremacy of
mind to account for reality at the expense of matter). This clearly is the intention of the first
two passages in Vasubandhu's auto-commentary on the *Vijnaptimatratasiddhi*, commentary,
whose origin I consider rather suspect. This is because the two passages do not occur in the
original Sanskrit version edited by Sylvain Levi. As a result, Levi had to reconstruct the
Sanskrit from the Chinese and Tibetan versions. This would mean that before the text was
translated into these two languages, the original passages of Vasubandhu's work were deleted
and new paragraphs were inserted which were subsequently translated into Chinese and
Tibetan. Here I provide the English translation of only the first paragraph, since it clearly
expresses the metaphysical idealists' view. I render the term as "conception", because it is a
nominal form derived from the causative verb, the conception being what makes consciousness known.

> A mere conception of the threefold elemental world is established in the
> Great Vehicle. It is based on [the statement in] the discourse: "O sons of the
> Conqueror, it is mere thought, namely, the threefold elemental world."
> "Thought, mind, consciousness and conception are synonyms." Mere
> thought" is intended to be associated [with others]. "Mere" is for the pur-
> pose of denying the object (see Levi, p. 3).[10]

"Mere thought" should remind the reader of its occurrence in the most extreme idealist
text of the *Lankavatara Sutra*, a Mahayana work dating from perhaps the fourth century or
before. However, nowhere else in Vasubandhu's auto-commentary on the *Vimsatika* – stemming from the fourth century – did he make any statement conveying any such a meaning.

---

10. Levi, S. (Ed.).(1925). *Vimsatika Vijnaptimatratasiddhi*. Paris: Libraire Ancienne Honoré Champion.

Interestingly, Vasubandhu's auto-commentary on the *Trimsika* is also not available. Instead, we are left with the commentary by Sthiramati – an author from the sixth century – who was interested in making Vasubandhu a metaphysical idealist in hindsight.[11] Thus, the metaphysical view of the Buddha's way became supreme and influential in the heydays of Mahayana and in its dissemination into China and the Himalayas.

---

11. See my *The principles of Buddhist psychology*. Albany: State University of New York Press, 1987, p.192 ff.

Chapter 4

Buddhist Psychology: Exploring Practical And Theoretical Aspects

Padmal de Silva

Introduction

The Early Buddhist Theravada literature is in the Pali language and poses problems of translation. Pali is nowadays not a spoken language and consists of:

A. The original Buddhist canon – generally accepted standard of what the Buddha had taught – was put together soon after his death and committed to writing in the first century BCE. It consists of three "baskets" or parts (*pitaka*): the Sutta Pitaka that contains the discourses of the Buddha on various occasions throughout his teaching life, the Vinaya Pitaka that contains the rules of discipline for the Bhikkhus and Bhikkhunis, men and women devoting their entire life to studying and practicing the Dharma, and the Abbidhamma Pitaka that contains highly systematized philosophical and psychological analyses, which were finalized in their present form about 250 BCE, later than the material in the other two parts.

B. The early Pali commentaries on the Canon that were composed in their present form by the end of the fifth century. These include major texts such as *Sumangalavilasini* (commentary on the DN), *Papancasudani* (commentary on the MN), and *Dhammapada-atthakatha* (commentary on the *Dhammapada*), which were all compiled in Sri Lanka.

C. Other Pali texts of the same period, which are best described as expository and interpretive works. The early expository and interpretive texts include, among others *Visuddhimagga* ("The Path of Purification" by Buddhaghosa, 5th century), *Milindapanha,* ("Milinda's Questions" from the 1st century or later) and *Nettippakarana* (a guide how to interpret the discourses, from the 2nd or 1st century).

A full account of the Pali canon and related texts is given by Von Hinüber (1996). For an account of Theravada, see Gombrich (1988), and for a discussion of the different Buddhist schools, see Reat (1994).

The Entire Pali Canon, and the majority of the commentaries and expository works, have been translated into English and published by the Pali Text Society (PTS) in London, and – in more recent years – by other publishers as well. However, English versions are often beset with problems of translation and interpretation. For example, the term *Dukkha* (Sanskrit *Duhkha*), has been translated by many as "suffering". This translation had led to the Buddhist teachings being described as essentially pessimistic, as *Dukkha* is stated as characterising all existence. Some authors have offered alternative translations such as "unsatisfactoriness", "disharmony", and "painfulness" (e.g. Gunaratna, 1968; Mathews, 1983). None of these offers a precise rendering of the original term, and Rahula (1967) among others, leaves the term untranslated. Another example is the term *papanca* (Sanskrit *prapanca*). Several scholars (e.g. Kalupahana, 1987) have translated this as "obsession". This is a problematic translation (because of its specific meaning as an anxiety disturbance in psychopathology), although the official *Pali-English Dictionary* of the PTS (Rhys Davids & Stede, 1921-1925) also offers "obsession" as one rendering of this word. *Papanca* is a key term in Buddhist Psychology and has been variously translated as "impediment", "prolific tendency" and "imagination", among others. This topic will be returned to in a later paragraph.

It should now be clear that the problem of translation can be an obstacle to understanding the Theravada teaching or indeed any other ancient system of thought. The material in this chapter is drawn solely from the original Pali texts.

The Buddha's teachings

Before focussing on Buddhist Psychology, it is necessary to make few introductory comments on the teachings as conveyed in Pali. The Buddha, whose name is derived from the root *budh*, which means "to know" or "to comprehend" and – literally means "the awakened one" – lived in the foot-hills of the Himalayan range of mountains in Northern India from 563 to 483 BCE. (For excellent accounts of the Buddha's life, see: Kalupahana & Kalupahana, 1982, and Schumann, 1989; a useful brief account is available in Guruge, 1999). The main teachings of the Buddha are contained in the "Four Noble Truths", which refer not to what is usually understood as "truth", something absolute to believe in, but rather refer to propositions of "the Noble One" (see Guruge, 1999, and Rahula, 1967, for a fuller discussion of main tenets of the Dhamma), i.e.:

(i) life is characterized by "suffering" and is unsatisfactory (*Dukkha*);

(ii) the cause (*Samudaya*) of *Dukkha* is craving or hankering (overdesire) (*Tanha*);

(iii) *Dukkha* can be ended (*Nirodha*), *via* the cessation or extinction of craving or hankering – this is the state of *Nibbana*; and

(iv) there is a way (*Magga*) to achieve this cessation, which is called the Eightfold Path.

The Eightfold Path is also called the Middle Path, as it avoids the extremes of a sensuous and luxurious life on the one hand, and a life of rigorous self-mortification on the other hand. The eight aspects of the Path are: right understanding, right thought, right speech, right action, right livelihood, right effort, right mindfulness and right concentration. The person who undertakes a life based on this path, renouncing worldly attachments, hopes eventually to attain the *Arahant* state, which may be described as a state of "perfection". The word *Arahant* literally means "the worthy one" (for s/he has defeated her/his "inner enemies" and is thus worthy to be respected). This state marks the attainment of *Nibbana*. The other major teachings of Buddha include the negation of a permanent and unchanging self (*anatta*), and the notion of the impermanence or transience of things (*anicca*). Buddhist teachings also exclude the notion of a god. There is no creator or a supreme being who rules and purveys the universe. Thus, there is no absolutism in the teachings either in the form of an eternal god or in the form of an unchanging universe or an unchanging soul.

For the laity, the vast majority of people who did not renounce worldly life to devote themselves to the immediate quest for *Nibbana*, the Buddha provided a sound and pragmatic social ethics. They were expected to lead a life characterized by restraint and moderation, respecting the rights of others and being dutiful to those around them. Such a restrained and dutiful life was considered not only to be a necessary prerequisite for one's ultimate aim of liberation; it was also valued as an end in itself. For example, the Buddha advised his lay students to abstain from alcoholic beverages because alcohol indulgence could lead to demonstrable ill-effects such as loss of wealth, proneness to socially embarrassing behaviour, unnecessary quarrels, disrepute, ill-health and eventual mental derangement (*Sigalovada Sutta*, DN III). This empirical and pragmatic approach is a prominent feature of the ethical stance of the Buddha's teachings. Detailed considerations of Buddhist ethics are available in several sources, including Harvey (2000) and Kalupahana (1995).

The psychology of Dhamma: theory

The considerable and still growing interest shown by psychologists in the Buddhist teachings is understandable in view of the fact that it contains a great deal of psychology. Some parts of the canonical texts, as well as parts of the later writings, are examples of explicit psychological theorising, while many of the other parts present psychological assumptions and much material of psychological relevance. For example, the *Abhidhamma* contains a highly systematised psychological account of human behaviour and mind, and the translation of one of its books, the *Dhammasangani*, was given the title *A Buddhist Manual of Psychological Ethics* by its translator, Caroline Rhys Davids, when it was first published in 1900. Buddhist practice and way of life involve much in terms of psychological change. The ultimate personal goal of the *Arahant* state both reflects and requires major psychological changes. The path leading to the achievement of this goal, the Eightfold Path, includes steps which can only be described as psychological (e.g., right thought and right understanding). As the goal is attainable essentially through one's own efforts, it is not surprising that the teachings have much to say about one's thinking and behaviour. As noted above, there is no god one can turn to for one's salvation. Nor did the Buddha claim to be able to guarantee his students the attainment of the goal. On the contrary, the Buddha explicitly stated that he was only a teacher who would show the way, and that the actual task of achieving the goal required and depended upon individual effort. A much-quoted passage in the *Dhammapada* (which is part of the KN) says: "The task has to be accomplished by yourselves. The Enlightened Ones only teaches the way."

In the following paragraphs, some of the main psychological aspects of the Dhamma will be considered and I shall go into some basic notions, namely: motivation, perception, and cognition.

Motivation

Perhaps the most logical starting point in a discussion of Buddhist Psychology is the theory of motivation. What drives people in their behaviour? What motivates human action? The unawakened person's behaviour, it is said, is governed and driven by *tanha*, or craving, which as noted in the previous paragraph, is given as the cause of "suffering" or "unsatisfactoriness". *Tanha* is classified into three basic forms: *kama tanha* (craving for sensory gratification), *bhava tanha* (craving for self-preservation) and *vibhava tanha* (craving for self-annihilation) (e.g., SN V).

These three primary drives in the Buddhist teachings have been compared, by some authors, to the Freudian notions of libido, ego and thanatos respectively (M.W.P de Silva, 1973, 1978, 2005). Like the Freudian theory, this account of motivation may be seen as a primarily reductionist one: all actions have as their source a small number of basic drives. While craving is seen as the source of "suffering", the term *tanha* is not exclusively used in a negative sense. There are several instances in the Buddhist literature where it is acknowledged that one can also develop a *tanha* for the cessation of "suffering". Thus *tanha* can take the form of, or can be turned into, a desirable force. For example, the expository text *Nettippakarana* says:

> Here, craving is of two kinds, wholesome and unwholesome. While the unwholesome kind goes with the unsatisfactory worldly existence, the wholesome kind leads to the abandonment of craving.

Perhaps the difference lies in the distinction between desire and overdesire. In a further analysis of motivation, the Dhamma identifies three factors that lead to unwholesome, or undesirable, behaviour. These are: *raga* (passion or lust), *dosa* (hatred or malice) and *moha* (delusion or false belief) (e.g., AN I; AN II). All unwholesome action is seen as deriving from a set of fundamental roots. In fact, the texts explicitly refer to these as "roots" (*mula*). They are called *akusalamulas*: unwholesome or unprofitable roots. It is not made explicit whether these always operate at a conscious level.

On the other hand, certain clearly non-conscious factors also have a part to play in determining behaviour. One such group of factors mentioned is *anusaya*, translated as "latent tendency", "latent bias", "predisposition" and "latent disposition". The PTS Dictionary adds that these meanings are "always in bad sense" (Rhys Davids & Stede, 1921-1925, p.44). The term itself (from *anu* + *si*, to lie down or lie dormant) indicates that these are non-conscious factors. It is clear that they are not transient mental states as these are dispositional factors which are part and parcel of one's personality, acquired through past experience; it is also clear that they play their part in influencing one's behaviour and contribute to the perpetuation of the cycle of "suffering". Seven types of *anusaya* are often mentioned. The list given in SN V, is as follows: tendency to seek sensory pleasure, tendency to anger, tendency to speculation, tendency to doubt, tendency to conceit, tendency to crave for continuous existence or growth and tendency to ignorance. Another group of factors which are clearly non-conscious and which influence one's behaviour are the *asavas* (Sanskrit *asrava*, from the root *sru*, to flow or ooze). The term *asava* has been translated as influx, bias, taint, and canker. These are factors that affect the mind so that it cannot rise higher. It is said that they "intoxicate" and "bemuddle" the mind (Rhys Davids & Stede, 1921-1925, p.115). They colour one's attitudes and thwart one's insight. In one's endeavour for self-development, one has to excise them, and this is achieved through insight, restraint of the senses and so on. The influxes are described as arising from different factors: sensuality, aggression, cruelty, body, and individuality are given in one account (DN II). Other lists include, among others, gain, loss, fame, disrepute, and evil intentions (AN IV).

Motives for good, wholesome actions are usually expressed in negative terms. The most consistent account is the one which gives *araga* (non-passion or absence of passion), *adosa* (non-hatred or absence of hatred) and *amoha* (non-delusion or absence of delusion) as the roots of good action – the opposite of the roots of unwholesome behaviours (AN I). Occasionally, they are described in clearly positive terms: as *caga* (renunciation), *metta* (loving kindness) and *panna* (wisdom, understanding) (AN III). It is stated that one must strive to develop these in order to combat and overcome their opposites.

Buddhist texts also refer to a particularly interesting aspect of motivation, termed "deceptive factors" (*vancaka dhamma*). They may be seen in effect as unconscious motives. M.W.P. de Silva (1978) has called them "desires in disguise". Essentially it is said that unwholesome mental states can emerge, and lead to action, through the guise of wholesome mental states. A detailed analysis of these, based on Pali texts such as the commentary on the *Nettippakarana*, has been given by the Venerable Chandavimala in a publication in Sinhala (Chandavimala, 1994). M.W.P de Silva (1978, p.64) has given the following illustrative hypothetical example of this phenomenon:

> A married man of deeply religious nature... is attracted to a woman who is beautiful, but, stricken with dire poverty. He has compassion for this poverty-stricken woman, but in reality, his compassion is due more to his love for her than to her poverty-stricken state. It is possible for passion to take an acceptable form by the outward appearance of compassion.

The author goes on to say:

> This is a very subtle mechanism and a great deal of honest introspection and self-criticism is necessary to safeguard one from it.

Perception and cognition

Perception is based on twelve gateways or modalities (*ayatana*), six of these being of five sense organs plus the mind, or the "inner sense", and the other six being the objects of each of these (SN II). The status of mind (*mano*) is special. It has the ability to reflect on the objects of the other senses, so in this way it is linked to the activity of all the senses (Kalupahana, 1987). Each combination of sense organ and its objects leads to a particular consciousness (*vinnana*); for example, visual consciousness arises because of the eye and material shapes. When consciousness is added to each of the pairs of modalities, one gets eighteen factors of cognition, referred to as *dhatus*, or elements. These are presented in Table 1. It is said that the meeting of the sense organ, object, and consciousness (e.g., eye, material shape, and visual consciousness) constitutes contact, because of this contact feeling arises, and what one feels, one perceives (MN I).

Table 1. The Eighteen Factors of Cognition

SENSE ORGAN	OBJECT	CONSCIOUSNESS
Eye	material shapes	visual consciousness
Ear	sounds	auditory consciousness
Nose	smells	olfactory consciousness
Tongue	tastes	gustatory consciousness
Body	tangibles	tactile consciousness
Mind	mental objects	mental consciousness

This is a fairly straightforward account of how perception takes place. However, the Buddhist exposition goes beyond this. The account continues:

> What one perceives, one reasons about. What one reasons about, 'one turns into *papanca*. What one turns into *papanca*, because of that factor, assails one in regard to material shapes recognizable by the eye belonging to the past, future and the present... (MN I).

It will be recalled that the term *papanca* was cited earlier as an example of a word posing particular difficulties for the translator. In this passage, the verbal form *papanceti* is used. Thus, the final stage of the process of sense-cognition is *papanca*. An examination of the term in various contexts related to cognition shows that it refers to the grosser conceptual aspect of the process, as it is consequent to *vitakka* (reasoning). Once an object is perceived, there is initial application of thought to it, followed by *papanca*, which in this context is best taken to mean a tendency to proliferation of ideas. As a result, the person is no longer the perceiver who is in control, but one who is assailed by concepts generated by this prolific tendency. The person is overwhelmed by concepts and linguistic conventions. One's perception is, in this way, vulnerable to distortion and elaboration due to the spontaneous proliferation of thoughts. This proliferation is said to be linked to *tanha* (craving), *mana* (conceit) and *ditthi* (dogma, or rigidly held views) (*Maha Niddesa, I*). They are all bound up with the notions of "I" and "mine". This marks the intrusion of the ego into the field of sense perception. In Buddhist Psychology, there is no self (*atta*; Sanskrit *atman*), but the delusion of self affects all one's behaviours (*Sutta Nipata*).

The Arahant state

One of the aims of personal development is to enable oneself to see reality as it is, without the distortions arising from the various factors that characterize the unenlightened person's functioning. A major aspect of reaching the state of *Arahant* is the freeing of one's perceptions from these distorting influences. When one reaches a state of "perfection", one's perceptions become free of distortions, and allow direct appraisal of the objects.

It is perhaps appropriate at this point to consider the *Arahant* state and its attainment. The religious goal of a Buddhist is to attain this state, which marks the end of the cycle of "suffering". This requires a process of personal development, involving disciplined conduct (*sila*), serious meditative efforts marked by concentration (*samadhi*), and wisdom (*panna*) which is attained through such efforts. But what does it mean to say that someone is an *Arahant*? There are numerous descriptions of an *Arahant* in the texts. For example:

> The *Arahant* has destroyed the cankers, lived the life, done what is needed to be done, set down the burden, achieved well-being, shattered life's fetters, and is freed by perfect knowledge. He has applied himself to six things: to dispassion, to detachment, to harmlessness, to the destruction of craving, to the destruction of grasping, and to non-delusion. (AN III)

In psychological terms, the *Arahant*'s actions do not emanate from the common basic motives of passion, hatred and delusion. The person is, however, capable of joy or positive sentiment. He or she has loving kindness (*metta*) to all and compassion (*karuna*). He or she indulges in nothing, and is restrained in his or her behaviour. Nine standards of behaviour are listed which an *Arahant* cannot and does not transgress: taking life, stealing, sexual contact, uttering falsehoods, enjoying comfort of wealth and going astray through desire, through hate, through delusion and through fear (ANIV). They contribute to society by being teachers and advisers, and are no burden on their fellow beings. A detailed discussion of the characteristics of the *Arahant* is found in Katz (1982).

It was noted above that the attainment of the *Arahant* state requires personal development based on both restrained conduct and meditative efforts. This explains why meditation is given a key place in Buddhist texts. In addition to numerous canonical discussions, large sections of Buddhaghosa's *Visuddhimagga* are devoted to a consideration of this subject in detail. It is significant that the Pali word for meditation, *bhavana*, etymologically means "development" or "cultivation". Detailed discussions are available in many sources; e.g. Analayo (2003) or Sole-Leris (1986). A particularly lucid discussion of the psychological aspects of Theravada Buddhist meditation has been given by Harvey (1997). As there is a large body of literature on this subject in English, only a few brief comments will be made here.

Some therapeutic aspects of Buddhist Psychology

Buddhist personal development is realized through meditation. Two forms of meditation are prescribed: the first is called *Samatha* (tranquillity), and the other *Vipassana* (insight). While further forms of meditation have been developed in later periods, and these include various Tibetan and Zen techniques, *Samatha* and *Vipassana* represent the earliest Buddhist techniques. It should be noted that meditation of the *Samatha* type is also found in some other ancient Indian systems, while *Vipassana* is uniquely a Buddhist development (Rahula, 1967).

The word *Samatha* means "tranquillity" or "serenity". *Samatha* meditation is aimed at reaching states of consciousness characterized by progressively greater levels of tranquillity and stillness. It has two aspects: (a) the achievement of the highest possible degree of concentration and (b) the progressive calming of all mental processes. This is done through increasingly concentrated focusing of attention; the mind withdraws progressively from all external and internal stimuli. In the end, states of pure and undistracted consciousness can be achieved. The *Samatha* meditation procedure starts with effort at concentrating the mind on specific objects, and progresses systematically through a series of states of what are called *jhanas*, or mental absorption (Buddhagosa's *Vissudhimagga*).

Vipassana, or insight meditation, also starts with concentration exercises using appropriate objects on which one focuses. In this procedure, however, once a certain level of concentration is achieved so that undistracted focusing can be maintained, one goes on to examine with steady, careful attention and in great detail all sensory and mental processes. Through this contemplation, one becomes a detached observer of one's own activity. The objects of this contemplation are classified as fourfold: body, sensations, mental states, and "mental objects", for example, various moral and intellectual subjects. The aim is to achieve total and immediate awareness, or mindful awareness, of all phenomena. This eventually leads, it is claimed, to the full and clear perception of the impermanence of all things and beings (MN I, SN V)

Benefits of meditation

Meditative exercises of both types, when properly carried out and developed, are claimed to lead to greater ability to concentrate, greater freedom from distraction, greater tolerance of change and turmoil around oneself, and sharper awareness and greater alertness about one's own responses, both physical and mental. They also lead, more generally, to greater calmness or tranquillity. While reaching the ultimate goal of perfection normally require a long series of regular training periods of systematic meditation coupled with major restraint in one's conduct, the more mundane benefits of meditation are available to all serious and persistent practitioners. An excellent account of how "mindfulness meditation" can be used for enhancing the quality of life has been provided by Bhante Henepola Gunaratana (1993).

From a present-day perspective, Buddhist meditation techniques may be seen as an instrument for achieving certain psychological benefits. Primarily, meditation has a role as a stress-reducing strategy comparable to the more modern techniques of relaxation. There is a substantial literature in present day clinical psychology and psychiatry which shows that meditation can produce beneficial effects this way (e.g., Kwee, 1990; Shapiro, 1982; West, 1987). Studies of psychological changes that accompany meditation have shown several changes to occur which, together, indicate a state of calmness or relaxation (Woolfolk, 1975). These include: reduction in oxygen consumption, lowered heart rate, decreased breathing rate and blood pressure, reduction in serum lactic acid levels, increased skin resistance and changes in blood flow. These peripheral changes are generally compatible with decreased arousal in the sympathetic nervous system. There are also certain central changes, as shown by brain wave patterns. The amalgam of these physiological changes related to meditation has been called "the relaxation response" by Benson (1975). Interestingly, the Buddha himself advocated meditation for what we would today term clinical problems. For example, he advocated that meditation be used to achieve trouble-free sleep and as a way of controlling pain (Vinaya Pitaka I; SN V).

It is perhaps worth dwelling briefly on the use of mindfulness meditation for pain control. In a much-cited paper Kabat-Zinn, Lipworth and Burney (1985) reported that a group of chronic pain patients who were trained in mindfulness meditation in a ten-week stress-reduction programme showed significant reduction in pain and related symptoms. A control group of patients who did not receive meditation training did not show such improvement. The rationale for selecting this strategy for the treatment of pain is explained as follows:

> In the case of pain perception, the cultivation of detached observation of the pain experience may be achieved by paying careful attention and distinguishing as *separate* events the actual primary sensations as they occur from moment to moment and any accompanying thoughts about pain. (Kabat-Zinn, et al., 1985, p. 165).

In another paper, Kabat-Zinn (1982) has given an even more detailed account of the rationale for using mindfulness meditation for pain control. He shows how mindfulness meditation can enable one to focus on sensations as they arise, rather than attempt to escape from them. It helps to recognise the bare physical sensation, unembellished by psychological events. This "uncoupling" has the effect of changing one's overall experience of pain. To quote:

> The nociceptive signals (sensory) may be undiminished, but the emotional and cognitive components of the pain experience, the hurt, the suffering, are reduced. (p.15)

It is this detached observation of sensations which mindfulness meditation helps one to develop, that makes such meditation a particularly well-suited strategy for pain control. In fact, the references in the Buddhist texts to pain control by mindfulness meditation make this very point. For example, it is stated that the Venerable Ananda, the Buddha's personal assistant, once visited a householder named Sirivaddha who was ill. On hearing from the patient that he was in much pain and that his pains were getting worse, Ananda advised him to engage in the meditation of mindfulness. Similarly, it is recorded that the Buddha himself visited two ailing Bhikkhus, Mogallana and Kassapa, who were in pain, and advised each of them to engage in mindfulness meditation. Perhaps the most impressive and most explicit in terms of the rationale for this use of meditation, is the account given of the Venerable Anuruddha. He was sick and grievously afflicted. Many Bhikkhus who visited him, finding him calm and relaxed, asked how his "painful sensations evidently made no impact on his mind". He replied: "It is because I have my mind well-grounded in mindfulness. That is why the painful sensations that come upon me make no impression on my mind." The implication here is that meditation can reduce, or "block out" the mental aspect of, the pain; while physical sensations may remain intact, one's vulnerability to subjectively felt pain is reduced. The above accounts are all from the SN IV, which states this position quite explicitly in a different passage:

> The untrained layman, when touched by painful bodily feelings, grieves and lament... and is distraught... But the well trained disciple, when touched by painful bodily feelings, will not weep, nor grieve, nor lament... nor will he be distraught... The layman, when touched by painful bodily feelings... weeps... He experiences two kinds of feelings: a bodily one and a mental one. It is as if a man is hit by one arrow, and then by a second arrow; he feels the pain of two arrows. So it is with the untrained layman, when touched by a painful bodily feeling, he experiences two kinds of feeling, a bodily one and a mental one. But the well-trained disciple, when

> touched by painful bodily feeling, weeps not … He feels only one kind of feeling: a bodily one, not a mental one. It is as if a man is hit by one arrow, but not by a second arrow; he feels the pain of one arrow only. So it is with the well trained disciple; when touched by painful bodily feeling, he feels but one feeling, bodily pain only.

The view of pain contained in this expository account is clear: physical pain sensations are usually accompanied by psychological correlates, which are like a second pain. The student, trained in mindfulness meditation sees the physical sensations as they are and does not allow himself to be affected by psychological elaboration of pain. Thus his experience is limited to the perception of the physical sensation only. It is this account of pain that provides the rationale for the instances cited above, where those in pain are advised to engage in mindfulness meditation.

Other behaviour change strategies

In addition to meditation, Theravada Buddhist literature also contains a wide range of behaviour change strategies, which were used and recommended by the Buddha and his students. This aspect of the Dhamma has not been explored by modern researchers until relatively recently and it is only in the last 25 years or so that these strategies have been discussed (e.g., P. de Silva, 1984) and highlighted as being remarkably similar to several of the established techniques of modern Behaviour Therapy and Cognitive-Behaviour Therapy. The ways in which the overall approach of behaviour modification and that of the Buddhist teachings may be seen as broadly similar, have also been discussed by Mikulas (1981, 2002). Some areas of similarity highlighted by Mikulas are: the rejection of the notion of unchanging self or soul; focus on observable phenomena; emphasis on testability; emphasis on techniques for awareness of certain bodily responses; emphasis on "living in the here-and-now", dissemination of teachings and techniques. Given these broad similarities and given the general empiricist/experientialist attitude of the Dhamma, it is not surprising that specific behaviour change techniques were used and recommended in the Early Buddhist teachings. Its empiricist/experientialist approach is exemplified by the *Kalama Sutta* (AN I), in which the Buddha advises a group of inquirers not to accept anything on hearsay, authority or pure argument, but to accept only what is empirically and experientially verifiable. It is also entirely consistent with the Buddhist pragmatic social ethic, which recognises the importance of behaviours conducive to one's own and others' well-being as a goal in its own right. Behaviour changes, both in oneself and others, were to be affected through the use of specific techniques.

The range of behavioural and cognitive-behavioural strategies found in the literature of the Dhamma is wide. The strategies include: reducing fear through graded exposure and reciprocal inhibition; using rewards for promoting desirable behaviour; modelling appropriate behaviours to induce behavioural change; applying stimulus control to eliminate undesirable behaviour; training social skills; practicing self-monitoring; controlling intrusive thoughts by distraction, by switching/stopping, incompatible thoughts, and by prolonged exposure to the unwanted intrusions; using intense, covert focussing on the unpleasant aspects of a stimulus or the unpleasant consequences of a response, to reduce attachment to the former and eliminate the latter; using a graded approach to the development of positive feelings towards others; use of external cues in behaviour control; use of response cost to aid elimination of undesirable behaviour; involving family members for carrying out behaviour change programmes; and so on. Since these strategies have been considered in detail in previous publications (P. de Silva, 1984, 1986, 2001), which also give references to the original texts, an example, rather than a full discussion will be offered here.

The *Vitakkasanthana Sutta* of the MN offers the disciple five different techniques for dealing with unwanted, intrusive cognitions, each to be tried if the preceding one fails to produce the desired results. Such unwanted, intrusive cognitions, which particularly hinder one's meditative efforts and can be a major problem for a Buddhist, several strategies are recommended. These are presented in a hierarchical fashion, each to be tried if the preceding one fails.

(1) Switch to an opposite or incompatible thought. The first is to reflect on an object which is associated with thoughts which are the opposite of the unwanted thought. This means that if the unwanted cognition is associated with passion or lust, one should think of something promoting lustlessness; if it is associated with malice, one should think of something promoting loving kindness; and if it is something associated with delusion or confusion, one should think of something promoting clarity. This exercise of switching to a thought that is incompatible with the unwanted one, "like a carpenter getting rid of a coarse peg with a fine one", is claimed to help eliminate the unwanted intrusion.

(2) Ponder on harmful consequences. If, however, the unwanted thought still keeps arising, one is advised to ponder on the perils and disadvantages of the thought; that is, to consider its harmful consequences. This would help one to rid oneself of the thought in question, "like in the case of a young man or woman, who is eager to look nice and clean, who would be revolted and disgusted if one finds the carcass of a snake round the neck and would immediately get rid of it".

(3) Ignore and distract. If that, too, fails, the technique of ignoring an unwanted thought is recommended. One is to strive not to pay attention, "like a man who closed his eyes or looks in another direction in order not to see a visual object that he does not wish to see". It is suggested that various distracting activities may be used in order not to pay attention to the unwanted cognition. These include: recalling of a doctrinal passage one has learned, concentrating on actual concrete objects, and engaging in some unrelated physical activity.

(4) Reflect on removal of causes. If the problem still persists, then a further strategy is recommended, this is to reflect on the removal or stopping of the causes of the target thought. This is explained with the analogy of a man walking briskly who asks himself "Why am I walking briskly?", then reflects on his walking and stops and stands; then reflects on his standing and sits down, etc.

(5) Control with forceful effort. If this strategy, too, fails, then a fifth

method is advocated, which is forcefully to restrain and dominate the mind. This use of effort is likened to "a strong man holding and restraining a weaker man", One is to use the "effort of one part of the mind to control the other."

The significance of the presence of these techniques in the Buddhist texts is manifold. Firstly, it reflects the fact that Buddhism is not only concerned with one's endeavours to achieve the ultimate religious goal by a process of self-development. It also has something to offer in the area of day-to day management of psychological problems, often as a goal in its own right, for reasons of one's own and one's fellow beings' benefit and happiness. Thus these techniques are applicable irrespective of whether or not one has committed oneself to a life devoted to the aim of personal development and, ultimately, the state of *Arahant*-hood. Secondly, being clearly behavioural and/or cognitive-behavioural, these techniques are well-defined, easy to use and empirically testable. Indeed, the Buddhist approach is one of trying out various strategies until one that is effective is found. Thirdly, the techniques are for use on oneself as well as helping others; numerous examples are found in the texts for both types of use. The Buddha's advice to the Kalamas, noted above, reflects and embodies this approach (AN I):

> Do not accept anything from hearsay, because of tradition, or because of the reputation of the teacher. Accept what you can see for yourselves as valid … When you have verified for yourselves that this is wholesome and that is not, this is blameless and that is blameworthy, this is conducive to well-being and happiness and that is conducive to suffering and illness, then you will choose this as your practice and reject that.

Indeed, the Buddha's own quest for awakening followed this path: having tried out various methods and teachings available at the time, he rejected all of them as each failed to lead him towards his goal.

Relevance of Buddhist strategies for therapy

Buddhist meditative practices and other behaviour change strategies have a clear relevance to present-day therapeutic practice. A wide range of clearly defined techniques is available for use with common psychological problems. Some of the strategies are closely similar to modern cognitive-behavioural techniques and this means that their validity and utility are now apparently established in both an eastern and a western sense, as many of the cognitive-behavioural techniques have recently been the focus of clinical trials (Butler, Chapman, Forman, & Beck, 2006). There is a strong case, too, for those Buddhist strategies that, so far, have no counterpart in modern therapy, to be empirically tested using clinical-experimental research methods. If clinical trials show them to be effective in western contexts, they can be fruitfully incorporated into the repertoire of techniques available to the present-day therapist.

It can also be argued that these techniques, which already have value in indigenous Buddhist groups will have particular value in the practice of therapy with Buddhist client groups in the West. One of the problems that arise in using methods derived from western science with client populations of a different cultural background is that the techniques offered may seem alien to the culturally different group. Thus, they may not be readily accepted or, if accepted, compliance with therapeutic instructions may be poor. These cultural difficulties in therapy and counselling have been fully recognised by many authors (e.g., Mikulas, 2002). On the other hand, if the techniques that are used and offered, although they may form an integral part of a western psychological system, are shown to be similar to ideas and practices that were accepted historically by the client's home culture, then therapists would have a greater chance of gaining a client's compliance and success. The use of meditation techniques as a stress-reduction strategy with Buddhist groups in several places provides an example of this phenomenon. A case in point is the use of Buddhist meditation in a psychiatric setting in Kandy, Sri Lanka (P. de Silva & Samarasinghe, 1998). Mikulas (1983) has also commented on the favourable reception accorded to the ideas and techniques of behaviour modification in another Buddhist country, Thailand.

A role in prophylaxis

A further application of Buddhist Psychology lies in the area of prophylaxis. Prophylaxis or prevention of psychological disorders, is an important aspect of mental health practice (see Albee, 1982; Caplan, 1964). Theoretically, there is much scope for this, both with Buddhist client groups and with others. Several Buddhist techniques appear to have a potential role to play in the prevention of certain kinds of psychological disorders. For example, training in meditation, leading to greater ability to achieve calmness and tranquillity, may help enhance one's tolerance of numerous inevitable stresses in modern life. One may, in other words, achieve a degree of immunity against psychological effects of stress and frustration (cf. stress inoculation training of Meichenbaum, 1985). The facility and skill in the self-regulation of behaviour is well documented (Baumeister & Vohs, 2004). The overall self-development that the Dhamma encourages and recommends also has something to offer for prophylaxis. For example, if one trains oneself not to develop intense attachments to material things and to those around one, one is less likely to be vulnerable to psychological distress and disorders arising from their loss, including abnormal and debilitating grief reactions. Some of the meditation exercises and other personal development endeavours found in Buddhism can potentially enable a person to develop an outlook on life and patterns of response which, in turn, will help them to cope better with the problems of living and minimise the chances of breakdown or dysfunction. This kind of primary prevention is certainly worth exploring.

Many Buddhist ideas and practices are also relevant to secondary prevention. Secondary prevention seeks to intervene early, as soon as problems begin to appear and prevent them from turning into more serious difficulties. It also includes endeavours to avoid relapse of disorders that have been overcome – in other words, to prevent further episodes. Perhaps the best modern example of secondary prevention comes from the work of a team of present day psychologists who have used mindfulness meditation as a way of preventing relapse in people with a history of depression. Segal, Williams, and Teasdale (2002) have reported the results of a large clinical trial. In this trial, Mindfulness-Based Cognitive Therapy, carried out in a group setting, was shown to be a promising and cost-effective psychological approach to the prevention of relapse in recovered, depressed patients with a history of recurrent episodes. This was a large multi-centre study, which involved a substantial number (145) of patients. Why was mindfulness meditation applied in this context? As pointed out by Segal and colleagues, increased mindfulness is relevant to the prevention of relapse of depression as it allows the detection of relapse-related patterns of negative thinking, feelings and physical sensations, so that they can be "nipped in the bud". Further, entering a mindful mode of processing at such times enables the person to disengage from the relatively "automatic" ruminative thought patterns that would otherwise promote the relapse process (Segal, et al., 2002). This highly impressive empirical study demonstrates the relevance of Buddhism in a major clinical area, aiding, and promoting secondary prevention. The results could be corroborated in a replication study by Ma and Teasdale (2004). There is clearly scope for much new work along these lines, using specific Buddhist strategies for preventive purposes in well-controlled clinical studies.

In this context it is useful to refer to M.W.P de Silva (2005), who has provided a valuable discussion of how Buddhist ideas can make a significant contribution in relation to positive mental health. The relevant areas are: reality orientation, attitude towards self, self-knowledge, voluntary control and autonomy, ability to form sensitive and satisfying relationships and body-mind integration. Buddhist teachings can contribute to positive mental health in each of these domains. The point here is that the Dhamma not only offers notions and strategies that can help in the remediation and prevention of psychological disorders; it also provides a framework for the active promotion of positive mental health and overall psychological well-being.

Conclusion

This chapter highlights several psychological aspects of Theravada Buddhist teachings. Buddhist Psychology includes detailed theoretical accounts of human behaviour and experience and practical measures for personal development including behavioural and cognitive change strategies. They have relevance to present day mental health practice, both in terms of therapy and in terms of prevention of psychological disorders. In addition, Buddhist Psychology can also make a significant contribution to the promotion of positive mental health. The strong psychological content of the Buddhist teachings has been acknowledged by many present day scholars in psychology and in related disciplines. More research on Buddhist Psychology is now being undertaken, especially from a therapeutic perspective, in different parts of the world. The growing study of the Buddhist teachings as a psychology is likely to open up many fresh possibilities.

Part II

The Dharma As An Upaya Of Communal Construction

In Chapter 5 Van der Velde makes the point that *Upayakaushalya*, an innovative and surviving force to reinvent the Dharma in changing circumstances, was inherently present in the Dharma and already propagated by the Buddha himself. That is why the Dharma can be interpreted and transformed as a religion, as a philosophy, as a way of life, and as a 21st century social constructionist "social-clinical-neuro-psychology" like in this book. The Dharma could withstand the ravages of time due to the unique Buddhist skilful methodology of adjusting its teachings to the students' cultural and intellectual backgrounds particularly because the Dharma is a communal happening. Down the ages meaning is particularly derived from telling and retelling about the Buddha's narrative. From this narrative fresh stories emerge which are connected to one's idiosyncratic life experiences. Thus, the narrative is a discursive metaphor – i.e. a form of discourse that is more than a metaphor of storytelling about the Buddha as a doctor, a liberator, and so on – which eventually might become a view and a path. It helps to organise, structure, cohere, and account for events which lead to an understanding of human nature, our intentional joint-actions, and the processes of our "selves". The self is at best a linguistically constructed concept that merely exists in dialogical relationships. Such a communally constructed dialogical-narrative self, i.e. a "social constructivist" self, remarkably corresponds with the Buddhist view of a non-foundational "empty" self.

Pemarathana's Chapter 6 is about a salient feature of *Upaya*. The Dharma does not cling to concepts and views; words and images cannot replace one's unspeakable meditative experiencing. The Buddha recognized the relative and pragmatic value of all thinking and languaging in the process of realizing awakening to Dependent Origination, selflessness, and pro-social action. Awareness and insight in the Dependent Origination of the mind provide guidelines to deal with the activity of the mind; these guidelines include the admonishment not to become attached, not even to the words of the Buddha. A pervasive dimension in the Buddha's Dependent Origination is the contextual basis of knowledge and meaning which emphasizes communal construction through social exchange and continuous dialogue and negotiation between people across time. This implies a liberating move away from trying to locate the origins of knowledge and meaning in individual authorship toward a perspective that ideas, beliefs, and attitudes are "multi-authored" in interrelationships.

Premasiri's Chapter 7 submits that the Dharma is a complex system comprising elements of religion, philosophy, and psychology grounded in the Buddha's awakening and liberation. The author proposes a Dharma as a way of life and a psychology for the "dis-eased" mind, a therapy which in principle leaves no room for metaphysics or godly rules for what is absolute good or bad. This way of life is guided by Buddhist ethics which are not based on commandments as Buddhists are basically non-theistic free thinkers, not blind followers. The Buddhist view of morality is practical and is foremost a means leading to end experiential suffering and to promote communal happiness. Such practice originates in contextual/relational interdependence through a generative-transformational languaging process with an uncertain outcome. This concurs with Gergen's (2009) "non-foundational morality of collaborative practice" which is not an "anything goes" moral relativism but an ethics that involves joint responsibility and accountability. Rather than absolute and fixed objective rules, Buddhist ethics are a communal activity, something done together, within universal and local contexts. It thus becomes intelligible that Robin Hood's morals are different from those of the sheriff's.

Chapter 5

The Buddha's Biography, Navayana, And Upaya

Paul J.C.L. van der Velde

Introduction

The Buddhist Dharma is not a unity; it is not "one religion" or "one philosophy". That is why the term Buddhism is a misnomer. There are and have been numerous schools that may, on the surface, have very little in common. Moreover, nowadays we may even find a discussion going on whether the Dharma actually is a religion, a philosophy, or a way of living, etc. We may even hear it being designated as a "secular religion". This is remarkable as in the original languages of India it is very hard to find a word for religion or philosophy. There are words such as "Dharma" or "Darshana", and these may come close to the western concept of religion, yet these are not equal to "religion". While they may resemble "religion", Dharma is not so much about "believing in Buddhism", it is rather about "practicing the Dharma", in whatever form. Yet there are two aspects that all forms of the Buddhist Dharma have in common: a link to the Buddha's life history and a claim that one knows for certain what the Buddha has meant.

The Dharma will always be linked to the life history of the Buddha. One may find this link not simply within the various schools of Buddhist thought. Many individual and practicing Buddhists or people attracted to the Dharma will underline this relationship. The schools can be so very different that at times adherents may not even recognize each other as Buddhists. However, there will always be the link to the life of the Buddha. The Buddha's life is held to be the ideal perfection of existence. The paradigm thus held in common by all Buddhists is the life of the Buddha. Besides this template, each current of Buddhist thought, every school, claims to have direct access to what the Buddha is supposed to have really meant and taught his students. Some schools will simply say the others are wrong. Other schools are more careful and admit that there can be variations of the Dharma. Still other schools may claim that their teachings encompass all earlier teachings. Most schools will also claim that their practices can be linked back to a particular moment in the life history of the Buddha. Zen for instance connects with the flower sermon in which the Buddha showed only a flower to Kashayapa. This instance forms the basis of the foundation of a tradition that propagates a silent, wordless teaching. Many schools link their practices of meditation back to the life of the Buddha. For example, one may find near the Mahabodhi temple in Bodh Gaya a meditation path that consists of stones in the shape of lotus petals. Schools practicing walking meditation connect this particular exercise with the acts the Buddha himself is supposed to have performed in the weeks before and after his awakening. Allegedly, the Buddha practiced walking meditation along this path.

Whither genuine Buddhist teaching?

Tradition has it that the first Buddhist conference was held at Rajageha, a place now known as Rajgir, in Bihar, India, just after the *parinirvana* (final Nirvana, death) of the Buddha. Under the guidance of Kashyapa 499 Arhats, awakened Bhikkhus worthy to be respected, took part in the meeting. On that occasion Upali recited the Vinaya rules for the Sangha, Ananda recited the discourses of the Buddha (the suttas) and the *Abhidhamma* (the "higher teachings") was made public. According to legend, the latter consisted of lectures the Buddha had taught his mother. The Arhats came to know about these via Sariputra. It was told that the Buddha rose up to heaven every day for three months to teach her as she had died shortly after his birth. Every day he descended one time to convey to Sariputra the teachings that he delivered his mother (who resided as a "male deity in the heaven of the 33 gods") during that period. Based on the *Vinaya*, the *Nikayas* and the *Abhidhamma* – as recited at that first conference and which came down to the present day intact and unadulterated, as tradition tells us – the Theravada through their Pali writings claims to have direct access to the pristine and thus most authoritative teachings of the Buddha.

While the Arhats were reciting in Rajageha, the Mahayana tradition insists that there was a parallel conference of the Bodhisattvas on the Gridhrakuta, the Vulture's Peak, near Rajageha, an elevated rock where the Buddha used to come to teach to an audience or, according to Nagarjuna (who lived in the 2nd century), on another peak nearby, named Vimalasvabhava, situated to the South of Rajageha. This meeting breathes an airy atmosphere because it is populated by metaphysical figures. It was Samantabhadra who presided over the conference. Vajrapani recited the Mahayana Sutras, while Maitreya took care of the Vinaya. Manjushri is said to have recited the Abhidharma. Sariputra was allegedly present there – amidst these metaphysical Bodhisattvas – and this is the reason why we may find, for instance in the *Heart Sutra* that the Bodhisattva Avalokiteshvara could address Sariputra. It might be speculated that these sutras were already uttered during Sariputra's lifetime and therefore even before the conference of Rajageha, because it is stated that Sariputra (and Mahamaudgalyayana) passed into *parinirvana* before the Buddha. Based on the Mahayana Sanskrit sutras, allegedly already started very early in Buddhist history, Mahayanists claim that they have the direct access to the most authoritative Buddhist teachings. These sutras consist of the Buddha's "discourses" written down in Sanskrit (but most probably made by Arhats after the Buddha's lifetime).

The Vajrayana tradition (an extension of the Mahayana) also claims to have access to the original Dharma of the Buddha, by means of the so-called Terma texts. These are texts that the Buddha is supposed to have taught or handed over as manuscripts during his lifetime, but society in his lifetime was not yet ready for these particular messages. Therefore he delivered the lectures but hid them in stones or taught them to wondrous snakes who practically live for ever or taught them to other supernatural creatures such as celestial damsels. The texts were in later days, when the time was ripe, revealed by the snakes (to Nagarjuna as told in myths) or they were discovered by wondrous magicians. Two famous magicians were Padmasambhava, who lived in Swat, Tibet and Bhutan in the eighth century, and Pema Lingpa (1450-1521), who lived in Bhutan. Pema Lingpa is said to have discovered many Termas in Bhutan. Several of these are in the wondrous Khandroma script that according to mythology is a script developed by heavenly damsels in which one sign may have a thousand meanings. I saw one Terma text that was supposedly discovered by Pema Lingpa when I was in Bhutan in 2000. It was a short text simply written in Tibetan but considered to be written in Khandroma. In the printed form it was quite large due to its multiple interpretations. Likewise, it was told that Padmasambhava discovered countless texts and taught several secret messages to his two wives, Mandarava and Yeshe Tsogyal, who also discovered Termas. Both Mahayana and Vajrayana also claim to have access to the original message conveyed by the Buddha. All these traditions adjusted the Buddha's original message to their audience, time and environment. The idea was to develop teachings to replace those taught at the time of the Buddha and which were not considered suitable for delivery centuries later. In the case of the historical Buddha, he had to start teaching somewhere at a certain time. But new teachings based on the original essentials are needed to adjust to new circumstances. In the Mahayana-Vajrayana they are not exactly presented as "new". They are only discovered in a new time, when they were needed most to convey the Dharma to new people in new countries with different cultures. Obviously, the "discovery" is an Upaya tale to assure people that the essence of these new teachings is the Buddha's. In fact, all teachings are Upayas. These are skilful means and adjustments of the Dharma to changing external conditions. As skilful means they are conventions that are "not always true". This idea that Dharma teachings are adjustments to the convention of the new circumstances was contended by Nagarjuna.

Dharma and the West

Quite often modern people attracted to the Dharma say that it is not the present one that they are attracted to, because that is a "religion" with all kinds of superstitions, dogmas and rituals. What they want is what is named the "original Dharma of the Buddha". This is not a religion. It is a way to liberation or of healing. An already somewhat older example of this is Alexandra David Neel (1868-1969), who was at times attacked for her interest in Tibetan Buddhist teachings which were in her days considered to be perverted. It was then called "Lamaism" and was heavily frowned upon. Alexandra David Neel asserted that it was not about Lamas, but about the highly respected original teaching of the Buddha that she cared (Lopez, 2002, p.xxxiii).[1] Other famous examples are Madame Helena Blavatsky and Colonel Olcott who founded the Theosophical Society in 1875. They both travelled to Asia in order to protect the Dharma against the influence of Christian missionaries that they considered to be a threat to Asian cultures (Lopez, 2002, pp.xiv-xv). Once they arrived in India they converted to Hinduism. Olcott travelled on to Sri Lanka where he embraced the Early Buddhist Dharma. All the time, however, both Blavatsky and Olcott kept the idea that the Buddhist teachings of their days were a corrupted form of the original Dharma. The original message of the Buddha was hidden beneath countless forms of superstition and all kinds of outdated rituals. Thus, Olcott composed his Buddhist "Catechism" in Sri Lanka, which was at first warmly welcomed and

---

1.   Lopez Jr., D. (2002). *Modern Buddhism, readings for the unenlightened.* London: Penguin.

approved by the Sangha. It was only when he openly stated that the famous tooth of the Buddha that was kept under worship in Kandy was merely a piece of a deer's antler that he was opposed by the Singhalese Sangha. The approval of his Catechism was withdrawn (Lopez, 2002, p.xix). However, Olcott never recanted – he never accepted the tooth for real. The tooth is considered sacred because it heard the edifying words of the Buddha before they reached the ears of his students. Western Buddhists will state that the Asian Dharma is full of superstitions and rituals and is therefore a religion. One may often hear that the essential Dharma has been polluted with all kinds of traditions and religious practices. In Asia one simply says that these practices are part of the tradition. They are part of the living Asian Dharma as it is practiced in daily life. At present one may state that this has more to do with what westerners long for than with the Dharma as an Asian ancient tradition. Thus, the Dharma contains many paradoxes.

The original Buddhist teachings were and are a way to liberation. There were many teachers in the days of the Buddha, which was the period of the late Upanishads, when the fixed goals of the great Vedic rituals were quickly losing their appeal. Their workings were doubted by many and alternatives were sought for the static targets of life of the Vedic religion that were far too much earthbound for many. At the end of the 19th century Olcott and Blavatsky considered the Dharma to be a serious philosophy, not a "creed" (Lopez, 2002, p.xv). Moreover, the Dharma was said to be scientific: it was in accordance with human reasoning and with natural sciences (Lopez, 2002, p.xv). We have to keep in mind, however, that they were here addressing the Theravada, which they considered to be the original Dhamma of the Buddha, not the Mahayana Buddhist practices of North and East Asia. Olcott and Blavatsky considered these to be debased and corrupted transformations of the pristine teachings of the Buddha into religion and superstition. However, even the *Abhidhamma* teachings are not to be viewed as simply a hypothetical model of how the human mind works. Instead they must – with dogmatic flavour – be regarded to be elucidating what the mind is absolutely about and how it functions for real.

Nevertheless, in the last few decades we witness in the West that the Buddhist teachings are considered to be a philosophy or a non-dogmatic way of living, not a religion. Thus, while many Buddhist schools will admit that all teachings are conventional (provisional and relative), they are only valid in the context of teaching to that particular individual or group at a certain time and place. What is "true" one moment is not necessarily "true" the next moment, even though it refers to the scriptural parts of the Dharma. Recently, the Dalai Lama developed yet another idea. He has stated on various occasions that it is not necessary to convert to the Dharma to appreciate it. Another author, David Brazier, has stated that there are Buddhists amongst the adherents of all world religions. Thus, it seems that the Dharma has undergone various changes: from a way out of the world of suffering, into a religion and a religious identity, into a non-theistic religion, into a philosophy and philosophy of life, into a science, and now most recently into a state of mind and a spiritual disposition found within all world religions. Nowadays it seems that Buddhist adherents have come to be seen as ideally developed persons.

This is all the more remarkable since, as stated earlier above, many Asian languages do not even have different words for religion, philosophy, way of living or faith. These distinctions do not exist in Sanskrit or Pali. However, speaking from within the Buddhist tradition these utterances would be considered as nothing else but Upaya: skilfulness in means. To refocus on the "original" is part of the entire Buddhist tradition: it is a form of skilful means to discover the actual Dharma in the form of a skilful means. Part of this refocusing may be the iden-tification of one's essential experience of personal suffering and the discovering of the Buddha's quest. The connection between the ideal paradigm and experience of the Buddha and one's personal Dukkha experience is essential to acquire the Buddhist identity and to connect with the Dharma. Dukkha is an active factor in the world and so is the Dharma; to be fully active the two experiences need to interact and move toward awakening. In a way, every being lives in a Jataka metaphorical narrative at the end of which each and every being will one day touch the earth of Bodh Gaya and defeat one's personal Mara. The life one lives at present is just like one of the countless lives the Buddha passed through as narrated in the Jatakas (see below). This world is the place where one develops the wisdom that will eventually result in the experience of Nirvana.

Just like the Buddha discovered what many other Buddhas had discovered before him, each one of us will discover what he had discovered. This is the rationale. Therefore, the Dharma always has a connection to one's life history in whatever birth shape one may appear at the moment of reflection. In the Mahayana lore, the moment that one perceives the Dharma depends on the grace of Bodhisattvas or due to the karmic merits one has accumulated in the past, which may have invoked the grace of the Bodhisattvas. Even the gravest sinner will at some time be thus reborn to come across the Dharma. In modern Buddhist literature one may find the idea that Bodhisattvas are not etheric beings but beings of flesh and blood living amongst us as exemplary ideal persons like Mother Theresa or the Dalai Lama. The metaphys-ical Bodhisattva ideal implies that everybody will one day reach awakening, even mass mur-derers or war criminals and those guilty of genocide. Buddhists are advised to feel sorry for these persons as they will lead millions of lives of great suffering before their negative Karma will become extinguished. Even the Buddha is said to have committed "sins" for which he has suffered during his life as Siddhartha Gautama (Strong, 2001, pp.32-34).[2]

Navayana: the new vehicle

The term Navayana – earlier proposed in the 1930s by Captain J.E. Ellam and in the 1950s by B.R. Ambedkar, India's Dalit former secretary of justice – is here used to designate the Dharma as it has developed and continues to develop within western and westernized culture in recent times. It refers to Buddhist thought and practice as it is developing in modernity, above all in the West, in dialogue with the issues that play a part in this juncture of history. Particularly, Navayana is the result of the interaction between Asian/traditional and western/modern Buddhist ideas. It is still under construction as the process is in full swing. The three major vehicles – Theravada, Mahayana and Vajrayana – are in constant dynamic development as well, but the idea seems to exist, above all in the West, that these vehicles are quite static. They actually are not. One may recall the late Buddhadasa Bhikkhu, who was a great Theravada innovator in Thailand. As we are living in a global village, concepts, teachings and ideas from

---

2.   Strong, J.S. (2001). *The Buddha, a short biography*. Oxford: Oneworld.

the new developments born out of the interaction with the West find their way back to Asia to start a new or renewed life there. The name Navayana is also used here to indicate the fourth great vehicle in Buddhist thinking. One thing to keep in mind while using this term Navayana is that it is a name for various currents of thinking within the Buddhist Dharma and that there is hardly any "new" Buddhist who designates him/herself as a "navayanin" or something of the kind. Therefore, Navayana is an etic term only rarely used by Buddhists themselves. This sets it quite apart from the names of the other three vehicles that are widely used by the traditional Buddhists to identify themselves. Mostly, we find the new Buddhists in the West designate themselves as belonging to the schools of their teachers. It is within these teachings that characteristics, typical for the new vehicle can be found. If one were to use the term Navayana, however, some Buddhist opposition might be met with. Other authors prefer Neoyana, which is literally the same as Navayana; except that "neo" is Latin for the Sanskrit "nava", and the two words are Indo-European cognates. Still others prefer terms such as NeoZen. I prefer Navayana as the word is a compound of Sanskrit words, and is loyal to the Asian tradition whereas the term NeoZen is, in my opinion, too limited in its scope as it would first of all refer to the Sino-Japanese Zen schools.

Most Navayana Buddhists are to be found in the West. Asian Buddhists will usually identify themselves with currents of Buddhist practice as found in Asia. Most people who live in the West (i.e., America, Europe, Australia, and New Zealand) and are raised as Buddhists can be found amongst migrants from Asia. One will only rarely come across Buddhists of western origin who were raised as Buddhists. Buddhist of western origin for some reason became attracted to the Buddhist Dharma as adults. Some of them call themselves Buddhists (or "converted to Buddhism"), while others support the Dharma without calling themselves Buddhists. This probably has to do with leading Buddhist proponents, such as the Dalai Lama, who proclaim that one does not have to convert to the Dharma in order to experience peace of mind, to exert compassion and to be friendly. Moreover, as was discussed above, typically the western Dharma is usually not considered to be a religion. It is rather viewed as a way of life, a philosophy or an attitude towards life, and the like. One converts to a religion, not to a philosophy, nor to an attitude towards life. In spite of this, however, the Dharma did adopt religious features, even if it was not stated as such originally. In many instances Navayana Buddhists are quite eclectic in what they practice. After all, it is not a problem to make combinations of Tibetan Vajrayana, Japanese Zen, and Theravada Vipassana techniques of South-East Asia. On the other hand one may – just like in the traditional schools – come across Navayana Buddhists who contend and nourish the idea that the teachings of other schools are simply wrong.

Dharma and biography

The step in the turn to the Dharma for a western Buddhist is usually a logical extension of the context of her/his biographical narrative. A new Buddhist will have an account to tell about where and when s/he started with her/his quest for inner growth or "spiritual" development. At one moment in the person's life the Buddhist message came across and the person felt attracted to it. As the Dharma is part of an autobiographical narrative construction with an open end it is difficult to say whether it will be the person's final developmental stage.

The Buddha's biographical story is the ideal life narrative. It is the quest for the healing insight and wisdom of the Dharma that is able to bring about an end to the imperfection and suffering of life. The Buddha's life history, however, not only encompasses his life as prince Siddhartha Gautama, it also consists of the long way to Nirvana. According to tradition, in the night of his awakening Gautama remembered all of his "previous lives" before he came to his last life as the son of king Suddhodana. He was then challenged by Mara, the "demon of the world", to give up his quest. Mara asked him who could bear testimony of his right to Nirvana. The Buddha then realized the importance of his "past lives" and he touched the earth with the request to testify about all his merits. The "goddess earth" appeared to beat Mara's army. Thus, the Buddha remembered his past lives, but he did not tell all of these to his students; he only chose to discuss his past lives in demanding circumstances. In fact he discouraged the idea of bringing up the past too much as one can choose the path to Nirvana and liberation at this very moment.

It is of no use to look for answers for one's sufferings in the present by studying the past and one's ostensible "past lives". We all know that everything has a cause and that this cause has a cause as well. The path to liberation lies in the disruption of the chain of causes. Thus, do not let the present action be a cause for further reactions. It was only when telling about past lives was part of the present teachings as Upaya that the Buddha was willing to look for causes in the past. Otherwise, knowledge of past lives can lead to attachments to skills and idle acts. Another trap is that of having an excuse. One can say they are unable to do anything about the present situation because of demerits that originate from an unlucky past. Thus, the reason why the Buddha chose to tell a birth story is handed down for posterity. Moreover, identifications are given. Each character that plays a role in the Jataka is identified with a person of the last life of the Buddha as prince Siddhartha Gautama. Therefore, the Jatakas not only serve as an ideal example of one person's striving for liberation, they also serve as an illustration of how an entire group of beings eventually develops into human beings. Because each of them were – due to their virtuous acts – time after time ostensibly "reborn" in the close proximity of the awakened teacher, they at the end almost all reached awakening in his close company. Even Devadatta, the evil cousin of the Buddha – who tried to kill him – reborn in "hell" at the end, was born in the Buddha's company, because he was not all bad from the beginning (Strong, 2001, pp.18-19). Thus, the Jatakas consist of an entire group of idealised life histories of those people surrounding the Buddha.

Thus, one may conclude that virtuous acts will always result in a rebirth close to persons who are about to reach awakening, if not now in this life, in one of the many lives closely following this life.[3] The Buddha's life history from the very beginning till the awakening is in fact a metaphor for the possibly of a psychological healing process of an entire community. The number of lives it takes may at times seem to be quite large but compared to eternity and the suffering this implies it is limited. Once the Buddha passed through his process of perfection he is supposed to have changed entirely. Tradition has it that he then developed his 32 charac-

---

3. Typical for currents of thinking in Navayana is e.g. the question whether "life" and "rebirth" are to be taken literally or as psychological metaphors, as the life or lifespan of an emotional episode, for instance of "hell" (anger), and as the rebirth of an emotion.

teristic body marks, the so called 32 Lakshanas, completed with the 80 secondary marks, the Upalakshanas. Sometimes it is stated that he had these characteristics already at his birth and that it was due to these body marks that the great seers who were summoned to attend his father's court once the prince was born, were able to recognize his remarkable nature. It is often stated that at the moment of realizing what Nirvana implied his skin showed a golden hue, a lustre, that disappeared only to return when he was about to pass into the final Nirvana. His healing process started when he first met a living Buddha, Dipankara, and he came to his final result when he reached awakening arising from his unveiling of imperfection and suffering in the world and of the way to cease suffering. According to some sources he met not one but many Buddhas in succession in his "previous" existences (Strong, 2001, pp.20-21). It was the path to the awakening and other episodes like the mythological trip to the "heaven of the thirty-three" in order to visit his mother, who was allegedly reborn there after her death seven days after she gave birth to the Buddha, which transformed the Buddha into the "ideal therapist". He has been there, he has experienced it all and moreover he has remembered it all. The visit to the "heaven of the thirty-three" is seen by some as a psychological experience in which he, through therapeutic visualizations, went through a healing of what was beyond any doubt a traumatic blow of having lost his mother at such an early age.

Having experienced such misery, the Buddha was the ideal example of a healer. He is the ultimate healer for the very good reason that he went through the wounding and the healing process himself, at least his biographies tell us this. Of course, Buddha's life history is a "vita" and we do not know that much for sure if it comes to actual history. There is a lot of "imagining the Buddha", which may be considered to be a history to "live with" instead of a history as "it actually happened", even though few Asian Buddhists would doubt the actual historical value of the Buddha's life accounts as they are handed over in the ancient, miracle-filled biographies. Because he went through healing processes himself, he became a Bhisaja, a clever physician. His Dharma is the most completed medicine, it is Bhaisajyaraja. Because he lived "all lives", he knows all experiences of physical and mental suffering. His analysis of the world is that of a skilled physician. There is the disease Dukkha; there is the cause of the disease "tanha" or "trsna"; the cause of the disease can be removed "nirodhana"; and there is the medicine: the Eightfold Path of the Dharma. In the *Saundarananda*[4] the Buddha laid out his four-partite analysis to his half brother Nanda, once the latter had come to realize that his ultimate healing lays in the path his elder brother had developed (the insight came at the moment Nanda has gave up his primary reluctance to follow this path) (*Saundarananda*; XVI):[5]

(41) Therefore think about the truth of Dukkha as if it were a disease, in the

---

4.   In this contribution I at times refer to this text. It is a poetical biography of Nanda the half brother of the Buddha. The text was composed in Sanskrit by Ashvaghosha, a Buddhist autor who lived in approximately the second century. In this text the conversion of Nanda to his brother's Dharma is described. The translations quoted in this article are my own based on the edition of Johnston (1928).

5.   Johnston, E.H. (Ed. & Tr.).(1928, 1975). *The Saundarananda or Nanda the fair*. Lahore: Oxford University Press.

vices (*dosha*) lies the cause of disease, in the truth about putting it to rest lies the ultimate health and in the path lies the medicine

(42) Therefore you should understand that activities bring Dukkha with them and you should also understand that the vices (*dosha*) come forth out of the same activities, know that avoidance of activities is the antidote and know also that avoidance is the path.

The original healing powers of the Buddha live on in his teachings as they have been handed down by his students up to the present time. Tradition would say that the teachings live on like the Buddha's physical presence lives on in his relics and in the images that were produced to replace his presence and in the Dharma. Many stories show not only how a person developed into an Arhat, but also how the Buddha handled skilful means, the above mentioned Upaya.

According to Buddhist cosmology, a being can be "reborn" in six realms. In the "realm of the gods" (e.g., pride) life will be perfect, every experience will be glorious. As a god, however, one will not experience any suffering, and suffering is one of the main triggers for Buddhist advancement. After a life in heaven, a downfall may follow into the "demi-god realm" (e.g., envy) or in one of the deepest "hell realms" (e.g., hatred) , just for the mere fact that in heaven awareness of what one does is lacking. In hell life is suffering. There are cold and warm hells. If one is in a cold hell, one will desperately long for a warm hell and the other way around. Born in the "animal realm" (e.g., ignorance) one might be instigated by illusions/delusions, although in many Buddhist accounts animals can be very bright and intelligent, the Buddha himself was in many Jatakas reborn as an animal and so were his students, parents and others. Life in the "hungry ghost realm" (e.g., greed) is about suffering and lust and so is life as one of the angry demons. Beyond any doubt within the Buddhist tradition a birth as a human is considered to be the most fortunate. It is the ideal birth to reach the ultimate experience as a human being gifted with a great intelligence and a great memory. If reborn as a human being, one will experience the sharp contrasts between happiness and suffering and these experiences of contrasts will inspire one to realize what existence is about. With the help of human intelligence one may understand what is happening against the backdrop of memory that recollects what has happened in the past. One knows that one will die one day and one knows of the passage of time. In between one experiences what it is like to be a human and has the possibility to experience Nirvana.

Meeting a living Buddha will have the greatest impact if one is reborn as a human being. Meeting a living Buddha has developed into an ideal paradigm. Many credulous Buddhists believers do not strive after awakening through the difficult path of meditation. Instead, they hope that by means of the accumulation of virtuous Karma they will be reborn in one of the heavens in order to be born on earth as soon as the next Buddha appears on earth. If one hears a living Buddha teaching it is very easy to experience Nirvana. If one only utters a genuine resolution to become a Bodhisattva or expresses the intention to aim for Nirvana in the presence of a living Buddha, this is a powerful statement. In the *Saundarananda* (V) we read:

(48) It is just like a doctor who forcibly administers a medicine to a patient that may be disagreeable, likewise what I told you may be disagreeable, but the essence is true and leads to your fortune.

(49) Therefore fix your mind with skills on your wellbeing, as long as this fortunate moment is there, as long as death does not approach, fix it on methodical exercises [yoga] as long as your youth is there.

Therefore, birth as a human being is the most profitable. Embodiment may be impure, the body may consist of a "thin leather bag full of entrails, worms and impurity", yet embodiment as a human implies the above mentioned intelligence and memory, enabling Nirvana. Moreover, when the Buddha lived as a human being, he also met several Buddhas of the past and it was in their presence that he made the resolution to awaken, which he realized as a a human being.

In contemporary Dharma, it is not only the Buddha's life history that is of utmost importance. Parallels can also be drawn by adherents of present day Dharma between their life histories and those of present day teachers such as the Dalai Lama or Thich Nhat Hanh. They are in a way considered to be exponents of the original teachings and of the historical Buddha. Therefore, meeting them and next to that constructing analogies between one's own life and that of the revered example emphasises that it is a Jataka story wherein one lives. The personal account during which one has discovered the value and meaning of the Dharma is often connected to an actual encounter with a living Buddhist teacher who has taken hold of one's experience and this sets one's life apart. Thus, the discovery of the value of the Buddhist Dharma can be a logical step.

Clever use of expedient means

Reflections on the clever use of skilful or expedient means, *Upayakaushalya*, is first of all found in the Mahayana teachings. It refers to the adjustment of the Dharma to the student just like a physician adjusting his treatment to the patient's disease. As the Dharma mainly exists in the form of teachings and as they are part of manifold life histories, one might say that the Dharma as we know it today is the result of countless Upayas. In Nagarjuna's Madhyamaka it is stated that the Buddha's discourses were conventions in the first place. Just as any message starts with certain first utterances and acts, the Buddha started his first teachings with certain first words and first formulations as well. From this point of view the "Four Noble Facts" are no exception, and they became a convention over time. The turnings of the Dharma wheel, the origin of Theravada, Mahayana, Vajrayana and the present Navayana or Neoyana can all be viewed as Upayas. Buddhas and Bodhisattva teachers have countless Upayas at their disposal and have the clever ability to adjust the Dharma to their particular students.

The mythological tale that the Buddha hid certain teachings for which society in his days was not yet well prepared is a striking example of Upaya. Another example is the metaphorical healing through which the Buddha is actually connected to his students. Drawing the line further, these students became his "patients" or "clients", concepts that make the Buddha looks like a "clinician", a physician or a psychotherapist, who first diagnoses and subsequently designs a personalized treatment plan. In the Dharma this diagnostic analysis and adjustment of the treatment to the idiosyncrasies of the student is called Upaya. The Buddha is renowned for his excellent skilfulness in expediting teaching and fostering his students' understanding of it by his unique handling of *Upayakaushalya*. In a broader sense Upaya may also imply that the Dharma needs to be adjusted not only to a particular student but also to a particular time, culture and society. Here we find a traditional opening of numerous possibilities in the Dharma when adjustment of the original teachings is required to fit new circumstances. In all cases however the content of the treatment remains the same: it is the Dharma. The Dharma is the "medicine" with many forms and shapes that have developed over the time. The message is that the patient is never to be placed in a Procrustean bed. The antidote needs to be constantly adjusted to the particular dis-ease, to the person who is struck, as well as to the changing circumstances.

There are two important varieties of Upaya in the Buddhist tradition. It can be certain acts, even "miracles", or it may consist of teaching the Dharma. The Buddha's showing Kashyapa the flower during a discourse can be called Upaya and so can the mythological visit that the Buddha paid to heaven with his brother Nanda in order to show him the heavenly damsels in order to get his mind distracted from carnal desires and worldly passions. In the *Saundarananda* (XIII), the Upaya treatment of the Buddha is described as follows:

> (3) The hero guided some with a subtle word, others in a loud voice, and yet others in both ways.
>
> (4) Just like gold comes forward out of dirt and it is pure, free of filth and is shining, even if it lies in dirt, it does not get stained by filthiness.
>
> (5) Just as a lotus leaf that originates from the water remains in the waters, and whether it is above the water or underneath it, it does not get stained by it,
>
> (6) just so an (Arhat) is born in the world and he does what is pleasing to the world, for the reason of his status and purity he does not get stained by the figurations (*dharmas*) of the world.
>
> (7) On moments when he gives his advices he does so the one moment binding, with abandon, friendly, in a harsh way, with stories or with concentration, but for the reason of the treatment, not just because he feels that way then.
>
> (8) And he took on a body out of that great compassion: "May I in whatever way deliver the creatures of suffering!", because he experiences that much compassion with them.

The Buddha thus adjusts his treatment to his student and he does not instruct students harshly for instance because he is in a bad mood that moment. And if he is in a bad mood it is Upaya...

Upayakaushalya is also the concept that explains how some of the Buddha's teachings seem to be contradictory or opaque at first sight. The contradictions arise because of the unique personality of the student or characteristics of the group (the person or group might lack proper understanding) to whom the Buddha addresses his personalized message. Upaya may even imply an occasional little lie, but only if its intention is to help the suffering patient. Just like with clinical treatments, paradoxically the pains that arise out of a treatment can at first be worse than the disease, as was true for Nanda, addicted to sensual passions, who was led by the Buddha to passionless-ness by having his passions intensified at first. Again, one finds an analogy here of the Buddha's acts with those of a skilled physician (*Saundarananda*; X):

(42) Just like a man cleans a dirty piece of clothing by at first making it even dirtier by applying soda, just so the Wise One dragged him into even worse passions, but with the target of putting an end to this impurity, not out of the idea of causing more impurity to arise. Just like a doctor intent on banishing diseases from a body will at first exert himself to cause the patient to suffer more, exactly, in that very way the Wise One connected him with heavier passions, for the very reason of putting his passions to an end.

Thus, it seems to me that the concept Upaya has four meanings to which I would like to add a fifth meaning:

(1) the adjustment of the Dharma treatment for a suffering person depending on the particular diagnosis;

(2) the adjustment of the Dharma to a particular society in a particular period;

(3) the principle that explains any apparent contradictions in the pristine teachings of the historical Buddha;

(4) the principle that explains any apparent contradictions in the Dharma after the Buddha as changing conditions require adjusted ways of teaching;

(5) the concept by means of which local modes, morals, manners and customs can be integrated into the greater Buddhist tradition.

Thus, Upaya is an innovative force that has always been inherently present in the teaching itself. Even if the Dharma is transformed into a science and practice of psychology, the Dharma's transformation in itself is nothing new.

In conclusion

The Dharma as we know it all over the globe can be said to be the result of Upaya. Therefore, if it is considered to be a religion, it can be so. If it should not be seen as a religion, but rather should be seen as a philosophy or a way of living, it can be so. Even a "theistic" Dharma is not unthinkable, although there is no "god" in the Dharma. If it must be a way to final liberation, it can be seen as such. However, there seem to be two essential elements one needs to keep in mind: the connection to the Buddha's vita must be made and there must be a relation to the original teachings, the pristine Dharma, no matter the form. In these two instances the message is nothing else than Dharma, even when wrapped as a psychology.

Westerners who are interested in the Dharma are mostly attracted to the Buddha as part of their personal narrative. For instance one may hear: "First I was raised as Roman catholic, as a student I became a feminist, later on I joined a global movement dealing with the environment, then I got involved in spiritual matters and discovered Buddhism after my trip to Nepal." One may hear next why the Dharma is scored as attractive. In popular terms, the Dharma is said to deny hell, to have no dogmas and no punishing god, to offer equal chances for men and women. Furthermore, the Dharma does not disrespect the human body as many religions do. It is considered to be liberating in many respects; there is even a gay Buddhist movement. No doubt, it is certainly challenging for the Dharma to be involved in matters such as psychotherapy and ethical issues like euthanasia, animal rights, and so on. In fact, in certain philosophical circles the Dharma has become a system of ethics that identifies a particular set of recommendations for appropriate conduct. Moreover, it is in accordance with the latest discoveries of science, most of all psychology and cognitive neuroscience. In spite of the fact that one may say the Dharma is a religion, a philosophy, a way of living, a psychology, a therapy, or whatever, these features can be far removed from the practice one finds in Asia, where in most parts men and women are not equally valued at all and the human body is often considered to be extremely impure. For the credulous believer in the East, "heaven" and "hell" are definitely present as a cosmological "reality out there" and Karma serves as a reward or punishment that provides a ticket to where one travels to. Multiple interpretations for the Dharma are possible and due to the principle of *Upayakaushalya* individuals may find idiosyncratic fits, no matter where one lives on the globe.

In closing, wherever Buddhist teachings journeyed in Asia, they always become mixed with local religious or philosophical thoughts and cultural traditions. Thus, a "pure Dharma" seems not to exist, despite claims of various schools to have such "purity" at hand. If one school insists it is giving the pure teaching, then all other schools also may have the same right to claim purity. Mental and physical healing have always been part of the Buddhist teachings as the Dharma serves as the medicine par excellence against the prime source of suffering: Dukkha, the imperfection embodied in existence. Modelled after the Buddha, the Buddhist aim is the complete cessation of Dukkha. This is the Nirvana experience: the extinction of irrational cravings and its behavioural concomitants, grasping and clinging. So it is stated.

Chapter 6

Early Buddhist Insights In Proliferating Concepts And Views

Soorakkulame Pemarathana

Introduction

The Theravada analysis of knowledge offers a particular insight in the psychological genesis of cognitions based on concepts (abstract terms of analytic reasoning) and views (internal images of the functioning of the world). It recognizes the proliferating cognitive tendency of the mind, which leads the perceiver to construct sensory experiences in various ways. Thus, the conceptualization and visualization of a particular sensory input (e.g. seeing or hearing) serve as the basis for postulating and constructing ideas about perceived reality. The means, contents and goals of constructed ideas are necessarily socially originated. Sensory processes, even if handled carefully, undergo idiosyncratic influences due to cognitive-affective procliv-ities. Individual affective inclinations may condition one's cognitions of the perceived world and the reverse likely happens as well. The Dhamma regards sensory contact (*phassa*) with the perceived object as the prime ground upon which biased inferences of the object that lead to concepts and views are fabricated. Therefore, any observing or correcting of misguided or unwholesome thinking advisedly begins with recognition of this point in the chain of mindful events.

In the *Brahmajala Sutta* (discourse on the "Perfect Wisdom on the All Embracing Net"), the reader's attention is drawn to cognitions about the past and the future as well as to how they come about and what they entail.[1] Most importantly, the Buddha admonished in this text not to become attached to them, or to any other beliefs for that matter, as attachment is perpetuated by the three poisons – greed, hatred and ignorance – that hamper awakening. What is special about this teaching is that the Buddha also targeted his students' defending and thus clinging to their own Buddhist teachings, for instance the teaching that "the universe must be neither infinite nor limited but also neither not infinite nor not limited". In contrast to those who favour free inquiry which maximizes the probability of liberation, believers of any faith or religion are like fish in a pond – they swim within the trap of a fisherman's net of beliefs.

Beliefs, just like attitudes, are habitual ways of reacting that perpetuate Karma, one's

---

1.   The *Brahmajala Sutta* (D. 1.1), a Theravada discourse, discusses the precepts and 62 "irrational" beliefs (*ditthi*) on the past (18) (beliefs referring to eternalism, the universe, absolutism, causality) and on the future (44) (beliefs referring to perceiving after death, annihilationism, Nirvana)

intentional/cognitive-behavioural activity. Both beliefs and attitudes are "abbreviated emotions". A belief comes into being from perceived contact, when an object comes to be (re)cognized in a blip and evokes a certain sensory and affective feeling that proliferates cognitions (logical concepts and imaginary views). In the course of time, beliefs are evoked by events in one's internal world through concepts and views, both of which usually and eventually become habitual evaluating thoughts. A belief might also be called upon by memory. Clinging (to beliefs) results in the karmic vicious cycling of psychological suffering and in the continuous rebirths of craving and grasping. This is to be dispelled in daily practice. In this practice cessation depends on developing an understanding of the conditioned nature of sensory contact, the subsequent vicissitudes arising from the conditioning as just described, and the way habits come to be.

An attitude causes one to get habitual affective urges or emotional feelings just by the perception of events in the external world without being aware of one's habitual evaluating thoughts (concepts and views). This results in the impression that external things are the cause of one's emotions. As habitual response modes, both beliefs and attitudes immediately arouse the same habitual affective/emotional feelings, which can be very strong and intense and difficult to extinguish. Due to their habitual nature, one is mostly unaware of them. Unless one dispels ignorance and craving by being aware of one's habits of feeling, thinking and behaving, the emotional poisons of greed/grasping and hatred/clinging become caught in automatic self-perpetuating cycles that one is usually not aware of and that are difficult to extinguish on the journey toward Nirvana.

The mind's proliferating tendency

The Dhamma, the Early Buddhist teachings of the Theravada handed down in Pali, highlights the constructive role of the mind in cognitively organizing sensory experiences. It thereby recognizes and emphasizes the proliferating tendency of the mind that is the capacity of the mind to multiply thoughts, concepts, views, attitudes and beliefs at a fast pace anytime and anywhere. The Early Buddhist analysis of sensory processes points out how raw sensory data go through various mental discernments and cognitive categorizations in a dualistic subject-object mode of thinking. The Theravada analysis of sensory processes, cognitive events and activities, called *vitakka* and *papanca*, signify the mind's complex processes. While *vitakka* refers to the initial reasoning about the perceived sensory object, the subsequent cognitive event, *papanca*, refers to the tendency of the mind to proliferate thinking and reasoning about the perceived object via concepts and views (*sanna*).

Discrete cognitive micro-events – the smallest units of experience in the flow of the mind's "behavioural activity" – are known as *dhammas*. Under the influence of the mind's proliferating tendency, the sensory perception is initially assessed as a positive, negative or neutral experience and subsequently actively processed. Flowing through various channels of feeling, thinking and behaving, it becomes a psychological manifestation like for instance an emotional or Karmic act. Formed as contiguous products of sensory inputs, thoughts arise spontaneously in the stream of consciousness, proliferate during the ongoing cognitive process (*papanca sanna sankha*) and start to lead their own lives, such that one needs to keep them in check.

The following anecdote illustrates the minutes of mental proliferation:

A man wants to hang a painting in his room. He has a nail, but not a hammer. The neighbour has one, so he decides to borrow it. But then he starts to doubt: "What if he refuses? Yesterday he did not say hello. He seemed to be in a hurry or maybe only pretended. What if he dislikes me? I haven't done anything wrong to him. If someone wants to borrow a tool from me, I would give it immediately. Why wouldn't he? How can a fellow human being refuse such a simple request? People like him are a public pest. He thinks I depend on him, just because he possesses a hammer. I am fed up!" The man gets mad, rushes next door and rings. When the neighbour opens the door, he screams: "You can keep your rotten hammer!"

The pitfall lies in the fact that "me" was thinking all of this and moreover, because these are "my" thoughts, "I", being un-awakened and in a state of daydreaming, ignorantly assume they have to be real. Because the mind has the tendency to proliferate issues from an erroneous sense of "self" and due to the self-reflexivity of thinking, it is not a matter of course that one is aware of the "cognitive dysfunctions" while making inferences about others and the self. Thus, one may abstract erroneously as a result of distorting, reifying, dichotomising, elaborating or exaggerating. If automatically/habitually exerted in a personalized way, dysfunctional thinking and consequently unwanted feelings as well as illusory perceiving of self, may proliferate to become conditioned personality traits that are nonetheless useful "provisionally" (for daily life), but not useful "ultimately" (in learning to see emptiness or not-self).

The Dhamma points out that concepts and views are necessary "devices" to understand the flow of psychological experiencing, but they are not meant to reduce the experiential flow into fragments. They are not only employed as mere tools either because they impose content regarding what are "real" or "true". Whenever experience is being tapped from the flow, it is arrested by cognitive constructing and proliferating. The constructed concepts and views are invested with dualistic notions – like identity and difference – notions to which validity is thus ascribed. Psychologically, one takes these to be frozen entities, reifications, in a world of impermanence that, nonetheless due to ignorance, may develop to become absolutistic and rigid identities, experiences, which are clung to as if one lives in a world of permanence. Cognitive knowledge is embedded in this undue identification of reality with proliferated concepts and views.

The Early Buddhists have further shown that this kind of identifying of concepts and views tends to resolve itself into theorizing about experience. They further argue that the construction of such theories is undertaken based on and to shore up personal experience. Within a particular experience one selects some pattern or fragment and constructs certain concepts and views, which then form an idiosyncratic theory about the sensory experience. By proliferating, i.e. projecting, these concepts and views, the sense experience as conceived and theorized about – and not as originally perceived – becomes "reality" or "truth".[2] Thus by its abstract nature cognitive

---

2. The *Brahmajala Sutta* (*D I* 22) and the *Mahakamma Vibhanga Sutta* (*M III* 211) point out that many thinkers have formulated views and theories by projecting their experiences to the world and by elevating their experiences to the status of reality.

knowledge is flawed by a *pars pro toto*, a proclaiming that some part is the whole. Such distorted knowing is illustrated in the Buddha's famous parable of the blind men, who take their own limited experience of an elephant to adequately represent the elephant in its fullness.[3]

It is this flaw that is implied in the term *adhivuttipada*, which is employed in the Pali discourses to refer to speculative metaphysical theories. The term literally means "overstatement".[4] Characterizing metaphysical theories as overstatements shows the Early Buddhist take on concepts and views. It seems that these are taken as overstatements in two senses. One is in the sense of an exaggeration of a particular fragment of experience to the whole thing that could be experienced in totality but is not, and the other is in the sense of an extra valuation of concepts and views which then emerge as gross categories or patterns of thought. These limitations of cognitive knowledge are presented in the discussion on the duality of absolute affirmation and absolute negation. The Dhamma regards the following two statements as the extremes of ontological claims.[5] The claim, "all exists (in the absolute sense)" (*sabbam atthi*) and the claim, "nothing exists (in the absolute sense)"(*sabbam natthi*). The former represents eternalism (*sassatavada*) and the latter represents annihilationism (*ucchedavada*). Surprisingly, the world at large is said to lean upon one of these extreme views. Once the Buddha addressing Kaccayana said:

> This world [the worldlings], Kaccayana, mostly rests on a duality: upon the
> notion of "existence" and the notion of "non-existence." [6]

The Early Buddhist teachings seem to have emerged as a critical response to the mutual opposition of these two extremes. So it is repeatedly said,

> ...not following either of these extremes, the Buddha teaches his doctrine
> by the middle.[7]

It is worth noticing that two important terms used in the above statement are abstract nouns, i.e. "isness" (*atthita*) and "is-less-ness" (*natthita*). These terms render the abstract substantialist cognizing of existence and non-existence. Thus, Bhikkhu Bodhi remarks,

> In view of these explanations it would be misleading to translate these two
> terms, *atthita* and *natthita,* simply as "existence" and "non-existence" and then
> to maintain [as is sometimes done] that the Buddha rejects all ontological
> notions as inherently invalid. The Buddha's utterance at the *Puppha Sutta* (S
> III 139), for example, shows that he did not hesitate to make pronouncements

---

3.   Udana Pali III, 2
4.   Suggested by D.J. Kalupahana, *A history of Buddhist philosophy.* New Delhi: Motilal Banarsidass, 1994, p.30
5.   S II 17, S II 20, S II 76
6.   S II 16
7.   S II 16, S V 421

with a clear ontological import when they were called for. In the present passage *atthi*a and *natthi*a are abstract nouns formed from the verbs *atthi* and *natthi*. It is thus the metaphysical assumptions implicit in such abstractions that are at fault, not the ascriptions of existence and non-existence themselves.[8]

Our cognitive knowledge is generally embedded in the notions of absolute existence and absolute non-existence. Within this embedded context one is able to understand the actual flow of "reality". Furthermore, cognitive knowledge, i.e. views, concepts and theories, has the tendency to produce a habit of intellectualization that ties the individual to the level of ideation, that is, to overly reasoning. Making reasoning a priority may produce an ideational complacency which obstructs one's practical engagement in the actual state of everyday affairs. The ideational complacency tendency is reflected in the Buddha's parable of the man struck with a poisoned arrow (the *Culamalunkya Sutta*).[9] Largely conditioned by the proliferating tendency of the mind, cognitive knowledge represents the intellectual fabrications and speculations used to provisionally cope with the actual states of daily affairs. Provisional implies pragmatism here: as long as it works to attain whatever goal, the thinking is declared "correct". *Sanna* or cognitions (conceptual logic and imaginary views) are formed in the perceiver's mind as a result of continuous proliferating reactions to initial sensory data. These in turn influence the subsequent sensory experiences. Their continuous applications forming a "habitual conceptual framework" within the perceiver determine her/his construction of sensory experience. Our provisional cognitive knowledge regarding the actual state of everyday affairs is by and large embedded in this habitual framework of conceptualizing and viewing into the world. It requires deep meditation and contemplation of the Dhamma to understand not-self and to gauge the ultimate: emptiness.

Inner urges and psychological projecting

The Early Buddhists also address the deeper levels of the human mind, which govern the construction of cognitive knowledge for everyday social functioning transmitted culturally through concepts and views. Their findings unveiled the psychological motives and the men-

---

8. Bhikku Bodhi, *The connected discourses of the Buddha*. Boston: Wisdom Publications, 2000, p.734.
9. The parable of the man stuck with a poisoned arrow is as follows: Suppose, Malunkyaputta, a man were wounded by an arrow thickly smeared with poison, and his friends and companions brought a surgeon to treat him. The man would say: "I will not let the surgeon pull out the arrow until I know the name and clan of the man who wounded me; until I know the height and the skin colour of him and the village or town that he lives in; until I know whether the bowstring that wounded me was fiber or reed or sinew or hemp or bark;…whether the bow that wounded me was a long bow or a crossbow; whether the arrow that wounded me was hoof-tipped or curved or barbed." All this would still not be known to that man and meanwhile he would die. So too, Malunkyaputta, if anyone should say: "I will not lead the noble life under the Buddha until the Buddha declares to me whether the world is eternal or not eternal, finite or infinite; whether the soul is the same as or different from the body; whether or not an awakened one continues or ceases to exist after death," that would still remain undeclared by the Buddha and meanwhile that person would die. Abridged from the *Culamalunkya Sutta* (M I 427). Nanamoli Thera and Bhikkhu Bodhi (Tr.) *The middle length sayings of the Buddha*. Kandy, Sri Lanka: Buddhist Publication Society, 1995, pp.534-6.

tal dispositions serving as the basis for theoretical speculation. People provisionally formulate theories about the actual state of affairs partly on the basis of various "internal urges". These are personal and might amongst others be sensory (e.g., desires like hunger or thirst), cognitive (e.g., concepts like expectations or images like being a millionaire) or affective (e.g., emotions like anger or fear) and cannot thus always be valid or "real". By using language and generally accepted concepts and views, theoretical constructions (by content and implication) are by definition interpersonally conditioned and learned, and are therefore – although personalized and private – social, not solipsistic.

Psychological attempts to comprehend the nature of experiential reality can easily be influenced, directed or misguided by these inner urges (e.g., if hungry one might see restaurants everywhere). When angry, one may feel poisonous. In need of clothes, one may see clothing all over. The psychological mechanism underlying such working is called "projection": one reads into the world a bias via thinking (conceiving and viewing) and feeling (sensing and emoting). More difficult is it to see that in a world of impermanence and process one tends to project abstract identifications as rigid things, like for instance: "he is a thief" instead of "he is a fallible human being, who stole a loaf of bread yesterday". It is quite understandable that the latter expression, rather than the first, invites one to feel compassion. It seems that this particular tendency of the human mind to identify has also received western scholarly attention. For example, Stebbing claims:

> There seems to be a deep rooted tendency in the human mind to seek what
> is identical, in the sense of something that persists through change… Hence
> the search for an underlying entity, a persistent stuff, a substance… Hence
> the popularity of substance theories in science.[10]

If this is the case, scientific theories are in a bid to establish a base of relative constancy with regards to experiential reality evoking the fallacy of permanence. Such evoking not only applies to rocket science, but to reeling and dealing with daily hassles as well. One way of trying to achieve a base of constancy, which is provisional, functional, and handy for daily life, is to seek for "uniformities" in experiencing reality in one's outer and inner worlds. Visualizations and imaginations function together to formulate uniformities in conjunction with sensory, affective and behavioural proclivities. Eventually, this concerted process leads one to form a 'theory' on the actual state of daily affairs. This is nothing but human beings' evolutionary strategy to survive, which is a pragmatic psychological endeavour to understand experience from day to day, not a research program to penetrate the ontological nature of reality.

Theories to cope with everyday life – although calculated – are a speculative means by which human beings try to secure predictability when confronted with sensory events subsequent to external or internal cues. Ironically, theoretical speculating was considered by Early Buddhists to be a result of proliferating in the ideational realm. Concepts and views are regard-

---

10. Stebbing L S, *A modern introduction to logic*. London: Methuen., 1945, pp.404-5

ed as the most typical instances of *papanca* explained before. It appears ironic, because the formulation of such theories was to unify the discrete instances of experience over time to counter the ordinary mind's natural and unbridled tendency to proliferate. This unifying formulation constructs an abstract cognitive order out of the chaotic penchant that inheres in *papanca* when engaged in making experiential sense out of sensory events. Murti contends:

> The more one internally proliferates, the further he goes away from the actual situation... The more one conceptualizes the sense object the more it becomes otherwise. [The thinker sets himself far from the actual picture.] And herein lies its falseness, the immature deceptive phenomenon that it is.[11]

From an Early Buddhist perspective, whenever one theorizes, one does so largely heavily influenced, conditioned, by inner urges and their projecting. This is the case because cognitive proliferating is governed by them. Not only does conditioning distort thinking, but theories, concepts, views, attitudes, beliefs and even "perceptual cognitions" are by their abstract nature not capable to represent the way things "are". The latter, if possible at all, is most probably best approximated by mindful awareness characterised by an inner stillness of the proliferating tendency or silence, not words, as the Buddha has taught.

With the insight that inner urges have an impact on the construction of concepts and views, no theory can be regarded as a "pure objective" description of things. Rather, they seem to appear, in this light, as prescriptions to understand the nature of reality in a certain way. Murti takes up this theme in his interpretation of Nagarjuna's Madhyamaka. This is a second century Mahayana school that emphasizes emptiness (*sunyata*). All things are empty of self-nature/essence (*svabhava*) and have no intrinsic/independent reality apart from the conditions/causes from which they originate. He comments:

> Philosophy selects a particular pattern from among several exemplified in things, exaggerates it out of all proportion and universalizes it to infinity. The pattern or concept so selected and universalized becomes an Idea of Reason, as Kant calls it... But having chosen one, consciously or rather unconsciously, we universalize it and take it as the norm of evaluation. Though innocently stated as a description of facts, philosophical systems are an evaluation of things or a prescription to view them in a particular way.[12]

A question to be raised here is: what impels one to select a particular pattern or point of view. What determines the selection? The Dhamma hypothesizes that the selection is motivated by

---

11. T. R.V. Murti, *The central philosophy of Buddhism*. London: George Allen & Unwin, 1955, p.125
12. *Ibid.* note 11

and comes about from one's internal urges. One selects a pattern among several exemplified in things, the one which is most fitting to the patterns of one's inner urges. In this way, concepts and views are fabricated and proclaimed so that they are enabled to correspond with and "satisfy" certain inner urges.

Theravada displays a considerable concern for urges that might be called existential needs and they try to evaluate the role of these needs in giving rise to various theories on existence and the beyond. Theravada points out that philosophical theory particularly regarding metaphysical issues also emerge as a reaction to inner urges that pose various existential questions. The prominent "existential urge" can be understood as a variety of "craving" (*tanha*, literary meaning thirst). Craving is recognized as a three-fold process, namely as a craving for sensual pleasure, for existence and for non- existence. In discussing the connection between these existential urges and metaphysical views, Bhikkhu Bodhi aptly states:

> If we explore precisely how craving functions as a condition in relation to views, we can see the different types of craving will be instrumental in the formulation of different philosophical views. The most powerful craving in man is the craving for existence... to satisfy our yearning for continued existence we fabricate views proclaiming the immortality of the imagined core of our being.[13]

Most human beings believe in a certain metaphysical core of existence not just because experiential evidence seems to inform thus, but rather because one is impelled by a desire to "believe". From a Buddhist stance, craving for existence is at the very bottom of metaphysical theorizing that projects eternal existence of the self in a future life. Jayatilleke, in this regard, writes:

> The belief in soul and substance thus not only have their origin in our linguistic habits but are also rooted in a craving in us to believe in them.[14]

Even the opposite view, which rejects any metaphysical substance and eternalism, is also impelled and motivated by an over-desiring urge, although of a very different kind: annihilationism. How craving for non-existence relates to craving for sensual pleasure is also aptly contended by Bhikkhu Bodhi:

> When craving for sense pleasure is most prominent, it may lead to the annihilationist position asserting the extinction of self upon the break-up of the body at death; for this position gives license to untrammeled indulgence in sense pleasures.....The craving for non-existence endangers views proclaimed the reality of the annihilation that is yearned for. In its simplest

13. Bhikkhu Bodhi, The Buddha's survey of views. In K. Dhammajoti, et al. (Eds.), *Recent researches in Buddhist studies*. Hong Kong: Chi Ying Foundation, 1997, p.54.
14. K.N. Jayatilleke, *Early Buddhist theory of knowledge*. London: George Allen & Unwin, 1963, p.382.

form, this craving, the result perhaps of personal frustration and deprivation, issues in the wish for annihilation immediately after death.[15]

From a Buddhist perspective, both theories of eternalism and annihilationism emerge and are
fuelled by existential urges. The mutual opposition between these two theories is often referred
in the Pali discourses as "umbrella theories", on which most other theories lean upon. These
two opposing philosophies seem to represent the vacillation of the human mind. As
Karunadasa explicitly puts it:

> The mutual conflict between *sassatavada* [eternalism] and *ucchedavada*
> [annihilationism] represents not only the perennial conflict between the
> spiritual and the materialist theories of existence but also the human mind's
> oscillation between two deep-seated desires.[16]

It is safe to conclude that on the bottom line non-cognitive factors – i.e., feelings and moods
of an affective or emotional nature sparking the motivation to act – largely govern one's forming of theories, concepts, views, attitudes and beliefs. Cognitive knowledge is considered to be
embedded in the non-cognitive factors of personality, manifested in the psychological projections of inner urges. Though innocently stated as a description of facts, any theory, either philosophical or psychological, is an evaluation of things and often a prescription to look at them in
a particular way. The Buddha admonished not to become attached to any theory including the
Buddhist one and instead to rather to experience and find out for oneself what is wholesome
or unwholesome in order to end everyday Dukkha going forward in this-worldly life.

Entangled by views of self

The Early Buddhist analysis, which is a large body of literature, finally touches the very core of
the genesis of cognitive knowledge, particularly on its own theorizing. A hypothetically vast con-
strued tangle of concepts and views is ascribed to one particular superseding theory on the non
existence of an abiding permanent self. It recognizes "the egocentric perspective" as the core
which gives rise to variety of false views. Its theorizing starts at the level of ordinary sensory
experience, on the basis of which the mind uncritically accepts the notion of selfhood. Initially,
as a convenient device when sensory experiences occur, a fictitious "experiencer" is assumed.
This imposed primary notion becomes strong in the subsequent cognitive proliferation arising
from sensory experience and fuelled by desires an affective/emotional nature. It is then fully crystallized and justified at the cognitive level of concepts and views. Thus, the vicious cycle is round
and the wrong notion of "I" as identification is comprehended. It is this which then underlies the

---

15. Bhikkhu Bodhi, The Buddha's survey of views. In K. Dhammajoti, et al. (Eds.), *Recent researches in
    Buddhist studies.* Hong Kong: Chi Ying Foundation, 1997, p.56.
16. Y. Karunadasa, The Buddhist critique of *Sassatavada* and *Ucchedavada. The middle way, Vol.* 74:2, 1999,
    p.69.

subsequent sensory processes, etc. Indicating the deep rooted latent tendencies towards such "identification" with a fabricated – abstract and reified – self, Nanananda comments:

> From the standpoint of the average worldling, there is an ego as the agent
> or mentor behind the sum total of sensory experience... its reality as an
> incontrovertible self evident fact of experience, is readily granted. Even at
> the end of a thorough introspection, he is often tempted to agree with
> Descartes in concluding "cogito, ergo sum" (I think, therefore, I am).[18]

Karunadasa explicitly shows that this "self-identification" is presented in the Dhamma as the core of the origin of views.[19] It is through "self-identification" either through material-bodily-behavioural or psychological sensory-affective-cognitive experience or through metaphysical notions that one is driven to fabricate various theories regarding the nature of self and its relationship to the world. The process of identification can be manifested in three ways as shown in the following passage of the early Buddhist discourses.

> When [the] uninstructed individual is impressed by a sensation born of con-
> tact, the idea, "this is mine" occurs to him, the idea, "I am" occurs to him,
> the idea, "this is my self" occurs to him."[20]

There is a selection that takes place on the basis of the given components of experience, whether physical or metaphysical, and that becomes identified as "this is mine" (*etam mama*), this "I am" (*esoham*) and "this is my self" (*eso me atta*). When there is self-identifiecation in an absolute sense with metaphysical or physical components given in the experience, then one is "obliged" to perceive the constructed notion of self in accordance with the alleged nature of that component. If there is identification with some metaphysical entity, then one attributes the qualities of that notion (such as its being immutable and eternal) to so-called "self". Karunadasa explains that in materialism one identifies the "self" with a physical body. It consequently follows that with the breaking up of the physical body the so-called "self" is annihilated as well. He concludes:

> In the context of Buddhist teaching, however, what matters is not the per-
> manence or impermanence of the object of self-identification, but the very
> fact of self-identification. Thus, Buddhists view both eternalism (*sassatava-*
> *da*) and materialism or annihilationism (*ucchedavada*) as two varieties of
> self- theory (*atmavada*).[21]

---

17. Bhikkhu Nanananda, *Concept and reality*. Kandy, Sri Lanka: Buddhist Publication Society, 1971, p.31.
18. Y. Karunadasa, *op.cit*. p.71.
19. S III 46.
20. Y. Karunadasa, *op.cit*. p.71.
21. Y. Karunadasa, *op.cit*. p.71.

With this initial error of self-identification, whenever one reflects on the nature of self and its relationship to the world, one ends up constructing a vast tangle of (metaphysical) theories. Thus, daily knowledge is embedded in the inherent false belief in the cognition or image of a self that is provisionally functional for everyday life but subsequently gratifies the need for identifying with the idea of one's perpetual life.

The pragmatics of concepts and views

With the above given critical assessment of views, concepts and theories, one may ask whether and on what basis the Early Buddhists demolish all thinking without residue. Does this apply as well to the Buddha's "grand theory" with regards to Nirvana and the end of Dukkha? There was an instance in Buddhist history when a person named *Dandapani* questioned the Buddha in order to know his proclaimed "theory". The Buddha gave a decisive reply that he had no theory to declare other than that he had put an end to all theories and proclivities towards them.[22] It is further stated:

> When, one understands as they really are the origin and passing away of the six bases of contact, their satisfaction, danger, and the escape from them, then he arrives at a realization of "that which transcend all these views." [23]...

> The sage has abandoned all views, he has in this world shaken off every philosophical view.[24]...

> The sages neither formulate nor proffer theories. They do not say, "this is the highest purity." Giving up the bonds of attachment, they form no attachment anywhere in this world.[25]

It might appear to some readers that the Theravada, the only extant Early Buddhist teaching to date, which historically stands most near to the pristine words of the Buddha, promotes the complete demolition of concepts and views. Not relying on concepts and views might be taken as the utter denial of them implying all theoretical speculations, including all philosophies and religions. It should be noted that it is not about condemning any theory or viewpoint here. Rather, it describes what a theory or a view comes into being: how it is made up (structure) and how it is sustained in the mind (process) and how it is released (Kamma action) so that perception is wholesome.

The later Mahayana Buddhists consider a similar systematic critique of theories and views. Nagarjuna offered a similar assessment of philosophical theories and views highlighting the Early Buddhists' way of thought. Applying a dialectical approach, he exhibited the

---

22. D. I. 45.
23. S Verse 787.
24. S Verse 794.
25. T.R.V. Murti, *The central philosophy of Buddhism*. London: George Allen & Unwin, 1955, p.128.

inner flaw of each theory and view. Murti, in his interpretation of the Madhyamaka System, showed that Nagarjuna's attempt was to remove the artificial restrictions and accidental distortions, which concepts and views with their sentiment-based bias have placed on sensory experience. He further alludes:

> The Madhyamika dialect tries to remove the conflict inherent in Reason by rejecting both the opposites taken singly or in combination... Rejection of all views is the rejection of the competence of Reason to comprehend reality. The real is transcendent to thought. Rejection of views is not based on any positive grounds or the acceptance of another view; it is solely based on the inner contradiction implicit in each view. The function of the Madhyamika dialect, on the logical level, is purely negative, analytic.[26]

Thus, to reiterate: the emphasis in Buddhist analysis is not on pointing to theoretical errors or imperfections but rather on revealing the deeper levels of the human mind, which give rise to the theorizing itself and its subsequent sustaining. In the final analysis, thinking itself is tackled at its source.

Triggered by sensory input the mind tends to proliferate theories one is delighted about. Consequently, one hangs onto these thoughts and treats them as the "truth", while at bottom ignorance prevails. Next, there is a greed to confirm the theories and hate may be felt toward other beliefs and attitudes. Such unwholesome states of mind often lead to interpersonal conflict in all its varieties. The Buddhist advice is to recognize these as mere cognitions, concepts and views, provisional varieties of reality representations, and not to see them as the ultimate "truth" that remains unknown, thus: emptiness. To ward off *papanca* and to secure a wholesome psyche, mindful awareness meditation is the prescribed medication. This antidote is to shut off *papanca* by staying at the observational level of sensory experience and by noting which thoughts lead to trouble and unwholesomeness and which ones to sanity and wholesomeness. This requires patience, while distancing, observing, noting, acknowledging and detaching by stepping back, not battling or otherwise going into any form of thinking. Thus, the unavoidable running off of the mind in every direction is slowed down and one may become master of one's own brain functioning. By staying during this process in the present moment, one will able to ward off the mind's penchant to identify any sensing, thinking, feeling or acting with a self. Eventually, the mind is tamed: awakening, not-self and Nirvana (the extinction of unwholesome emotionality) are imminent.

The Early Buddhists, who walked and still walk the Middle Way, nowhere recommend to demolish thinking *in toto* or to consequently reject all theories and views. They contend like Nagarjuna (2nd century) to finally reject and give up all theories and views without exception, once the purpose of these useful tools is served. On the contrary, their analysis reveals the integrative function of cognitions – concepts, views or theories – with internal urges. It is simply

---

26. *Ibid.* p.160.

suggested that one must be aware of these internal influences and their probable distorting qualities. Although cognitions have the potency to delude and one is at the mercy of cognizing when analyzing and explaining experiences, it is up to each one of us to cognize without giving the absolute value to concepts and views and without getting into the trap of loaded urges. One might again pose a critique that the claim "all theories should be transcended" is itself a view. Madhyamaka argues that the critique of theories cannot itself be a theory or view:

> Criticism of theories is no theory. Criticism is but the awareness of what a theory is, how it is made up; it is not the proposing of a new theory. Negation of proposition is not one more position. Dialectic, as analysis, does not impose any new thing; it reveals rather than adds or distorts... The knowledge of what theories are cannot itself be a theory.[27]

The Early Buddhists provide different layered answers. The Dhamma allows one, initially, to hold the theory that all theories should be transcended, in order to see the inherent emptiness of all theories and views. It does however not recommend the demolition of all concepts and views indiscriminately. Rather, it promotes a gradual strategy by which the final stage is the transcendence of all theories and of all proclivities to theorizing. Recognizing the pragmatic and relative value of thinking and thoughts, it allows making use of them while not giving them an ultimate value.

Closing remarks

As concepts and views have deeper roots in the human mind, an intellectual alertness on their futility is, although necessary, not sufficient. As long as reflective awareness is limited, and confined within the intellectual level, it merely serves as a form of meta-view. That is an internalized self-reflective theoretical view that all views should be abandoned without residue. As remarked by Nanananda:

> the dialectician might sometimes develop a complex of his intellectual superiority and... might throw all ethics to the wind and lull himself into the belief that he has arrived at the Truth.[28]

The Theravada strategy aims at transcending concepts, views and proclivities to them both intellectually and existentially. Its concern is basically not about theoretical errors or contradictions of concepts and incompatible views, but on their contribution to distorting sensory experience that hampers liberation. The mere intellectual understanding of the inherent faultiness of concepts and views is therefore insufficient and would not fulfil the rationale of the Early Buddhist practice.

---

27. Bhikkhu Nanananda, *Concept and reality*. Kandy, Sri Lanka: Buddhist Publication Society, 1971, p.83.
28. M III 234 (my translation).

The Buddha's Middle Way itself relies on cognitive formulations outlining the steps of training, which are to be made use of with circumspection and detachment. That is why, even after critical assessment of views, the Buddhist Right View appears in the very beginning of any Buddhist practice to counter ignorance. This is in line with the recommendation to gradually transcend concepts and views toward emptiness. With Right View as the harbinger of practice, Buddhists will able to use cognitive strategies and for that matter also their linguistic structures without giving absolute value or becoming attached to them. As mentioned earlier, human beings are at the mercy of socially constructed cognitions that are not absolute, but are merely instrumental for communication. They possess a relative and pragmatic, not an absolute value. At this point it is helpful to consider the Early Buddhist guidance on the proper use of language to understand the practical attitude and approach toward handling the language of concepts and views. It is stated in the *Suttanipata* and in other instances, that,

> One should not insist on the usage of regional dialects, one should not override the usage of common parlance.[29]

This way of treating language is considered to be the "peaceful path" (*aranapatipada*) in contrast to the "pro-conflict path" (*saranapatipada*). With such stance there is aloofness toward extremist and apathetic attitudes. Language consists of merely socially constructed "empty" common conventions, which the Buddha makes use of without clinging to them.[29] It would be therefore unwise to become attached to the Buddha's words without pursuing the quest in daily life and practice.

---

29. D I 202.

Chapter 7

Buddhist Philosophy As A Way Of Life For The Therapy Of The Dis-Eased Mind

Pahalawattage D. Premasiri

Introduction

The question whether the Buddhist Dharma is a religion, philosophy or psychology has often been raised. The response of some to this question is that it is exclusively a religion. Others hold that it is not a religion but a philosophy. Still others maintain that the Buddha taught mainly about the human mind and that therefore, the Dharma is psychology. According to the most influential philosophical school in the modern English speaking world that developed and applied the method of philosophizing advocated in the later writings of Wittgenstein, the Dharma cannot be considered as a philosophy. It may be argued that there are certain elements in the teachings of the Buddha that may be considered philosophical in the traditional sense in which the term "philosophy" was used. One major objection to accommodating the Dharma within the discipline of philosophy is that in the traditional western way of doing philosophy, it is characterized by the method of rigorous argumentation. Such a method is not characteristic of the early teachings of the Buddha although it could be witnessed in the later development of the Buddhist doctrines which arose in interaction with other non-Buddhist schools as well as in the development of doctrinal differences within the fold of the Dharma itself. Several schools of Buddhist thought represented such doctrinal developments and they attempted argumentatively to establish and defend their own ideological standpoints. Looking at the entire Buddhist tradition in terms of the different stages of its historical development it is more reasonable and realistic to consider the Dharma as quite a complex phenomenon. It is only in terms of unwarranted generalizations that it could be strictly compartmentalized into a single category such as religion, philosophy or psychology. There are elements of all of these represented in what we generally recognize as the Dharma. The Dharma is complex and multifaceted, and cannot be unambiguously caught in a western category. This complexity and multifaceted nature of Buddhism is implicit in the early Buddhist teachings represented in a considerable section of the canonical scriptures known as the Pali Nikayas of the Theravada tradition.

Philosophy as a way of life

It needs to be pointed out at the outset that the terms religion and philosophy are western in origin, and exact equivalents cannot be found for them in eastern languages. In the West too, the connotation of these terms has not remained static or uniform. At one time for most thinkers in the West religion without god or a form of theism involving a creator and a supreme divine law-giver appears to have been inconceivable, although today most westerners would admit that Buddhism and Jainism can be viewed as religious systems even though the notion of a creator god is not admitted in them. The same is true of philosophy. Most western philosophers today are inclined to consider the speculative elements contained in the systems of traditional philosophers like Plato, Spinoza, or Berkeley as forming no part of genuine philosophical thinking. In contemporary western thought there is an increasing tendency to compartmentalize human knowledge and to think in a stricter and more rigid manner, thus establishing sharp boundaries between what is to be viewed as religion, philosophy and science. It is often pointed out that in the East, no such sharp distinction was made between philosophy and religion, and that they have often existed as one integrated system. This appears to be true of the Dharma too as it is the case with many other schools of Indian thought like Vedanta and Saikhya, and it has been so both in the origin of the Dharma and in later stages of its development. In the case of Buddhist thought philosophical and religious characteristics were intermingled from the very beginning. In the case of Christian thought, which started purely as a religion, philosophy entered in the theological speculations of the Middle Ages through the argumentative and rational methods which had been used in the pre-Christian Greek thought of Plato and Aristotle.

The Buddhist Dharma originated at a time when there was intense interest among intellectuals in fifth century BCE in India to reach an understanding of the nature of the universe and the human predicament which was characterized by impermanence suffering and death. Most thinkers during the time of the Buddha were disenchanted with traditional explanations regarding these matters as well as with the ways of life traditionally recommended. In this backdrop, the Buddha's independent system of thought attempted to open up new pathways of knowledge and to prescribe new modes of living. The Buddha himself was one among many intellectuals of this period who claimed to be awakened by his own effort to experiences, which in their opinion were of great significance and benefit to all rational beings. The Buddha's claim to have discovered original insights into certain realities was made in the context of a variety of competing claims made by other religious teachers, philosophers and sages of the time.

In India the term used to describe world-views asserted by the Buddha, and some of his contemporaries, was *darsana,* the term that is used as the present day equivalent for the English word philosophy. This term derived from the verbal root *drs* "to see" and was used to signify not only world views associated with certain beliefs about the holy and supernatural, ideals and goals of life and prescribed systems of ethical norms and codes of discipline for the conduct of life, but also a plain and simple materialistic view of life associated with the advocacy of a sensualist ethic. The nucleus of the teaching of the Buddha represented in the Pali Nikayas, which in terms familiar to the Indian tradition may be referred to as the *dhamma* or *darsana* can be recognized as philosophy in a sense familiar to the western tradition as well.

If one recognizes the fact that a variety of modes of philosophizing could be identified in the long history of the discipline known as philosophy extending over two and a half millennia, the Dharma in its earliest form fits in primarily with one of the principal modes of philosophizing which may be described as "Philosophy as a Way of Life". Nussbaum, who draws our attention to this mode of philosophizing observes:

The idea of a practical and compassionate philosophy—a philosophy that exists for the sake of human beings, in order to address their deepest needs, confront their most urgent perplexities, and bring them from misery to some greater measure of flourishing—this idea makes the study of Hellenistic ethics riveting for a philosopher who wonders what philosophy has to do with the world.[1]

Nussbaum further points out that

...the Hellenistic philosophical schools in Greece and Rome—Epicureans, Skeptics, and Stoics – all conceived of philosophy as a way of addressing the most painful problems of the human life. They saw the philosopher as a compassionate physician whose arts could heal many pervasive types of human suffering. They practiced philosophy not as a detached intellectual technique dedicated to the display of cleverness but as an immersed and worldly art of grappling with human misery.[2]

Wisdom has identified seven modes of intellectual activity that come near or within the area of what is called philosophy for the purpose of evaluating them, among which the last is considered as "philosophy as a way of life". He says:

Philosophy as a way of life is often an unarticulated idea with which young students approach the subject. And it is widely looked upon as falling outside the proper business of philosophy. Nevertheless, several examples make it quite clear that philosophy as a way of life began two thousand years ago and that this tradition has continued, even if in a minor way ever since.[3]

A close study of the teaching of the Buddha as preserved in its early form appears to offer an eastern alternative of the mode of philosophy referred to by Wisdom and Nussbaum and is likely to attract the attention of those who are engaged in the search for a philosophy that has direct relevance to human concerns.

There is a tendency on the part of some recent scholars influenced by the Wittgensteinian mode of philosophizing to consider the teachings of the Buddha purely as religion. In their opinion "Buddhism" consists of interesting subject matter for the philosopher of religion. All of its concepts are to be treated as items belonging to what they conceive to be the religious language game of the Buddhists, and meanings of those concepts are to be understood within the form of life in which the words in that language game play their part. If philosophy is conceived so parochially as the Wittgensteinian philosophers of the linguistic analysis school do,

1. Nussbaum, M.C. *The therapy of desire.* New Jersey: Princeton University Press, 1994, p.3.
2. Ibid.
3. Wisdom, J.O. *Philosophy and its place in our culture.* New York: Gordon & Beach, 1975, p.1.

then the Buddhist teachings cannot be said to contain anything philosophically important. However, the claim that linguistic analysis is the only function of philosophy has not gone unchallenged. Russell challenged it in agreeing with the critique of the linguistic method by Gellner.[4] It was Russell's view that linguistic philosophy amounts to an abandonment of serious thinking. It is an abandonment of a desire to understand the world.

An implicit assumption that goes with those who consider philosophy to be a merely second order activity confined to the analysis of concepts in different areas of human discourse is that no genuine knowledge of matters of fact can be gained by means of philosophy. Before the empirical sciences developed using their distinct methodology of scientific discovery (despite the fact that there are epistemological disagreements about this methodology itself) philosophical knowledge was conceived to be of utmost importance. For Descartes metaphysics was the root of all human knowledge and for Spinoza philosophical knowledge superseded all other kinds of knowing. The Logical Positivist School of philosophy which had a considerable influence on the philosophical thinking of the West in the second half of the twentieth century explicitly denied cognitive significance to all discourse that did not fall under the empirical sciences and the formal sciences like logic and mathematics. The denial of a cognitive character to all normative discourse in ethics and aesthetics also followed from the Logical Positivist analysis of cognitively meaningful discourse. Epistemologically, this approach placed reliance only on the data of the ordinary senses for the acquisition of factual knowledge about the world. All genuine knowledge was confined to scientific hypotheses, which had been highly confirmed by observation and experiment. Although philosophers of the linguistic analysis school did not accept the Logical Positivist theory of meaning the most significant aspect of positivist epistemology – that factuality is confined to the empirical sciences – was tacitly assumed. This assumption implied the denial of philosophical knowledge of matters of fact. It also implied the denial of the traditional view that it is within the function of philosophy to discover truths about the proper and desirable goals of human life and action.

However, if we grant that the philosopher is entitled to propose a synthetic world view based on the totality of elements of knowledge acquired by him by valid means, and to relate that synthesis of experience to a theory about desirable goals of human action, the Buddha could very well qualify as a philosopher. Wisdom which draws our attention to the "way of life" approach in philosophy, points out that it is an approach that presupposes many things.

> To work out a way of life is impossible without coming to terms with questions, such as "What is it all for", or the possibility of a future life, or the possibility that life is essentially absurd, and questions about the nature of human nature, what is man, what is the source of evil, is there a fixed relation between good and evil, and the like. Thus one has to consider what is man, what is the place of man in the universe, how does one conceive the relation of a man to other human beings. And many of these questions pre-

---

4.   Gellner. E. *Words and things.* London: Routledge & Kegan Paul, 1979.

suppose that one has given oneself tentative answers to some of the great enduring cosmologico-ontological questions.[5]

An inquiry into the content of the sutta literature in the Pali Nikayas representing the teachings of the Buddha shows that it is largely and precisely concerned with what Wisdom has outlined. It is probably in view of this fact that K.N. Jayatilleke proposed that early Buddhist Dhamma has the characteristics of a full-fledged philosophy, with a theory of knowledge, a theory of reality, a theory of ethics and a logical theory of its own.[6]

Religion versus epistemology

The question of the epistemological basis for an assertion, whether it is an assertion about the nature of the world and the nature of man, or about how a human being ought to conduct himself or herself, or about what is good and bad, right and wrong was thought to be of paramount importance during the Buddha's time. It is possible that this was due to the fact that many conflicting claims were made in this regard and inquiring persons considered it important to examine the rational basis of the claims. The Pali Nikayas show that the Buddha himself confronted this question when asked to explain the basis on which he propounds the principles of the "higher life" (brahmacariya).[7] The Buddha's answer shows that he had a clear awareness of the nature of epistemological questions. Most thinkers of that time founded their philosophy of life on beliefs about the nature of man, the nature of the universe, and the nature of human destiny. The means by which knowledge claims were made regarding these issues needed to be critically evaluated if any reliance was to be placed on such beliefs. Therefore in a thought system like the Buddha's, which was concerned with philosophy as a way of life, discussion of epistemological issues became relevant. The Buddha classified in this connection, all contemporary teachers into three classes as

(1) those who depended on authority or revelation (anussutika),
(2) those who depended on logic and reasoning (takki vimamsi) and
(3) those who depended on their own "supercognitive" experience (abhinna).[8]

The Buddha claimed to belong to the third group among them. The Kalama Sutta too mentions ten grounds on which philosophies of life were accepted as true. Each of those ten grounds can be included under either authority or reason. Here too, the Buddha insisted that ultimately one has to depend on personal knowledge, leaving aside authority of all kinds, traditional, scriptural or individual, as well as speculative reason.

---

5. Wisdom, J.O. *Philosophy and its place in our culture* New York: Gordon & Breach, 1975, p.60f.
6. Smart, N. (Ed.), *Message of the Buddha.* London: George Allen & Unwin, 1975.
7. Majjhimanikaya. Pali Text Society, London; Vol. 2, p.21.
8. For detailed discussion of these three epistemological positions see K.N. Jayatilleke, *Early Buddhist theory of knowledge.* London: George Allen & Unwin, 1963, p.170 f.

In his exhaustive analysis of the epistemology of early Buddhism, Jayatilleke argued that Buddhist epistemology considers the data of the senses as a dependable foundation for human knowledge. He also points out that according to the early Buddhist Dhamma the data of extrasensory perception (the data of the experience of *abhinna*) are also considered to be dependable and are even more important in ascertaining certain truths that cannot be established by ordinary sense experience. During the time of the Buddha there had been objections to categorizing the data of *abhinna* as a dependable source of information for making any claims about matters of fact. However, there is no philosophical reason why such experience should *a priori* be considered non-cognitive, unless one dogmatically assumes that ordinary sense-experience is the only dependable means of obtaining factual knowledge. Suppose someone claims to know the same facts that can be established by ordinary sensory means, by some other means, such as an extraordinary visual capacity like clairvoyance (*dibbacakkhu*). If this claim is consistently proved right, or proved right in a statistically significant number of cases, there is no reason to deny cognitive status to the claims made on such a basis. The perceptions aided by other material means that extend the capacity of our ordinary senses provide us with knowledge of entities not known to the unaided senses. We accept such perceptual data because they fit into a coherent pattern of our experiences. If the data of *abhinna* also fit into such a coherent pattern there is no reason why cognitive status should not be granted to those experiences. In fact, the early Buddhist argument is that it is impossible that the so-called extraordinary cognitive abilities are obtainable by a human being was rejected on the ground that it is like the blind saying that it is impossible to see colour and form merely because they do not have any visual experience of them.[9] From a Buddhist perspective a difference is recognized between entities determined purely by speculative reason and entities determined by supersensory capacities.

Hoffman who has considered the Dharma solely as a religious system which can only be treated from the point of view of philosophy of religion has argued that the Buddhist concept of *abhinna* does not stand for any significant cognitive experience. He rejects the view that *abhinna* can be interpreted as the epistemological basis of early Buddhism.[10] The view expressed by Hoffman is that the Dharma is proposing neither an epistemological basis which could be seen as an alternative to the epistemological bases of the theories of reality asserted by other contemporary systems of thought nor an epistemological theory comparable to or different from that of empirical science for making assertions about the nature of reality. He wishes to interpret all Buddhist concepts as having a distinctively religious meaning. It contains what contemporary philosophy of religion would call religious language. According to this interpretation, there is no sense in speaking about the early Buddhist epistemology. It is clear that Hoffman is attempting to impose upon the teachings of the Buddha the non-cognitivist analysis of what philosophers in the Wittgensteinian tradition called religious discourse. However this cannot be done without completely distorting the character of the early Buddhist

9.   Majjhimanikaya. Pali Text Society, London; Vol. 2, p.201.
10. Hoffman, F.J. *Rationality and mind in Early Buddhism*. Delhi: Motilal Banarsidas, 1987, Chapter 5.

Dhamma. And this distortion has been evidently done in chapter five of Hoffman's *Rationality and Mind in Early Buddhism*. This distortion extends even to the explanation of the etymology of Pali usages as is evidenced in the interpretation of the most crucial term used in the Pali suttas in contexts where *abhinna* is mentioned as a means of knowing. The relevant Pali usage is *sayam abhinna sacchikatva* (having verified or directly witnessed by means of one's own super-cognition). The etymology of the term *sacchikatva* is misinterpreted here by breaking the term into *sacca* (true) and *katva* (made or established).[11] However, the correct etymology suggests exactly what Hoffman seeks to deny. The Pali term *sacchikatva* is analyzable into *sva+aksi+krtva* meaning "having personally witnessed".

There may be philosophical or scientific reasons to dispute the Buddhist claim that truths could be verified by means of the extraordinary methods proposed in the early Dhamma. But to say that the Dharma as a whole is not making any such epistemological claim is a misguided attempt to fit it into a preconceived theory about how it should be characterized. A further point about the *abhinna* is that the most crucial one of the higher means of knowing recognized for the purpose of attaining the Buddhist goal of final liberation does not strictly require any mystical or extra-sensory mode of knowing. The goal itself is described as a profound psychological transformation of the person involving freedom from unwholesome emotions leading to psychological suffering and freedom ensured by a radical change in the way one cognitively responds to the sensory environment. The specifically Buddhist *abhinna* is called the knowledge pertaining to the destruction of corruptions, influxes or psychological cankers (*asavakkhyanana*) which is expected to be attained not by some mystical intuition, but by insight into the impermanent, the unfulfilling and unsubstantial nature of all empirical phenomena. The observations of the ordinary senses, considered in the light of analytical insight with a mind removed from various subjective biases and prejudices, and cleansed of all unwholesome emotions would suffice for its attainment. It is this kind of systematically trained insight that the Dhamma refers to as the knowledge pertaining to the destruction of corruptions.

Epistemology, not metaphysics

Insofar as the Buddha was concerned with setting out a way of life based on a certain theory of reality, he was also interested in putting forward an epistemological theory on which the model or system of reality was based. This model also implies certain views about what the human intellect could legitimately claim to know. The Buddha described certain metaphysical issues, which were commonly debated during his time as not resolvable. It was his view that no definitive answer can be given to certain questions of a metaphysical nature and that any attempt to give definitive answers is likely to end up in interminable conflicts. He saw the consequence of such attempts as dogmatic clinging to views, the truth or falsity of which can never be established by means of human experience. Questions regarding the ultimate origin of the

11. Ibid. p.94.

universe such as whether it is eternal or non-eternal or the ultimate spatial characteristics of the universe such as whether it is finite or infinite, and questions regarding the ultimate relationship between mind and matter were all considered by the Buddha to be undetermined or unanswered questions (*avyakata*). The last four questions relating to the existence or non-existence of the liberated person after death were also based on certain metaphysical presuppositions about the nature of the person. They were left aside for several reasons. The Buddha disregarded them primarily because they had no direct connection with the main practical issue of life with which he was concerned, namely, the problem of unsatisfactoriness. The Buddha was also aware that there was no experiential means of determining the truth or falsity of answers given to them. Thirdly some of these questions were based on unwarranted presuppositions and logical confusions.

One of the major contributions made by the Buddha to philosophy was his epistemological and psychological critique directed mainly at speculative metaphysics. Some renowned philosophers of the West had also considered philosophy to be the supreme science with the conviction that human reason unaided by experience could unravel the most profound philosophical realities about nature and existence by following the method of reasoning deductively from self-evident premises. The classical rationalist method of philosophizing in the western tradition exemplified in the philosophical systems of Descartes, Spinoza and Leibniz would clearly have been repudiated by the Buddha. These philosophical systems are based on "self-evident" premises, which were represented by, for instance the *"cogito"* argument of Descartes or the definitions and axioms of Spinoza. It was this method of reaching conclusions about the nature of reality that the Buddha characterized as making assertions based on logic, reason and self-evident premises. However, the classical rationalists were neither capable of arriving at unanimity regarding their ultimate philosophical truths, nor could they show how they could resolve their disagreements. The Buddha pointed out, as Kant did in the western tradition, that the consequence of this method of reaching conclusions about the nature of reality is the emergence of a multiplicity of mutually contradictory opinions with no basis for testing their objective validity. It is as a consequence of rejecting the rationalist notion of self-evident truths that the Dharma did not and does not admit into its system such metaphysical notions as the concept of "Being", "Substance", "God", "indestructible Atman" or "immortal Self". The notion of god as the cause of itself or as the uncaused first cause or that of which its essence involves its existence would be seen from the Buddha's point of view as mere dogmatic metaphysics.

Those who pursued the methods of empirical science leaving aside the speculative metaphysics of the traditional philosophers, were capable of establishing a commonly acceptable body of knowledge which at the same time made great strides in its ability to improve the material conditions of human life through the practical applications of such knowledge. We have already noted that the Buddha, in the context of the emerging diversity of religious views, ways of life, and philosophical doctrines in India of the fifth century BCE, observed that there were three fundamental grounds on which people depended for their convictions. Out of these the Buddha did not agree with the first ground, which consisted primarily of the authority of mystical revelations (*anussava*), and a body of traditionally handed down sacred doctrines (*parampara, pitakasampada*). He also did not agree with the second ground, which placed reliance on a person's skill in reasoning and speculation, the method commonly adopted by rationalist metaphysicians (*takki vimamsi*). He agreed with the third method followed by the experientialists, who depended on both sensory and introspective observation, taking into account both the observed data of the five physical senses and insights gained by a systematically trained mind. The Buddha claimed to have perfected this method for the purpose of attaining what he described as the noble knowledge (*ariyam nanam*) that produced the effect of eradicating all the corruptions of the mind, thus overcoming the psychological ills that human beings suffer due to their delusion. In the western world those who abandoned traditional authority and speculative metaphysics moved in the direction of establishing a body of scientific knowledge about the material world which was practically useful for fulfilling the material needs and desires of human beings. The Buddha abandoned speculative metaphysics to establish a body of knowledge pertaining to the workings of the human mind practically applicable to the overcoming of many pervasive forms of human suffering.

The Buddha asserted that the realities with which he was concerned are the four realities that, if understood, accrues "nobility", and which are traditionally known as "noble truths". These could be stated as "down-to-earth" unsatisfactoriness (Dukkha), its cause, its cessation and the way to its cessation. What kind of "truths" are they? Are they empirical, philosophical or religious? Our contemporary ways of thinking, which do not admit paradox, do not allow us to comfortably say that they can be all of them at the same time. But for the Buddhist way of thinking they are. Take the first truth of unsatisfactoriness for illustration of this point. It is, from the Buddhist point of view, a philosophical truth to the extent that it is a judgment based on the synthesis of the total experience of mankind. It is also based on philosophical assumptions like *that which is impermanent cannot be the basis of stable happiness*. That life involves suffering is often not a simple matter of direct empirical observation but a philosophical synthesis of experience coupled with human reason. The first truth is also an empirical judgment to the extent that actual frustration of desire and the impossibility of reaching a point of gratification in human life are given as supporting evidence for the judgment. This truth has a religious character to the extent that the emphasis on the recognition of the presence of suffering and the possibility of overcoming it by human endeavour introduces a particular value orientation to life. Neither suffering nor its cessation, were conceived as realities divorced from the immediate experience of human beings. The same could be said of the other two truths, the truths relating to the origin of suffering, and the path leading to its cessation. For the Buddha the speculative concerns of the earlier philosophers who were engaged in the pursuit of finding solutions to metaphysical problems by resorting to speculative reasoning should be replaced by the understanding of these truths. To this extent the early Dhamma is seen to be offering a philosophical critique of previous philosophical systems. This critique seems to apply to a large part of what was conceived as philosophy in the history of the western tradition as well.

The psychological perspective

The Buddha is referred to as an incomparable surgeon because he heals the festering psychological wounds by drawing out the poisoned arrow of greed and hatred that pierces the hearts of ignorant beings. The clinical/medico-psychological model for understanding the teaching of the Buddha is really appropriate because the classical expression of its essence in terms of the four truths taught by the Buddha represents that model. The relationship of the aims of the Dharma with the aims of medicine or rather psychotherapy is widely recog-

•

nized.[12] The Buddhist four truths follow the causal method of dealing with problems relating to health and illness. The Dharma, like Hellenistic philosophy, is concerned with the healing of the human mind. The Buddha's teaching recognized two kinds of diseases: diseases that affect the human body and those that affect the human mind According to the Buddha, the diseases that affect the human mind are much more common, frequent and widespread than those that affect the human body.[13] The Buddha also repeatedly emphasized that his teaching was confined to matters relating to human suffering and its cessation.[14] He wanted people who came to him seeking answers to perplexing philosophical problems to understand that he was not concerned with solving problems that are unrelated to his main concern.[15] They were told that some metaphysical questions raised by people to satisfy their curiosity should be left aside because they do not lend themselves to any satisfactory answers and that answering them would only lead to irresolvable disagreements.

The Buddha's epistemological critique of speculative philosophy pointed out that the method of reasoning from self-evident premises lead to consequences that do not accord with the observed facts. Such criticism is applicable to time honoured sacred doctrines as well, because teachings most faithfully handed down in sacred traditions may turn out to be void, useless and false whereas what is not so handed down may be in accordance with fact.[16] A belief cannot be taken as true merely because it has been faithfully handed down in a sacred tradition, or is a conclusion derived from flawless deductive reasoning from self-evident premises. The Buddha also drew attention to the frequent occurrence of irresolvable doctrinal conflict due to the mutually contradictory nature of the beliefs and world-views that were dogmatically affirmed by people who subscribed to divergent traditions of revelation, and by people who pursued the light of their own rational intuitions. Unverifiable dogmas that lead to serious ideological disputes could be the outcome of dependence on revelations and reason.

In the psychological critique of philosophical dogmatism the Buddha observed the influence of the emotions on people's views. He pointed out that clinging to a view is a latent tendency in the human mind (*ditthanusaya*), a corrupting influence (*ditthasava*), and a kind of passionate dogmatic grasping (*ditthi upadana*). People find it extremely difficult to give up their firmly grasped views because they have grasped them through the influence of their desires, inclinations and propensities, their individual preferences, likes and dislikes.[17] One clings strongly to the view in which one sees personal advantage.[18] Sometimes people give up one view only to cling to another like monkeys that let go of one branch only to cling to anoth-

---

12. See Keown, D. *Buddhism and bioethics*. New York: Palgrave, 2001 pp.1-2 and Keown's reference to Duncan, A.S., Dunstan, G.R., & Welbourn R.B. (1981), *Dictionary of Medical Ethics*. London: Daxton, Longman & Todd.
13. Anguttaranikaya. Pali Text Society, London; Vol. 2, pp.142-143.
14. Both earlier and now I refer to Dukkha and its cessation. Majjhimanikaya. Pali Text Society, London; Vol. 1, p.140.
15. Ibid. p.485.
16. Ibid. p.520.
17. Suttanipata Verse 781: How could one transcend one's own view, one has reached it being led by desire and preference. Reaching one's own conclusions one speaks in accordance with one's knowledge.
18. Ibid. Verse 797

er.[19] The Buddha also criticized the arrogance associated with people who grasp certain dogmas and condemn others because the others do not accept their own view. He observed that if anyone claims to be insightful and wise because one holds a particular philosophical thesis with great passion for it, then others also who hold a view with equal passion should be equally insightful and wise.[20] If someone condemns another as a stupid beast because that person does not approve of one's view then everyone should be a stupid beast because each one grasps one's own dogma.[21] The Buddha points out that people quarrel about the truth because they tend to measure themselves against others as inferior, superior or equal.[22] It becomes a source of pride, and conceit, which are unwholesome emotions that have to be eliminated in order to attain peace of mind. Some people during the time of the Buddha entered intensely into hostile debate with those who held different views about what is true and real producing much psychological tension within themselves eager to be judged victorious in such debates. They suffered immense frustration if their view was defeated because of their deep attachment to their dogmas.[23] Those who are intent on the appeasement of their passions do not see any value in the engagement with such ideological controversy. The Buddha maintained that there is one truth, the understanding of which puts an end to all philosophical controversies.[24]

Since the Buddhist interest in a world view was based on the practical consideration of the effective means of removing suffering or attaining emancipation from suffering, it discouraged clinging to philosophical dogmas while encouraging a wholesome philosophical outlook or a pragmatically sound world-view which it characterized as the right view (*sammaditthi*). The right view advocated by the Buddha involved a belief in the causal efficacy of human action and initiative which amounted to a denial of strict determinism and fatalism, an admission of the efficacy of moral and spiritual endeavour in achieving the goal of emancipation from suffering, and a rejection of the materialistic position that man is merely a byproduct of material elements which are annihilated at death.

In closing

It seems that the Dharma considers the search for the knowledge of right and wrong, ought and ought not, good and bad to be an imperative concern of the student who engages in philosophy as a therapy and philosophy as a way of life. For contemporary philosophers who confine themselves to the empirical sciences, genuine cognitions which add to the store of human knowledge, statements about right and wrong, ought and ought not, good and bad are all insignificant. Such statements are believed to be mere expressions of emotion or a variety of commands or prescriptions. The normative function of determining what is right and wrong,

---

19. Ibid. Verse 791.
20. Ibid. Verse 881.
21. Ibid. Verse 860.
22. Ibid. Verse 860.
23. Ibid. Verse 826.
24. Ibid. Verse 884.

and so on, is considered to lie outside the task of philosophy. But as a philosophy which demands commitment to a way of life, the Dharma avows that knowledge of what is right and wrong, and so on, is extremely significant, thus endorsing an ethical cognitivism. However, the basis of its ethical cognitivism differs from that of theistic religions in that moral principles are not looked upon as divine commandments. Instead the Dharma combines a consequentialist principle with what may be described as the Golden Rule as the rational foundation of morality to acquire peace of mind and attain the end of Dukkha. Accordingly, when faced with a situation demanding moral choice one ought to perform that act which is conducive to the happiness and well being of oneself and others and avoid that act which results in harm to oneself and others.[25] The Buddha asserted that it is an experientially verifiable fact that behaviour proceeding from greed, hatred and delusion or any other confusion of mind are harmful to oneself as well as to others. It appears to hold that when this consequentialist principle is combined with the principle involved in the Golden Rule, that is, the principle enjoining that one ought to behave towards others in the way that one would wish others to behave towards oneself, there is then a sound rational basis for moral decisions.

Some modes of philosophy have traditionally attempted to perform the role of guiding human beings in the choice of a good life. Today, science is exclusively engaged in the task of acquiring factual, practical knowledge. But in addition to factual knowledge human beings seem to be desperately in need of practical and moral wisdom. It is the wide expansion of scientific knowledge and technological skill unchecked and unguided by practical and moral wisdom that has resulted in most of the regrettable circumstances of contemporary life. It is in this context that the Buddhist philosophy of the Middle Way seems most significant. The Dharma has a crucial philosophical contribution to make towards initiating a process of wisely dealing with the proliferation of uncontrollable greed and craving. The lifestyles of people, specially in the so-called developed world, which seem to provide the model for all others, do not seem to suit the very natural conditions of the world that we live in. The consequence of this is that mankind is faced with unprecedented problems of great magnitude, such as problems of environment, depletion of non-renewable resources, population explosion, war, conflicts and violence, drug addiction, alcoholism and numerous forms of criminal behaviour. There is a great need for a philosophy of life which can serve as an antidote to these social and psychological trends. Unwholesome emotions that produce suffering and make people psychologically sick arise from lack of insight. The philosophical perspective contained in the Buddha's right view (*sammaditthi*) which he proposed against numerous metaphysical dogmas and philosophical extremes can still be seen as an effective therapy for the human mind's diseased condition that produces suffering in people's individual and social lives.

---

25. Majjhimanikaya. Pali Text Society, London; Vol. I, p.415 f.

Part III

The Buddha's No-Nonsense Empty-Self Psychology

In Chapter 8, Kariyawasam clarifies that the Buddha's alleged divine capacity of "omniscience" is a grave misconception. No such quality was claimed in the Buddha's discourses. Although the Buddha dismissed praises of omniscience, only a few centuries after his *parinirvana*, smart students applied the "pragmatics of omniscience" in debates with rivalling groups. In the same spirit of dismissing the "nonsensical", Kalupahana's Chapter 9 explains the Buddha's approach to miracles. Although the Buddha recognized psychokinesis and telepathy as miraculous, because they go beyond normal human capacity, he did not exploit their pragmatic value and wisely prohibited his students from practicing them. For the Buddha the instruction of his Dharma is a "miracle".

Chapter 9 clarifies that it was this educational psychology which made the Buddha one of the world's greatest teachers for more than 2500 years. However, there is nothing magical or mysterious about his method of teaching. The quintessence appears to be the Buddha's adjustment of his messages to the audience or person he is talking to (*upaya*). This implies a "withness", a two-way street and a joint activity, that starts with openness in order to come to understanding. From the discourses one might infer that the Buddha continuingly reflected a way of being in relationship and conversation with others in his thinking, talking, and responsive acting. For the reader of the Buddha's dialogical discourses this requires hermeneutics which suggests a generative process creating a new understanding while interpreting the Buddha's alleged words in the text and trying to arrive at the Buddha's intention and meaning. Thus, the readers' present explanatory meaning of the Dharma unavoidably implies a relational reconstruction of the Buddha's message across time in imaginary conversation with the Buddha of which one is not always aware. Obviously, language is the vehicle of this meaning-and-action making process.

In Chapter 10, Tilakaratne deals with Nirvana that, along with the topics of omniscience and miracles, is often misunderstood. The author argues that popular views of Nirvana as a mystical state or as a heavenly paradise to dwell in after death cannot be substantiated in the Pali discourses. The scriptures rather emphasize the non-metaphysical and experiential nature of Nirvana as the cessation or extinction of the flames of emotional suffering attained through a modified state of mind. This no-nonsense vocabulary meaning of Nirvana goes hand in hand with a relational meaning of Nirvana in that the end of emotional misery implies balanced relationships. Mostly, this refers to the cessation of anger at someone, fear of somebody, or sadness about some person.

From the editor's social constructional perspective the mind is a relational concept. The other person and self are linguistic creations only existing in dialogue and in relationship. Thus, the self and identity are dialogical-narrative constructions existing only in language and therefore only engaged in conversational construction, deconstruction, and reconstruction through continuous interactions in multiple relationships. Such I-me-mine/self is always (per)forming; I am as many potential selves as are embedded within and constructed through conversations. Identity and continuity, or what I think of as self-hood, become maintaining coherence and continuity in the stories I tell about myself. This self or rather self-narrative does not represent a single voice and is a multi-authored polyphony self. Since I-me-mine/self does not exist outside of language and discourse, there is no inner-core self and no fixed tangible self. Lacking a substantial/inherent self, the self is thus empty. Here at this point, the Dharma and the psychology of Social Construction are in a concatenated confluence. Does this view absolve the individual from responsibility? No! The individual, although provisionally seen as solitary, is of primary importance. As non-solitary "relational beings", we are confronted more, not less, with issues of social responsibility in striving toward Nirvana, here-and-now.

Chapter 8

Omniscience: The Buddhist Point Of View

Tilak Kariyawasam

Introduction

Omniscience – the capacity to know everything infinitely – is first and foremost a distinct characteristic of a "god". Thus, in all theistic religions god is described as being omniscient and hence, what "he" reveals, either through direct visions to devotees or through media to selected candidates, is taken as the gospel truth to be accepted and followed without questioning. Some religious founders have made claims to omniscience as well. Undoubtedly this was done to enhance their position as religious teachers and to give authority to their teachings. This had been especially the case with teachers, who did not accept divine revelation, but yet expected their followers to dogmatically cling to the views propounded by them, so that it would help to establish their authority and give sanctity to their teachings. This may even have been a necessity at a time when teachings propounded by teachers – who did not proclaim to be godly – had to vie with teachings considered to be of divine origin.

That this was the case in the sixth century BCE India is clearly seen from the Pali Nikayas (containing the Buddha's discourses that were first transmitted orally and written down on palm leaves for the first time in the first century BCE in Sri Lanka). These Buddhist scriptures that can be reasonably dated to early times specially refer to at least two teachers who had claimed omniscience openly on which basis they emphasized the necessity to accept their absolute authority. The two well-known teachers were Nigantha Nataputta, the Jaina leader and Purana Kassapa, whom the Buddhist texts portray as an Akiriyavadin (a teacher who did not deal with the consequences of karmic intentional action and is thus expounding a false teaching). Both of them are generally considered to be senior contemporaries of the Buddha. The Majjhima Nikaya[1] as well as the Anguttara Nikaya[2] very explicitly state that Nigantha Nataputta, also known as Jaina Mahavira, asserted that he was omniscient. Nigantha Nataputta's omniscience was/is one of the Jain fundamental dogmas. The Anguttara Nikaya[3] records two Brahmin metaphysicians visiting and reporting the Buddha:

---

1. MN, Pali Text Society, I, p.519, II, p.31.
2. AN, Pali Text Society, III, p.74.
3. AN IV, p.429.

Master Gotama, Purana Kassapa, all knowing, all seeing, professes unlimited knowledge and vision and says: "Whether I walk, stand, sleep or awake, knowledge and vision constantly and continually are present in me."

The same is said about Nigantha Nataputta. There are two predominant characteristics in this declaration of omniscience. One is its "all knowing" (*sabbannu*) and "all seeing" (*sabbadassavi*) nature implying a knowledge and vision that is infinite (*ananta*) and therefore encompasses everything (*sabba*). The other characteristic is its being operative at all times, constantly, continuously and even automatically, irrespective of whether one is asleep or awake. Perhaps, this is even a little wider in its ambit than the omniscience of a god, for it is not clear whether a god's omniscience operates in this manner. A characteristic of religions that upholds their founders' omniscience is the place given to dogmatism. It is surprising to see how in Jainism, which also developed an epistemological theory, omniscience had assumed the status of a fundamental dogma. Kalupahana, explaining this, says:

An [Awakened] One cannot make any mistake about one-to-one relation. Yet the epistemological theories of "possibilities" and "standpoints" leave Mahavira in a position where such mistakes are unavoidable if a person adopts any one of the possibilities or standpoints. Thus, if an [Awakened] One is to make no mistake whatsoever, he must adopt all the possibilities or standpoints each time he makes a prediction. This would account for Mahavira's recognition of "omniscience" (*sarvajnata*) as the highest form of knowledge. Indeed, Mahavira was the first religious teacher in India to claim such omniscience, which can be described as the most comprehensive way of reaching ultimate objectivity.[4]

According to Basham even Makkhali Gosala, one of the "Six Sectarian Teachers" – the Buddha's contemporaries conveying false teachings – also is said to have claimed omniscience. But as Basham himself admits, this claim is referred to only in later times.[5] There is however no evidence to show that Makkhali Gosala himself personally claimed omniscience. While some religious teachers of the sixth century BCE India claimed omniscience, others openly disclaimed it. Thus, the sceptics did not posit any such claim. The reason is that the sceptics held the human intellect as being limited. Therefore it was not possible for anyone to claim that someone can know everything. The Buddha openly had disclaimed omniscience in the *Kannakutthala Sutta*[6] by stating:

4. Kalupahana, D.J. (1992). *A history of Buddhist philosophy, continuities and discontinuities.* University of Hawaii Press, p.19.
5. Basham, A.L. (1951). *History and doctrine of Ajivikas.* London: Luzac, p.92.
6. MN II, p.127.

There is neither a recluse nor a Brahmin who at one and the same time can know all, can see all; this situation does not exist.

Omniscience, a misconception

According to the Nikayas this idea of omniscience is a misconception. As pointed out above, the Buddha could not agree with the idea of knowing everything at once. According to the Buddha the highest form of knowledge achievable by human beings is the so-called "threefold knowledge" (*tevijja*). Rationally, this comprises: the knowledge how to attain Nirvana, the insight in the cyclical nature of the dependent origination/ceasing of mental phenomena, and the memory of their daily "births". Thus, "he can recollect previous existences as much as he likes."; MN I, 482). Similarly this applies to a "higher" form of knowledge known as the "divine eye" (a metaphor for the ability to see how states of being originate and cease depending on the intentional/karmic activity invoked). Although these types of knowledge are peculiar, it does not necessarily mean that they connote omniscience. On particular subjects the Buddha as well as his students can extend their knowledge as much as they like. According to the *Pasadika Sutta*, "with regard to the past the Tathagata's consciousness follows in the wake of his memory". He recalls as much as he likes; with regard to the future the Tathagata ("the-thus-come-thus-gone", a nick name for the Buddha) has the knowledge resulting from awakening "that is the final rebirth". Concerning the future the Buddha did not contend that he had unlimited knowledge; to him the future is indeterminate as well. The latter illustrates the Buddha's human nature in spite of being awakened.

According to Purana Kassapa's and Nigantha Nataputta's statements, they were omniscient in the sense that they had an all embracing knowledge at all times. The Buddha vehemently denied their claims. The Anguttara Nikaya mentions that two Brahmins skilled in metaphysics had visited the Buddha, saying:

> Master Gotama, Purana Kassapa, all knowing, all seeing, professes unlimited knowledge and vision: "Whether I walk, stand, sleep or wake, always ever, knowledge and vision are presented." And he has thus declared: "With infinite knowledge I abide knowing, seeing a finite world." Master Gotama, the Nigantha Nataputta, all knowing, all seeing, also professes unlimited knowledge and vision, but he has declared thus: "With infinite knowledge I abide knowing, seeing an infinite world." (AN IV, 429)

It appears that their statements are contradictory, whereas if they were omniscient their statements should be the same. In the *Brahmajala Sutta*[7] it is said that the Buddha declared that this view of the world as infinite or as finite is mistaken. Hence, the two religious leaders' statements about their omniscience are wrong. The Buddha clearly denies that one can be all know-

---

7.   DN, Pali Text Society, I, pp.22-23.

ing and all seeing all at once (MN II, 127), and illustrates his point by means of a parallel that a man cannot know everything in the world up to the end of the world, as follows:

> Four men standing at the four corners of the world, each man endowed with supreme pace and speed with the supreme length of stride – as an archer, mighty with bow, skilled, deft, a marksman, may wing with ease a slender shaft across a palm tree's shadow – let such be their speed; as western sea from eastern sea – such their stride. Now suppose the man standing at the eastern corner were to say: "By walking I'll reach the end of the world." Though man's life span were a hundred years and he lived a hundred years and walked for a hundred years – save when eating, drinking, chewing, munching, answering nature's calls and dispelling fatigue by sleep – he would die before he reached the end of the world. So the men at the other three corners.[8]

This parable explains the impossibility of knowing everything in the world.

Though Brahma is supposed to know everything, according to the *Kevaddha Sutta*, he was unable to answer the question, "where do these great elements... completely cease to be?" (DN I, 223). In the *Brahmajala Sutta* (DN I, pp. 39-44) Brahma is shown as a person holding a mistaken position. The passage below speaks for itself:

> There is a time when this world system dissolves. And when this happens beings are mostly reborn in the world of radiance, and there they dwell made of mind, feeding on joy, radiating light from themselves, traversing the air, continuing in glory; and thus they remain for a long period of time. And there comes also a time this world-system begins to re-evolve. When this happens, the mansion of Brahma appears, but it is empty. And some being or other, either because his span of years has passed or his merit is exhausted, falls from that world of radiance, and comes to life in the mansion of Brahma...
>
> And there also he lives made of mind, feeding on joy, radiating light from him, traversing the air, continuing in glory; and thus does he remain for a period of time. Now there arises in him, from his dwelling there so long alone, a dissatisfaction and a longing: "O, would that other beings might come to join me in this place." And just then, either because their span of years has passed or their merit was exhausted, other beings fall from that world of radiance, and appear in the mansion of Brahma as companions to him, and in all respects like him...

---

8.   AN IV, pp.428-430.

The one who was first reborn, thinks thus to himself: I am Brahma, the Great Brahma, the Supreme One, the Mighty, the All-seeing; the Ruler, the Lord of All, the Maker, the Creator, the Chief of All, appointing to each his place, the Ancient of Days, the Father of All that are and are to be. These other beings are of my creation. And why is that so? A while ago I thought, "would that they might come." And on my mental aspiration, behold! The beings came...

And those beings themselves, too, think thus: This must be Brahma, the Great Brahma, the Supreme One, the Mighty, the All-seeing; the Ruler, the Lord of All, the Maker, the Creator, the Chief of All, appointing to each his place... we must have been created by him. And why? Because, as we see, it was he who was here first and we came after that...

The one who first came into existence there is of longer life, and more glorious, and more powerful than those who appeared after him. It might well be that some being on his falling from that state should come hither. And having come hither he might go forth from the household life into the homeless state. And having thus become a recluse, he by reason of ardour of exertion of application of earnestness of careful thought, reaches up to such rapture of heart that, rapt in heart, he calls to mind his last dwelling-place, but not the previous ones...

He says to himself: That illustrious Brahma, the Great Brahma, the Supreme One, the Mighty, the All-seeing; the Ruler, the Lord of All, the Maker, the Creator, the Chief of All, appointing to each his place, the Ancient of Days, the Father of All that are and are to be, he by whom we were created, he is steadfast, immutable, eternal, of a nature that knows no change, and he will remain so for ever and ever. But we who were created by him have come hither as being impermanent, mutable, limited in duration of life.[9]

The Buddha clarified that Brahma, the highest of gods, is not omniscient. He was the first born in that particular world, and thus he mistakenly thinks that he is the creator and that he knows everything.

---

9.   DN I, pp.17-18.

Omniscience and the undetermined questions

In the Nikayas there are ten so-called classical "unanswered" or "undetermined" questions, about which the Buddha wisely kept silent.[10] These are as follows:

1-2   Is the world eternal or not?
3-4   Is the world finite or infinite?
5-6   Is the soul identical or different from the body?
7-10 After his death does the Tathagata exist, both exist and not exist, nei-
      ther exist nor not exist?

According to the Buddha, men hold divergent views regarding these questions, which eventually result in violent controversy. As Jayatilleke suggests, these questions were probably discussed in studious circles in the Buddha's time, with different schools coming to different conclusions.[11] The interest here is with regard to the relation of these questions to the issue of the Buddha's omniscience. Did the Buddha know the answers to these questions? There are four possibilities to be considered:

> (a) The questions are answerable in principle but the Buddha simply did not know the answers. This view taken by Keith and Jacobi is, as we shall see, the only one which counts against the claim that Buddha was omniscient. However, there is little or no evidence to support such a view. On the other hand, there is evidence to suggest that it is simply wrong, to which we now turn in considering the second possibility.

> (b) The questions are answerable in principle, but the Buddha, though he knew the answers, did not give them because such information was irrelevant to the crucial issue of following the path to awakening and Nirvana. The Buddha used to say of such questions that is not important for the seeker's life.[12]

There is evidence in the Nikayas indicating that the Buddha knew the answers, at least to the first six questions. In his discourses about causality, we are frequently told that the teaching of dependent origination takes the middle way between the extremes of eternalism and annihilationism, existence and non-existence, unity and plurality. What is important is that this treatment is extended in the Nidanavagga of the Samyutta Nikaya[13] to the question whether or

---

10. Tilakaratne, A. (1993). *Nirvana and ineffability.* University of Kelaniya, Sri Lanka: Postgraduate Institute of Pali and Buddhist Studies. (pp.117-123)
11. Jayatilleke, K.N. (1963). *Early Buddhist theory of knowledge.* London: George, Allen & Unwin, pp.243-250.
12. MN I, p. 431, DNI, p. 187-189, SN, Pali Text Society II, pp.223-224.
13. SN II, pp.17.

not the soul is identical with the body. In other words, the Buddha actually answered the third pair of "unanswered" questions by avoiding the two extremes and teaching his Middle Way. There seems to be no reason why we should not, as Warder[14] suggests, extend this argument to the first four questions and conclude that: "There is no continuing (infinite) or totally destroyed (finite) universe, there is no such entity, there is only the sequence of dependent origination." We might then say that though the Buddha knew the answer to these questions, he dealt only with the one which is most important – the question about body and soul – and left the questions about the universe aside as idle speculation not conducive to awakening.

The other two possibilities are:

(c) The questions are unanswerable in principle, because the answer can only be intuitively related and is wholly beyond the grasp of human intellect and empirical investigation. As Jayatilleke puts it: "It is not that there was something that the Buddha did not know, but that what he 'knew' in the transcendent sense could not be conveyed in words because of the limitation of language and of empiricism."[15]

(d) The questions are unanswerable in principle, because the questions are logically meaningless or rather, they are not real questions, and they are wrongly put, in which case it is nonsensical to speak of answers. Indeed in one place Buddha said that the undetermined questions arise because of wrong considerations.[16]

One might suggest that this possibility applies to the last four questions about the nature of Parinirvana (final Nirvana of death). Since all that can be said to exist in any person are the five impermanent aggregates (Skandhas or modalities: sensation-affect-thought-behaviour-awareness) which are by definition removed by *parinirvana*, further questions about whether or not the Tathagata exists after death would seem to be meaningless. From such considerations it seems clear that the fact that the Buddha left certain questions unanswered does not mean that he was not omniscient. He may have known the answers and been unable or unwilling to give them, i.e. (b) and (c), or the questions are so absurd, which means that it is not due to the limitation on the knowledge of the Buddha that he does not answer them.

What is the Buddhist position with regard to claimants of omniscience? Did the Buddha himself claim omniscience? With regard to the first question it is clear that the Buddha did not endorse the claims to omniscience as made by either Nigantha Nataputta or Purana Kassapa. To reiterate: in the *Kannakatthala Sutta*[17] the Buddha had said: "There is neither a recluse nor a Brahmin who once and the same time can know all, can see all; this situation does not exist."

14. Warder, A.K. (1970). *Indian Buddhism*, Delhi: Motilal Banarsidass, p.40.
15. Jayatilleke, op. cit. p.473f.
16. AN V, p.187.
17. MN II, p.127.

As stated earlier, this rejection of two reputed teachers' claim to omniscience clearly shows that the Buddha did not accept the position that one can have knowledge and vision regarding everything continually, continuously and that omniscience operates automatically. With regard to the second question, whether the Buddha himself claimed omniscience, the opinions differ. Such reputed scholars as Keith[18] and De la Vallée Poussin (quoted by Jayatilleke (op. cit. p. 377), held that the Buddha claimed omniscience. Jayatilleke (op. cit. p. 376f) quite rightly points out that such views are put forward by scholars "without distinguishing the question as to whether this was a claim of his or of his (students), immediate or of a later time." Further he says (loc. cit.) that De la Vallée Poussin in support of his view quotes only the *Milindapanha* – a Theravada work that narrates a dialogue between a Bhikkhu called Nagasena and the Greek king Menander (or Milinda in Pali), who ruled in North-West India in 153-150 BCE – which is undoubtedly of a later date than the Buddha's discourses.

Some consider the incident recorded in the *Kevaddha Sutta*[19] as evidence showing the Buddha's claim to omniscience. Therein it is said that the Buddha knows the answer to a question, which the Brahma failed to answer. The purpose of this incident is to bring to light Brahma's ignorance, though he claims to be all-seeing, and it is not at all intended to show the Buddha's omniscience. However one has to take note of the fact that in the *Kannakatthala Sutta*[20] the Buddha was recorded as saying that:

> ...those who maintain that the Buddha holds the view that there is neither a
> recluse nor a Brahmana who, all knowing, all-seeing, can claim all-embrac-
> ing knowledge and vision are misrepresenting the Buddha.

This seems to suggest that there can be beings who are omniscient. However, the Buddha is clarifying his position by saying that there is neither a recluse nor a Brahmin who at one and the same time can know all and see all (loc. cit.). Thus the crux of the sutta is that the Buddha is denying the type of omniscience claimed by Nigantha Nataputta and Purana Kassapa.[21] References such as the "Parable of the Simsapa Leaves"[22] show that the Buddha knew much more than what he taught his students. Therein he explained that what he actually teaches is only what one needs to know to awaken, the amount of which is comparable to a limited number of leaves in his hand (while his understanding of existence is comparable to all the leaves in a forest). His attitude in dealing with the "unanswered" questions strengthens this view. Yet, knowing more than what he taught is not the same as being omniscient. Therefore, such evidence cannot be considered sufficient to show that the Buddha claimed omniscience.

It is also clear that while the Buddha declared that he had knowledge regarding many

18. Keith, A.N. (1923). *Buddhist philosophy in India and Ceylon.* Oxford: Clarendon Press, p.35.
19. DN I, pp.222-223.
20. MN II, 127.
21. Toshiichi, E. (1997). *Buddha in Theravada Buddhism.* Dehiwala, Sri Lanka: Buddhist Cultural Centre., p.59.
22. SN V, 437-438.

more things than he taught his disciples and listeners, he also quite openly maintained that he possessed only the threefold knowledge, pointed out in the previous paragraph, that constitutes the last three items of the "six super cognitive abilities". This claim is put forward in the *Tevijja Vacchagotta Sutta*.[23] These three are: retrocognition (the ability to perceive one's own past history), clairvoyance (or "divine eye": the ability to see how states of being originate depending on the intentional/karmic activity invoked), and the knowledge regarding the destruction of influxes (warding off unwholesome afflictions ensures liberation from further rebirths of cankers). It is safe to conclude that the possession of these three forms of knowledge do not qualify one for being omniscient in the sense it is generally understood.

Elsewhere[24] I have outlined a metaphoric interpretation of the term *sabbannu*, that has been used as an epithet for the Buddha, basing my argument on the special Buddhist use of the term *sabba*. Therein I have pointed out that in the Nikayas the term *sabba* is employed to denote the whole world of sense experience, thus: not the world "out there" (considered flat in the Iron Age), but the world "in here".[25] My inference finds plausible corroboration in the Samyutta Nikaya, wherein the Buddha explained:

> What brethren, is the all (*sabba*). It is the eye and object, ear and sound, nose and scent, tongue and savours, body and tangibles, mind and mind-states. That brethren is called the all. (loc.cit)

The term is used in a similar sense in the *Mulapariyaya Sutta*.[26] Taken in this sense "the all" (*sabba*) means six sense-spheres. Thus, it is seen that the Buddha had explained also the arising of the world (*loka*) on the basis of sense-spheres.[27] These explanations about the term *sabba* and *loka* throw much light on the Buddhist conception of *sabbannu*. On this evidence it can be reasonably surmised that having knowledge of everything or omniscience (*sabbannu*) means having knowledge of the sense-fields, and that this knowledge of sense-fields is nothing but the knowledge regarding the world and everything in it. This knowledge of the world of sense experience is much narrower in scope than "all" or "everything" meant by Nigantha Nataputta or Purana Kassapa. Besides, the Buddha did not claim that cognitive experience both sensory and extra-sensory – including everything in the past, present and future – is of unlimited scope. The Buddha did not make any claim to absolute knowledge, particularly regarding the future. The Buddha speaks about the future by resorting to inductive inference, whereby the future possibility of an event is inferred through several experiences. These experiences do not make it possible to make an absolutely certain prediction, but only one of a high degree of probability.

All of this shows that the Buddha did not claim omniscience like the other contemporary

---

23. MN I, 482.
24. See my chapter The development of omniscience in Buddhism, in Y. Karunadasa (Ed.).(1990), *Essays in honour of Ananda W.P. Guruge*. Colombo: Unpublished, pp.223-236.
25. SN IV, 15; MNI, 3-4.
26. MN I, 1.
27. SN II, 73.

teachers of his time did. If he did claim to possess some type of omniscience, it was in the sense of the new interpretation he gave to *sabba*. Yet later Pali Buddhist texts explicitly state that the Buddha was omniscient and that he had knowledge of everything; i.e. of all that is conditioned and unconditioned without remainder. For example, the *Patisambhida Magga*, "Way of Analysis" (KN), a late Pali scholastic treatise definitely made after the Buddha's lifetime in the style of the *Abhidhamma* (worked on during many centuries by later students – which together with the Buddha's discourses [Nikayas] and the Buddhist commune rules [Vinaya] – form the Tipitaka, the three canonical books of the Theravada). Why these early Buddhists made such turnaround is a quest for the next paragraph.

Omniscience in the Theravada

The *Patisambhida Magga* gives many details of the Buddha's omniscience in answering the question: "What is meant by the omniscience of the Tathagata?" It begins by stating that his omniscience consists in "knowing everything, conditioned and unconditioned, without remainder." This omniscience is said to be unobscured by hindrance and consists of forty-seven aspects, explained as follows:

1-3	Knowing everything in the past, future, and present.
4-8	Knowing everything about the organs of vision, hearing, smell, taste, and touch and about their respective objects.
9	Knowing everything about the mind-organ *mano* and its objects i.e. *dhammas* (italics added; i.e., the smallest unit of psychological experience).
10	Knowing everything as far as the various aspects of impermanence, suffering and non-self are concerned.
11-15	Knowing everything about the five *skandhas* as far as the various aspects of impermanence, suffering and non-self are concerned.
16	Knowing everything about the eye as far as the various aspects of impermanence, suffering and non-self are concerned.
17	Knowing everything about decay and death as far as the various aspects of impermanence, etc. are concerned.
18-22	Knowing everything concerning intuitive knowledge and its various aspects... full understanding and its various... abandoning and its various aspects... meditation and its various aspects... realization and its various aspects.[28]

---

28. *Itivuttaka* ("This was said by the Buddha", p.106), Intuitive knowledge of everything involves full understanding of suffering, the abandonment of its case, meditation as the path and realization of *nirodha* (the unmaking of sensory craving and conceptual clinging).

23-25   Knowing everything concerning the aggregates (the five *skand-has*) and their various aspects... the elements and their various aspects... the sense fields and there various aspects.

26-27   Knowing everything concerning the conditioned and its various aspects... the unconditioned and its various aspects.

28-30   Knowing everything concerning wholesome (*kusala*)... unwholesome (*akusala*)... and neutral *dhammas*.

31-34   Knowing everything concerning *dhammas* belonging to the realm of craving... the realm of form... the realm of the formless... and concerning those which are un-included.

35-38   Knowing everything concerning the Four Noble Realities (propositions or or facts, better known as "Truths" of the "Noble One") aspects (there is existential suffering, there are causes for this, there is a way out, and this way is the Eightfold Path: right effort, action, intention, understanding, speech, livelihood, concentration and mindful awareness).

39-42   Knowing everything concerning the fourfold "Analytical Knowledge" and their various aspects. (This refers to knowledge of effect/result [e.g., awakening], cause [e.g., the Eightfold Path], language [e.g., interpretation of the suttas] and knowledge of analytical knowledge and its function).

43   Knowing everything concerning the knowledge of what goes on in the senses and intentions of others.

44   Knowing everything concerning the knowledge of the hankering of beings.

45   Knowing everything concerning knowledge of the miracle of the "double appearance". (Thus called because the magical illusion was created in twins or pairs of opposites like fire and water; the Buddha wisely discouraged his students from performing such miracles.)

46   Knowing everything concerning the knowledge of the attainment of great compassion.

47   In the world with its *Devas* (common gods as joyful states), *Maras* (destructive demons as angry states) and *Brahmas* (upper gods as blissful states) all that is seen, heard, felt, discerned, accomplished, striven for, or devised in mind by the being of the "world-gods" or men, recluses or Brahmins ("holy" men) – knowing all this is an aspect of omniscience.

The *Patisambhida Magga* is one of the first attempts, undertaken after having compiled the Nikayas, to show that the Buddha was omniscient. This account tries to show the Buddha's omniscience by radically departing and breaking from the Nikayas by attributing the claim that "he knows everything in the future." As Jayatilleke[29] contended, this kind of omniscience was clearly not accepted by the Buddha himself. Apart from the idea of knowing everything in the future, the rest of the omniscient aspects falls within the main tenets of the Buddhist path. That is to say that the Buddha's omniscience includes knowing everything about all conditioned and unconditioned *dhammas*, the aggregates, the four elements, the six sense-fields, the three marks of existence (suffering, impermanence and not-self)), the Four Noble Facts, and so on. Thus, it seems that the *Patisambhida Magga* largely follows the definition of omniscience given in the Nikayas. Thus, according to the *Patisambhida Magga*, only the Buddha was omniscient. Because the omniscient aspects, apart from knowledge of the future, were explained on the basis of the Buddhist type of awakening, the Buddha's omniscience was different from that of others. This is further explained in the definition of his all-seeing ability that implies the "Fourteenfold Buddha Knowledge" of which the first eight (the knowledge of the Four Noble Facts [35-38] and the Fourfold Analytical Knowledge [39-42], as indicated above) was achieved by the Buddha and can be achieved by all students of the Dhamma. The remaining belong only to the realm of the Buddha:

> ...these are knowledge of what goes on in the senses and intentions of others, of the craving of beings, of the twin miracles, and of the attainment of great compassion along with omniscience, and knowledge unobscured by hindrances."[30]

In the *Milindapanha* there is another late Pali discussion about the Buddha's omniscience. According to the *Milindapanha* the Buddha was omniscient, but his knowledge and vision was not constantly and continuously present. The Buddha's omniscient knowledge was dependent on his mind's adverting. When he adverted, he got to know whatever it would please him to know.[31] This explanation of the Buddha's omniscience did not satisfy King Milinda (who reigned in the 2nd century BCE), so he responded: "Revered Nagasena, the Buddha was not omniscient if his omniscient knowledge was due to searching."[32] In order to explain the Buddha's omniscience, Nagasena subsequently described the differences between the seven kinds of mentality, as follows:

> 1. The mental state of ordinary persons. The mentality of these persons arises with difficulty, proceeds sluggishly, because that mentality has attachments, aversions, confusion, the defilements, their body is not developed for meditation, their moral habit is not developed, their mentality is not developed, their intuitive wisdom is not developed.

29. Jayatilleke, op.cit. p.381.
30. *Patisambhida Magga* (PS), Pali Text Society, p.134.
31. Trenker, V. (Ed.).(1928). *Milindapanha*. London: unknown.
32. Ibid. p.102.

2. The mental state of the "Stream Enterer". Such person's mentality – of someone who entered the stream ending in the ocean of Nirvana – upraises quickly, proceeds quickly as far as the first three of the ten stages toward awakening are concerned (to let go of believing in a permanent self, of doubting in the Buddhist way, and of clinging to rules and rituals), but the higher planes arise with difficulty, proceed sluggishly, because of utter purification of the three first stages, and because of not having got rid of the fetters (psychological afflictions/defilements).

3. The mental state of the "Once Returner". His mentality upraises quickly, proceeds quickly as far as the five stages are concerned (the three fetters above plus the letting go of craving and "ill-will" or insufficient motivation), but the higher planes arise with difficulty, because of utter purification of the fourth and fifth stages and because of not having got rid of defilements.

4. The mental state of the "Non-Returner". His mentality upraises quickly, as far as the first five of the ten[33] stages are concerned (s/he can let go the first five fetters completely, not yet of the last five), but the higher planes arise with difficulty, proceed sluggishly, because of utter purification of all of the ten stages and because of not having got rid of the defilements.

5. The mental state of the "Awakened One" (Arahant). The mentality of the Arahants - whose cankers are destroyed, whose stains are vanished, whose defilements have been left behind, who have lived the life, done what was to be done, laid down the burden, attained their own welfare, utterly destroyed the fetters of becoming, won the analytical insights, and are utterly purified in the students' planes – arises buoyantly, proceeds buoyantly in the student's range, upraises with difficulty, proceeds sluggishly in the planes of one who is a "Buddha by and for himself", because of utter purification in the student's range and because of the lack of utter purification in the range of one who is a "Buddha by and for himself". (This final advance can be made after having broken all fetters, the last five of which are: craving for material and/or immaterial existence, conceit, restlessness and ignorance. There are no more rebirths of hate, greed, ignorance, envy and arrogance, extinguished due to a virtuous life of confidence, awareness, perseverance, concentration and wisdom. The person is liberated from the cycle of rebirths (*samsara*) of emotional negativity and experiences Nirvana.)

---

33. Although mentioned here as the "ten stages", the "Non-Returners" have only got rid of the five fetters.

6. The mental state of the "Buddha-by-and-for-himself" (*paccekabud-dha*). The mentality of those who are "Buddhas by and for themselves" (lone Buddhas who are on their own and not teach others), self-dependent, without a teacher, faring along like the horn of a rhinoceros, their minds utterly purified and spotless in their own range, arises buoyantly, proceeds buoyantly in regard to their own range, (but) arises with difficulty, proceeds sluggishly as regards the planes of an "Omniscient Buddha", because of utter purification in his own and because of the greatness of the range of an "Omniscient Buddha".

7. The mental state of the "Omniscient Buddha" (*sammasambuddha*). The mentality of those perfect Buddhas (who are not on their own and teach others to become *sravakas* [hearers]), is omniscient. They are the bearers of the "Ten Powers", confident with the confidences, possess the "Eighteen Buddha Qualities", and are the conquerors of the unending. Their knowledge is unobstructed, arises buoyantly everywhere because it is everywhere utterly purified. The eighteen special inner qualities – that include the powers – refer to behaviour (6), realization (6), awakening and awareness (6), and are the following < www.berzinarchives.com >:

1. Being calm, wherever and no matter who stands in front.
2. Speaking in a balanced and calm way without any extreme talking.
3. Not forgetting anything experienced or anyone met earlier.
4. A continuous absorption in emptiness without exemption.
5. A deep and sharp empathy on others' actual existential states.
6. Watching whether someone needs help to find her/his way.
7. A non-declining intention to care out of compassion like a mother.
8. A non-declining joyful perseverance to guide people to end suffering.
9. A non-declining focused attention for each one's particular situation.
10. A non-declining awareness of concentrative absorption.
11. A non-declining awareness of emptiness.
12. A non-declining liberation from any obscuration of the mind.
13. A deep awareness while physically active
14. A deep awareness while verbally communicating
15. A deep awareness while sensory experiencing
16. An insight in the antecedent factors of karmic events.
17. An insight in the consequent factors of karmic events.
18. An insight in the present emotional/behavioural impact of karmic events.

In order to show how quickly the Buddha's "omniscience" functioned, Nagasena refers to the "twin miracles", referred to earlier. However, according to the Early Buddhist tradition this concept of the "twin miracle" is a later addition to the description of the Buddha. It appears in the later parts of the Tipitaka. According to the *Patisambhida Magga* the "twin miracle" is only for *sammasambuddhas* and not for Arahants or for *paccekabuddhas*. It looks invalid and far-fetched to use the "twin miracles" as substantial evidence for the Buddha's "omniscience". The *Milindapanha* puts the explanation forward that whenever the Buddha wanted to know anything, he only needed to open his mind to get to know it. One can understand that because of this reasoning Buddhist writers of later times came to attribute omniscience to the Buddha. The conspicuous feature which differs from the religious leaders' claims of omniscience is that the Buddha's omniscient knowledge depends on "adverting". It seems that the later Buddhist authors did not like to accept the idea that their Buddha was not omniscient (in the sense of not knowing everything). However, they could not escape from the Tipitaka framework, so they stated smartly that the Buddha was omniscient, but he could know things only when he chose to know them.

Omniscience in the early Mahayana

Mahayanists used the idea of omniscience in order to explain emptiness as the ultimate reality experience (*sunyata*) and the concept of Bodhisattva (a "Buddha-to-be" that can be earthly or transcendental). The earthly Bodhisattva follows certain rules of conduct to attain various degrees of "perfection" (the *paramitas*). Among these practices are: generosity, righteousness, forbearance, energy, meditation, wisdom, skilfulness, resolution, strength, and erudition/wisdom. Thus, the Bodhisattva will also achieve "omniscience". As written down in the "Perfection of Wisdom in 18000 lines": "It is thus that a Bodhisattva who courses in perfect wisdom comes near to omniscience."[34] And in the "Perfection of Wisdom in 25000 lines" it is explained that "Endowed with omniscience a Bodhisattva sees, in each of the ten directions, Tathagatas as many as sands of the river Ganges, hears their demonstration of Dharma, honours their community, and sees purity of their Buddha fields."[35] This is the ability he has as an "omniscient person". In the early Mahayana literature, especially in the "Perfection of Wisdom" sutras, we can find the division of omniscience in relation to a hierarchical taxonomy of Buddhist sages. The author of these *Prajnaparamita Sutras* is unknown, but it is quite certainly written by anonymous Bhikkhu brotherhoods as from the first century BCE until the 2nd century and commented by Nagarjuna (2nd century). Three divisions of omniscience are discerned therein as follows:

1. Knowledge of all modes of a Buddha (*sarvakarajnata*)

2. Knowledge of the modes of the path (*margakarajnata*)

3. Omniscience (*sarvajnata*)

34. Mitra, R.E. (Ed.).(1888). *Astasahasrika Prajnaparamita Sutra* (Perfection of Wisdom in 8000 lines).Calcutta: Asiatic Society. Tr. E. J. Conze (1958), *Perfection of Wisdom in 8000 Lines and its Verse Summary*. Calcutta: The Asiatic Society of Calcutta (Bibliotheca Indica, p.11.
35. Dutt, N. (Ed.).(1934). *Pancavimsatisahasrika Prajnaparamita Sutra* (Perfection of Wisdom in 25000 lines). Tr. E.J. Conze (1961), *The large sutra on perfect wisdom*, Part I. London: Luzac, p.76.

This threefold division is a development introduced in early Mahayana texts to distinguish the omniscience of the Buddha from that of an Arahant (awakened students of the *sammasambuddha*) or a *pratyekabuddha* (Sanskrit for *paccekabuddha*), as explained earlier. If what is meant by omniscience is knowledge regarding the six sense spheres, then all Arahants also could claim omniscience. Hence, the Mahayanists found it necessary to distinguish the Buddha's "omniscience" from that of his students. To achieve this, they added the knowledge of all modes of a Buddha, which only the Buddhas can achieve. This addition made the Buddha's omniscience "all-encompassing" (meaning transcendental) and hence, wider in scope than that possessed by the Arahants and *pratyekabuddhas*. The knowledge of all modes of a Buddha's omniscience is thus higher than the *sarvajnata* type of omniscience. According to the explanation given in Perfection of Wisdom literature, this threefold division of omniscience relates to the three kinds of Buddhist sages. According to these three divisions, the sages are graded in parallel as follows:

1. Knowledge of all modes of a Buddha (*sarvakarajnata*): Buddhas

2. Knowledge of the modes of the path (*margakarajnata*): Bodhisattvas

3. Omniscience (*sarvajnata*): Arahants and *pratyekabuddhas*

The Arahants and *pratyekabuddhas* only achieve the limited omniscience feasible for human beings (*sarvajnata*), but do not realize the knowledge of the modes of the path, nor do they realize the knowledge of all modes of a Buddha. The Bodhisattva realizes the knowledge of the modes of the path that includes *sarvajnata*, but he does not realize the knowledge of all modes of a Buddha. A Buddha realizes all of them.[36] According to the "Perfection of Wisdom in 8000 lines" the reason for the differentiation is that everything that there is, *dharmas* (Sanskrit for *dhammas*) evoked by both inner and outer inputs, has been cognized by the Arahants and *pratyekabuddhas*, but not all the paths and not all of their aspects. Knowing all *dharmas*, Arahants and *pratyekabuddhas* are said to be "omniscient".

However, they have not yet realized the knowledge of the modes of the path and the knowledge of all modes of a Buddha. The first means the understanding of every path. It is said, however, that the Bodhisattva should produce and cognize all paths, including the paths of the Arahants and *pratyekabuddhas*. Those paths should be fulfilled and through them should be done what ought to be done, without losing a sense of reality. The "Perfection of Wisdom in 18000 lines" explains the knowledge of all modes of a Buddha according to the *sunyata* point of view (i.e., total emptiness of non-self). It says that all modes are modes of calm. *Sunyata* is explained by way of *santa*, a word that can be inferred in many ways. In the Tipitaka we can find the word santi that refers to Nirvana: deathless calm. The word Nirvana can also mean eternal (SN IV, 204), as well as a perfect peace void of fear (AN II, 24). We can also see

---

36. Conze, E.J. (Ed. & Tr).(1962). Astadasasahasrika Prajnaparamita Sutra (Perfection of Wisdom in 18000 lines). London: George, Allen & Unwin, pp.147-148.

the word *santa* used to define Nirvana in the sense of reality.[37] It can be used to define reality in the early Mahayana Sanskrit literature. Thus, we see that Nagarjuna used the word *santa* to define reality, which refers to the total emptiness of non-extinction, non-destruction, non-permanence, non-identity, non-differentiation, non-origination, and non-ceasing. It is said in the *Mulamadhyamakakarika* (Nagarjuna's commentaries of the Perfection of Wisdom sutras) that "Any entity which exists by virtue of relational origination is quiescence in itself, therefore, the presently originating and arising per se are likewise in the nature of quiescence."[38]

In the *Lankavatara Sutra* (from a later Mahayana period, dating perhaps from the 4th century), *santi* is explained as oneness of objects, it is the highest *Samadhi* (total meditative absorption) from which grows an inner perception by supreme wisdom. It is formulated as:

> O, Lord of Lanka, he who sees thus, sees rightly; if seen otherwise, it is carrying on discrimination, because here is discrimination which leads to dualism. It is like seeing one's own face in water, or like seeing one's shadow in the moonlight or by the lantern, or listening to an echo of one's own voice in a valley, wherein discrimination takes place leading to attachment.

In like manner, to separate "Dharma" (the Buddhist way) from *adharma* (this antonym means: which is not of the Dharma) is only due to discrimination. On account of this, one finds it impossible to do away with the discrimination, thereby creating all forms of falsehood. One is thus unable to realize tranquillity (*santi*), by which is meant "oneness of the awareness of *dharmas*", the highest *Samadhi*, from which grows an inner perception by supreme wisdom.[39]

Thus we can understand that the knowledge of all modes of a Buddha means the realization of emptiness. At the same time we can find in the Perfection of Wisdom literature this knowledge of "all modes of a Buddha" described in terms of perfection of wisdom in various degrees and in all other various descriptions of the emptiness experience. The "Perfection of Wisdom in 25000 lines" conveys that

> It is thus that a Bodhisattva, who courses in the perfection of wisdom, should investigate all *dharmas* as empty in their essential original nature. He should survey them in such a way that there is no mental apperception of any dharma. This is the concentration-circle (*Samadhi mandala*) of the Bodhisattva which is called the "non appropriation of all dharmas", vast, noble and fixed on infinitude, to which all Arahants and *pratyekabuddhas* have no claim, and in which they have no share. Dwelling in this concen-

---

37. *Mulamadhyamakakarika* (Nagarjuna's verses on the his Mahayana Middle School system). Pali Text Society, XVIII, p. 9.
38. Ibid. PTS VII. P.16.
39. D. T. Suzuki, D.T. (1932).(Tr.). *The Lankavatara Sutra* (Descent on Lanka), based upon the 1923 Sanskrit edition of B. Nanjo. London: Routledge, p. 20.

tration-circle, a Bodhisattva will go forth to the knowledge of all modes. But also that knowledge of all modes cannot be appropriated, on account of the emptiness of the subject, and all the other kinds of emptiness."[40]

In the explanation given above on the early Buddhist interpretation of omniscience I have said that the Buddhist way of understanding the world is the understanding of the five aggregates or psychological modalities. If omniscience is the understanding of the world, one has to understand these modalities of sensation-affect-thought-behaviour-awareness. Therefore, mindful awareness of and understanding these functions in their true nature is the achievement of the Buddhist "omniscience". The "Perfection of Wisdom in 8000 lines" also mentions that these aggregates comprise "the world". Although this explanation differs from that of the Nikayas (which point out the reasons for the emptiness of aggregates) in saying that the aggregates should be understood from an emptiness point of view, there is no essential difference in the two stances. It is said that:

> The perfect wisdom of the Tathagata has pointed out the five skandhas as "the world", because they do not crumble, nor crumble away. For the five skandhas have emptiness for their own being, and as devoid of own being, emptiness cannot crumble nor crumble away. It is in this sense that perfect wisdom instructs the Tathagatas in this world. And as emptiness does not crumble, nor crumble away, so also the signlessness, the wishlessness, the unaffected, the unproduced, non-existence, and the realm of dharma.[41]

According to both the "Perfection of Wisdom" in 25000 lines[42] and in 18000 lines[43] we may take omniscience as the understanding of emptiness. Understanding emptiness is the understanding of the five modalities in their true nature as being empty.

As explained earlier, we might understand that the knowledge of all modes of a Buddha means understanding emptiness as "reality limit" or "ultimate reality". Only the Buddha has this kind of knowledge. When one realizes the knowledge of all modes of a Buddha, one will have purified one's Buddha-field and will accomplish fully awakening. In order to obtain full awakening one needs to abandon the hindrance of passions and the hindrance of knowledge: the obsessive idea that things "must" be known. Of these two, Arahants and *pratyekabuddhas* achieve only the abandonment of the hindrance of passion, but not the abandonment of the hindrance of knowledge. This is the main difference between a Buddha on the one hand and Arahants and *pratyekabuddhas* on the other hand. The latter only realize the not-selfness of the person. In the Mahayana perspective, by achieving both kinds of abandonment, Buddhas real-

40. Conze (1961), pp.132-133.
41. Conze (1958), p.256.
42. Conze (1961), pp.132-133.
43. Conze (1962), pp.148-149.

ize not only the not-selfness of the person (regarding the inner world), but the non-selfness of all *dharmas* (regarding the outer world) as well. The result of these two kinds of abandonment comprises the Buddhist "omniscience".[44]

Conclusion

To wrap up the above, in the early texts of the Theravada school no claims whatsoever were found that the historical Buddha was omniscient, but in the later Pali writings and Mahayana Sanskrit traditions it is voiced – most probably for pragmatic reasons – that the Buddha was "omniscient" after all. In short, except of a glitch that the Buddha was allegedly able to foresee the future, the Pali tradition emphasizes omniscience in reference to self-understanding, while the Mahayana traditions primarily refer to the emptiness experience. It is safe to conclude that based on the Early Buddhist Pali scriptures, the Buddha himself did not claim to possess the capacity to know everything infinitely.

---

44. D.T. Suzuki (Tr).(1932). *The Lankavatara Sutra.* London: Routledge & Kegan Paul, p.241.

Chapter 9

Miracles: An Early Buddhist View

David J. Kalupahana

Introduction

In theology a miracle is defined as an event or effect that apparently contradicts known scientific laws, hence thought to be due to supernatural causes, especially to an act of god. The Buddha's teaching, even though well known as an oddity among the wisdom traditions in that it does not contribute to a conception of god, continues to recognize the possibility of miracles. Yet, this admission of the possibility of miracles is seen to conflict with the Buddha's theory of existence that is founded on human knowledge and understanding based on human experience. The question is: How can the Buddha, while being an empiricist in epistemological matters, continue not only talk about miracles which are out of the ordinary but, in fact, be able to perform them? The early discourses refer to three kinds of miracles: (1) the miracle of psychokinetic power, (2) the miracle of telepathy, and (3) the miracle of instruction (DN 1.212-215). The first two – referred to before – were already part and parcel of the pre-Buddhist religious traditions. The third seems to be purely a Buddhist version of a miracle.

Even though it is not actually a form of knowledge but a "power" (i.e. perceptual capacity), *psychokinesis* is listed as the first of the six forms of "higher" knowledge achieved by the contemplative. The contemplative, after s/he has attained the first four preliminary stages of meditation when the mind becomes concentrated and supple, if s/he so wishes, can direct thoughts to the enjoyment of psychokinetic capacities. These are necessarily within the realm of the Buddha's "All and Everything" that – as emphasized above – does not exceed the faculties of the six senses. Within imagery, experiencing could include the ability to make oneself appear in various forms or in different places at the same time; to move unobstructed by physical objects as if one were traversing the empty space; to dive into and emerge from earth as one does in water; to walk on water as if on earth; to traverse the air in a cross-legged posture; to touch the awesome and enormously powerful sun and moon with the hands; and to extend one's physical prowess as far as the world of Brahma. The so-called miracle of *telepathy* is the third among the higher forms of knowledge. The ability to read thoughts of another person is to be achieved in several different ways. Firstly: by observing the physical appearance, especially the countenance of a person. Secondly: by listening to the voice or speech of a person. Thirdly: by listening to the vibrations produced by the reflections and thoughts of a person. And finally, one is able to do so by directly perceiving the thought processes of another. The *miracle of instruction* does not constitute a form of higher knowledge but refers to the entire system of instruction, especially relating to the applied psychology of living. "Reflect thus, do not reflect thus; be intent thus, be not intent thus; renounce this, cultivate this." (AN 1.171) So goes the miracle of instruction.

In addition to the reference to these three specific forms of miracles there are more than ninety references in the discourses to what may be called the "miraculous," understood in the sense of the "wondrous" or the "unusual". The three specific forms of miracles are also described in the same literal way (AN 1.171-172). If taken literally, the first two miracles described earlier do indeed come under the category of "miracles proper". Even though they are not looked upon as events caused by an external power, a "supreme being" or a god, they are indeed the "activities of the superior human" (VP 1.209; DN 1.211; MN 1.68, etc.). However, the question is: Are these events or effects that apparently contradict known scientific laws?

Miracles and relativity

If by scientific laws are meant the deterministic laws of physics or even equally deterministic laws of scientific psychology that adhere to logical positivism, these miracles do indeed contradict such strictness. But the Buddha did not commit himself to absolute laws. As David Hume argued, miracles appear to be genuine miracles as long as we are steeped in the belief in absolutely inviolable physical and psychological laws of uniformity. Hume was challenging the very idea of "necessary connection" between cause and effect on the basis of which the laws of uniformity were formulated by the determinists. Unfortunately his criticism went too far in denying any empirical causal relation except proximity or contiguity. The Buddha avoided both determinism and indeterminism when explaining causal relations. The reason why he was able to adopt a middle standpoint between these two extremes is epistemological. The unmitigated desire on the part of rational human beings to predict with certainty the occurrence of an event from a given cause also turned out to be a victim of the Buddha's wholesale destruction of desire (DN 2.61, etc.). Having eliminated such desire, he was willing to confine his investigation to what has already occurred or is dependently arisen. Whatever theory he formulated is thus grounded on the limited range of human experience, and such a theory, therefore, will be sufficiently flexible and receive a minimum jolt and maintain maximum continuity (to use a model from William James, see Burkhardt, p.35)[1] when the unusual or the unanticipated occurs. Thus, his theory of dependent arising (pratityasamutpada) can easily accommodate the so-called miracle, which, as mentioned earlier, is defined as the "unusual" and hence the reason for it being considered "wondrous".

The Buddhist will admit that the most "unusual" relating to the life of human beings, especially their psychological life, occurred with the Buddha's attainment of awakening (bodhi) and freedom (nibbana). The Buddha himself recognized the "unusual" nature of his attainments. Hence his initial reluctance to communicate to the outside world what he had achieved. It is also reflected in the attitude of the very first human being, Upaka, whom the Buddha met on his way to Varanasi in search of his erstwhile friends. Upaka observed the "unusual" appearance of the Buddha, the brightness of his faculties, the purity of his skin-colour, etc., and inquired about the

---

1.   Burkhardt, F. (Ed.).(1975). The works of William James. Cambridge, MASS: Harvard University Press.

Buddha's teacher or the spiritual guide. When the Buddha replied that he had no teacher and that his attainments were the results of his own effort, Upaka, steeped in his Brahmanical tradition, could not believe the Buddha and left him, saying "Let it be so, friend." (VP 1.6) The Buddha was also not unaware of the manner in which the "unusual", when it occurs, becomes the "usual" in no time. Thus, the life of the Buddha, his awakening, and the first enunciation of his way which are often referred to as something previously unheard of, (SN 5.422), all of which are described in one place as the "wondrous" and the "unusual" (MN 3.116-124), are presented elsewhere as the "usual" or the "natural" (DN 2.12 ff).

There are occasions when the Buddha gave arguments for his considering the "unusual" as the "usual". Once he argued that when a ball of iron is heated for a whole day it becomes light, not heavy, even so when the mind with which the body is associated is concentrated, as in the four preliminary stages of meditation, the weighty body itself becomes light and buoyant enabling the practice of psychokinesis such as levitation (SN 5.422). Such activities can be "unusual" or miraculous only in the context in which the dependence of the mind on the body is upheld as an absolute law, and the dependence of the body on the mind is assumed to be impossibility. In other words, psychokinetic activities appear to be miraculous only in the context of physical and behavioural models of explanation relating to the human person. Another alternative would be to consider the psychokinetic as the royal road to spiritual power and well-being, a position that is generally favoured by the spiritualist. As is often the case where the Buddha adopted a middle standpoint between extremes, here too he opted for a Middle Path in evaluating the meaning and significance of miracles.

Thus, in spite of the Buddha's ability to perform the first two forms of miracles (in the metaphorical sense, because he consequently insisted to be nothing more than a human being), and his accommodating them in the category of higher knowledge, he was not unaware of the response of the ordinary human beings to such phenomena. The awakened student may be able to adopt the more philosophical attitude outlined above. But for the ordinary unawakened person, it is "wonder" pure and simple. It is the mysterious, the exotic, and the magical. It contradicts everything he has considered to be normal. When he is grounded in such a belief, it becomes impossible for him to understand its meaning and function. As such he can get enamoured with it. The confidence and faith that he generates will be without a basis, and not grounded on a correct understanding of the phenomenon. Hence the Buddha's acceptance of the view that the first two forms of miracles appear to be of magical nature (AN 1.72). For this very reason he discouraged his students from performing such miracles indiscriminately (VP 2.111-112). Interestingly, the Buddha even spoke of the evil consequences of these two types of miracles (DN 1.213).

The miracle of instruction

The third of the miracles under discussion is the miracle of instruction . It does not constitute a form of higher knowledge as do psychokinesis and telepathy. It refers to the entire system of instruction, especially relating to the psychology of his way. Analyzing the first two miracles, I mentioned earlier that even though the Buddha recognized the possibility as well as the value of these miracles, he was not very enthusiastic about them, especially because of their possible harmful effects. On the contrary, he had no reservations whatsoever about the miracle of instruction. In fact he considered it to be the best form of miracle. The miracle of instruction is manifold. Instruction involves at least three important things: an instructor, the method and content of instruction, and the goal achieved through such instruction. Someone named Vessavana refers specifically to these three when he says: "It is wondrous,… it is unusual that there is such an excellent teacher (*sattha*), that there is such an excellent exposition of the Dhamma (*dhammakkhana*) and that there is such excellent realization of distinction (*visesadhigama*)." (DN 2.218) Let us examine them in that order.

First is the miraculous instructor. Even though many of the Buddha's leading students who had attained awakening and freedom continued to instruct others, the term teacher is reserved in the early discourses to refer primarily to the Buddha. The reason for this may be found in the statement of the Buddha that there was no difference between himself and his awakened students in regard to attainments, the only difference being that he was the teacher and the others followed in his footsteps (MN 3.8). The students were thus reluctant to appropriate a title that is the only one that distinguished the Buddha from themselves. References to the miraculous character of the teacher can be examined under two headings, the moral and the physical. Teachers whose ideas give birth to new movements naturally earn the deep respect and devotion of their followers as well as the wrath and enmity of those who are not comfortable with their ideas. The Buddha was not an exception. Yet he did not allow his students to entertain groundless faith in him, insisting instead that if someone were to speak well of the Buddha, the doctrine and the community, the Bhikkhus should not be gladdened and elated on that account. Similarly, if someone were to speak ill of the Buddha, the way and the community, the Bhikkhus should not be angry and unhappy. The Buddha instructed that appreciation as well as criticism need to be checked for their veracity, for whether these are true in relation to the teaching as well as practice (DN 1.2-3). If this advice was generally followed by his students, whatever they perceived as being "miraculous" relating to the Buddha, the way, and the fruits gained by practicing the way could not be exaggerations.

The Buddha was a strong advocate of the idea that a balanced psychological life of virtue protects the one who cultivates it (DHP 168). Indeed his teaching would be meaningless if its practitioner were to face the same obstacles, constraints and suffering in the same way as a psychologically imbalanced person would experience them in the world. This idea is *symbolically* represented by two of the incidents considered to be miraculous. When the water in a stream was muddied by the wheels of a caravan of carts, and the Buddha who was in the vicinity needed a drink of water, Ananda insisted upon his moving a little further where clean water could be found. However, the water in the river suddenly turned pure enabling the Buddha to quench his thirst. Again, when the Mallas, who did not like the Buddha visiting them, covered their drinking wells, the water overflowed its covering so that he could use it (*Udana* 78, 83). However, these could also have been coincidental events.

In addition to the wondrous and the unusual physical characteristics such as the marks of a great being (DN 3.142 ff; AN 2.37), the Buddha is generally accredited with the possession of bright faculties and a pure complexion (MN 1.170). However, toward the end of his life he was ageing, with the purity of his complexion disappearing, his limbs becoming cold and wrinkled, his body bending forward and his physical faculties deteriorating. This is when the Buddha, in spite of his moral and spiritual attainments, could not overcome the forces of particle physics. Yet, this fact was also looked upon as the wondrous and unusual (SN 5.216). This viewpoint may seem rather strange because decay and destruction of psychophysical personality is considered to be usual even according to the Buddha's own teachings. However, it was a cause of wonder for those who had a different conception of the Buddha, namely, one that did not accommodate change and impermanence but one that implied a state of permanent and eternal existence. Even some of the modern interpreters of the Buddhist teachings may experience "wonderment" when they learn of this particular reference. So much for the miraculous instructor.

Let us now consider the miraculous character of the method and content of instruction. Whilst the Buddha recognized the protective power of a virtuous life, he also relied upon the effectiveness of a psychological approach to solving human problems. One of the most important characteristics of a genuine teacher is his ability to understand the different inclinations of his audience. The Buddha was endowed with this wondrous and unusual quality (DN 1.2). One of the best examples, again referred to as the wondrous and the unusual, is the Buddha's conversion of Agulimala, the murderer. When everyone, including the royal army, dreaded Angulimala who assassinated human beings in order to obtain their fingers with which he made a garland, the Buddha realized that this person was not motivated by tendencies that would normally lead to killing and destruction of life, namely, greed or hatred. Instead, he was driven by a magical belief in the efficacy of wearing a garland of human fingers. Therefore the Buddha confidently approached Angulimala. The story of what happened, as related in the discourses, is interesting and I will relate it for the sake of those who are unfamiliar with it. It goes as follows (MN 2.98-100):

> Angulimala was surprised to see the Buddha passing his residence all alone. He thought to himself: "The strongest of men in Kosala have avoided this road. Even the king's men have kept away from this path. How is it that this ascetic dares to come along unaccompanied? Maybe he is destined to die and provide me with fingers to extend my garland." Taking his sword, Angulimala went after the Buddha. He was not ready to swing his sword at the Buddha without asking him some questions, for it must have been unbelievable courage that induced the Buddha to come along this path. Going behind the Buddha, he said: "Stay there, [Bhikkhu], stay there. I want to talk to you." The Buddha continued as if he did not hear Angulimala. Angulimala stopped and yelled at the Buddha at the top of his voice. "Stop, [Bhikkhu], stop." "I have stopped, Angulimala. Don't you want to stop?" asked the Buddha as he continued on his way. Angulimala was confused. He thought. "These [Bhikkhus], sons of the Sakyans, speak truth and assert truth. But though this [Bhikkhu] is walking, he says he has stopped. When I have stopped here, he assumes that I have not. He probably means something." He questioned the Buddha who continued to go on his way. "[Bhikkhu], you say you have stopped and yet continue to walk. When I have stopped, you assume that I am walking and have not stopped. What do you mean?" "Angulimala, I have stopped for ever hurting any living being, and therefore have stopped this continuous roaming and running in *samsara* [cyclical existential suffering), in existence. As for you, with all this violence committed against innocent beings, you will continue to flow along like a boat without rudder and anchor in a fast moving stream. Disaster lies ahead for you unless you are ready to stop now."

When Angulimala heard about the possible consequences of his actions he was greatly agitated and after listening to the Buddha's admonitions, he became a Bhikkhu and soon attained awakening and freedom. Many incidents like these are reported in the discourses.

Method and content of instruction

Often we find the Buddha's method of instruction described in four terms (MN 2.55). These are generally understood as synonyms and translated into English simply as "instructed and gladdened." In fact these four terms describe the Buddha's method of instruction in four gradual stages. The *first stage* is represented as "pointing out", that is, indicating the problem. If it is a reference to an individual, the Buddha would explain that person's present situation. If it concerned an event, thing or phenomenon, he would explain the problem as it existed. During the *second stage*, the Buddha would attempt to create some "agitation" by emphasizing the absence of anything permanent or eternal, something like a self or soul (*atma*) in the individual or something like an unchangeable substance or nature or even a law in the outside world. How frightening it would be to think that one day we will be in a grave or that the law of gravitation, which is not absolutely perfect, is failing and this beautiful earth of ours is getting attracted toward the sun and will be barbecued. This denial of self or substance (*anatta*) is popularly known. If the discourse is concluded at this point, the person to whom it is addressed will be left in a state of anxiety. During the *third stage* the agitation is immediately calmed or appeased by pointing to a way out of the problem. This is often achieved by indicating the possibility of attaining freedom and happiness through a gradual path of mental culture toward psychological balance that begins with the cultivation of simple virtues such as sympathy, generosity, charity, etc., which enables a person to reduce his greed and hatred until they are totally eradicated through knowledge and understanding. The *fourth stage* is when the person gains confidence and accepts the Buddha's solution to his problem. In other words, he gets "converted". Even though this did not involve the secret transmission of a mysterious doctrine, the manner in which people embraced the teachings of the Buddha caused consternation among the competing teachers of religions, especially the Brahmanical and Jaina teachers. They warned their disciples of the Buddha's "magical power of conversion" and recommended that they stay away from him (MN 1.375). In one place this power of conversion was described as a miracle (DN 1.2). This constitutes the Buddha's method of instruction.

In addition to what can be achieved through the proper method instruction, the Buddha also admitted the possibility of a psychological transformation of an ordinary person when confronted by a character of mental preponderance. In the eyes of those who are prone to thinking that psychological events have no sovereignty over the physical, it would appear to be a miracle if someone suffering from an ailment could be cured as a result of a psychological change taking place in that person by coming face to face with a charismatic teacher. Such is known in contemporary psychology as the placebo effect: hope and expectation may lessen mental stress and other mental ills. The reference in the Vinaya Pitaka (2.18) [one of the three canonical books that contains rules and regulations of communal living] that a big wound on a person's body was healed by the mere sight of the Buddha could be taken as an example of a placebo. To this may be added the story of Suppavasa, the daughter of a Koliyan, who, after giving birth to seven still-born babies, was finally able to give birth to a healthy baby as a result of her confidence in the Buddha and the Buddha's own wish that she be able to do so (*Udana*

15-16). There are many such instances where asseveration of truth in the presence of a pregnant woman relieved her of severe pains and facilitated the birth of her child. These have contributed to the formation of a ritual called "protection" that is popular among some of the Buddhist communities (see: De Silva, pp.139-150)[2]

Now I come to the content of instruction, the so-called curriculum, which is even more unusual and miraculous than the method, for it was a total revolution in human thinking in India during the sixth century BCE, and, interestingly, seems to remain such even in the twenty-first century. In order to make matters easy, I shall concentrate primarily on one aspect of the doctrine, even though it is rather pervasive in character. This is the Middle Path. Name the area of interest, whether one is a physicist, astronomer, biologist, a medical person, environmentalist, politician, sociologist, economist, linguist, logician, ethicist or a spiritualist, the Buddha will prescribe a middle standpoint that one could follow in order to be successful and happy. In a short presentation like this, it would not be possible to explain what the middle path would look like in all these different disciplines. Therefore, I will focus on four major areas that would cut across all of them. These will include epistemology or human knowledge, ontology or the theory of existence, ethics or moral philosophy and the philosophy of language.

In the area of epistemology, the Middle Path consists of avoiding the two extremes of absolute certainty and equally absolute scepticism. I tried earlier to explain how the Buddha treated even such exotic phenomena like psychokinesis without being overly enthusiastic or unduly sceptical about them. Human knowledge, he claimed, is grounded in sensory experience. When the sensible world is presented to our consciousness, which is what happens on occasions of sense experience, it comes as a "big, blooming, buzzing confusion." Mindful awareness is unable to deal with it without being selective. This selection is done in terms of a person's interest. Those aspects of the sensible world the person is not interested in, get ignored, those that the person is interested in receive her/his attention. Without such simple interest, consciousness cannot function and knowledge becomes impossible. Often this simple interest, referred to as *sankhara*, can grow into monstrous proportions. In the context of knowledge, such compound interest is called prejudice or bias. The elimination of that prejudice, as mentioned earlier, enables the person to see things in a proper perspective. This represents a middle standpoint in which one does not renounce sense experience altogether, either by looking for a transcendental intuition or by relapsing into total scepticism. Sense experience, strengthened and purified by concentration, provides a springboard for limited inferences relating to the remote past and into the future, areas in which we have no direct experience.

Based upon this middle standpoint in epistemology, the Buddha formulated his theory of existence or ontology. It avoids the extremes of permanent existence and absolute non-existence, strict determinism and chaotic indeterminism (SN 2.17). As mentioned earlier, the middle is represented by the principle of dependent arising/origination that is applicable in every sphere of existence, physical, psychological, sociological, or ethical. The world of experience

---

2.   See Lily de Silva's The Paritta ceremony of Sri Lanka, in: Kalupahana, D.J. (Ed.).(1991). *Buddhist thought and ritual.* New York: Paragon House.

is in a constant flux; it undergoes change and transformation. Things arise and pass away, not according to a fixed law or at random, but in an orderly fashion conditioned by various factors. Yet to claim knowledge of each and every condition operative in a given context, that is, to know everything with absolute certainty, is to claim omniscience which is a capacity not of humanity. The principle of dependence is formulated on the basis of utility or functionality and relativity, not absolutely incorrigible knowledge. Relying upon this knowledge and understanding, the Buddha recommended a Middle Path in ethics (SN 5.421 ff). In this case, the two extremes are self-indulgence described as being low, vulgar, individualist, ignoble, and unfruitful, and ascetic self-mortification characterized as being ignoble and painful. The middle is the eightfold path, involving comprehensive knowledge, conception as well as practical application. It is intended to bring about happiness for oneself as well as for others. Presenting the Middle Path is this form, the Buddha is not only avoiding possessive individualism but also suicide or self-immolation. It is a combination of self-culture and social service that is reflected in the Buddhist "moral principle". This is not an absolute law, but rather a pragmatic guide to be treated like a raft (MN 1.134). One utilizes this raft in order to cross over the ocean of suffering and unsatisfactoriness, not as a decorative device to be carried on one's shoulders after one has crossed over.

The ideas referred to above were meant neither for non-verbal transmission nor for expression through a special technical vocabulary of precision. The belief in non-verbal transmission may not have been as popular as it came to be subsequently, even among some of the Buddhists. Yet the very idea of sitting close to a teacher (which is the literal meaning of the term *upanisad*), when combined with the view that the ultimate reality (*atma*, Brahma) is a mysterious principle that is not easily communicated, led to the belief in non-verbal transmission. In addition, there was a move in the opposite direction of constructing an absolutely perfect language in order to express this ultimate truth. The development of Sanskrit (literally meaning "the well-done") was the end product of this process. The Buddha following a middle path remained with the ordinary spoken language, Prakrit (meaning the "natural"), allowing his students to use whatever language they were familiar with in order to understand and disseminate the teaching. When our knowledge, our theories about the nature of the world, and our conceptions of good and bad, right and wrong, are not precise and are flexible there is no need to look for a language of precision. A concept expressed by a term or a word in language can have a variety of meanings, and these meanings are often contextual and relative. Therefore, to grasp on to linguistic conventions as being absolute or to reject them as being totally useless are two extremes to be renounced if one is to avoid any conflict in the world (MN 3.234 ff). The only aspect of language that the Buddha generally avoided is the use of the active voice, now a widely propounded Buddhist way of expressing suggesting the absence of substantiality. In fact, one can notice a profuse use of the passive forms in the early discourses. The reason for this was that he wanted his language to be consistent with the very essence that he taught, namely: not-self or non-substantiality (*anatta*).

Previously unheard of

However, the most significant quality considered to be wondrous and unusual, is the manner in which the Buddha as instructor and the students as the instructed were able to deal with meaning and expressions, i.e. language. There certainly were occasions when a student would misinterpret the meaning of a term or expression, the most prominent case being one that involved a Bhikkhu named Sati who had only one meaning for the term consciousness, understanding it as implying a transmigrating personality that is permanent and eternal (MN 1.257 ff). Generally, the Buddha and his students were credited with the ability to relate and harmonize meanings with meanings and words with words (SN 4.397; AN 5.320). This means that either their conceptions of meanings or their use of terms were not rigid and absolute but rather fluid and flexible so that they were able to avoid contradictions or antinomial conflicts. This is applicable even with regard to the conception of the highest state, which is freedom (*nibbana*) (SN 4.379). It is this very same characteristic that enabled them to lead a life of non-conflict or peace (MN 3.234 ff). It may now become clear why the method and content of instruction was referred to as something previously unheard of. It is also for this reason that the realization at the bodhi-tree in Gaya and first enunciation in Sarnath were looked upon as being unusual, out of the ordinary and hence miraculous.

Finally, we come to the third aspect of the miracle of instruction which is the achievement of distinction or the fruits reaped by following the instructions. In the "Discourse on the Fruits of Recluseship" (*Samannaphala-suttanta*) (DN 1.47 ff), the fruits of the way of life in the Buddha's dispensation were placed in the background of the teachings of six heterodox teachers. The contents of this discourse are then repeated in another discourse in identical words, and a person named Todeyyaputta declares them to be "wondrous and unusual (DN 1.204 ff). These consisted of the perfection of virtues (*sila*), concentrative absorption (*Samadhi*), and wisdom (*panna*) culminating in the attainment of awakening and freedom, the ultimate goal of the Buddha. Regarding the interpretation of Nirvana controversies are plentiful. In a brief presentation like this, I do not expect to get involved in any such controversy. I have been part of it for the past decades and suffice here by briefly examining the concept as it occurs in the early discourses. If I am not mistaken about what I said so far regarding the nature of the teachings, its theory of knowledge, its view of human existence and psychology to live, then it would not be proper for me to assume that the conception of the ultimate goal of life, which is Nirvana, transcends everything human and represents an eternal and permanent state of existence. Everyone who attained Nirvana, including the Buddha, is subjected to ageing, decay, and death. This would mean that constraints imposed by some aspects of "particle physics" are not overcome even by the Buddhas. As such the meaning and significance of the Buddha's conception of Nirvana have to be sought elsewhere.

According to the Buddha, Nirvana is the cessation of greed, hatred, and confusion. Examining the statements in the discourses regarding the status of the person who has attained Nirvana, it is possible to trace at least three types of transformations taking place in such a person. I would call them epistemological, behavioural and psychological. First is the epistemological. Speaking about sensory experience, I refer to the manner in which simple human interest, which is a necessary condition for knowledge, can be compounded and grow into monstrous proportions and appear in the form of lust, greed, attachment, and so forth. The elimination of the latter does not mean the abandoning of the former as well, because the elimination of interest would be epistemological suicide. It is human interest that keeps the vehicle of knowledge rolling. However compound interest is what produces ideological constraints, that is, the mental blocks created when someone upholds any idea, view or theory as being absolutely true or valid. *Bodhi* or awakening is precisely this epistemological transformation, that is, a change from being a dogmatist or a sceptic to one who is open-minded. Furthermore, simple interest is also a necessary condition for living. Elimination of interest is suicide pure and simple. The Middle Path of psychological balance and a virtuous life, it was mentioned, avoids the extremes of self-indulgence and self-mortification, and the latter includes self-immolation or self-destruction. The one who is liberated continues to live in the world without generating greed or hatred either for oneself or for the outside world. Such a person remains unsmeared by the world of gain or loss, good repute or disrepute, praise or blame, happiness or suffering (DN 3.260). S/he is like the lotus that grows in the muddy pool but remains unsmeared by the dirt therein (AN 2.37-39). This constitutes the behavioural transformation that takes place in the person who has attained Nirvana.

Finally, with the elimination of greed, hatred, and confusion, a freed person enjoys a stable and non-fluctuating happiness and peace of mind, which is the psychological transformation of personality. The effect of this psychological transformation is one that was most misunderstood during the entire Buddhist history, especially during modern times. There is no doubt that the effect of this is happiness (*sukha*). *Sukha* is a term occurring in the pre-Buddhist literature, and more often meant the happiness achieved as a result of attaining union with the permanent and eternal ultimate reality (Brahma). It is this association of happiness associated with the attainment of union with an ultimate reality that prevented some of the contemporaries, as well as some of the later Buddhists from understanding the nature of happiness recognized by the Buddha. The Buddha's conception of happiness could not be understood unless placed in the context of his conception of suffering or *dukkha*. Like many other terms that the Buddha utilized, the term *dukkha* was not in the Indian vocabulary before the Buddha. This again justifies the Buddha's claim that what he discovered under the bodhi-tree is something "unheard of before". A great linguist as he was, he realized the term *sukha* is derived from the term "kha", meaning "axle-hole," with the prefix "su" which means "good. Therefore, literally, the term would mean a "good axle-hole." Keeping this in mind, he seems to have coined the term *dukkha*, which would literally mean "a bad axle-hole." A bad axle-hole is one that does not properly align with the axle. It is either too loose or too tight. When it is too loose, the wheel will wobble. If it is too tight, the wheel will get heated and burn up. This is precisely what *dukkha* means in the life of a person. That person is either unsteady or wobbly in her/his behaviour, or that person is often under stress and tension. In contrast, a well-aligned axle and an axle-hole will provide for a smooth ride. This is certainly what the Buddha meant by happiness or *sukha*. Thus, freedom or *nibbana* is one that enables a person to lead a smooth flowing life, as is emphasized in the popular "Discourse on the Great Auspiciousness" (*Mahamangala Sutta*):

> Whose thought, when in contact with the worldly phenomena, does not tremble, who is sorrowless, without blemish and peaceful, this is the highest blessing.

This is further exemplified by the Buddha's statement (SN 3.138): "[Bhikkhus], I do not conflict with the world. Yet the world conflicts with me." It is also embodied in the life of one who lives without conflict mentioned earlier.

If it is the wheel, as described above, that symbolizes the life of happiness, then the best wheel, according to the Buddha, will be the "virtuous wheel". It is this wheel that he set rolling with his first discourse to the world at Varanasi, especially to the five ascetics with whom he practiced austerities before his awakening and Nirvana (VN 1.11-12; SN 5.423). In addition, the Buddha maintained that, if there were to be a lay person who follows the teachings of the Buddha, but who prefers to live in the household life and would like to lead the world, he would be a king. He becomes the guardian of the "wheel of law" which he sets rolling, always according to the principles of Buddhist virtue. He is called the Universal Monarch (DN 3.58-79). The above is the ultimate goal of the virtuous life. However, the goal does not represent a quantum leap from the way. It is simply the culmination, the crown. Hence it should not be separated totally from the way. For if it were, this would mean that when a person is traversing this way s/he is continually achieving some form of psychological distinction, and that is not the way.

In addition to the concrete psychological achievements obtained by adhering to the Buddha's instructions, there are other aspects of the teachings that produced social change. These changes seem to have been so radical that they were looked upon as being "wondrous and unusual." A good example is the Buddha's definition of the social classes. Questioned by a Brahman named Janussoni, the Buddha presented a description of the social classes in terms of their intentions, interests, aspirations, commitments, and goals which were contrary to the theory provided by the Brahmanical contemporaries, especially their theory of caste based primarily on birth (AN 3.363). This example represents a social goal of instruction.

In conclusion

In conclusion, I would like to refer to specific metaphors which are used to describe the eight "wondrous and unusual" qualities of the entire dispensation, qualities which are compared with those of the great ocean (AN 4.206-208):

> (1) Just as the ocean reaches its deepest level gradually, not abruptly, even so is the Buddha's dispensation where the highest realization is reached through a gradual path, not abruptly.

> (2) Just as the great ocean has remained steady and does not abandon the waves, even so the disciples have remained faithful to the recommended virtues and do not abandon them.

> (3) Just as the ocean never retains a dead body and quickly carries it over to the shore and leaves it on the ground, even so whosoever is of evil conduct and is secretive, he is not retained by the community. The community remains aloof from him.

> (4) Just as the great rivers, Ganga, Yamuna, Aciravati, etc., when reaching the ocean abandon their former names and are known as the great ocean, even so the four castes: the *ksatriyas, brahmas, vaisyas,* and *sudras,* upon renouncing the household life abandon their former names and are known as the ascetics who are followers of the Son of the Sakyans.

> (5) Just as, when the rivers flow into the ocean and rain falls from above, the ocean does not appear to be diminished or overfilled, similarly, even though many have attained the state of freedom while living, by that the state of freedom is neither diminished nor overfilled.

(6) Just as the ocean has only one taste, namely, the taste of salt, so is the doctrine possessed of one taste, namely, the taste of freedom.

(7) Just as the ocean is filled with a variety of precious jewels, such as pearls, gems, lapis lazuli, shells, quartz, corals, silver, gold ore, rubies, and cat's-eyes, even so this teaching is filled with precious jewels such as the four states of mindfulness, four states of exertion, the four bases of psychic power, five faculties, five powers, seven factors of awakening, and the Noble Eightfold Path. And finally:

(8) Just as the great ocean is the abode of great beings, large fish, excessively large fish, the *asuras* [demons], *nagas* [sea serpents], *ghandhabbas* [heavenly musicians], and the like, even so is this dispensation the abode of great human beings, the stream-enterers, once-returners, non-returners, and *Arhats*.

In these discussions I have utilized only a small portion of the ninety references in the early discourses to the miraculous specifically defined as the "wondrous and unusual". It is apparent that the terms miracle and miraculous were used by people who were experiencing a sense of awe and wonder about events or occurrences or phenomena as a result of these being contrary to what they took to be the normal. Buddha had no difficulty allowing them to perceive these phenomena in that form so long as they did not make them the reason for their confidence in the teaching. However, the other side of the coin is that these are really not miraculous as long as they are perceived in the context of the Buddha's explanation of the nature of existence. The third form of the miraculous, namely, the miracle of instruction, highlights the originality in the teachings of the Buddha and not any mysterious character. It is precisely because some of his contemporaries failed to understand the reasons for the effectiveness of the Buddha's teaching that they perceived him as one who knows the "magic of conversion".

To conclude, my hope is that students in the down-to-earth, secular and sober teachings of the Buddha as exposed above understand the superfluity and redundancy of metaphysics and other-worldly inferences of miracles and other mysteries in explaining experiential phenomena according to the principles of the Buddha's psychology of education toward awakening and Nirvana.

Chapter 10

Nirvana Of The Healthy Mind

Asanga Tilakaratne

Introduction

"May the golden gates of the city of Nirvana[1] be open for you" - this statement in Sinhala language is commonly seen in Sri Lanka on banners raised to honour the dead. Rahula (1978) in his well-known work *What the Buddha Taught* referred to a more elite version of a similar belief when he wrote some popular inaccurately phrased expressions like "The Buddha entered into Nirvana or *parinirvana* after death" have given rise to many imaginary speculations about Nirvana (p.41). In this manner, for the ordinary Buddhists Nirvana may well represent a city they enter after death and where they live happily ever after. For the educated it could well be a mystical state entered after death. In either belief Nirvana is essentially a phenomenon that has its validity in the life after and not much to do with one's lived reality.

The questions such as "what is Nirvana" and "what happens after death to one who has realized Nirvana" continue to be as pressing as they were even during the time of the Buddha. As we will see later in the discussion there are some good psychological reasons for these Nirvana-centred worries. The purpose of the present paper is to reiterate the early textual positions that Nirvana is not a metaphysical state that one achieves after death and not a city those lucky people enter upon death, but is a positive psychological experience and a state of mind. Although such an interpretation may seem to be at odds with the scholastic interpretation subsequently developed by commentators, in developing this interpretation I do not think that I am presenting a new picture of Nirvana against the tradition since it is one which can be derived from the early discourses, An exposition of Nirvana developed following the basic discourses of the Buddha will show Nirvana to be a purified state of mind and not a mystical metaphysical state. Next I will look at some textual passages that have been understood as supporting what I would like to call a transcendental interpretation of Nirvana.

---

1. In this chapter I use the term Nirvana, the Sanskrit language form, instead of Nibbana, the Pali language form, for the former is more familiar to the western reader although all the discourses and the commentaries I make use of in this chapter are in Pali language which most probably comes closest to the language the Buddha had spoken.

Nirvana: the cessation of suffering

In the Four Noble Truths, the third is that of cessation of suffering, which is Nirvana. The *locus classicus* of the Four Noble Truths, the *Dhammacakkappavattana-sutta* does not use the term Nirvana. It simply describes the cessation of suffering as

> the residue-less detachment and cessation of the very same thirst,[2] giving it
> up, letting [it] go, release [from it] and non-attachment [to it].[3]

The "very same thirst" is what is described as the cause of suffering under the second Noble Truth of the origin of suffering. If the thirst (for pleasures, existence and destruction) is the cause of suffering, the eradication of the cause is the cessation of suffering and that is simple enough logic to follow.

Of the Four Noble Truths the first is described in experiential terms as birth, decay, disease, death, to be associated with the unpleasant, to be dissociated from the pleasant and not getting what one craves. Finally, the whole series of experiences is summarized as "the suffering associated with the five elements of (psycho-physical) existence characterized by clinging." This is the problem the teaching of the Buddha is meant to solve. It is the problem intimately connected to existence; in particular, in so far as the self-consciousness of the individual who undergoes that suffering is concerned, it is a human problem more than a problem of any other being although all other beings, who are not awakened, are subject to it. With this emphasis on suffering as a human problem, what I try to drive at is that it is not a "metaphysical" or imaginary problem but a real problem of real human beings. The second Noble Truth locates the source of the problem right within the human being her/himself. The thirst cannot exist anywhere else other than in human (or any other *samsaric*) beings, who are subject to the cycle of daily psychological "rebirths" of emotional events.

This point is well illustrated in one of the discussions the Buddha had with a naked ascetic called Kassapa. The dialogue between the two ran in the following manner:

> Kassapa: Is suffering done by oneself?
>
> The Buddha: Do not say so.
>
> Is suffering done by other?
>
> Do not say so.
>
> Is suffering done by both oneself and other?
>
> Do not say so.
>
> Is suffering, done by neither, arisen for no reason?

---

2. This is the literal translation of the term *tanha* in Pali (*trshna* in Sanskrit), which is usually translated as overdesire or craving (or in many other similar terms).
3. Samyutta Nikaya V, pp.420-24. (For a translation: see Bhikkhu Bodhi. 2002, Vol. II, pp.1843-1847).

Do not say so.

Is it the case that suffering does not exist?

It does exist.

Is it then the case that you do not see it?

I do see it.

Subsequently the Buddha explains how suffering arises depending on causes and conditions which are ignorance, constructions, consciousness, psycho-physical personality, six sensory bases, contact, feeling, thirst, grasping, becoming, birth, decay and death; these are the twelve aspects that form the standard explanation how karmic suffering intentionally arises.

There are several important insights we can derive from this analysis based on the teaching of dependent co-origination. One is that the metaphorical thirst (i.e., mental craving) given as the reason of suffering is explained in a broader context of human psychological function, which ultimately leads to the generation of suffering. In fact thirst alone is not all; it is one in a series which is also dependently arisen. Another very important insight is that thirst is essentially an aspect of human psychological functioning. One cannot talk about thirst as an entity that is there in one's mind permanently. The whole point of dependent co-origination-based analysis is that all these phenomena including the thirst are arisen dependently, which means that they arise depending on conditions and cease depending on the cessation of conditions.

The third Noble Truth is "the complete cessation of this very same thirst", which has three main manifestations. The first is the thirst for pleasures, namely pleasures one enjoys through one's senses, eye, ear, nose, tongue, skin/body and brain/mind. The respective pleasures are physical forms, sounds, smells, tastes, touches, and concepts/views. This type of thirst represents the most common and the most gross from. It is also a very forceful, if not the most forceful, motivation of ordinary human behaviour. (This motivation is common to animal behaviour too with the possible exception of concepts/views as mental objects.) The second is the thirst for continued existence or the perpetual desire to "be" something. The third and last is the thirst to be annihilated or the (self and other) destructive face of human craving. The eradication of these three forms of thirst is called the cessation of suffering. The fourth Noble Truth describes the path leading to the cessation suffering, namely, the Noble Eightfold Path.

The description up to this point illustrates that the key teaching of the Buddha, namely, the Four Noble Truths, is a straightforward scheme which does not involve anything metaphysical or mystical. Nevertheless, it is a fact around which many metaphysical speculations have been developed, particularly about the state of Nirvana, which the Buddha simply described as the cessation of suffering. It is important to emphasize this, as the Buddha described the ultimate goal of his blissful life in terms of processes and events and not as entities, and his path to realization of cessation of suffering did not involve any metaphysical or mystical elements.

Purity and freedom

The two most common terms used in the discourses to refer to the final goal are purification (*visuddhi*) and emancipation (*vimutti*). In the *Dhammapada* the insight into the three *signata*, namely, impermanence, sorrowfulness, and non-substantiality, are described as "the path to purification".[4] This reminds us of Buddhaghosa's monumental work, the "Path of Purification" (*Visuddhi-magga*), detailing the path to cessation of suffering. The concept of emancipation (*vimutti*) is equally used in the discourses to refer to the release one achieves by freeing the mind from influxes. In the *Theragatha* and the *Therigatha*, in which the joyous utterances of the liberated Bhikkhus and Bhikkhunis are recorded, it is almost customary for these people to describe their attainment as "liberation of mind from influxes".[5] The Buddha and the Arahants (those who have realized the cessation of suffering) are described as spending their leisure time "experiencing the happiness of emancipation".[6]

These two concepts respectively refer to defiling phenomena, which are usually described by such terms as defilements (and related concepts) and hindrances,[7] and binding phenomena, described as influxes, cankers, bondages and engagements.[8] Defiling and binding phenomena are basically attachment, hatred and delusion, and related phenomena. The five factors that obstruct the smooth practice of the path, namely, sensual desire, extreme aversion, sloth and torpor, confusion and regret, and doubting mentality are called hindrances. The concept of purification becomes meaningful in the context of these defiling phenomena. In addition to being a deep psychological analysis, the two mutually related concepts reveal how the Buddha gave a new meaning to the deep-rooted belief in ritualistic purity and impurity prevalent among the Brahmins during his time. The concept of emancipation derives its meaning from the presence of influxes or characteristics of mind that infatuates it, binds it or enslaves it to pleasures. The predominant character of these phenomena is to create bondage or bounded nature in the human mind. Emancipation is to liberate one's mind from these phenomena. The Buddha's analysis of these two phenomena, purification and emancipation, and the related characteristics made his teaching the only psychological one of all other teachings that attend a way of life hitherto available.

In addition to purification and emancipation, the final goal has been described in the discourses frequently as "comprehensive extinguishment". The relevant Pali term is *parinibbana* which is intimately connected with the idea of Nibbana. It is important at this juncture to review this idea in some detail. The term *parinibbana* or *parinirvana* (in Sanskrit) is usually used in current Buddhist parlance to refer to the passing away of the Buddha or an Arahant. The mistaken idea (as we saw in Walpola Rahula's remarks at the beginning of this chapter) is that the Buddha or an Arahant really attains Nirvana along with his *parinirvana*, which is understood to be the death of such *awakened* person. In fact, the discourses make it quite clear that the idea of *parinibbana* is basically connected to what happens to one who realizes cessation of suffering. Let me give some examples: the *Rathavinita-sutta* of the Majjhima Nikaya

---

4. When one sees with wisdom that all the constructed phenomena are impermanent, then he becomes disgusted in suffering; this is the path to purification. When one sees with wisdom that all the phenomena are sorrowful... when one sees with wisdom that all phenomena are non-substantial... this is the path to purification. *Dhammapada*, pp.277-279.
5. Mind was freed from influxes or similar expressions. D II, p.35; M I, p.501.
6. Vinaya I, p.3.
7. Concepts such as *kilesa, upakkilesa, sankilesa* (all meaning different shades of defiling factors) and *nivarana* (hindrances) are some examples.
8. *Asava, sannojana, bandhana, yoga* are some examples.

(24) records a discussion between two great students of the Buddha, Sariputta and Punna Mantaniputta, on the issue of the purpose of the wholesome life lived under the Buddha. When questioned by the former on this, the latter admits that this life is lived not for the sake of any one of the seven types of purification.[9] When questioned further as to what the purpose is if it is not for any one of the seven purifications, Punna Mantaniputta answers by saying that it is for the sake of "comprehensive extinguishment without clinging."[10] The point of the discussion is to show that each of the seven purifications leads to subsequent purification and all seven together lead to the final goal, which is comprehensive extinguishment without clinging. The use of the concept in this context shows that the goal, comprehensive extinguishment without clinging, is achieved within this life and its attainment does not mean or necessitate the physical death of the person. In many instances, the discourses describe the attainment of the final goal as "mind was liberated from influxes without clinging."[11] The concept of *parinibbana* without clinging and the concept of liberation without clinging, no doubt, are synonymous in these contexts. The *parinibbana* concept has been used in the same sense in places such as: "That Exalted One, being himself comprehensively extinguished teaches the doctrine for comprehensive extinguishment."[12] And, "comprehensively extinguished in this life itself."[13] The goal of being without thirst is to be achieved "before the break of the body."[14]

The path

The non-mystical and non-metaphysical character of the final goal may be demonstrated by analyzing the path to be followed in order to achieve it. In earlier discussion we saw that the Buddha described the path as the fourth Noble Truth and presented it as an eightfold procedure. The technical details of this procedure are given in many other discourses varying in length depending on the special circumstances of such elaborations. In this discussion I would use the elaboration found in the *Samannaphala-sutta* of the Digha Nikaya, where the Buddha

---

9. The seven purifications outline the gradual process of purification taught by the Buddha. They are: purification of virtue *(sila-visuddhi)*, mind *(citta)*, view *(ditthi)*, overcoming doubt *(kankha-vitarana)*, and knowledge and vision *(nana-dassana)*, purification by knowledge and vision of what is the path and what is not the path *(magga-amagga-nanadassana)*, purification by knowledge and vision of the way *(patipada-nanadassana)* and purification of knowledge and vision *(nanadassana)*.
10. In their translation Bhikkhu Nanamoli and Bhikkhu Bodhi (1995/2001) translates *anupada-parinibbana* as "final Nibbana without clinging". I would, however, translate *parinibana* not as "final nibbana" but as "comprehensive extinguishment", which is closer to the original etymology.
11. The relevant Pali phrase is: *anupadaya asavehi cittam vimucci.* D II, p.35; M I, p.501.
12. D III, p.55.
13. S IV, p.102. Also look at the usage, by the Buddha, of the concept *parinibbana* in the *Sallekha-sutta* of the Majjhima Mikaya (8): "That one who is himself untamed, undisciplined, (with defilements) *unextinguished,* should tame another, discipline him, and help *extinguish* (his defilements) is impossible; that one who is himself tamed, disciplined, (with defilements) *extinguished,* should tame another , discipline him, and help *extinguish* (his defilements) is possible. So too: A person given to cruelty has non-cruelty by which to *extinguish* it..." (emphasis added). (Translation from Bhikkhu Nanamoli and Bhikkhu Bodhi, 1995/2001. p.130)
14. The relevant concept is *vita-tanho pura-bheda* (before break-up) and found emphasized in the *Purabheda-sutta* of the *Suttanipata, 853.*

details the fruits of the noble life to King Ajatasatthu. On being questioned by the King on "the fruits of the noble life *in this very life*" (italics added, see note 15) similar to the fruits enjoyed in this very life by those engaged in various professions, the Buddha lists such fruits and consequently, the discourse is a detailed analysis of attainments at different levels of the path. In this context, I would like to highlight the significance of the idea that what is being described are "the fruits of noble life *achieved in this very life.*"[15] Also note the pragmatic character of the King's question, comparing the noble life to professions followed by people for living, and the Buddha's taking it obviously in the same spirit and undertaking to answer it.

The path begins with virtue described under three categories, namely, small, medium, and large, and covers the ethical behaviour to be developed in him/herself by one who lives the noble life. Being virtuous is thus the first fruit of the noble life. What one gets out of this is described in the following words:

> And then, Sire, that [Bhikkhu] who is perfected in morality sees no danger from any side owing to his being restrained by morality, just as duly-anointed Khattiya king, having conquered his enemies, by that very fact sees no danger from any side, so the [Bhikkhu], on account of his morality, sees no danger anywhere. He experiences in himself the blameless bliss that comes from maintaining this Aryan morality.[16]

This account shows that virtue is not understood merely as a training but as training providing moral stability and a sense of being blissful.

Subsequently it lists the steps of the noble path leading to the second stage, namely, concentration of mind. The requisites for the second stage are: being a guardian of sensory faculties, being accomplished in mindfulness and clear awareness, and being contented. With these psychological qualities in him, the Bhikkhu "sits down cross-legged, holding his body erect, and concentrates on keeping mindfulness established before him" and abandons the five hindrances in him. The process of abandoning the hindrances has been described in the following manner, when...

> [a]bandoning worldly desires, he dwells with a mind freed from worldly desires, and his mind is purified of them. Abandoning ill-will and hatred... by compassionate love for the welfare of all living beings his mind is purified of ill-will and hatred. Abandoning sloth-and-torpor... perceiving light, mindful and clearly aware, his mind is purified of sloth-and-torpor. Abandoning worry-and-flurry... and with inwardly calmed mind his heart is purified of worry-and-flurry. Abandoning doubt, he dwells with doubt left behind, without uncertainty as to what things are wholesome, his mind is purified of doubt.[17]

---

15. *Sanditthikam samannaphalam* is the relevant Pali term.
16. Translation from Walshe (1987, p.100).
17. Translation from Walshe (1987, p.101).

Note how salutary attitudes are developed at the abandonment of the five hindering factors. The state of the mind resulting from the abandonment of these hindrances is described by five similes which underscore the freedom and the sense of relief the practitioner gets from it. The state of mind without hindrances is compared to the feeling one gets when one repays, upon successful development of his business, a loan taken to develop his business; to the feeling one gets when he regains health after a severe sickness; to the feeling a prisoner gets when he is released from prison; to the feeling a slave gets when he is freed from his slavery; and to the feeling one gets when one safely crosses a dangerous desert. Being with hindrances is compared to being in debt, unhealthy, in prison, in slavery, and in a desert. And absence of hindrances is winning freedom, release and relief, illustrated by quite mundane and day-to-day comparisons.

The next step in the path is the attainment of serene states of mind described as *jhana* in the texts. The *jhanic* attainments have been good candidates for being described as mystical states by those who are not sufficiently familiar with them. A study of the nature of serene states and the process of attaining them reveals that this mystical states viewpoint is not the appropriate. The Buddha describes the process leading to *jhana* in the following words:

> And when he knows that these five hindrances have left him, gladness aris-
> es in him, from gladness comes delight, from the delight in his mind his
> body is tranquillised, with a tranquil body he feels joy, and with joy his
> mind is concentrated.

The first, second, third and the fourth *jhanas*, characterizing gradually increasing sense of aloofness from sensory experience and the resultant joy, or equanimity in the case of the fourth *jhana*, are attained on this basis. The first *jhana* is "with thinking and pondering, born of detachment, filled with delight and joy." Once the practitioner is in the state of...

> ...delight and joy born of detachment, (it) *so suffuses, drenches and fills
> and irradiates his body that there is no spot in his entire body that is
> untouched by this delight and joy born of detachment.* (italics added)

This is compared to when...

> ...a skilled bathman or his assistant, kneading the soap powder which he
> has sprinkled with water, forms from it, in a metal dish, a soft lump, so that
> the ball of soap-powder becomes one oleaginous mass, bound with oil so
> that nothing escapes.

The second *jhana* is a result of subsiding of thinking and pondering, which yields to inner tranquillity and oneness of mind. Its characteristics are absence of thinking and pondering, being born of concentration and filled with delight and joy. Exactly as in the first *jhana*, in this experience, too, the body of the practitioner is suffused so that no spot remains untouched with the delight and joy born of concentration. This is compared to a lake to which rain water flows and gets mingled with its cool water so that no part of the pool is untouched by it.

The third *jhana* arises when delight fades away, joy is retained, and the practitioner becomes imperturbable, mindful and clearly aware. Equanimity and mindfulness are the characteristics of this state, "and with this joy devoid of delight he so suffuses his body that no spot remains untouched." This state is compared to the lotuses in a pond that remain completely suffused with the cool water of the pond.

The fourth *jhana* arises in a Bhikkhu who gives up pleasure and pain and whose former gladness and sadness disappear. The experience is beyond pleasure and pain and purified with equanimity and mindfulness "...and he sits suffusing his body with that mental purity and clarification so that no part of his body is untouched by it." This state is compared to a man who covers himself totally with a white sheet so that all parts of his body are covered by that sheet.

The most impressive character of these *jhanic* experiences is that they combine intimately both mind and body. They seem to be neither purely mental nor purely physical for they cover the totality of the person. The state of mental purity that serves as the basis for this experience, as we saw earlier, is again an example of mutual influence of mind and body: delight of the mind tranquillizes the body; a tranquillized body generates joy; and with joy, mind becomes concentrated. The *jhanic* states follow as natural results. The *jhanas* in this manner are states of serenity and tranquillity and are not mystical states in which one "communicates with" or is "filled with feelings from" the unknown. Also it is noteworthy how at the end of the exposition of each experience the physical aspect of it has been highlighted.

In addition to the four *jhanas* just discussed, which are called "fine-material" *jhanas*, it is useful at this juncture to mention that there are four further *jhanas* called "non-material" (they were not mentioned in this particular discourse). Briefly, they are: the sphere of infinite space, the sphere of infinite consciousness, the sphere of no-thingness, and the sphere of neither perception-nor-non-perception.[18] These, similar to the first four *jhanas*, are states of meditative experience characterized by gradually ascending aloofness from sensory perception, the final stage of which has almost no perception at all. The conclusion of this process is described in the discourses as the cessation of perception and what is felt, at which stage or point the practitioner seems to become a totally devoid of any perceptive or cognitive process at all for a limited period of time. Whereas the states beginning with the first fine-material *jhana* represent gradually increasing aloofness and the resultant serenity and joy, this state of cessation is the culmination of the process marked by total absence of any connection with any sensory data. Obviously one cannot be in this state for a long time. This looks like a situation in which one stops one's entire psycho-physical activity temporarily.

Certain discourses describe the path to cessation of suffering through these attainments. Some modern commentators seem to have understood this process as the attainment of cessation as directly resulting in cessation of suffering. Moreover, continuing in their understanding, they seem to understand the Nirvanic experience in terms of the cessation of perceptions

---

18. This state is discussed in such discourses as *Cullvedalla-sutta* of the Majjhima Nikaya (44) (Bhikkhu Nanamoli and Bhikkhu Bodhi: 1995, 2001, pp.396-403; & S IV 293-295) and in the *Visuddhimagga*. For a comprehensive modern discussion on it see: Paul J. Griffiths, *On being mindless: Buddhist meditation and the mind-body problem.* La Salle, Illinois: Open Court, 1985.

and feelings. In fact what the discourses say is that once arisen from the attainment of cessation, the practitioner directs his mind to insight and consequently "having seen through wisdom his influxes are eradicated."[19] As the *Mahanidana-sutta* of the Digha Nikaya (15) explains, a practitioner may first practice and master what are called "the eight liberations" of which the last five are the four non-material *jhanas* and the attainment of cessation, and subsequently get the knowledge of destruction of influxes, which we come across in many other discourses including the *Samannaphala-sutta* under discussion. Cessation, which is the cessation of perceptions and feelings, and the non-material *jhanas* are neither necessary nor sufficient conditions for the realization of cessation of suffering although these states may be achieved in the process by the practitioner.

Coming back to the *Samannaphala-sutta*, after the *jhanas* the Buddha outlines some attainments that can be achieved based on the *jhanic* experience:

> With the mind concentrated, purified and cleansed, unblemished, free from impurities, malleable, workable, established and having gained imperturbability...

the practitioner directs his mind towards, *knowing and seeing*, which is the first of such attainments. With this ability he sees the relationship between his physical body and his consciousness "which is bound to it and dependent on it." This act of distinguishing is compared to easy distinguishing between a pure gem and the cord strung to it by a man with good eye-sight. Subsequently, the practitioner directs his mind with characteristics described above to *making mind-made bodies*: "out of this body he produces another body, having a form, mind-made, complete in all its limbs and faculties." This is compared to a man's drawing out a reed from its sheath, drawing a sword from its scabbard, and drawing a snake from its (old) skin. The next is to direct one's mind to various *supernormal powers* such as

> ...being one he becomes many; being many he becomes one; he appears and disappears; he passes through fences, walls and mountains unhindered as if through air; he sinks into the ground and emerges from it as if it were water; he walks on the water without breaking the surface as if on land; he flies cross-legged through the sky like a bird with wings, he even touches and strokes with his hand the sun and the moon, mighty and powerful as they are; and he travels in the body as far as the Brahma world.

This is compared to a skilled potter or his assistant making any form that he wishes with well-prepared clay; skilled ivory-carver or his assistant making any object with well-prepared ivory; and a skilled gold-smith or his assistant making any article with gold. The next attainment is

---

19. M I., p.175.

the *divine-ear* with which "he hears sounds both divine and human, whether far or near." This is compared to one distinguishing between the sounds of big drum, small drum, conch, cymbals, or a kettle-drum. The last among these attainments before attaining the three knowledges, is the *knowledge of others' minds*. "He knows and distinguishes with his mind the minds of other beings or other persons", namely, the mind with passion to be mind with passion or mind without passion to be without passion, etc. This act is compared to a woman or a man or a young boy, fond of one's appearance, examining one's face in a brightly polished mirror or in water and knowing whether there was a spot there or not.

What is described next are the three "sciences" or knowledges, namely, knowledge of (one's) previous existences, knowledge of arising and passing away of beings and the knowledge of the destruction of the influxes. In the standard explanations of the final stage of the path to cessation of suffering these three knowledges are invariably included, and they are given as following the four *jhanic* attainments described above. What was described in-between, from the state of knowing and seeing to the knowledge of others' minds are abilities the practitioner may or may not cultivate for they are neither necessary nor sufficient conditions for the realization of the final goal. In this particular discourse they have been described in the context of the King's question as to the fruits of the noble life. The point of my discussion of these aspects in this paper is to show that even some of these abilities representing supernormal powers have been understood in the system not as mystical but as deriving as its natural results from purified, concentrated and well-practiced mind.

The first of the last three knowledges is about one's previous existences. By means of this knowledge the practitioner comes to know his past existences with all the details, extending into several eons. This cognition is compared to a man's going from his village to another and having returned recollecting how he left his village, did things in the other village and how he has now returned to his own. The second is the knowledge of passing away and arising of beings. With this knowledge – "with the divine eye, purified and surpassing that of humans" – the practitioner sees beings passing away and arising depending on the good and bad Karmas committed. This knowledge is compared to seeing by a man, standing at a lofty building situated at a crossroads, people entering or leaving the building, walking in the street or sitting in the middle of the crossroads.

The final and most important among the three is the knowledge of the destruction of influxes. It is the knowledge that produces the ultimate realization of the cessation of suffering. This knowledge has been described in the following words:

> And he, with mind concentrated, purified and cleansed, unblemished, free from impurities, malleable, workable, established and having gained imperturbability, applies and directs his mind to the knowledge of the destruction of the influxes. He knows as it really is: "This is suffering", he knows as it really is: "This is the origin of suffering", he knows as it really is: "This is the cessation of suffering", he knows as it really is: "This is the path leading to the cessation of suffering". And he knows as it really is: "These are influxes", "This is the origin of the influxes", "This is the cessation of the influxes", "This is the path leading to the cessation of the influxes."

This is the knowledge that ultimately produces the liberation from suffering. The nature of this knowledge and its subsequent implications are described in the following manner:

> And through his knowing and seeing his mind is delivered from influx of sense-desire, from the influx of becoming, from the influx of ignorance, and *the knowledge arises in him: "This is the deliverance!"*, and *he knows*: "Birth is finished, the holy life has been led, done is what had to be done, there is nothing further here." (italics added)

This crucial knowledge has been further described with the following simile:

> Just as if Sire, in the middle of the mountains there were a pond, clear as a polished mirror, where a man with good eyesight standing on the bank could see oyster-shells, gravel-banks, and shoals of fish on the move or stationary. And he might think: "This pond is clear,... there are oyster-shells..." Just so with mind concentrated... he knows: "Birth is finished, the holy life has been led, done is what had to be done, there is nothing further here."

The Buddha concludes his discussion with the King on the fruits of the noble life, emphasizing that there is no more excellent or perfect fruit than this last. What is significant in this entire discussion and in the description of the last in particular is the non-mystical character of the entire process. The simile of the man seeing what is in the clear water pool is very important in this context. It highlights the clarity of the understanding at this stage. The deliverance is from the influxes headed by the influx of desire, which is none other than what is described as the origin of suffering. This shows that the path culminates in the realization of deliverance of mind from the influxes or the causes of suffering. Once the mind is delivered from these influxes it knows that it is liberated, and this is the most crucial aspect of this whole process. The ultimate realization arises from a clear process of cognition, the key characteristic of which is clarity. When this knowledge arose in him the Buddha described it as: "the eye was born; knowledge was born; wisdom was born; science was born; and light was born."[20] These expressions reveal the non-mystical character of the ultimate goal.

Textual controversies

Our discussion is not complete unless we refer to some instances in the early canonical texts that have been interpreted by commentators, both ancient and modern, as supporting a metaphysical interpretation of Nirvana.[21] One of the oft-quoted instances in this connection is the

---

20. S IV, pp.420-424.
21. In this context I will not make a detailed analysis of these textual instances which I have discussed in detail elsewhere; see Tilakaratne (1993, pp.75-82).

following, which is known as U.80 (referring to page 80 of the Pali Text Society edition of the *Udana*, one of the texts in the Khuddaka Nikaya):

> There is [Bhikkhus], that sphere wherein there is neither earth nor water nor fire nor air; there is neither the sphere of infinite space nor of infinite consciousness, nor of nothingness, nor of the sphere of neither perception nor non-perception; where there is neither this world nor the world beyond, nor both together; nor moon nor sun; this I say is free from coming and going, from duration and decay, there is no beginning no establishment, no result, no cause; this indeed is the end of suffering...

> [Bhikkhus], there is not-born, not-become, not-made, not-compounded. [Bhikkhus], if that not-born, not-become, not-made, not-compounded were not, no escape from the born, become, made and compounded would be known here. But [Bhikkhus], since there is not-born, not-become, not-made and not-compounded, therefore an escape from the born, become, made and compounded is known.

What is described in the first passage is a "sphere" which has no connection to any of the very advanced fine-material mental states or to any worldly categories such as this world or world after and so on. The Buddha finally equates this sphere with the cessation of suffering. In the next paragraph what is described as "not-born, not-become, not-made, not-compounded" seems to refer to Nirvana although the specific word is not mentioned there. Now the problem is this: why has Nirvana been described in such terms as these, terms which apparently betray a sense of metaphysical entity?

These statements taken as they are, no doubt, are open to both metaphysical and non-metaphysical interpretations. The fact that there is textual ambiguity cannot be denied. The language used when viewed superficially betrays a metaphysical sense. Depending on this type of sporadic instance, whether we should undermine the wide-spread "naturalist" characterization of Nirvana is open to debate.   As the Buddha himself mentioned in the *Mahaparinibbana-sutta* of the Digha Nikaya, the criterion to judge whether or not any particular statement belongs to the Buddha is its consistency and coherency with the rest of the Dhamma. Viewed from this criterion, the statements in the U. 80 have to be interpreted to be consistent with the predominant interpretation of Nirvana given in almost all other discourses. Accordingly, the first statement can be interpreted as distinguishing Nirvana, as an experience, from all other worldly experiences and states of mind. Hence, reference to fine-material states and other extreme categories. The second statement can be understood as referring to Nirvana as absence of birth, becoming, actions and constructions, characteristics of worldly existence.

The other debated issue pointing in a metaphysical direction is the answer to questions about the post-mortem status of the liberated person, the Arahant. Among the well-known unanswered questions, the last four are on the post-mortem status of the Arahant, whether he exists, does not exist, both or neither. In the *Culamalunkyaputta-sutta* of the Majjhima Nikaya, the *locus classicus* of these questions in the Pali canon, the Buddha did not answer these questions. He did not answer them on the clear ground that they are not pertinent to the realization of the goal.[22] The well-known parable of the man hit by an arrow is described by the Buddha in order to drive the point, namely, the irrelevance of the knowledge of the answers to these questions for the goal.

The question "What happens to the Arahant after his death" seems to have bothered many. In particular this existential anxiety makes sense in the context of the thirst we discussed earlier, for it is the thirst for enjoyment of pleasures (thirst for pleasures) and the thirst to continue to do it (thirst for existence) which are fundamental to worldly human existence or any form of existence for that matter. Consequently, uncertainty about one's continued existence is one of the most existentially important issues any person will have to reconcile with her/himself. The most popular solution to this anxiety is given by theistic religions in the form of an eternal life without death in a blissful plain. As the Buddha has enumerated in the *Brahmajala-sutta*, the very first discourse in the Digha Nikaya, the collection of the long discourses of the Pali canon, there are four eternalist views that hold eternity of the world and the self on four different grounds, and partly-eternalist and partly non-eternalist views that hold the world and the soul to be partly eternal and partly non-eternal on four different grounds, grounds that can be regarded as the result of this anxiety.

In the same discourse the Buddha enumerates views on post-mortem existence. According to this account there are sixteen views relevant to 'conscious post-mortem survival', namely, self after death is healthy and conscious and (1) material, (2) immaterial, (3) both material and immaterial, (4) neither material and nor immaterial, (5) finite, (6) infinite, (7) both, (8) neither, (9) of uniform perception, (10) of varied perception, (11) of limited perception, (12) of unlimited perception, (13) wholly happy, (14) wholly unhappy, (15) both, and (16) neither. There are eight views on 'unconscious post-mortem survival', namely, self after death is healthy, unconscious and (1) material, (2) immaterial, (3) both, (4) neither, (5) finite, (6) infinite, (7) both, and (8) neither. And similarly there are eight views on "neither conscious nor unconscious survival" on eight grounds as mentioned above. Now all these views, believed to have been held by different religious groups or people, can be regarded as philosophical expressions of the existential anxiety regarding the question of post-mortem survival.

The Buddha's analysis of the belief in self, which is the basis for all types of anxiety, is found in many discourses. In the *Alagaddupama-sutta* of the Majjhima Nikaya the Buddha describes vividly how taking the five aspects of personality, material form, feeling, perception, construction and consciousness and the views as "this is mine, this I am, this is my self" causes suffering and agitation. In particular, the view mentioned here is the self-view, namely,

> ...that which is the self is the world; after death I shall be permanent, everlasting, eternal, not subject to change; I shall endure as long as eternity.

This clearly shows that the root-cause of the problem of suffering is the desire to be till eternity, which means, endlessly. Subsequently, the Buddha explains what happens in a person

---

22. This issue has been discussed so much by scholars that a fresh discussion at this point seems redundant. See Tilakaratne (1993, Ch.9, pp.109-124) for a detailed discussion and references.

who holds this belief when he hears the Buddha teaching:

> ...for the elimination of all standpoints, decisions, obsessions, adherences, and underlying tendencies, for the stilling of all formations (constructions), for the relinquishing of all attachments, for the destruction of craving, for dispassion, for cessation, for Nibbana. He thinks thus: *"So I shall be annihilated! So I shall perish! So I shall be no more! Then he sorrows, grieves, and laments, he weeps beating his breast and becomes distraught."* (italics added)[23]

It is very clear that what causes anxiety about the post-mortem survival of the person who has realized Nirvana is the deep-rooted desire to last forever.[24]

There is an instance in the Suttanipata, a text believed to be older than other texts and belonging to the Khuddaka Nikaya (collection of minor anthologies), where the question has been put to the Buddha directly:

> ...the person who has ceased to exist – does he not exist or *does he exist eternally without any defect*; explain this to me well, Venerable Sir, as you understand it (1075).

As the italicized phrase highlights, the issue is whether or not the Arahant exists without any defect after his demise. (Although the actual words used do not directly mean Arahant, the context makes clear that what is meant is the person who realized the goal.) In other words, this is to ask whether or not Nirvana is an everlasting state. The Buddha's answer to the question was as follows:

> The person who has ceased to exist is without measure; he does not have that with which one can speak of him. When all the phenomena are destroyed all ways of speech too are destroyed (1076).

This statement does not provide a direct answer to the question on Arahant's eternal existence. It seems to say that we cannot talk about a person who has reached this state. To paraphrase the late Prof. Jayatilleke this means that the transempirical cannot be empirically described or understood, but it can be realized and attained. The Tathagata freed from the conception of form, sensation, ideas, dispositions and consciousness is said to be deep, immeasurable and

---

23. Translation from Bhikkhu Nanamoli and Bhikkhu Bodhi (1995/2001, pp.229-231).
24. The other side of this desire, the utter denial of death, has been expressed by a modern writer in the following words: "I do not want to die – no; I neither want to die nor do I want to want to die; I want to live for ever and ever and ever. I want this "I" to live this poor "I" that I am and that I feel myself to be here and now, and therefore the problem of the duration of my soul, of my own soul, tortures me": Miguel de Unamuno (1864-1936), as quoted by Brian Davis (1993, OPUS, p.231).

unfathomable, like the great ocean.

Discussing this matter further he says that what the Buddha knew in the transcendent sense was beyond verbal articulation due to the limitations of language and empiricism. I have discussed Jayatilleke's position elsewhere in detail and am not going to do it again. Nevertheless, it is important to reflect on the particular discussion of the Buddha on which Jayatilleke's comments are based. In this discussion Vacchagotta, a wandering ascetic, questions the Buddha on the ten issues that were "kept aside" by the Buddha without answering. The last four of these questions are on the posthumous existence of the enlightened person. The Buddha answered him by saying that expressions such as "is born" or "is not born, et cetera, do not apply to such a person. The Buddha takes the fire burning by them as an example and illustrates how the fire that was burning due to grass, sticks, and so forth, will be extinguished once the fuel (such as grass sticks, etc.) is consumed. Once the fire is extinguished it is not proper to ask where has the fire gone, to the East, West, North or South, and the proper explanation is that

> ...the fire burned in dependence in its fuel of grass and sticks, when that is used up, is reckoned as extinguished when it does not get any more fuel.

The Buddha sums up the explanation in the following words:

> So, too, Vaccha, the Tathagata has abandoned that material form by which one describing the Tathagata might describe him, he has cut it off at the root, made it like a palm-stump, done away with it so that it is no longer subject to future arising. The Tathagata is liberated from reckoning in terms of material form. Vaccha, he is profound, immeasurable, unfathomable like the ocean. The term "is born" does not apply, the term "is not born" does not apply, the term "both is born and is not born" does not apply, the term "neither is born nor is not born" does not apply.[25] [The same is repeated about the other four aspects of personality.]

The discussion highlights two important matters the first of which is that the awakened person is extinguished when the "fuel runs out", and that he does not have any more the five aspects of personality with which one can speak of him. The fire simile is quite straightforward and what is said is clear: like fire that was extinguished the Arahant is no more. What happened to him is like what happened to the fire. If this is a matter for consternation that is our problem as we look at it while still being "on this shore". The second matter that the discussion highlights is that an Arahant who attains such a state is "profound, immeasurable and unfathomable". This is not as clear as the fire simile: does this mean that he attains a position characterizable in such terms as these after his physical death or is it an account

---

25. M I, p.487. The translation adapted from Bhikkhu Nanamoli and Bhikkhu Bodhi, 1995/2001, p.593.

of his nature while still he is alive? Since an Arahant has five aspects of personality while he is living this assertion cannot be about a living Arahant. If this describes the state of the Arahant after his physical death, which obviously seems to be the case, the after-death state of the Arahant has to be taken as something more than simple extinguished fire. He is like the fire in the sense that in extinguishing due to lack of fuel the fire has not gone anywhere to return later. But, on the other hand, what happened to the Arahant is not as simple as what happened to the fire for the process of making an end to all the fuel in the case of an Arahant is a complex activity involving development of mind to advanced levels of purification.

In discussing this matter we need to appreciate the mentality behind Vaccha's question. It is a question that arises basically from the existential anxiety of being forced to imagine a universe without ones own existence. The religions that offer eternal heaven clearly cater to this deep rooted need, for in that state nothing happens without one's knowledge or in one's absence for one exists for ever. To believe that the story is over from death is to concede to materialism with a sense of loss, bewilderment and grudge. Malunkayputta's and Vaccha's and many others' query over the posthumous existence of the Arahant is a result of this mentality characterized by the desire for continued existence, which we discussed as the "thirst for existence" at the beginning of this discussion. In the entire canon I have not come across one single instance where an Arahant raises this set of questions as something causing existential anxiety for them, except for a few short discourses containing, without any context, the typical question and the answer, (short discourses of this nature being abundant in the canon). Usually Arahants have never raised this query as an existentially nagging question of their own. It is also interesting to see that the Buddha has never tried to give an easy answer to these minds in order to give the desired comfort.

It is quite clear that the Buddha did not say that one is eternal or annihilated after death. Not only about an Arahant but also about any ordinary person, the Buddha did not make this claim. It is plainly because "an individual in true and substantialist sense is not available", the precondition for either eternity or annihilation to be postulated. But the claim about the ordinary "worldling" has not been understood as ruling out his discontinuation in the *samsara*; it is understood that such a person undergoes birth and death repeatedly. The problem, however, rests on what happens to the Arahant who has got rid of the idea of self by eradicating all forms of thirst: if his *samsara* is over and if he would not continue in the *samsara*, his *samsaric* existence must be over. Whether or not there is an extra-*samsaric* existence, another form of becoming (*bhava*), has never been suspected, for the Buddha has quite clearly denied any such existence. When an Arahant attains physical death there is nothing that exists or does not exist.

Conclusion

This brings us back to the question with which we started this discussion, namely, what is the nature of the experience that is characterized by purity and freedom? In the early texts we have numerous instances of those venerable men and women, in addition to the Buddha, who realized it and talked about it. (Earlier in this essay I referred to the verses attributed to them, i.e. the Theragatha and Therigatha.) As one final example let us allow one who realized the cessation of suffering to talk about it. As occurring the Vinaya literature the speaker is Sona Kolivisa who entered the Sangha from a very affluent social background and had to be advised by the Buddha to balance his over-zealous approach to the practice. Having attained Arahanthood, he came to the Master and described how desire, hatred and delusion are gone away from one who has destroyed cankers, and further articulated the implications of this on one's lived experience in daily life:

> Thus, Venerable Sir, even if physical forms cognizable by the eye come very strongly into the field of vision of a [Bhikkhu] whose mind is wholly freed, they do not obsess his mind for his mind comes to be undefiled, firm, won to composure, and consequently he notes its passing. [The same is said for the sounds cognizable by the ear, scents cognizable by the nose, tastes cognizable by the tongue, touches cognizable by the body and mental objects cognizable by the mind.] It is as if, Venerable Sir, there were a rocky mountain slope without a cleft, without a hollow, of one mass, and as if wild wind and rain should come very strongly from the eastern quarter [western, northern and southern quarter] it would neither tremble nor quake nor shake. Even so, Venerable Sir, if physical forms cognizable by the eye... mental objects cognizable by the mind come very strongly into the field of vision [etc.] of a [Bhikkhu] whose mind is wholly freed, they do not obsess him...

This is what the liberated mind means in terms of the lived experience of daily life: it is characterized by stability and unshakability.

The Buddha frequently refers to this state as "health". Once he claimed that he was one of the few people who could claim health in the psychological sense. In an illuminating discussion with a very old householder student couple, Nakuala-mata and Nakula-pita, who complained that they were quite indisposed and old, the Buddha advised them to preserve their mental health for total physical health is a near impossibility. What he seems to have meant by mental health in this context is the total mental health resulting from eradicating all defilements from one's psyche. As we saw in our discussion this metaphor of gaining health was used by the Buddha even in his account of getting rid of the five hindrances. In the ultimate sense, however, in the early Buddhist discourses "health" is a term used to describe Nirvana. This makes the realization of Nirvana tantamount to achieving health in a deep and comprehensive sense.

Those who are healthy are naturally happy. On this, let me quote Rahula again:

> There are two ancient Buddhist texts called the Theragatha and Therigatha which are full of joyful utterances of the Buddha's [Bhikkhus], both male and female, who found peace and happiness, in life through his teachings. The king of Kosala once told the Buddha that unlike many a [Bhikkhu] of other (ways of life) who looked haggard, coarse, pale, emaciated and unprepossessing, his [Bhikkhus] were "joyful and elated, jubilant and exultant, enjoying the spiritual life, with faculties pleased, free from anxiety, serene, peaceful and living with a gazelle's mind, i.e. light-hearted." The king added that he believed that this healthy disposition was due to the fact that

"these venerable ones had certainly realized the great and full significance of the Blessed One's teaching."[26]

The Buddha has been described by his contemporaries as "ever with a mild smile" (*mihita-pubbangama*); the above account by the King suggests that this smile was "infectious"!

---

26. W. Rahula (1978, p.28).

Part IV

Digging Into The Mind The Buddhist Way

Chapter 11, by Karunadasa, draws on the *Abhidhamma*, the third canonical book of the Theravada. He zeroes in on the subject of looking inside the mind through an inner telescope called meditation. What one sees in refined grades of awareness are the smallest units of experience, technically known as *dharmas*, which might be called "perceivables" and "knowables", and which are by any means socially constructed, as anything that can be named is inescapably textual and changing over time, and thus ultimately empty. This ultimate emptiness discards eternal truth or reality, but does not exclude the existence of "truthfulness" or of a local "reality" of a community. Notwithstanding the absence of absolute certainty, somebody can be truthful. "Truth" is in trouble Gergen (2000). As language cannot represent or picture an independent reality, there is a need to discern a conventional or "provisional reality" of the Dependent Origination of *dharmas* and an "ultimate reality" of emptiness that is language independent and which includes people's minds and selves. I-me-mine/self exists by virtue of language; without forms of speaking there is no experience, thus the only way to be is to "inter-be".

In Chapter 12, Yao connects to the field of cognitive science to explore the twilight zone of memory lane, its impact on self-construction, and the Buddhist self-deconstruction. Inspired by Vasubandhu (4th century), he particularly links the field of neurophenomenology with ancient Buddhist wisdom in the spirit of an on-going constructive dialogue. Like the previous chapter, this chapter is presented in an "aboutness" theoretical mode. It seems that without having a full intellectual explanation of the mysteries of human life and memory, we can relate with each other satisfactorily, find our way about within life, and move on without grappling with the ineffable beyond emptiness. Memory strikes as a function of relationships, a relational construction identifying oneself through generative narratives of a personal history, rather than as abiding physiological correlates lodged in-between the ears. The physiology of memory is difficult to establish at present due to the mere impossibility of indexing when memory occurs. Although genetically provided and universal within the human species, memory processes within our minds are in our daily functioning foremost a socially designated discursive achievement. Remembering itself points at a narrative and at actions with a relational meaning within the tradition one lives. Thus, when the Buddha remembered his "past lives aeons ago", this might refer to a metaphorical/cultural meaning wherein "life" equals a period of a karmic emotional episode, since the Buddha discarded metaphysics.

In Chapter 13, P.M.W. de Silva goes into the mind's "architecture", illuminates its cognitive, emotional, motivational, and attentional facets, and illustrates his practice with a vignette on alcohol addiction. Mindfulness, enabling to break through stimulus-response vicious cycling mechanisms, makes the Buddhist contribution unique. Alas, mindfulness has also become a commercial slogan in the West. A pioneer in Buddhist Psychology, the author presents an erudite in-depth analysis on emotions, a neglected subject in the Dharma. The reader gets to know about the healing of addictions, a condition ripe to be tackled by a Buddhist approach par excellence. This pathological variant of attachment, which finds its roots in craving, grasping, and clinging, were dealt with for 2600 years in the Dharma and yet remains obviously still actual, and in dire need of emotion-focused change. The world suffers from many kinds of addictions, occurring in all layers of society and causing much trouble worldwide. The numbers of addicts to drugs, alcohol, and food are mushrooming and some people are addicted otherwise; they are "rage-o-holics" or "fear-o-holics". From a Buddhist stance, the Dependent Origination of these stubborn habits needs to be unveiled. Addicts are basically "greed-o-holics" and "hate-o-holics" who are ignorant about karmic self-chosen meaning, intention and action, modifiable at any time.

Chapter 11

On "dhammas": The Building Blocks Of Psychological Experience

Yakupitiyage Karunadasa

The world of Dhamma

During its long history of over 2500 years, the Dhamma gave rise to a large number of schools and sub-schools all resulting in an immense variety of interpretations. In this situation one pertinent question that can be raised is whether we can identify the core teaching which, while uniting all schools of Buddhist thought, separates the Dhamma from all other streams of thought and thus whether we can speak of a unity that transcends all school differences.

In this connection it is worth examining why the Dhamma gave rise to a wide variety of schools. One relevant reason is that the Dhamma is a means to an end and not an end unto itself. In the "Parable of the Raft" the Buddha compared the Dhamma to a raft. It is for the purpose of "crossing over" and not to be grasped as the "truth". The Dhamma has instrumental value that is relative to the realization of a goal. As an extension to this idea, it is also recognized that the Dhamma as a means can be presented in many ways. As recorded in the *Bahuvedaniya Sutta* of the Majjhima Nikaya, when two students of the Buddha, a Bhikkhu and a layman, had a fierce argument on the nature of feeling, the Buddha told them that both of them were correct because they adopted equally effective approaches to the subject. It is on this occasion that the Buddha told Ananda that the Dhamma has been presented in many different ways and forms. What "works" needs not to be repeated in the same way as a holy hymn. It can be restated in many different ways, for the Dhamma is not something esoteric or mystical. The more one elaborates it the more it shines. In connection with this, what we need to remember is that the Dhamma is not "actuality" as such, but a description of actuality and a conceptual model or framework that describes the nature of actuality. We find this idea formally expressed in a Pali commentary contending that the nature of actuality has been presented as a conceptual model through the symbolic medium of language, words and meaning as concepts. What is actual can be stated in many ways. Thus here, as elsewhere, the Dhamma avoids absolutism. There is no one absolutist way of presenting the Dhamma which is valid for all times and climes. Thus, we can consider different schools of Buddhist thought as different conceptual models. This applies to the Dhamma as a psychology as well.

If we approach the different schools of Buddhist thought in this manner, we need to identify the basic or essential Buddhist teaching that unites them. Of course there can be more than one that can be so considered, but in my opinion it is the teaching of not-self (*anatta*) that is eminently qualified as a candidate for this choice. From its very beginning, the Buddha was aware that the teaching of *anatta* was not shared by any other contemporary systems of thought. In fact this has been clearly recognized and expressed in one of the early Buddhist discourses. In the *Culasihanada Sutta* of the Majjhima Nikaya it is said that there are four kinds of clinging: to sense pleasures, to speculative views regarding the self and the world, to rules and observances (i.e., to external rules, rituals and austerities in the belief that they lead to liberation) and to a doctrine of self (i.e., to a view of a truly existent self). The sutta goes on to say that there could be other teachers, who would recognize only some of the four kinds of clinging and that at best they might teach the overcoming of the first three forms of clinging. What they cannot teach, because they have not comprehended this for themselves, is the overcoming of clinging to a self, for this is the subtlest and the most elusive of the group. Thus *anatta* is the unique discovery of the Buddha and is crucial in separating his teaching from all other systems. The title given to this sutta, *Culasihanada*, means the "Shorter Discourse on the Lions Roar". This intended to show that the Buddha's proclamation of the *anatta* teaching is "bold and thunderous like a veritable lions roar."

The status of the view on *anatta* as the most crucial insight that separates the Dhamma from all other currents came to be recognized in the subsequent schools of Buddhist thought as well. Yasomitra's *Abhidharmakosavyakhya*, for instance, categorically asserts that in the whole world there is no other teacher who proclaims a teaching of not-self. Buddhaghosa (a 5th century Theravada scholar) stated that the characteristics of impermanence (*anicca*) and suffering (*dukkha*) are known whether Buddhas arise or not; but the characteristics of not-self are not known unless there is a Buddha, for the knowledge of not-self is the province of none but a Buddha. The Blessed One shows no-selfness in some instances through impermanence, in some through suffering and in some through both. Why is that? While impermanence and suffering are evident, not-self is not evident; its characteristics seem obscure, arcane, impenetrable, hard to illustrate and hard to describe. In the history of Buddhist thought there has never been a Buddhist school that openly acknowledged a theory of self. If there is one teaching every school is committed to defend, it is the teaching of not-self. What is more, every Buddhist school has been very sensitive to the charge of being criticized as upholding some sort of self theory. At the same time, some Buddhist schools may have developed certain theories that amounted to some kind of veiled recognition of a self theory. For instance, the *Vatsiputriyas* admitted a sort of quasi-permanent self, neither identical with nor different from the mental states. However, what matters here is the fact that they vehemently denied that their theory is a veiled recognition of self. Despite their protests and denials, they nonetheless came to be rather sarcastically referred to by other Buddhists as "heretics".

It is obvious that the teaching of not-self is unique to the Dhamma. Most importantly, the teaching of not-self not only separates the Dhamma from all other views and metaphysical speculations, it also provides a comprehensive explanation as to causal genesis. The idea of self has a psychological origin. In every cognitive act, which consists of a series of cognitive events, the latent tendency in consciousness to possess an ego awakens and gradually solidifies, eventually becoming fully crystallized at the final stage. Buddhists call this process conceptual proliferation. Once the ego consciousness has arisen it cannot exist in a vacuum; it needs concrete form and content. Then, the unawakened worldling identifies her/his ego-consciousness in relation to the five aggregates or psychological modalities (in short: body, sensation, cognition, affect and awareness). The process of identification takes the following form: This is "mine", this "I am" and this is "my self". Of these, the first is due to craving (*tanha*), the second to conceit (*mana*), and the third to wrong views (*ditthi*). What is called self-conceit arises at a pre-rational level, whereas the idea of self, although conditioned by craving, arises at an elementary reflective level, also called the personality view. It affirms the presence of an abiding self in the psychophysical organism in one of many ways – as either identical with, possessing, contained within or containing one or another of the five aggregates that constitute the individual personality. But once the self view has arisen, it becomes the basis for a count-less number of cosmological, metaphysical, theological and speculative ideologies. Thus we read in the Samyutta Nikaya that as to those diverse views that arise in the world, it is owing to the personality view that they arise and if the personality view exists not, they do not exist.

In the remainder of this chapter, the core teaching of the Dhamma on the reality of not-self will be illuminated according to what I have called: "*dhamma* theory".

The world of "*dhammas*"

The *dhamma*[1] theory (with small d as opposed to Dhamma with capital D that denotes here the Buddha's teachings as promulgated by the Theravada school) was not peculiar to any one Buddhist school but penetrated all the early schools, stimulating the growth of their different versions of the *Abhidhamma*. The Sarvastivada theory (Sarvastivada is a 3rd century Early Buddhist school that expounds a theory of "all that exists") together with its critique by the Madhyamikas (a 4th century Mahayana school championed by Nagarjuna), has been critically studied by a number of modern scholars. The Theravada version, however, has received less attention. There are sound reasons for believing that this Pali *Abhidhamma* (one of the three baskets that together comprise the Teaching of the Elders' "canon", the other two deal with the Buddha's discourses and commune rules) contains one of the earliest forms of the *dhamma* theory, perhaps the oldest version. This theory did not remain static but evolved over the cen-turies as Buddhist thinkers sought to draw out the implications of the theory and to respond to problems it posed for the critical intellectuals. Thus, the *dhamma* theory was repeatedly enriched, first by the *Abhidhamma* commentaries and later through the exegetical literature and medieval compendia of the *Abhidhamma*, the so-called "little finger manuals" such as the *Abhidhammattha-Sangha*, which in turn gave rise to their own commentaries.

In this chapter I will attempt to trace the main stages in the origin and development of the *dhamma* theory and to explore its implications. The first part will discuss the early version of the theory as represented by the *Abhidhamma*. At this stage the theory was not yet precisely articulated but remained in the background as the unspoken premise of *Abhidhamma* analysis. It was during the commentarial period that an attempt was made to work out the implications of early *Abhidhamma* thought, and it is this development that I will treat in the second part. Finally, in the third part, I will discuss two other topics that received scholarly attention as a consequence of the *dhamma* theory, namely, the category of the nominal and the conceptual (*pannatti*) and the theory of the twofold reality. Both of these were considered necessary meas-

---

1.   The term *dhamma* denotes not only the ultimate data of empirical existence but also the unconditioned state of Nibbana. In this study, however, only the former aspect is taken into consideration.

ures to preserve the validity of the *dhamma* theory in relation to our routine, everyday understanding of ourselves and the way we perceive the world in which we dwell.

The early version of "dhamma" theory

Although the *dhamma* theory is an *Abhidhammic* innovation, the antecedent trends that led to its formulation and its basic ingredients can be traced to the Early Buddhist scriptures which seek to analyze empiric individuality and its relation to the external world. In the Buddha's discourses there are five such modes of analysis. The first, the analysis into mind or psyche (*nama*) and soma/body (*rupa*),[2] is the most elementary in the sense that it specifies the two main components, the mental and the corporeal aspects, of the empiric individual. The second analysis is that into the five aggregates (*khandhas* or Skandhas in Sanskrit): corporeality (*rupa*), sensory feeling (*vedana*), cognition/imagery (*sanna*), affect/behaviour (*sankhara*), and consciousness/awareness (*vinnana*).[3] The third is that into six elements (*dhatus*): earth (*pathavi*), water (*apo*), temperature (*tejo*), air (*vayo*), space (*akasa*) and consciousness (*vinnana*).[4] The fourth is that into twelve avenues of sense-perception and mental cognition (*ayatanas*): the eye, ear, nose, tongue, body/skin, and mind/brain; and their corresponding objects: visible form, sound, smell, taste, touch, and mental objects.[5] The fifth is that into eighteen elements (*dhatus*), an elaboration of the immediately preceding mode obtained by the addition of the six kinds of consciousness, which arise from the contact between the sense organs and their objects. The six additional items are the visual, auditory, olfactory, gustatory, tactile and mental consciousnesses.[6]

The Buddhist purpose in using these analyses is varied. For instance, the main purpose of the *khandha*-analysis is to show that there is no ego either inside or outside the *khandhas* which could make up the so-called empiric individuality. None of the *khandhas* belongs to "me", they do not correspond to "I", nor are they "my self"[7] Thus the main purpose of this analysis is to prevent the intrusion of the notions of "mine," "I," and "my self" into what is otherwise an impersonal and ego-less congeries of psychological and physical aggregates. On the other hand, the analysis into eighteen elements is often resorted to in order to show that consciousness is neither a soul nor an extension of a soul-substance but is a psychological phenomenon which comes into being as a result of certain conditions: there is no independent consciousness which exists in its own right.[8] In similar fashion each analysis is used to explain certain fea-

---

2. The reference here is to its general sense. In its special sense *nama-rupa* means the following psychophysical aspects: "Sensation, perception, will, contact, and attention – these are called nama. The four material elements and the form depending on them – this is called rupa" (S II, 3). In the oft-recurrent statement, *villanapaccaya namarupat*, the reference is to the special sense.
3. See e.g. S III, 47, 86-87; M III, 16.
4. See e.g. S II, 248; III 231.
5. See e.g. D II, 302; III, 102, 243; A III, 400; V, 52.
6. See e.g. S II, 140; D I, 79; III, 38; A I, 255; III, 17.
7. S III, 49
8. Cf. M III, 281.

tures of sentient existence. It is, in fact, with reference to these five kinds of analysis that the Buddhist teachings frame its fundamental tenets. The very fact that there are at least five kinds of analysis shows that none of them can be taken as final or absolute. Each represents the world of experience in its totality, yet represents it from a pragmatic standpoint determined by the particular theme, which it is intended to illuminate.

The *Abhidhammic* theory of *dhammas* developed from an attempt to draw out the full implications of these five types of analysis. If each analysis is examined in relation to the other four, it is found to be further analyzable. That the first, the analysis into psyche and soma, is further analyzable is seen by the second, the analysis into the five *khandhas*. For in the second analysis, the psychological component of the soma is analyzed into sensation, cognition, affect and awareness/consciousness. Analysis into *khandhas* (meaning "groups" or modalities), too, can be further analyzed. This is shown by the analysis of soma into six elements: earth, water, temperature, air, space and consciousness. These six are also further analyzable as seen from the fact that consciousness, which is reckoned here as one item, is made into four in the *khandha*-analysis. The same situation is true of the analysis into 12 modes of sense perceiving (6) and object cognising (6) and by the next analysis into 18 elements, which includes the former 12 modes plus six types of corresponding consciousnesses. The latter is an elaboration of the former. Can this analysis be considered final? This supposition must be rejected, because although consciousness is here itemized as six-fold, its invariable concomitants and refinements are not separately mentioned.[9] It will thus be seen that none of the five analyses can be considered exhaustive. In each case one or more items is further analyzable.

This is the line of thought that led the Abhidhammikas to evolve still another mode of analysis, which in their view is not amenable to further analysis. This new development, which is more or less common to all the systems of *Abhidhamma*, is the analysis of the world of experience into what came to be known as *dhammas* (Pali) or *dharmas* (Sanskrit). The term *dhamma* looms large in the discourses of the Buddha. It is found in a variety of senses and its meaning has to be determined by its specific context. In the Abhidhamma, however, the term assumes a more technical meaning, referring to those items that result when the process of analysis is taken to its ultimate limits. In the Theravada *Abhidhamma*, for instance, corporeality *khandha* is broken down into 28 items called *rupa-dhammas*. The next three aggregates – sensation, cognition and affect – are together arranged into 52 items called *cetasikas*. The fifth, consciousness, is counted as one item with 89 varieties and is referred to as *citta*.[10] Thus the *dhamma*-analysis is an addition to the previous five modes of analyses. Its scope is the same, the world of conscious experience, but its divisions are finer and more exhaustive. This situation in itself does not constitute a radical departure from the earlier tradition, for it does not as yet involve a view of existence that is at variance with that of the Early Buddhist teachings There is, however, this situation to be noted: Since the analysis into *dhammas* is the most

---

9. Such as sensation, perception, cognition, conception, visualisation, intention, conation, motivation, and emotion, all relevant terms and topics of psychological science (editor).
10. See *Dhammasangani*, 5ff.

exhaustive, the previous five modes of analysis become subsumed under it as five subordinate classifications.

The definition and classification of these *dhammas* and the explanation of their inter-connections form the main subject matter of the *Abhidhamma*. The Abhidhammikas presuppose that to understand any given item properly is to know it in all its relations, under all aspects recognized in the theoretical and practical discipline of the Dhamma. Therefore, in the *Abhidhamma*, they have classified the same material in different ways and from different points of view. This explains why, in the *Dhammasangani* and other *Abhidhamma* treatises, one encounters innumerable lists of classifications. Although such lists may appear repetitive, even monotonous, they serve a useful purpose, bringing into relief, not only the individual characteristic of each *dhamma*, but also its relations to other *dhammas*.

With this same aim in view, in bringing out the nature of the *dhammas*, the *Abhidhamma* resorts to two complementary methods: that of analysis *(bheda)* and that of synthesis *(sangaha)*. The analytical method dominates in the *Dhammasangani*, which according to tradition is the first book of the *Abhidhamma* for here we find a complete catalogue of the *dhammas*, each with a laconic definition. The synthetical method is more characteristic of the *Patthana*, the last book of the *Abhidhamma* for here we find an exhaustive catalogue of the conditional relations of the *dhammas*. The combined use of these two methods shows that, according to the methodological discipline employed in the *Abhidhamma*, "a complete description of a thing requires, besides its analysis, also a statement of its relations to certain other things."[11] Thus, if analysis plays an important role in the *Abhidhamma*'s methodology, no less important a role is played by synthesis. Analysis shows that the world of experience is resolvable into a plurality of factors; synthesis shows that these factors are not discrete entities existing in themselves but inter-connected and interdependent nodes in a complex web of relationships. It is only for the purpose of definition and description that things are artificially dissected. In actuality the world given to experience is a vast network of tightly interwoven relations.

This fact needs emphasis because the *Abhidhammic* theory of *dhammas* has sometimes been represented as a radical pluralism. It is mostly Stcherbatsky's writings[12], based on Sarvastivada sources, which have given currency to this not admissible incorrect interpretation. "Up to the present time," observed Nyanaponika Thera, "it has been a regular occurrence in the history of physics, metaphysics, and psychology that when a whole has been successfully dissolved by analysis, the resultant parts come again to be regarded as little wholes."[13] This is the kind of process that culminates in radical pluralism. As we shall see, about a hundred years after the formulation of the *dhamma* theory, such a trend surfaced within certain schools of Buddhist thought and culminated in the view that the *dhammas* exist in all three periods of time. But the Pali *Abhidhamma* did not succumb to this error of conceiving the *dhammas* as

---

11. Nyanaponika Thera (1976). *Abhidhamma studies: Researches in Buddhist Psychology.* Kandy, Ceylon: Buddhist Publication Society (p.21).
12. Cf. *The central conception of Buddhism and the meaning of the word "Dharma".* London: Asiatic Society, 1923; *Buddhist Logic* (Vol.1, Introduction). New York: Dover Publications, 1962 (reprint).
13. Nyanaponika Thera (1976, p.41).

ultimate unities or discrete entities. In the Pali tradition it is only for the sake of definition and description that each *dhamma* is postulated as if it were a separate entity; but in reality it is by no means a solitary phenomenon having an existence of its own. This is precisely why the mental and material *dhammas* are often presented in interconnected groups. In presenting them thus, the danger inherent in narrowly analytical methods has been avoided; the danger; namely, of elevating the factors resulting from analysis to the status of genuinely separate entities. Thus if analysis shows that composite things cannot be considered as ultimate unities, synthesis shows that the factors into which the apparently composite things are analyzed are not discrete entities.[14]

This *Abhidhammic* view of existence, as seen from its theory of *dhammas*, cannot be interpreted as a radical pluralism, neither can it be interpreted as an out-and-out monism. For what are called *dhammas* – the component factors of the universe of experience of phenomena within us and outside us – are not fractions of an absolute unity but a multiplicity of co-ordinate factors. They are not reducible to, nor do they emerge from, a single reality, the fundamental postulate of monistic metaphysics. If they are to be interpreted as phenomena, this should be done with the proviso that they are phenomena with no corresponding *noumena*, no hidden underlying ground. For, they are not manifestations of some mysterious metaphysical substratum, but processes taking place due to the interplay of a multitude of conditions.

In thus evolving a view of existence, which cannot be interpreted in either monistic or pluralistic terms, the *Abhidhamma* accords with the "middle view" that avoids both the eternalist view of existence, which maintains that everything exists absolutely[15] and the opposite nihilistic view, which maintains that absolutely nothing exists.[16] It also avoids, on the one hand, the monistic view that everything is reducible to a common ground, some sort of self-substance [17] and, on the other hand, the opposite pluralistic view that the whole of existence is resolvable into a concatenation of discrete entities.[18] Transcending these two pairs of extremist views, the middle view explains that phenomena arise dependent on other phenomena without a self-subsisting *noumenon* serving as the ground of their being.

The inter-connection and inter-dependence of *dhammas* are not explained on the basis of the dichotomy between substance and quality. Consequently, a given *dhamma* does not inhere in another as its quality, nor does it serve another as its substance. The so-called substance is only a product of imagination. The distinction between substance and quality is denied because such a distinction leaves the door open for the intrusion of the theory of a substantial self with all that it entails. Hence, it is with reference to causes and conditions that the interconnection of the *dhammas* should be understood. The conditions are not different from the *dhammas*, for it is the *dhammas* themselves that constitute the conditions. How each *dhamma* serves as a condition for the origination of another is explained on the basis of the system of conditioned

---

14. *Visuddhi Magga*, 137.
15. S II 17, 77.
16. Ibid.
17. S II 77.
18. Ibid.

genesis.[19] This system, which consists of 24 conditions, aims at demonstrating the interdependence and dependent co-origination of all *dhammas* in respect of both their temporal sequence and their spatial concomitance.

Development of "*dhamma*" theory

The foregoing is a brief summary of the earliest phase of the *dhamma* theory as presented in the books of the Pali *Abhidhamma*, particularly the *Dhammasangani* and the *Patthana*. About a hundred years after its formulation and as a reaction against it, there emerged what came to be known as personalism (*puggalavada*),[20] a theory that led to a further clarification of the nature of *dhammas*. Now here it may be noted that according to the Early Buddhist discourses there is no denial as such of the psychological concept of the "person" (*puggala*), if by it is understood not an enduring entity distinct from the five *khandhas* nor an agent within the *khandhas*, but simply the sum total of the five causally connected and ever-changing *khandhas*. From the point of view of the *dhamma*-analysis, this can be restated by substituting the term *dhamma* for the term *khandha*, for the *dhammas* are the factors obtained by analysis of the *khandhas*.

However, this way of defining the concept of person did not satisfy some Buddhists. In their opinion the *dhamma* theory as presented by the Theravadins led to a complete depersonalization of the individual being and consequently failed to provide adequate explanations of such concepts as rebirth and moral responsibility. Hence these thinkers insisted on positing the person as an additional reality distinct from the *khandhas* or *dhammas*. As recorded in the *Kathavatthu* ("Points of Controversy"), the main contention of the Puggalavadins (Personalists) is that the person is known in a real and ultimate sense.[21] Against this proposition a number of counter-arguments are adduced, which need not concern us here. What interests us, however, is that in denying that the person is known in a real and ultimate sense, the Theravadins admit that the *khandhas* or *dhammas* are known in a real and ultimate sense. Thus, in their view what is real and ultimate is not the person but the *khandhas* or *dhammas* that enter into its composition.[22]

Now the use of the two words, "real" (*saccikattha*) and "ultimate" (*paramattha*) as indicative of the nature of *dhammas* seems to give the impression that in denying the reality of the person the Theravadins have overstressed the reality of the *dhammas*. Does this amount to the admission that the *dhammas* are real and discrete entities existing in their own right? Such a

---

19. For a short but lucid description, see Narada Thera, *A manual of Abhidhamma* (Vol. II, pp.87ff). Colombo, Ceylon: Yajirarama, 1957.
20. See: Demievielle, P (trans.), L'origine des sectes bouddhiques d'apres paramartha. *Mélanges Chinois et Bouddhiques*, Vol. I, 1932, pp.57ff; Masuda, J. (trans.), Origin and doctrines of Early Indian Buddhist schools (translation of Vasumitra's Treatise). *Asia Major,* Vol. II, 1925, pp.53-57; Conze, E. *Buddhist thought in India* (pp.122ff). London: Unwin, 1962; Warder, A.K. *Indian Buddhism* (pp. 289ff). Delhi: Motilal Banarsidass, 1970.
21. *Kathavatthu,* 1ff. See too the relevant sections of its commentary.
22. Ibid.

conclusion appears untenable. For if the *dhammas* are defined as real and ultimate, this means not that they partake of the nature of absolute entities, but that they are not further reducible to any other reality, to some kind of substance which underlies them. That is to say, there is no behind the scenes" substance from which they emerge and to which they finally return. This means, in effect, that the *dhammas* represent the final limits of the *Abhidhammic* analysis of empirical existence. Hence, this new definition does not erode the empirical foundation of the *dhamma* theory as presented by the Theravadins. This view is consonant with the statement occurring in the earlier texts that the *dhammas* come to be without having been and disappear without any residue.[23]

Why, unlike the *dhammas*, the person is not recognized as real and ultimate needs explanation? Since the person is the sum total of the causally connected mental and corporeal *dhammas* constituting the empiric individual, it lends itself to further analysis. What is subject to analysis cannot be an irreducible datum of cognition. The opposite situation is true of the *dhammas*. This brings into focus two reality levels: that which is amenable to analysis and that which defies further analysis. Analyzability is the mark of composite things; non-analyzability is the mark of the elementary constituents (*dhammas*).

Another controversy that has left its mark on the Theravada version of the *dhamma* theory is the one concerning the tri-temporal existence. What is new about this theory, advanced by the Sarvastivadins, is that it introduced a metaphysical dimension to the doctrine of *dhammas* and thus paved the way for the erosion of its empirical foundation. For this theory makes an empirically unverifiable distinction between the actual being of the *dhammas* as phenomena and their ideal being as *noumena*. It assumes that the substances of all *dhammas* persist in all the three divisions of time – past, present and future – while their manifestations as phenomena are impermanent and subject to change. Accordingly, a *dhamma* actualizes itself only in the present moment of time, but in essence it continues to subsist in all the three temporal periods. This tri-temporal existence theory resulted in the transformation of the *dhamma* theory into a "theory of own-nature" (*svabhavavada*) and paved the way for a veiled recognition, if not for a categorical assumption, of the distinction between substance and quality. What interests us here is the fact that although the Theravadins rejected this metaphysical theory of tri-temporal existence, including its qualified version as accepted by the Kasyapiyas,[24] it influenced the Theravada version of the *dhamma* theory. This is to be seen in the "post-canonical" literature of Sri Lanka where, for the first time, the term *sabhava* (Sanskrit: *svabhava*) came to be used as a synonym for *dhamma*. Hence we have the recurrent definition: "[d]hammas are so called because they bear their own nature"[25] The question is this: Did the Theravadins use the term *sabhava* in the same sense as the Sarvastivadins? Did the Theravadins assume the metaphysical view that the substance of a *dhamma* persists throughout the three phases of time? Does this amount to the admission

---

23. Cf. *Patisambhida Magga,* 76 and *Visuddhi Magga,* 512d.
24. See Karunadasa, Y. Vibhajyavada versus Sarvastivada: The Buddhist controversy on time. *Kalyani: Journal of Humanities and Social Sciences*, Vol.II, pp.16ff, 1983.
25. Cf. e.g., *Maha Niddesa Atthakatha,* 261; *Dhammasangani Atthakatha,* 126; *Visuddhimagga Sannaya,* v.6.

that there is a duality between the *dhamma* and its *sabhava*, between the bearer and the borne, a dichotomy which goes against the grain of the Buddhist doctrine of not-self (*anatta*)?

This situation has to be considered in the context of the logics used by the Abhidhammikas in defining the *dhammas*. This logic involves three main kinds of definition. The first is called agency definition because it attributes agency to the thing to be defined. Such, for example, is the definition of *citta* (consciousness) as "that which thinks".[26] The second is called instrumental definition because it attributes instrumentality to the thing to be defined. Such, for example, is the definition of *citta* as "that through which one thinks".[27] The third is called definition by nature, whereby the abstract nature of the thing to be defined is brought into focus. Such, for example, is the definition, "The mere act of thinking itself is *citta*."[28] The first two kinds of definition, it is maintained, are provisional and as such are not valid from an ultimate point of view.[29] This is because the attribution of agency and instrumentality invests a *dhamma* with a duality when it is actually a unitary and unique phenomenon. Such an attribution also leads to the wrong assumption that a given *dhamma* is a substance with inherent qualities or an agent performing some kind of action. Such definitions are said to be based on tentative attribution[30] and thus are not ultimately valid.[31] It is as a matter of convention and for the sole purpose of facilitating the grasp of the idea to be conveyed[32] that a duality is assumed by the mind in defining *dhamma*, even though *dhammas* are actually devoid of such duality.[33] Thus both agency and instrumental definitions are resorted to for the convenience of description and as such they are not to be understood in their direct literal sense. On the other hand, definition by nature is admissible in an ultimate sense.[34] This is because this type of definition brings into focus the real nature of a given *dhamma* without attributing agency or instrumentality to it, attributions that creates the false notion that there is a duality within a unitary *dhamma*.

It is in the context of these implications that the definition of *dhamma* as that which bears its own nature has to be understood. Clearly, this is a definition according to agency and hence its validity is provisional. From this definition, therefore, one cannot conclude that a given *dhamma* is a substantial bearer of its qualities or "own-nature". The duality between *dhamma* and *sabhava* is only an attribution made for the convenience of definition. For, in actual fact both terms denote the same actuality. Hence, it is categorically stated that apart from *sabhava* there is no distinct entity called a *dhamma*,[35] and that the term *sabhava* signifies the mere fact

---

26. See *Abhidhammatthasangaha Vibhavini Tika,* 4.
27. Ibid.
28. Ibid.
29. Ibid.; cf. *Visuddhi Magga,* 141.
30. Cf. *Abhidhammavatara,* 117; Ibid. 16.
31. *Visuddhi Magga,* 484.
32. Ibid. 491.
33. *Dighanikaya Tika,* 28.
34. *Abhidhammavatara,* 16; *Abhidhammatthasangaha Vibhavini Tika,* 4.
35. *Abhidhamma Mulatika,* 21.

of being a *dhamma*.[36] If the *dhamma* has no function distinct from its *sabhava*,[37] and if *dhamma* and *sabhava* denote the same thing,[38] why is the *dhamma* invested with the function of bearing its own-nature? For this implies the recognition of an agency distinct from the *dhamma*. This, it is observed, is done not only to conform with the inclinations of those who are to be instructed,[39] but also to impress upon us the fact that there is no agent behind the *dhamma*.[40] The point being emphasized is that the dynamic world of sensory experience is not due to causes other than the self-same *dhammas* into which it is finally reduced. It is the inter-connection of the *dhammas* through causal relations that explains the variety and diversity of contingent existence and not some kind of trans-empirical reality, which serves as their metaphysical ground. Nor is it due to the fiat of a creator god[41] because there is no divine creator over and above the flow of mental and material phenomena.[42]

Stated otherwise, the definition of *dhamma* as that which bears its own-nature means that any *dhamma* represents a distinct fact of empirical existence which is not shared by other *dhammas*. Hence, *sabhava* is also defined as that which is not held in common by others,[43] as the nature peculiar to each *dhamma*[44] and as the own-nature is not predicable of other *dhammas*.[45] It is also observed that if the *dhammas* are said to have own-nature this is only a tentative device to drive home the point that there is no other-nature from which they emerge and to which they finally lapse.[46] Now this commentarial definition of *dhamma* as *sabhava* poses an important problem, for it seems to go against an earlier Theravada tradition recorded in the canonical *Patisambhida Magga*. This text states that the *khandhas* are devoid of own-nature.[47] Since the *dhammas* are the elementary constituents of the aggregates, which are empty, this should mean that the *dhammas*, too, are devoid of own-nature. What is more, does not the very use of the term *sabhava*, despite all the qualifications under which it is used, give the impression that a given *dhamma* exists in its own right? And does this not amount to the admission that a *dhamma* is some kind of substance?

The commentators were not unaware of these implications and they therefore took the necessary steps to forestall such a conclusion. This they sought to do by supplementing the former definition with another, which actually nullifies the conclusion that the *dhammas* might be quasi-substances. This additional definition states that a *dhamma* is not that which bears its own-nature, but that which is borne by its own conditions.[48] Whereas the earlier def-

36. Ibid. 70.
37. *Abhidhammavatara*, 210.
38. *Abhidhamma Mulatika*, 121.
39. *Dighanikaya Tika*, 76.
40. Ibid. 673; cf. *Abhidhamma Mulatika*, 66; see also *Visuddhimagga Sannaya*, V 184, *Visuddhi Magga*, 484.
41. *Visuddhi Magga*, 513.
42. Ibid.
43. *Visuddhi Magga*, 482.
44. *Abhidhammavatara*, 393.
45. *Visuddhi Magga*, 482.
46. *Abhidhammavatara*, 123.
47. *Patisambhida Magga*, II 211.
48. *Abhidhammavatara*, 414; *Dhammasangani Atthakatha*, 63; *Patisambhida Magga*, 18; *Mohavicchedani*, 6.

inition is agent-denotation, because it attributes an active role to the *dhamma*, elevating it to the position of an agent, the new definition is object-denotation because it attributes a passive role to the *dhamma* and thereby downgrades it to the position of an object. What is radical about this new definition is that it reverses the whole process, which otherwise might culminate in the conception of *dhammas* as substances or bearers of their own-nature. What it seeks to show is that, far from being a bearer, a *dhamma* is being borne by its own conditions.

Consonant with this situation, it is also maintained that there is no other thing called a *dhamma* than the "quality" of being borne by conditions.[49] The same idea is expressed in the oft-recurrent statement that what is called a *dhamma* is the mere fact of occurrence due to appropriate conditions.[50] In point of fact, in commenting upon the *Patisambhida Magga* statement that the *khandhas* – and, by implication, the *dhammas* – are devoid of *sabhava,* the commentator observes that since the aggregates have no self-nature, they are devoid of own-nature.[51] It will thus be seen that although the term *sabhava* is used as a synonym for *dhamma,* it is interpreted in such a way that it means the very absence of *sabhava* in any sense that implies a substantial mode of being.

Another common definition of *dhamma* is that which bears its own-characteristic (*salakkhana*).[52] Since this is used in the same sense as *sabhava*, this definition carries more or less the same implications. That each *dhamma* has its own characteristic is illustrated with reference to colour, which is one of the secondary material elements. Although colour is divisible as blue, yellow, etc., the characteristic peculiar to all varieties of colour is their visibility.[53] Hence, it is also called "individual characteristic".[54] As in the case of *dhamma* and *sabhava*, so in the case of *dhamma* and *salakkhana*, too, their duality is only a convenient assumption made for the purpose of definition. For, it is a case of attributing duality to that which has no duality.[55] And since it is only an attribution it is based on interpretation[56] and not on actuality.[57] Hence, the definition of the earth element – as that which has the characteristic of solidity[58] – is said to be invalid from an ultimate point of view, because of the assumed duality between the element and its characteristic. The correct definition is the one stating that solidity itself is the earth element, for this does not assume a distinction between the characteristic and what is characterized thereby.[59]

As the own-characteristic represents the characteristic peculiar to each *dhamma*, the universal characteristics are the characteristics common to all the *dhammas*. If the former is indi-

49. *Abhidhamma Mulatika,* 21; Ibid. 22.
50. *Visuddhimagga Tika,* 462; see also *Abhidhammavatara,* 116; *Visuddhimagga Sannaya,* v.132.
51. *Patisambhida Magga,* III 634.
52. *Vibhanga Atthakatha,* 45; see also *Visuddhimagga Sannaya,* v.273; *Visuddhi Magga,* 359.
53. *Patisambhida Magga,* I 16; *Visuddhi Magga,* 24.
54. *Samyutta Atthakatha,* II 213; *Visuddhi Magga,* 520.
55. *Abhidhammatthavikasini,* 156.
56. *Visuddhi Magga,* 362.
57. *Abhidhammatthasangaha Vibhavini Tika,* 32; *Abhidhammatthasangaha-Sannaya,* 52.
58. *Visuddhi Magga,* 321.
59. Cf. *Visuddhi Magga,* 362.

vidually predicable, the latter are universally predicable.[60] Their difference goes still further. As the own-characteristic is another name for the *dhamma*, it represents a fact having an objective counterpart. It is not a product of mental construction,[61] but an actual datum of objective existence and as such an ultimate datum of sense experience. On the other hand, what is called universal characteristic has no objective existence because it is a product of mental construction, the synthetic function of mind, and is superimposed on the ultimate data of empirical existence. On this interpretation, the three characteristics of conditioned reality – namely, the origination, cessation and the alteration of that which exists – are universal characteristics. Because they have no objective reality they are not elevated to the status of *dhammas*. If they were to be so elevated, that would undermine the very foundation of the *dhamma* theory. If, for instance, origination, subsistence and dissolution[62] are postulated as real and discrete entities, then it would be necessary to postulate another set of secondary characteristics to account for their own origination, subsistence and dissolution, thus resulting in an infinite regress.[63] This is the significance of the commentarial observation: "It is not correct to assume that origination originates, decay decays, and cessation ceases because such an assumption leads to the fallacy of infinite regress."[64] The difference between the particular characteristic and the universal characteristic is also shown in the way they become knowable, for while the particular characteristic is known as a datum of sense perception, the universal characteristic is known through a process of inference.[65]

In what sense the *dhammas* represent the final limits into which empirical existence can be analyzed is another question that drew the attention of the Theravada commentators. It is in answer to this that the term *paramattha* ("real and ultimate") came to be used as another expression for *dhamma*. It was noted earlier that the use of this term in this sense was occasioned by the Theravadins' response to the Puggalavadins' assertion that the person exists as real and ultimate. In the *Abhidhamma* this term *paramattha* is defined to mean that which has reached its highest,[66] implying thereby that the *dhammas* are ultimate existents with no possibility of further reduction. Hence own-nature (*sabhava*) came to be further defined as ultimate nature (*paramattha-sabhava*).[67] The term *paramattha* is sometimes paraphrased as "the actual".[68] This is explained to mean that the *dhammas* are not non-existent like an illusion or mirage or like the soul and primordial nature of the non-Buddhist schools of thought.[69] The evidence for their existence is not based either on conventions or on mere scriptural authority.[70] On the

60. *Dighanikaya Tika*, 105; cf. *Samyutta Atthakatha*, II 291.
61. See *Abhidhammatthasangaha Vibhavini Tika*, 32.
62. These are the three phases of a momentary *dhamma*, according to the Theravada version of the theory of moments.
63. See *Abhidhammatthavikasini*, 288; *Mohavicchedani*, 67.
64. *Mohavicchedani*, 67–68.
65. *Dighanikaya Tika*, 105.
66. *Abhidhammatthasangaha Vibhavini Tika*.
67. *Abhidhammatthasangaha-Sannaya*, 3.
68. *Mohavicchedani*, 258.
69. Ibid.; *Abhidhammatthavikasini*, 123.
70. *Mohavicchedani*, 258; *Kathavatthu Atthakatha*, 8.

contrary, their very existence is vouchsafed by their own intrinsic nature.[71] The very fact of their existence is the very mark of their reality. As observed in the *Visuddhi Magga*:

> [*Dhamma*] is that which, for those who examine it with the eye of under-standing, is not misleading like an illusion, deceptive like a mirage, or undiscoverable like the self of the sectarians, but is rather the domain of noble knowledge as the real un-misleading actual state.[72]

The kind of existence implied here is not past or future existence, but present actual and veri-fiable existence.[73] This emphasis on their actuality in the present phase of time rules out any association with the Sarvastivadins' theory of tri-temporal existence. Thus, for the Theravadin, the use of the term *paramattha* does not carry any substantialist implications. It only means that the mental and material *dhammas* represent the utmost limits to which the analysis of empirical existence can be pushed.

The description of *dhammas* as *paramattha* means not only their objective existence, but also their cognizability in an ultimate sense.[74] The former refers to the fact that the *dhammas* obtain as the ultimate, irreducible data of empirical existence. The latter refers to the fact that, as such, the content of our cognition can also be finally analyzed into the self-same elements. This is not to suggest that it is only the *dhammas* that become objects of knowledge; for it is specifically stated that even concepts, which are the products of the synthetical function of the mind and hence lack objective counterparts, are also knowable.[75] In point of fact, in the tech-nical terminology of the *Abhidhamma*, the term *dhamma* is sometimes used in a wider sense to include anything that is knowable.[76] In this sense, not only the ultimate realities – the *dham-mas* proper – but also the products of mental interpretation are called *dhammas*. To distinguish the two, the latter are called "*dhammas* devoid of objective reality".[77] The use of this term in this wider sense is reminiscent of its earlier meaning as used in the Pali Nikayas, where in a very general sense it includes all cognizable things on the empirical level. However, there is this situation to be noted: Although both *dhammas* and concepts constitute the content of knowledge, it is into the *dhammas* that the content of knowledge can be finally analyzed. Thus, there is a close parallel between the *dhammas* on the one hand and the contents of knowledge on the other. That is to say, the ultimate irreducible data of cognition are the subjective coun-terparts of the ultimate irreducible data of objective existence. If the term *paramattha* brings into focus the irreducibility of the *dhammas*, the term *aviparitabhava* shows their irreversibil-ity.[78] This term means that the essential characteristic of a *dhamma* is non-alterable and non-

---

71. *Mohavicchedani*, 259.
72. Bhikkhu Nanamoli. *The path of purification* (p.421). Colombo, Ceylon: A. Semage, 1956.
73. *Visuddhi Magga*, II, 159.
74. See *Visuddhi Magga*, 227; *Mohavicchedani*, 258; *Itivuttaka Atthakatha*, 142.
75. *Abhidhammatthavikasini*, 445.
76. Cf. *Abhidhammavatara*, 445.
77. *Abhidhammatthavikasini*, 346; cf. *Visuddhi Magga*, 539.
78. *Abhidhammatthavikasini*, 4; *Visuddhi Magga*, 225.

transferable to any other *dhamma*.[79] It also means that it is impossible for a given *dhamma* to undergo any modification of its specific characteristic even when it is in association with some other *dhamma*.[80] The same situation remains true despite the differences in the time factor, for there is no modification in the nature of a *dhamma* corresponding to the divisions in time.[81] Since a *dhamma* and its intrinsic nature are the same (for the duality is only posited for purposes of explanation), to claim that its intrinsic nature undergoes modification is to deny its very existence.

The relative position of the *dhammas* is another aspect of the subject that requires clarification. Do they harmoniously blend into a unity or do they divide themselves into a plurality? In this connection we may do well to examine two of their important characteristics. One is their actual inseparability,[82] the other their conditioned origination.[83] The first refers to the fact that in a given instance of mind or matter, the elementary constituents (i.e., *dhammas*) that enter into its composition are not actually separable one from another. They exist in a state of inseparable association forming, so to say, a homogeneous unity. This idea is consonant with an earlier tradition recorded in the early Buddhist discourses. For example, in the *Mahavedalla Sutta* of the Majjhima Nikaya it is said that the three mental factors – sensation (*vedana*), cognition (*sanna*) and consciousness (*vinnana*) – are blended so harmoniously that it is impossible to separate them from one another and thus establish their identity.[84] The same idea finds expression in the *Milindapanha*.[85] When Nagasena Thera is asked by King Milinda whether it is possible, in the case of mental factors which exist in harmonious combination, to separate them out and establish a plurality as: "This is contact, and this sensation, and this mentation, and this perception", and so on, the elder answers with a simile:

> Suppose, O king, the cook in the royal household were to make a syrup or a sauce and were to put into it curds, and salt, and ginger, and cumin seed, and pepper and other ingredients. And suppose the king were to say to him: "Pick out for me the flavours of the curds and of the salt, and of the ginger, and of the cumin seed, and of the pepper, and of all the things you have put into it." Now would it be possible, great king, separating off one from another those flavours that had thus run together, to pick out each one, so that one could say: "Here is the sourness, and here the saltiness, and here the pungency, and here the acidity, and here the astringency, and here the sweetness?" [86]

---

79. *Abhidhammatthasangaha Vibhavini Tika*, 62.
80. *Mohavicchedani*, 69.
81. *Visuddhi Magga*, 197; *Abhidhammatthasangaha Vibhavini Tika*, 123.
82. *Visuddhi Magga*, 376, 381; *Abhidhamma Mulatika*, 43; *Tikapatthana*, 59.
83. *Tikapatthana*, 62ff.
84. M I 480.
85. *Milindapanha*, 58–59..
86. T.W. Rhys Davids (Trans.). *The questions of King Milinda* (p.97). New York: Dover, 1963 (reprint).

In like manner, it is maintained, we should understand the position of the mental *dhammas* in relation to one another.[87]

This situation is true of the material *dhammas*, too. In this connection Buddhagosha's *Atthasalini* adds that the material *dhammas*, such as colour, taste, odour, etc., cannot be separated from one another like particles of sand.[88] The colour of the mango, for instance, cannot be physically separated from its taste or odour. They remain in inseparable association. This is what is called positional inseparability.[89] On the basis of this principle of positional inseparability it is maintained that there is no quantitative difference among the material elements that enter into the composition of material objects. The difference is only qualitative. And this qualitative difference is based on what is called "intensity or extrusion".[90] To give an example: As the four primary elements of matter are invariably present in every instance of matter, for they are necessarily co-existent and positionally inseparable,[91] the question arises why there is a diversity in material objects. The diversity, it is maintained, is not due to a difference in quantity, but to a difference in intensity.[92] That is to say, in a given material object one primary element is more intense than the others. For instance, in a relatively solid thing such as a stone, although all the primary elements are present, the earth element is more intense or "extruded" than the others. So is the water element in liquids, the heat element in fire, and the air element in gases.[93] The best illustration for the relative position of the material elements is given in the *Visuddhi Magga* where it is said:

> And just as whomsoever the great creatures such as the spirits grasp hold of [possess], they have no standing place either inside him or outside him and yet they have no standing independently of him, so too these elements are not found to stand either inside or outside each other, yet they have no standing independently of one another.[94]

This explanation is justified on the following grounds: If they were to exist inside each other, then they would not perform their respective functions. If they were to exist outside each other, then they would be resolvable.[95] The principle of positional inseparability is also resorted to as a critique of the distinction between substance and quality. Hence it is contended that in the case of material elements, which are positionally inseparable it is not possible to say: "This is the quality of that one and that is the quality of this one."[96] The foregoing observations should show that

87. For other illustrations, see *Dhammasangani Atthakatha*, 273; M II 287; *Abhidhammatthavikasini*, 293.
88. *Dhammasangani Atthakatha*, 270.
89. See *Abhidhammatthasangaha*, 28; *Visuddhimagga Sannaya*, 389.
90. See *Visuddhi Magga*, 451; *Abhidhammatthavikasini*, 273.
91. See *Tikapatthana*, 3, 14, 16; *Abhidhammatthasangaha*, 28.
92. *Visuddhi Magga*, 451; *Abhidhammatthavikasini*, 273.
93. See Y. Karunadasa. *Buddhist analysis of matter* (p. 26). Colombo, Ceylon: Dept. of Cultural Affairs, 1967.
94. *Visuddhi Magga*, 387.
95. *Visuddhi Magga*, 364; see also *Abhidhammatthavikasini*, 248.
96. *Visuddhi Magga*, 444-445.

the mental as well as the material *dhammas* are not actually separable one from another.

In the case of the mental *dhammas*, the term used is "conjoined"; in the case of the material *dhammas*, the term used is "inseparable". This raises the question why the *dhammas* are presented as a plurality. The answer is that although they are not actually separable, they are distinguishable one from another.[97] It is this distinguish-ability that serves as the foundation of the *dhamma* theory. Hence it is often mentioned in the Pali sub-commentaries that the real nature of the things that are distinguishable can be brought into focus only through analysis.[98] This distinguish-ability is possible because although the *dhammas* are harmoniously blended in reality, they are cognized severally[99] and are thus established as if they were separate entities. It is, however, maintained that material *dhammas* are much more easily distinguished than mental *dhammas*.[100] For instance, the distinction between colour, odour, taste, touch, etc., is easy even for an ordinary person to make, while to distinguish mental phenomena one from another is said to be the most difficult task of all. This situation is well illustrated in the following reply given by Nagasena Thera to King Milinda:

> Suppose, O king, a man were to wade down into the sea, and taking some water in the palm of his hand, were to taste it with his tongue. Would he distinguish whether it were water from the Jumna, or from the Aciravati, or from the Mahi? More difficult than that, great king, is it to distinguish between the mental conditions which follow on the exercise of any one of the organs of sense, telling us that such is contact, and such sensation, and such idea, and such intention, and such thought.[101]

The other characteristic, which was referred to earlier, is the conditioned origination of the *dhammas*. This is akin to the conception discussed above, for it also seeks to explain the nature of the *dhammas* from a synthetic point of view. In this connection five postulates are recognized as axiomatic, either implicitly or explicitly:

> (i) It is not empirically possible to identify an absolute original cause of the "*dhammic*" process. Such a metaphysical conception is not in accord with Buddhism's empirical doctrine of causality, the purpose of which is not to explain how the world began but to describe the uninterrupted continuity of the *samsaric* process whose absolute beginning is not conceivable.[102] In this connection it must also be remembered that as a system of philosophy the *Abhidhamma* is descriptive and not speculative.

---

97. See e.g., *Abhidhammatthasangaha Vibhavini Tika*, 5; *Visuddhi Magga*, 21; *Abhidhammatthavikasini*, 22.
98. *Abhidhammatthavikasini*, 22; *Visuddhi Magga*, 470.
99. *Milindapanha*, 58-59.
100. M II 287.
101. *Questions of King Milinda*, p.142.
102. S II 178.

(ii) Nothing arises without the appropriate conditions necessary for its origination. This rules out the theory of "fortuitous origination".[103]

(iii) Nothing arises from a single cause. This rules out theories of a single cause.[104] Their rejection is of great significance, showing that the *Abhidhammic* view of existence rejects all monistic theories, which seek to explain the origin of the world from a single cause, whether this single cause is conceived as a personal god or an impersonal godhead. It also serves as a critique of those metaphysical theories, which attempt to reduce the world of experience to an underlying trans-empirical principle.

(iv) Nothing arises singly, as a solitary phenomenon.[105] Thus on the basis of a single cause or on the basis of a plurality of causes; a single effect does not arise. The invariable situation is that there is always a plurality of effects. It is on the rejection of the four views referred to above that the *Abhidhammic* doctrine of conditionality is founded.

(v) From a plurality of conditions a plurality of effects takes place. Applied to the *dhamma* theory, this means that a multiplicity of *dhammas* brings about a multiplicity of other *dhammas*.[106]

One implication that follows from the conditionality of the *dhammas* as discussed so far is that they invariably arise as clusters. This is true of both mental and material *dhammas*. Hence it is that whenever consciousness (*citta*) arises, together with it there arise at least seven mental concomitants (*cetasika*), namely, contact (*phassa*), sensation (*vedana*), cognition (*sanna*), volition (*cetana*), one-pointedness (*ekaggata*), psychological life (*arupa-jivitindriya*), and attention (*manasikara*). These seven are called "universal mental factors", because they are invariably present even in the most minimal unit of consciousness. Thus a psychic instance can never occur with less than eight constituents, i.e. consciousness and its seven invariable concomitants. Their relation is one of necessary co-nascence. We thus can see that even the smallest psychic unit or moment of consciousness turns out to be a complex co-relational system. In the same way, the smallest unit of matter, which is called the basic octad, is in the ultimate analysis a cluster of (eight) material elements, namely, the four primary elements – earth, water, fire and air – and four of the secondaries, colour, odour, taste and nutritive essence. None of these eight material elements arises singly because they are necessarily co-nascent and positionally inseparable.[107] It will thus be seen that in the sphere of mind as well as in the domain of matter there are no solitary phenomena. It is in the light of these observations that the question

---

103. D I 28; *Udana*, 69.
104. *Dhammasangani Atthakatha*, 78.
105. Ibid. 79.
106. Ibid. 78ff.
107. See Narada Thera, *A manual of Abhidhamma* (pp.79ff). Colombo, Ceylon: Vajirarama, 1956; Y. Karunadasa. *Buddhist analysis of matter* (pp.155ff). Colombo, Ceylon: Dept. of Cultural Affairs, 1967.

posed earlier as to whether the *dhammas* exhibit a unity or a plurality has to be discussed. The answer seems to veer towards both alternatives although it appears paradoxical to say so. In so far as the *dhammas* are distinguishable, one from another, to that extent they exhibit plurality. In so far as they are not actually separable, one from another, to that extent they exhibit unity. The reason for this situation is the methodological apparatus employed by the Abhidhammikas in explaining the nature of empirical existence. As mentioned earlier, this consists of both analysis and synthesis. Analysis, when not supplemented by synthesis, leads to pluralism. Synthesis, when not supplemented by analysis, leads to monism. What one finds in the *Abhidhamma* is a *combined use* of both methods. This results in a philosophical vision, which beautifully transcends the dialectical opposition between monism and pluralism.

Concepts (*pannatti*) and the two realities

What emerges from this *Abhidhammic* doctrine of *dhammas* is a critical realism, one which (unlike idealism) recognizes the distinctness of the world from the experiencing subject yet also distinguishes between those types of entities that truly exist independently of the cognitive act and those that owe their being to the act of cognition itself. How does this doctrine interpret the "common-sense" view of the world, which is a kind of naive realism in the sense that it tends to recognize realities as more or less corresponding to all linguistic terms? In other words, what relation is there between the *dhammas*, the ultimate elements of existence, and the objects of common-sense realism? What degree of reality, if any, could be bestowed on the latter?

It is in their answers to these questions that the Abhidhammikas formulated the theory of concepts or designations (*pannatti*) together with a distinction drawn between two kinds of reality, conventional and ultimate. This theory assumes significance in another context. In most of the Indian philosophies, which were associated with the *atma*-tradition (of selfness) and subscribed to a substantialist view of existence, such categories as time and space came to be defined in absolute terms. The problem for the Abhidhammikas was how to explain such categories without committing themselves to the same metaphysical assumptions. The theory of *pannatti* was the answer to this. What may be described as the first formal definition of *pannatti* occurs in the *Dhammasangani*.[108] Here the three terms, *pannatti, nirutti* and *adhivacana* are used synonymously and each term is defined by lumping together a number of appropriate equivalents. In Rhys Davids' translation:

> That which is an enumeration, that which is a designation, an expression (*pannatti*), a current term, a name, a denomination, the assigning of a name, an interpretation, a distinctive mark of discourse on this or that *dhamma*.[109]

---

108. *Dhammasangani,* 110.
109. Rhys-Davids, C.A.F. *Buddhist manual of psychological ethics* (p.340). London, The Royal Asiatic Society, 1923.

Immediately after this definition, a "predication of equipollent terms",[110] it is observed that all the *dhammas* constitute the pathway of *pannattis*.[111]

As shown by this definition, designation is the *pannatti*; what is designated thereby is the *pannatti-patha*. Whether the term *pannatti*, as used here, denotes the individual names given to each and every *dhamma* only, or whether it also denotes names assigned to various combinations of the *dhammas*, is not explicitly stated. It may be noted that according to the *Abhidhamma* every combination of the objectively real *dhammas* represents a nominal reality, not an objective reality. The fact that the term *pannatti* includes names of both categories, the objective and the nominal, is suggested not only by what is stated elsewhere in the *Abhidhamma*,[112] but also by the later interpretation. We may conclude then that according to the *Dhammasangani* definition *pannatti* denotes all names, terms and symbols that are expressive of the real existents as well as of their combinations in different forms. Another important fact that should not be overlooked here is that according to the later inference *pannatti* includes not only names (*nama*) but also ideas corresponding to them. Since the assignment of a designation creates an idea corresponding to it, we may interpret the above definition to include both. It is true of course that the *dhammas* do not exist in dependence on the operation of the mind, on their being designated by a term and conceptualized by mind. Nevertheless the assignment of names to the *dhammas* involves a process of conceptualization. Hence *pannatti* includes not only the names of things, whether they are real or nominal, but also all the concepts corresponding to them.

This theory of *pannatti*, presented as ancillary to the doctrine of *dhammas*, is not a complete innovation on the part of the *Abhidhamma*. Such a theory is clearly implied in the early Buddhist analysis of empirical existence into the aggregates, sense bases, and elements, and the only really new feature in the *pannatti* theory is its systematic formulation. Accordingly, the term "person" becomes a common designation (*sammuti*) given to a congeries of dependently originated psycho-physical factors:

> Just as there arises the name "chariot" when there is a set of appropriate
> constituents, even so there comes to be this convention "living being" when
> the five aggregates are present.[113]

There is, however, this important difference to be noted: The early Buddhist idea of *sammuti* is not based on a formulated doctrine of real existents. Although what is analyzed is called *sammuti*, that into which it is analyzed is not called *paramattha*. This development is found only in the *Abhidhamma*, as we have already seen. We should also note that in the *Abhidhamma* a clear distinction is drawn between *sammuti* and *pannatti*. *Pannatti*, as we have seen, refers to terms (*nama*) expressive of things both real/ultimate (*paramattha*) and conven-

---

110. Ibid.
111. *Dhammasangani*, 110.
112. Cf. *Kathavatthu* controversy on the concept of person (*puggala*).
113. S I 135..

tion-based (*sammuti*) and the ideas corresponding to them. In contrast, *sammuti* is used in a restricted sense to mean only what is convention-based. It is this meaning that finds expression in the compound *sammuti-sacca* (conventional reality). That for the *Abhidhamma sammuti* is not the same as *pannatti* is also seen by the fact that in the *Dhammasangani* definition of *pannatti* quoted above, the term *sammuti* does not occur among its synonyms.

Although the theory of *pannatti* is formally introduced in the works of the *Abhidhamma* basket, it is in the *Abhidhamma* commentaries that we find more specific definitions of the term along with many explanations on the nature and scope of *pannattis* and on how they become objects of cognition. For example, because *pannattis* are without corresponding objective reality, the commentaries call them "things without a real nature" (*asabhava-dhammas*) to distinguish them from the real elements of existence.[114] Since *sabhava*, the intrinsic nature of a *dhamma*, is itself the *dhamma*, from the point of view of this definition what is qualified as *asabhava* amounts to an *abhava*, a non-existent in the final sense. It is in recognition of this fact that the three salient characteristics of empirical reality – origination, subsistence and dissolution – are not applied to them. For these three characteristics can be predicated only of those things which answer to the *Abhidhammic* definition of empirical reality.[115] Again, unlike the real existents, *pannattis* are not brought about by conditions. For this same reason, they are also defined as "not positively produced". Positive production is true only of those things which have their own individual nature.[116] Only a *dhamma* with a beginning and an end in time, produced by conditions, and marked by the three salient characteristics of conditioned existence, is positively produced.[117]

Further, *pannattis* differ from *dhammas* in that only the latter are delimited by rise and fall; only of the *dhammas* and not of the *pannattis* can it be said, "They come into being having not been; and, after having been, they cease."[118] *Pannattis* have no own-nature to be manifested in the three instants of arising, presence and dissolution. Since they have no existence marked by these three phases, such temporal distinctions as past, present and future do not apply to them. Consequently they have no reference to time.[119] For this self-same reason they have no place in the traditional analysis of empirical existence into the *khandhas*, for what is included in the *khandhas* should have the characteristics of empirical reality and be subject to temporal divisions.[120] Another noteworthy characteristic of *pannattis* is that they cannot be described either as conditioned or as unconditioned, for they do not possess their own-nature (*sabhava*) which is necessary to be so described. [121] Since the two categories of the conditioned and the unconditioned comprise all realities, the description of *pannattis* as exempt from these two categories is another way of underscoring their unreality.

---

114. *Abhidhammatthavikasini*, 346.
115. See *Kathavatthu Atthakatha*, 198-199.
116. *Abhidhamma Mulatika*, 114ff.
117. Ibid. 116.
118. *Visuddhi Magga*, 210.
119. Cf. *Abhidhammatthasangaha Vibhavini Tika*, 36.
120. M II 299.
121. Cf. *Kathavatthu Atthakatha*, 92.

What the foregoing observations amount to is that while a *dhamma* is a truly existent thing, a *pannatti* is a thing merely conceptualized.[122] The former is an existent verifiable by its own distinctive intrinsic characteristic,[123] but the latter, being a product of the mind's synthetic function, exists only by virtue of thought. It is a mental construct of things and hence possesses no objective counterpart. It is the imposition of oneness on what actually is a complex that gives rise to *pannattis*.[124] With the dissolution of the appearance of unity,[125] the oneness disappears and the complex nature is disclosed.

Thus, as when the component parts such as axles, wheels, frame, poles, and so on, are arranged in a certain way, there comes to be the mere term of common usage "chariot", yet in the ultimate sense, when each part is examined, there is no chariot, and just as when the component parts of a house such as wattles, etc., are placed so that they enclose a space in a certain way, there comes to be the mere term of common usage "house", yet in the ultimate sense there is no house, and just as when trunk, branches, foliage, etc., are placed in a certain way, there comes to be the mere term of common usage "tree", yet in the ultimate sense, when each component is examined, there is no tree, so too, when there are the five aggregates (as objects) of clinging, there comes to be the mere term of common usage of a "being", and a "person", yet in the ultimate sense, when each component is examined, there is no being as a basis for the assumption "I am" or "I".[126] The imposition of oneness on what is complex should be understood in a similar way. So, two kinds of *pannatti* are distinguished. One is called *nama-pannatti* and the other *attha-pannatti*. The first refers to names, words, signs or symbols through which things, real or unreal, are designated: "It is the mere mode of recognizing by way of this or that word whose significance is determined by worldly convention."[127] It is created by worldly consent and established by worldly usage.[128] The other, called *attha-pannatti*, refers to ideas, notions or concepts corresponding to the names, words, signs or symbols. It is produced by the interpretative function of the mind and is based on the various forms or appearances presented by the real elements when they are in particular situations or positions.[129] Both *nama-pannatti* and *attha-pannatti* thus have a psychological origin and as such are devoid of objective reality.

Nama-pannatti is often defined as that which makes known and *attha-pannatti* as that which is made known.[130] The former is an instance of agency definition and the latter of object definition. What both attempt to show is that *nama-pannatti*, which makes *attha-pannatti* known, and *attha-pannatti* which is made known by *nama-pannatti*, are mutually interdependent and therefore logically inseparable. This explains the significance of another defi-

122. *Abhidhammatthasangaha Vibhavini Tika*, 52-53.
123. *Vissudhi Magga*, 198.
124. Ibid. 137.
125. *Dighanikaya Tika*, 123.
126. Bhikkhu Nanamoli (1956, p.458).
127. *Visuddhi Magga*, 225
128. *Abhidhammatthasangaha Vibhavini Tika*, 53.
129. *Abhidhammatthasangaha Vibhavini Tika*, 151; *Abhidhammatthavikasini*, 317ff; *Milindapanha*,7-8.
130. *Abhidhammatthasangaha*, 39; *Abhidhammatthasangaha Vibhavini Tika*, 151; *Sahassavatthu*, vv.37ff.

nition, which states that *nama-pannatti* is the relationship of the term with the ideas and that *attha-pannatti* is the relationship of the idea with the terms.[131] These two pairs of definition show that the two processes of conceptualization and verbalization through the symbolic medium of language are but two separate aspects of the same phenomenon. It is for the convenience of definition that what really amounts to a single phenomenon is treated from two different angles, angles which represent two ways of looking at the same thing. The difference is established by defining the same word, *pannatti*, in two different ways. When it is defined as subject it is *nama-pannatt*, the concept as name. When it is defined as object it is *attha-pannatti*, the concept as meaning. If the former is that which expresses, the latter is that which is expressible.[132 133] Since *attha-pannatti* stands for the process of conceptualization it represents more the subjective and dynamic aspect, and since *nama-pannatti* stands for the process of verbalization it represents more the objective and static aspect. For, the assignment of a term to what is constructed in thought – in other words, its expression through the symbolic medium of language – invests it with some kind of relative permanence and objectivity. It is crystallized into an entity.

Now the definition of *attha-pannatti* as that, which is made known by *nama-pannatti*, gives rise to the question as to what its position is in relation to the real existents (*dhammas*). For if the real existents, too, can be made known (*attha-pannatti*), on what basis are the two categories, the real and conceptual, to be distinguished? What should not be overlooked here is that according to its very definition *attha-pannatti* exists by virtue of its being conceived and expressed. Hence it is incorrect to explain *attha-pannatti* as that which is conceptualizable and expressible, for its very existence stems from the act of being conceptualized and expressed. This rules out the possibility of its existing without being conceptualized and expressed. In the case of the *dhammas* or real existents the situation is quite different. While they can be made known by *nama-pannatti*, their existence is not dependent on their being known or conceptualized. Where such a real existent is made known by a *nama-pannatti*, the latter is called *vijjamana-pannatti*,[134] because it represents something that exists in the real and ultimate sense (*paramatthato*). And the notion or concept (equals *attha-pannatti*) corresponding to it is called *tajja-pannatti*, the verisimilar or appropriate concept.[135] This does not mean that the real existent has transformed itself into a concept. It only means that a concept corresponding to it has been established.

While the doctrine of *dhammas* led to its ancillary theory of *pannatti* as discussed above, both in turn led to another development, that is, the distinction drawn between two kinds of truth as *sammuti-sacca* (conventional reality and *paramattha-sacca* (absolute reality). Although this distinction is an *Abhidhammic* innovation it is not completely dissociated from the early Buddhist teachings, for the antecedent trends that led to its formulation can be traced

---

131. *Abhidhammatthasangaha-Sannaya,* v.53.
132. *Abhidhammatthasangaha-Sannaya,* 159.
133. *Abhidhammatthasangaha-Sannaya,* v.54.
134. *Sahassavatthu,* v.68; M I 55.
135. Ibid.

to the early Buddhist scriptures themselves. One such instance is the distinction drawn in the Anguttara Nikaya between *nitattha* and *neyyattha*.[136] The former refers to those statements, which have their meaning "drawn out" (*nita-attha*), that is, to be taken as they stand, as explicit and definitive statements. The latter refers to those statements which require their meaning "to be drawn out" (*neyya-attha*). The distinction alluded to here may be understood in a broad way as the difference between the direct and the indirect meaning. The distinction is so important that to overlook it is to misrepresent the teachings of the Buddha:

> Whoever declares a discourse with a meaning already drawn out as a discourse with a meaning to be drawn out and (conversely) whoever declares a discourse with a meaning to be drawn out as a discourse with a meaning already drawn out, such a one makes a false statement with regard to the Blessed One.[137]

It seems very likely that it is this distinction between *nitattha* and *neyyattha* which has provided the basis for the emergence of the *Abhidhammic* theory of double reality, and, in point of fact, the commentary to the Anguttara Nikaya seeks to establish a correspondence between the original sutta-passage and the Theravada version of the two kinds of reality.[138]

One interesting feature in the Theravada version of the theory is the use of the term *sammuti* for relative reality. For in all other schools of Buddhist thought the term used is *satvati*. The difference is not simply that between Pali and Sanskrit, for the two terms differ both in etymology and meaning. The term *sammuti* is derived from the root *man*, to think, and when prefixed with *sam* it means consent, convention and general agreement. On the other hand, the term *satvati* is derived from the root *va*, to cover, and when prefixed with *sam* it means covering, concealment. This difference is not confined to the vocabulary of the theory of double reality alone. That elsewhere, too, Sanskrit *satvati* corresponds to Pali *sammuti* is confirmed by other textual instances.[139] Since *sammuti* refers to convention or general agreement, *sammuti-sacca* means truth based on convention or general agreement. On the other hand, the idea behind *satvati-satya* is that which covers up the real nature of things and makes them appear otherwise.[140]

The validity of the two kinds of statement corresponding to *sammuti* and *paramattha* is set out as follows:

> Statements referring to convention-based things (*sanketa*) are valid because they are based on common agreement; statements referring to ultimate cat-

136. A II 60.
137. Ibid.
138. A II 118.
139. See e.g. *Bodhisattvabhumi*, Ed. U. Wogihara (Tokyo, 1930-1936), p.48; see *Abhidhammatthasangaha-Sannaya*, 159.
140. See *Bodhicaryavatara-panjika* (Bibliotheca Indica, Calcutta, 1904-1914, p.170). For a detailed account of the theories of reality as presented by various Buddhist schools, see L. de la Vallée Poussin, *Les deux, les quatre, les trois verités: Mélanges Chinois et Bouddhiques*, Vol. V, pp.159ff..

egories (*paramattha*) are valid because they are based on the true nature of the real existents.[141]

The distinction between the two realities depends on the distinction between *sanketa* and *paramattha*. *Sanketa* includes things which depend for their being on mental interpretations superimposed on the category of the real.[142] For instance, the validity of the term "table" is based not on an objective existent corresponding to the term, but on a mental interpretation superimposed on a congeries of material *dhammas* organized in a particular manner. Although a table is not a separate reality distinct from the material *dhammas* that enter into its composition, nevertheless the table is said to exist because in common parlance it is accepted as a separate reality. On the other hand, the term *paramattha* denotes the category of real existents (*dhammas*), which have their own objective nature (*sabhava*). Their difference may be set out as follows: when a particular situation is explained on the basis of terms indicative of the real elements of existence (the *dhammas*), that explanation is *paramattha-sacca*. When the self-same situation is explained on the basis of terms indicative of things which have their being dependent on the mind's synthetic function (i.e., *pannatti*), that explanation is *sammuti-sacca*. The validity of the former is based on its correspondence to the ultimate data of empirical reality, which validity is based on its correspondence to things established by convention.

As pointed out by K.N. Jayatilleke in his *Early Buddhist Theory of Knowledge*, one misconception about the Theravada version of double truth is that *paramattha-sacca* is superior to *sammuti-sacca* and that "what is true in the one sense is false in the other."[143] This observation that the distinction in question is not based on a theory of degrees of truth will become clear from the following free translation of the relevant passages contained in three commentaries:

> Herein references to living beings, gods, Brahma, etc., are *sammuti-katha*, whereas references to impermanence, suffering, ego-lessness, the aggregates of the empiric individuality, the spheres and elements of sense perception and mind-cognition, bases of mindfulness, right effort, etc., are *paramattha-katha*. One who is capable of understanding and penetrating to the [reality] and hoisting the flag of Arahantship when the teaching is set out in terms of generally accepted conventions, to him the Buddha preaches the doctrine based on *sammuti-katha*. One who is capable of understanding and penetrating to the [reality] and hoisting the flag of Arahantship when the teaching is set out in terms of ultimate categories, to him the Buddha preaches the doctrine based on *paramattha-katha*. To one who is capable of awakening to the [reality] through *sammuti-katha*, the teaching is not presented on the basis of *paramattha-katha*, and conversely, to one who is capable of awakening to the [reality] through *paramattha-katha*, the teaching is not presented on the basis of *sammuti-katha*.

141. A I 54; *Kathavatthu Atthakatha*, 34; D I 251.
142. See *Sahassavatthu*, vv.3ff.
143. Jayatilleke, p.364

There is this simile on this matter: Just as a teacher of the three Vedas who is capable of explaining their meaning in different dialects might teach his pupils, adopting the particular dialect which each pupil understands, even so the Buddha teaches the Dhamma adopting, according to the suitability of the occasion, either the *sammuti-katha* or the *paramattha-katha*. It is by taking into consideration the ability of each individual to understand the Four Noble Truths that the Buddha presents his teaching either by way of *sammuti* or by way of *paramattha* or by way of both. Whatever the method adopted, the purpose is the same: To show the way to "immortality" through the analysis of mental and physical phenomena.[144]

Conclusion

As shown from the above quotation, the penetration of reality is possible by either teaching, the conventional or the ultimate, or by the combination of both. One method is not singled out as superior or inferior to the other. It is like using the dialect that a person readily understands, and there is no implication that one dialect is either superior or inferior to another. What is more, as the commentary to the Anguttara Nikaya states specifically, whether the Buddhas teach according to *sammuti* or to *paramattha*, they teach only what is real, only what accords with actuality, without involving themselves in what is not real (*amusava*).[145] The statement: "The person exists" (equals *sammuti-sacca*) is not erroneous, provided one does not imagine by the person a substance enduring in time. Convention requires the use of such terms, but as long as one does not imagine substantial entities corresponding to them, such statements are valid.[146] On the other hand, as the commentators observe, if for the sake of conforming to the ultimate reality one would say, "The five aggregates eat" or "The five aggregates walk", instead of saying: "A person eats" or "A person walks", such a situation would result in what is called *voharabheda*, that is, a breach of convention resulting in a breakdown in meaningful communication.[147] Hence in presenting the teaching the Buddha does not exceed linguistic conventions,[148] but uses such terms as "person" without being led astray by their superficial implications.[149] Because the Buddha is able to employ such linguistic designations as "person" and "individual" without assuming corresponding substantial entities, he is called "skilled in expression"[150] The use of such terms does not in any way involve falsehood.[151] Skillfulness in the use of words is the ability to conform to conventions (*sammuti*), usages (*vohara*), designations (*pannatti*) and turns of speech (*nirutti*) in common use in the world without being led astray by them.[152] Hence, in understanding the teaching of the Buddha one is advised not to

---

144. A I 54–55; D I 251–52; *Samyutta Atthakatha,* II 77.
145. D I 251.
146. See Jayatilleke, p.365.
147. *Samyutta Atthakatha,* I 51
148. *Kathavatthu Atthakatha,* 103
149. Cf. *Kathavatthu Atthakatha,* 103.
150. S I 51.
151 Cf. M 125.
152 D I 251.

adhere dogmatically to the mere superficial meanings of words.[153]

The foregoing observations should show that according to the Theravada version of double reality, one kind of reality is not held to be superior to the other. Another interesting conclusion to which the foregoing observations lead is that as far as the Theravada is concerned, the distinction between *sammuti-sacca* and *paramattha-sacca* does not refer to two kinds of reality as such but to two ways of presenting reality. Although they are formally introduced as two kinds of reality, they are explained as two modes of expressing what is real. They do not represent two degrees of reality, one of which is superior or inferior to the other. This explains why the two terms, speech (*katha*) and discourse (*desana*), are often used with reference to the two kinds of reality.[154] In this respect the distinction between *sammuti* and *paramattha* corresponds to the distinction made in the earlier scriptures between *nitattha* and *neyyattha*. For, as we saw earlier, no preferential value judgment is made between *nitattha* and *neyyattha*. All that is emphasized is that the two kinds of statement should not be confused. The great advantage in presenting *sammuti* and *paramattha* in this way is that it does not raise the problem of reconciling the concept of a plurality of realities with the well-known statement of the *Suttanipata*: "Reality is indeed one, there is no second".[155]

---

153 *Abhidhammavatara,* 88.
154 A I 54; *Abhidhammatthavikasini,* 324.
155 *Suttanipata,* V 884.

Chapter 12

On Memory And Self

Zhihua Yao

Introduction

There has been a growing interest amongst scholars in the constructive engagement between cognitive science and phenomenology in recent years. Among them is the late Francisco Varela, who coined the term "neurophenomenology" and initiated a series of dialogues engaging western scientists and Buddhist scholars. Various publications of this forum sparked and brought together up-to-date research from various fields of experimental research, especially from psychology, cognitive science, and Buddhist philosophy. These multidisciplinary reflections and discussions were inspiring to examining a puzzling issue with regard to memory and personal identity in the framework of mindful observation and awareness meditation. Particularly, the present author addresses the question whether memory determines one's personality or self? Or is it rather the other way around: Is it one's self that makes memory possible? This chapter covers an attempt to explore the relationship between memory and self by drawing sources mainly from the Yogacara Buddhist scholar Vasubandhu (4th century) who is often considered as a Buddhist psychologist. Having discussed the ambiguous meaning of the Sanskrit term *smrti* (mindfulness), Vasubandhu's views are introduced. These views encompass the conditions of memory and the store-consciousness as the basis for memory and include criticism of his position by Madhyamaka, a competing school founded earlier by Nagarjuna (2nd century). Through this study, the hope is to complement the new field of neurophenomenology with observational insights from Buddhist meditation and ancient wisdom, and to thus contribute to the on-going constructive dialogue between the various disciplines that are involved in the Dharma.

Memory: an information-processing model

In the field of cognitive psychology, there is a current model of mind referred to as the "information-processing model", shown in Figure 1.[i] In this hypothetical construction, information from the external world is pictured as flowing into the senses and, mediated by attention, into the "very-short-term memory", "short-term memory", and "long-term memory", thence to be used in problem solving and decision making, eventually resulting in manifest behaviour,

---

1.   J.W. Hayward & F.J. Varela, Eds., *Gentle bridges: Conversations with the Dalai Lama on the sciences of mind.* Boston: Shambhala Publications, 1992, p.99.

observable in the external world.

In this model of mind, various types of memory plays an important role. On the encoding side, there is the very-short-term memory, also called iconic memory or the sensory register. It has been determined that whenever a stimulus object enters through the sense organs, for example the eyes, it is held in storage in its raw form for a very brief period, for about a quarter of a second. Therefore, experimental psychologists assume that there must be a brief storage system, one that lasts under 250 milliseconds during which visual information is held and within which one's attention can be directed to parts of the information, and from which the information disappears after that brief storage period.[2] According to these researchers, some information from the very-short-term memory that has not been erased or lost and has been the object of attention moves on to the short-term memory that might last up to 20 seconds.

However, neither the sensory register (very-short-term memory) nor the short-term memory is what most people refer to when they speak of memory. They rather mean the long-term memory that might last anywhere from half a minute up to the rest of one's life and which mostly includes what is termed a person's autobiographical memory, knowledge, habits, motives, and so forth. It is usually represented as an independent stable storage structure like a warehouse or a bank. In this view, memory itself is actually a higher level process of remembering which connects the single stored items into a phenomenological whole and into a "memory" of either a fact (declarative memory) or an episodic (autobiographical or self-aware memory). These source memories are usually represented as being housed in an independent stable storage structure like a warehouse or a bank, a metaphor that already occurred to Vasubandhu who elaborated on this subject.

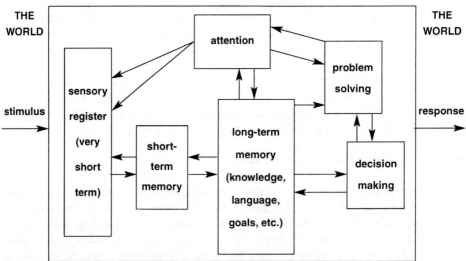

Figure 1. An Information Processing Scheme of Memory (Hayward & Varela, 1992, p.99)

---

2.   Ibid., p. 101.

The information model under scrutiny is an abstraction of mechanisms which does not explain how it is possible to have such a long-term memory. From this storage-bank view there is not much of an idea of impermanence or intention either, which is essential for a Buddhist account. To complement what is missing here, forgetting also needs to be explained. One may speculate about different ways of forgetting: (1) items in long-term storage might decay over time and/or (2) items might be pushed out of memory by new information. Alternatively, (3) there might be no forgetting at all. Despite the passage of time, items might stay in storage "permanently" and more correctly one may then postulate that what may actually be lost is the access to the stored items. Hayward and Varela argue that this possibility cannot be disproved:

> Every time you remember something that you had previously forgotten, it counts as proof of the theory. But when you cannot remember something, even if you never remember it your whole life, you can always say that you have just lost access to it rather than that it is gone from your memory.[3]

Moreover, when one refers to the unconscious of Freudian or Jungian theory, which contains many memories that have been pushed beyond the preconscious – often events, thoughts, fantasies that one does not wish to remember – it is even harder to disprove that what is lost is access to a stored memory rather than the memory itself. All of the discontinuities or forgetting counted to be evidence of the impermanence of memory can be denied or discounted by referring back to a presumably continuous unconscious. This is a great challenge to the experimental method of science, for one of the important canons of scientific investigation is that theories must be disprovable. But neither one's losing access to memory nor the unconscious can be observed directly. As a result, to some, the long-term memory becomes a kind of metaphysical assumption.

On the other hand, none of the researchers would deny that the long-term memory is based in matter, in the human brain, in an organ that is subject to the wear and tear of life and which is thus not permanent at all. The dawn of neuroscience makes it more persuasive than ever before that memory is a brain phenomenon. The neuroscientists' effort is to try to reduce mental phenomena to the physiological activities of neurons and to locate the emergence and action of mental abilities in certain areas of the brain. Making a materialistic assumption – that the brain is the only basis of memory – they avoid posing some other relevant questions, like: "who is remembering?" or "what determines memory?" With regards to the issue of personality, they contend that a person builds one's personality on the basis of memory and that in loosing memory one loses oneself, as stated by Hayward and Varela:

> It is due to the fact that memory accumulates, and it is on the basis of that recollection of memory of a causal sequence stored in the brain somewhere that I can say that's me.[4]

---

3. Ibid., p. 103.
4. Ibid., p. 118.

Understood conventionally, the personality or self is static and solid. It seems to possess a value of reality through a sensed continuity in time. For instance, I can say not only that "I am" a teacher, but that "I was" in India last year, and so forth. For more than thirty years, in some sense, I have had the same abiding self. I may not have so much memory of my first three years of life, but I, as well as others, believe that it is still "me." There are some puzzling issues here, i.e. whether the self or self-identity is based on memory? Whether the self defines memory or makes memory possible? And, whether memory is based on the brain or, perhaps, has some other basis? It seems to me that the scientific approach is limited in its capacity to solve these problems, for it tends to equate the mind with the brain and the person/self with memory.

Smrti: memory and mindfulness

Many types of mental activities were examined carefully by various Buddhist schools throughout history. This is because they took meditative practice to be their central concern. Theoretical reflections serve the purpose of guiding practice and, in its turn, these are based on experience gained in practice. However, it is interesting to notice that fairly little has been written in the Buddhist literature on the subject of memory, with the exception of few passages on the recollection of "past lives", which may be a good place to start. In the very first watch of the night that he awakened, the Buddha allegedly experienced the following:

> When my concentrated mind was thus purified, bright, unblemished, rid of imperfection, malleable, wieldy, steady, and attained to imperturbability, I directed it to knowledge of recollection of past lives. I recollected my manifold past lives, that is, one birth, two births, three births, four births, five births, ten births, twenty births, thirty births, forty births, fifty births, a hundred births, a thousand births, a hundred thousand births, and many aeons of world-contraction, many aeons of world-expansion, many aeons of world-contraction and expansion: "There I was so named, of such a clan, with such an appearance, such was my nutriment, such my experience of pleasure and pain, such my life-term; and passing away from there, I reappeared elsewhere; and there too I was so named, of such a clan, with such an appearance, such was my nutriment, such my experience of pleasure and pain, such my life-term; and passing away from there, I reappeared here." Thus with their aspects and particulars I recollected my manifold past lives.[5]

This is a classical example of how one recollects one's "past lives" in the Buddhist tradition. Recollection of "past lives", or the memory of one's own "former lives", is known as one of the six "super-knowledges" (*abhijna*) in the Buddhist literature. This memory occurs as a

---

5.   Majjhima Nikaya 1.4 (Bhayabheravasuttam). English translation by Bhikkhu Nanamoli & Bhikkhu Bodhi, *The Middle Length Discourses of the Buddha (Majjhima Nikaya)*. Boston: Wisdom Publications, 1995, p.105.

constituent of the awakening of both the Arhat and the Buddha, and is, presumably, accessible to others who practice meditation that aims to lead to "super-knowledge".

The content of the Buddha's memory of former abodes, like all memory, is a reconstruction of the past. It is a remoulding of the past for the purpose of the present. To account for memory, people tend to believe that a memory-image – in the interval between the perceived occurrence of an experience and its recall – has been stored up, allegedly in the brain. This familiar assumption is not quite as cogent as it may seem. For example, one may sneeze on Monday at 3.30 PM and on Tuesday at 4.30 PM, and nevertheless no one would ask where the memory of the sneeze has been for twenty-five hours during the interval. As Conze points out,

> ...in a memory it is not the perception, feeling, etc., which recurs. The act
> of remembering is a new, different act of consciousness, to which the old,
> remembered experience contributes as one condition.[6]

In this sense, memories are always present and the one who is doing the retrieving and recollecting is not the same as the one who lived in that "previous life", otherwise the remembering agent would be a permanent factor. It is through the memory of his alleged earlier existences that the Buddha

> ...destroys the past as a source of identity and attachment and replaces it
> with the memory of an existence that is happily abandoned.[7]

On the other hand, according to the Buddhist literature, memories of past abodes are a common "by-product" of deep levels of concentration, which can be experienced even by non-Buddhists. As we learn in the above passage, "concentrated mind" is a precondition to recollect proverbial "former lives." To some extent, we may say that the memory of "former lives" is possible only through concentration or *samadhi*. For, as anyone can experience in meditation, meditative mindfulness can set up a condition for memory and recollection of any kind. Interestingly, *sati* in Pali or *smrti* in Sanskrit has two basic meanings: recollective memory, or more generally, memory of the past, and what is most often rendered as "mindfulness." In a practical manner, Griffiths explains how one word can bear two meanings:

> When one engages in the practice of mindfulness one pays close attention
> to whatever one is taking as the object of one's meditational practice... the
> very act of paying close attention to the present contents of one's mind
> makes it possible to recall those contents at some later time.[8]

6.   E. Conze, *Buddhist thought in India.* The University of Michigan Press, 1973, p.100.
7.   D.S. Lopez, Memories of the Buddha, in J. Gyatso, Ed., *In the mirror of memory: Reflections on mindfulness and remembrance in Indian and Tibetan Buddhism.* Albany: State University of New York Press, 1992, p.37.
8.   P.J. Griffiths, Memory in classical Indian Yogacara, in J. Gyatso,1992, p.114.

However, it is debatable whether mindfulness should be considered as a type of memory or vice versa. Some, like Griffiths, hold that *smrti* mainly denotes active attention and has no essential reference to remembering past events. Others, e.g. Cox, suggest that recollection of the past as such is in fact understood in some Buddhist schools to be a subtype of mindfulness. To avoid the controversy, Kapstein has adopted English terms based on the Greek root *mna-*, which, like the Sanskrit *smr-*, can mean recollection as well as mindfulness.[9] Actually, the ancient Tibetan and Chinese translators adopted the same strategy. The Tibetan word *dran* means both memory and mindfulness; the Chinese word *nian*, literally "present mind", carries both the meanings of being mindful in the present moment and remembering the past.

Keeping in mind that memory, inferred as based on the root *mna-*, can be understood in a sense broader than usual, it could accommodate various meanings including recollection, reminding, mindfulness, holding in mind, memorizing, recognition, and commemoration. In this sense, there are two main types of memory: that of holding in mind and that of recollecting of what was previously experienced. Only in this sense can the word memory cover the variety of the phenomena of memory in the Buddhist tradition, such as recognition or the mind's ability to store data, memory of innumerable "past lives", memorization of vast volumes of text, holding an object in mind in meditative concentration, commemoration of the Buddha in the practices of devotion and visualization, and so on.

Conditions of memory

Smrti is frequently defined as a technical term in the Abhidharma texts. In the *Mahavibhasa*, *smrti* is viewed to be one of the mental factors present in all states of the mind. According to this view it is not possible to be conscious without having memory functioning.[10]

The analysis was later further developed by Vasubandhu, who, in his *Abhidharmakosabhasya*, defined *smrti* as the "retention of" or "not letting drop the object".[11] Here he did not specify whether the term object in this definition refers either to something in the past or to something in the present and he thus left open the possibility that *smrti* could mean either memory of the past or mindfulness of the present. In his *Pancaskandhaka-prakarana*, Vasubandhu defined *smrti* more in its sense of memory. He wrote:

> What is memory? It enables the mind not to forget a range of events towards which there is acquaintance, and it has the nature of repeatedly addressing.[12]

---

9.   J. Gyatso, Introduction, in Gyatso, 1992, pp.4-5.
10. The *Mahavibhasa* (Taisho 1545: 220a) takes *smrti* to be the eighth *mahabhumikas*.
11. *Abhidharmakosabhasya* II. 24.5.
12. *Pancaskandhaka-prakarana* (Taisho 1612: 848c). Thanks to Dr. Li Xuezhu for allowing me to use the yet unpublished Sanskrit version of the text.

Since *smrti* carries both meanings of mindfulness and memory, it is impossible to define memory without mentioning cognition. Mindfulness and memory are pre-conditions of each other. Vasubandhu elaborated this point further in his *Vimsatika*:

> Remembering takes place from that ["from that" means "from the cognition"]. A mental cognition arises with the discrimination of a visible, [hearable, touchable] etc. when that appearance is linked with memory, so an experience of an [external] object cannot be demonstrated through the arising of a memory.[13]

In his *Karmasiddhi-prakarana*, Vasubandhu asked himself:

> In that case, when one has studied a text, and after a long time has elapsed, a memory still arises regarding it, and memories arise in regard to other objects that have been seen, etc., what is the event [*dharma*] through which this memory later arises for [this object] which has been studied or seen, etc.? At what moment does it actually arise?[14]

Here Vasubandhu asked himself a profound question, namely, "How is memory possible?" As we know from our everyday experience, memory is an experiential fact, but questions still remain: how is it possible, how can I remember, how can I recognize? And if we refer to the Buddhist teaching of no-self, more questions arise: if the self is not real, who then remembers, who recognizes things, who recites and memorizes the texts? All these questions require a phenomenological approach to the experience of memory, an approach through which we may reveal the mechanism of memory and its conditions or basis.

Vasubandhu is one of the few Buddhist scholars who examined the mechanism of memory. In his *Abhidharmakosabhasya*, he provided detailed discussions on the conditions of memory. According to him, five conditions are required for memory:

> (1) There should be "bending" of the mental activity, i.e. a turning of attention towards that object (*tadabhoga*);

> (2) Mental activity should have an ideation (conceptual identification), which resembles the ideation of the past object. For example, a memory of a fire seen in the past aroused by its resemblance to the conceptual identification of a fire in the present (*sadrsa-samjna*);

> (3) Mental activity should have a conceptual identification suggesting a relation to the past object. For example, a memory of a past fire aroused by

---

14. *Karmasiddhi-prakarana* (Taisho 1609: 783b). Yamaguchi Susumu, *Seshin no jogoron,* Kyoto: Hozokan, 1975, p.14.

the conceptual identification of smoke seen in the present (*sambandha-samjna*);

(4) Mental activity should have a certain resolution. For example, "I shall remember this at a certain time." (*pranidhana*);

(5) There should be no impairment of the mental activity on account of bodily pain, grief, or distraction, etc. (*anupahata-prabhava*)

These five conditions are necessary, but they are not adequate to produce a memory. Both factors, namely, connection to the previous conceptual identification and a suitable state of mind, are needed for the emergence of a memory. A mental state other than this is incapable of evoking memory.[15]

Vasubandhu took *smrti* to be a special type of mental activity, a representative cognition of the past object. In memory, the present consciousness with a present conceptual identification has to connect itself with a past concept, either on the basis of a resemblance or a relationship between the two concepts. In other words, an object, once forgotten, can be recollected when stimulated by repetition, by a similar object, or by circumstances conducive to recollection. The mental activity in which the original object was experienced and in which it is remembered must be part of the same mental continuum. The specific mental activity in question must be causally related to a previously experienced object in a non-accidental way. Therefore, memory requires a single causally connected, that is, a homogeneous stream of experiences. But if, according to the Buddhist observation of impermanence, all factors are momentary, then the past concepts must be considered to have perished and thus be inaccessible to the present mental activity. So how is the present linked with the past? Could it be possible that one mental event has perceived the object and another remembers it? Can we say that Yajnadatta, for instance, remembers an object perceived by Devadatta? Vasubandhu responds:

No, [Yajnadatta cannot remember the object that Devadatta has perceived]. Because there is no connection [between Devadatta and Yajnadatta]: They are not connected in a relationship of cause and effect, which is the case for [minds] belonging to the same continuum.[16]

Vasubandhu applied the Buddhist teaching of causality to the case of memory and maintained that there is a "causal" or rather functional or correlational relation between the previous perception and present remembering. Elsewhere in the *Ahhidharmakosabhasya*, Vasubandhu applied the metaphor of "seeds" to explain memory. He contended:

---

15. *Abhidharmakosabhasya* IX. See Padmanabha S. Jaini, "*Smrti* in the Abhidharma literature and the development of Buddhist accounts of memory of the past", in J. Gyatso (1992, pp. 49-50).
16. *Abhidharmakosabhasya* IX.

What is a seed? It is the capacity to bring forth defilements in a particular person, a power that comes from [previous] defilements. In just the same way there is a power to bring forth memory, a power that comes from [previous] experiential awareness.[17]

He viewed the defilements (*klesa*) in their dormant stage to be in the form of seeds, which under certain conditions will bring forth defilements in reality. This is like the capacity to produce the rice plant is engendered by the rice seed and carried through various stages in between. Vasubandhu held that memory works the same way, and that it is brought forth by the seeds of stored memory.

The store-consciousness

The use of such an analogy immediately raises further questions: where, for example, are the seeds located while they are ripening? According to the Yogacara theory that Vasubandhu adopted later in his life, these seeds are located not in any of the active consciousnesses (*pravrttivijnana*), but rather in the store-consciousness (*alayavijnana*), the "*non-intentional consciousness*" wherein all seeds are stored. Actually, one of the major epithets applied to this store-consciousness in virtually all Yogacara texts is "that which possesses all seeds", which certainly include the seeds of memory. The occurrence of a memory-event is thus presented as a process of maturation of one's seeds of memory that is located in individual consciousness.

In the system of Yogacara philosophy, there are eight categories of consciousness. The first five are the consciousness related to the usual five senses. The sixth consciousness or *mano-vijnana* is the aspect of the brain-based mind that coordinates the data of the sense-consciousness so that, for example, the smell, shape, and colour of an object are all related to the same object. The seventh consciousness or *manas* is the defiled mind ("our inner demons") that instigates subjectivity or the self. It carries an embryonic sense of duality between subject and object. The eighth consciousness is the store-consciousness that is also often referred to as "foundation consciousness" of memory storage. The following is a description of the store-consciousness to be found in Sthiramati's *Trimsikabhasya*, which is a commentary to Vasubandhu's *Trimsika*:

> Here, maturation is that consciousness which is called "store," the container of all seeds.... [The phrase] "which is called "store" identifies that consciousness which is known as the store-consciousness with the transformation which is maturation. It is a store because it has the quality of being the place in which all defiled seeds are located.... [The store-consciousness] is an instance of consciousness because it cognizes; it is called "maturation" because it has the quality of bringing to maturity good and bad karma

---

17. *Abhidharmakosabhasya* V.2a.

among all spheres, destinies, wombs, and births. And it is called "the container of all seeds" because it has the quality of being the basis of the seeds of all *dharmas*.[18]

In this view, memory is only possible on the basis of the store-consciousness. The residual impressions from past moments are stored in the form of seeds in the store-consciousness. The latent impressions are a constantly changing series of moment-events, which will gradually, if conditions allow, give rise to a memory. The relationship between consciousness-moments and seeds is symmetrical, since each consciousness-moment leaves an impression in the consciousness-series and this "seed"-series influences all future consciousness. Without the store-consciousness, memory cannot be explained. On the other hand, the possibility of memory is considered to be a proof of the store-consciousness.[19]

Being the basis of memory and the abiding locus for impressions, the store-consciousness is "stable" only in the sense that it forms a continuous, never greatly altered series. Yogacara theorists consistently deny that the store-consciousness is an enduring substance and that anything endures therein. The store, in their account, is no more than the totality of the causal powers of its constituent events. The store-consciousness is not anything over and above the seeds that it contains. From the viewpoint of causality, the store-consciousness is that which acts as the agent that stores, i.e. executes the process of possessing seeds. If considered from the viewpoint of the effect of the cause, the store-consciousness is that in which all *dharmas* are being stored up and organized.

Then how is the store-consciousness different from the self? If the self is understood to be single and devoid of action, then it has nothing to do with this constantly changing mental process. If, on the other hand, one holds that there are transformations within the self, then the store-consciousness would be identical to this conventional self. As it is stated by Vasubandhu: "[Question] Why not admit a self (*atman*) existing in and of itself as the base of the six consciousnesses? [Answer] What is the characteristic of this self admitted by you? If this self, like the store-consciousness, is a series of productions and destructions which transforms itself in accord with conditions, then what is the difference between the two?"[20]

The conventional self

By adopting the metaphors of the "store consciousness" and "seeds," Yogacara theory provides an explanatory model of how and where the latent memories persist. But in the eyes of many critics, the store-consciousness would seem to amount to an enduring substance with attributes – "a self by any other name" – and might hence be inferred as a surrender of the Buddhist basic view of no-self. For this reason the Yogacarins have been criticized at length by the

18. *Trimsikabhasya* 2cd.
19. P.J. Griffiths, On being mindless: Buddhist meditation and the mind-body problem. La Salle: Open Court, 1987, p.134.
20. *Karmasiddhi-prakarana* (Taisho 1609: 785b). *Yamaguchi*, 1975, p.26.

Madhyamikas. As summarized by the 14th Dalai Lama, who is a Prasangika Madhyamika:

> In brief, this foundation consciousness, or storehouse consciousness, is believed to be the repository of all of the imprints or *bag chags* [Tibetan term], the habits and latent propensities that one has accumulated in this and former lives... I totally refute the existence of the foundation consciousness... because they [Yogacarins] were philosophers who believed that phenomena must exist substantially. They wanted to believe that the self was findable under critical analysis.... They were compelled to formulate this consciousness because of their rational presuppositions, rather than through empirical investigation or realization.[21]

The Madhyamaka school consists of two major sub-schools, i.e. the Svatantrika Madhyamaka school and the Prasangika Madhyamaka school. Based on the doctrines of Bhavaviveka, the Svatantrikas hold that it is not necessary to posit a foundation consciousness. For, the continuum of mental consciousness itself will act as a repository for the residual impressions or imprints (*bag chags*).[22] Proponents of the other school, the Prasangikas, go one step further by contending that one does not need to posit even the continuum of mental consciousness as the repository of latent imprints. In fact, they think, all of these problems arise because of an underlying essentialist assumption that something, i.e. the self, must be findable under analysis. The Prasangika system refutes the existence of any "I" that is findable under analysis, for it regards the self as something imputed on the basis of the collection of the Skandhas, the aggregates of the mind and the body. Not identified as being among the five aggregates, it is merely a label or designation. Moreover, the very notion of an unchanging self, when applied to the self as an agent of action and to the self as the experiencer, is a contradiction. Thus, Prasangikas hold that the self as well as the mental continuum and the stored imprints exist only conventionally, not substantially, which is the Theravada's as well as Nagarjuna's contention. This is the concept of "mere-I" (Tibetan: *bdag-tsam*).[23]

The "mere-I" is not a substantial self in the following sense: it is non-stop in the process of transformation and it is not a single independent entity. For example, there are many different selves appearing in one's memory: one might be the self of ten years old, another is right here and now, and there is the one that says I am all of them. None of them is a permanent single entity or soul, indivisible and without "parts". In this sense, one does not "have" the same self as one did "have" many years ago. Here the important point is that there is continuation in the person, yet what is continuing is also continuously changing from moment to moment. It makes no sense to say the self of a ten years old child is exactly the same as the self of an old person.

---

21. F.J. Varela, Ed., *Sleeping, dreaming, and dying: An exploration of consciousness with the Dalai Lama.* Boston: Wisdom Publications, 1997, pp.86-88.
22. *Ibid.*, p.88.
23. This Tibetan expression may have source in the Pali idiom "*ahan-neva*" as found in the *Milindapanha*.

According to the Prasangika view, the "mere-I" is not something tangible and really to be found. It is merely something that is designated on various levels of abstractions. The "I" can be designated on the basis of the gross aggregates (e.g., the faculty of cognition) or the subtle aggregates (e.g., thinking: "I am a bad person."). In the same sense, the "mere-I" can be a designation on the basis of gross consciousness or subtle awareness. In this view the memory or the imprints are stored in the "mere-I" of the conventional person (who on a deeper or ultimate level is empty of "intrinsic nature" [*svabhava*]). Thus, the "mere-I" can be considered to be a learning experience as in the following quote:

> One way of looking at this statement, that the mere-I is the repository of mental imprints, is to look at it from a conventional point of view. When a person has done an action that leaves certain imprints, he now has a certain propensity due to that experience. That's all there is to it. You don't need to posit a substantial basis that exists as the repository for that propensity. That is the Prasangika Madhyamaka view.[24]

Conclusion

In my view, the Madhayamikas are not sharply distinctive from the Yogacarins at this point. They both admit that there should be a basis for memory, either the store-consciousness or the conventional self, which is provisional. Both of them share the common feature of being in consistent transformation and having a pluralistic character. They are very different from the self or *atman* in its strict sense that is inherently existing, substantial/single, and devoid of action. In this sense none of the schools has violated the Buddhist assumption of no-self. They only nourish different opinions on how memory is related to personality. After all, they are all Buddhists, who hold that the person or the self is momentarily changing and inseparable from the process of memory. They base their views on the observation of impermanence and no-self which is to be experienced and understood through meditation.

My initial quest was inspired by a disprovable postulate of memory in the information-processing model and my intention was to seek Buddhist philosophical arguments in favour of the neurophenomenological study of memory. But now it seems that I am just substituting one disprovable method for another: it is a matter of subjective experiencing rather than of objective experimenting. Instead of getting answers, more questions now emerge. Which method or principle is most helpful to uncover the secret of memory? Or will we get stuck in speculation? Should we introduce the concepts of self or no-self to study memory? Should science accept metaphysical assumptions? Probably most scientists would like to stay with the material assumption considering the brain to be the only basis of memory and will avoid questioning "who is remembering" or "what determines memory." Still many others believe that though memory is a brain phenomenon, it is definitely not limited to just grey matter.

---

24. F.J. Varela, 1997, p.90.

Definite answers will not to be found in the foreseeable future, I am afraid, but who knows, one day science fiction might become part of our daily lives and the controversy could be solved by successfully transplanting grey matter from one body to another. We would then be able to observe whether the person with a new brain will be able to remember her/his past or not. If s/he remembers, s/he will keep her/his identity; if not, s/he has become someone else. Time will tell...

Chapter 13

Buddhist Architecture Of The Mind: Cognitive, Emotional, Motivational And Attentional Facets, Exemplified By A Case Study

Padmasiri de Silva

Locating emotions from a Buddhist stance

When we use Aristotle's tripartite division, perception (*sanna, vinnana*) representing the cognitive dimension of the mind, feeling (*vedana*) representing the affective dimension of the mind, and volition/dispositions (*sankhara)* representing the conative aspect of the mind, we get a clear picture of the Buddhist architecture of the mind.

Four of the Five (Body) Mind Aggregates:

Sanna _____
Vinnana _____ } Cognitive Facet

Vedana_____   Affective Facet

Sankhara_____   Conative or Volitional Facet

Even though this traditional picture of the mind is useful, we need not place absolute reliance on it. All four *khandas* (Pali) or Skandhas (Sanskrit) are present in all states of consciousness and experience. The body as a Skandha is crucial, especially playing part in the physiology of emotions. A crucial point in Buddhist Psychology, then, is the reciprocal relationship between the mind and the body. Cartesian dualism or reductionism attempting to reduce the mental into the physical, and vice versa, is avoided. Taking a specific emotion as an example, all five aggregates (including the body) are inseparably associated with each other. Another feature is that the mind is seen as a dynamic continuum; both mind and body are seen as completely interwoven processes. The Buddha rejects any concept of a permanent entity and views the person as a psycho-physical continuum of processes working on (and in the midst of) a number of causal factors, as this psycho-physical process is inextricably enmeshed in causality of Dependent Origination.

According to Dependent Origination, sensory contact conditions feeling, feeling conditions craving, craving conditions grasping, and these links help to appreciate the dynamic interplay of factors at play in the emergence of emotions. The Buddhist conception of the mind also makes a reference to mental activity at subliminal levels. Threshold consciousness is open to six "sense doors" through which stimuli reach us, stimuli we perceive via seeing, hearing, smelling, tasting, touching, and via remembering and thinking. Able to control the senses (*indriyasamvara*), one remains unaffected by these stimuli, but the mind is subject to attraction and aversion, and thus to subliminal proclivities such as those associated with aversion, lust, and conceit. This view helps to understand the emergence of anger, greed, envy, jealousy, and deep rooted attitudes like arrogance and vanity.

Now that we have located emotion in the Buddhist architecture of the "bodymind", the rest of this first part will be about understanding the affective dimension of our lives: emotions. The study of emotions has been neglected for many years for a number of reasons. Within the natural and social sciences, the study of emotions was not given its due recognition, as emotions were associated with a kind of "subjectivism", which is considered unscientific and not suited to the emerging "objective" research methods of psychology. Emotions have also been relegated to the realm of the irrational. They were considered by many to be antithetical to our cognitive skills of thinking, reasoning, and understanding. Emotions were considered to be states that interfered with the development of "good" character. Even in routine life, emotions are said to interfere with calm and rational decisions. To add to these irrational prejudices, great harm was done to emotion studies by the consistent refusal across disciplines, even among philosophers, to confer the concepts of responsibility and choice on human emotions. At the psychological level, emotions were considered as states of imbalance.

Considering the multifaceted negative attitude to emotion studies, it is necessary to place before the reader the thesis that while most of us are subject to conditions of emotional agitation, during certain periods of our life, there is sufficient space within us for mature emotional growth and development. The emerging new perspectives may be summarized in the words of the neuroscientist Damasio (1994):

> ...reason may not be as pure as most of us think it is or wish it were... emotions and feelings may not be intruders in the bastion of reason at all: they may be enmeshed in its network, for worse and for better (p.xii).

On the one hand, emotions "partially shape and determine what we value", wrong to consider them as unintegrated and irruptive sources of motivation (Goldie, 2002, p.48), on the other hand we should not over-intellectualise emotions by trying to *always* make them fit into the moulds of logical rigour. Some times emotions are like, "geological upheavals in a landscape, they mark our lives as uneven, uncertain, and prone to reversal", but at times, "they are suffused with intelligence and discernment, and thus a source of deep awareness and understanding" (Nussbaum, 2001).

The study of emotions is important not merely as a subject of academic and scientific interest, but also as a subject of great practical importance in the conduct of our lives and in understanding other people. Emotions have a rich complexity and contribute to widening the horizons of self-understanding, as well as developing sensitivity to the people and the world around us. During the last three decades, there has been a significant revival of interest in emotion studies due to new developments in neuroscience, biology, psychology, and more broadly in cognitive science as well as in medicine. This revival also had a significant impact on philosophical studies of emotion, which attempt a critical integration of these findings without falling into the traps of reductionism. In fact the most recent research projects in the Dalai Lama's influential Mind and Life Institute provide an ideal context for reflecting on the Buddhist philosophy of emotions. The illumination of the interface between emotions in the western and Buddhist traditions is a very significant turn of events, especially clearly seen in the current research projects of the Mind and Life Institute. For instance Ekman (2003), who is a prominent member of this project says that emotions have evolved to respond to our flight and fight mechanisms and that they produce automatic and reflex behaviour, especially where there is a need for quick response and hardly any time for deliberation. But Buddhist Bhikkhus are so well trained in meditation, that they can develop a readiness to encounter such situations, and can "recognize the spark before the flame". The phenomenon of the demonization of emotions seen alongside the development of new perspectives for looking at the past in order to deal with guilt and self-hate and to convert despair and emptiness into positive insights, presents an important area for the study of emotions and for the conduct of psychotherapy. Ekman points out the value of the development of the mind for preventive work, whereas traditional western psychotherapeutic approaches tend to focus on damage control after a person is already "burning up". Within the multifaceted techniques in the Buddhist tradition for managing emotions, this prior training for calming the mind and refining the emotional sensibility is a very basic feature of controlling and moderating emotions. Though the work of the institute has been specially directed towards practitioners of the Tibetan *(Vajrayana)* Buddhist tradition, they apply equally to all Buddhist traditions, and especially to the Pali Buddhist tradition from where I draw most of my research material.

In his book *Emotions revealed*, Ekman (2003) said that if we develop the "habit of being attentive" or in Buddhist terminology develop mindfulness practice, we develop the skill to observe ourselves during an emotional episode, ideally before more than a few seconds have passed. We can also recognize when we are emotional and consider whether our appraisal of the situation is justified and re-evaluate our appraisal. Most emotions involve judgments. In fact, as I shall explain in the discussion that follows, according to the Buddhist analysis, the germinal state of what later develops to an emotion with great speed is found in pleasurable, painful, or neutral feelings (*vedana*). Then with the addition of thought, appraisals, desires, and the excitement of our deep-rooted tendencies towards attachment, aversion, and conceit, including social and cultural filters, etc, it is clear that what emerges as an emotion is a *social construction*. So, the important point to be made is that we can in fact "put our brakes on" at any point on the development of this sequence from its inception as elementary affect to its experience as a full emotion. Ekman cites especially knowledge about causes and emotion triggers and bodily sensations. As we develop the skill of being attentive we are able to moderate our emotional behaviour, from our facial expressions to our speech and to our actions. In fact, one of the ground breaking insights that have emerged especially from the work of Davidson and his co-workers (2003) is about Buddhist meditation and the plasticity of the brain. Brain parts correlating with emotional experience like the frontal lobes, the amygdala, and the hippocampus may change due to the impact of the repeated emotional experience and meditative experience can bring about positive changes (Goleman, 2002).

Emotions in the Buddhist tradition

Apart from my general interest in emotion studies, this analysis is basically written with the hope of developing a Buddhist contribution to understanding emotions and their relevance for leading meaningful and good lives. In addition to recognizing the moral and social dimensions of the Buddhist discipline, understanding emotions in terms of a meditative and spiritual life is important. The Buddha was considered the "incomparable charioteer for the training of persons". The understanding and management of negative passions or emotions in an intelligent and wise manner opens to us the path towards liberation. The passions defiling our mind are nourished by certain psychological bases or roots (*mula*). They are the roots of addiction (*lobha*), reaction (*dosa*), and a narcissistic self image which clouds our perception *(moha)*. *The Middle Length Sayings* give a list of defilements *(upakkilesa)*. Most of them are negative passions and states related to them: greed, covetousness, malevolence, anger, malice, hypocrisy, spite, envy, stinginess, deceit, treachery, obstinacy, impetuosity, arrogance, pride, conceit, and indolence (M I, 36-37). These defiling passions also exist at dormant and subliminal levels, and become manifest in the presence of suitable stimuli. It is because we need a systematic path to deal with the defilements that the Buddha introduced the Noble Eightfold Path. This path combines the diligent practice of the moral life, the practice of meditation and the development of wisdom. Along this path there is the development of emotional harmony, balance, and maturity. In the West, Plato (4th century BCE) also used the image of the charioteer when looking at human passions; emotions are unruly and need to be controlled by *reason.* In a recent study, Blackburn (1998) comments,

> Here is the classic dualism of heart and head, desire and reason, with reason in control so long as things are going well. Apollo rules in the light, Dionysus rules in the dark (p.238).

According to Blackburn, Plato's celebrated model was "dramatically turned upside down by Hume." Hume said that reason ought to be the slave of the passions and it is the task of reason to serve and obey the passions. The Dutch philosopher Spinoza entertained the attractive notion that we can use a positive emotion to rectify a negative one, like using compassion as an antidote for anger. Spinoza also had an insightful theory that emotions had "thought components" and that these are useful in the classification and discrimination of emotional states, and the development of "reflexive knowledge" for use in changing those states. If we follow Spinoza and accept that emotions involve beliefs, we logically conclude that by changing beliefs we can transform negative emotions (Neu, 1977). Aristotle, who came after Plato, emphasized the importance of training and character development, which I shall discuss in the section on emotions and ethics.

In contrast to these western views, while the Buddha did value the importance of reason as well as the importance of looking at the thought components of emotion, he discerned that reason by itself was not in a position to handle human afflictions and negative passions. Thus the Buddha went beyond the contrasting images of reason and passion found in Plato and Hume to discover fresh resources in the power of mindfulness practice. Even the thoughts that contribute to the building of an emotion are more clearly seen in meditative reflection, than rational analysis. Emotions help us to find resources to live in today's complex multi-cultural society, developing the required empathy, tolerance, and care towards others. Rhys Davids observed as far back as 1914, that this was a neglected area in Buddhist studies and that there was an "archaic silence" on the subject.

> We must now abandon this incomplete survey of the extent to which the books, reckoned oldest in the Buddhist culture, analyse the nature of mental procedure. If we have found something, there is much we have not found, for instance, the image and the conditions of its reinstatement, an analysis of the emotions, instinct as compared with volition. (Rhys Davids, 1914, p.133)

The Buddhist concept of emotions

Etymologically, the term *emotion* is derived from the Latin "e+movere" meaning to migrate or move from place to place. Also used to refer to agitations, it is this metaphor that has become associated with the word. As pointed out by Averill (1980), the word *passions* was used for approximately two thousand years, from the ancient Greeks to the middle of the eighteenth century, and as the derivation from the Greek *pathos* (passion) and the Latin *pati* (to suffer) conveys, emotions came to be associated with *passivity*.

> At the root of these concepts is the idea that an individual or (physical object) is undergoing or suffering some change, as opposed to doing or initiating change. Thus in ordinary discourse, we speak of being "gripped", and "torn" by emotion. (p.38)

Averill also observed that the "passivity" experience is an illusion, and can be seen for what it is by widening the area of self-awareness and developing greater insight into the sources of one's actions. Metaphors used in every day life like, "drowned by sorrow", "driven by anger", and "plagued by remorse" tend to confirm the image of passivity that we attribute to emotions. This process of self-attribution helps individuals to abjure responsibility for the consequences of emotional action.

It is true that emotions are linked to our bodily-felt sensory feelings, especially feelings of pain and pleasure, attraction and aversion. But to experience an emotion like anger or fear is not just having some unique inner feeling. As they are not just occult inner happenings, they come within the public interaction and interpersonal responses, it may be said that emotions are about a state of affairs. In short emotions presuppose certain cognitions:

> ...we are not afraid of x unless we take x to be dangerous; we are not angry at x unless we take x to be acting contrary to something we want; we do not have remorse over having done x unless we regard as unfortunate that we did x. (Alston, 1967, p.481)

Thus, emotions have these thought components. While emotions involve thoughts, beliefs, and judgments, they also refer to objects. The objects may be existing ones like a snake in the case of fear or the death of a friend in the case of sadness or the infuriating behaviour of a thug in the case of anger. But the object of fear may be even imaginary or rooted in the unconscious as Freud described in certain forms of anxiety. As there is a "formal object" of emotion, we use the term *intentionality*, directed towards situation or object.

For example, a person is walking on a forest track and is suddenly alerted to a *sound* and then a *shape*, which is recognized as a snake. The person also has the belief that snake venom is poisonous and is a threat to his life. Now this belief is the cognitive core around which the person makes the appraisal "danger". Assuming that our description is like a slow motion film, the perception of the situation and its evaluation generates certain physiological changes and bodily reactions in the autonomic nervous system: release of adrenaline, pounding of the heart, change of breathing patterns, and related visceral responses. The motivational aspect is seen in these manifestations of a drive for survival. The emotion of fear is very much related to the emergency alarm of the flight-fight-freeze mechanism. There will be changes in facial expression and behavioural changes, a sort of action readiness for flight. Some of the more basic emotions like anger, fear, and sadness have clear physiological and biological facets but not all emotions have them, conceit, for example, does not. Emotions with an interpersonal orientation have a socio-cultural dimension. In emotions like anger, lust, envy, and jealousy, we look for the notion of human agency, choice, and responsibility. The Buddhist notion of intention *(cetana)* contains these features, thus making these emotions the object of moral criticism. This analysis takes us to the central Buddhist concern with awareness and mindfulness, which will be taken up as we proceed with outlining the Buddhist concept of emotion.

In the ongoing research in the West these different facets of an emotion are studied at various levels of expression. Emotions are linked to the electrical activity of the brain, the visceral-glandular system, the circulatory system, and the respiratory system; they are reflected in the dynamics of our motives, drives, and the appetitive aspect of our being; they are closely related to the ways we respond to and evaluate external situations; and they are linked to our beliefs and bound to our socio-cultural relationships. There is an initial affective response to sensory and ideational stimuli, which develops in to a full emotion. In the Buddhist perspective on emotions, these different facets of an emotion are all recognized: feelings as affective response to sensory stimuli, desire, beliefs, appraisals, behaviour, and physiology, as well as socio-cultural conditioning. Most important is the moral dimension of emotions and the concept of ethical responsibility. To clarify, the *Pali* term *vedana* has to be distinguished from the English term *emotion*. In fact in Buddhist Psychology, there is no generic term "emotion" as used in the English language. Instead there are varied discussions of the emotion family members like anger, greed, fear, sadness, and conceit. As Nyanaponika Thera (1983) says,

> It should be first made clear that, in Buddhist psychology, "feeling" [Pali: *vedana*] is the bare sensation noted as pleasant, unpleasant and neutral. Hence [feeling] should not be confused with emotion, which, though arising from the [basic] feeling, adds to it likes or dislikes of varying intensity, as well as other thought processes. (p.7)

In the contemporary literature in the West on emotions, one who follows the writings will notice a continuing debate among those who advocate different conceptions of emotions, and today the debate has become polarized between the cognitive theories versus the physiological arousal theories. I have discussed these controversies in great detail in *Twin Peaks: Compassion and Insight* (de Silva, 1992a). Basically, the Buddha does not push these conceptual issues beyond their specific context and it would, therefore, be consistent to take a wholistic stand on the nature of emotions. In his dialogues, the Buddha says that one should use names, turns of speech, and designations according to their contextual usage and not to go astray (D I, 202). At a deeper level, in the practice of meditation, we are encouraged to see emotions like anger and fear as having no essence, as empty, and as projections of the mind. But in other contexts, we might see emotions as strong phenomenological present and persistent.

Emotions at their subliminal and unconscious levels

The Buddhist concept of the mind also involves a reference to mental activity at subliminal levels (*anusaya*). The term *anusaya* is defined in the Pali-English Dictionary as, "Bent, bias, proclivity, the persistence of a latent disposition, predisposition, tendency". *Anusayas* are dormant passions that are roused into activity by suitable stimuli. Because of their tenacity, they provide the base for the emergence of states like greed, anger, and pride. There are seven *anusayas*: sensuous craving, anger, conceit, erroneous opinion, scepticism, craving for existence, and ignorance. In recent times, the claim that affective reactions could take place without conscious awareness of stimuli is a theme greatly explored in a ground breaking work, *The Emotional Brain*, by Ledoux (1998). His important finding is *that the emotional meaning of a stimulus may be appraised by the emotional brain, before the perceptual systems have fully processed the stimulus.* In a way this corroborates the Freudian analysis focussed on the dark, traumatic, and inaccessible facets of the unconscious (de Silva, 1992). Firstly, unconscious motives imply that a person is not aware of the real motives of action, as routine life is a tangle of desires. Secondly, our lives are dominated by unreflective habits and there is a large habit dominated area in our mental architecture. Thirdly, in the Freudian sense, motives are fashioned under unpleasant circumstances and we would like to forget them. Important differences between western and Buddhist models of approaching the unconscious emerge in the methods used for managing and gaining autonomy from the spell of the unconscious. A most important point in the context of our present study is that in the western tradition, since Aristotle, the most frequent antonym of passion has been reason. The Buddhist tradition sees the management of the passions as a three-factor situation: emotion, reason, and mindfulness. Although gaining momentum, there are few psychologists using Buddhist techniques in their therapies. The implications of using mindfulness meditation for managing emotions are relatively unknown to mainstream psychology (de Silva, 2002, pp.188-193).

The Buddha describes the mind as wavering and restless, difficult to guard and restrain. It is said that a wise person straightens his mind as a maker of arrows makes the arrows straight (*Dhammapada*, 33). In another context, the Buddha compares the mind to a monkey moving from branch to branch, only releasing the feet over one branch after having grasped another. But life itself unfolds with momentous challenges, upheavals, and uncertainties; it is only a trained and tamed mind that can deal with these challenges. Buddhist practice refines our level of awareness and gives us a better understanding of emotional functioning. With this comes a great skill, the ability to open our minds without any closure, denial, or repression, and thus to tolerate and manage a wide variety of emotional experiences.

An issue in emotion studies that has been a problematic perennial controversy is the mind-body relationship. To some extent, the conflict between cognitive theories and physiological arousal theories has emerged in a kind of polarization in contemporary emotion theories around body-mind relationship and this dichotomy is one way of locating the current tension in emotion theories (Solomon, 2004). The Buddha considers the human being as a psycho-physical complex. There is no attempt to reduce mental processes to physical processes or vice versa. The mind and the body have a conditioned existence and they emerge within a dynamic continuum of a variety of relations. Specifically, Buddhist teachings uphold neither a dualistic nor a monistic position, either of the materialistic or idealistic variety. Within this non-reductionist framework, the Buddha makes contextual distinctions, like "feelings can be physical or mental". As the teachings are focussed towards practice, the Buddha advises his students not to push useful contextual distinctions beyond necessity and not to get entangled in theoretical battles. In a deeper sense, the question of whether the mind is identical with the body or is independent from the body is one of the questions which the Buddha left as a "classical undetermined question". The view that the mind (jiva) and body are the same is "materialism", and the view that they are different, where the soul is considered as a spiritual principle existing independent of the body, is "eternalism" (MI, 485). Working within the contextual conventions of the mind and body relationship, the Buddha accepted a two-way reciprocal relationship. The relationship between mind and body (nama-rupa) is compared to two bundles of reed supporting one another (S II, 114). It is this reciprocal relationship of the body and mind with a two-way feedback that best helps us to understand emotions from a Buddhist stance (de Silva, 2005, pp.153-181).

Self-control and "moral weakness"

The focus here is on the general nature of moral weakness and addictions with special reference to alcohol addiction, on the philosophical, psychological, and therapeutic frontiers of moral weakness and addictions, and on examining the Buddhist therapeutic resources for understanding and managing addiction issues at the cognitive, motivational, and attentional levels, and address the "paradigm clash" between the *abstinence* and *controlled drinking* models. Following up the section on addiction theory, I will describe my personal attempts to develop a therapeutic methodology in relation to clients, focus on alternative models of therapy for drug addiction, and discuss a case study..

The self-control of emotions and behaviours is the virtue of living according to one's values, insofar as one has the capacity to do so by exercising courage and persistence, supplemented by wise understanding, motivation, and mindfulness. Lack of self-control is described as "weakness of will". Such weakness may be occasional or habitual and limited to specific vices, and would come within different degrees of control and awareness. The puzzle is: Why do people knowingly court self-defeating forms of behaviour? The irresistibility of addictions is seen in the areas of gambling, smoking, drug and alcoholic addiction and irresponsible sexual behaviour. Uncontrollable anger, though not a form of addiction, also comes within the domain of moral weakness and weakness of will. In strict Buddhist ethical discourse, abstinence is the ideal moral norm (Padmal de Silva, 1983). But in therapeutic contexts other models prevail; for instance Marlatt (2002) developed what he calls the "Harm Reduction Model". This model is based on compassionate pragmatism rather than on imposing any moral ideal. It recognizes that a minority of people has always abused alcohol and always will continue to do so. It doesn't condone this behaviour, but seeks to reduce its incidence and the harm it does produce. Marlatt has been greatly influenced by Buddhist techniques which confer the ability to choose on the individual and offers a harm reduction model to clients who are unable or unwilling to adopt an abstinence goal. He also sees many parallels between Buddhist and cognitive-behavioural approaches to addictions treatment.

The "Four Exertions" and the "Spiritual Maladies" show the Buddhist approach:

> There are these four exertions. Which four? There is the case where a monk generates desire, endeavours, arouses persistence, upholds and exerts his intent for the non-arising of evil, unskilful qualities that have not yet arisen… for the sake of abandoning of evil, unskilful qualities that have arisen…for the sake of arising of skilful qualities not yet arisen…and for the maintenance, non-confusion, increase, plenitude, development and culmination of skilful qualities that have arisen. These are the four right exertions. (Kindred Sayings, XLIX.1)… Guarding and abandoning, developing and maintaining, these are the four exertions. (Gradual Sayings, IV.14)

> Through spiritual or physical tiredness, through accident, through weakness of body, through illness, through general apathy, through despair, through inability to concentrate, through a feeling of uselessness or futility, and so on, one may feel less and less motivated to seek what is good. One's lessened desire need not signal…that there is less good to be obtained or produced… Indeed, a frequent added defect of being in such "depressions" is that one sees all the good to be won or saved and one lacks the will, interest, desire, or strength. (Stocker, 1979, p.744; Stocker, 1996, pp.244-245)

Nature of alcohol and drug addictions

As Martin (2007, p.190) contends:

> Self-control is the virtue of living according to one's values, insofar as one has the capacity to do so by exercising courage, persistence or simple discipline. Lack of self-control often takes form of *weakness of will* in which we judge that we ought to do something, have the power to do so, but fail to do so; when the judgment is specifically moral it is *moral weakness.*

Stocker (1979) observed about people in moods of apathy, tiredness, and even despair, that one sees all the good to be won or saved and one lacks the will, interest, desire or strength. Such weakness may occur in a dramatic form where one gives in to temptation knowing that one would very soon get into a miserable state or in a more humdrum, occasional or habitual manner; it may be regional, for example a student's failure to stick to a regular timetable, even though he exhibits no such laxity in other areas of life like keeping to promises or not falling a victim to irresponsible sexual pleasures, gambling, smoking, drug, and alcoholic addiction. An agent who has self-control in all regions of life would be a remarkable accomplishment.

Self-control may be a matter of degree, rather than an all or nothing situation.

Greeks like Socrates and Aristotle used the term *akrasia* to refer to weakness of will and *encratia* for self-control. According to Aristotle, weakness of will or incontinence of greed and lust need to be condemned when compared to the incontinence of anger and loosing one's temper which is a common frailty. It is also interesting to note that according to him, the vicious man who has bad moral principles is hard to educate compared with the incontinent man who has good moral principles but fails to stick to them and is aware of this limitation. In fact, it has been observed that *akrasia is the price that virtue pays to vice.*

Socrates presented a time-honoured axiom that "virtue is knowledge" which is a puzzle and a paradox since those who have genuine moral knowledge and are bound to produce good conduct, do, in many instances, the opposite and give into temptation. Also, one may say there is an illegitimate passage from the "is" to the "ought": the knowledge that a person has about moral rules is descriptive of his state of knowledge but there is no logic dictating that such a person will stick to the rules. These issues about the irresistibility of addictions have been the subject of behavioural science and psychological research especially by experts like Jon Elster, George Ainslie, Alfred Mele and Stanton Peel, and have been the subject of active clinical studies with a Buddhist perspective by Allan Marlatt, Thomas and Beverly Bien. In consuming drugs, alcohol and cigarettes, and engaging in compulsive gambling, people knowingly choose the things they will regret. It is necessary to understand these forms of *self-defeating behaviour. Why do people knowingly court disaster?* Socrates thought that to know what is morally right is to do it. Aristotle diverged from Socrates and thought that the "self-controlled" person can master the passions to which weak people fall victim. Thus, Aristotle emphasizes the motivational factors in addition to the cognitive factors.

But the clear limitation with both Socrates and Aristotle is that the agent's faculty of self-control is identified with the agent's faculty of reason, and it is here that understanding the focus on *attentional factors* (mindfulness) becomes crucial.

> I follow Aristotle in understanding self-control and *akrasia* as two sides of the same coin. However, I distance myself from him on a metaphysical matter. Aristotle identifies the *self* of self-control with the agent's "reason" (faculty). I identify it, holistically with the person, broadly conceived. An agent's desires and emotions that run counter to her best judgments are rarely plausibly seen as alien forces (Mele, 1996, p.100).

While the Buddhist tradition certainly considers reason to be an important ally in self-control, it is the power of mindfulness that helps one to handle negative desires, thoughts, and emotions. The Buddhist method also presents a wholistic analysis of factors bearing on weakness of will: cognitive, motivational, emotional, and attentional factors. At the cognitive level, while the Buddhist method accepts wisdom as a refined spectrum of knowledge, it also accepts degrees of awareness and knowledge in ordinary life. The most important of these is the knowledge that one is free to make decisions, and thus free to refrain from taking to various types of substances and succumbing to behaviour abuse. Mindfulness brings into this free choice context a greater awareness and acceptance of immediate experience, which can help to prevent relapse. It has been observed that awareness and acceptance may help to deal with risk factors like negative emotional states and the tendency to attribute failure (to abstain) to personal weakness (Marlatt & Chawla, 2007, p.252):

> A more accepting approach may not only encourage greater tolerance with
> regard to emotional states but also support a more compassionate and bal-
> anced evaluation of one's own actions, reducing the likelihood of spiralling
> into a relapse following a brief setback or stressful event.

Mindfulness practice also helps the process of rebuilding, the move to distance oneself from addiction, by acting as an antidote to craving. People, who do not want to be alive to their problems or to find solutions, often take the path of alcoholic addiction. This feature has been described as a form of "experiential avoiding".

It is also important to be aware of the moral and social implications of one's behaviour. While abstinence is the Buddhist ideal moral position, some one moving from addiction to controlled drinking would be able to appreciate the fact that s/he is not wrecking her/his life and family. One is also expected to be sensitive to facts of psychology, and even of medicine and science, when such knowledge is available, as such information throws light on the risk that people take when they fall a victim to addictions. But it is the practice of mindfulness and attentional factors that make the Buddhist contribution unique. From a Buddhist perspective the *cognitive dimension is not synonymous with the rational faculty*. Aristotle said that an *akratic* is like a city that has good laws but does not implement them. In the Buddhist tradition too, the practical qualities of commitment, persistence, courage in the face of adversity and ardency (*viriya*), presence of mind (*sati*) and *sampajanna* (the rationale for our activities), all play an important role in helping people to guard against unskilled states not yet arisen, abandon unskilled states already arisen, develop skilled states not yet arisen and maintain the skilled states already arisen. The motivational factors of commitment and sticking to one's commitment through fair and foul weather refer to factors of ardency and effort *(atapi, viriya)*. In this context, motivational counselling assumes an important role in current therapies for addictions.

Above all, the Buddhist approach considers free will as a necessary background condition for moral assessment. Leaving out the actions of a person with a deranged mind, all other instances of weakness of will, recklessness, and even compulsive behaviour come within moral assessment. There may be degrees of unwholesomeness depending on the intention/volition behind the action as well as degrees (or various kinds) of knowledge relating to it. Thus, both motivational and cognitive factors play a dual role. Intention and intentional agency (*cetana)* are central to Buddhist Psychology and ethics. An action emerging from an intention is a legitimate subject of moral evaluation as wholesome and unwholesome.

According to Groves and Farmer (1994), what distinguishes the disease model of addiction from the Buddhist model is the ability to choose and take responsibility:

> Buddhism offers a spiritual but non-theistic alternative to the theism implic-
> it in the 12-steps approach. This may be important for not just Buddhists
> with an addiction problem, but also the many addicts who reject a theistic
> approach. Also unlike the disease model, people are seen as having the abil-
> ity to choose and take responsibility for their actions. The attempt to
> change, unlike much contemporary therapy, is not primarily problem ori-

ented. The main focus is creating well-being through practicing skilful behaviour and cultivating skilful mental states. (p.191)

Classifying intentional actions

Harvey (2000, pp.53-58) has offered the following useful classification:

> An action done without intending to do it, like accidentally treading on an ant without any thoughts of harming would not incur blameworthiness and bad *karmic* results... A type of action which is performed by an agent who knows it to be evil, but does it while he is not impassioned and not in full control of himself. Such an action may be a lesser evil. The person is "out of mind, agitated" (*visanna*). A possible example is a monk who breaks a monastic rule in an abnormal state of mind... An evil action carried out when one is not clear about the object affected by the action. This is moderately blameworthy... An action done with full intention, fully knowing what one is doing, and knows that the action is evil. This is the most obvious of wrong actions, especially if it is premeditated... An evil action where one intends to do the act, fully knowing what one is doing but does not recognize that one is doing wrong. This is seen as the worst of actions.

This useful classification helps to overview the place of intention/volition and different types of knowledge and ignorance that play a role in developing a concept of moral weakness. Now, if one looks at the last category, we may cite the difference between a matter of fact, where one does not know one is harming someone, and the more spiritually blatant ignorance, where one does not know that harming a sentient being is wrong, which is a kind of spiritual ignorance. Also one may know that it is evil to harm sentient beings and yet do it. While Harvey's categories are useful in getting an overall picture of the degrees and types of culpability on the issue of culpability and moral weakness, paying heed to contextual factors is important.

Aristotle made a difference between those cases where, (i) having deliberated, we decide to do something, and then we fail to do that thing or do something else instead (last-ditch *akrasia);* and (ii) without having deliberated, we rush into doing something which, if we had deliberated, we would not have done (impetuous *akrasia*). Apart from rational deliberation, emotions or our affective side have significant links with moral weakness: emotions like lust and anger feed incontinence, whereas affects like compassion, caring, and gratitude may strengthen a strong will and contribute to clear perception. I have shown in a number of Buddhist studies on emotions, the role that emotions play in human behaviour and also that humans are responsible for behaviour related to emotions (de Silva, 1992, pp.3-4). Phrases like, "driven by anger", "plagued by remorse", "struck by a cupid's arrow", and "aroused by temptations" tend to give a very passive picture of the human mind in emotions. Averill (1980, p.38) says this kind of self-attribution allows the individual to abjure, to a limited extent, the responsibility for the consequences of his actions.

The etymologies of *pathos* and *pati* tended to make the passions central to our emotion vocabulary for a long period of time. The Buddhist vocabulary does not have a word for emotions but only for feelings *(vedana)*, which is a very early stage of affectivity as pleasure, pain, and neutral feelings. But it is with the addition of desires, thoughts, and volitional activity *(sankhara)* that we see a full-blown emotion, where intentions and responsibility are important features (de Silva, 1995, p.109). The determinism and free-will debate among philosophers in the West, in the context of addictions and *akrasia*, has been the subject of number of papers. A clear and a comprehensive study defending the role of free-will in the context of moral weakness can be found in Kennett's work on *Agency and Responsibility* (2001). While the scope of the present study does not give a context and space to discuss some of the interesting issues raised in this work, the work is useful for giving a glimpse into the relative role of motivational and cognitive factors in *akrasia*, both in the context of Greek thinkers and contemporary philosophical studies.

In the light of these observations on self-control, addiction, and the Dhamma, it is necessary to emphasize that there are scholars working in the field of addiction studies who do not have a clear understanding of the Buddhist perspective on addictions. This impression is clearly seen in Ainslie's comments:

> Buddhism, for instance, concerns itself with emancipation from "the bond ofworldly passions", and describes five strategies of purification, essentially: having clear ideas, avoiding sensual desires by mind control, restricting objects to their natural uses, "endurance", and watching out for temptation in advance. However, the ways that non-western religions enumerate causes of and solutions to self-defeating behaviors seem a jumble from any operational viewpoint of trying to maximize a good. (2001, p.5)

He also observes that despite all the attention paid to the subject, not many really new ideas have appeared over the years. He has taken this reference from *The Teachings of the Buddha* by Kyokai (1996, pp.228-342).

There are a number of critical points to be made regarding Ainslie's approach. First the reference he has taken from Kyokai is not accurate, and if one reads the discourse in the *Middle Length Sayings (the discourse on all the influxes, asava)* that refers to these methods, there are seven methods and these need to be broadly located on the Buddhist path of liberation. These methods refer not merely to the "bond of worldly passions" *(kamasava)*, but to the attachment to becoming *(bhavaasava)* and to the attachment to wrong views *(ditthasava)* as well. Regarding the methods it is said that these cankers or influxes may be got rid of by *vision*, by *control*, by *use*, by *endurance*, by *avoidance*, by *elimination*, and by *development*. While the purpose of these methods goes well beyond merely dealing with self-defeating behaviour, it is unlikely that Ainslie understood the complete context of this discourse.

Regarding the operational value of the methods cited here and what I have summarily described as guarding, abandoning, developing, and maintaining in the context of our lives, the recent use of mindfulness in therapy has in no uncertain terms shown the value of the innumerable techniques for leading a good and harmonious life. Also there have been a number of studies of the use of Buddhist techniques specifically directed towards addictions. *Mindful Recovery: A Spiritual Path to Healing from Addictions* by Bien and Bien (2002) is a product of extensive clinical work across many years. From my own practice as a counsellor,

I have succeeded in using Buddhist techniques for addictions in clients, as well as presenting these ideas to a larger group as an educational venture. Marlatt's contribution to addiction studies and Buddhism also point to the profound limitations of Ainslie's observations. Peel (author of number of works on addiction), commenting on Bien and Bien, submits,

> Mindful Recovery combines two hitherto unrelated worlds – that of cognitive therapy and Buddhist reflection. The connection makes incredible sense since Buddhism is not a religion in the traditional sense so much as it is a method for directing one's thoughts and experiences. By centering oneself in one's here-and-now, lived experience, addicts can avoid the infantilism, the regrets, the efforts to seek unrewarding rewards that are the basis for self-destructive behavior. (Peel, in Bien & Bien, 2002, p.1)

Mindfulness remains as the main ingredient of the recipe for awakened living.

The third point, I wish to convey is that in spite of his misunderstanding of Buddhist contributions to addiction studies, Ainslie has made an important contribution. In fact, one of his claims is that if one falls a prey to addiction in spite of a general commitment to self-control, one falls a prey to a momentary pleasure close at hand and ignores the long-term suffering. But human beings need not be at the mercy of the effects of the proximity of rewards, they can bring it about that they act for a larger, later reward in preference to a smaller one. This is very much in line with Buddhist insights, where the Buddha emphasizes the ignorant person's tendency to fall a prey to momentary and passing pleasures.

There is also the more recent work using Buddhist insights but directed towards a pragmatic ideal of moderation for addicts, and which is described as the Harm Reduction model (Marlatt, 2002). This is a very compassionate approach to tidy and re-arrange the lives of problem addicts, even if they cannot achieve complete abstinence. Even Bien and Bien (2002), who present a Buddhist model par excellence and thus would encourage addicts towards reaching the ideal of abstinence, appreciates the half-way pragmatic goals of moderation, where complete abstinence is not possible, except on the treatment route for limited periods of time.

In general, according to the Buddhist approach, a multiplicity of factors has a bearing on moral weakness and the need is for educating the victims of incontinence so that they can become stable people with rigour and ardency in their moral lives. It may not be enough simply to hold the conviction that some behaviour types like gambling, smoking, drug, and alcohol addiction or loose sexual impulses are destructive for the person and for others, unless these beliefs have strong motivational roots. As the psychologist Atkinson (1975) points out,

> The magnitude of response and the persistence of behaviour are functions of the strength of motivation to perform the act relative to the strength of motivation to perform competing acts. (p.361)

Mele (1996) points out that mere good judgments offer "no motivational magic" when we act intentionally to do what we are strongly motivated to do. Perceived proximity of prospects for desire-satisfaction also plays a role and that is why the Buddha advocated people to find suitable places of calm, stillness, and solitude for meditation. In active normal life, one's attentional stance is important and the practice of mindfulness in daily life helps one to be heedful about exciting contexts and situations. Thus, we need to emphasize as Mele does that there may be a misalignment between our assessment of desired objects and the motivational strength of our desires. This is the approach required to diffuse the Socratic paradox that "virtue is knowledge" and perhaps there is really no *akrasia*, and that if you really know that something is bad, you may not fall a victim to it. While the Buddhist approach accepts a higher level kind of wisdom which analytically rules out wrong-doing (as in Socrates), between the lower limits of normal secular life and the upper reaches of spirituality, there is a whole spectrum of emotional, motivational, and cognitive variation, and richness open for locating the nature of moral weakness or incontinence. I have discussed in detail Buddhist perspectives on cognition, motivation, desire, and emotions (de Silva, 2005). The Buddhist approach makes a distinction between *conventional* and *absolute* knowledge. Absolute knowledge may cover something like the Socratic notion of wisdom which analytically leaves out wrong-doing, the epistemic power of a refined form of spiritual knowledge. Conventional knowledge allows us to do what is wrong, while knowing that it is wrong, and is a self-defeating form of behaviour. One is knowingly courting disaster.

The preventive aspect

Another important facet of the Buddhist perspective is the *preventive aspect*: as Ruden (2000) observed in *Craving Brain*,

> Buddha's clever solution was not to fight the craving response once it occurred, but instead to prevent the pattern recognition process before it began. (p.87)

This stance implies restraint at the sensory level: guarding the senses keeps out incoming stimulation. He also recommends the combining of biobalance and mindfulness practice. It is when the biobalance is disturbed that the brain initiates a complex chain reaction making the body generate substance craving. In fact, Elster (1999), in a comprehensive study of addictions from the viewpoint of a social scientist and philosopher, presents a strong focus on the place of craving in addictions. He says that apart from the fact that addictive substances modify the physiological state of the organism; the craving for hedonistic pleasure is a central variable:

> The hedonic and non-hedonic effects jointly influence the state of *craving*, which is the central explanatory variable in the behavioural study of addiction and its consequences. (p.194)

The discourses of the Buddha contain many references to the unwholesome consequences that follow the consumption of alcohol, and it is basically on grounds of heedlessness that the Buddha makes the primary criticism. Apart from the negative impact of alcohol on psyche, he mentions six other consequences: loss of wealth, increase in quarrels, susceptibility to disease, earning a bad reputation, proneness to acts of immodesty, like exposure of one's body and a weakening of the intellect. Padmal de Silva (1984) has presented a useful paper on the

Buddhist ethical outlook on alcohol. An important dimension of the ethics of alcoholism is the social parameter of alcoholic consumption which is the same with other addictions like gambling.

Social dimensions of *akrasia*

While the individual is important, society does play a key role in moving towards an education for healthy recovery. Rorty (1998), writing on the ethics, the socio-pathology and the politics of *akrasia* makes the following observations:

> (1) The structure of the *akrasia* of anger differs from that of desire, but the explanation of its obduracy and entrenchment is similar.

> (2) Both *akrasia* of anger and *akrasia* of greed are typically dispositional rather than episodic, and both express conflicts among entrenched habits.

> (3) Because a good deal of *akrasia* is sustained and reinforced by socio-political and economic arrangements, patterns of *akrasia* are often a common form of social pathology.

> (4) The most effective reform of *akrasia* lies in the reform of its epidemiological sources – its socio-political and economic origins – rather than in the attempt to correct the immediate beliefs or desires that prompt individual cases. There is a need for a diagnosis of the social roots of *akrasia.*

Today drug and alcohol addictions, as well as compulsive gambling, are gradually taking epidemiological proportions and Rorty's point is important. Peele also brings out the social dimensions of addictions.

In the world where the Buddha lived, the kind of expectations and unending spiral of pseudo-desires and the spell of consumerism did not exist at a rampant scale as today. As I have emphasized in *Buddhism, Ethics and Society*, today the Buddhist temple and educational institutions have a key role in counteracting the moral blindness (inability to see moral issues), moral silence (reluctance to articulate one's moral stand), and moral apathy (lack of ardency about moral concerns) which runs through society. We have done a pilot project on these concerns in a summer school for forty young people at the Dhammasarana Temple in Keysborough, Melbourne, with very good results. Both the good and the bad are infectious. A morally vibrant social awareness is a necessary ally to deal with the increasing load of social *akrasia.*

The place of the body in addictions

According to Caldwell (1996, p.51):

> We threaten our lives when we introduce large amounts of toxins into our bodies. We damage our lives when we practice addictions that cause long-term illness or break the fabric of our families and societies. We limit our

lives when we fail to grow, when we keep ourselves sedated or distracted, when we fail to contribute to others. We promote life when we commit to our happiness and the happiness of others. Moving from life-threatening to life-promoting actions is a tremendous step.

Body-centred psychotherapist Caldwell, in a work titled, *Getting Our Bodies Back*, presents an admirable case for the innate capacity of the whole body-mind for healing. The Buddhist view on body-mind linkage (de Silva, 2005, pp.142-152) allocates to the body a central role in Buddhist meditation practice and therapy by focusing on the mindfulness of breathing and physical postures. The Buddhist approach also presents a psychological perspective emphasizing body-mind integration. As I have also shown in the same work (de Silva, 2005, pp.1153-1181), the Buddhist view has a wholistic view to interpose in the conflict between physiological arousal versus cognitive theories of emotions. Thus, this important front on addictions that Caldwell developed supplements the work of cognitive therapy in counselling and therapy.

Caldwell's plea to "reclaiming our bodies" in the context of addictions has found expression in a ground-breaking work of our times, *The Molecules of Emotion* by Pert (1997). She submits that emotions are the real link between the mind and the body or in Buddhist terms the psycho-physical complex (*nama-rupa*):

> By getting in touch with our emotions, both by listening to them and by directing them through the psychosomatic network, we gain access to healing wisdom that is everyone's natural biological right. (p.285)

Her pioneering research deals with the chemicals within our bodies and how they form a dynamic information network, linking mind and body. While making contributing to cancer and AIDS research, she also threw light on addictions and emotions. Pert, a molecular biologist is credited with the discovery of the opiate receptor and several other peptide receptors in the brain and the body. She could alter the old standpoint that the brain directs the flow of molecules and bring about the recognition that the flow of chemicals arises simultaneously from several systems: the immune, the nervous, the endocrine, and the gastrointestinal systems. These nodal points form a vast superhighway of information exchange. This is a picture emphasizing the importance of recognizing what may be called the "wisdom of the body". Against this theoretical background, the Sophia College counselling program has developed a Buddhist influenced body-based psychotherapy (Sherwood, 2005).

Alcohol/drugs may be used for medical, recreational and work enhancement purposes. Peer pressure, social interaction and curiosity, especially the desire to experiment, are factors that push some people to take drugs, and the social setting is as important as the physical and psychological dimensions of drug addiction.

The paradoxes of drug/alcohol addiction

Ven. Nyanavira (1987) – who discussed how he as a layman found a way to get out of an addiction to smoking, saying that the only way to give up smoking is to give up, which sounds like a tautology, observed:

> Unlike a "normal person" who may take a drug once in a while for the novelty or pleasure of the effect, and who at that time becomes "abnormal", the confirmed addict is "normal" only when he has taken a drug, and becomes "abnormal" when he is deprived of it. The addict reverses the usual situation and is dependent upon the drug to keep him in his normal integrated state. (p.7).

In a deeper sense he is pointing out that the addict is in a vicious circle and if he can understand this vicious circle as an outsider, and holds to the right view that his drugged state is not normal, he will be able to put up with temporary deprivation. He refers to the fact that a similar mechanism often works in the vicious circle of sense desire. He cites a *sutta* where a man with a skin disease is fiercely scratching the skin with his nails for temporary relief, and then it becomes worse (M I, 506-8). Nyanavira concludes that the addict has to be intelligent to understand this vicious circle and willing to make the necessary effort. A good response to breaking through such a vicious circle is found in the trial and error learning model developed by Marlatt.

Positive concepts of mental well-being

As the former president of the American Psychological Association, Seligman, pointed out, "the exclusive focus on pathology that has dominated so much of our discipline results in a model of a human being lacking positive features that make life worth living" (quoted in Ladner, 2004, p.xiv). Ladner also observes that historically the focus on pathology grew out of the disease model of looking at human beings, in which we try to repair damage rather than promote positive mental health. Ladner claims that the Buddhist tradition is different; it has an overarching focus on the positive (de Silva 2005, pp.126-128). Therapists working with addicts aim not merely in bringing them back to normal routine life, but also explore ways of enhancing their well-being, widening their life goals, and bringing back "the magic of the ordinary", the sense of liveliness and the elegance in the moment to moment flow of life.

A very recent study discussing Buddhist positive concepts of mental well-being works out in detail the conative, attentional, cognitive, and affective dimensions of *Mental Balance and Well-being* (Wallace & Shapiro, 2006). This study presents well-being as something that transcends transient and stimulus-driven pleasures. By the term conation they refer to intention and volition basically represented in the Buddhist concept of *sankhara* and *cetana, motivated and purposeful activity.* I use the concept "motivational" to cover such intentions and volitional activity as well as desires and drives. Conative balance entails intentions and volitions that are conducive to our well-being. Also, "A conative deficit occurs when people experience an apathetic loss of motivation for happiness" (Walace & Shapiro, 2006, p. 694). In the context of *akrasia*, enthusiasm and ardency to develop skilful activities and refrain from unskilful activities are important. Developed very much in the context of meditation and extended to its presence in routine life, attentional focus as shown in this article is sustained voluntary attention and is a feature of meaningful activity that features optimal performance and mental health. Mindfulness is a quality that can break through the stimulus-response mechanism of addictive behaviour. Cognitive balance refines our perception of things and situations without distortions, assumptions and projections. When people are out of touch with reality, absent-minded or seeing the world through their prejudices and bias, there is a cognitive deficit. Affective balance has played an important role in recent psychology with the development of the concept of emotional intelligence (Goleman, 1996). Wallace and Shapiro cite affective deadness, affective hyperactivity, and affective dysfunction as instances of the loss of affective balance.

Therapeutic perspectives from a counsellor's diary

The technique that I have used may be described as a kind of cognitive therapy infused with the Buddhist practice of mindfulness in routine life. The guidelines from cognitive therapy are the following:

> (1) Alcoholism (a word to be avoided with the client) is not a disease. It is a label used to describe one who drinks to excess.

> (2) Excessive drinking (a better term to use) is an acquired set of bad habits that condition behaviour.

> (3) These bad habits are linked to maladaptive and self-defeating ways of coping with inner and outer pressures.

Once the self-defeating patterns are identified and their causes are made clear, the client will be able to learn new and more adaptive coping strategies, without the immoderate use of alcohol. The technique emphasizes the trial and error learning aspect by getting the client used to short and then much longer periods of abstention, with the possibility of gradually becoming comfortable with controlled drinking. It is a hard road but it often works. Clarity of aim, persistence and a bit of passion combined with mindfulness make a big difference to some one who could have wrecked his life and those of his family. A loving and encouraging backing from home, friends, and the therapist are great blessings in this journey of self-transformation. Issues in the client's social, occupational, and marital life may add to his problems but they do not directly cause it. It takes time to sort out the different factors aligned to his drinking habits. Basically the focus is on high risk factors that generate excessive drinking, on continuous awareness, and on being mindful of testing situations. Moments of early failure to keep to temporary phases of abstentions are crucial and people in the home front need to have great deal of patience, compassion, and hope to aid the client.

Clinical vignette

While there is a strong link between emotions and addictions, as Elster has shown in *Strong Feelings: Emotion, Addiction and Human Behaviour* (1999), and though a detailed perspective on emotions is presented here, my case study basically focuses on the interaction of cognitive and motivational factors. While the emotional factors having an impact on the client (both negative and positive) will be kept in the background, the emotional deficits of anger, self-blame, guilt, despair, and depression, as well as the assets of acceptance, hope, confidence, joy of recovery, and the "magic of the ordinary" are the crucial facets of the below study.

The greatest bliss of a recovery is the joy of coming back to normal life... The client, Patrick, is a British migrant to Australia who spent several years in Middle East. There were certain positive factors on the client's side. He had no sense of underachievement or low self-esteem as he was doing well, and often presented himself as though he was a workaholic. He earned a good living and supported his family well. He had close friends and enjoyed their company. He was extremely generous. During the time that he spent in the Middle East, he had taken to smoking as there were restrictions on drinking and also as his family budget was small. At the time of entering treatment he was quite prosperous and had no financial or other restrictions on drinking. As he worked hard, the drinking habit took root for relaxing and getting together with friends. This went beyond routine enjoyment. But there was no awareness that he was going beyond the limit till a major incident nearly cost him his life. Since then anxiety entered his life, along with his drinking and a certain amount of reactive anger in the home front. Reactive anger in the home front was basically due to fear and to Patrick's inability to discuss his drinking problem at home. Drinking to respond to this reactive anger is a self-destructive path, and this is something that he realized in the early sessions. Drinking due to anger is different from drinking for enjoyment, drinking to forget worries or drinking because of the inability to solve problems. Patrick's leisure time was not profitably organized, had no variety, depth, and direction. Being in his mid-fifties and having grown-up children, he had no sexual striving but did have a need for love, understanding and compassion. Love and compassion was certainly there for many years, but excessive drinking had generated lot of misunderstanding and incessant bad feelings at home. This is a profile of a beautiful person, if not for the habit of excessive drinking.

We worked on a number of fronts: replacing ruminative negative thought patterns of temptation with decentering skills and seeing them more as impersonal patterns that come and go, that have no solidity, and that are not imperatives. With mindfulness, passing thoughts about having a drink may be put aside, Patrick learned to direct more awareness towards the stimulus to drink from time to time and to change perspectives from the fear of failure and poor self-confidence to developing some commitment towards a short term phase of abstention. He also developed an acceptance of his emotional deficit of anger, self-blame, guilt, and mild depression. There was a feeling of relief when bottled up thoughts were released during counselling and when I explained to the client the way that the process of such catharsis works. While there was some improvement, the client had a number of relapses. Then it was discovered by the client that the real issues emerged "during the empty hours in the evening after work, when you don't know what to do". Gradually he discovered that he could relax in the evening without a drink and could center himself in the here-and-now of immediate experience, what Kabat-Zinn calls the vividness of daily living and what Thich Nhat Hanh calls the "miracle of the ordinary". Patrick discovered he could enjoy the simple things in life like: making a cup of tea, cleaning the kitchen, doing a bit of gardening, cooking a meal, and watching a TV drama or film.

In conclusion: giving confidence and trust in oneself

In my counselling practice, I use to work on the following principles and help clients to understand their importance: responsibility, motivation, strength of purpose, mindfulness and attention, and alternatives.

(1) First, people can recover to the extent that they decide to take charge of their lives. Taking responsibility for one's own life is the starting point.

(2) Next, people can recover to the extent that they believe that an addiction is hurting them and wish to overcome it. They realize that this addiction causes pain and suffering. Here one has to work at the cognitive level, changing the way one perceives addictions. This perspective may be refined over several sittings.

(3) Then, after refining one's perception of addictions and their harm, developing motivational strength is crucial. As Mele (1996) observes mere judgments do not have "motivational magic". The clients need to feel enough efficacy and confidence that they can manage their withdrawal and life without the addiction. This is the level at which the motivational and intentional aspects may be developed. The secret of this level lies in taking small and effective steps, and one may say that the *devil is in the details.*

(4) Mindfulness and the attentional stance are key ingredients for success. The clients are given simple exercises in mindfulness practices which are to be developed to break through the stimulus response mechanism in addiction. If they find alternative ways of spending their leisure away from the hustle and buzz of hectic workaday life and enjoying the stillness of an evening at the temple or home, it becomes possible to break through that emptiness that comes during evenings for many addicts. Music, gardening, and enjoying long walks help them to generate energy. In fact, the walking meditation has a wonderful therapeutic potential. A healthy attentional stance, slowing down the speed and automatism of daily living, and enjoying movements of stillness, helps clients to slow down and gradually change their life style:

> It stands to reason that by becoming conscious of our options in stressful situations and being mindful of the relevance and effectiveness of our response in those situations, we may be able to exercise control over our experience of the stress and thereby influence whether or not it would lead to disease. (Kabat-Zinn, 1990, p.239)

In these accelerated times, working with computers, statistics and programs of varying accuracy, speed and rigour, people get baffled when they encounter uncertainty, sudden setbacks, ambiguity and paradox in their lives (Claxton, 2000). The new learning model of complete absorption and joy is called the "flow": "the state in which people are so involved in an activity that nothing else seems to matter" (Csikszentmihalyi, 1991). Why is this idea important? Sometimes, clients agree to stick to a period of abstention so that they can gain a certain amount of physical desensitization and after a long period get back to normal life. My own experience with clients is that once having them stick to a successful phase of abstention, a void then invades them, as they do not have sufficient activities for leisure, to keep them absorbed, especially in the evenings: "When you stop using your drug of choice, there is a hole in your life where the drug used to be. Suddenly you are left with empty hours that you don't quite know what to do with." (Bien & Bien, 2002, p.37) Some try to fill the void with a whole package of entertainment. A better way than trying to fill all your moments is to become aware of the fullness that each moment already offers. For instance, one of my clients found doing a bit of cooking in the evening, washing dishes, and studying recipes quite fascinating. This is the "magic of the ordinary" and is about mindfulness while eating a mandarin. This fascination can be extended to taking a shower, brushing teeth, making a cup of tea, folding laundry, and so on.

(5) The final principle is that clients must find and learn to value sufficient alternative rewards to make life worthwhile. Recovery is within oneself and is often slow, but it is possible to maintain steady progress. Issues of meaning are important to a person struck by futility and depression. It is within our power to make life interesting, absorbing and meaningful. One has to move out of the spell of separateness and develop connectedness and healing relationships. It is also necessary to tolerate uncertainties and changes that are a part of the world around us. In the last analysis, the greatest bliss that recovery brings to a client is "the joy of coming back to normal life".

Part V

Buddhist Psychology Expanding From Within The West

Chapter 14 by Mikulas reports on western psychology's embracing the Dharma. The author was the first to note the remarkable similarity between Behaviour Therapy and the *4-Ennobling Realities* in the 1970s. Now he coins the term "Essential Buddhism", a container term which refers to the pan-Buddhist tenets attributed to the historical Buddha and recognized by all Buddhist schools. These form the basis for a Buddhist Psychology that is linkable to cognitive science, behaviour modification, psycho-analysis, and Transpersonal Psychology. The emphasis is on mindfulness that has been successfully incorporated into Cognitive-Behaviour Therapy to overcome suffering. The various voices in western psychology share the idea that there is a self, while Buddhist Psychology only recognizes a "provisional self". To date, the only psychology that concurs with the Buddhist emptiness of "ultimate self" is Social Construction. The key premise is that knowledge and language are communal-relational and generative-transformative. Buddhists and social constructionists share the postmodern view that reality is in a flux and its referential semantics are non-abiding. In such impermanence, emptiness is ubiquitous and pervades the self. The implication for practice is that while evidence-based therapies are effective, this effectiveness might be enhanced by the therapist's "not-self way of being". Paradoxically, this way is "with-ness"-oriented, a collaborative approach requiring intensive dialoguing and conversations, i.e. communicating, talking, thinking, seeing, and acting *with* the people we work. This is entering a shared space of "uncertainty and not knowing" wherein partners work, learn, and create new perspectives to view things "for the first time".

The recommended "with-ness"-way-of-being surely also applies when training clients in Schulz's Autogenic method as described in Chapter 15 by Naylor. Unlike western therapies, it is not an analytic method that fixes what is broken, but is rather a skill of mental balance learned in observational silence with compassion over time. This homeostatic self-healing helps one become aware, perceive, and know the habits of emotion, thought, and behaviour. This sounds like mindfulness meditation. The intersection between Autogenics and Buddhist Psychology particularly emphasizes a confluence which is concatenated in the 12 steps of Karma and the 12 possibilities of karmic change by autogenic means to switch and shift in order to arrive at self-healing.

Chapter 16 by Fleischman is a gem, a timeless pièce de résistance. The author presents a wise, erudite, and outspoken essay which vilifies the present alienation, i.e. the professionalization, medicalization, and commercialization of Vipassana that includes mindfulness. For the loyal student of Goenka, the currently hyped western-ized mindfulness-based approaches that are separated from the Dharma have become a disgrace to a rich tradition that views Vipassana as a free gift of the Buddha to lib-erate everyone in the context of "Relational Interbeing". Because Vipassana is not a possession it can only be transmitted free of charge, not because of some socialistic attitude but because it is a gift of love. Should it stay that way? Poignantly remarked, if sold the seller could not get the experience of the open handed generosity which is characteristic for the non-attached meditator. Vipassana literally means clearly see-ing, perceiving, sensing, observing, watching, regarding, investigating, and the like. The Buddhist epiphany is that we are all interconnected: meaning and action are rela-tional. Our individual practice of Vipassana only seems to be a solipsistic encase-ment, for the greatest insight of all is that what we see inside are constructions of multiple relationships. The present western psychiatrist's *crie de coeur*, advancing Buddhist Psychology from within the West, finds resonance in less assertive Asian Buddhist psychologists. In an antithetical move, some of them attempt to re-embed mindfulness in various ways. Their views can be found in the next Part VI.

Chapter 14

Integrating Buddhist Psychology And Western Psychology

William L. Mikulas

Introduction

This chapter provides a western psychological interpretation of the fundamentals of Buddhist thought with special attention to integration with cognitive science, behavior modification, psychoanalysis and Transpersonal Psychology (Mikulas, 2007). To help, a few conceptualizations are drawn from the author's integrated psychology, called Conjunctive Psychology (Mikulas, 2002). The expression "Essential Buddhism" (EB) was invented to mean the fundamental principles of Buddhist thought, traditionally attributed to the historical Buddha, and recognized as basic to all Buddhist major schools. Insightful understanding of the essential Buddhist teachings has been continually stressed from the Buddha through to the current Dalai Lama.

EB is not religion or philosophy. Relative to religion, the Buddha did not claim to be other than a human being; he did not suggest he was a god or a god manifested in human form; he did not claim inspiration from any god or external power; and he discouraged veneration of himself. EB has no personal deity or impersonal godhead, no creeds or dogmas, no rituals or worship, no savior and nothing to take on faith; rather it is a set of practices and free inquiry by which one sees for oneself the truthfulness and usefulness of the teachings. The Buddha clearly did not want to establish a religion. And the Buddha's community was educational, not religious; the members were prohibited from involvement in religious practices and were not to compete with the Brahmin priests. Similarly, the Buddha avoided philosophizing and debates with philosophers. He particularly avoided speculative metaphysical questions. For example, he would not discuss whether the world is eternal, whether the soul is the same as the body, or whether a Buddha exists after death. He did not consider such philosophizing as useful to the path; rather it is more important to clean up one's life and train one's mind. Practice is more important than philosophy.

If EB is not religion or philosophy, although usually confused and confounded with them, then what is it? Clearly it is psychology, for it deals with topics such as sensation, perception, emotion, motivation, cognition, mind and consciousness (e.g., Wallace & Shapiro, 2006). The Buddha said his primary work was to reduce suffering, and the Dalai Lama continually stresses that his Buddhist approach is about increasing happiness. Padmasiri de Silva (2000) points out how more attention is given to psychology in the Buddhist teachings than in any other major spiritual discipline. Levine (2000) suggests a number of commonalities between the Buddhist discipline and western psychology: Both are concerned with alleviating human suffering. Both focus on the human condition and interpret it in natural rather than religious terms. Both see humans as caught in a matrix of forces, including cravings and drives, based in biology and beliefs. Both teach the appropriateness of compassion, concern and unconditional positive regard toward all beings. Both share the ideal of maturing and growth. And both acknowledge that the mind functions at a superficial and deep level.

Basic constructs

Next are described basic constructs of EB. These were all first introduced in the Buddha's classic discourse about the Four Noble Truths, which includes the Eightfold Path (Rahula, 1974). Although the discussion here is from a western psychological perspective and different from what is found in the traditional Buddhist literature, everything is totally compatible with EB.

Dukkha

A very broad and central concept in Buddhist Psychology is Dukkha (Claxton, 1992), which is usually translated as "suffering"; but actually means something closer to "unsatisfactoriness." Literal translations include: hard to bear, off the mark, and frustrating. It includes anxiety as described in western psychology. A very common example is when perceived reality does not match how one wants or expects reality to be. This discrepancy can be part of a feedback mechanism to guide behavior (Miller, Galanter, & Pribram, 1960). Dukkha arises when the discrepancy causes an undesired emotion, such as anxiety, anger, frustration, or jealousy. Dukkha then often impairs one's behavior, such as one's thinking. For example, if one's child or co-worker is not acting as one wants, then this discrepancy may cause one to act in ways to influence the other person. But if the discrepancy also causes anger, then one may think less clearly and thus be less effective.

One may compare one's image of one's self with an ideal or possible self as a basic feedback mechanism for behavior change and personal growth (Stein & Markus, 1996). But this comparison may result in Dukkha, such as anxiety or depression (Higgins, 1987; Rogers, 1961). One then acts to reduce the Dukkha (escape conditioning). This negatively reinforced behavior may be desirable; or it may be problematic, such as many cases of self-deception, lying to oneself or denying oneself certain information. Another common form of Dukkha is a sense of personal and/or spiritual unsatisfactoriness, possibly including the feeling that things are not quite right, the sense that real happiness is continually out of reach, and/or the conviction that one can't get free. This Dukkha is often part of the motivation that leads people to religion, spirituality, drugs, psychotherapy and other possible cures. At the existential level one often encounters a form of Dukkha based on a feeling of isolation, not being related to the whole (Yalom, 1980), and/or a threat to one's existence as a self (May, 1967).

A third common source of Dukkha, particularly in the US, results from the "more is never enough" trap. This occurs when one believes that collecting more of something (e.g., possessions, money, power, or fame) is the path to happiness and fulfillment. When this doesn't work, there can be profound Dukkha, such as a mid-life crisis. Dukkha is a very general concept that cuts across many domains and levels of being. This generality makes it particularly useful in integrating Buddhist and western psychologies. The strength of the concept is that all of Dukkha is explained in terms of one dynamic: clinging.

Clinging

The mind has a tendency to crave for and cling to certain sensations, perceptions, beliefs, expectations, opinions, rituals, images of the self, and models of reality. In EB, this craving and clinging is the cause of Dukkha. A possible cause of a midlife crisis is the clinging to an unrealistic image of how one's life should be at some point, even when realistically one has a good life. In the Buddhist teachings one of the "three marks of existence" is impermanence (*anicca*), the principle that everything changes. If one clings to something as it is at some time (e.g., one's relationship to child or spouse, a restaurant or vacation place, one's youth), then one will suffer Dukkha when it changes. If one doesn't cling, there is no Dukkha and one can go along with the change and perhaps influence it (e.g., allow a relationship to evolve, find a new vacation place, age gracefully).

If one clings to certain ideas or opinions, one will suffer Dukkha when one is wrong, and will probably have trouble recognizing one is wrong and changing one's mind. Instead one may come up with reasons why one is not really wrong after all. Clinically, it is common for people to cling to some behavior patterns even when they are not working well, in some cases because the people define themselves in terms of these behaviors and cling to those self-images. Clinging results in psychological inertia, a resistance to change, even when the change would make the person's life more effective and happier. Hence, clinging impairs behavior change and personal growth (Maul & Maul, 1983) and reducing clinging improves growth (Mikulas, 2004b).

In addition to Dukkha and resistance to change, clinging may also produce distortion in perceptions (e.g., seeing things in ways to fit one's beliefs) and impairment in thinking (e.g. holding on to some assumptions, decreased mental flexibility). This relates clinging to the dynamics of many psychological theories, such as psychodynamic defense mechanisms, cognitive dissonance theory, the "new look" in perception and schemas in cognitive psychology, which is beyond the scope of this chapter. In Buddhist Psychology, clinging is always detrimental, even though what one clings to may be judged desirable or not by various practical, psychological, ethical, and legal considerations. Glasser (1976) suggested there are some "positive addictions", such as for running or meditating; this is disputed in Buddhist Psychology. To be motivated and committed to jog every possible morning may be good for one's biological and perhaps psychological health; but if one clings to this, then one suffers Dukkha when one cannot jog, as when prohibited by the weather.

Four Noble Truths

In the Buddha's first major discourse, he described the Four Noble "Truths" (Rahula, 1974), or rather hypotheses, propositions, or facts, which one needs to rediscover for oneself every time and again. The first one is that life is filled with Dukkha. The second one is that the source of Dukkha is craving (which leads to clinging). The third one is that Dukkha ends when craving ceases. At this point, it is said that one is fully in the present, joyful, peaceful and compassionate. A common misunderstanding is that this will result in a person being apathetic or unemotional. This is not the case; one can still have preferences and goals without clinging. One's behavior becomes motivated more by compassion and appropriateness, rather than security, sensation, and power. In this sense Buddhist Psychology is more humanistic than

Freudian; it is postulated that the basic nature of people is sane, clear, and good. It is a matter of getting free from defilements, such as the three poisons of the mind, identified in Buddhist Psychology as greed (over-desire), hatred (anger), and ignorance (delusion).

The fourth "Truth" is the way to get free from craving and defilements, the Eightfold Path (Das, 1997). The first is right view or understanding; understanding the situation one is in (e.g., the Noble Truths and empirical marks of existence) and resolving to do something about it. The second is right intention or thought, including no lust, ill-will or cruelty. The third is right speech, including being constructive and helpful and avoiding lying, gossip and vanity. The fourth is right action, including being moral, compassionate, precise, and aware, and avoiding aggression. The fifth is right livelihood, not creating suffering. The sixth is right effort, actually doing what should be done. The seventh and eighth are: right awareness (mindfulness) and right attention (concentration), which are discussed in more detail next. The nature, function, and cultivation of mindfulness is one of the Buddha's great contributions to world psychology.

"Behaviors of the mind"

The construct "behaviors of the mind", unique to Conjunctive Psychology (Mikulas, 2002), is helpful in clarifying the nature of and differences between concentration and mindfulness. A critical distinction is between contents of the mind and behaviors of the mind. Contents of the mind include the various objects that arise in a person's consciousness, such as perceptual experiences, verbal and visual thoughts, reconstructed memories, attributions and beliefs, and cognitive aspects of emotions and attitudes. Behaviors of the mind are those processes of the mind (or brain if one prefers) that select and construct the contents and that provide awareness of the contents. Behaviors of the mind occur prior to, during and in response to any particular contents. Western psychologists and philosophers often confuse and confound contents of the mind with behaviors of the mind. Behaviors of the mind can be defined operationally, studied directly and through interactions with other behaviors, operantly and respondently conditioned, and shown to differ neurophysiologically (Dunn, Hartigan, & Mikulas, 1999; Mikulas, 2000, 2002). There are three fundamental behaviors of the mind: clinging, concentration, and mindfulness. Clinging, discussed above, refers to the tendency of the mind to grasp for and cling to certain contents of the mind. Concentration refers to the focus of the mind; and mindfulness involves the awareness of the mind, including properties of breadth and clarity.

Concentration

Concentration is the learned control of the focus of one's attention; it is the behavior of keeping one's awareness, with varying degrees of one-pointedness, on a particular set of contents of the mind. In western psychology concentration is generally seen as one aspect of attention (Moray, 1969), sometimes discussed in terms of focused attention, controlled attention, sustained attention, or vigilance. However, these literatures usually refer more to the readiness and/or ability to detect the critical signal, rather than the skill to maintain the desired focus of attention.

The world literature on meditation-produced concentration, some western research (Murphy & Donovan, 1997) and anecdotal reports suggest that developing concentration can have a wide range of applications in therapy, education, sports and art. Students can learn how to keep their minds from wandering while studying. Listening skills can be improved in counselor training and communication therapy. Athletes can learn to not be distracted by the crowd and stay focused on the sport (e.g., keep one's eye on the ball). Artists can learn to fully immerse themselves in their creations. Concentration training is a significant addition to our psychological technology. One of the most obvious potential applications of concentration training is in attention disorders, including ADD/ADHD (attention deficit disorder, perhaps with hyperactivity), self-focused attention (Ingram, 1990) and attentional bias (Dalgleish & Watts, 1990). ADD/ADHD is usually treated with drugs, perhaps combined with behavior modification for hyperactivity. To what extent and how could concentration training help some of these people?

If a person sits quietly and practices a concentration form of meditation, then the mind becomes calm and relaxed, which often relaxes the body. This biological relaxation is, by far, the most researched effect of meditation in the western literature (Andresen, 2000; Murphy & Donovan, 1997). If a western psychology text mentions meditation, it is usually in terms of relaxation and/or stress reduction. Concentration-produced relaxation can be an effective treatment for anxiety (DelMonte, 1985). This quieting of the mind that comes from concentration gives the practitioner more control over thoughts, an effect with great potential significance for western psychology. For example, unwanted intrusive thoughts occur in almost everyone in varying degrees (e.g., Freeston, Ladouceur, Thibodeau, & Gagnon, 1991). Clinically, these thoughts may lead to and/or exasperate problems such as anxiety, worry, depression, and anger. Western therapies have had very limited success at reducing these thoughts, with attempts to control or suppress the thoughts often being counterproductive (Clark, 2005).

In the Buddhist teachings concentration has a more profound purpose, the dis-identification with contents of the mind and creating space for insight knowing. If one does not quiet the mind, then one will probably stay lost in the contents most of the time; one's reality is the contents and one believes one's self to be the self-related contents (e.g., reconstructed memories involving the self, self-concept). From a Buddhist perspective, there is an existential freedom that comes when one no longer identifies oneself with mental contents; but this is hard to accomplish without quieting the mind. Relatedly, mindfulness-produced insight, the goal of Buddhist practice discussed later, is difficult without quieting the mind. Hence, concentration is part of the Eightfold Path. The yogic/Buddhist literature describes eight different levels of concentration and absorption called *jhanas* (Buddhaghosa, 1975; Khema, 1997). Before he became the Buddha, Gautama studied and mastered all eight levels. He later argued that the *jhanas* could only suppress defilements, while mindfulness could destroy them. And optimal mindfulness only requires some degree of concentration.

Mindfulness

Mindfulness, as a behavior of the mind, is defined as the active maximizing of the breadth and clarity of awareness. It is the behavior of moving and sharpening the focus of awareness within the field of consciousness. This definition corresponds to how mindfulness is usually described in EB. Other times in the Buddhist literature mindfulness is described more as a property of the mind, in which case the above definition corresponds more to the cultivation of mindfulness, rather than mindfulness itself. Mindfulness involves simply observing the contents and processes of the mind; it is just being aware, bare attention, detached obser-vation, and choiceless awareness. It is not thinking, judging, or categorizing; it is being aware of these mental processes. The essence of mindfulness training is noticing whatever arises in consciousness while minimizing the occurrence of and getting lost in related thoughts, reactions and elaborations. Traditionally, mindfulness is cultivated during sitting and walking meditation, as found in the Theravadin Vipassana literature (Goldstein, 1993; Hart, 1987; Mahasi Sayadaw, 1978, 1980). "Vipassana" means clear seeing in new, varied and extraordinary ways. Vipassana meditation is often called "insight meditation" because in EB it is held that cultivation of mindfulness leads to a form of insight called *panna* (Pali) (*prajna,* Sanskrit), an immediately experienced intuitive wisdom. *Panna*-based knowing is different than sensory knowing or conceptual knowing, although when it is later thought about, conceptual knowing is involved. *Panna* involves mindful and penetrating seeing into the fundamental nature of things in a way that transforms one's being, the ultimate purpose of meditation in EB. For example, insightful seeing of impermanence leads to a reduction of clinging.

In a therapeutic situation, mindfulness training would focus on clinically significant fac-tors, such as thoughts and feelings related to anxiety. Mindfulness could be assessed in terms of its effects on the clinical problem (e.g., anxiety) and/or via a mindfulness questionnaire geared toward general mindfulness (Baer, Smith, & Allen, 2004; Brown & Ryan, 2003; Mikulas 1990) or mindfulness of a specialized domain (e.g., DeMaria & Mikulas, 1991). Mindfulness is critical to developing optimal behavioral self-control (Mikulas, 1986, 1990). When one is aware of a less preferred behavior and/or a sequence of events leading to a less preferred behavior, then one utilizes an intervention strategy to disrupt the sequence, decrease the undesired behavior, and/or increase a desired alternative behavior. Mindfulness training helps one become more aware of the critical environmental cues, body sensations, feelings and thoughts. Particularly important is moving the mindfulness back earlier and earlier in the chain of events. For example, it is easier to avoid anger with a self-control skill when one is starting to get angry or is becoming predisposed to anger, then to try to stop anger when it is occurring. In western research, Kristeller and Hallett (1999) suggested that increased mindfulness of sati-ety cues and eating-related social, emotional, and physical cues may help in binge eating; and a similar argument has been made for cues related to substance abuse (Breslin, Zack, & McMain, 2002; Groves & Farmer, 1994).

In the last decade, mindfulness has become very popular in western approaches to thera-py, including psychotherapy (Boorstein, 1997; Germer, Siegel, & Fulton, 2005; Horowitz, 2002; Segall, 2005) and cognitive behavior therapy (Baer, 2003; Smith, 2004; Witkiewitz, Marlatt, & Walker, 2005). Mindfulness has been identified as a "core psychotherapy process" (Martin, 1997) and a theme "across schools of psychotherapy" (Horowitz, 2002). What is lit-tle known in western psychology is how mindfulness can be developed as a generic skill, over and above its application in specific domains.

The Buddha and his disciples practiced and recommended mindfulness for pain control (de Silva, 1996). More recently Kabat-Zinn developed a stress reduction clinic at the University of Massachusetts Medical Center to treat stress and pain (Kabat-Zinn, 1990). Treatment components of the program, now called "Mindfulness-Based Stress Reduction" (MBSR), include mindfulness meditation and homework assignments, mindful yoga practices, body scans (slowly sweeping attention through the body noticing sensations), awareness of breathing and stress, noticing sensations and thoughts non-catastrophically, developing concentration, communication training, and discussion of stress and coping. Research within this clinic has shown the effectiveness of the program for pain Kabat-Zinn, 1982; Kabat-Zinn, Lipworth, Burney, & Sellers, 1987) and anxiety (Kabat-Zinn et al., 1992; Miller, Fletcher, & Kabat-Zinn, 1995).

Research by other groups on programs based on Kabat-Zinn's MBSR have provided supporting positive results (e.g., Astin, 1997; Reibel, Greeson, Brainard, & Rosenzweig, 2001; Shapiro, Schwartz, & Bonner, 1998; Speca, Carlson, Goodey, & Angen, 2000). However, in all this research mindfulness has not been well-defined, measured and factored-out (Baer, 2003; Bishop, 2002). Of all the components of the MBSR program, including mindfulness, it has not been determined their relative weights and contributions to the overall effectiveness of the program. This includes the program components listed in the previous paragraph plus group support, instructor modeling and reinforcement and non-specific effects such as expectations and demands. At first, psychologists were interested in how MBSR reduces stress and pain. Now researchers are considering how MBSR-type programs can be applied to other domains, such as relationship enhancement (Carson, Carson, Gil, & Baucom, 2004) and Mindfulness-Based Cognitive Therapy (MBCT), discussed later.

Meditation

Worldwide, meditation is the most recommended and utilized practice for improving the health of body, mind and spirit; it is the central practice of EB. There is a large western research literature on meditation (Andresen, 2000; Murphy & Donovan, 1997) and a fast growing interest in the psychotherapeutic uses of meditation (e.g., Kwee, 1990; Marlatt & Kristeller, 1999). There is no agreed-upon definition of "meditation", and in the US the term is often used for guided imagery, deliberation, and daydreaming.

In Conjunctive Psychology, the practice of meditation is divided into four discrete components: form, object, attitude, and "behaviors of the mind". Form refers to what one does with one's body during meditation. The Buddha suggested four basic forms: sitting, walking, lying and standing. Object refers to the primary stimulus of one's attention, such as one's breathing, an external visual or auditory stimulus, a sound or phrase said to oneself, or an imagined being or scene. The object determines whether a meditation practice is primarily religious, therapeutic or something else. Attitude is the mental set in which one approaches meditation, including moods, associations, expectations and intentions. Optimal practice involves persistent dedication, a welcoming openness to experience, a readiness to let go, letting be rather than trying to accomplish something, making friends with oneself and being in the here and now.

The behaviors of the mind component refers to the fact that all the major meditation traditions in the world stress the development of concentration and/or mindfulness (Goleman, 1988; Ornstein, 1986); hence this would be part of an ultimate definition of meditation. All the major meditation practices contain both concentration and mindfulness, but most emphasize concentration. The emphasis given to mindfulness is the Buddhist strong contribution; but in some Buddhist meditation practices and/or an individual's practice at a certain time, concentration is emphasized. Because meditation is often done within a religious context and/or with a religious object, all of meditation is often seen as a religious practice and thus irrelevant or inappropriate to some western psychologists. But meditation can be psychotherapy when in a therapeutic context with a therapeutic object (examples will be given in the section on behavior modification). Also, it is necessary to explore a wider range of forms, including ones individualized for clients, such as running, swimming, fishing, craftwork, and listening to music.

Confusions and confounding

There are a number of very common confusions that permeate all the literatures related to behaviors of the mind, including research and theories about mindfulness, cognitive behavior therapy and meditation. Mindfulness, especially of cognitions, is often experientially confused with thinking. Consider a mindfulness of thoughts continuum: On the low side of the continuum is a person who notices a thought and then has thoughts about the thought and perhaps has thoughts about thinking about the thoughts. This is basically thinking with a small amount of mindfulness, although experientially it may seem quite profound. On the high side of the continuum is a person who has learned to quiet the mind and disengage and step back from the thoughts, the experience being of a passive witness watching thoughts pass through consciousness. The person on the low end of the continuum is readily pulled into the thoughts, particularly those with high affect and/or personal significance; the person on the high end can more easily maintain some distance from the thoughts, recognize them as "just thoughts", and more easily alter them (e.g., stop, challenge, replace). Beginners in mindfulness meditation (Vipassana) often confuse thinking with mindfulness of thoughts, until they experience the difference. Similarly, some cognitive therapy and western mindfulness programs include descriptions suggesting mindfulness of thoughts, when it is actually just more thinking, such as nonjudgmental reflection.

Mindfulness and concentration are often confused and confounded. One reason is that they are usually cultivated together and a change in one usually produces changes in the other. For example, it is usually easier to be mindful when the mind has been quieted and focused through concentration; and one of the things one can become mindful of is how concentrated the mind is, which facilitates developing concentration. Some Buddhist meditation programs begin with an emphasis on concentration and then gradually shift the emphasis to mindfulness, other programs always emphasize mindfulness. In western psychology, mindfulness and concentration are often confused and confounded because, although in the last few years there has been a moderate interest in mindfulness, there has not been a corresponding interest in concentration. Hence, many mindfulness-based programs are actually cultivating both concentration and mindfulness, but all results are attributed to mindfulness. In some cases more attention to cultivating concentration might improve the successfulness of the program. Concentration and mindfulness are often confused and confounded with clinging, since they all influence each other. For example, as discussed earlier, cultivation of mindfulness is an important part of developing a self-control program to reduce craving and clinging. And reducing clinging can improve mindfulness by reducing distortion and/or by allowing awareness to move into new areas.

We need clearer understanding of the three behaviors of the mind and how they differ and interact. And this is probably best done by people who have at least a moderate amount of experience working with the behaviors in themselves.

Western disciplines

Next will be considered how EB relates to four very different schools of western psychology: cognitive science, behavior modification, psychoanalysis, and Transpersonal Psychology.

Cognitive science

In academic psychology, the dominant and usually exclusive cognitive science is the information-processing computer-simulation model. In this theory humans are information processors, the brain is the major or only vehicle for this processing, and computers are models for how the brain functions. Behaviors of the mind are an alternative cognitive science with the strength of obvious implications for therapy, personal/spiritual growth, education, sports, and art. The Buddhist discipline in general has much to offer western cognitive science (e.g., Varela, Thompson, & Rosch, 1991) including a very comprehensive cognitive science in the *Abhidhamma* (deCharms, 1997; Lancaster, 1997).

The *Abhidhamma* ("ultimate teaching") is the third collection of books in the Pali canon. It is the further philosophical and psychological development of EB (Bhikkhu Bodhi, 1993). For some people, the expression "Buddhist Psychology" refers to the *Abhidhamma*. This Buddhist cognitive science includes a detailed dissection of mental processes and experiences, plus an explanation for how they all fit together. On the practical side, it is held that this analysis can facilitate the development of insight (*panna*), and it is the basis for some meditation practices. The *Abhidhamma* is a critically-analyzed, detailed map of the mind, broken down into sequences of conscious and mental factors. This involves dissecting experience into *dhammas*, elementary essences of conscious reality experiences. A *dhamma* is a irreducible atom of expression, such as a single characteristic or quality. For example, a triad of *dhammas* is related to feeling: pleasant, unpleasant, or neutral. Dhammas include momentary forces, defined in terms of function, that create conventional reality. One classification of *dhammas* is by the five aggregates or "heaps" (Pali: *Khanda*), currently best known in the West by the Sanskrit term *Skandha*. The *Skandhas* are collections of *dhammas* that comprise entities such as a person. The five *Skandhas* are form (elements of matter, the five physical senses and their objects), feeling, perception (discernment of an object, beginning of concept formation), mental formations (mental contents other than feeling and perception) and consciousness.

The *Abhidhamma* includes many different systems of categorizing and grouping *dhammas* and other basic components of the mind and consciousness. One is the 52 mental factors (*cetasikas*), components associated with consciousness. Seven of the factors are "universals" since they are found in all consciousness and are needed for basic cognition of an object (Bhikkhu Bodhi, 1993):

(1) Contact, consciousness mentally touches object;
(2) Feeling, experience of affect;
(3) Attention, making object present to conscious;
(4) One-pointedness, concentration;
(5) Perception, recognition of object via its features;
(6) Volition, willing, actualization of goal;
(7) Mental life faculty, vital making and maintaining associated with mental states.

The *Abhidhamma* also includes lists of unhealthy factors and healthy factors (Goleman, 1988). These factors impair or help meditation, and can be the basis for personality and mental health. Therapy consists of cultivating healthy factors that offset unhealthy factors. For example, cultivating the healthy factors of insight and mindfulness reduce the unhealthy factor of delusion, which could be causing paranoia. The unhealthy factors include delusion, perplexity, shamelessness, remorselessness, egoism, agitation, worry, greed, avarice, envy, contraction, and torpor. The healthy factors include insight, mindfulness, modesty, discretion, rectitude, confidence, non-attachment, non-aversion, impartiality, and composure. The above is a small sample of how the *Abhidhamma* provides a dissection of mental processes and experiences; but it also includes how these components fit together, as described by the Four Noble Truths and Dependent Origination. Perhaps the most profound, and certainly the least understood, theory of EB is the theory of Dependent Origination (*paticca-samuppada*) (Buddhadasa, 1992), also called "co-dependent origination" and "causal interdependence". This elaboration of the Four Noble Truths, which was originally taught by the Buddha and detailed in the *Abhidhamma* (Bhikkhu Bodhi, 1993), is very relevant to western cognitive science (e.g., Kurak, 2003).

The principle of Dependent Origination is that everything arises through dependence on something else (Macy, 1991). This is expressed in many ways, such as: with X as a condition, Y arises; because X exists, then Y arises; and through X, Y is conditioned. In the most popular version of Dependent Origination there are 12 links in a circular chain, with every link depending on the previous link. The 12 links are ignorance, formations, consciousness, name and form, six senses, contact, feeling, craving, grasping, becoming, birth and death. Ignorance includes biases, blind spots and absence of right understanding (first of the Eightfold Path). With ignorance as a condition, formations arise. Formations include bodily, verbal, and mental formations, plus volitional predispositions. Next is consciousness, the five types of consciousness associated with the five physical senses plus the mental consciousness of perceptions, thoughts, and memories. The associated state of mind is often restless, little concentration. Next to arise is name and form, mentality and materiality, self and not-self, and a sense of personal experience. This leads to the six senses, the senses associated with the six types of consciousness, such as the eye sense with visual consciousness. With the six senses as a condition, contact arises, the sense organ makes contact with the object of the sense. The apparent world now arises, with sensing and thinking. Contact leads to feeling, the immediate quality of the sensation, whether it is positive, negative, or neutral. With feeling as a condition, craving arises, including approaching the positive and avoiding the negative. Craving leads to grasping which leads to clinging, as discussed earlier. Grasping conditions becoming, the arising of sense of a personal self and will plus predispositions for certain behaviors. Becoming leads to birth, the occurrence of behaviors, and to identification of the self with various experiences and actions. And birth is followed by death as everything is impermanent and eventually comes to an end.

The links of the six senses through grasping correspond to two factor theory in learning (Mikulas, 2002). According to two factor theory, respondent variables provide the initial motivation and/or consequent reinforcers/punishers for much of operant behavior (Levis, 1989). The senses and contact lead to feeling: positive, negative or neutral. This basic affect could be a natural property of the stimulus or it could be based on respondent conditioning as described by evaluative conditioning (Martin & Levey, 1978). Evaluative conditioning, as opposed to the better known CS-UCS contingency learning, is the simple conditioning of positive or negative affect to stimuli. This affect may later be experienced or interpreted in many ways (e.g., love/hate and excitement/fear). The affect leads to craving, the motivation for an operant response to consume or escape. Craving leads to grasping, including the operant responses to hang on to some things and avoid and fight against others. In the presence of the discriminative stimuli related to feeling and craving, one makes an operant approach or avoidance response (grasping). One theory of drug addiction is that the escape and avoidance of negative affect is the major motive for addictive drug use (Baker, Piper, McCarthy, Majeskie, & Fiore, 2004).

In the Buddhist literature, when Dependent Origination is discussed, it is almost always described as a model for rebirth and Karma; ignorance and formations apply to the "past life", the next eight links apply to the "present life", and birth and death to the "future life". This may be true but it is outside the domain of this chapter, unless life refers to a this-worldly and non-metaphysical episode of an emotional event. It should be understood that this was not the emphasis given by the Buddha (Buddhadasa, 1992), Rather, the Buddha's explanation refers more to how the sense of a personal self may arise at a particular time, and how the principles of dependent origination apply to everything that arises in consciousness. Hence, for any one person, hundreds or more such cycles occur every day (Buddhadasa, 1992). These are the cycles of interest to psychologists and cognitive scientists. When a cycle of dependent origination is producing undesired overt behaviors, cognitions or feelings, then the question is how to break the cycle; the chain can be theoretically broken at any link. Intervention at the link of contact might be done via stimulus control, such as getting liquor bottles out of the house. Some Vipassana practices are aimed at bringing mindfulness back through the chain to feelings, as a point of intervention. Perhaps the best point of intervention for western psychologists is at the links of craving and grasping (Mikulas, 2004b); many western therapies apply here.

The interrelationships between cognitive science and the *Abhidhamma* are just beginning to be explored; there are great opportunities. In comparing and combining Buddhist psychology and cognitive science, we can re-evaluate some of our theoretical and practical assumptions, such as the strengths and weaknesses of the computer simulation model.

Behavior Modification

The term Behavior Modification is used here in the broadest sense to include Behavior Therapy, Cognitive-Behavior Therapy, and Applied Behavior Analysis. Similarities between EB and behavior modification discussed in an early article (Mikulas, 1981) include the following: both stress perceiving reality as it is with a minimum of distortion and interpretation, avoiding theoretical and metaphysical constructs that are difficult to measure or have questionable usefulness. Both are primarily a-historical with a focus on living more fully in the here and now, historical information is primarily useful in understanding current conditions. Both encourage increased awareness of body, mind, and emotions, and the importance of learning related self-control skills. Although teachers, peers, and others may help in various ways, it is usually best when one takes responsibility for one's life, including one's behavior. In doing this one learns to not identify one's self with one's behavior. Both recognize that everything changes and offer models for how this change takes place. And both focus on reducing attachments, seen in terms of clinging and/or habits. Padmal de Silva has many publications interrelating EB and western psychology (e.g., 1996, 2003), including two articles describing how the Buddha and other early Buddhists utilized and advocated practices that today would be called behavior modification (1984, 1985).

Since the beginning of the field of behavior modification, counter-conditioning has been a basic approach to reduce respondently-based behavior, particularly unwanted emotions such as anxiety. Although there is no agreement about how counter-conditioning works, it is clear how to do it (Mikulas, 1978): In the presence of stimuli that elicit the undesired behavior, an incompatible and dominant response is elicited or emitted. Response dominance is ensured through increasing the strength of the incompatible response and/or by gradually encountering stimuli along a hierarchy of increasing response strength. Counter-conditioning is traditionally done with imagined scenes and/or in vivo, but can also be done in other ways including modeling, stories and virtual reality. Counter-conditioning is also a major and prevalent practice in EB. One example, mentioned above, is the use of healthy factors to reduce unhealthy factors. When counseling lay-people, Thai Bhikkhus commonly offer advice such as cultivating friendliness to offset ill-will or sympathetic joy to offset jealousy. Another example, common in the Buddha's time, was to meditate in charnel grounds on dead bodies in varying degrees of decay, as a way to reduce body-related craving, such as lust or vanity. Counter-conditioning also naturally occurs during meditation; when a thought or memory with negative affect arises, if the meditation-produced calm or relaxation is dominant to the negative affect, counter-conditioning will occur.

A popular and powerful example of Buddhist counter-conditioning is loving kindness (*metta*) meditation, which takes many forms (Salzberg, 1997). For example, one person has a hierarchy of people beginning with someone who is very loved, moving through people liked to people disliked and ending with a hated person. The practice consists of gradually going through the hierarchy, meditating on the people, while maintaining a feeling of loving kindness. This is obviously very similar to the counter-conditioning therapy of systematic desensitization, except that the first item on the loving kindness hierarchy is very positive rather than neutral, and negative feelings are being counter-conditioned by love rather than anxiety by a response such as relaxation.

Based on Kabat-Zinn's MBSR program, described earlier, Segal, Williams, and Teasdale (2002) developed MBCT, which they found reduced relapse in depression (Ma & Teasdale, 2004; Teasdale, et al., 2002; Teasdale, et al., 2000). The core skill that this program "aims to teach is the ability, at times of potential relapse, to recognize and disengage from mind states characterized by self-perpetuating patterns of ruminative, negative thought" (Segal, et al., 2002, p. 75). It is suggested that mindfulness training facilitates "early detection of relapse-related patterns of negative thinking, feelings, and body sensations" when they are easier to stop, which is facilitated by "disengagement from the relatively automatic ruminative thought patterns" (Ma & Teasdale, 2004, p.34). These results are probably due to cultivation of mindfulness and concentration, where the concentration quiets and focuses the mind, which allows one to step back from cognitions.

For the past few decades the major behavior modification organization in North America has been the Association for Behavioral and Cognitive Therapies (ABCT), previously called the Association for Advancement of Behavior Therapy. In the last few years, two of the most popular topics in ABCT have been mindfulness-based therapies and acceptance-based therapies, primarily Hayes' Acceptance and Commitment Therapy (Hayes, Strosahl, & Wilson, 1999). As a result, mindfulness and acceptance have become heavily intertwined within ABCT. Publications, talks, and workshops by prominent ABCT members usually define mindfulness in terms of acceptance, with acceptance being seen as a critical component of mindfulness, sometimes the most important component. A number of therapeutic approaches combine mindfulness and acceptance (e.g., Gardner & Moore, 2004; Hayes, Follette, & Linehan, 2004; Orsillo, Roemer, & Barlow, 2003; Roemer & Orsillo, 2002). In EB mindfulness and acceptance are separate and very different. Mindfulness has nothing to do with accepting or rejecting, it is simply awareness of these processes. This distinction has important implications for therapy and personal/spiritual growth, such as when it is important for the person to be mindful of not accepting; this should be particularly important for acceptance-based therapies. If mindfulness training suggests that acceptance is part of mindfulness, then the person will be biased against being mindful of non-acceptance and this could generalize to related domains and thus impair overall mindfulness. Acceptance is part of the attitude component of meditation, discussed earlier, and it affects all three behaviors of the mind, particularly clinging. Thus, acceptance reduces clinging, which then improves mindfulness.

"Equanimity" is a very important concept in EB (Pandita, 1992), a concept related to acceptance. It is equal acceptance and receptivity toward all objects of consciousness, an evenness of mind in which one is not more interested in or drawn to some objects of consciousness than others. One way of producing equanimity is by quieting the mind via concentration, with equanimity gradually increasing with increasing concentration, until it is at full strength at the fourth *jhana* (Goleman, 1988). Equanimity is one of the seven factors of awakening (Pandita, 1992); the other six factors are mindfulness, concentration, investigation, effort, rapture and calm. Again, it can be seen that mindfulness, concentration and equanimity are all different, but related. Mindfulness is considered primary, as it facilitates the awakening, strengthening and keeping in balance of the other six factors.

Behavior modification and EB package very well and can profit from more integration. Current interest in mindfulness has been heuristic and helpful, next is to include more attention to concentration and clinging and how all three behaviors of the mind interact.

Psychoanalysis

There is a large diverse literature comparing psychoanalysis and the Buddhist teachings (e.g., Aronson, 2004; Epstein, 1995; Molino, 1998; Rubin, 1996; Safran, 2003; Suler, 1993), with a major part of the literature focusing on Zen (e.g., Brazier, 1995; Magid, 2005; Twemlow, 2001). Similarities between psychoanalysis and EB that are commonly mentioned include the following. Both are primarily concerned with reducing the suffering of everyday life. Both utilize an experiential approach to explore the dynamics of the personal reality, including perceptions, emotions and the sense of self. Both cultivate clear perceiving, knowing reality, and insight into the nature of the self, in ways that transforms one's being. And both encourage personal development and freedom from oppressive forces. Epstein (1995) suggests that the Buddha may have been the first psychoanalyst, and both Freud and the Buddha applied their procedures to themselves (de Silva, 1992).

There are also important similarities between psychodynamic inquiry and mindfulness-based inquiry, as in Vipassana meditation. Both often use a sitting or a lying form (e.g., sitting in a chair or on a cushion, lying on a couch or on the floor), as a way to simplify the situation for inner discovery, restrict action and acting out, and minimize escape. In both the journey is guided by well-established instructions and practices, such as free association in psychoanalysis and looking for specific mental dynamics in Vipassana (e.g., the interplay of mind and body, or the rising and falling of mental contents in consciousness). Both encourage people to open their consciousness to new and repressed material and to actively notice what arises. And both may lead to the transpersonal, discussed later.

There are, however, important differences between psychodynamic inquiry and Vipassana. In psychoanalysis the therapist is more involved with the client during inquiry, interacting with the client and encouraging and guiding the client; while in Vipassana the meditator usually works alone, based on instructions and feedback between meditation sessions. Vipassana is more concerned with the processes of the mind than the content, while psychoanalysis is often very concerned with content (Epstein, 1995). In psychoanalysis, the client is often encouraged to engage and work through contents, rather than simply notice them as in most mindfulness practices. When clients should immerse in the contents and when they should mindfully disengage is an important clinical issue (Cortright, 1997). And resulting insight in psychoanalysis is usually more verbal and rational, while Buddhist insight (panna) is more non-verbal and non-conceptual.

Meditation by client and/or therapist can facilitate the psychoanalytic process. If the client meditates, it may allow formerly unconscious material, including some that was repressed or suppressed, to arise in consciousness; then some of the related content and issues can be addressed via psychotherapy (Epstein, 1995). If through meditation the client develops a position of detached mindful observation of the contents of the mind, then this might facilitate ego development (Boorstein, 1997). In addition, Rubin (1996) suggests that when this objective witnessing is applied to contents of the mind that were previously equated with the self, this may lead to greater freedom and openness related to self-structures, more flexible relatedness to self and others and a decrease in self-recrimination. And Epstein (1995) suggests that mindfulness complements psychotherapy by facilitating surrender into direct experience, being in the here and now with present experience and how to be with emotions. Meditation by the therapist facilitates being more mindful of the client, listening better and being more fully present with the client; this includes reduction of distracting cognitions, such as premature treatment planning and categorizing. Rubin (1996) suggests that fully present listening is a form of compassion and unconditional acceptance. Freud recommended that therapists cultivate a stance of "evenly hovering attention" (Epstein, 1984), which includes mindfulness, equanimity and reduced cognitive reacting. Although Freud did not suggest positive ways to cultivate this attentional stance, it appears to be like the results of developing concentration and mindfulness, as via meditation (Epstein, 1984, 1995; Rubin, 1996).

Psychodynamic defense mechanisms and the clinging behavior of the mind produce many similar results, such as distorted perceptions and memories, decreased awareness and resistance to change. An open question is to what extent various functions of defense mechanisms can be explained in terms of clinging; this has important practical implications. More generally, there are many ways EB and psychoanalysis can complement each other. Psychoanalysis could learn from Buddhists about levels of being and development beyond the current psychoanalytic limits, Buddhists could learn about unconscious interferences with meditation and personal/spiritual growth and the influence of the person's overall psychological and social development (Rubin, 1996; Suler, 1993). And Buddhists "long ago perfected a technique of confronting and uprooting human narcissism, a goal that western psychotherapy has only recently begun even to contemplate" (Epstein, 1995, p. 4). Buddhists postulates three unwholesome roots of motivation: craving/greed, aversion/hate and illusion/delusion; Freud suggested two primary forms of motivation: *eros* and *thanatos*. There are similarities between craving/greed and *eros* and between aversion/hate and *thanatos*; and the id deals with craving/greed and aversion/hate, while the ego deals with ignorance/delusion-illusion (de Silva, 2000; Metzger, 1996). An important difference is that in Freudian theory *eros* and *thanatos* are innate, while in the Buddhist teachings they can be overcome.

A major issue in integrating psychoanalysis and the Buddhist teachings is related to the nature of the "self" (Engler, 2003). Across psychoanalytic theories there is no agreement on exactly what is meant by "self"; sometimes it is the same as "ego", and sometimes it is very different. But the self is usually a central construct in psychoanalysis; and self-work might include making the self more effective, distinguishing the real self from false selves, uncovering disowned or rejected parts of the self, integrating the self or restructuring the self. In EB, one of the marks of existence is egolessness or not-self (*anatta*). The assertion is that a separate independent self-entity does not exist. This is not an article of faith, but a discovery of mindfulness. In Vipassana one takes a mind trained in concentration and mindfulness and turns it inward in pursuit of the "self." One finds no constant entity of a self, but rather a set of mental processes, including clinging and memories, to which a sense of a self is assigned. As elaborated on in the *Abhidhamma*, the self is a changing process put together from the five *Skandhas*. This self vs. not-self distinction appears to be a fundamental difference between psychoanalysis and the Buddhist teachings, but the difference decreases upon closer inspection. First of all, few if any psychoanalysts would assume the self to be a fixed entity, rather than a functional changing entity, as observed in Vipassana. Second, it may be that the self of psychoanalysis and Humanistic Psychology is at a different level of reality or being than the not-self of the Buddha (Engler, 2003; Fontana, 1987); this is the position of Conjunctive Psychology described in the next section. If self and not-self are at different levels, then there may be developmental issues (Fontana, 1987; Wilber, 2000); a person may first have to resolve personal self-related issues before transcending the self to not-self. Engler (2003), who was the first to elaborate this point, includes therapeutic examples where one should first do self-work and an early emphasis on self-transcendence could be therapeutically harmful.

Continuing the comparison of psychodynamic inquiry and Vipassana, in Vipassana one does not stop when one finds the dynamic processes taken to be the self. Rather, one sees through these processes to the transpersonal and dis-identifies with the opinion that these processes are the essence of one's being. Insightful seeing (*panna*) of the truth of not-self (*anatta*) is a central part of the Vipassana path to awakening. In psychodynamic inquiry when one encounters the dynamics of the self, it is a vehicle for self-work, rather than a way to get beyond the self. However, psychodynamic self work may result in the transpersonal spontaneously arising and in psychodynamic depth approaches one goes deep inside past the personal self until a fundamental sense of presence or essence emerges (Almaas, 2004; Cortright, 1997). All of this requires an understanding of the transpersonal.

Transpersonal

In North America, Transpersonal Psychology is the branch of psychology that deals with levels of development and being beyond ("trans-") the personal self-centered level (cf. Cortright, 1997; Walsh & Vaughn, 1993; Wilber, 2000); this includes experiences that "encompass wider aspects of humankind, life, psyche, and cosmos" (Walsh & Vaughn, 1993, p.3). In the Buddhist teachings uncovering the transpersonal is fundamental. All other benefits of Buddhist practice are subordinate to this goal.

In Conjunctive Psychology it is argued that everyone exists at four totally intertwined levels of being: biological, behavioral, personal, and transpersonal (Mikulas, 2002). The biological level is the domain of the body, including the brain; and the behavioral level is the domain of overt and covert behaviors, including cognitions. The personal level is the domain of the learned, conscious, personal reality, intermittently inhabited by a self or selves that periodically experience a sense of willing actions. The transpersonal level includes forces and domains of being that are superordinate to and/or prior to the self-centered personal reality, including the dynamics that create the personal reality and the sense of self. The personal level is self-centred; the transpersonal is beyond this self, "beyond" in a superordinate inclusive sense, not separate. The personal level focuses on contents of consciousness, including self as object (e.g., self concept, self-esteem); the transpersonal focuses on processes of consciousness and consciousness per se as an aspect of the fundamental ground. Psychoanalysis and Humanistic Psychology are primarily concerned with the personal level, Transpersonal Psychology with the transpersonal level, and Conjunctive Psychology with all levels and their interactions.

During development and personal growth, people become lost in the personal level of being; they confuse the content of their minds with some assumed concrete reality, and they identify themselves with the functional personal level selves. In EB clinging to this self is seen as a major source of delusion and Dukkha. Awakening, the goal of EB, is simply getting free from this clinging and waking up to a broader reality that includes the transpersonal. The Buddha made no claims about himself other than he woke up; the word "buddha" means "awakened one."

In Conjunctive Psychology it is argued that the transpersonal level of being is always already present; there is nothing one has to do to acquire it, just uncover it (Mikulas, 2004a). Thus, everyone is already awakened, even if the personal level self does not realize it. There is nothing one has to do to awaken, but one must utilize spiritual practices to free oneself for the full realization of this truth. An important point is that the personal level self cannot become enlightened, since awaking involves disidentification with the personal self. What often happens to people involved in spiritual practice is that the personal self converts the journey into a self-adventure, which cannot work.

A very common misunderstanding among spiritual practitioners of many traditions, including the Buddhist tradition, is that one must undo or kill the personal level self in order to awaken; but this is not necessary or desirable. There is no problem with the existence of the personal level self; and it may be important to focus therapy on this self, for many reasons, including setting the stage for later transcendence. Awakening does not eliminate or devalue this self; rather, it is a disidentification with this self, which, according to Buddhists, leads to freedom and peace of mind. If one surveys all the major world spiritual traditions, one will find little consensus at the level of religion, philosophy and cosmology. But if one looks at the level of practice, what one should do to awaken within each tradition, then one finds consensus (Mikulas, 1987). One orders life along moral and practical guidelines; and one utilizes one or more of the four universal practices: quiet the mind, increase awareness, open the heart and reduce attachments. In Conjunctive Psychology these four practices are called universal somato-psycho-spiritual practices, since they strongly impact all levels of being. In EB, quieting the mind is primarily accomplished by cultivating concentration, increasing awareness by cultivating mindfulness and reducing attachments by reducing clinging. EB approaches opening the heart through practices such as loving kindness meditation. The Buddhist Mahayana tradition adds more attention to cultivation of compassion.

EB obviously has much to contribute to Transpersonal Psychology. This includes many detailed descriptions of the nature and process of awakening, plus related maps of higher levels and states of development and consciousness, such as those related to advanced cultivation of concentration and mindfulness (Buddhaghosa, 1975; Goleman, 1988). Buddhists have been doing applied research in these areas for over 2500 years and across various disparate cultures.

Conclusion

Buddhist Psychology has much to offer western psychology, including new conceptualizations, theories and practices. In the process western psychologists have a chance to reconsider and refine basic constructs and dynamics and move into new domains. And western psychology has much to offer Buddhist Psychology and practices. A few examples were given here, but there is much more. An integration of Buddhist and western psychologies should yield a much more comprehensive psychology with more powerful and more applicable therapies. Finally, these can be integrated with other world psychologies, health systems and wisdom traditions to generate an even broader and more powerful psychology (Mikulas, 2002).

Author note
Special thanks go to colleague and production assistant Connie Works.

Chapter 15

Some Intersections Between Autogenic Training, Cathartic Autogenics, and Buddhist Psychology

Ruth Tiffany Naylor[1]

Introduction

In practice, teaching Autogenics begins with teaching a person about the inextricable link between stimulus (whether internal or external), body-mind (including thoughts, feelings, intentions, drives, emotions, and so on), action (wilfully or conditioned and "automatic"), and cyclical response cycles (Hayward, 1965). From a Buddhist perspective, Autogenics practice can be seen as an indirect way of teaching people about karmic cycles, about the actual intentionality of the mind, the cognitive/affective processes, in developing and maintaining thought/action cycles. The cognitive/affective processes are larger than just thoughts and feelings – they extend to "holding" and "releasing" memory throughout the body-mind and speech (Body/Mind/Speech). The release, or "discharge" in AT terms, happens in all the senses and in the mental contents, spontaneously, and at its own pace, when people pay attention to the Body/Mind/Speech in a contemplative and compassionate way. AT is a meditative approach which starts with concentration and culminates in insight. There is a "switch" or "release" during practice itself, and an uptake of a mindfulness approach along with the release process which generalises to everyday life. A western shorthand way of talking about the "autogenic switch" or shift is: decrease and turn off the "stress response" and turn on and increase the "relaxation response". In other words, turn off the unwholesome conditioned (automatic) responses and turn on the wholesome unconditioned, natural responses.

While the didactic, whole system the Buddha worked out is not made fully explicit in Autogenics, the bare bones are there, and the variety of experiences which have been reported by practitioners over the last 80 years attest both to its usefulness and its convergences with

1.   Acknowledgement: I am completely indebted to my late husband Brian Harold Naylor, who helped me by being, by listening and thinking along with me, and by translating Schultz's Das Autogene Training for me in the weeks before his sudden death. I am grateful also to my colleague, friend and guide, Tamara Callea, DiplPsych (Heidelberg), Clinical Psychologist and Autogenic Psychotherapist, and Monika Sanson, linguist, for their detailed review of my work and her helpful and essential translations of books, interviews, and papers on Autogenic methods which originally appear in German, Italian, and French.

Buddhist practices. The basic or "small" Autogenics, Autogenic Training, or "AT", as it is fondly called by practitioners and trainers was developed in mental health settings and is foundational for all the other applications of the Autogenic method in various settings. It has been extensively studied in clinical and research settings since its beginnings in the early 1900s. Schultz's colleague, Wolfgang Luthe, expanded basic AT in the early 1960s by adding what he called "cathartic" exercises, which also have much in common with Buddhist practices. They focus people on freely expressing nonsense movement and sound, putting the body through expressions of anger, anxiety, and grief, and facing fears of vomiting and death. Many contemporary AT practitioners also include cathartic exercises which focus on expressing laughter, appreciation, and love. Today, westerners are easily able to discern AT's connections to eastern methods since meditation-based practices have thoroughly entered the cultural mainstream via western education and medicine, first through Transcendental Meditation, then through Henry Benson's efforts, and today with the general uptake of Yoga, Tai Chi, Qi Gong, and similar practices across the board. As Russell Cassel, a prominent American educator and proponent of AT throughout his working life, remarked in 1995 (p.251): "In 1990 Fourth Force Psychology, Transpersonal Psychology, and Autogenics came of age... Autogenics, of course, tracing its history back to early Eastern philosophic meditation techniques."

Would it be too bold to suggest that Schultz's disciplined approach, which engages and trains observation and the body in a context of compassionate acceptance, when applied either by itself or with Luthe's cathartic practices, is a few buds nestled in the Buddha's whole bouquet? Or perhaps to suggest, that the footprint of (Cathartic) AT fits neatly within the Buddhist footprint?

Autogenics background

For readers who are not familiar with basic Autogenic Training (AT), here is a brief synopsis. AT was developed by Dr. Johannes Schultz, a psychiatrist and neurologist, at his Berlin-based mental health clinic. In 1932 he published his seminal work on the method, including its connections with related religious, psychological, and philosophical methods, both eastern and western. Autogenic methods are now used clinically and prophylactically worldwide. In its youth during the first half of the 20th century, AT went through the same developmental phases that other meditation based western practices have gone through during the latter half of the century: pilot and case study work to show the method was promising, followed by psychophysiological exploratory work (e.g., EEG, EKG, GSR), and dissemination of the method worldwide. However, by today's standards, the development of the Autogenics' evidence base was severely hampered not only by technology's limits but also by the simple political and geographic facts that AT was presented in the late 1920's and early 1930's, during Hitler's rise. AT was non-ideological, non-religious, and presented no apparent threat to the regime, so it seems that practitioners of the method were able to continue their work unhampered within Germany. Wider dissemination of AT did not take place until after WWII, just as the Randomised Control Trial (RCT) research paradigm came into prominence, and well after Autogenics as a basic practice was fully developed. After the war, Autogenic Training, and methods built upon it, were embraced in Europe as Schultz intended, in its foundational form as a "small" (*kleine*) psychotherapy, and in its advanced forms as a complete, "big" (*grosse*) psychotherapy. The recently launched *European Journal of Autogenic and Bionomic Studies* clearly sets out how Schultz's method was influenced in Italy, Spain, and Germany over the last 50 years, and Ranty (2008) writes specifically about the situation in France as it stands today. It may be because of the parallels between Autogenics and Buddhist Psychology that AT was rapidly taken up in the East and continue to flourish there, and to be built upon today as the ground there is fertile for this approach. Naruse (1965), for example, noted that AT, neutral hypnosis, Zen-training and Yoga-exercises have a "state of meditative concentration" in common. In the East, Autogenics have long been taught as a "do" (*doh*) (equivalent to the Chinese "tao", which means "way") process – an individually tailored coaching method – and have also been well integrated into psychosomatic medicine, psychotherapy, and bodywork programmes since the 1960s (cf. Weidong, Sasaki, & Haruki, 2000). In the English speaking world, particularly in North America, where the traditions of behaviourism dominated through much of the 20th century, Autogenics were often stripped back, diluting the essentials they share with Buddhist meditative methods. Abbreviated AT has been used in the brief talking therapy context, especially cognitive behaviour therapy variants, as a way to quickly relax highly anxious individuals before therapy proper begins (e.g., Benson 1974; Hayward 1965; Linden 1980; Smith 1980). More radical stripping of the method was undertaken in the biofeedback context, when AT was adopted and then adapted with a variety of instruments and methods in order to exert control over physiological processes. A variant of these exercises used by NASA astronauts was patented in the USA in 1997 (Cowings 1977). Aspects of Autogenic meditative techniques have also been used in other therapeutic techniques, often without reference to their origins (Smith 2004).

Autogenics has been in use in the British National Health Service (NHS) since the early 1960s in both mental and psychosomatic settings and continues in use today. In the mid-1980s Schultz's student and colleague, Dr. Wolfgang Luthe, who practised in Canada in his later years, invigorated further uptake of the method in Britain, and his contributions have been influential in the way AT and the other Autogenic methods are taught in the UK today. We learn both Schultz AT and Luthe's Cathartic AT which was designed specifically to support the uptake of Schultz AT practice when resistances are met. Cathartic exercises are specific contemplative and physical practices designed to put the body-mind-and-speech through the expression of emotion, usually without tapping directly into the "triggers" or the "feelings" which accompany these triggers in ordinary waking life, and always in a context of compassionate self-acceptance. For example, a "crying" exercise involves simply rocking the body gently and making the whimpering or wailing sounds of grief, but does not involve actually producing tears or the feelings of sadness or grief. This is because the aim of the exercise is to "offload" stored tension relating to unexpressed emotion, regardless of how the tension is held. The aim is not to surface or analyse specific triggers, or dysfunctional thought patterns, or even the outcomes of the experience, or the reasons for suppression of the emotion, and so on. The emotional range addressed by the cathartic exercises has been broadened considerably by contemporary AT trainers (Kermani 1990; Naylor & Marshall 2007) who also focus some trainees on expressing laughter (joy), appreciation (kindness) and love (compassion). Again, the goal is to support and enable the trainee who often does not understand the links between "positive" and "negative" emotions, and who fears risking the full-on expression of felt emotions, to directly teach themselves by experience and in short bursts that internal experience of and outward expression of appropriate emotion can be easy, acceptable, fruitful, calming, moral, kind, productive, joyful, safe, and so forth. When trainees train themselves using these practices, they learn to feel safe experiencing and expressing a wide range of emotions more deeply. They are then able not only to live in the present more successfully, but also to alter their circumstances, their viewpoints and their reactions more easily in order to create new experiences and to live more balanced lives. They are more "ready" to benefit from Schultz-type AT practice, too.

AT is easily presented to the public as an accessible, cost-effective, non-pathologising, pro-homeostatic stress reduction technique that is a simple, easy to learn "package" of standardized, subvocally repeated phrases about the body. Instead of contemplating a single body process (breath) and a single thought (mantra), as in Transcendental Meditation (TM™), Benson's Respiratory One Method (ROM), Carrington's Clinically Standardised Meditation (CSM), and Zen, with AT contemplation shifts passively from one body part and its qualities to the next body part, in a specific order, in other words, in a series of "moving mantras" which are called the "six standard exercises". Taking passive awareness to the body parts, we notice feelings of heaviness and warmth in the musculoskeletal system, saying to ourselves, for example, "Arms and legs, heavy and warm". In a similar way, we say very short phrases to ourselves about the regularity of breath and heartbeat, about warmth emanating from the solar plexus, and about coolness gently caressing the forehead. We pay attention to our body, and begin to notice what is happening to it, whether emotions or feelings are arising and where they arise from, whether things are changing, different or the same from side to side, different from the last practice, and so on, much like in Buddhist mindfulness meditation. Contrary to popular misconceptions about AT, this is not a hetero-hypnotic or self-hypnotic position – the goal is not to produce heaviness, warmth, or coolness: quite the opposite. Non-striving contemplation of the body, of feelings arising within the body, of thoughts arising in the mind in relation to the body, of stories being told in the mind, and so on, is intermittently interspersed with affirmations of peace, quiet, and calm. To train attention and non-judgmental awareness, trainees are encouraged to simply notice and, if necessary, to label other thoughts, feelings (emotional and somatic), and desires, and – much like in Buddhist breathing meditation – to gently return their attention to awareness of the body. Practitioners learn to neither accept nor dispute Body/Mind/Speech content during AT practice, whilst outside practice, they often find they can more appropriately dispute the irrational and accept the rational, either by themselves or as they work within the therapeutic hour with their trainer. A more pleasurable and deep self acceptance quickly results for most trainees.

The whole method can be learned over the course of two to six months in only eight one hour group meetings or individually in as little as 15 minutes per meeting, depending on the skill of the therapist and the readiness of the trainee. By "readiness", we mean in essence the trainee's patience, optimism, and motivation to practice. It is not surprising, therefore, that AT helps at all stages of life, from frail nursing home trainees (Kircher, Teutsch, Wormstall, Buchkremer, & Thimm, 2004) to young children and their families (Goldbeck & Schmidt 2003), and with a broad range of psychosomatic and mental health problems, from migraine (Zsombok, 2003) to depression relapse (Krampen, 1999).

Wallnöffer, the elder statesman of Autogenics since Schultz's and Luthe's deaths, remarked in a video interview (Guttmann, 2002) that biologically AT rests on these simple concepts: "We are conditioned, relaxation leads to calmness, the body behaves as if the mere thought of muscle movement would cause a reaction, and all of this readjustment activity takes place in the context of psyche, of depth psychology." This viewpoint brings another western method immediately to mind, Edmund Jacobson's Progressive Muscle Relaxation (PMR) especially as it has been reported to induce "trance" states in some people, and particularly as it is implemented in clinical practice today in a cognitive behaviour therapy context as Applied Relaxation (McGuigan & Lehrer, 2007). So it is important to emphasise that AT is not foremost or simply a somatic relaxation intervention, a viewpoint which has been promulgated in America for many years. Instead, the emphasis is on engaging sensory, cognitive, and emotional processes in a holistic way, in a context of compassionate self-acceptance, and this is why the practice has an immediate impact on both psyche-and-soma. Keeping this emphasis in mind, experiments which offer 20 minutes of training in one or the other type of relaxation therapy or contemplative or insight meditation practices in order to garner support for the cognitive/somatic specificity hypothesis (Rausch, Gramling, & Auerbach, 2007, for example), or for other hypotheses, appear to be completely beside the point as the theories of personality and methods which underpin the practices are ignored from the outset. What is coming clear in western approaches which use methods similar to eastern ones is that once the whole person is engaged fully in objectively observing life in the now in a compassionate way, profound changes at all levels are bound to spontaneously arise. For westerners, or for anyone for that matter, who has scruples about techniques labeled either "hypnosis" or "philosophy" or "religion", AT and its cathartic extension is an acceptable approach.

Some Autogenic and Buddhist intersections

Schultz was a neuropsychiatrist in Berlin from 1909 to 1970. He took a holistic, dynamic, systems approach to his work, developing Autogenics in clinical practice from this vantage point. It was very important to Schultz, who was educated in Vogt's laboratory and familiar with hypnotic methods, that people learn to know themselves through education and self-training, and that they not expect the teacher or physician to "offer a magic pill or have a magic answer" for alleviating their personal suffering. Instead, he insisted that they experience for themselves through their own "Kritische" or objective, detached yet accepting observation of their own bodies, feelings, and minds to break the cycle of automaticity or conditioning, regardless of how the conditioning arose in the first place. It is immediately obvious that Schultz and the Buddha shared a key value, education, and turned their backs on its opposites, the appearance of magical and miraculous healing. As the Buddha made clear in the *Honeyball Sutta* (MN 18), each one of us must examine ourselves by ourselves to discover for ourselves our "underlying tendencies" to "delight, welcome and hold on to" our own conditioning, whether it is wholesome or unwholesome being beside the point insofar as understanding is concerned. So Buddhist meditation and AT practice share this: contemplation of our Body/Mind/Speech in what amounts to our own personal cognitive (in the widest sense of the word) laboratory and the practices are taught without any hetero-hypnosis, guided imagery, or suggestion at all. Also like the Buddha, Schultz was a pragmatist. During the AT training course, whether with individuals or groups, after instruction in the practice, appreciative enquiry surfaces each person's response to the practice. This is for ethical and medical reasons, and so that the trainer can tailor the course to the participants' requirements. Learning also comes by example and there are no didactic lectures about passivity, or contemplation, or non-judgment, or acceptance, or awareness and there are no lectures on philosophy or psychology. In some training courses, trainers may decide to simply write the Autogenics practice phrases on a piece of paper and

leave the room while trainees practice by themselves. This is done first of all to make absolutely certain there is no hetero-suggestion and second of all to teach the trainee by their own experience that they must find out for themselves. It is for these kinds of reasons that for the most
part AT trainers use the *do* method (Sakairi, 2000, pp. 205-212), meaning that they expect the
trainee to follow instructions to the letter as a set task in order to learn for themselves, as while
this may be unexpected and unfamiliar to westerners, it is in fact the approach that Schultz
found works best.

As people become proficient in using AT's series of six moving mantras, or "six standard
exercises", and as they develop a consistent AT practice, their awareness opens up to observe
all kinds of mental and physical states – all kinds of sensations, emotions, behaviours, and
thoughts – as they originate, arise, subside, and cease in co-dependence anywhere in the whole
organism. A spirit of appreciative enquiry pervades the training process, with the trainer asking for feedback about practice in such a way that the trainee is enabled to learn for themselves
in a compassionate way. In advanced Autogenic practice, the trainee is asked to contemplate
specific mental objects in a specified order and in a progressively more complex form. Onda
(1965, pp.251- 257) wrote specifically about the differences between Zen and Autogenics, noting that these are difficult to "express precisely". He notes that the postures are different and
says there is no equivalent to walking or standing Zen; but the way AT is taught today does
include a number of walking, standing, and sound/breath centering practices. For example, one
of the Schultz practice mantras is repeated with eyes open while either walking or standing,
and this brings with it not only calmness but also grounded awareness in the present. One of
the Luthe practices is to move the body, gently shaking it in whatever way it "wants" to go,
whilst making accompanying sounds as they spontaneously arise. Otherwise, as Onda notes,
AT is usually done with eyes closed. It must also be pointed out that although standard AT practice may be described as or experienced as "giving direction", which is contrary to Zen practice, the method is in actual fact taught to be practised in an opposite way. One is to be passively aware without trying to make anything at all happen, so the only "conscious control" is
either to bring the mind gently back to the moving mantra ("passive concentration" stage) or
to gently contemplate everything that arises in the Body/Mind/Speech without holding any of
it, making stories about it, or "running away with it". A gentle expansion of awareness ensues,
rather like being an eagle flying in the Grand Canyon or rather like being on a raft in the white
water, without a paddle! Unlike Zen, there is also no effort at all in AT to consciously pay attention to the breath in- and outflow, or to regulate it – as this happens all by itself. We now know
that "regular" breath is in fact not metronomically regular at all, so the point of the untimed,
unregulated AT breath phrases (e.g., "breathe calm and regular"), that breath regulation does
happen "all by itself", is physiologically sound. As Onda (1965, p.256) says: "AT seems to lead
to a specific psycho-physiologic state by degrees, from passive concentration to meditative
concentration. At this point, we can find similarity between Zen meditation and AT." Along
similar lines, there are reciprocal links between mind, body, and emotion, like sides of a pyramid or triangle, so that physical changes shift mental states and feelings, and vice versa.
Finally, like Buddhist practice, Autogenics is not an analytic method, it is a method learned
experientially, over time, in silence, and with compassion. AT's non-judgmental, passive,
observational, letting go stance over time, and with consistent practice, enables people to move
from an automatic, reactive state to a more disciplined, autonomous, proactive, responsive
state where insight and action are better balanced, and more and more consonant with right

ways of seeing and thus of behaving.

So we can see some shared understandings in Buddhist and Autogenic psychologies – the whole system is dynamic and radically changing from moment to moment, everything is variable, insubstantial, and socially conditioned. The whole changes when one aspect of it changes, all that happens is conditioned, and through contemplation of the parts, as a unitary totality, people can uncover and release their own conditioning. Whilst Buddhist Psychology talks of "no-self", Autogenic psychology talks of the "loss of ego", the transformation and disintegration of form and meaning, and shift of ego boundaries to release from conditioning. With Autogenics, it is not that the person is broken and needs fixing, which is the traditional western medical model of psychotherapy; instead, with Autogenics, it is that the person is bound, and naturally, bionomically, seeks release, intuitively knowing and sensing the boundedness, the conditioning, and the resultant suffering. For Schultz, the brain, that is, the neurology or wherever emotion, affect, thought, feeling, mind, and so on, are held in the organism, simply "knows" what it needs to loosen, to let go of, to release in order to be free, in an organic sense of the word. In other words, with consistent practice of AT, what Schultz called the "switch", the "breaking the circle of conditioning" or the karmic circle, occurs and a release happens to the whole person.

It is very clear in Schultz's description of the "switch", the "autogenic shift", that the goal is to release what in Buddhist Psychology is called Karma, the intentional acts of Body/Mind/Speech (whether they be internally experienced only, or also find expression externally) which are circular, the cause-effect cycles arising from habit and conditioning. Intention in this sense is that which is "done", the existential experience of one's life, and so on. For Schultz, this intention, or Karma, extended to the moment to moment coherence of the sense of "I-ness", which disintegrates during AT practice, just as it does with meditative practices in general. It is this disintegration which has the potential to forever change the practitioner. How does the "switch" come about? The most difficult part of the process is the beginning, the first effort, the "agreement" to be passive, to focus awareness and attention, and to enter a state of "critical self-observation".

Wallnöfer has also remarked in a video interview (Guttmann, 2002): "AT provides ongoing passive self-control: 'I allow something to happen to me'. It aims to help cope with reality better. With AT, all becomes equally valid". This is a "double entendre", a play on words, in German: *gleichgueltig*, meaning "indifferent", and *gleich gueltig*, meaning "of equal value". People who begin AT often do it to "learn to relax" or "be more productive" or "get in touch with artistic creativity" and the like, not realising immediately that what they will learn about themselves will be much larger and go much deeper. It is in this way that Autogenics is accessible, and has come of age in the West. By observing my own practice, and the practice of many people whom my colleagues and I have trained together, I have learnt that passive agreement to begin, in Schultz's sense, develops and deepens slowly over time. It is an awareness that is without becoming, without goals, without choices, and without judgement; a gentle, unbounded awareness that is understood only by practice.

Table 1.
The Concentrative (Authentic/True/Real) Experience of the Switching

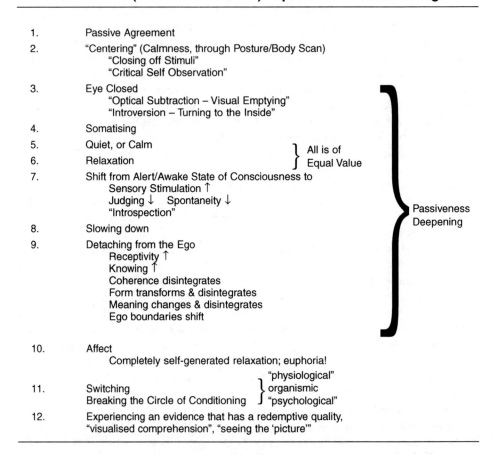

1.	Passive Agreement
2.	"Centering" (Calmness, through Posture/Body Scan)
	"Closing off Stimuli"
	"Critical Self Observation"
3.	Eye Closed
	"Optical Subtraction – Visual Emptying"
	"Introversion – Turning to the Inside"
4.	Somatising
5.	Quiet, or Calm } All is of
6.	Relaxation } Equal Value
7.	Shift from Alert/Awake State of Consciousness to
	Sensory Stimulation ↑
	Judging ↓ Spontaneity ↓
	"Introspection"
8.	Slowing down
9.	Detaching from the Ego
	Receptivity ↑
	Knowing ↑
	Coherence disintegrates
	Form transforms & disintegrates
	Meaning changes & disintegrates
	Ego boundaries shift
10.	Affect
	Completely self-generated relaxation; euphoria!
11.	Switching } "physiological" organismic
	Breaking the Circle of Conditioning } "psychological"
12.	Experiencing an evidence that has a redemptive quality,
	"visualised comprehension", "seeing the 'picture'"

(Passiveness Deepening)

To break the cycle of conditioning Schultz knew we needed a switching, shifting process, a Body/Mind/Speech action with a different grammar, one that is different to Body/Mind/Speech grammar of the vicious cycle as M.G.T. Kwee clearly describes in this volume. Schultz describes the twelve step switch/shift process which AT induces as "Das Konzentrative Umschaltungserlebnis", or "The Concentrative Authentic Suggestive Experience of the Switching through AT". This process evolves and deepens a person's natural developmental tendencies, with modifications of consciousness and conditioning naturally ensuing when the method is consistently practiced. Nakamura (2000), Sasaki (2000), Ikemi (2000) and many others agree with Schultz, who thought that life itself has inborn aims, which while constrained in space-time, seek actualization through self-guided recovery from the conditioning which inevitably limits right perception, thought, affect, and action. Table 1, "Das Konzentrative (Echt Suggestive) Umschaltungserlebnis" (Schultz, 1973, p.322), sets out the 12 key points in the switching process. Concentrative absorption deepens over time until there is a break from the circular patterns of conditioning and a euphoric release from the "conditioned co-arising" (or

Dependent Origination causality hypothesis). This de-conditioning process begins as soon as a person consciously brings their Mind/Speech into their Body, to experience the unitary totality of sensation/body states, thought/speech and feeling/emotion in the present moment, in the now.

AT practice at work

Here I propose there may be some useful points of contact between Schultz's 12 key points of the circular/spirals-switch/shifting process and the *pratityasamutpada* (Dependent Origination) model of the "conditioned co-arising" postulate. Schultz's preliminary emphasis on the body accompanied by deepening passivity, non-judgmental "agreement" to objectively observe, at the early stages of Autogenics practice immediately helps people to "unpick" the "stuckness" of pain, pleasure and neutrality arising on sensory contact with initial sense impressions and from arising/subsequent desire (see Table 2; Lusthaus, 2002, p.69).

Table 2. *Pratityasamutpada* Model of the 12 Links

Link 1	*Avijja*	Ignorance
Link 2	*Sankara*	Embodied conditioning
Link 3	*Vinnana*	Ignorance emerging into consciousness
Link 4	*Nama-rupa*	Consciousness is "embodied conditioning" instantiating as a sensorial body
Link 5	*Sad-ayatana*	Sensorial body is consciousness channelled into the six sensorial realms
Link 6	*Phassa*	The six sensorial realms are a way of speaking about a sensorial body experiencing sensory contact
Link 7	*Vendana*	Sensory contact consists of the six sense spheres engaged in pleasurable, painful, or neutral sensations
Link 8	*Tanha*	*Vedana* is the precipitation of sensory contact as desires
Link 9	*Upadana*	Desire is a euphemism for how pleasurable and painful conditioning manifest as appropriational activities
Link 10	*Bhava*	Appropriation describes how desire becomes on-going behaviour
Link 11	*Jati*	The on-going coalesces, giving birth
Link 12	*Marana*	To consequences of appropriational trajectories; birth is the on-going leading to its inevitable conclusion, death

AT Switching Point 1

Usually it is dramatic life changes (Links 12 or 11), or ongoing painful behaviour (Link 10), or feelings of lacking or wanting or changing (Link 9) which bring people to an Autogenic therapist. Most are uncomfortable in their skin, if in fact they actually inhabit it. They want to get back to basics, to the beginning, to a unity which they cannot lexically describe. Whilst conscious sensory contact (Link 5) is in the first instance an intermediate therapeutic goal, we must work backwards, first by actively agreeing (Link 8) to learn the method, and more importantly by passively agreeing, by engaging, by starting (Link 7). This is the "way" to the "switch".

AT Switching Points 2-4

Stimuli are limited by taking specific postures, scanning the body, and closing the eyes. A posture which we find very conducive for trainees to firmly engage with the autogenic process is the lying-down posture, which is identical to *savasana*, the "Yoga dead pose". In this pose, complete relaxation develops, blood flow to the extremities increases, and the person and the mind rest. This is a way directly through the body, a non-verbal way, to return to the mother, to unity, to the safe, protective, posture associated with repose. As Schultz says: "Furthermore, the experience of restricting to the internal field and "collecting" oneself thusly, is very substantial and is favoured by an inward turning to an experience of the body... significant external irritations [do not disturb]... and the [trainee] slides passively, feeling [her way] into her body experience, somatising herself, as it were." (1973, p.12) This connects to Link 6, the six sensorial realms experience sensorial contact... The somatisation, the focus on the body, brings spontaneous emergence of conditioned "unconscious contents". People report everything from a cacophony of thoughts to flowing cinematic images, to feeling the body floating, undulating, disappearing, sinking, merging, expanding, and to the whole body becoming a mouth. This connects to Link 5, consciousness is channelled to the body...

In contemporary Italian practice, preliminary to this phase of AT, the first three training weeks for groups of five to eight people who meet for three hours weekly are called Somatic AT. Gastaldo and Ottobre (1994, p.30) set out the following instructions to be given at the start. "Several times a day, LISTEN to the sensations in your body at the following times – first week, while you are walking towards a goal, when you are simply walking without a specific goal, and when you are accomplishing an habitual task in your work; second week, when you can stop for a moment during your activities, and, choosing a comfortable position, simply dedicate yourself to listening to your body." These instructions resonate with the instructions given in Kabat-Zinn's mindfulness training and in the outworking of this training in cognitive therapy settings (Kabat-Zinn, 1990; Teasdale, Segal, & Williams, 2004). Becoming comfortable with sensory contact in this new way, a way that is observant with reactions noted but not outwardly acted upon, is work that is preliminary and necessary to fixing attention, to contemplation in the Buddhist sense, and is a very important step for westerners to take within safe boundaries. Luthe's first two cathartic AT exercises, motor movement and nonsense noise, assist in preparing people to listen to their bodies during standard AT practice.

For many, consciousness of this sensory contact work needs to take place over a number of years before sufficient progress is made to move forward with Buddhist methods. We are reminded of the gentleness of the way Autogenics is introduced to trainees and also of the practice difficulties Engler (1986), Luthe (1984), Otis (1984), Wilber (1986), and others reported when people who reacted negatively to TM, as it swept North America during the 1970s and 1980s, came to them for help. Many people, whose personalities were fragmented, and who were not sufficiently prepared, suffered, believing that if they could simply discover and become one with the "not-self" advertised in the West as a form of Buddhist Nirvana, they would not have to develop a cohesive sense of self in the first instance. Carl Jung (1969, pp.532-3) makes the point quite clearly: while "introversions [like yoga and other Eastern meditative processes] ...lead to peculiar inner processes which change the personality", it is difficult, if not impossible, to expect a westerner to understand with his "heart, belly, and blood" that *prana* means more than "breath". This sensibility must be nurtured, and Autogenic practice is a wonderful vehicle for westerners in this regard. The beauty of the Autogenic way is that it arose within the West and is eminently suited to the western mind. As Farnè and Jimenez-Muñoz (2002) have demonstrated in clinical research, AT does in fact change personality. Not everyone is ready for this development without significant support. As Schultz said, "Indeed, systematic concentrative relaxation leads to 'sinking' [toward dissolution of ego boundaries], without any suggestive moments, or directive, outside influences, and needs only an empathic teacher to impart the method." (1973, p.295)

"Critical self-observation", Schultz's second step in the switching process, involves the mind. In Buddhist terms, this is the sixth sense-base and the objects of the mind, which are its own thoughts and ideas fuelled by its feelings, experiences, and the sensory objects of the other five sense-bases. The operation of the six sense-bases (described in Links 5 and 6), or capacities, which are all we have with which to construct our understanding of the world, comes clearer when we critically observe ourselves. This is an objective stance, it is a stepping back stance, to a place of non-judgement, in other words, to a place where we acknowledge and observe proliferating thoughts. As thoughts arise, we learn how to not follow them – we are not on a high speed train, we are watching, listening, witnessing, and observing.

AT Switching Points 5 & 6

We become observant of everything in a calm way. Our passivity is deepening, all is of equal value, and we are quiet and relaxed. This connects to Link 4 – this is unusual and new in the chain; we begin to experience the karmic chain in another way...

AT Switching Point 7

Intellect and sensation meet here in a new state of consciousness. Autogenic discharges spontaneously emerge. They appear and subside in the internal field – they are gustatory, visual, kinaesthetic, auditory, olfactory, vestibular, motor, and sensory. The brain knows what needs to be "unchained", the brain continuously presents this disturbing material to itself, and change occurs discontinuously and only as and when brain, mind-and-body, the "Unitary Totality", the whole open system, are ready and poised for practical action. A grounded experience of the body more fully inhabited arises as one attends to the multiple, varied and hitherto unrecognised or acknowledged discharges from various bodily organs. Recently, Nicholson (2002, 2004) has presented compelling evidence for the origin of the visual images induced during meditation (ranging from visions of outer space to "Indra's Net", the interconnectedness of Body/Mind/Speech across the board, particularly in the interpersonal/social realm), a finding they originate in sub-clinical seizures and paroxysmal brain activity arising in pre-sleep states or by induction during advanced meditation wherein the vision and attention areas of the brain are "awake" whilst the rest of the "Unitary Totality" is "tricked" into acting as though it is entering sleep.

AT Switching Point 8

We slow down, we re-discover the sensorial nature of our bodies and the constant *mis*-taking of interpretations for actual reality comes clearer and clearer. We discover that we do not have to react to pain or to pleasure or to neutrality by moving away, by moving toward, or by changing in any way – we can simply be.

AT Switching Point 9

A process of ego detachment, largely in a most pleasant way, ensues. The object disappears. Subject-object dualism disappears. Form transforms and disintegrates, meaning changes and disintegrates, ego boundaries shift. This connects to Links 3 and 2 – the conditioning embodied in the ego shifts. This is a new state of consciousness/awareness. Schultz describes it thusly: "Relaxation and 'sinking' are different. In 'sinking' have we an original, unique reaction before us, which is broadly analogous to the problem solving character of the 'falling asleep experience.'" (1973, p.296). This analogy is very apt, as although physiological study of AT, meditation, and sleep states shows differences between them, recent research also shows that it is in pre-sleep states that memories can be recalibrated (Hobson, 2002; Stickgold, 2002). The emotions and the impetus to hold on, release their grip.

AT Switching Point 10

We are in a relaxation euphoria for moments at a time, 'bliss' is often reported.

AT Switching Point 11

The Switching. The vicious cycle breaks on an organismic level. This connects to Link 1: Ignorance ensues, in the nicest possible way – not "knowing"', simply being.

AT Switching Point 12

Things look different now. Behaviour changes. Awakening. People see the picture, a redemptive, self-generated, self-healing comprehension emerges.

AT experiences

With Autogenic practice, different exercise phrases trigger the "switching" in different people at different times and to different degrees and practice will accelerate, intensify and make the switching process more secure. During introductory practice of the "Dominant Arm Heavy" phrase, a woman fearing that early exposure to toxic chemicals on the forearms and hands may have caused her arthritis, experiences her arms as "skinned" and "raw", like the frozen legs of lamb she hands out in autumn to her customers. This brings with it a dawning realisation of the complexity of her conditioning and the depth of her held stress. A young man fearing death from brain cancer reports complete release from his fear after experiencing many sneezing bouts during a week of practising the sixth practice phrase, "Forehead Fresh or Cool". An emergency services telephone operator finds renewed confidence for taking action in everyday life after a loud auditory discharge during the first training session which contemplates a "Heavy Musculoskeletal System". People enter the switching cycle at different points, too. They can be experienced almost simultaneously, inclusively, circularly. And the work continues beyond the actual time of practice. A young mother attending university reports seeing pyramids and triangles during first moments of silent AT practice. As trainers, we listen, we accept, with permission we ask questions, and we are silent. As with Buddhist practice, silence is fundamental. A week, two weeks, and three weeks later, the mother finds words to describe her unfolding experience in the present of her life now. She reports no longer feeling wound up tighter than a drum, no more intense arguments with her husband, and a child learning to get attention by saying "I love you" instead of by fighting and screaming. The pressures of university haven't changed. The ways of processing the post-traumatic stress, the flashbacks from childhood abuse, and the anger have changed.

As the awareness shifts according to the sequence of standard practice phrases and also when the sequence is complete, the field of focus naturally expands to the entire internal field. The process of focusing in the here and now of consciousness, of accepting its whole reality without judgement, and of letting go of each moment, each thought, each feeling, each sensation, and each "distraction" from the outside world, as the next emerges, immerses people in a journey of self-discovery by directly engaging them with the processes, modalities, and contents of their own Body/Mind/Speech and eventually the beginning-middle-end of all mental contents and all processes. The perceptual illusion of sameness is laid bare, without fear. And this process is what leads to the dissolving of conditioning and liberates us. Onda (1965, p.257) describes this well: ...both Autogenic Training and Zen meditation aim at the control of body and mind. In Zen meditation there act the dynamics of body à mind (adjustment of body, adjustment of respiration à adjustment of mind) or mind à body (adjustment of mind à regulation of physical functions). And in autogenic Training there act (sic) the dynamics of mind à body (passive concentration on parts of body à meditative concentration à physiological change) or body àmind (somatosensory change à change of feeling).

There must be more than a bit of karmic humour in the way AT is talked about, taken up, and attached to by its many practitioners – AT is significant and meaningful for them because of its presence and its outcomes, and the consequences arising from practice in their lives. As people get on in years, of necessity they are glad to reap all the physiological shifts accruing to normalising arousal, stabilising heart rates, reducing cholesterol levels, and so on, that come with contemplative practice. And because AT works for the good, practice is kept. Invisible presuppositions become visible. Speculation gives way to observation and reality testing. Slowly, it becomes more and more alright to observe, to see – to see the variable, the transitoriness, the mutable, the interdependence of everything in life. This is a more comfortable view. New karmic links to new chains are formed, links and chains which are more open, kind, and loving. For those who consistently practice AT, Schultz's "small" psychotherapy does generalise to mindful living of everyday life. And this living is more and more often a positive, centered "no-self" experience, too.

Chapter 16

Beyond Mindfulness:
Complex Psychological Development
Through Vipassana

Paul R. Fleischman

Introduction

In my contacts with meditators and health professionals both in the US and around the world, I have noticed the need for a specific kind of explanation of Vipassana meditation, one that clarifies the difference between Vipassana and stress-reduction and other healing techniques associated with "mindfulness". Mindfulness is a very important aspect of Vipassana, but only one of many. Vipassana offers its students a potential for complex psychological development. For this potential to be actualized, Vipassana needs to be accurately understood, preserved, and practiced in its fullness. Information about its unique profile of action can help students appreciate its specific qualities. Vipassana can be explained from both traditional, eastern descriptive psychology, as well as from the concepts provided by western psychology and psychiatry.

Unfortunately, as Vipassana has flowered around the world, its rapid spread and enthusiastic reception have made it subject to distortion. The distortion has occurred through attempts to reduce it to shorter and easier forms of practice or to commercialize and market the well being associated with it or to medicalize it and make it an adjunct to healing and health professions. In fact, Vipassana is only tangentially related to "mindfulness" and "stress reduction," and to its other fragmentary derivatives intended for sale or for treatment of illness. These partial forms of meditation utilize a key feature of the whole, but delete many of the other valuable and enriching attributes of Vipassana has endured the millennia because it freshens, focalizes and organizes life. The cherished salience of Vipassana will not become palpable to persons appending a single aspect of it as a convenient afterthought to an otherwise uninvolved lifestyle. Brief and compartmentalized trainings in components of meditation are in many ways antithetical to Vipassana, which aims at calling up and developing realizations that direct a way of life.

Mindfulness in isolation from the totality of meditation may well help people and may form an approachable entry way into the great old traditional path, and in this limited sense may constitute a welcomed first step. It may in itself soothe and it may facilitate further inquiry and progress. But the presentation of "mindfulness-based" healing may also create customers out of potentially serious meditation students, refocus efforts onto post-hoc healing rather than onto pre-emptively awakened lifestyles, leach off spirituality, which is based on the inevitability of death, and instead augment narcissistic preoccupations, and obscure the origins and depth of the traditions that discovered and amplified mindfulness to be the prow in a much greater voyage.

Vipassana is the continuation of a tradition, an ancient path that is based upon the transmission of compelling personal experience. Preservation of the depth of Vipassana experience remains important, in the way that a constitution underpins specific legal statutes. For those who receive it experientially and who accordingly become inheritors of its fruits, Vipassana, like an heirloom, ceases to be a hand-me-down that can be modified for convenience. No curator of a cultural inheritance feels free to re-paint Van Gogh's and Rembrandts. One hundred years ago Rabindranath Tagore, India's great poet and the first non-European to be awarded the Nobel Prize for literature, predicted that when meditation would be brought to the West, it would be re-interpreted as a "mechanical training of the brain". Today his prognostication has been fulfilled by healers embossing their advertisements, and even by spokespersons for ancient traditions who imagine that mechanistic reductionism and brain imagery can help them expand their popular support.

The error of scientizing meditation lies in the misapplication of the proper domain of scientific inquiry. There is no science that can reduce experience to the machinery of the brain or body in which it occurs. There can be a science of what prevents certain experience, but not a brain-based science of experience itself, which would be recreating the old error of reducing complex systems to the additive functions of their underlying parts. Complex systems gain new functions through higher and more complex levels of organization. While destruction of certain brain areas or body functions can eradicate certain experiential possibilities, those loci are necessary but not sufficient to account for experience. Science does nowhere near understand the complexity of thought and feeling of the intact human being, which may well rest not only upon intact physiology, but also upon infinitely subtle neuronal remodeling, synaptic chemistry, and even molecular resonances. Experiences are not assessable or measurable through the visualizable physiological activities that accompany them.

The attempt to reduce meditation to what happens in the brain as a person meditates derives from a fundamentally demeaning attitude towards the activity. There are as yet no scientists who wire up their fiancés to an MRI to see if the poor dear is really worthy of marriage. No scientist has attempted to degrade poetry and painting by proving the obvious fact that the arts also use neural circuitry, which can be seen on the screens of imaging technology. Of course the brain is necessary for poetry, art or meditation, but experience cannot be reduced to the functioning of its substrate. Meditation experience is fulfilling personally and culturally; it does not need a neurologist to sanctify or bless it, any more than do art museums or poetry readings. Deep human feelings generated through activities like poetry, art or meditation exceeds the merely functional biological aspects that can be measured as they are unfolding. The meanings of marriage cannot be reduced to what happens while two people balance the same check book. Similarly, Vipassana differs from its dismembered applications or its neurological preconditions.

No one feels free to say they have re-written and improved upon Hamlet. Because meditation originated in Asia, some westerners of no distinction feel free to claim possession over it and imagine they are improving it in their own image of what they want it to be, without pausing first to learn it in its fully established, complex, and textured traditions. There is a long history of westerners attempting to co-opt and devalue meditation-based cultures of Asia. In British Ceylon, for example, policies were made to "discountenance... confront... and discomfort" Buddhists, whose culture became the basis to deny them schools or even the legitimacy of their children who were not products of a church-blessed marriage. Unconsciously repeating this cultural hierarchy, some western professionals and healers appoint themselves to pick apart aspects of meditation, which are then applied superficially without knowledge of their matrix. Part of the rush to medicalize meditation is economic and due to the fact that it can be used without criteria or certification. How we would feel if professionals from a foreign culture learned how to listen to the heart through a stethoscope and after a few sessions call themselves doctors?

For more than two thousand five hundred years Vipassana has been treasured as something requiring the devotion of a lifetime to learn. It has always been understood as interfacing with personality at numerous facets and angles. Modern psychological analysis concurs, revealing Vipassana to be an epic journey of insight and wisdom.

The goal of Vipassana

Vipassana addresses the humanness in us, the suffering, and the aspiration towards understanding and wisdom, illuminating life. Focused on holistic apperception rather than on a strategic attainment, Vipassana's goal is to reduce suffering through realism. The practice is based upon neutral observation of our selves, mentally and physically: to augment love and compassion, to reduce hate, fear and delusion, and to cross beyond materialism to realities that cannot be ritualized, named, or owned but which impacts the establishment of harmony and compassion in individuals and in their social surrounding.

By "Vipassana meditation" I am referring to something specific, a form of meditation that is preserved, taught, and practiced on three criteria of validation. First, it is based upon the original texts in the Sutta Pitaka of the Pali Canon where the teaching of the Buddha is stated and where the term, "Vipassana" is coined. Vipassana means: insight derived from systematic observation of mind and body as a field of arising and passing vibrations. Second, it is taught by qualified teachers, who were taught by qualified teachers, a chain of certification and investiture. Third, it is manifested by its practitioner community with a sense of respect for continuity and integrity that extends back to its origins in revelation and free person-to-person non-commercial transmission.

Vipassana can be apprehended only in a wholeness that circumambulates its interlocking complexity to reveal the seriousness, quality, and richness of this form of meditation when it is practiced properly, as it was designed to be practiced, and as it has been handed down over the generations, without adding to or deleting from its original discovery. An approach that is authentic, appealing and respectful may generate the intrigue and curiosity that are necessary preconditions for making the vigorous effort that is required to actually test its worth.

Prerequisites

It is necessary for a student to bring to Vipassana practice certain developmental attributes. Some psychological tools need to be in place before Vipassana can be utilized and certain psychological tasks need to have been mastered and integrated into personality before Vipassana can be productively practiced. Meditation has its own demands and ardors, and its practitioners require certain abilities before they begin.

The student needs to be able to understand and attend to verbal instructions, which are to be received during meditation itself. One must be able to follow instructions on one's own over sustained periods of hours, across the varying times of day with their differing states of wakefulness and satiety. One must persevere in this application to oneself of auditory instructions for days at a time, while encountering some degree of learner's difficulties and frustrations. Since meditation occurs in the privacy of one's own mind and body, the new student of the technique will need autonomous concentration, frustration tolerance, industriousness, freedom from perfectionism, capacity for self-acceptance and a touch of humor. Since the practice is introduced in meditation halls, in group learning circumstances, the student will need to be able to participate in structured, privately apprehended yet publicly situated education, without succumbing to distraction, despair, or disruption. As the instructions emanate from an impersonal authority, the student will have to proceed without undo "negative transference", that is, without becoming blocked by suspicion, doubt, defeat, personal demands or cynicism.

Certain states of mind prevent meditation. One needs freedom from acute, severe, overwhelming pre-existing feelings accompanying life crises or which often coexist with delusions, mania, depression, panic, or alcohol or drug withdrawal. All people bring with them the turmoil and existential pain which is not only compatible with meditation but which may well provide motivation to learn it. But just as one would not implement a fitness program for beginners by climbing Mt. Everest, it is foolhardy to commence meditation in states of mind requiring Herculean effort to work with or which by their very nature preclude the insight necessary for these states to enter the purview of Vipassana.

An integrated whole

The complexity and depth of Vipassana works as a functioning and integrated whole, as if it were a living body. Just as a medical student might study anatomy and physiology in serialized compartments with the ultimate necessity of creating a unified knowledge, this chapter will describe Vipassana's active ingredients in conceptually constructed sections that are not isolated entities but tissues in a living practice. Heuristically, Vipassana's modes of action can be divided into three groups, each in turn with multiple parts. The first comprise five psychosocial actions (values-based education, cognitive restructuring, group participation, cultural immersion, and causal thinking), three psychobiological actions (insight, body-mind integration, and biochemical integration), and four psychospiritual actions (purification, ecstasy, transcendence, and transmission). These twelve actions are variables interacting in a complex way.

(1) Values-based education. Vipassana is values based, not values neutral. It emphasizes the necessity of pro-social attitudes and commitments. The training begins with vows of five moral precepts – not to kill, lie, steal, use intoxicants or commit sexual misconduct. These formalities of moral positioning form a platform from which meditative observation can subsequently occur. This is in line with the contemporary scientific understanding, derived from "the uncertainty principle", that observation is never "neutral" and that the position of the observer partly determines what will be observed. Just as a naturalist focuses his binoculars on the watering hole at dawn and dusk rather than at high noon, so that his observations are not random time samples, but attempts to actually witness antelopes drinking and lions stalking them, so Vipassana begins with a particular region of focus. The five vows spring from the position: "do what helps others; refrain from harming others". This attitude is exhortative and educative. It performs meditation as an activity that necessitates social values, and which immediately links relief from personal suffering to apprehension of the common ground of the suffering of

all beings. The goal of Vipassana is to observe as objectively as possible, but also to observe with a goal of insight into suffering, its cause, and its elimination. Vipassana commences with a didactic assertion that a morally principled life is essential to personal equanimity.

However, the values-education of Vipassana is not limited to moralizing. As the practice evolves, the student is provoked towards questions and observations about the direct psychological impact of values in one's own life. The practice develops meditation-derived, personal insights into the ironically selfish benefits that accrue to altruistic values. The dichotomous concepts of "selfish" and "altruistic" are dissolved through realizations, which highlight the mutually synergistic interaction of generosity and well being. The thermostat in the human emotional apparatus, that tells us whether our life is going well or not, is observed to be pre-set for social attunement. The meditator cultivates his or her own welfare and happiness through internalization of identificatory values. Vipassana is not mere idealism. It does not deny narcissistic striving nor inveigh against self-concern. It does not preach self-abnegation. Instead, it harnesses self-interest into a realistic assessment of the quality of life that derives from positive social engagement, as seen through the lens of intense meditation.

(2) Cognitive restructuring. En route to dispelling ignorance and cultivating wisdom, Vipassana augments and reinforces particular cognitions while selectively reducing others. A change in (increase and utilization of) particular mental sets is intrinsic to meditation. Neutral observation, free of judgment, nevertheless requires mental skills that exist as ideas and attributes. Meditation is choiceless observation, but the suspension of judgment and the requirement of focused attention make it a vigorous exercise. The cognitive restructuring that occurs during meditation is based on will, determination, renewal, autonomy, self-responsibility, diligence, balance, relaxation, modulation, acceptance, realism, and appreciation.

Meditation evokes will, to sit still, pay attention, cultivate habits of observation, turn away from habitual thinking and to turn towards observation of bodily sensations, all of which are, at least initially, effortful. This is the attribute of mindfulness, the intention to be alert and aware of the object of meditation, which in Vipassana means the sensations of the body. When mindfulness is given one specific focus, such as the sensations at the base of the nostrils, the effort is to concentrate. When meditation is given moving foci, such as a sweep of all of the sensations of the body, the effort is for a fluid and tracking awareness, like a spotlight at an airport. In all cases, intention, focus, determination, renewals of effort are ideas that are valued and exercised. The solitary, independent, internal activity reorders the mind, towards self-responsibility and self-control. The expectation, opportunity, and necessity of returning to mindfulness and abandoning distraction, prioritizes vigor and self-mastery. Meditation is training in cognitive ideals.

Because there is no one to blame or acquiesce to, the playing field of the mind in meditation is a level of autonomy and self-agency. Vipassana training is built upon the ideal of diligence. Vipassana is a form of mental work. It is not just letting things be, not a drifting, pointless, undirected mind. At the same time, meditation will not be successful if it becomes tense or clutched. No one can meditate perfectly or even very well without practice, so that acceptance of varying levels of success becomes as essential as exertion. Along with diligence, there must be relaxation. Just as a guitar string sounds a sharp note if it is tuned too tight, or sounds flat if it is not stretched tightly enough, so meditation is a practice of balancing diligence with relaxation, tuning up or down the effort of the mental work to find the enduring and reliable realm of focus without depletion. Meditation teaches the ideal of self-awareness coupled to self-regulation.

The ideal of modulation is not limited to the realm of proper effort. It is applied as well towards attitudes regarding the contents of the mind. Much of psychic life contains a tension or dialectic between action and suppression. Should I do what I want to do or feel impelled to do, or should I put aside that idea, forget about it, squash it or deny it? In the realm of Vipassana, a middle path is advocated between action and suppression. The training is to observe with full awareness, free of denial, but also free of action: just observation. This education, in belaying impulse without denying its existence, becomes a learned stance that generalizes into daily life. A classical image likens the meditator to a well-trained horse who can run to win but who never does so without permission from his beloved and commanding rider.

Vipassana is forward looking; an education in living and a path of development, but this focus on self-improvement could become unbalanced if self-acceptance were not also part of the practice. Just as the guitar string of effort must be tuned into key by combination with relaxation, so growth on the path is counter weighted by pragmatic, realistic acceptance of one's own strengths, limitations, abilities and deficits. Realism is inculcated, replacing aggrandizement or defeat. We grow, but we do not all become our own idealized self over night. There is no limit to what you might attain tomorrow, but today is done: time for sleep. The numerous changes in ideation that are a part of Vipassana create a cognitive restructuring that forms one of the active psychological ingredients of the practice. This change in attitude and thought has appreciation as its fulcrum. The meditator is walking the path, going forward, progressing if ever so slowly or not according to some naively preconceived schedule, but still embracing a lifelong activity of ascent. Vipassana inculcates a sense of opportunity. There is a widespread misconception that meditation derives from passivity and resignation, the mere acceptance of situation as Karma. In fact, Vipassana trains the mind to apprehend the world through observation, responsibility, effort, diligence, modulation, positive expectation, progress and the crystallization of all of these in well-chosen action. Although the activity of meditation appears from the outside to be sedate, it feels psychologically vital and energetic, a fundamentally active experience that one creates one's own subjective world.

(3) Group participation. Vipassana is taught and practiced in groups. While the dynamism of meditation occurs within the individual, the psychic and internal world is buffered, contained, and sustained by affiliation with a living community. Meditation is people. Despite the stereotype of meditation as solipsistic activity, it is essentially a gathering of friends. Meditation is as involved with creating and sustaining "friendship on the path" as tennis requires someone else on the other side of the net. Meditation, discovered by people, has been handed down person to person, is learned from people, and resonates at its most tuneful in groups of like-practicing companions. One of the active psychological ingredients of Vipassana is membership in a fluid, world-wide, nonsectarian, multiethnic, no-due, no-cards, no-appeals network, built upon a cross-cultural Gestalt. As Vipassana swept around the world in the second half of the 20th century, the benefit of global community magnified.

Vipassana always produces social learning. Group meditation inculcates prudent, tested, trust in leadership. As an activity of repetition and renewal, experience becomes the best teacher, but suggestions can reduce misguided thrashing around, so the suggestions of a teacher can be salutary. Groups produce a holding environment. They lead to a balance of autonomy with participation. In a group of meditators, each individual receives the proximate warmth of everyone else, and contributes his or her own presence back to the others. Giving and receiving in silence, and via meditation, replace the aridity of merely personal and solitary auto regulation. Like an orchestra, groups are most harmonious with a conductor. Like a chamber quartet, small groups may practice together and cohere in mutually enhancing vibration. Vipassana is an experiential training in "positive group transference". Students benefit from flexible long-term continuity in a sustained connection of positive mutual regard. Human relationships kindled by meditation form a branching network around the individual, and these relationships not only are contemporaneous, but also include an ancestry, and future generations to be considered and cared for. Meditation ultimately includes the maintenance of facilities, courses, and the practice itself. Meditation properly practiced is opposite from the stereotype of the stone icon seated in immobile solitude. Vipassana is the journey from individual encasement to communion.

(4) Cultural immersion. Vipassana is located at a confluence of cultures. A culture is an eager practice of elevating relationships, a widely shared prescription for living. The values, cognitions and communities that form the psychosocial action of Vipassana, are located within a wider net of interactions, activities, skills, attitudes, practices, properties, architecture, and psychic states that are treasured, taught, and distributed among persons and across generations. The people who maintain the living steam of Vipassana easily mingle, with nonviolent values, absence of intoxicants, consideration of the ethical basis of their livelihood, attempts at courteous interactions, distance from divisive ideologies, and reverence for life and for the practice. Much of this culture is not unique to Vipassana but blends into a wider pool of cultures with which it shares features. Vipassana collects from what is held in common a compilation of ways of being human, and adds the unique components of it. Some of its value and power derives from immersion in this way of life that is old, surrounding and enduring, like the ocean. Recognition of ancestry, of community, and of embeddedness makes true meditation very different from a merely self-administered psychological self-maintenance.

The culture of meditation is one in which containment, reflection, and calm are systematically cultivated. There is an attempt to reduce agitation or stimulation for its own sake, such as exists in many forms of entertainment. Ignorance, understood as the root cause of suffering, is diminished by placing meditation at the beginning and ending of every day's activities, promoting a culture of self-examination and self-soothing. This ethos is universal, as western as it is eastern, and shares with Greek philosophy the postulate that the unexamined life is not worth living. Meditation becomes a field of play and relaxation. The mind is a space that can be explored subjectively and objectively, and its contents are understood to be mental products, not facts. Ideologies, taken to be constructed things in the atelier of mind, are subject to reversal by further information and experience. The culture of meditation is observational, cautious of opinion and social positioning. Mental contents are useful tools, but not mirrors of an external reality. Meditation, not thought, is granted primacy as the ultimate media of knowing.

Because meditation is based on realization of impermanence and mortality as the common ground of life, the culture of meditation recognizes all lives as related. All living beings share the same fundamental conditions. Everything that lives, dies, and all living things can recognize their own hopes and fears in the eyes of others. Why harm someone who is only trying to be happy, just as are you and I? Reverence for life is a natural correlate of the universal kinship that is found throughout the processes of creation and dissolution. Vegetarianism is not enjoined, but is a common expression of this ethos. Sobriety is emphasized in the moral precepts of Vipassana, and a mind free of even psychic intoxication is axial to the culture of meditation. By psychic intoxication I mean the over excitements, obsessions and revilements that sweep aside equanimity for which meditation is practiced in the first place. True enthusiasms remain a part of the culture of meditation, and are given expression through their endurance, depth and commitment, rather than through their flurry or vehemence. For the lifelong meditator, excitement becomes sublimated into devotion despite winter and cross winds.

In a world of causality, impermanence and kinship, universalism, rather than insularity, is the cultural stance. So is non-sectarianism and tolerance, but not a tolerance that acquiesces to intolerance or that fails to stand up and speak clearly. Personal empowerment and freedom of conscience are rooted in autonomy of experience – the person who returns systematically to silent meditation creates a private laboratory in which to formulate the right approach for tomorrow, but not forever. The meditator becomes a private investigator of his or her own conscience and position. The conventions of surrounding cultures, their amusements, amphitheatres, politics and gods, may be politely nodded to, but are recognized as temporary theatre sets subject to change.

The culture of Vipassana is built on modulation of personal style, and sensitivity to the vulnerabilities of others, rather than on intrusion or righteousness. Meditation heightens awareness of one's frailties, and that helps us empathize with others. We are all partial and temporary. Giving back to community is the cultural correlate of knowing that meditation does not exist independently of "friendship on the path". Meditation floats in a culture of gratitude that supplants the fantasy of being a "self-made-man". Today's opportunities were prepared by previous generations. We are derivatives of people in the past. Meditation is understood to be received, upheld and carried forward. It is a gift, a family property. Pragmatism is a cultural value that manifests realism, and freedom from ideology and delusion. Vipassana is practiced to augment well-being here and now. Participation in all these cultural norms of Vipassana leads to a relocation of psychosocial identity within a nexus of meditation-derived attributes. Everywhere there are people like me, many of whom are pillars holding up the vision we have in common. The culture of Vipassana gives us team strength. Vipassana comes from, participates in, and amplifies a world of human interactions and meanings. The serious meditator has roots in the past, branches that reach outward and a flowering into the future. Vipassana culture is a tissue of creative, long-lasting community that receives, shares, and perpetuates its answer as a living tissue does, with many enzymes flowing from cell to cell.

(5) Causality. Vipassana practice and the culture in which it is embedded are based on a world-view of causality. This is empiricism, out of which science derived and which is the opposite of magical, superstitious, self-referential thinking or the belief in divine intervention. Vipassana is differentiated from much of religious or spiritual thinking, because it does not postulate for its followers special privilege or cozy exemption from universal law. The Vipassana experience unfolds like this: everything in the visible and tangible world follows the rules of understandable causality; our minds and bodies, just like the rest of the material universe, follow laws and principles of causality; we can understand and develop ourselves through rigorous application of the knowledge of causality to our selves.

Vipassana is a volunteer-run, non-professional enterprise, so it does not generate data for publication in scientific journals, but its emphasis on a causal universe makes it co-terminate with the scientific worldview. Undoubtedly this emphasis partly accounts for the spread of Vipassana in the 20th century. It is acceptable to educated and to scientifically trained people, and compatible with (post-)modern ethos. Vipassana tempers people into self-observers. Utilizing systematic self-observation, meditators appreciate how their thoughts and actions participate in the construction of their sense of self. The sense of self is caused; it is a creation. It can be recreated through changed perceptions and actions, but it also can be deconstructed through Vipassana. Static conceptual self referents prevent accurate insight into the fluid life process that one actually is.

Throughout the human community, both in individual life stories, or in organized religion, or in nationalism, or in other groups inflated with self importance, we find exaggerated self-reference, fantasies of passive receipt from higher powers, magical thinking based on false, casual correlation between unrelated events and other pathologies of thought. These errors function to seemingly exempt the self from the rule of natural law. Vipassana reveals the inconsistency and irrationality that contribute to these epidemics of individual or group self-promotion. By immersing oneself in observation of cause and effect as they function in the psychological construction of self-percepts, one can emerge from them into a more concept-free realism. One can become more insightful, less burdened by ideation, and freer to live pre-emptively, choosing and self-regulating. The emphasis on observing causal connections between events places Vipassana closer to science and humanism than to theology or deism. That the sense of self is caused, self-causing and potentially self-liberating is one of the key observational foci of Vipassana.

(6) Psychological insight. Meditation practice often begins in a paradoxical manner. Rather than calm and peace, there is an upwelling of physical, mental, and emotional reactions, the way a hard rain stirs up the bottom of the pond. This turbulence is vivid, dramatic and memorable. Memories, daydreams, wishes, fears, past and future fantasies are unveiled. Nothing new is being created but what was present and shrouded now becomes visible. Mere observation does not change who you are, but it does uncover it. Meditation acts as if it were a mirror to both manifest and latent aspects of personality. For this authentic mirroring, one must practice properly enough, and for sustained enough periods of time, and with an attitude anchored in observation rather than reaction. There is no attempt to manipulate, create, or erase psychic worlds. A meditator sees him/herself boldly, with clarity, complexity and depth, "Know thy self".

The attempt of the meditator is to delve below the river of thought, vision and emotion, to not drown in it nor become distracted away from the meditative observational focus. Nevertheless, this exposure almost always provides an evocative, educative, and transformative awareness of the content of one's psyche. Here is its history, anticipations, aspirations, repulsions, and orientations. This is an experience of insight into the vicissitudes of personality and motivation. Some of the insight into mental content that I am discussing so far in this section is not absolutely unique to Vipassana. It may not essentially differ from the experiences of self-reflective intellectuals, or long-distance hikers alone on the ridge tops for a month, or analysands free-associating on the psychoanalytic couch. Some features of meditative psychological insight derive from unbroken awareness of conscious mental imagery. This is often helpful.

There is also a more unique component of insight that springs up from the focus on sensations of the body. Memory and experience are stored not only in the brain but in the whole body. Meditation that utilizes as its focus systematic investigation of the entire soma unveils a rich layer in the archeology of self. Unlike mental imagery that was previously conscious but is now more clearly observed, observation of sensations often catalyzes awareness of mental contents that had not previously been available to awareness. This uniquely Vipassana layer of meditation brings into consciousness aspects of oneself that had been stored in somatic code. Vipassana translates them from sensation-based memory into greater accessibility as thoughts, feelings and images that are "the other side of the coin" of sensations. These layers of psychological insight are often useful to the meditator in areas like abandoning convenient old self-deceptions, or rekindling dim memories, or constructing better future plans, because they expand self-definition beyond its previous corral. But the meditative function of this arena of insight is not retrospective, analytical, nor anticipatory. It provides a factual inventory out of which the sense of self is not only amended but also deconstructed. The uniquely Vipassana layer of insight clinches the realization that conscious self-definition is never rich enough to contain the welter of the mind's storehouse. We are always more than what we remember or define of ourselves. The reality of ourselves is not well served by our definition of our self. We are longer in the making and suffused out among many experiences and forces. We are not properly known within a circle. This layer of self-discovery also provides a catalogue, using which causality is more deeply understood, from which greater freedom becomes possible.

We are not who we think we are. We are all that we are. We cannot wish ourselves free of the past, but we can walk forward with heightened awareness of who we have been, how we have gotten here, and how to progress towards our goals. No one leaves a ten-day Vipassana course without a new understanding of themselves at the psychological level of personal history, formative events and freshly recognized opportunities.

(7) Psycho-physical integration. Vipassana directs attention towards the sensations of the body in interaction with which the mind is found. This choice of focus is part of the definition. The sensations on the body are a storehouse of mental content, and mental content is a pictorial representation of body sensation. They are two sides of the coin of mind-and-body life. The contact of the two *is* life. Both are expressing forms of energy, which are encoded and stored in the organism. Sensations of the body and contents of the mind are both the activity of atoms, molecules, and cells, the ripples of the physics and chemistry that we call life, matter in unique vitality. We are alive at the intersection of mind and body, the crossroads of body sensations and mental activity. To observe and to understand the tightness of the interconnection between bodily and mental life lies at the center of Vipassana meditation.

When the meditator is able to extract attention away from the captivation with mental contents, s/he can at last observe the subtle bodily basis of concurrent mental states. Physiological and psychological activity is observed to be one entity. Mind and body are experienced as integrated and co-dependent. Previously unconscious causality can now become manifest such as when thoughts produce body sensations or when reactions to sensations produce thoughts. It is this focus on sensations that diminishes the careening mind stream and commences the possibility for systematically cultivated objectivity and decreased reactivity. The attempt of the mind to observe the mind is like the finger trying to touch itself, but the mind can objectify and observe sensations on the body just as a finger can touch a finger on the other hand. Because of the unbroken, days-long attention directed to this task, Vipassana offers a profound sense of integration of the body and the mind. Imbalanced over-identifications with either mental or physical self-aspects can be reduced by practiced apperceptions of these two as integrated wholes. Watching the mind and body connect during long hours of meditation reveals their resonance. They play upon each other, producing conscious life. Steady observation of these events, which lie deeper than one's previously conscious sense of self, opens the door to observation without reaction, which is the gateway to equanimity.

All of Vipassana comes down upon this point. It is realization and apprehension of one-self as a process embedded within the physics and chemistry of the universe, from which one gains true insight into who one is. From this, realistic appreciation, realistic detachment, deep equanimity can occur. I am a product of the laws of the universe, a temporary cloud of parti-cles and energies, caused from the past, creating effects into the future, devoid of any endur-ing ether or title, without any exemption from the universal arising and passing away of all things. There is no social club, ethnic affiliation, vehement attestation, warring pack, religious or philosophical belief, or book that can change these facts. I am the same as every raindrop, wolf or flower, except that I can understand this reality and so I can stop imprisoning myself in identification with this temporary collection of biological events in which my sense of self rides. Beyond all matter there may be the non-material realities. My personal body-and-mind isn't that.

(8) Biochemical-psychological re-integration. Practiced, sustained, continuous, objective, observation of the myriad subtle and ceaselessly varying body sensations leads to powerful, new, meditation-derived emotional memories. It is as if these revolutionary experiences were the opposite of trauma. They produce new orienting points for a new way of life. They imprint in mental-physical memory a re-integration of self-experience that occurs at the level of sen-sation-based self-awareness that was previously below the observational threshold. For this to be a life transforming experience, sensations below the level of the gross and obvious ones need to enter into conscious awareness. That is why deep and continuous meditation is the hall-mark of Vipassana. Only through sustained observational effort can breakthroughs in aware-ness lead to breakthroughs in experience, leading to breakthroughs in self-definition.

A new sense of reality about the world and one self is deeply experienced, re-experienced and internalized. What was before seen as real now seems to be a superficial interpretation. Systematic meditation practice, with its sustained inward focus, reveals a dynamic, flexible, changing, flow of matter beneath the artificially static construct of self. The meditator devel-ops the capacity to re-locate in biological tissue the biochemical vibrations of molecular insub-stantiality. Oneself and all reality are apprehended to be changing and impermanent. The avail-ability of this layer of meditation experience explains two things that might have previously appeared arbitrary. It explains the focus of Vipassana on fleeting and subtle body sensations, which is the only zone in which a person can directly experience the simultaneous arising and passing of phenomena. It is this immersion into impermanence at the millisecond, molecular level that defines Vipassana and differentiates it from vaguely similar meditation practices that are limited to more didactic and ideational presentations of impermanence. Secondly, this layer is the media which catalyses freedom from suffering with the basis of insight into reality as it is.

(9) Purification. When the essential impermanence of body-and-mind is repeatedly real-ized in deep meditation, and is understood to be universal reality, and is observed without reac-tion, many previously conditioned reactive discharges are de-conditioned. Impermanence is not only an insight. When encountered in one's own self, it becomes a cleansing of many for-mer problems. I have been reacting all along to a dim awareness of, and fear of impermanence. The dissolution of one's self is a bedrock human fear. In the past, I used to be reacting to intu-itions of impermanence that I was contacting in my body, and to which I was responding below the threshold of consciousness. I have lived in reactivity to my own body-and-mind without awareness that I was constantly doing so. I have tried to create a reality that is independent of

the change that underlies everything. Different states of the sensorium of the body were being abhorred or desired, on the basis of whether they helped me maintain the fantasy that I was not destined to disappear. Now the somatic basis of so much fear and desire is revealed and conscious.

The change in the body-and-mind occurring constantly implies how transitory my life and my self are. So many of my past physical and emotional reactions were about impermanence, and each reaction utilized as the vehicle of reaction more impermanent chemical messages. Thoughts and feelings depend upon the movement of molecules. Reaction patterns that trigger chemical flows of neurotransmitters or other hormonal messages are impermanent reactions to impermanence. They are responses to and participants in the flow, constituting life. Unconscious reactions to impermanence in the body become further impermanent reactions in the body, a vicious cycle of reactivity constituting unexamined living. With Vipassana, I can notice and understand this process of generating reaction to change with more reactive change. Meditation enables insight-derived decrease in reactivity. There is a diminution of thoughts and emotions based upon reaction to the perception of impermanence in the body-and-mind: less internal psychic chatter and a quieter mind. Fears and cravings for particular kinds of sensation, for particular excitations or dysphorias, become conscious and easier to regulate. They can be understood at the root level, and can be lessened or even entirely abandoned.

Vipassana develops equanimity, a reduction in fear or craving for one's own particular psychophysical, biochemical states. One observes, does not react to the flow of life and so becomes not only calmer in the moment, but also lets go of old habit patterns of reaction. One becomes less murky to one's self, purer. Equanimity becomes re-locatable and reproducible as a physical as well as a mental state. A self-rewarding feedback loop, an auto-regulation of calm at the actual level of modulated neurotransmission, is practiced. Self-experience shifts from anxiety-driven and desire-driven. Equanimity derived from Vipassana means a life of reduced fear and craving, and this learning occurs at the intellectual, somatic and biochemical levels. Vipassana is experienced at and acts upon all the organizational levels of the organism. This cybernetic complexity and penetration account for the power of Vipassana experience. It explains how meditation develops insight that is far more self-interactive than conscious belief alone.

At the core of this learning is the observation that the self is an arbitrary construct, superimposed upon the malleable, adaptive, responsive, but ungraspable, impermanent and transitory body-and-mind. The self is a static conceptualization incapable of accurately describing a fluid world. Realism about human life and self-harmony becomes increasingly reproducible experiences. Unrealistic impositions are dropped. This is an education, a practice teaching freedom at the level of chemistry, biology, and psychology. Without contact with the subtle biochemical level of one's body, the idea of impermanence remains conceptual rather than deep, personal, and total. Through Vipassana, the subtlest sensations of the body enter awareness with insight into their essential impermanence. One listens to oneself absolutely. The truth is within one's self. Reality is that all sensations that constitute the body, the mind, and the self are insubstantial, temporary, and ungraspable. Through objective observation and attunement to feedback, one is taught calm, simply by the very act of observing accurately. One learns to balance on impermanence and change as experienced within the body-and-mind.

Whatever leads to agitation, anger, fear, or hate is a source of strong chemical flow of neurotransmitters beneath the thoughts and emotions. It is unskillful to continue to stir up these storms of thought-emotion-molecules-chemicals, for one's own sake if not for any one else's. It is skilful to let go of the attitudes, beliefs, and behaviors causing these perturbations within the biosystem. Whatever leads to calm, dispassion, peace and harmony, intrinsically and automatically reduce turbulence within the being. It is skilful to cultivate these mental states in both thought and in lifestyle. Attitudinal changes create bodily changes by changing neurochemical activity. Harmonious and social emotions like love and compassion are the pure water states. They ride above salubrious vibrations in the body from which mental states can be apprehended and transcended. They do not catalyze somatic turbulence. They are not merely calming mentally, but also neurochemically.

Cynicism, bitterness, and self-righteousness produce somatic intensifiers. It is as if they enclose and obscure the heavens, producing noise that obscures anything else. The meditator now can experience them not only as mental anguish, but also as hurricanes of sensations in the body, that are caused by biochemical storms which are the flow of neurochemicals that accompany these particular ideations. Meditation leads to a purification of mind and body as a byproduct of the peace, harmony and joy that the practice brings into focus as wisdom. Wisdom is not profound thoughts, but a life of peace caused by realistic self knowledge.

(10) Ecstasis. Systematic, non-reactive self-observation cultivates ecstasy, standing outside oneself, and seeing oneself from the same angle as one views the rest of the phenomenal world. This self-detachment reduces the egocentric melodrama of self. Every thought and feeling you have is temporary. Your life is temporary. The centrality of one's self is recognized to be a perceptual distortion based on proximity. It is as if a red ball had been one inch away from your face and had been all that you could see; but then the red ball is placed on the ground one mile away and is seen in perspective. Relinquishment of narcissistic perspective reveals an originless, unending world of time and space. There are no boundaries to the fact of change everywhere and always. Personal death is inevitable. You see the world free of imaginary fortresses and heavens. For the recipient of this cherished gift of ecstasy, self-referential contortions of the culture of narcissism disappear. The glossy magazines in the health food store that prescribe meditation as medicinal palliation appear silly. The goal of meditation lies far beyond doctoring or psychotherapy. Similarly, the conventions and obligations that may have bound in the past are apprehended from a new perspective.

Vipassana permits a revolutionary re-entry into possibility. Everything called "reality" has occurred within my body, mind, and senses. It is not that Vipassana reveals these events to be wrong or "unreal", they are limited. They may well be real enough at one layer of reality, but they are not the entire story. To the meditator, it cannot be credible that the sensory apparatus of one little body-mind organism accurately transmits all "truth". Vipassana admits the possibility of realizations from beyond the apparatus of self, unknowns exceeding thought, language, feeling or any other body-or-mind-based confinement. The meditator develops beyond viewpoints based on perspectives grounded in an ephemeral self. A non-self-referential understanding holds in abeyance conclusions based upon parochialism. The need to reduce reality to definitions and certainties fades away. The world is witnessed as evolving, lawful, horizonless. Convictions, certainties, opinions, gods – how can you claim to know them, who cannot claim any objectivity beyond your own body? Outside of the small-minded, self-inflating myths of the collectivities, are the great unknowns, sources of awe and reverence. If you can name it within some linguistic, conceptual category, you are pretending to hold the wind in a cage.

Realism and objectivity are more numinous than are stories invented a few thousand years ago under roofs and within walls. Readiness to receive and readiness to change are the best routes to reverence. From the experiences of deep Vipassana meditation, you do not define a new reality, but stop accepting the old definitions. You are not the centre of the world. Your contemporaries do not define ultimate truth with their narratives. Allow yourself permission to receive more. There may be a purpose to your life that does not require you to fight, argue, believe or pretend to know. Standing aside from the drumming may be the best way to hear more clearly the music of the spheres.

(11) Transcendence. The direct, recurrent, meditative encounter with ceaseless change and impermanence leads to a de-mythologized universe. The meditator brushes shoulders with, takes a dip into, de-semanticized knowing, whose dimensions and protean nature are not adequately recounted by religion, philosophy, science or any other language-based narrative. The meditator enters the stream of experiential apprehension of reality transcending definition.

But if everything is so "beyond" and life is so impermanent, doesn't that devalue friends, family, work, society, the everyday? Isn't meditation also a narcissistic trap? It could be! But important correctives to this danger should already be in place. First, there is the long development of social values and ways of life already bolted into the bridges of the Vipassana path, as discussed in so much detail in this article. You can't get to the top of the mountain without having climbed its lower slopes. Secondly, static self-satisfaction won't long endure the overturning and reviving renewal that continues through ongoing Vipassana practice. As long as there is life, the practice remains fertile, rejuvenating, and challenging to yesterday's assumptions and conclusions.

Transcendence of culturally sanctioned reality-narratives does not devalue contextual daily living. Insight at any level does not obviate the need for food, shelter, family and factuality. Development in meditation is not a license for professional advancement, an entitlement, nor an exemption from the vicissitudes of realistic and responsible living. Each day becomes treasured as an occasion for further awakening. Pragmatism and skillful coping underpin a non-sectarian faith in the value of life as a path. If you stop moving and growing you can't call it the path. There is yet another dimension beyond today. Keep letting go of what you have attached. Transcendence is not based on self propulsion but on effacement. Service suffused with a feeling of reverence is its upper slopes. The word "transcendence" properly applied to Vipassana is not a self important excitement, but a detachment from self based knowing. It is not an attainment, but a detachment from. It is not a new, strident worldview, but an intelligent distance from all pretense of ontology and cosmology. It is not a more cogent argument but a recognition of the limits of the value of disputation. Transcendence is not union or communion with gods or mystical states, but a recognition of them as illusions of sensoria. Transcendence is not ecumenism, but a-theological, a-theoretical modesty and empiricism.

The use of the word "transcendence" does not mean that the meditator is necessarily fully enlightened, free of suffering or never beset by ordinary problems. Just as a person can be well fed, but still need sleep, so a person can be free of suffering in some moments and to some significant extent, but not entirely so. Transcendence means freedom from both belief and skepticism. On the path with fellow meditators, who are established in and devoted to the practice, on the path alone inside one's own experience, one transcends each arising sensation, each arising thought, each arising emotion. Transcendence brings clarity, immediacy and expectation of change. You let go of sensations, thoughts and feelings. You keep letting go. Releasing your grasp, you rise above clutching at things as they pass.

(12) Transmission. Meditation is taught and learned, not only through rules, schedules, and instructions but also through atmosphere. Vipassana is transmitted with attitude. If it is sold, then it is given as part of exchange and you feel you have purchased the right to own it. That is not transmission. The teaching of Vipassana can only be for free, not because of some socialistic attitude but because its maintenance and movement from person to person across time and history is a gift of love. It is a transmission and reception of a mode of relationship. A gift leaves you in debt, and the feeling of debt is intrinsic to the need to transmit the gift across the generations into the future. Like the wisdom of culture that we share with our children, like the children themselves who our bodies give to the future generation, Vipassana is given. Reducing Vipassana to a possession, a commodity, or even a professional skill, it looses its essential ambiance. Transmission of the vibration of Vipassana is blocked when the student needs to claim personal possession of it as a professional accoutrement. This professionalizing of meditation derives from the culture of narcissism that seeks to gain economic rights over public treasure. A mother does not demand recompense for the time she put in teaching and helping us. A housekeeper does. Because it has been given freely with compassionate love, an emotional inheritance enters us more deeply than does a clean floor.

In this short life of ours, we can join the illimitable reality beyond ourselves through four doors: love, joy, compassion and equanimity. Vipassana can only become its whole potential when it is given in keeping with these. You can't purchase the whisper of wind in aspen leaves. If you paid for it, you did not get Vipassana. Whoever sold it has never experienced its unattached, impersonal, universal open-handedness. Why would you pay someone to feel the breeze? How can you imagine that the entrepreneur you are tipping has experienced the gift of self transcendence?

You know that you have received transmission of Vipassana when you have assigned yourself to maintenance of the path with a task appearing in the basin of your own attainments, limitations, and situation. Feeling stewardship free of possession, you have received the path. With such a rich complex of actions and such deep and unique experiences, Vipassana inspires people to preserve it in the unmodified wholeness with which they received it. You experience the path as steppingstones placed by great and admirable guides. Their voices continue to murmur along the trail. They left directions like blazes on trees when they walked across this planet long ago. You feel inspired to preserve the ancient path that leads through the wilderness. To keep it clear, you place your footprints, one after another, on the ground. Surrounded by the loneliness of your individual and mortal self, you join the path. As you decay you dissolve into the stream.

The destination and conclusion

The destination of the path is Nibbana, the unconditioned, "beyond the wind", or "without a flickering flame". Any practice aiming towards less is not Vipassana. Everything is changing, but there is an unarising, unchanging, to be found beyond body, mind, books, religions, ideas, beliefs, concepts or any other form of grasping. This freedom from grasping at anything is called liberation. To be this free of clinging, one needs to have relinquished attachment to oneself and to have moved past the suffering which derives from holding onto an impermanent sense of "I". This is a rare attainment.

Mindfulness is a tool on the path and a prerequisite to awareness of the full array of the body's sensations, their integration with mind, the development of equanimity, purification of lifestyle and exalted states of ecstasy, transcendence and the receipt of transmission. Any committed meditator will grow beyond the mere tool of mindfulness, and beyond medical or commercial utilization of that and will flower with love and compassion, radiating them with a deep sense of personal fulfillment, while at the same time ripening in devotion and gratitude towards the complex and holy garden of Vipassana, filled with ancestors, friends, guides, texts, courses, centers, teachers and future practitioners, a flowering that is perennial, blooming century after century, a world of deep and meaningful experiences.

Vipassana is a treasury of the rational, numinous, and sacred, whose essence is to relinquish personal possession of it. It is a practice, a path, and a communion. Those who enter its gates ingenuously find religious feeling without religious ideology. As you practice it, it continuously opens up around you, exfoliating beyond any station you have reached. The old familiar reality you had constructed dissolves. Meditation reveals simultaneous guidance from many angles as an interrelating, logical, magical gift from awakened minds.

Part VI

Mindfulness Issues In Psychotherapy Along Buddhist Lines

In Chapter 17 Myint, who stems from the Burmese Theravada tradition, points at the *8-Fold Balanced Practice* that embeds mindfulness – as attention and awareness – alongside the other practices aimed at balancing views, intentions, speech, actions, living, and efforts. We need to examine how these interlinked components of mindfulness practice translate into the language of psychology. Calm stability and insightful understanding of the phenomena at hand seem to have got lost in translation. Is the current application a sophisticated technique or will it lapse into a self-help cliché? As the outcome evidence is still slim and controversial, sceptics see hallmarks of another fad. Translating the complete method as the Buddha taught it into a scientific language and replicating its effects in research for comparison with the current western approaches might be a remedy. Unlike western modes of mindfulness which see mindfulness as attention control training, intentional control of attention, or metacognition training, the pristine mindfulness does not result from cognitive training, linguistic deconstruction, or reframing of phenomena, but rather emerges from the coming together of: cognition of wise worldview and thought, embodiment of ethical feeling and action, and behaviour of choiceless observation and reflection. An insightful understanding of the phenomenon emerges from reflection of nonjudgmental knowledge. Thus, the wise cognition, the ethical affect and the choiceless behaviour support each other interdependently like a tripod for the emergence of mindfulness and clear comprehension. As the author remarked, we are languaging, interpreting, and meaning making beings; thus we also have the ability to become mindful "humane" beings.

Rapgay's Chapter 18 signals a Buddhist's concern about the misrepresentation of mindfulness in the western clinical-research community. Since many called for the original practice, the author, who stems from a Tibetan Vajrayana tradition, introduced "Classical Mindfulness" and innovated "Classical Mindfulness-Based Integrative Cognitive-Behavior Therapy" to treat anxiety disorders, particularly Generalized Anxiety Disorders. His approach differs from the "mindfulness-based" approaches which fail to discern attention from awareness and which include acceptance and nonjudgmental conceptions and approaches, thus hampering the cultivation of bare experience. It seems that mindfulness works to help anxiety by regulating the reactivity involved with anxiety. For instance, it tends to decrease vital body functions such as breathing; and if breathing rate goes down metabolism also begins to regulate itself and the proclivity to react to anxiety and discomfort in a fight or flight mode will subside. The benefits are foremost at the cognitive and emotional levels. One learns to separate the sensations that comprise anxiety from the cognitive associations or affective associations, and the imaginary projections on the fear.

Sik's Chapter 19 raises the same issue, namely that mindfulness attention-and-awareness meditation is a not an isolated technique, but rather a process embedded in six quintessential steps of the Buddha's awakening, uncovering Dependent Origination and paving a Middle Way to cease Duhkha. The author, who stems from a Mahayana denomination, thus proposes a "Dharma Therapy", a six phase parallel program in the Buddha's footsteps with mindfulness as one of the key components to help seeking clients. The rationale of the steps is that one needs to be aware of the suffering, to develop a desire to be liberated, to investigate the cause of suffering, to mindfully observe the conditions of suffering, and to take the necessary steps to end suffering with insight and wisdom. It should be noted that the Dharma's aim is not per se to cure pathology but to liberate from existential suffering. Therefore any claims of the Dharma as a therapy needs to be scrutinized against the backdrop of existing treatments "as usual" which were already applied with success.

Chapter 17

Mindfulness Ain't Enough In Psychotherapy: Case Study Of Meditation Classes

Aung Myint

Introduction

Current apparently mindless application of "mindfulness" to psychotherapy has been questioned as to whether it will become a sophisticated therapeutic technique or whether it will lapse into a self-help cliché. Sceptics see this as hallmarks of another fad (Carey, 2008). Kabat-Zinn (1982) first secularised part of tranquillity meditation, namely "mindfulness of breathing", as a palliative pain control technique called Mindfulness-Based Stress Reduction (MBSR) at the University of Massachusetts hospital in Worcester in the 1970s. Though he originally learnt from Asian Buddhist teachings, he excluded seven other interdependent components of mindfulness practice (Thich, 1999). Kabat-Zinn may have initially done this for purely a self-admitted reason of scientific acceptability. All components of mindfulness can be grouped into three categories; namely cognitive views *(panna)*, affective behaviours *(sila)* and "stable mind" *(samadhi)*. Kabat-Zinn (2003b), himself taught through the tradition of tranquillity, emphasizes mindfulness as:

> ...the awareness that emerges through paying attention on purpose in the present moment, and non-judgementally to the unfolding of experience moment by moment (p.145).

He uses the breath as an object of meditation to calm the mind for the examination of phenomena transpiring in the body and the mind. Subsequent researchers, who followed Kabat-Zinn's (1990) *awareness* and *acceptance* premise, extended and added their own theoretical orientations which yielded similar inconclusive findings (Hayes & Smith, 2005; Linehan, 1993; Witkiewitz & Marlatt, 2007).

Scientific evidence is still slim. Early research data on pain relief using MBSR (Kabat-Zinn, Lipworth, Burney, & Sellers, 1987; Kabat-Zinn, Lipworth, & Burney, 1985; Kabat-Zinn, 1982), and treatment and prevention of depression and suicidal relapses using Mindfulness-Based Cognitive Therapy (MBCT; Williams, 2000; Segal, Williams, & Teasdale, 2001) show that the science behind mindfulness is debatable. Review of 22 studies using the MBSR or the MBCT which includes MBSR as a component concludes that the MBSR is probably efficacious (Baer, 2003) and strongly recommended for serious research (Bishop, Lau, Shapiro, Carlson, Anderson, et al. (2004). Further, meta-analysis of studies which included control groups showed that mindfulness interventions significantly improved both mental and physical health indicators for patients across a wide variety of diagnoses (Grossman, Niemann, Schmidt, & Walach, 2004). Despite methodological limitations noted in all of these studies (e.g., Smith, 2004), the analysis suggests that mindfulness is helpful for patients with a wide variety of medical conditions. For instance, the practice of MBSR during classes was found to have decreased psychological distress and improved well-being for rheumatoid arthritis patients (Pradhan, 2007), and that they increased the immunity of HIV infected patients respectively (Robinson, Mathews, & Witek-Janusek, 2003). In addition, similar increases in well-being were demonstrated amongst volunteers and medical students to those shown in patient populations after 10 weeks of MBSR training (Rosenzweig, Reibel, Greeson, Brainard, & Hojat, 2003; also: Shapiro, Schwartz, & Bonner, 1998). In a pilot study MBSR is associated with improved glycemic control in type2 diabetes mellitus (Rosenzweig, Reibel, Greeson, Edman, Jasser, et al., 2007). A review of 10 studies also showed that mindfulness has positive effects on neurophysiology although its mechanisms of action were not clear (Lazar, Kerr, Wasserman, Gray, & Greve, 2005).

Recently, Huynh, Gotay, Layi, and Garrard (2007) identified 127 published studies of mindfulness that are based on Kabat-Zinn's (1990) MBSR, including 50 randomized controlled trials on cancer patients including learning of MBSR via an online course. They concluded that mindfulness was a promising intervention, but that mindfulness research needed to be replicated and extended (Ospina, Bond, & Karkaneh, 2007; Speca, Carlson, Goodey, & Angen, 2000; Carlson, Speca, Faris, & Patel, 2007; Carlson, Speca, Patel, & Goodey, 2003; Carlson, Ursuliak, Goodey, & Speca, 2001; Ott, Norris, & Bauer-Wu, 2006). Further research with cancer patients can only confirm that MBSR has potential as a clinically valuable self-administered intervention, not as a cure (Smith, Richardson, Hoffman, & Pilkington, 2005). In addition, more recent studies in mindfulness and mental health suggested that MBCT could be effective at relieving patients with insomnia, anxiety, depressive symptoms, and suicidal ideation or behaviour (William, Teasdale, Segal, & Kabat-Zinn, 2007) among bipolar participants and participants in the unremitted depressive phase of bipolar disorder (Kenny & Williams, 2007). Again, the preliminary findings warrant further study (for a bibliography on mindfulness studies from 1975-2008, see: < http://marc.ucla.edu >.

In general, mindfulness as a technique has been applied and tested in a number of contexts, e.g. education (Shapiro, Schwartz, & Bonner, 1998) and sports (Jackson, 1995). Though such applications show a wide and growing interest in mindfulness and related techniques, the reports indicate that considerable additional rigorous research is still needed to understand more fully the potential contributions of meditation practices to health and other areas of human services. It appears from available data that the meagre results are unlikely to be caused by the poor research design. Research into Kabat-Zinn's mindfulness approach has been conducted out of the interdependent context and there was no effort at all to identify what aspects of the multicomponent MBSR program might be implicated as an active ingredient. Hence, further research on a fully contextualised mindfulness program is warranted. This program should fully translate all components of mindfulness into psychological terms, and examine the results. One of Siddhartha Gautama's contributions to humanity about 2600 years ago is a fully contextualized methodology of simultaneous and successive causality. On the other hand, science still holds a linear and sequential causation, even in systemic thinking. In addition to a necessary method, clients or subjects also need to be sufficiently briefed on the knowledge of whether they will be learning tranquility (Samatha) or insight (Vipassana) meditation or both. Emphasis on a particular meditation depends on the provider who studied the method to a particular level of theoretical understanding and practical experience. An understanding of such nuances may also lead to different results (Germer, Siegel, & Fulton, 2005).

Purpose of this study

The purpose of this study is to describe and explain how mindfulness arises together with seven other interacting components. In addition, it seeks to clearly illustrate how the interdependent connection between the "Four Truths", the "Eightfold Path" or "Practice" and the postulate or principle of "Interdependent Arising", better known as "Dependent Origination" (Figure 1) compares to psychotherapy's metaphysical, epistemological, and moral conflicts or sufferings within cognitive, behavioural, and affective domains.

This study emerged from three sources: naturalistic observations, feedback from participants of meditation classes, and feedback from psychotherapy clients. In experimental studies, scientists usually isolate an independent variable to examine its effect. They may also secularize what is deemed as the rituals out of religion. Unfortunately, current researchers appear to have extracted mindfulness practice from its interdependent context and this study, which uses a grounded theory approach, seeks to remedy this lack.

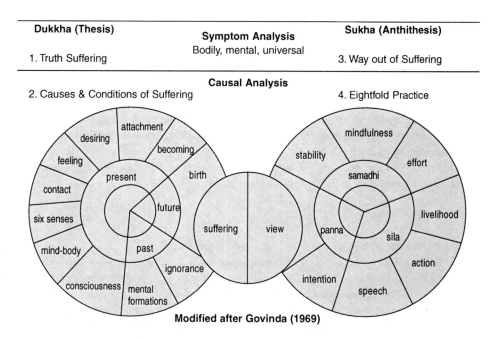

Fig.1. Interdependence between the "Four Truths", the principle of "Dependent Origination" and the "Eightfold Practice"

Table 1. Interdependence between "Dependent Origination" and the "Eightfold Practice" (in English and *Pali,* modified after Govinda, 1969)

The Principle of Dependent Origination	The Eightfold Practice
Suffering *(Dukkha)*	Right View or Understanding *(samma dhitthi)*
'Subconscious' Mental Activities *(sankhara)*; Ignorance *(avijja)*	Right Intention or Thought *(samma samkappa)*
Consciousness *(vinnana)*	Right Speech *(samma vaca)*
Mind-Body *(nama-rupa)*; Sense organs *(salayatana)*	Right Action *(samma kammanta)*
External Contact *(phassa)*	Right Livelihood *(samma ajiva)*
Feelings or Emotional impulses *(vedana)*	Right Effort *(samma vayama)*
Attachment or Craving *(tanha)*	Right Mindfulness *(samma sati)*
Becoming *(bhava)*; birth or nature *(jati)*	Right Stability of Mind or Concentration *(samma Samadhi)*

Ignoring or discounting the importance of seven other components of mindfulness practice produces inconclusive results. These components are neither the contents of cultural baggage nor the irrelevant impositions of a religious practice. They belong to cognitive, behavioural, and affective domains of action, which uniquely belong to evolved human values. We are languaging, interpreting, and meaning making beings in contrast to our animal ancestors. Hence, we should make every effort to examine seriously how the seven other components of mindfulness practice translate into the language of psychology, but also how they interface with the *cognitive, behavioural*, and *affective* domains of psychotherapy. A "grounded theory" approach of induction rather than deduction enables this type of deeper inquiry. Table 1 shows how Buddhist Psychology elaborates the psychology of suffering and the alleviation of such states through an integrated practice. It should be noted that the Pali word *jati* in Table 1 does not necessarily mean *birth* of a human being. It also means *origin*. Therefore, it could be interpreted that the "present becoming" contributes to "the birth or the origin of future phenomena" at hand, which allude to psychological experiences.

The cognitive domain

The cognitive domain comprises "right" view and "right" intention.

1. Right view. Without the commitment to maintain the proper ecology between self, other, and the environment or what the Buddha referred to as right or wise view, mindfulness practice does not have a basis for beginning. The question of whether mindfulness and its components are to be considered as a religious, philosophical, psychological, or ethical practice can be succinctly answered. As an experience and a practical way of self-realisation mindfulness and its components is a religion, as an intellectual formulation of one's experience it is a philosophy, as a systematic self-observation it is a psychology, as a norm of behaviour resulting from inner commitment and attitude and a principle of outer conduct it is ethics and morality

(Govinda, 1969). Right view is understood to be the cognitive aspect of wise understanding. Right view begins with an experiential insight that materiality and immateriality in the world are subject to change, and that desires for a lasting state lead to suffering. Right view culminates in complete understanding of the reciprocal conditioning between causes and consequences. Since our views, our cognition, interact with other thoughts, and with feelings and actions, the right view will yield the right thought and the right action.

Metaphysical pain in psychotherapy. In contrast, psychotherapy endures conflicting philosophical worldviews and models of psychological existence and reality. The scientist-practitioner model of psychotherapy focuses on enabling and accepting a third person external observer's conceptualization of the directly embodied experience of the first person client's suffering. At the outset this formulation begs the metaphysical questions of how subjective experiences are different from objective reality, how they relate to each other in the mind-body problem, whether they obey the law of causation or conflict with the notion of free will and determinism, and whether they can be studied using the same epistemological method and criteria as hard sciences use. Psychotherapy relies on an unexamined belief in the exercise of free will, but the psychological theories that guide the exercise are primarily deterministic. While psychoanalysis follows psychic determinism, biological and behavioural therapies adhere to genetic or environmental determinism. On the other hand, humanistic-existential and transpersonal psychologies take an extreme position of free will as the determining factor in psychotherapy. However, human behaviour is purposeful or teleological and constantly challenging the "nothing but" reductionist ideology in biology, socio-biology, psychology, neuroscience and information science. In Dawkins' (1976) socio-biology, the "selfish" genes make conscious moral choices by assuming humans have diverse language, culture, and decision-making processes built on the history of human life that is constructed on the interdependence matrix of self, other and environment. This is misappropriation of language to describe how the phenotype develops from the genotype in such a way as to imply that genetic survival constitutes the whole explanation of particular human qualities. Similar reductionist approaches can also be found in the fields of neuroscience (Crick, 1994) and artificial intelligence (Newell & Simon, 1972).

Psychotherapy is said to be a process between two or more people leading to the reconstruction of old meanings and the creation of new ones. Many who characterise their positions as constructivists, narrativists, social constructionists, or postmodernists help their clients re-conceptualise and re-interpret the meaning of their stories or narratives (Neimeyer, 1995; Rosen, 1996). However, what therapists may miss is that clients not only make causal interpretations of what triggered their experience, but also interpret some life experiences as good and others as bad. Such value judgments and moral issues are usually dealt with by religions. Nevertheless, the scientist-practitioner model of psychotherapy shies away from finding commonalities and complementarities with religious practices. Both psychotherapy and religion deal with an interface between emotion and cognition when helping clients live a valued and meaningful life. There is a complementary and interconnected relationship between psychotherapy and religion. Religions teach moral decisions that cannot be derived without emotion, while psychology sees emotion as functional and even rational rather than disruptive (Watts, 1996). Science is not value free. It interprets data within a particular context or paradigm. Thus, "all data is theory-laden" < http://loyno.edu/~folse/Hanson.html > (Hanson, 1958). All scientific knowledge is, therefore, provisional and open to reinterpretation.

Similarly, religious knowing should also be subject to reinterpretation and reintegration with the science of clinical psychology.

Practice pain in psychotherapy. Practice pain relates to misunderstandings and misapplications in integrating meditation principles to psychotherapy. The misuse of mindfulness by applying it as a single meta-cognitive skill together with other supportive techniques speaks for itself. Researchers succeeding Kabat-Zinn have also left out the interdependent components. Consequently, clear perception *(sampajanna)* to allow the emergence of conceptual understanding of the given phenomenon may not arise. Therapy without mindfulness does not provide individuals with a neutral-space-in-between to commute to and from in understanding the phenomenon at hand. Teaching mindfulness alone, without involving right affect and behaviours, would end up as an exposure or cognitive acceptance technique to endure the suffering with awareness. Mindfulness resembles the Rogerian notion of "unconditional positive regard" and Freud's notion of "evenly suspended attention". However, the qualitative difference between these two notions and mindfulness requires that with mindfulness the therapist must see the client's desires, beliefs, and behaviours, as they really are with skilful attention (*yoniso manasikara*) and to understand the client's experience and meaning making in reflection.

2. Right intention. Since our views interact with our thoughts, we intend or aspire to take valued actions. Wise, right or healthy thought contains a dynamic quality of "intention", "attitude", and "aspiration" towards oneself, others and environment. Right intention derives from aspiration developed in a social context, aspiration to overcome unhealthy desires, e.g. shamelessness (*hiri*) and recklessness (*ottappa*), and has direct reference to rebalancing social ecology. On the other hand, western notions of guilt refer to an internalized conceptual control of socially imposed expectation. Aspiration, here, incorporates healthy desire, motivation and virtue. Virtue is the unique evolution to humans against the background of genetic and animal heritages, is connected with sympathetic physiology and the concept of self-esteem that many psychotherapists consider to be an important factor in optimal mental health, and is founded on social trust (Ridley, 1996) as one worries over others' evaluation which is considered the foundation of adult morality (Smith, 1959). Guilt arising from hurting others has become an essential part of the human repertoire, perhaps because humans are one of the few species able to kill large numbers of their own kind. In short, humans interpret and value situations in complex and symbolic ways and have feelings of guilt, shame, and the desire to feel good and virtuous, which are qualities not present in animals.

The natural world presents itself as fact, not value or virtue. Virtues support social ethics that lead to moral thought and emotion. Although clinicians must observe ethical standards in working with clients, psychotherapy does not directly address the ways the client's ethical behaviours lead to his own suffering. The client's ethical views and thoughts are regarded as "private matters". Freud, on the other hand, considers a sense of morality as an internalized superego based on the external constraint of civilization. A related concept to virtue, one popularized by Maslow (1968) and called "self-esteem" also translates to having the "right view" and the "right thought". This approach rests on the idea that each individual subconsciously computes an average of the distance between each of his or her important qualities and the associated ideal. Self-esteem represents that average. Ridley (1996), a Darwinian, insists that no individual acts unless he stands to gain some external prize. However, the symbolic private assurance that one is virtuous – given by the self to the self – is an attractive prize that humans seek and this price is absent in the most cooperative non-human species. Therefore, it is a serious conceptual error to claim that humans are driven by a unitary desire to maximize pleasure. Unlike other animals, humans constantly evaluate the moral implications of their views, thoughts and behaviours. Even the cleverest ape cannot be conditioned to react with anger upon seeing one animal steal food from another; surprise or fear may be possible but anger or guilt is not.

Epistemological pain in psychotherapy. In psychotherapy, the belief in *efficient causation* (sinking billiard balls metaphor) creates and underpins the confusion between *rational* (causal) *theories* of treatment, which considers that only *rational reasoning* can push away irrational emotions, and the *rational* (scientific) *method* of studying change in emotions and cognitions. Currently, this problem is further confounded by cost-conscious government and insurance driven health care systems, which demand scientific evidence of the efficacy of any treatment approach before they will fund or approve it. Consequently, clinical and academic psychologists use random control trials and related research designs to validate theories and develop robust evidence-base practice. These studies focus on manipulating independent variables often in artificial treatment contexts. This efficient manipulation totally obscures the research hypotheses developed to validate the theories of both *formal cause* – "association" as well as a *final cause* – "intention". However, recent research has shown that affective-intentional factors of the learner, instead of the learner's associative mechanisms are effective in learning and retention of learnable items (Rychlak, 2000). The main epistemological pain in psychotherapy is that of confused conceptualizing of "causality" and ignorance *(avijja)* of making intentional "choices" within the given context of self, others, and environment when one faces difficulties. These difficulties challenge the morally related questions of free will and determinism.

Pain of abstraction in psychotherapy. Epistemological pain of science in general is succinctly characterised as that of the passion to an abstraction free of all constraints. The famous controversy between Einstein and Bohr is a good example. Einstein believed that reality consisted of substances whose properties were unaffected by their relationship with observers, while Bohr considered nature as consisted of relationships between substances. Therefore, from Bohr's point of view no measurement could reveal an autonomous aspect of an event because every measurement was a relationship between substances. Kagan (1998) suspects that psychologists who study human personality and emotions are friendly to Einstein's position. For example, many students of emotion write about "fear" as if it were a single psychological-cum-physiological state, knowable through measurement of brain activity, peripheral physiological responses, self-report, facial expressions, or overt behaviours despite cultural, age, sex, language, context, and species differences between their subjects. This is the danger of ignoring specificity in favour of generality (Ekman, 2003; LeDoux, 1996; Izard 1993).

The behavioural domain

The behavioural domain comprises "right" speech, "right" action, and "right" livelihood.

3. Right speech. Speech plays a prominent role in daily activities whether one is engaging in self-talk or interacting with others. Right speech, as well as social ethics, interactively guides moral principles and supports mindfulness. Purifying one's mind from defilements and developing a steady or stable state demand right speech. Words can be helpful or harmful, make enemies or friends, start war or create peace. Hence, one needs to refrain from the false speech detailed in the Eightfold Practice.

4. Right action. Action, like speech, validates the actor's intention through visible and embodied experiences in the actor and the receiver. Unhealthy actions cultivate unsound states of mind, while healthy actions enculture sound states of mind. The importance of this practice encourages one to take training in refraining from harming self and others, taking what is not given and sexual misconduct.

5. Right livelihood. Right livelihood encourages one to take training in leading a livelihood and way of living that does not harm others, e.g. dealing with weapons, raising animals for slaughter as well as slave trade and prostitution; working in meat production and butchery, selling intoxicants and poisons, such as alcohol and drugs, occupations that would violate the principles of right speech and right action.

Moral pain in psychotherapy. The Buddha sees suffering as the result of the final *(intentional)* causation through proliferation of ethically unhealthy thought, feeling and behaviour. Margolis (1989) who examines the issues of whether or not psychotherapy is value-neutral finds that *psychotherapy is a moral enterprise.* Suffering can only be overcome by practicing healthy *moral* behaviour while paying particular attention to releasing the *metaphysic*al illusion of eternal existence and by skilfully exercising *epistemological* understanding. Thus, the Eightfold Practice, unlike psychoanalysis for example, uses suffering as the turning point for to changing the tragic plot of a confused life into a romantic plot of freedom into life.

The affective domain

The affective domain comprises "right" effort, "right" mindfulness, and "right" stability.

6. Right effort. Mental energy is the force behind right effort and it arises in either healthy or unhealthy states. The same energy that fuels desire, envy, aggression, and violence can on the other hand fuel self-discipline, honesty, benevolence, and kindness. Right effort involves the application of energy as guided by right attitude or intention and by right view, the view that leads to move toward the goal of liberation. Right effort takes training:

> to prevent the arising of unbidden unhealthy states,
> to let go of unhealthy states that have already arisen,
> to arouse healthy states and
> to maintain healthy states already arisen.

Prevent unhealthy states. Unarisen unhealthy states are known as the "five hindrances" (*pancanivarana*) to mindfulness. The first hindrance, sensual desire, refers to agreeable sights, sounds, smells, tastes and touches including the broader craving for wealth, power, position and fame. The second hindrance covers hatred of any object – self, others, or environmental contexts. The third hindrance shares the common feature of mental dullness and drowsiness. At its opposite extreme is the fourth hindrance, restlessness that displays itself as agitation and worry. The fifth hindrance, doubt, manifests itself as chronic lack of commitment to the teacher (the therapist), the teachings, and the method.

Let go of unhealthy states. Despite the effort to protect the senses, unhealthy thoughts and emotions can surface from the depths and disrupt mindfulness. The Buddha provided several methods for countering each of these hindrances, e.g.: expel the defiled thought with a healthy thought, i.e. meditation on impermanence; use social tools such as shame (*hiri*) and moral dread (*ottappa*) as antagonistic responses; redirect attention to something else, and away from unhealthy thoughts; confront the unwanted thought by scrutinizing and investigating its source; and, as a last resort, push out the unwanted thought using the power of the will.

Arouse healthy states. The Buddha summarizes these healthy states as the "seven factors of awakening". These are: mindfulness, the investigation of phenomena, energy, rapture, tranquillity, concentration, and equanimity. These factors lie on the path to freedom from suffering.

Maintain healthy states. This last of the four right efforts called "endeavour to maintain" aims at guarding the object of concentration. In doing so, the seven enlightenment factors increase their stability and gradually increase in strength until they give birth to liberating realization.

7. Right mindfulness. Right mindfulness is the mental ability to "See Things As They Really Are", with clear awareness. Usually, the cognitive process begins with an impression induced by perception or thought, but it does not stay with the mere impression. Instead, the mind conceptualises sense impressions and thoughts immediately. It interprets them and sets them in relation to other thoughts and experiences, which naturally go beyond the quality of the original impression. The mind then posits concepts, joins concepts into constructs, and weaves those constructs into complex interpretative schemes. All this happens only half consciously, and as a result we often see things as through a glass darkly, obscured. Right mindfulness is anchored in clear perception and it attends to impressions without getting carried away. Right mindfulness enables us to be aware of the process of conceptualisation in such a way that we are able to actively observe and understand the way our thoughts process themselves. The Buddha presented the *Four Foundations of Mindfulness* for guidance: contemplation of the body, contemplation of the feelings, contemplation of the states of mind, and contemplation of the phenomena of the mind. In mindfulness, the mind keeps at the level of bare attention, a non-attached observation of what is happening within and around us in the present moment. It is a "choiceless observation" an observation that does not become entangled with discriminating thoughts. The mind is trained to remain in the present space, open, quiet, and alert. All judgments and interpretations are suspended or if they occur, they are acknowledged and abandoned. Mindfulness is the practice of staying in the present or staying in the here-and-now.

8. Right Stability. Together with other components, e.g. right intentional effort and steady attention to a single mental object, right stability of the mind is facilitated and upheld. In this state, the meditator is supposed to have already countered and overcome hindrances of dullness and drowsiness by the initial application of the mind *(vitakka)*. The sustained application of the mind *(vicara)* has also driven away doubt. Rapture *(piti)* has shut out ill will, happiness *(sukha)* has excluded restlessness and worry, and one-pointedness *(ekaggata)* has let go of desire.

Tranquillity or insight meditation?

With the strengthening of mental stability, material and immaterial absorptive states *(rupa* and *arupa jhanas)* of tranquillity arise. However, the tranquil states alone are not enough to attain insight. Conversely, mindfulness alone is not a sufficient condition either. Tranquillity is a conditioned process of "becoming". Therefore, such experiences change in the end. However, insight meditation allows us to be mindful and let go of everything and accept uncertainty, silence and the cessation of conditions. The result is the experience of complete peace, rather than tranquillity alone. In short, mindfulness reinforces tranquility and vice versa. This phenomenon is verified by feedback from meditation students and psychotherapy clients. Those who perceived mindfulness as keeping themselves aware of single meditation object (tranquility instruction), breath for example, reported they could not concentrate or focus on the single object form moment to moment as they could not stop thinking about other things. The harder they concentrated the more they became prone to headaches. On the other hand, those who began with single object focus but switched to paying attention to many objects as they appear to the mind (insight instruction) reported that mindfulness was not so hard after all. It was just like stepping aside and witnessing a daydream or streams of consciousness non-reactively.

Some queried, however, whether they were really meditating at all. This is due to widely held confusion between tranquillity (Samatha) meditation and insight (Vipassana) meditation. Tranquillity subdues the distracting thoughts and feelings. Nevertheless, when one stops practicing tranquillity, defilements will surface again. Insight takes an open approach to watch whatever comes along. In reality, both tranquillity and insight have to be practiced together like two wings of a bird. The reason why awareness and acceptance of mental object(s) in psychotherapy do not progress further is due to lack of wisdom conditions. Wisdom, according to Tejaniya (2008), works like information technology: awareness gathers data; our innate wisdom channels the data into streams of information; comparing and contrasting streams of information create knowledge; wisdom then uses knowledge about the interaction of physical and mental processes in skilful ways in order to positively influence events. When wisdom understands the extent of causes and effects, it knows how to work on causes and conditions. Hence, awareness and acceptance alone are not sufficient; wisdom needs to be present for insight to arise.

Conclusion

Thus, in psychotherapy mindfulness has been used as a tool for reaching awareness of and acceptance of human suffering. Both MBSR and MBCT have developed their own mindfulness formulations. Research findings on the effectiveness of both MBSR and MBCT have not been conclusive. This chapter argues that the reason this has happened for the past three decades is that both approaches and similar studies have not resolved their metaphysical, epistemological, and moral issues, nor have the therapies themselves. On the other hand, the Eightfold Practice coherently addresses the universal flux of change connected with human suffering; interdependent causes and conditions of such experience; and the cessation out of such suffering through an integrated practice within cognitive, behavioural, and affective domains of psychotherapy.

Reluctance of the researchers to conduct the Eightfold Practice research appears to be related to a wrong view, at least, on two possible accounts: seeing the rest of mindfulness practice as religious rituals and/or interpreting the principle of Dependent Origination as something to do with the belief in after live(s). Again, the Pali word *jati* in Dependent Origination does not necessarily mean human *birth*. Also meaning *origin*, it could be inferred as the origin of future psychological phenomena. What this case study clarifies is the striving towards a peaceful and ecologically balanced living *in this very life* which is irrefutably taught by the Buddha. Hence, the "Right View" of the Eightfold Practice interfaces with the suffering factor of Dependent Origination in order to counter this suffering and to break the cycle of ignorance as depicted in Figure 1 and Table 1.

Beside this wrong view, psychotherapy supported by westernized mindfulness completely misses the philosophical and ethico-behavioural underpinnings of interdependent arising, the core of Buddhist teachings. Telling oneself to be mindful is not enough. The wrong cognitive view of what it means to not "Seeing Things As They Really Are" in Vipassana likely leads to wrong mindfulness. Similarly, wrong affect and behaviours of greed *(lobha)*, hatred *(dosa),* and ignorance *(moha)* will also lead to wrong mindfulness. Finally, psychotherapy undermines the integrated practices of mindfulness not only by ignoring the Buddhist teachings' foundations of the principle of Dependent Origination, the Four Truths, and the Eightfold Practice, but also by completely excluding the importance of a combined practice which alternates appropriately and effectively between the tranquillity and mindfulness meditations.

Chapter 18

Classical Mindfulness: Its Theory And Potential For Clinical Application

Lobsang Rapgay

Introduction

The past two decades witness an increasing interest in mindfulness as an intervention for a wide range of psychological and medical conditions as well as for enhancing general well-being. Mindfulness forms a significant part of the so called "third wave" of Cognitive-Behavior Therapy (CBT; Hayes, Strosahl, & Wilson, 1999). A main reason for the prominence attributed to mindfulness is that it challenges the conventional western psychotherapeutic emphasis on controlling dysfunctional thoughts, feelings, and behaviors by positing an alternative way of changing through accepting non-judgmentally. Preliminary research support the concept that trying to control psychopathological states, such as anxiety, actually reinforce the aberrant condition, whereas giving up control by accepting the anxious experience non-judgmentally helps to reduce anxiety. As the preliminary evidence of the effectiveness of mindfulness began to emerge, attempts among researchers and practitioners to further psychologize and secularize mindfulness gain momentum. Proponents assert two reasons: (1) in order to assess outcome, mindfulness must be made suitable to conform to a research paradigm and (2) if mindfulness is to meet the cultural needs of the western mindset, associations with the underlying Buddhist teachings (the Dharma) must be eliminated. From a Buddhist point of view the cost of such an approach is high. By disassociating the Dharma from contemporary clinical mindfulness, the Buddhist underlying theory of perception and cognition is grossly ignored. Without an in-deep understanding the Buddhist conceptualization of mindfulness, there is no way one can accurately translate, correctly practice, and effectively apply mindfulness in psychotherapy. This is comparable to applying cognitive therapy without understanding and subscribing to its theoretical underpinnings. Can someone honestly say s/he is practicing psychoanalysis without being informed by Freudian theory?

A growing number of leading Buddhists scholars/practitioners has expressed concern about the potential damage by misrepresenting or under-representing the pristine teachings of mindfulness. However, as yet most of them have been reticent to openly confront the clinical and research communities about this matter. As a consequence, false notions remained unchallenged, perpetuating the idea that mindfulness (Satipatthana) is equivalent to insight meditation (Vipassana) and that mindfulness has got nothing to do with concentration and calm-abiding meditation (Samatha). Analayo (2003), a Pali scholar asserting the Theravada viewpoint, confirmed the strong allegiance between mindfulness and concentration/calming. This author intends to explore and elucidate the original Buddhist version of mindfulness to enrich the clinical application of mindfulness as in Mindfulness-Based Stress Reduction by proposing Classical Mindfulness (CM). The following will cover the theoretical conceptualization of CM, its clinical practice, and its differences with Mindfulness-Based Stress Reduction (MBSR); this chapter will also critically review MBSR and the CBT of Generalized Anxiety Disorder (GAD). A clinical case study will illustrate how CM targets specific anxiety symptoms which MBSR and CBT fail to do and show how CM facilitates a favorable outcome.

Background of CM

According to the Buddhist literature the initial goal of meditation is to refine levels of knowing through which one develops reliable and valid internal states that can be used to access higher states of awareness. The Theravada scriptures explain two major ways of knowing (Analayo, 2003): (1) direct experience associated with perception and (2) discriminative observation/analysis associated with cognition. Concentration, the main way to achieve calm-abiding (Samatha), is to acquire direct experience, while discriminative observation/analysis is to acquire insight (Vipassana). Knowing fear first hand through direct experience provides a sensory quality of knowing which differs from knowing through detached observation or abstract analysis. Direct sensory experience can be acquired in various levels of refinement and can be sustained by training. Sensory awareness training enables the experience of freshness and bareness of the object at hand, i.e. stripped from its projected meaning (Thera, 1973). For instance, refined direct experience allows one to hear the bang in one's ears on the street as a series of varying vibrational sensations. This is in sharp contrast to the habitual tendency to instantly interpret the sound as a car accident. Since we habitually tend to respond reactively to (external and internal) stimuli in a biased way, learning how to inhibit evaluative processes in order to directly experience the stimulus is critical. Discriminative observation, on the other hand, involves watching an event unfold and evaluating what was observed to acquire insight into the nature of the event. Discriminative analysis is an appropriate way of knowing phenomena which are conceptual and abstract like the interrelated antecedent triggers for anxiety and its consequent behaviors.

After the Buddha passed away, some groups of adherents shifted the integrated practice of mindfulness into primarily an insight oriented approach to such an extent that eventually mindfulness/Satipatthana became synonymous with insight/Vipassana. However, there is virtually no substantial evidence in the canonical texts for equating mindfulness and insight (Sujato, 2003). The scriptures associate mindfulness primarily with calming/Samatha and the integration of the two as evidenced by the repeated linking of mindfulness to states of absorption (Jhanas) acquired through mindfulness as a practice of Samatha. When the Buddha was asked which of the different ways of knowing he associated himself with primarily, he replied that it was with direct experience associated with concentration rather than with discriminative observation/analysis associated with insight (Analayo, 2003). There is more evidence in the discourses associating mindfulness with concentration than associating mindfulness with insight. In the Eightfold Path mindfulness is subsumed under concentration, not under insight.

Scholars of the Buddha's discourses (*Nikayas* and *Agamas*) share the view that mindfulness is a combination of Samatha/calming and Vipassana/insight, citing several references to the Buddha teachings wherein mindfulness is an integration of calm-abiding and insight. They go on to tell that for all practical purposes the two meditations were originally never separated into two distinct practices (Sujato, 2003). It is critical to define mindfulness as a practice based on the various texts on *Satipatthana* in the Nikayas. There, mindfulness is described as a practice using a breathing technique to develop refined levels of perceptual and cognitive skills so that mindfulness' four foundations (the body and its feelings and the mind and its contents) can be understood. Since these four foundations involve the attending of objects in various levels of subtlety, it implies that varying states of mind are required to perceive and cognize them. Thus, mindfulness is used to develop both sensory perceptions (direct experience) and discriminative cognitions (observation/analysis) to access and comprehend its four foundations.

This is a direct challenge to many contemporary proponents' penchant to view mindfulness as solely a Vipassana practice and to their argument that Samatha is a totally distinct practice from mindfulness. Furthermore, discerning Samatha and Vipassana does not make mindfulness distinct from Samatha (Sujato, 2003).

Some basic distinctions between CM and MBSR

During the last decade efforts to secularize and simplify MBSR by researchers and clinicians have resulted in equating mindfulness to the function of being mindful itself – that is, to the act of paying attention and being aware of each moment of experience (Roemer & Orsillo, 2002). However, understanding mindfulness simply as a state of being mindful of each experience runs the risk of minimizing the traditional complexity of and the potential effectiveness of the practice as presented in the suttas. It is, therefore, important to understand some of the major differences between the MBSR type of mindfulness and CM skills and practices. In the traditional literature, mindfulness is described not only and not simply as a technique of attending and observing. It is much more deeply and broadly defined in terms of a number of processes each of which has specific functions and objectives (Thanissaro, 1997). Thus, defining mindfulness as an attention and awareness practice is misleading. These are not an end in themselves, but a means to acquire levels of perceptual skills enabling the practitioner to carry out progressively more complex mental processes as to meet short and long term objectives.

Conversely, MBSR defines mindfulness as a process of being aware of whatever arises in the present moment in a non-judgmental way. By asserting that non-judgmental awareness of the present moment is the essence of the practice, the idea that the mindfulness practitioner has goals to strive towards is rejected (Baer, 2003; Roemer & Orsillo, 2003). Observing events unfold in a non-judgmental manner certainly has benefits since the process is an alternative to the habitual, reactive way of responding. However, according to Buddhist Psychology, change can only occur when dysfunctional thoughts, feelings, and behavior decrease and corresponding functions increase. Non-judgmental awareness does not possess mechanisms to change deeply entrenched thoughts, feelings, and behaviors even though such awareness may provide some relief from negative thoughts, feelings, and behaviors. Buddhists view non-judgmental awareness much like relaxation and positive affirmations; while they may have therapeutic benefits, they certainly do not have the capacity to change the underlying distorted thoughts and beliefs maintaining psychopathology.

Modern and classical presentations also differ on the nature of mindfulness. Modern versions associate the practice of mindfulness with cognitive and affective features. Several authors equal mindfulness to acceptance, while others describe it as a meta-cognitive process (Wells, 2002). In these versions, subjects are instructed to engage in cognitive processing such as experiencing music as a pleasant sound or thoughts as thoughts, not facts process (Brown & Ryan, 2004). CM, on the other hand, is primarily a perceptual process toward a heightened awareness. Perception involves the bare experience of an event; thus, the police siren is simply a sound qua sound without associating and qualifying the sound as being loud, threatening, or coming from a police car. Any form of cognitive processing associated with mindfulness such as "it is merely a thought, not a fact" is discouraged since cognitive processes inhibit the effort to develop attention and awareness as a perceptual process. The suggestion that repeated observation of thoughts and feelings (affect, emotion and sensation) will lead to cognitive insight such as "thoughts are not facts" or "my feeling that I am a bad person is simply a thought", etc. is from a Buddhist stance unlikely. Such cognitions would at the best lead to an intellectual understanding that may have the benefit of positive affirming, but will be unable to change ingrained dysfunctional beliefs, e.g. that thoughts are facts. According to Buddhist Psychology, to be truly convinced that thoughts are not facts requires a challenging of the underlying deep-seated beliefs which are unlikely to change by repeating memos that thoughts are not facts.

The CBT literature on modern versions of mindfulness makes no clear distinction between attention and awareness and this has led to considerable confusion about the nature of mindfulness. Researchers have not only failed to provide clear definitions of attention and awareness, but have also used the two interchangeably (Baer, 2004; Bishop, Lau, Shapiro, Carlson, Anderson, et al., 2004). In their effort to define mindfulness, the latter group of authors describes it as focused attention at one instance and at another instance as an invitation to and awareness of any experience arising in the field of consciousness. Brown and Ryan (2004) rightly pointed at the impossibility to focus attention on the breath fully while inviting and being aware of extraneous thoughts and feelings at the same time.

In the traditional Buddhist literature, attention, as a function, is the act of focusing single pointedly on a selected object to the exclusion of other experiences for an extended period of time. As a state, it is narrow and focused. Awareness as a function is the act of observing, while as a state it is spacious and expansive with a containing capacity (Rabten, 1992). Contemporary researchers and clinicians like Teasdale, Segal, and Wells define mindfulness as a meta-cognitive function and state. However, Brown and Ryan (2004) raise the question whether mindfulness can be regarded as a meta-cognitive process, i.e. as a cognition or thought of another thought. They argue that mindfulness is a perceptual process. According to the classical Buddhist literature, the initial phase of mindfulness is primarily a perceptual state and not a meta-cognitive state. However, in order to encode experience acquired through the first phase of mindfulness and contrary to what Brown and Ryan (2004) suggest, CM in a later phase does reinstate meta-cognitive processes. The need for meta-cognitive or detached discriminative observation as an integral part of mindfulness is evidenced in the four foundations of mindfulness mentioned in the Satipatthana texts. Since the 4th foundation phenomena (the contents of mind) are more subtle and abstract than phenomena of the preceding foundations (the mind, bodily feelings, and the body), they cannot be known via perceptual or direct experience and therefore accessed by means of discriminative processes.

A major difference between MBSR mindfulness and CM is on acceptance as a feature or function of mindfulness. MBSR definitions of mindfulness, e.g. as proposed by Bishop, et al.

(2004), posit acceptance as one of the two central features and functions of mindfulness. This idea is not classical. It is contrary to the traditional theory and practice of mindfulness since acceptance is a preconception that interferes with the cultivation of direct perceptual experience, the first phase objective of mindfulness. Justifiably, the centrality of acceptance in mindfulness as a distinct construct separate from attention and awareness has been challenged. Factor analysis showed that acceptance does not provide any separate advantage over attention and awareness, thus appearing to be functionally redundant in mindfulness (Brown & Ryan, 2004).

In Theravada, mindfulness is characterized as the ability to achieve *direct experience* of an object of attention (Analayo, 2003). This is the experiencing of either an object or event without any preconceptions, thoughts, attitudes, or emotional tones interfering with pure experience. Any preconceived values such as acceptance and MBSR's non-judging interfere with the ability to engage with the stark, bare experience of an object. Mindfulness practices enable people to develop *bare attention* (used here synonymous to direct experience) so that all of these preconceptions are eliminated from the experiencing of an object. In order to experience the "bare" sound of a police car, the sound must be stripped off of its ascribed meaning of threat, so that *awareness becomes free from any and all preconceptions*. Similarly, to experience negativity such as an aversive sensation, the sensation must be stripped off of all projections in order to experience it as it is. Thus, the intent to accept the sensation must also be inhibited since it interferes with the experience of the sensation as it is in the moment.

Openness to whatever experience arises in consciousness as a function of MBSR is also in contrast to CM training instruction. Thanissaro (2002) states that an ability to be open to whatever experience occurs without judgments and reactivity is achieved much later in mindfulness training and, therefore, during the initial training phase, the client should be aware of functional versus dysfunctional thoughts, feelings, and behaviors. There is also the danger that openness and curiosity can obstruct the development of attention and awareness skills. Since the goal of mindfulness is to learn how to reduce sensitivity to external stimuli in order to access internal ones often not available in conscious awareness, encouraging curiosity and inviting experiences is likely to increase preoccupation with contents of thoughts and feelings, the very thing that one tries to overcome in mindfulness.

Researchers, e.g. Baer (2003), suggest that mindfulness is a state of non-striving without any specific objective. She argues that the therapeutic benefit of such an approach is an alternative to the habitual process and demand of working towards goals. However, CM has specific goals in various phases of its practice (Bodhi, 2006). All Buddhist teachings have the explicit overall goal of eliminating unwholesomeness (thoughts, feelings, and behaviors) and to replace them with wholesome ones. Consequently, every major aspect of mindfulness involves the identification of specific goals, means to achieve them, and methods to assess the outcome.

MBSR and other forms of western mindfulness highlight the centrality of present moment experiences. Roemer and Orsillo (2002) even go to the extent of suggesting that past memories and future fears should be avoided during mindfulness. While the breath is used as the anchor to develop attention and awareness, all past, present, and future experiences are treated as distractions that the patient identifies and labels and then returns to the attention and awareness of the breath. CM on the other hand involves mindfulness of present, past, and future experiences. In CM, being in the present moment is simply understood as being aware of whatever contents arise during attention and awareness on the breath. In fact, trying to sup-press past and future experiences could act as a negative reinforcement of anxiety, the very problem the authors seek to eliminate.

The modern authors have further suggested that mindfulness facilitates emotional experi-ence and regulation. Hayes and Feldman (2004) see mindfulness as an emotional balancing technique to regulate mood and increase clarity of affect. They quote teachers like Chödron (2001) to describe how mindfulness can be used to feel the full force of an emotion as a way to overcome it. Linehan (1993), as well as Kabat-Zinn (2000), imply that mindfulness involves affective related practices such as compassion. However, in the Buddhist literature exploring affective states such as compassion is an entirely separate practice introduced only after devel-oping skills in mindfulness (Pabongka, 1997). Using mindfulness to experience powerful emo-tions in their full force is contraindicated for the simple reason such would obstruct the devel-opment of sustained attention and awareness, the primary goal of mindfulness. When affect arises in CM, it is observed and immediately labeled as feeling; subsequently, the client returns to the primary task of experiencing the breath. The objective is to observe the arising of emo-tion and instantly identify the emotional triggers as well as the subsequent consequences. The experiential insight thus gained on the emotional triggers and consequences helps to newly regulate habitual reactive patterns and to increase adaptive ways of responding.

Introduction to CM

In the last few years a concerted effort has been made to define and operationalize mindful-ness resulting in a number of instruments measuring mindfulness. Some of them have been constructed by individuals with little knowledge of the concept's complexity and mindful-ness practice (Grossman, 2008). Most of them assume that mindfulness is a construct much like attention. However, treating mindfulness as a mental construct or function is more than misleading. To better understand mindfulness, it is important to sort out the various contexts in which mindfulness is used and understood in the original Buddhist texts. As a function of recall or retention, mindfulness (*sati*) is understood as a mental construct much like the men-tal construct of attention (Rabten, 1992). On the other hand, when the suttas describe mind-fulness (*sati*) in the context of the four foundations, they describe mindfulness as a practice involving the use of a breathing technique to generate direct experience with the help of con-centration. This is to know the initial foundations familiar with direct experience on the one hand and on the other hand to develop insight with the help of discriminative observation/analysis as to understand the subsequent foundations (Thanissaro, 2000). Mindfulness as a practice cannot be operationalized like psychoanalysis or CBT, except its various constructs and processes.

Though direct experience is a usual occurrence and we all experience it repeatedly every day, it is a so fleeting experience we are not aware of the experience. Mindfulness is designed to train an individual to use attention and awareness to bring direct experience under awareness control to modify maladaptive thoughts, feelings, and behaviors into adap-tive ones. Discriminative observation is also a common experience. Generally, however, our discriminative observation is heavily colored by cognitive biases. The insight aspect of mindfulness is designed to teach how to refine observational skills. This requires the ability to inhibit evaluative processes, to discriminatively watch an event unfold, and to draw conclusions when the same process occurs repeatedly. Instead of immediately concluding that someone is judgmental because s/he made a critical remark, one learns to discriminatively watch for further evidence before forming an opinion.

Grounded in clinical experience, the author recommends the application of mindfulness as a skill-based intervention rather than as a non-specific intervention. This author proposes several processes associated with CM namely, attention, awareness, labeling, exposure, disengagement from threatening stimuli, and discriminative observation/analysis. The first five are associated with the first phase of using attention and awareness in developing direct experience, while the last skill is associated with developing insight. Patients are trained in each of the processes till they acquire a level of mastery/skill. Once the skill is acquired, they are trained to apply it to target the symptom. The advantage of a skill is that the technique can be dispensed with as soon as it is acquired. The patient has now the flexibility and adaptability to apply the skill in a way that is most appropriate for her/his particular needs and disposition.

Another advantage of a skill-based mindfulness is that a particular skill can be matched with a specific clinical symptom and measured to determine its effectiveness. For instance, the skill of disengagement from threatening stimuli can be applied to reduce selective attention to threatening stimuli and can be assessed with the "Stroop" test and the "Dot Probe" test. Similarly, the skill of habituation to threatening stimuli is applied to reduce experiential avoidance of threatening stimuli and can be measured with the "Action and Acceptance Scale".

The six processes and skills associated with CM

CM's processes are: attention, awareness, labeling, open ended exposure, disengaging from threatening stimuli, and discriminative observation/analysis.

1. Attention. Attention involves training in sustaining focus on a single object to the exclusion of everything else. The goal is to gradually reduce distraction to other stimuli while increasing the ability to focus on the totality of target object for prolonged periods of time. The purpose is to develop the skill to apply sustained attention to facilitate full engagement with the totality of the object of attention. Direct experience, i.e. engagement with the totality of the object helps to reduce selective attention on a particular real or perceived feature or characteristic of the object. For instance, anxious patients tend to instantly selectively focus on the threatening aspect of a situation even though the threat is very unlikely to occur. Repeated training in engaging in the totality of the stimulus employing sustained attention will help the patient to experience the threatening aspect in the context of experiencing the totality of the experience.

2. Awareness. Awareness as a state involves experiencing expanded spaciousness, a capacity of consciousness. Awareness training involves generating external and internal fields of spaciousness. This involves the capacity of containing which facilitates mental flexibility and adaptability. Such a state helps patients to contain experiences including aversive ones within them rather than to resort to habitual patterns of expelling them instantly. Without being able to contain and hold experiences, it is impossible to process them. Just like a blood sample that must be stably located on a slide under the microscope, anxiety must be held in one's awareness to enable its examination. An anxious thought or feeling being expelled cannot be accessed or processed; it needs to be held steady in consciousness first.

3. *Labeling.* When distractions occur during training in sustaining attention and awareness, these are labeled accordingly. However, the contents of the thoughts and feelings are not labeled but the mental process generating the contents is labeled. Thus, instead of labeling the content of the anxious thought "I am going to fail", the process that generates the thought which is "thinking" is labeled. By labeling the mental process such as thinking, feeling, emoting, sensing, doing, and so on, the client learns to become aware that it is the mental processes that generates the contents and realizes that by changing thinking and feeling, one changes the contents of thoughts and feelings. On the other hand, labeling content such as "I am going to fail" as failure thoughts is likely to generate associative thoughts and feelings such as "What will happen next?" or "Will I be rejected?", and so on, resulting in increasing preoccupation with maladaptive thoughts and feelings.

4. *Open ended exposure.* Repeated direct engagement with the totality of the threatening stimulus while learning to tolerate the presence of secondary threats in the peripheral field of awareness helps to develop habituation. Open ended exposure is a flexible process. While the patient seeks to develop sustained exposure to the threat, s/he is required to engage in any distraction that occurs and label it accordingly before returning to the primary threat. Rather than seeking to extinguish the fear, mindfulness exposure seeks to habituate the client to the primary and secondary threatening stimuli. In effect this is a learning process of attending to a primary task in the presence of threatening stimuli without being interfered by them.

5. *Disengaging from threatening stimuli.* By helping the client sustain direct engagement with the totality of the threatening stimulus, s/he becomes habituated to the primary threat and to other secondary ones. Habituation in turn helps with disengagement from the threatening stimulus and with subsequent interferences in one's experiencing. Being able to disengage from a preceding stimulus, in turn, helps to fully orient to a new stimulus and, by reducing the potential of the preceding threatening stimulus from interfering with the activity, to be fully engaged with it.

6. *Discriminative observation/analysis.* Having engaged in direct experience as a way to know anxiety, the patient reinstates evaluative processes to discriminatively observe and analyze what has been learned about anxiety from direct experience. Determining the knowledge acquired from direct experience requires discriminative observation and analysis which allows developing conceptions of what was learned. Encoding direct experiential knowledge into conception facilitates growth by combining it with other related concepts which in turn leads to the formulations of concepts that can be tested by the "behavioral experimentation" of trial and error.

Through regular practice of mindfulness, these six processes are refined into skills. For patients the level of mastery expected should be significantly different from that expected from non-clinical individuals. If necessary, the order of clinically applying the two phases of direct experience and insight may be reversed in the clinical situation. For some patients it may be necessary to teach them how to apply discriminative observation/analysis to their disorder prior to introducing direct experience. Furthermore, discriminative observations may be applied when engaging in daily individual activities, such as walking in the park, but also when engaging in interpersonal activities while interacting with other people.

Treating GAD by CBT and Interpersonal Psychotherapy: a brief review

Rather than relying on narrow range "imported" practices like the "mindfulness-based" approaches, the application of mindfulness to treat GAD will be advanced when the traditional Buddhist way of applying mindfulness is also systematically evaluated in an evidence-based research framework. Designed to complement CBT, CM strategies, inhering in a strong theoretical potential for targeting GAD symptoms, will be outlined and contrasted to MBSR approaches. A case study will illustrate CM's specific method. The author recognizes that this is a first attempt to introduce a CM and CBT integrated approach to treat GAD. CM is a potentially fruitful method because it manages features of GAD not adequately controlled heretofore.

According to research studies in the past two decades, CBT for GAD has evolved progressively through a number of developmental phases resulting in a better understanding of GAD's triggers and maintaining factors. In the early phase, GAD was treated with Beck's Cognitive Therapy which was originally designed to treat clinical depression. The treatment is non-specific to GAD (Leahy, 2004). Borkovec, Robinson, Pruzinsky, and DePree (1983) were among the first to develop a CBT protocol specific for GAD. They identified excessive, uncontrollable, and pervasive worry as a critical symptom of GAD and modified the general CBT approach to specifically target GAD symptoms. This included a strategy to cope with avoidance of actual emotional distress and future oriented threatening events. However, CBT's value to reduce and regulate uncontrollable worrying proved to be limited. GAD patients continue to find oceans of worry (Dugas, 2000). Wells (1995) suggested that the poor outcome of CBT for GAD is a result of CBT's only targeting the contents of worry, so-called "type I worry", and CBT's failing to address meta-cognitive beliefs, such as "worrying about worry", so-called "type II worry". He hypothesized that "type II worry" was the primary cause maintaining GAD. Changing meta-cognitive beliefs and accompanying behaviors is crucial for CBT's effectiveness. According to him, it is the patient's habitual use of worry as a coping strategy to avoid threatening thoughts, feelings, and behaviors which leads to the negative meta-beliefs about worrying. The failure to resolve "type I worry" through planning and problem solving results in emotional distress and processing problems, triggering worrying about worrying. As a result, there is an increase in threat appraisals accentuating anxiety. By reverting to "type I worry" as a means of resolving the anxiety the patient creates a feedback loop that reinforces worrying. Preliminary studies show that targeting meta-cognitive appraisals and beliefs is effective for treating GAD.

Dugas, Gagnon, and Ladouceur (1998) argue that treating the cause of uncontrollable worrying is central to successful treatment of GAD. Rather than focusing on the maintaining factors of worrying such as described by Wells, they propose that "intolerance of uncertainty" is the core cause of uncontrollable anxiety. Chronic patients prefer to experience negative outcomes rather than facing uncertainty about future threats; they thus create an illusion of certainty and predictability. Like all GAD patients, these patients use their tactics to avoid events resulting in the non-recurrence of the avoided threat which they then see as evidence that worrying helps to prevent threats. Even though CBT interventions help GAD patients develop more realistic probability estimates of feared outcomes through cognitive restructuring and exposure, dealing with these causal factors is critical for success.

There has been increasing evidence that emotional processing and interpersonal conflict is associated with GAD. Studies show that GAD patients rate interpersonal issues as the main source of their worry (Borkovec, et al., 1983). In another study, GAD patients report significantly more insecure attachment to primary caregivers than those without GAD (Lichtenstein & Cassidy, 1991). Other studies provide evidence that GAD patients associated their early trauma experience primarily to friends and family as compared to those without GAD (Molina, Roemer, Borkovec, & Posa, 1992). Based on these data, clinicians have developed an interpersonal psychotherapy for GAD which forks out in three major directions. The first involves the study of a standardized interpersonally oriented psychodynamic therapy model for GAD (Crits-Christoph, Gibbons, & Crits-Christoph, 2004), the second is a standardized model of interpersonal, psychodynamic, and CBT integrated treatment protocol (Newman, Castonguay, Borkovec, & Molnar, 2004), and the third is a CBT emotional processing intervention (Moses & Barlow, 2006). Tracing the origins of the condition to early childhood patterns of attachment, the first two models base their understanding of GAD on an interpersonal perspective which serves as the foundation for the individual's core views of self and others.

The *first model* hypothesizes that GAD is rooted in early threatening and anxiety producing experiences that lead to the formation of basic wishes, expectations, beliefs, and feelings about self and others. These are associated with the need for safety, trust, stability, and love. However, when the patient connects to these needs, the process is disrupted by the activation of fears (of rejection, abandonment, or abuse). The fear is so overwhelming that one not only avoids the anxiety triggering threats but the unfulfilled positive needs, experienced as distressing, as well. These dynamic schemata, then, become the template for the patient's future relationships. The *second model* integrates CBT and psychodynamic principles and practices. Emotional and interpersonal sources of danger and the learned avoidance of them are identified by conducting a functional analysis. These are subsequently systematically targeted by a treatment strategy comprising Socratic questioning, emotional exposure, modeling and skills training, applied in sequences of interpersonal and CBT interventions to facilitate research. Compared to a CBT package alone, CBT co-administered with psychodynamic components resulted in significantly better outcomes (Newman, et al., 2004; Newman, Castonguagy, & Borkovec, 1999). Larger studies are required to confirm these initial findings. The *third model* is consistent with CBT. Addressing GAD in a structured way, Moses and Barlow (2006) suggest that emotional dis-regulation not only affects functioning but is also responsible for GAD, as studies show that emotional suppression and maladaptive ways of managing emotions often produces negative consequences. According to the authors a standard emotional regulation approach can be used to treat a range of emotional disorders. They identify three stages of treatment: (1) the restructuring of distorted cognitive appraisals, (2) the identification and treatment of emotional dis-regulation based behavior, and (3) the targeting of emotional avoidance with exposure to facilitate emotional expression and processing.

The early psychoanalytical literature includes a number of different explanations of anxiety. Freud's initial presentation traces early sexual repression, later followed by the signal theory of anxiety; subsequent analysts further elaborated upon the psychodynamic basis of anxiety. Horney (1950), Sullivan (1953), and Fromm-Reichmann (1955) presented an interpersonal perspective for anxiety. For clinicians of the object-relations school, like Fairbain (1952), anxiety is rooted during infancy's separation conflict of dependency (the fear of being engulfed) versus the fearful loss of identity. Klein (1975) on the other hand, proposed that the roots of anxiety lay in feelings of being persecuted which result from failing to evoke the primary caretaker's affection and subsequent feelings of incompetence to repair damaged relationships. From a psychodynamic perspective, it is questionable whether GAD can be treated on the basis of emotional dis-regulation rooted in attachment problems. According to the Psychodynamic Diagnostic Manual (2006), GAD is a complex condition involving signal, separation, moral, and annihilation factors depending on the severity of the disorder. Relying entirely on CBT and interpersonal strategies may not be adequate to address the underlying factors associated with anxiety.

In summary: evident from extensive CBT-GAD studies, a number of key considerations emerges. Firstly, cognitive, verbal-based, and restructuring strategies appear limited in reducing uncontrollable worry, a cardinal symptom of GAD. Secondly, intolerance of uncertainty and avoidance of experiencing anxiety and disengaging from threatening stimuli maintaining the anxiety are not adequately dealt with by the available strategies. Thirdly, interpersonal factors related to attachment issues appear important to address in any comprehensive treatment of GAD.

Research review and considerations for including mindfulness to treat GAD

The best known and most researched form of using mindfulness as a component in a treatment package is MBSR (Kabat Zinn, 1990). MBSR uses a modified form of insight (Vipassana) practice to suit the western mindset. A wide body of studies has shown the efficacy of MBSR for a wide range of medical and psychiatric conditions (e.g., Segal, Williams, & Teasdale, 2002; Bishop, et al., 2004). In the first study on the effects of MBSR on a variety of anxiety disorders including GAD, Kabat-Zinn, Massion, Kristeller, Peterson, Fletcher, et al. (1992) conducted an uncontrolled study with 22 patients. They showed significant improvement on several standard measures of anxiety and depression at post-treatment and at a three month follow-up (on virtually all reported anxiety symptoms). A subsequent separate three year follow-up study of the same participants showed that treatment gains were maintained (Miller, Fletcher, & Kabat-Zinn, 1995). However, the outcome for GAD was not as significant as for other disorders and furthermore, the studies lacked active control groups. Due to constraints of the experimental design, it is problematic to ascribe the outcome to MBSR. Moreover, when an active control group was included to determine interaction effects of MBSR on anxiety and depression in a psoriasis study, no significance was found (Toneatto & Nguyen, 2007; Kabat-Zinn, Wheeler, Light, Skillings, Scharf, et al., 1998).

A study combining mindfulness with CBT in four GAD patients (Roemer, Orisollo, & Barlow 2003) showed significant pre- and post-treatment results. Nevertheless, the data indicate that the patients individually continued experiencing moderate levels of GAD symptoms after treatment. This raises the question whether the mindfulness employed added anything relevant to CBT's partial reduction of GAD. Roemer, et al. (2003) based their treatment on the view that avoidance is a core problem underlying GAD and minimized or ignored other critical symptoms central to GAD. These include: (a) the excessive, pervasive, and uncontrollable nature of worrying; (2) the maintaining factors of worrying and anxiety, such as positive and negative beliefs and assumptions about the role of worrying; (c) the selective attention to threatening stimuli; (d) the intolerance of ambivalence and uncertainty, and (e) the increasing evidence on the emotional dis-regulation and interpersonal conflict underlying GAD.

Acceptance and Commitment Therapy (ACT), which incorporates a modified version of MBSR with a stark emphasis on the acceptance of anxiety, showed significant improvement on a number of outcome measures. Notwithstanding, the conclusion was that larger studies are needed to corroborate the effectiveness of mindfulness in GAD (Hayes, Strosahl, & Wilson, 1999). Given the potential of mindfulness for treating GAD, a number of anxiety researchers theorized that underlying processes of GAD might be impacted by ACT and MSBR resulting in symptom reduction (Roemer & Orsillo, 2002; Wells, 2002; Hayes & Feldman, 2004). The primary benefit of mindfulness for GAD is subsumed under four categories: (a) acceptance, (b) attention and awareness, (c) cognitive change, and (d) present moment experience. A brief critique of the existing literature on mindfulness for the treatment of GAD follows.

Acceptance, identified as a primary therapeutic agent of mindfulness, is described as a non-judgmental, non-evaluative state of experiential openness of present moment experiences (Hayes, 2002; Bishop, et al., 2004). By instructing patients to adopt this state of openness without any specific training, mindfulness becomes a cognitive or self- talk strategy. Roemer, et al. (2003) combine acceptance and mindfulness integrated into a CBT protocol targeting the primary cluster of GAD symptoms, i.e. experiential avoidance. Based on the theory of ACT (habitual attempts to control internal experiences is the major cause of GAD), acceptance is conceptualized as an alternative response facilitating immediate contact with aversive experiences with the potential to break through and replace anxiety maintaining avoidance patterns. By cultivating willingness to experience the threat as it is, rather than as either good or bad, patients learn to tolerate threatening events. As greater tolerance develops, patients are more amenable to pursue and engage in valued behavior (Roemer, et al., 2003). However, there is no conclusive evidence that acceptance is able to extinguish fears about future oriented threats. Studies of selective attention to threatening information associated with GAD demonstrate that the threat often operates outside awareness (Martin, Williams, & Clark, 1991). It is, therefore, very unlikely that acceptance might adequately access and process aspects of the anxiety such as deep-seated beliefs and schemata inaccessible to conscious recall.

The conceptual basis of acceptance in treating GAD was also criticized by Craske and Hazlett-Stevens (2002) who point out that simply accepting threat and danger signals inherent in GAD is in conflict with the human proclivity to value fear as a protection against danger. They also raise the point that acceptance could be another subtle form of control which challenges Roemer and Orsillo's (2002) premise that psychopathology is rooted in the attempt to control internal experiences. Much of CBT's success in treating anxiety disorders is primarily based on control. Roemer and Orsillo also suggest that mindfulness replaces rigid ways of responding with more flexible ones (flexible regarding cues, responses, and contingencies). Others speculate that mental flexibility applied to anxiety and worry helps to reduce patterns of cognitive rigidity by inhibiting secondary processes through elaborating on thought and feeling (Wells, 2002). Wells, Martin, and others suggest further that awareness acquired through mindfulness helps patients detach from the habitual way of responding to negative and threatening stimuli. Detached awareness is helpful in developing a meta-cognitive mode to view thoughts as mental events to be processed rather than as facts. However, they do not explain how learning to detach from habitual experience can help reducing excessive, pervasive, and uncontrollable worry and anxiety. Given the nature of the worry and anxiety of GAD, it is unlikely that simply learning to observe in a detached way while temporarily providing relief – comparable to the effect of relaxation and positive affirmation – can undo entrenched distortions.

Orsillo and Roemer (2003) like many others claim that mindfulness of present moment experiencing reduces anxiety of future-oriented threats. Training a GAD patient to be mindful of present moment experiences prevents from thinking about future fearful events. This comes about by developing flexible ways of responding to environmental contingencies (as opposed to the fear-evoking rigid, verbal, rule-governed cognitive processes). However, they did not explain how focusing on present moment experience might stop GAD thoughts and feelings. Given the nature of anxiety, it is likely that focusing on present moment experience and avoiding engaging in future oriented experiences could result in negative reinforcement of anxiety.

The above critiques about the therapeutic benefits of mindfulness for GAD highlight the need to further explore the range of mindfulness approaches, so that their therapeutic potential might be fully realized. As yet, it remains unexplained which features of MBSR accomplish therapeutic effects, reason for this author to present CM. CM is not meant to replace MBSR or other mindfulness approaches tested in CBT, but builds upon them by expanding the mindfulness to include the full array of Buddhist tenets.

Targeting GAD symptoms: CM's specific ways

CM skills-training possess an intrinsic stronger theoretical potential to effectively alleviate GAD than MBSR or CBT, alone or in combination. For example, one of the main features of GAD is excessive self-verbalization and thinking that contributes to maintaining of uncontrollable and excessive worrying (Freeston, Dugas, & Ladouceur, 1996). CBT strategies such as logical-empirical disputation, problem solving, and exposure may inadvertently encourage patients to continue worrying by finding many other threat occurring probabilities. The skill to engage sustainably with target stimuli might help to reduce self-verbalization due to inhibiting the tendency to label experiences. The full engagement with the totality of an experience inhibits excessive self-verbalization. Brain imaging studies confirm that excessive verbalization is a major factor in maintaining GAD. These studies show excessive activation of the left inferior frontal cortex and the speech area in GAD patients. Brain activity decrease can be brought about by both CBT and pharmacotherapy. A GAD feature not covered by CBT is the narrow, constricted, and rigid state of anxiety restricting attention to threatening stimuli to the exclusion of neutral and pleasant stimuli. It is seems that CBT strategies are not particularly effective in reducing worry and anxiety in GAD patients when the anxiety state is rigid and confined to selective attention (to threatening stimuli). CM involves awareness training which involves learning to expand the mind into an open, expansive, and flexible state which enables containing functional and dysfunctional thoughts and feelings. Training such a skill eventually results in converting the narrow and rigid state of anxiety into a more open and flexible mind state capable to attend neutral and pleasant stimuli with reduced interference from threatening stimuli. Research shows that vigilance and problems of disengaging from threatening stimuli are mechanisms of anxiety disorders (Koster, Geert, Verschuere, & Houwer, 2004). Selective attention to threat maintains the overestimation of risk and danger, eventually overriding the patient's mental ability to regulate thoughts and emotional responses. Thus, the patient becomes overly sensitive to threat related cues and signals (Matthews & Mackintosh, 1998). Training patients to reduce vigilance and to disengage from threatening stimuli can be done by helping them to learn how to sustain full engagement with the totality of a threatening stimulus. This ability to sustain engagement with the totality of the threatening stimulus helps to develop habituation to the threat. The effective disengagement from the threatening stimulus facilitates an orienting toward and a fully engaging in new non-threatening stimuli. Experiential avoidance, another major clinical feature of GAD, has not responded to conventional CBT exposure either. It seems likely that CM's habituation-based exposure is a more appropriate and beneficial intervention. Why? Probably because one of the major problems identified when using conventional exposure to target GAD triggers is that the nature of these triggers is multiplicity and that many of these triggers are internal, often not immediately present in consciousness. Conventional exposure works well in other anxiety disorders, such as in phobias, because the fear trigger is circumscribed and tangible (e.g., heights, elevators, or spiders). CM provides an alternative form of exposure by developing habituation of threatening stimuli instead of directly extinguishing them. Habituation comes about by repeatedly training the mind to attend to the totality of the primary stimulus rather than just attending to the threatening aspect of the stimulus. CM skills include learning to be simultaneously aware of the secondary threats in the peripheral field of experience. Habituation is acquired through repeated open ended exposure to the primary and secondary threats.

Integrating CM with Integrative CBT: an illustrative case study

Integrative CBT (ICBT) integrates various practices of CBT. It is a clinical approach applying strategies from CBT and CM, and also includes some psychodynamic insights to account for clinical disorders. ICBT consists of interventions most appropriate and effective for targeting particular symptoms. The following case study, lasting 15 sessions, illustrates the practice of CM in an ICBT framework. *Subject.* The patient is a divorced Caucasian woman in her mid 30s, who lives with and works to earn a living for her mother as well. Her father died about two years before and she claims to have recovered from his death. She recalls that in her short marriage her husband was verbally and emotionally abusive towards her. However, she could not muster the courage to leave him; eventually, he left her. She remembers being anxious as a child and always trying to take care of family members. The complaints include daily uncontrollable and excessive worry, "every hour"; furthermore, she reports a number of present and future concerns with underlying emotions of anger, frustration, resentment, guilt, and sadness. In her account, worrying is beneficial, because it makes her feel to be better prepared for fearful situations. She has little control over worries about her long standing conflicts with her mother. These anxieties are often accompanied by additional symptoms of restlessness, feelings of being on edge, concentration difficulties, increased irritability, tensed muscles, and breathlessness. This distress interferes with attending work, performing at work, socializing, and carrying out many daily activities. She tends to procrastinate and finds it difficult to make decisions and to stick to them. No other psychiatric disorders are present and there are no medical factors contributing to her anxiety. A history of major depression exists during college, but this had been treated successfully with medication and psychotherapy.

Table 1. Step 1 (Sessions 1-3)

1.	**Assessment:** Mini-psychiatric diagnostic questionnaire, Beck's Anxiety Inventory and Beck's Depressive Inventory
2.	**Psycho-education:** The psycho-education of the patient involves information about the triggers and maintaining factors of her anxiety and how classical mindfulness combined with Integrative Cognitive Behavior Therapy helps to treat GAD.
3.	**Psycho-physiological regulation:** Involves the use of the preliminary practice of classical mindfulness to reduce the physical tension and arousal associated with anxiety.

Treatment Protocol. Step I (Sessions 1-3): Assessment, psycho-education and self-regulation of arousal and distress (see Table 1). The patient contracted for 15 sessions of CM/ICBT including regular compliance with daily assignments and completion of self-monitoring sheets. Her chief assignment was a daily 30 minute practice of the CM skills six days a week. The goal was to progressively develop each of the skills sequentially in daily practice during the first six weeks. She was taught the synchronized inhalation and exhalation with the movement of the abdomen; the goal was to master the process so that she could regulate her breathing with the movement of her abdomen rather than through conscious mental control. When the breath became slower and finer to the point where she did not have to consciously think about it, she was taught to immerse herself into the sensation of the breath to the point that she could sense the variations in breathing not only during exhalation and inhalation but also during the beginning, the middle, and the end of exhalation and inhalation. The skill of letting the breath occur spontaneously and utilizing the attentional resources to immerse in the breath helped her develop control abilities without consciously seeking to do so. Developing control skills without making such an effort enabled her to disinvest in fighting or fleeing from the physical tensions activated by her anxiety.

Assessment. Assessment included the administration of the mini-psychiatric diagnostic questionnaire with a comprehensive 90 minutes clinical interview as well as the Beck Anxiety Inventory (BAI) and the Beck Depressive Inventory (BDI). The pre-treatment BAI score was 44 and 16 on her BDI. Both questionnaires were also administered post treatment for evaluating outcomes. Ongoing assessment also included regularly monitoring the severity, frequency, and duration of the symptoms. She was instructed to practice CM 20 minutes daily. A further 10 minutes daily were spent completing the self-monitoring sheet on severity, duration, and frequency of symptoms to measure the effectiveness of the mindfulness basic skills and CBT in reducing GAD.

Psycho-education and psycho-physiological regulation. Psycho-education involved orienting the patient to the potential causes, triggers, maintenance factors, reasons why standard treatment could not work, and how and why CM helps increasing ICBT's effectiveness. After psycho-education, she received the initial instructions for the first phase of treatment. This involved training in synchronized breathing with the movement of the abdomen for regulating physiological arousal associated with anxiety. By being able to regulate breathing with the movement of the abdomen rather than through conscious control, she reported a gradual reduction in arousal. The synchronized breathing achieved the same results as progressive muscle relaxation (Wolpe, 1973) and may have required less time.

Step II (Sessions 3-7): Sequential CM and CBT procedures for treating pervasive, excessive and uncontrollable worrying and anxiety, the patient's chief complaints. As research has shown that restructuring of cognitive distortions underlying GAD does not necessarily result in significant reduction in uncontrollable worrying and anxiety, it is here hypothesized that trying to restructure the maladaptive, anxiety related thoughts, assumptions, and beliefs without first converting the associated constricted and rigid state of consciousness into a more open and adaptive one, prevents her from learning how to initiate voluntarily redirecting attention to neutral and positive information. Since, by definition, anxiety of GAD results from reflexive orientation towards threatening stimuli, its sequelae triggers the patient's excessive and uncontrollable worry. An initial modicum of voluntary control of attentional processes must first be restored before cognitive restructuring and other strategies requiring attention and awareness can be initiated. This was achieved by having the patient train herself to achieve the processes of mindfulness and by applying them to GAD (in steps II and III).

For example, the patient first learned to recapture some voluntary control of attentional processes. This resulted from learning the key skill of *containing threatening stimuli without resorting to the automatic pattern of expelling them instantly.* This containment skill consists of connecting to the containing capacity within by generating an internal sense of spaciousness. This was learned in practice sessions by focusing attention either on the sensory experience of the external space of the room or within a circle while in a calm state of mind. Then she practiced internalizing this sense of spaciousness to be within the mind itself. Once this containment skill was well practiced, it could be applied to anxiety experiences. Generating a sense of spaciousness during anxiety enabled her to disrupt the narrow, rigid state of anxiety and to move into creating an open and flexible state of consciousness. The patient was then able to engage with the primary anxiety provoking stimuli without expelling them, thus disrupting the GAD attentional processes of being automatically directed towards the threat. Thus, she gained greater voluntary attentional resources which she could make available for attending towards other aspects of the primary threatening stimulus. In the course of several practice sessions, the patient learned that excessive worrying with the contents of the distractive thoughts and feelings resulted in increased preoccupation with them and in shattering the open, flexible, and expansive state of mind she had achieved. Her loss of spaciousness resulted in fixations on the trigger event again with a reverberating of secondary global meanings of threat.

Having developed the initial capacity to contain threatening stimuli without resorting to the habitual pattern of expelling them instantly, the patient took the second step of repeatedly practicing this to strengthen the containment skill. Once strengthened, she had the ability to inhibit the tendency to form evaluative and reactive responses such as global labels to the primary threatening stimuli evoking excessive worry. Through further practice she learned to contain all anxiety related forms of distractions (primary threat and automatically triggered secondary excessive worry) as events in a spacious field of awareness. She began to discover that the anxiety, distractions, and worry occurred within a spacious field and that they arose and disappeared on their own without further effort. Repeated training of directing attentional resources to other features and functions of the stimulus, rather than being caught in the automatic selective attention to its threatening aspects, enabled her to get the direct experience of the stimulus, since it was stripped of its threatening aspects and global labels.

When the patient began to effectively apply the mindfulness skill of containment reducing cognitive biases and restored some voluntary control of her attention, she was introduced to CBT restructuring strategies relating to the primary cognitive distortions of GAD. The strategies comprise seeking evidence for and against the likelihood of the feared events occurring followed by a cost and benefit analysis to determine alternative, realistic ways of thinking instead of the old ways of appraising future threats. Cognitive restructuring of the overestimation of risks and catastrophic thinking was consolidated by behavioral strategies of setting up specific worry time and worry free zones in order to help her develop control over uncontrollable worry and anxiety.

Step III (Sessions 7-10): Open ended exposure, behavioral experimentation, and problem solving. Since CBT based exposure has been shown to be of limited value to GAD even though it is highly effective for other anxiety disorders, mindfulness based open ended exposure was used to help her develop habituation of both the anxiety and its triggers. Consistent with the pervasive nature of anxiety and worry in GAD, mindfulness involves open ended exposure to varying types of anxiety and their triggers. This approach is unlike conventional CBT exposure which targets a single, tangible behavior in order to extinguish the fear. In the mindfulness exposure she was trained to develop habituation of the presence of multiple threats by repeatedly training her to allocate 80% of her attentional resources to the totality of the primary threatening stimulus associated with the anxious affect and 20% of the resources to the secondary threats in the peripheral field of awareness. The patient was repeatedly exposed to thoughts and feelings triggering anxiety and avoiding anxiety. Allowing thoughts and feelings arising on their own (without the pressure to engage in exposure for a prescribed period of time) provided her the freedom to eventually develop familiarity and tolerance to threatening stimuli. As the fear of the threat decreases, the avoidance behavior also diminished. In fact, habituation serves the ultimate function of response prevention.

After the patient developed greater habituation to threatening stimuli, she was trained in the mindfulness skill of disengaging from threatening stimuli rapidly by making use of her voluntary attentional resources. This was done by means of repeated training in engaging in the threatening stimulus and disengaging from it by rapidly orienting and engaging with neutral and pleasant stimuli. The patient was able to reduce vigilance towards threatening stimuli by developing the skill to engage with the totality of the stimulus for extended periods of time. Decreased vigilance helped her to disengage from the stimulus, a process which was further facilitated by redirecting attention towards the next new experience. For instance, when she could disengage rapidly from the anxious thoughts of a conflict with her mother, she could orient herself more readily to a more realistic and positive thought about her fears. When the patient was able to disengage rapidly from threatening stimuli, she was then recommended to carry out behavioral experiments to test her deep seated fears about specific situations.

Step IV (Sessions 10-14): Resolving underlying emotional and interpersonal conflict, the source of intolerance of uncertainty. The next five sessions were devoted to the patient's identifying the unfulfilled need from the other, the actual or perceived response of the other, and the response of the self to the other. The first step was to help her identify the primary emotion of intense repressed anger in which she wanted to scream at her mother and shake her to shut up. Recreating and reliving her past anger helped her recognize the depth of her anger, the resistance, and the complex feelings of fear and guilt it activated. In exploring the underlying source of her anxiety, she experienced a mother who was demanding and critical. She was disappointed and noticed that that this might quickly turn into anger and resentment. Feelings of resentment and anger in turn activated feelings of guilt and the fear of mother's retaliation.

The ambivalence of her relationship was maintained by the fact that there was a part of her deeply wanting her mother to accept her unconditionally (evidenced by her efforts to do everything to please her mother). However, her inability to resolve the ambivalence between her negativity towards the bad mother and her as the angry resentful child and her desire for a good mother and her as the perfect child lead to intolerance of any ambivalence and uncertainty of future threats. As a result, she could not live fully in the present moment of experience; she constantly maintained a state of vigilance about future threats. Nor could she fully take advantage of the various strategies to manage her fears because she lived in a fantasy that there exists no future free from all forms of threats. Thus, the patient was educated about the role of intolerance, ambivalence, and uncertainty and interpersonal conflicts. She was introduced to be mindful of experiential insight strategies designed to help her recognize that mental experiences are constantly subjected to change from moment to moment. This was done as a way to help her become tolerant of ambivalence and uncertainty. Consequently, change was not the problem per se but rather how she perceived, appraised, and reacted to change (the underlying factor). Through experiential insight how the perception and appraisal of a trigger of anxiety determine the subsequent reaction and consequent behavior, she became aware how changing perception and appraisal of anxiety triggers could result in reducing fearful reactions and subsequent behaviors. Having recognized that the meaning ascribed to an event is the basis of anxiety, she then also recognized that if no such meaning was actively ascribed, the event was experienced as an occurrence in the field of awareness dissolving into the spaciousness on its own.

Step V (Session 15): Relapse prevention. At the end of session 15, her post-treatment BAI score was 17 and her BDI score was 10. She reported significant improvement in GAD symptoms and an increased ability to regulate them, though some problems remained in a number of situations. For example, there were fewer triggers so that anxiety reactions were few; she felt confident to live separately from her mother and hoped to find a new job and a new relationship. She reported reacting with much less intense physical tension and somatic symptoms to anxious thoughts and concerns, when they did occur. She was also able to prevent uncontrolled worrying most of the time by applying the strategies she had learnt. Interpersonally, she could better regulate her reactions to her mother and thus verbalize directly to her mother not only her concerns but her needs as well. Furthermore, she was encouraged to recognize that anxiety could still persist, but now she has tools to cope with it, she did not have to live in constant dread. She was reminded that during major stress events, she could anticipate an increased degree of distress and disruption, and could timely apply her skills.

In closing

CM/ICBT offers an alternative way to apply mindfulness for treating GAD. Its strength lies in teaching the patient skills to refine the two ways of perceiving and appraising with the help of mindfulness in order to replace dysfunctional thoughts, feelings, and behaviors with functional ones. However, little is known about CM in the clinical and research community. The UCLA Clinical Research Program in CM/ICBT for anxiety disorders is probably the first academic effort to explore, develop, and study CM. The program has developed manuals for GAD and Obsessive Compulsive Disorder and is currently working towards standardizing the manuals. This author recognizes that CM warrants further empirical investigation in order to determine whether it can help durably. Introducing CM to the professional community is an ongoing process that requires adherence to the demands of evidence-based research and it is hoped that others will further study CM and explore its potential to help cure and free patients from their suffering going forward.

Chapter 19

Dharma Therapy: An Intervention Program With Mindfulness As One Of Its Key Components

Hinhung Sik

Background

In recent years, the relevancy of Buddhist teachings to psychology and psychotherapy has been of increased interest to academia and many respected scholars. The breadth of research and studies related to these topics vary from studies of Buddhist Psychology, as presented in canonical texts (Kalupahana 1987) to neuroscientific research and to the Tibetan Lamas' degrees of happiness. Interesting and encouraging results have emerged recently (Davidson, Kabat-Zinn, Schumacher, Rosenkranz, Muller, et al., 2003). These include the use of mindfulness meditation training in the management of stress and chronic pain, pioneered by Kabat-Zinn (1982, 1990), and Mindfulness-Based Cognitive Therapy (MBCT) for depression as developed by Segal, Teasdale, and Williams (Teasdale 2003).

In a review summarizing the literature on mindfulness training as a clinical intervention, Baer (2003) noted that the use of mindfulness training as a clinical intervention is described with increasing frequency, and its popularity appears to be growing rapidly. As of 1997, over 240 hospitals and clinics in the United States and abroad were offering stress reduction programs based on "mindfulness training" (Salmon 1998). Kabat-Zinn (2003) suggests that this increasing interest in studies of mindfulness and its clinical application is being driven primarily by the realization that new dimensions of therapeutic benefit and novel insight into mind/body interactions might accrue through its exploration. However, in the same article, he warned that:

> …it becomes critically important that those persons coming to the field with professional interest and enthusiasm recognize the unique qualities and characteristics of mindfulness as a meditative practice, with all that implies, so that mindfulness is not simply seized upon as the next promising cognitive behavioral technique or exercise, decontextualized, and "plugged" into a behaviorist paradigm with the aim of driving desirable change, or of fixing what is broken (p.145).

Furthermore, Kabat-Zinn (2003), emphasizing his intention in developing Mindfulness-Based Stress Reduction (MBSR) back in 1979, added that,

> ... [although] MBSR as an intervention needed to be free of the cultural, religious, and ideological factors associated with the Buddhist origins of mindfulness... the program needed to remain faithful in both spirit and substance to the universal dharma dimension alluded to, which, as noted, lies at the very core of the gesture of mindfulness. (Kabat-Zinn 2003, p.149)

In the same issue of *Clinical Psychology: Science & Practice*, Teasdale, Segal, and Williams (2003) also raised the point that

> ...mindfulness has always been used as only one of a number of components of a much wider intervention, or path, itself grounded in a clear formulation of the origins and cessation of suffering, rather than as an end in itself .(p.159)

These separate components of this path to ending suffering, integrate and interact in ways that allow the impact of the whole path to become more powerful than the sum of its parts. Based on this reasoning, Teasdale and associates (2003) suggest that

> ...contemporary clinical applications of mindfulness training would similarly benefit from theory driven integration within a wider intervention.

Answering the call of both Kabat-Zinn and Teasdale and associates, this essay will formulate and present a therapy, the Dharma Therapy, that applies the universal Dharma as its theoretical foundation and that puts mindfulness back in its original place, where it plays a role as one among several key components. Hopefully, by presenting the theoretical foundation of Dharma Therapy in a language that is familiar to clinicians, the suffering elimination model discovered by the Buddha can be more easily understood and more appropriately assimilated by western practitioners and researchers. Furthermore, by putting mindfulness meditation back into the context from which it was taken, and allowing all of the components of the path to interact coherently, Dharma Therapy promises to be a much more effective intervention than methods which use mindfulness alone and out of its original context.

Dharma Therapy: theoretical foundations

Dharma is a Sanskrit word that has many meanings including the following two: (1) The teachings of the Buddha, and (2) The concept of Dependent Origination of all things. Hence, Dharma Therapy implies a therapeutic model built on the teachings of the Buddha; and, it can also mean a therapeutic model based on Dependent Origination, which, in the Buddhist teachings is not a proposition to be taken for granted but rather a postulate to be discovered on an experiential level. According to the Buddha, his teachings are a "suffering elimination model" built on Dependent Origination, which he experienced while meditating under the Bodhi tree. It was his discovery of Dependent Origination that enabled the Buddha to propose a comprehensive teaching that could eradicate suffering.

Before going further into the working of Dharma Therapy, it is necessary to recapitulate the Buddha's awakening experience under the Bodhi tree and to explain in detail the concept of the Dependent Origination, which is the theoretical foundation of Dharma Therapy.

The Buddha's awakening experience and the concept of "Dependent Origination"

The Buddha's awakening experience is the crucial factor that brilliantly distinguishes the Buddha from ordinary human beings, and it is from this experience that the Buddha discovered the concept of Dependent Origination and the path to end suffering. The following is a brief description of the steps that the Buddha took to awaken:

Steps 1 & 2: Become aware of the suffering and unsatisfactory condition of the current situation and develop a desire to be liberated from the suffering. While sitting under the Bodhi tree just before attaining awakening, the following questions came to the Buddha's mind:

> This world has fallen into trouble, in that it is born, ages, and dies, it passes away and is reborn, yet it does not understand the escape for this suffering. When now will an escape be discerned from this suffering? (Bodhi 2000, p. 601)

Just as any successful psychotherapeutic counselling, the path of recovery and healing begins with the candidate seeing the unsatisfactory condition of the situation and developing a desire to be free from the suffering. Because of his sensitivity and mindful observation, the Buddha's understanding of suffering was much deeper than that of ordinary people. He saw that existence and the endless process of rebirth is one whole mass of suffering that was unacceptable to him. Therefore, for the Buddha, true liberation comes only when the bondage of the endless process of rebirth ceases.

Step 3: Question and investigate the cause of suffering. With this desire to be free from suffering in mind, the Buddha questioned: "When what exists does aging-and-death come to be? By what is aging-and-death conditioned?" With this investigative frame of mind, the Buddha wanted to know: what are the conditions that lead to the suffering of aging-and-death. While investigating, he noticed,

> ...through careful attention, there took place in me a breakthrough by wisdom: "When there is birth, aging-and-death comes to be; aging-and-death has birth as the condition." (Bodhi 2000, p.601)

What the Buddha noticed was that phenomena come to be conditionally, that is, the coming to be of one phenomenon will bring about the arising of the next phenomenon. As long as there is birth, aging and death are inevitable. This awareness of the Dependent Origination nature of phenomena is the theoretical foundation of all Buddhist teachings. Furthermore, the Buddha also pointed out that it was "a breakthrough by wisdom" that enabled him to realize the Dependent Origination nature of phenomena.

Step 4: Observe and learn by paying careful attention to suffering and the cause of suffering. As the Buddha proceeded further into his investigative search of how birth and suffering come to be, he saw clearly that life is a process of cyclic existence supported by twelve links where one leads to the arising of the next and are ultimately interdependent on each other.

The twelve links of this cyclic existence of life and death are: aging and death, birth, existence, grasping, attachment, feeling, contact, the sense spheres, mind-and-matter, consciousness, volitional action and ignorance.

Step 5: Develop insight and wisdom on suffering and the causes of suffering. The Buddha saw clearly that among these twelve links: birth leads to the arising of aging and death, existence to the arising of birth, grasping to the arising of existence, attachment to the arising of grasping, feeling to the arising of attachment, contact to the arising of feeling, the sense spheres to the arising of contact, mind-and matter to the arising of sense spheres, consciousness to the arising of mind-and-matter, volitional action to the arising of consciousness, and ignorance leads to the arising of volitional action. With this observation of the causal chain of the twelve links, the Buddha realized that the impulse of craving, clinging and Karma, working under the influence of ignorance is the fuel of this mass of bondage and suffering.

Step 6: With insight and wisdom, take the necessary steps to bring an end to suffering. On the other hand, the Buddha also noticed that with the cessation of ignorance, all the factors dependent on ignorance likewise would draw to a close, and this whole chain of bondage and suffering would cease to be. This is the inverse order of the interdependent causal chain of life and death. Hence, the key to end suffering is to eliminate ignorance by the development of Buddhist knowledge and wisdom. When there is "true" knowledge and wisdom, suffering will cease to be. This short description of the Buddha's investigation into the cause of suffering, lists out the Buddhist pathological explanation of the cause of suffering and the remedy for dealing with it. The Buddha observed that ignorance is the root of suffering and that eliminating ignorance through the development of knowledge and wisdom is the remedy to eliminate suffering.

A deeper understanding of the concept of "Dependent Origination": the interdependent triangle of "mind-and-matter" and "consciousness"

To deepen the understanding of the process of cyclic existence supported by the twelve links, the Buddha noticed that among the twelve links, the interdependent triangle of "mind-and-matter"[1] and "consciousness" is most peculiar and important in understanding the arising and coming to be of existence and suffering. In order to explain the working of this interdependent triangle, it is necessary to first explain the Buddhist understanding of a person. The Dharma sees a person as being composed of five aggregates, namely: form, feeling, thoughts, volitional action, and consciousness. Form is matter, the physical body. Feeling, thought, volitional action, and consciousness are the psychological functions of a person. Apart from representing the physical and psychological aspects of a person, the five aggregates can also be divided and understood from another perspective, the interdependent phenomena of the consciousness and the objects of consciousness, namely the other four aggregates – matter, feeling, thought, and volitional action. In the interdependent triangle of mind and matter and consciousness, mind

---

1.   Mind-and-matter: is sometimes translated as name-and-form.

represents the aggregates of feeling, thought, and volitional action. Therefore, together with matter and consciousness, the interdependent triangle of mind-and-matter and consciousness comprises the five aggregates that form a person.

In the Samyutta Nikaya, the Buddha explained his observation of the interdependent nature of the triangle (Bodhi, 2000, p.601):

> When there is consciousness, mind-and-matter comes to be; mind-and-matter has consciousness as its condition.

On the other hand,

> When there is mind-and-matter, consciousness comes to be; consciousness has mind-and-matter as its conditions.

From this observation, the Buddha concluded that:

> This consciousness turns back; it does not go further than mind-and-matter. It is to this extent that one may be born and age and die, pass away and be reborn.

It is quite easy to see that without consciousness, there is no way for a person to be aware of and conceptualize any aspect of anything. On the other hand, without the arising of the concept(s) of matter and/or mind in the mind-body, consciousness cannot arise due to the absence of something to be conscious of. In order for consciousness to arise, there needs to be at least an awareness of a concept of something to be conscious of. This is what the Buddha meant by,

> This consciousness turns back; it does not go further than mind-and-matter.

It is on the basis of this particular observation that the Buddha ruled out the possibility of an independent consciousness or the existence of a universal consciousness that transcend all phenomena.

Furthermore, because of the Buddha's practical and empirical approach to finding a remedy for the problem of suffering, one could argue that the Buddha's teachings are based on empirical observation, and hence, do not entertain metaphysical discussion.

In many Buddhist teachings, this interdependent triangle of mind-and-matter and consciousness is often compared to three sheaves of reeds leaning against each other to form a standing pyramid to illustrate their interdependence.[2] Only with consciousness there can be mind-and-

---

2.   In the Chinese translation of the Samyutta Agama, Sutra 288, three sheaves of reeds were used as an illustration. However, in the equivalent version of the Pali text, Samyutta Nikaya, II 112, two sheaves were used as an illustration.

matter, and only with mind-and-matter there can be consciousness. When the triangle of mind-and-matter and consciousness comes to be, suffering and the whole endless process of cyclic existence, supported by the twelve links of Dependent Origination, also come to be.

With this knowledge, the Buddha proclaimed:

> "Origination, origination" – thus, in regard to things unheard before there arose in me vision, knowledge, wisdom, true knowledge, and light. (Bodhi, 2000, p.601)

It is at this point that the Buddha awakened to Dependent Origination, which he later on summarized as:

> When there is this, that comes to be; with the arising of this, that arises.
> When there is not this, that does not come to be; with the cessation of this,
> that ceases. (Nanamoli 1995, p.655)

Armed with this new insight and wisdom, the Buddha realized that he had found the way to bring an end to suffering, that is to say: directly from the understanding of the interdependent nature of mind-and-matter and consciousness, a person's attachment to there being an independent and permanent self in the form of either mind-and-matter or consciousness ends. Furthermore, with the cessation of mind-and-matter comes the cessation of consciousness; with the cessation of consciousness comes the cessation of mind-and-matter; with the cessation of mind-and-matter, the whole mass of suffering might cease to be, as from the observation of the twelve links of cyclic existence, the Buddha realized that consciousness ceases when ignorance and volitional action ceases. Therefore, with the wisdom and knowledge developed from apprehending Dependent Origination, and the working of the twelve links of cyclic existence, the Buddha eliminated ignorance, and as a result, all factors that depend on ignorance ceased to be. Hence, for the Buddha, the cessation of all suffering was attained.

From the above description of the Buddha's experience of awakening, we can identify six steps that the Buddha took to attain the eventual liberation from suffering:

(1) Becoming aware of the suffering and unsatisfactory conditions of the current situation.

(2) Developing a desire to be liberated from the suffering.

(3) Questioning and investigating the cause of suffering.

(4) Observing and learning by paying careful attention to suffering and the cause of suffering.

(5) Developing insight and wisdom into suffering and the causes of suffering.

(6) With insight and wisdom, taking the necessary steps to bring an end to suffering.

These six steps to liberation that the Buddha took are basically consistent with the framework of the teachings that he taught his students. Although, in Dharma Therapy we are not trying to help clients to eliminate their ultimate bondage of life and death, these six steps that the Buddha took to eliminate suffering can still be an efficient model to help clients to remedy their problems and suffering in today's world. Therefore, these six steps are adopted as the basis for the therapeutic model of Dharma Therapy. Their content and application in a psychotherapeutic environment are elaborated later in this essay.

The significance of "Dependent Origination" and its derivative implications: no-self, "Karma", and the "Middle Path"

To understand the significance of Dependent Origination and its therapeutic implication, we need to study and analyze separately both the concept itself and the nature and characteristics of the phenomena that arise from the conditions set by Dependent Origination. The relationship between Dependent Origination and the arising phenomena is this: Dependent Origination is the generalized formula or principle of the process of how phenomena arise and cease to be. From studying Dependent Origination, one can understand and see the nature and characteristics of the phenomena only on a conceptual level. To understand Dependent Origination truly, i.e. on the experiential level, one needs to observe empirically and pay careful attention oneself to the operation of phenomena. Thus, one will gain direct insight and comprehension of Dependent Origination. The Buddha's discovery of Dependent Origination came from paying careful attention to the actual phenomena in relation to the arising and cessation of suffering as described in the twelve links of cyclical existence.

Insight in "Dependent Origination"

From the above description of the Buddha's experience of awakening, it is obvious that Dependent Origination is not the Buddha's creation; it is simply "uncovered" by the Buddha by observing and paying careful attention to the arising and cessation of suffering. In fact, the Buddha pointed out that with or without the Buddha, before and/or after his appearance, Dependent Origination persists and is applicable at all times. Furthermore, it prevails and is applicable to all things in every circumstance. The Buddha had only directly awakened to it, declared it, taught it, and set it forth. He revealed it, explained it, made it plain, and said,

See! With birth as condition, aging-and-death. (Bodhi, 2000, p.551)

Dependent Origination resembles a law of nature which validity is shared by adherents in the particular scientific community. Through Dependent Origination one is able to explain the phenomena of the world at different levels of abstraction, like how a person comes to be or how a person's psyche functions. That is why Dependent Origination is the foundation of Dharma Therapy. Although at first appearance, Dependent Origination seems easy to understand, its meanings and implications are deep and profound. Allegedly, the Buddha himself had said that Dependent Origination is deep and difficult to see (Walshe, 1987). Furthermore, the Buddha declared that those who see Dependent Origination see the Dharma. The Dharma forms together with the Buddha and the Sangha the Triple Gems, in which all Buddhists take refuge.

The phenomena: impermanence and no-self

As already pointed out, Dependent Origination describes the arising and cessation of all phenomena in the world; hence, all phenomena share a common nature and characteristics which can be described as due to the influence of Dependent Origination. Understanding Dependent Origination will help us to see the nature and characteristics that are common to all phenomena. According to Nanamoli (1995, p.655) the Buddha alluded to Dependent Origination as: "When there is this, that comes to be; with the arising of this, that arises." When a cause and the necessary conditions are there, a phenomenon will come to be. It is because of this observation that the Buddha did not accept that there was an ultimate creator of all things. There is no place for a creator, because a phenomenon cannot be "created". One can only work on the necessary conditions to facilitate the arising of phenomena, once a cause is there. When the causes and conditions are ripe, phenomena will come to be. For example, we cannot create a flower, but we can plant the seed, facilitate its growth by working on the necessary conditions, like providing water, fertile soil, enough sunlight, and so on. When the seed and the necessary conditions are there, a flower will bloom naturally. On a psychological level, although – according to Dependent Origination – we cannot create happiness, we can, however, learn to develop gratitude and emotional intelligence, improve interpersonal relationships, and so forth. In other words, happiness will come naturally when there is a cause and the necessary conditions.

It is also worthwhile to point out that when a phenomenon comes to be, nothing new or substantial has been created because phenomena are the "mere" coalescence of causes and conditions. Apart from the causes and conditions, there is no such thing as "the thing itself". For example, one can say that "my legs, eyes, memory, feelings, thinking, etc. belong to me". However, one cannot pinpoint something as being "the thing" that is the ultimate and real "me". This reality of not being able to identify the existence of something substantial and independent that we can pinpoint as "I" or "me" – other than through emotional and sentimental attachments developed from an illusion or a delusion – is the main reason why the Buddha pointed out that phenomena are inherently empty in nature, i.e. are empty of self: there is "no-self". Thus, the Buddhist proposition is that phenomena are empty of self- nature. Although the concept of "no-self" may sound daunting, it is liberating. When phenomena and events in life have "no-self", there is hope that things can be changed for the better. Pain and suffering in life come to be from causes and conditions. When the conditions end to be, suffering and pain will end to be.

"Karma" and the "Middle Path"

Antecedent events are often a "causal" factor if they have the potential power to determine the outcome or "effect" over time. Thus, only a sunflower seed can lead to the blooming of sunflowers. If the necessary conditions are in place, these conditions support the cause by facilitating the healthy growth of the sunflowers' seed. Conditions may also hamper the cause to take effect by negatively influencing the sunflowers' blooming. This relationship between the seed and the flower or fruit, i.e. the cause and effect, is the basic idea of Karma, which can be thought of as corollary of the concept of Dependent Origination. When we come up with an idea to make something, we might see the relationship between an idea and the product as similar to the relationship between a seed and its fruit. For example, having the idea to draw a particular painting, we collect the necessary colour paints, paintbrushes, and paper to nurture the idea into tangible reality. The painting is nothing more than the colour paints arranged according to the idea and imagination of our minds. Nothing extra has been created nor has anything been destroyed. What has changed is that the paints have now been rearranged in a certain way to reflect the influence of the thoughts and ideas. But, unlike a seed and its fruit, we like to call the painting our creation and we become attached to it. The creative idea is not the same as the painting and the creation painting is not identical to the idea. However, apart from the idea (the seed), there would not be the possibility of the coming to be of a new painting (the fruit). The seed is not the same as the fruit, nor is it independent of the seed.

This "neither the same, nor different" relationship of the seed and the fruit holds in all cases, and is the deeper meaning of the Middle Path, which is one of the most important derivative implications of Dependent Origination. With a correct understanding of the Middle Path, we can avoid falling into extremes; more importantly, we avoid developing a rigid attachment to the notions of duality: "there definitely is" or "there definitely is not". Dependent Origination implies that all phenomena exist only relatively and interdependently, as illustrated above.

The implication and application of Buddhist teachings in therapy

Having explained the theoretical foundation of Dharma Therapy, we can now examine its implication and its application in a psychotherapeutic environment. Apart from trying to present the suffering elimination model discovered by the Buddha in a manner that is familiar and applicable in the psychosocial discipline, this is also an attempt to present a holistic use of mindfulness by putting the practice back into the context and theoretic foundation from which it was taken. Therefore, the specific details of "how to" and "why" of the practice of mindfulness will not be discussed in detail here, rather, a more general framework of the major steps of Dharma Therapy will be presented to give an integrated picture. Furthermore, Kabat-Zinn (1990), Teasdale and associates (2003), and many other meditation masters have written clearly and extensively on the usage and application of mindfulness in clinical settings. Readers are recommended to study their pioneering works to supplement their knowledge on mindfulness. Therapists training people in MBSR and MBCT practice mindfulness themselves and therapists who intend to become Dharma Therapists need to be practitioners of mindfulness themselves as well. Without practicing mindfulness personally, a therapist will lack the skill and experience to guide clients through the learning process of mindfulness, which is a major component of Dharma Therapy.

As stated earlier, Dharma Therapy is based on the six steps that the Buddha took to attain liberation from suffering and is therefore divided into the six steps as outlined earlier and discussed below. However, in addition to these steps, introduction and preparation sessions are needed to build communication and trust between therapist and clients, to introduce the psychology of Dharma Therapy, and to let the clients know what will be expected from them if they wish to participate in a course of Dharma Therapy. During these introduction and preparation sessions, the practice of mindfulness should also be introduced to the clients.

The introduction and preparation sessions

Introductory and preparatory sessions with each prospective client can be held either individually or in a group setting, in small classes. There are three main purposes in having these sessions:

(1) *Clarifying the client-therapist's relationship.* In Dharma Therapy, the therapist takes the roles of a teacher and of a compassionate friend. The therapist as a teacher guides the client through the process of therapy and advises her/him to be aware of possibilities and potentials. As a compassionate friend, the therapist encourages and accompanies the client in difficult times during therapy. However, clients should be made aware that due to Karma, we are all responsible for our own thoughts and actions. Therefore, the ultimate motivation and responsibility to heal and transform must come from our own self. It must be emphasized here that, just as in any other type of therapy, Dharma Therapy has its limitations and may not be applicable to some clients, especially those who have a serious difficulty concentrating and who cannot think in a logical and coherent manner.

(2) *Guiding clients to develop faith and motivation by explaining the theoretical foundation of Dharma Therapy and by reassuring them that they too have the potential to transform and heal.* To help clients to develop faith and motivation, the therapist should explain to the clients that, as pointed out by the Buddha in the teachings known as the Four Noble Truths, suffering is a part of our life. Even though the suffering that the clients are facing maybe very real and very painful, it is normal and common for people to have difficulty in life. Furthermore, like all phenomena in the world, suffering comes to be because of causes and conditions. When those causes and conditions change in certain ways, suffering will cease to be. Suffering is also impermanent and empty in nature, just as it is for all phenomena in the universe. Nobody is nor can be condemned to eternal suffering, although sometimes it may feel that way. There is always hope for a better future. It is a goal in Dharma Therapy to help clients to first develop an understanding and a peaceful relationship with their suffering instead of generating additional anguish from fighting and/or denying it. From this understanding and by developing a peaceful relationship, clients can then use their newly learned skill of mindfulness to examine and comprehend the cause and conditions of their suffering. However, at this point in the therapy, it is not advisable to lead the clients to explore immediately the causes and conditions of their suffering. Clients may not be ready for this at this point in the therapy.

(3) *Helping clients to build a "spiritual oasis", which they can use as a base to understand and deal with their emotions through the practice of mindfulness.* Emotions always have a feeling of urgency and importance associated with them. The more intense the emotions, the more urgent and important the person feels the need to do something in accordance with the direction set by the emotions. Added to generating motivational drives, emotions also influence and distort our perception of the world and ourselves. When a person is overwhelmed by an emotion, it seems as though bugs have been planted in the neurons in the brain, bugs that would influence the person to perceive everything prejudicially and in accordance with the direction set by the emotion. For example, when a person falls deeply and reciprocally in love, self-esteem is most likely to be enhanced and the world might seem to be a better place. However, with a broken heart, the opposite effect likely takes place.

Because emotions influence us in many ways, they need to be dealt with properly to prevent damaging side effects from developing. Furthermore, the damage of these side effects can be significantly magnified if they become a habit of our minds. A series of broken hearts can lower a person's self-esteem in such a way that can induce the mind to think in a habitually pessimistic manner that might eventually lead to a depression. As pointed out above, the Buddha observed that ignorance is a root of suffering and that eliminating ignorance through the development of knowledge and wisdom is the remedy to eliminate suffering. Therefore, to handle emotions intelligently, one needs to pay careful attention to them in order to develop the necessary knowledge and wisdom. In his book *Emotional Intelligence*, Goleman (1997) pointed out that awareness is the most important factor in enhancing emotional intelligence. The more we are aware of the reality of something, the more our ability to deal with it will increase appropriately and in proportion. For example, if we can develop a keen awareness of the illusory nature of our thoughts and emotions, and understand that their manifestations are conditional and subject to change, their importance and urgency to drive us to "listen" to them will decrease significantly. It is for this reason that mindfulness practice, as a means of developing awareness, insight, and wisdom on the working of our mind, is the crucial factor in the practice of Dharma Therapy.

Mindfulness training is best introduced to clients as a tool to develop awareness and insight of their mental habits, and also to manage and transform emotions. Clients learn to practice mindfulness in order to develop a "spiritual oasis" where there is concentration, awareness, and clarity. Using this "spiritual oasis" as a platform, the clients' ability to develop insight and to deal with problems can be greatly enhanced. The exact method and know-how of mindfulness taught to the clients will depend on the therapist's own training. However, during these introductory sessions, clients are only to breathe peacefully and learn to enjoy and be mindful of their own breathing. Being able to breathe peacefully and enjoy one's breathing is quite important because without peacefulness and enjoyment, it is not possible to build a spiritual oasis.[3]

I. Becoming aware of the suffering and unsatisfactory condition in the current situation

This is a step where the therapist and the client explore together the current unsatisfactory situation of the client's problems. It is also a chance for the therapist to gather data and background information on the problems that the client is facing. The objective of the exploration is not to cure or deal with the problems, but to assess the situation and to let the client reflect on the current situation so that motivation to strive for a way out develops quickly. For those clients who are already facing a lot of stress or suffering, the reflection process need not be too deep because the main objective of this step is to help the clients to see and use suffering as a means to develop a sincere motivation. However, for those clients who are not aware of the suffering or the problems that they themselves have, or the suffering and problems that they are inflicting on other people, then a deeper reflection process will be needed in order to motivate the client to develop a strong determination to deal with the problems.

The therapist starts every session with five minutes of mindfulness breathing together with the client in order to set the stage for a therapeutic session conducted in an atmosphere of mindfulness. At this juncture, the therapist tells the clients the Buddhist narrative of the two

---

3.   Just as the therapists in MBSR program and MBCT, Dharma therapists need to be seasoned practitioners of mindfulness themselves.

darts of suffering (Bodhi 2000, p.1263), so that the client can have a clear picture of the type of suffering that s/he is experiencing. In the teaching of the two darts, the Buddha explained that when the "well-taught noble disciple" and "untaught worldling" encounter a stimulus through their senses, both will experience pleasant, painful, or neutral feelings in their primary states. However, if the untaught worldling experiences a painful feeling, he "worries and grieves, he laments, beats his chest, weeps and is distraught". He thus experiences two kinds of feelings, bodily feelings and mental feelings. It is as if a man was pierced by a dart, and following the first piercing, he was hit by a second dart. But in the case of a well-taught student, when he is touched by a painful feeling, he will "not worry nor grieve and lament, he will not beat his chest and weep, nor will he be distraught." He experiences one kind of feeling, a bodily one, but not a mental feeling. It is as if a man were pierced by only one dart, but was not hit by a second. From this teaching of the two darts, the therapist can guide the clients to see what kind of suffering they are experiencing.

There are painful events in life that we have no choice but just have to live with. Events like sickness, old age, death, and painful experiences that have already happened; we just have to learn to live with them so that we do not breed additional mental suffering (the second dart). However, there is another type of suffering, suffering of the nature of the second dart, which we can avoid by learning to reinterpret the painful situation (the first dart) in a more constructive way or develop a deeper understanding of it. This simple two tier classification allows clients to have a better idea about the suffering that can be eliminated by developing a better understanding and insight into the situation and about the suffering for which there is no alternative but to learn to live with it.

II. Developing a desire to be liberated from suffering

Cultivating the following insights helps a person develop a sincere desire to be free from suffering:

(1) *Seeing that life without suffering is a better alternative.* On the surface, having this insight seems easy enough. However, very often people hide behind their suffering and/or find a safe haven in the suffering for some complicated and deep-down reason. To develop a sincere desire to be free from suffering, it is not necessary to go immediately into exploring these deep reasons at this stage. Instead clients are helped to generate a more general and global determination to learn to be more understanding and mindful of the suffering that they are experiencing.

(2) *Developing a compassionate attitude toward oneself and an understanding that suffering can be eliminated.* Compassion is the wish or desire to liberate someone from pain and suffering, and is an important Buddhist practice. In a psychotherapeutic setting, clients often need to cultivate an understanding and compassionate feelings toward themselves in order to get a sincere desire to work diligently for their own rescue. This seems like a simple task, but for clients, who hold a very critical and judgmental attitude toward themselves, cultivating understanding and compassion toward themselves is quite hard. In order to develop compassion, a person has to learn to be mindful of her/his own suffering. The awareness of suffering can induce compassion and empathy. Clients should be introduced to the Buddhist value that we are all equal, in the sense that we all have the potential to be happy and excel, and ultimately become a Buddha. There is no reason why we should treat ourselves harshly and inflict pain

and suffering on ourselves. Furthermore, practicing mindfulness and learning to become detached from emotions will help clients to see that they are more than just the intense emotions which they are experiencing at this moment. Detachment and awareness nourish people's confidence and self-efficacy to deal with the emotions intelligently.

(3) *Realizing that eliminating suffering is a worthwhile objective that is achievable.* Suffering too is dependently originated and subject to the conditions that facilitate its coming to be. It too has that quality of emptiness. Therefore, suffering can come to be, and more importantly, it certainly can disappear as well. Although, as pointed out in the teaching of the two darts of suffering, there is a type of suffering that we will have to live with, a major portion of our daily suffering can be eliminated. If our practice of mindfulness becomes stronger, even suffering which we did not choose for and with which we need to learn to live might become our teacher and boost our motivation to excel. As it is often said in the Dharma, lotus flowers do not grow in the highland and on solid ground, but only bloom in humble and muddy soil. Today's garbage contains the compost and fertilizer of the flowers of tomorrow.

III. Questioning and investigating the cause of suffering

Once we have developed a desire to do something about our suffering, the next question arising automatically is: "What can I do and how should the problem be tackled?" At this point, fate and destiny may appear in the minds of some clients. Questions and beliefs like, "Is this suffering my fate?" or "I am condemned, there is no way out!" may arise. However, if someone truly understands the Dharma, these questions will not arise in this form as the concepts of fate and destiny erroneously denote that events in life have been predetermined by an "ultimate creator". Because of Dependent Origination the Buddha ruled out the possibility of a god.

As pointed out in the *Discourse of the salt crystal* (Thanissaro, 1998), the course of one's life is *not totally* controlled by past Karma. The Buddha explained that if two people performed a similar unwholesome deed, one may end up in experiencing hell, but the other may barely feel an effect. The sort of person ending up in hellish emotions is

> ...undeveloped in [contemplating] the body, undeveloped in virtue, unde-
> veloped in mind, undeveloped in discernment: restricted, small-hearted,
> dwelling with suffering. (Thanissaro, 1998, AN III 99, p.250)

However, for those people who are

> ...developed in [contemplating] the body, developed in virtue, developed in
> mind, developed in discernment: unrestricted, large-hearted, dwelling with
> the immeasurable. (Thanissaro, 1998, AN III 99, p.250)

the effect of the deed could be very small. The Buddha used the simile of putting salt crystals in a small cup and putting the same amount of salt crystals in the Ganges to illustrate the different between the two people. The water in the cup would be too salty to drink. On the other hand, the salt crystals would not make much difference to the Ganges. It must be pointed out here that the above explanation is not ruling out the relationship between cause and effect. What the Buddha was telling us was that between cause and effect, there is also the influence of the conditions. The formula should be "cause + conditions = effect". An insignificant cause nourished by favourable conditions can bring about a large result. On the other hand, a significant cause with unfavourable conditions may only have a minimal effect. This discourse gives us a clear message that no matter what we did in the past, we can still work diligently to improve the conditions for good seeds to flourish and make the conditions harder for bad seeds to develop.

In the introductory sessions, clients should be educated to see that according to Karma, we are all responsible for our own thoughts and actions. Therefore, we cannot pass on our responsibility of looking after our own suffering because they are of our own making. In the famous *Dhammapada*, the Buddha explained that a person's thoughts and actions are the cause and conditions that will shape one's future.

> Mind is the forerunner to all things. It directs and makes them. If someone speaks and acts with a deluded mind, suffering will follow him, as the wheels follow the footsteps of the animal that draw the cart. Mind is the forerunner to all things. It directs and makes them. If someone speaks and acts with a pure mind, happiness will follow him, as the shadow follows the body.

In these few verses, the Buddha spelled out clearly the relationship between our mind and our well-being. If someone speaks and acts with a deluded mind, a mind that is deluded by greed, hatred, and ignorance, suffering will follow. On the other hand, if someone speaks and acts with a pure mind, happiness will also follow. Our minds and actions will influence and determine our well-being. This is the basic teaching of Karma: volitional action will generate karmic energy that will manifest in the future when the necessary conditions are present to nurture it into fruition.

If we accept that our mind and actions are responsible for our suffering, the next problem is to find out what exactly did we do wrong and what is the root of the problem. In most situations, we were not mindful as to what happened in our mind and what kind of karmic seeds was planted in our consciousness. Therefore, we need to investigate, pay careful attention to, and become aware of what is happening in our minds: the minds' habits, attachments, reactions to stimuli, thoughts and emotions, the relationship between thoughts, emotions, actions, and so on, in order to develop the insight and wisdom that are necessary to transform our suffering.

IV. Observing and learning by paying careful attention to suffering and the causes of suffering

All living beings have some kind of consciousness. What differentiate them are their awareness, insight, and wisdom. These attributes make all the difference in the world. For example, a cat can sit in front of the TV and watch the images of a horror movie on the screen without developing too much feeling. However, if young children watch the same horror movie, they could be horrified because the images on the TV screen would be experienced as real. Alternatively, if a TV technician watches the same horrifying programme, because of insight and awareness about the illusory nature of the images on the screen, he is not deluded by the horrifying images. As a result, he has a lot more freedom to deal with the horror images. He can watch the whole programme, turn off the TV or admire the wonders of the electrons on the screen. What is different among the three examples is not what appears on the TV screen, but the awareness, insight, and wisdom of each of the viewers.

Awareness, insight, and wisdom can be developed from the practice of right mindfulness, which sometimes has been translated as "careful attention". However, the term "mindfulness" is more appropriate to describe the mindset that is needed to develop awareness, insight, and wisdom. For example, the child who watched the horror movie on TV was paying careful attention to the screen, but lacked the reflective and regulatory power that would be present if mindful. This is the prime reason that in Dharma Therapy, the practice of mindfulness is an important key component. Through mindfulness practice, clients are taught how to observe and learn by paying careful attention correctly.[4]

In the *Mahasatipatthana Sutta*, the Buddha's Discourse on the four foundations of mindfulness, the Buddha explained the essentials of practicing mindfulness. The Buddha allegedly said,

> A [Bhikkhu] abides contemplating the body as body, ardent, clearly aware and mindful, having put aside hankering and fretting for the world. (Walshe, 1987, p.335)

In this short sentence, the Buddha illustrated the necessary mindset and conditions to practice mindfulness. To elaborate further on the topic, these five phrases will be discussed in more detail below: "abides contemplating", 'body as body", "ardent", "clearly aware", and "mindful".

"Abides contemplating" implies that the person should be at ease and comfortable with the objects of mindfulness. The mind should not wander, it should be concentrating. Without concentration, it is difficult to develop understanding and insight. "Body as body" means that when contemplating on the body (or feelings or mind), the person should not differentiate and add on any subjective connotation or interpretation to what has been observed and comprehended. Although this may sound easy, in reality, not too many people can do it without the practice of mindfulness. Too often we are absentminded as to what we are doing and what is happening in our minds. Even if we can become aware of a feeling through our senses, we usually mix it together with old habitual thinking patterns, drives, past experiences, etc., and turn the feeling into a muddle phrase of either "I am very happy" or "I am very upset". That is why during the practice of mindfulness, the Buddha emphasized that we should observe without tagging on the notions of "my body", "your body", and the feelings of good, bad, desirous, or repulsive, etc. "Ardent" is the attitude that one should have when practicing mindfulness. That is, one needs to practice mindfulness with diligence and enthusiasm so that the mind does not wander and we are calmly able to actively monitor our thoughts so that unwholesome and distracting thoughts cannot disturb our mindfulness. Very often feelings of joy and ecstasy arise while practising; these are feelings which can help practitioners remain ardent in mindfulness practice. "Clearly aware" is related to the development of knowledge, insight and wisdom. When practicing mindfulness,

---

4. According to Kabat-Zinn (1994, p.4), the definition of mindfulness is "paying attention in a particular way: on purpose, in the present moment, and non-judgementally". To observe the body just as the body, or observe the object just as the object is what Kabat-Zinn likely meant by: "...in the present moment, and nonjudgmentally."

apart from the developing of concentration, there is also the development of awareness and comprehension of the nature and characteristics of the object of mindfulness. This development of awareness and comprehension facilitates the development of knowledge, wisdom, and insight.

In order to comprehend a phenomenon clearly, we need to see the phenomenon and all its aspects clearly, including the relationship between the object and the observer of the object. In the Samyutta Nikaya (connected discourses) there is the following passage on knowledge (Bodhi, 2000, p.1281):

> "These are feelings": thus, [Bhikkhus], in regard to things unheard before, there arose in me vision, knowledge, wisdom, true knowledge, and light.
>
> "This is the origin of feeling": thus, [Bhikkhus], in regard to things unheard before, there arose in me vision... and light.
>
> "This the way leading to the origination of feeling": thus, [Bhikkhus], in regard to things unheard before, there 'arose in me vision... and light.
>
> "This is the cessation of feeling": thus, [Bhikkhus], in regard to things unheard before, there arose in me vision... and light.
>
> "This the way leading to the cessation of feeling": thus, [Bhikkhus], in regard to things unheard before, there 'arose in me vision... and light."
>
> "This is the gratification in feeling" ... "This is the danger in feeling" ... "This is the escape from feeling": thus, [Bhikkhus], in regard to things unheard before, there arose in me vision... and light.

From this passage, we can see that when being mindful of feelings, the Buddha saw feelings as feelings and he also saw the different aspects of feelings: their origins, the way leading to the origination of feelings, their cessation, the way leading to the cessation of feelings, and the gratification, danger, and the escape from feelings. Without understanding these characteristics of feeling, we are slaves to experienced feelings. However, when we are aware of these characteristics of feelings, we are in a much better position to handle them. "Being mindful", apart from all the qualities that have been discussed above, or mindfulness, sati in Pali, literally means "remembering". When something passes through our consciousness, very often we let it slip through our mind without making an impression. However, when we are mindful of something, what passes through our consciousness makes an impact and gets clearly registered. This quality of mindfulness enables the mind to learn and to remember from the experiences of our awareness, and, as a result, enables us to differentiate and discern what is truly beneficial and skilful and what is ultimately harmful and unskilful.

V. Developing insight and wisdom on suffering and the causes of suffering

One first learns of an object through awareness and from awareness feelings and concepts develop. With feelings and concepts working together, supporting each other, numerous other subjective thoughts and feelings arise. Because of the influences of these subjective thoughts and feelings, one loses the ability to comprehend an object objectively. If the person holds on to these feelings and thoughts as real, and lives in a world of her/his own creation, and then generates more thoughts and feelings from this illusory world, s/he will certainly suffer when the reality of the real world catches up with the person. If the wake-up call from suffering cannot wake one up, and the person continues to dwell in the world of her/his own creation, then the stress from suffering and the conflict between the two worlds will soon lead to psychological problems.

Thus, the objective of Dharma Therapy is to help clients develop knowledge, insight and wisdom, each of which will enhance their ability to accept and face up to reality, sort out complications, deal with difficult situations in life and increase their ability to weather stress. In the above quotation from the Samyutta Nikaya on knowledge, we know that when the Buddha was contemplating on feelings and the different aspects of feelings, in every instance, he developed vision, knowledge, wisdom, true knowledge, and "light". These five qualities of perception and insight, discussed in more detail below, are the foundations of mental health.

Vision

Vision is the function of being able to be aware of and recognize an object. It also has the meaning of illuminating, of becoming aware of, and gaining recognition of objects that heretofore were out of sight. Being an ordinary person, we are accustomed to focusing our attention onto objects in the outside world. That is why we are easily influenced and swayed by what we see, hear, smell, touch, etc. However, the Buddha taught us that, if we are to develop true knowledge, insight, and wisdom, we must be mindful of objects closer to home. In the *Satipathanna Sutta*, the Buddha pinpointed four foundations or objects of mindfulness that we need to focus on and to be aware of in order to overcome sorrow and suffering; these are: the body and its feelings, and the mind and its thoughts.

In Dharma Therapy, clients should always be taught to start their mindfulness practice on the body because when we focus our attention on the body, either by being mindful of our breathing or practicing walking meditation, we ground our focus and awareness onto something solid and tangible. This is especially important and beneficial for clients who have been living in their own illusory world for too long. Furthermore, as it has been pointed out during the discussion of the theoretic foundation of Dharma Therapy, body-mind, and consciousness come to be in Dependent Origination. Thus, when stress and suffering exist in the mind and in consciousness, they will somehow be reflected and experienced as tension and stiffness in the body. When we get in touch with the body through mindfulness, we therefore also influence the psychological side of the person. If we can relax the tension and stiffness of the body by being mindful of it, mental stress and suffering will also decrease. Another advantage of beginning our practice of mindfulness on the body is that the body is an easier and more stable object to focus on than feelings and consciousness. By practicing mindfulness on the body, feelings and thoughts automatically become more apparent as they distract us from our practice of mindfulness on the body. When they become apparent, we can then learn to be mindful of them in the more grounded, safe setting of our mindfulness practice.

Knowledge

With the awareness and recognition gained from balanced vision, forms and concepts will manifest in the mind. With forms and concepts, words and phrases can be coined and assigned.

With all these tools, the mind will have what it needs to think, differentiate, reflect and learn. What has been learned will become knowledge. That is why we can say that the information gathered from vision is the foundation of knowledge. However, if delusion and subjectivity have distorted the process of vision, the subsequent knowledge gained will also be in error. This is why the Buddha emphasized that when practicing mindfulness on the body, we should observe the body as just body, feelings as just feelings, etc, as explained above.

To help clients to accumulate knowledge and develop insight and wisdom to overcome psychological problems, clients should be taught to be mindful of their feelings and emotions from two different angles: (1) the relationship between one's own mental attitude (i.e., greed, hatred, and delusion), emotions (the second dart) and the events that have happened (the first dart) and (2) the emptiness and illusory nature of feelings and emotions (the second dart). Clients need to be guided to be aware of the interdependent nature of the emotions and the mental attitude that are being held in regard to the events that took place. With such and such an attitude, such and such emotions will arise automatically as hypothesized by Dependent Origination. Further, and as explained in the theoretical foundation section, even pain and suffering come to be from the coming together of causes and conditions. When the causes and conditions change, like all phenomena in the world, pain and suffering will also wither away. There is always hope for change and a better tomorrow. Thus, clients are advised to concentrate on changing and improving the causes and conditions that are affecting them here and now.

Wisdom

Wisdom is the ability to differentiate, sort out confusion, and make decisions. Generally speaking, in Buddhist teachings, there are three types of wisdom: wisdom from education, wisdom from reflecting, and wisdom from practicing. "Wisdom from education" is the wisdom that we gain from learning from the wisdom and experience of others through conversation, books and other communication media. In a way, it is a second hand learning experience, but it is still necessary because it shortens the learning process tremendously. The guidance and instruction that the therapist gives to the clients is a form of wisdom from education for the clients.

"Wisdom from reflection": is the wisdom that arises from reflecting on the wisdom and knowledge acquired from education and/or awareness and recognition. For example, from seeing and reflecting on the relationship between the interdependent nature of emotions and mental attitude, clients can develop new insight and choose to change attitudes towards past events.

"Wisdom from practice": is the wisdom gained from firsthand experience, such as observing the object directly. This firsthand experience and/or observation of the object should be guided by the wisdom acquired from the previous two types of wisdom, but without the use of diction and cognitive reasoning. Like playing tennis, as long as the player keeps his eyes on the ball, without thinking and reasoning, he can still hit the ball skilfully and appropriately. The reason that he can do so is because of the interaction between what he has learned and the additional information he is gathering while paying attention to the ball. Similarly, once clients have gained enough knowledge and wisdom on the illusory nature of feelings and thoughts, they can be aware of the arising and fading away of their feelings and thoughts without developing any attachment to them.

True knowledge

As above, the functioning of vision, knowledge and wisdom rely on the information acquired during awareness and recognition. True knowledge is illuminating and leads to developing insight from information gathered during the process of vision, knowledge and wisdom. For example, when we are being mindful of the arising and fading away of feelings, we see that when there is a pleasant sensation, there arises a happy feeling and when there is an unpleasant sensation, there arises an unhappy feeling. If the pleasant sensation fades away, the happy feeling also fades away; and when the unpleasant sensation fades away, the unhappy feeling also fades away. From the observation of the interdependent relationship between sensations and feelings, we develop the insight and knowledge: "When there is this, that comes to be; when this fades away, that also fades away." This knowledge of Dependent Origination comes from the insight gained from the awareness and recognition of the arising and fading away of sensations and feelings. Although all feelings, emotions and sensations, are impermanent and empty in nature, the applicability of Dependent Origination regardless of time and space needs to be experienced. Hence, "true knowledge" arises when we can comprehend and develop insight from being mindful of the working of phenomena in our worlds of experience.

When we can comprehend and have insight into the working and functioning of things and events in our experiential worlds, our ability to manage and deal with them will be greatly increased. For this reason, when clients comprehend and develop insight on the working and functioning of feelings and emotions, their ability to deal with and manage them can be greatly improved.

Light

Light is illuminating and a function of wisdom. When there is light, we can see the rocks and puddles on the ground. If we can see the rocks and puddles, the mind does not need to deliberately make an effort to avoid them and we can still walk safely. Similarly this applies for the "light of wisdom". When we can truly comprehend and have insight into the working of our feelings and emotions, we will automatically sail through all the rocks and puddles of greed, hatred, and ignorance without any deliberate effort. It should be emphasized here that the purpose of being mindful of feelings and emotions is not to ignore or eliminate them, but to understand and comprehend them better. With this understanding and comprehension, we can handle them better, and eventually transform the unwholesome emotions (i.e., fear, hatred, greed, etc.) into wholesome affect like compassion, empathy, and love. Without feelings and emotions, it would be difficult to make decisions and find meaning in life. This is why Dharma Therapy emphasizes that the root and foundation of the Dharma are both built on the ground of compassion, not on a mind of blank nothingness.

VI. Taking the necessary steps to end suffering with insight and wisdom,

We put this newfound insight and wisdom, acquired from being mindful, into action and solidify the learning. For example, from understanding the relationship between mental attitude, emotions, and the events, it is necessary to transform those mental attitudes that bring about the unwholesome emotions. This transformation may come automatically, as explained, if there is the development of the light emanating from wisdom. When this happens, behavioural changes in the client usually come automatically as a result of the change in attitude. However, sometimes the depth of awareness may not be enough to bring about the development of the light of wisdom. In that case deliberate behavioural and environmental changes may be needed to solidify the transformation. At this point, the therapist needs to work with the client in order to come up with the necessary changes.

Conclusion

Although in recent years research in psychological science has made considerable progress, with the ever-increasing number of mental health related problems, new angles and perspectives as to how we can manage psychological issues will continue to develop. This chapter is an attempt to present the Buddhist way of dealing with suffering adjusted to a psychotherapeutic environment. The Buddhist way of dealing with suffering is based on the principle that our minds and actions dictate our well-being. Deluded minds and dysfunctional behaviours fuelled by ignorance are considered to be the major cause of pain and suffering. Dharma Therapy is based on helping the client to develop comprehension, insight, and wisdom regarding the causes and conditions that lead to the arising of suffering. When there is insight and wisdom, there is no ignorance. When there is no more ignorance, the cause of suffering will cease to be. The application of mindfulness is the tool that can break the tyranny of ignorance. By re-integrating the practice of mindfulness into the theoretical foundation from where it was derived, Dharma Therapy can be a promising intervention for clients, who are suitable for and comfortable with this quite demanding approach to therapy. Although, the practice of mindfulness and the process of developing insight and wisdom were originally prescribed by the Buddha to serious practitioners who strove for the ultimate liberation from life and death, laymen who practice accordingly in order to develop insight and wisdom to handle day-to-day psychological problems can also derive considerable benefits. By being aware of feelings and emotions, and/or the relationship between mental attitude, emotions and the events that occur, even if approached retrospectively, clients will be able to identify them and to see the dynamic relationships between them. From this comprehension, the mind will be able to manage feelings and emotions more skilfully and then gradually reach a higher level of peacefulness and clarity, and improve the clients' overall mental health.

In this chapter, I have presented the theoretical foundation of Dharma Therapy and drawn up a framework of how to apply the theory in a clinical environment. Although the Dharma was taught by the Buddha and practiced by many accomplished masters for centuries, we still need to put the therapy into clinical trials and document our findings to substantiate its effectiveness. Finally, this chapter was an attempt to repackage the Dharma so that it is readily accessible for clinicians and can be used as a psychotherapeutic intervention for those who are in need.

Part VII

Toward Karma Transformation By Selfless Dialogue

In Chapters 20 and 21 Kwee and Kwee-Taams present a coaching system to transform Karma, meaningful/intentional action, which is a collaborative practice requiring the meaningful interaction of teacher/trainer/clinician and student/trainee/client. The coach skilfully supports, encourages, and nurtures the apprentice's wholesome affective/relational performances. Both parties are engaged in a "transformative dialogue", a unique facilitating conversational encounter wherein each tries to locate oneself within the other thus finding inflection points effecting positional shifts going forward and opening up new territories. This social constructionist dialogue is a venture whose effective transformational outcome depends on the mutual affirmation of evolving realities, thus creating new wholesome narratives of reality. To engage in such a dialogue requires communication skills of listening to the implication of what is said (content) and to how it is said (the relational meaning).

Postmodern social constructionist psychology, collaborative practice, and transformational dialogue do not rule out empirical research. There is, however, a major refiguring of the place of quantitative research and its potentials. Modernist attempts to study phenomena of the self-contained mind (such as self, emotion, affect, cognition, perception, motivation, beliefs, or attitudes) deal with ephemeral social constructions. If history is our guide, the ideal of cumulative knowledge is a fiction (Gergen, 1996). Nonetheless, traditional empirical study does have actuarial value by virtue of its power to predict various recurring behavioural patterns emerging out of the wellspring of human conduct, among others: the reliable prediction of various social indicators (e.g., accidents) and health indicators (e.g., obesity). Its potential includes outcome studies of cognitive-behavioural techniques providing pragmatic evidence as a "never settled" basis to idiosyncratic practice. Empirical evidence of efficacy is the prevailing benchmark in science-oriented cultures and generally preferred above irrational practices based on magic or the supernatural. The use of evidence-based procedures does not imply that the person is a robot; psychotechnology only takes hold in a harmonious relational match.

Austin's Chapter 22 adds lustre to this anthology by dealing with neurological explanations of meditation. His chapter completes the social-conctructivist-clinical-neuro-Buddhist-Psychology theme of this book. While endorsing the non-esotericism of the "humane" being, the author presents an intriguing, inspiring, and instructional text of insight-wisdom that fits in the concept of this volume. Awareness and awakening to selflessness by promoting internal atonement involve neural connections, which are interesting to know about as we are after all Body/Speech/Mind. The author's "neuro-Zen" food for thought is made edible for the reader by figures and a glossary of technical terms. Brain imaging shows how brain portions become activated in reference to the self and how grey matter attends preferentially to self-centred interests in a quite different way from how it attends to other things in the outside world. The reader decides for her/himself whether this "brain-based stream of consciousness trip" on meditating selflessly helps to drop off personal thoughts of self along with the barriers separating the self from the environment in Dependent Origination. It requires effort to tune into a flow and have a stilled and blank mind focus on the act of reading as an attending effort to empty the mind by the mind.

•

Chapter 20

The Collaborative Practice Of Karma Transformation: Cyclical Emotional Episodes And Their Sequential Rebirths

Maurits G.T. Kwee & Marja K. Kwee-Taams

Introduction

Although the Dharma has been qualified as a psychology for more than a century, it is only since the pioneering work in the 1970s and 1980s of Mikulas (1978), De Silva (1984), and Kwee (1990) that specific connections between the Buddhist teachings and Cognitive-Behaviour Therapy (CBT) were made explicit. Indeed, there are significant commonalities linking the Dharma with the evidence-based practices of Behaviour Therapy and Cognitive Therapy, commonalities which are grounded in the experimental paradigm of an *S-O-R* psychology and in the social cognitive interpretation of learning through classical (Pavlov), operant (Skinner), and vicarious conditioning principles (Bandura, 2001). *Viewed from a social constructionist perspective, this positivist underpinning is not about accuracy or substance but about the potential of opening up a reservoir of action; that is, cognitive behavioural concepts are viewed as provisional narratives and metaphors on a microscopic level of abstraction to guide action of transforming human conduct.*

To luxuriate in the mechanical metaphor of the *Stimulus-Organism-Response* model, a *Stimulus* impinges on the *Organism* that subsequently chooses to emit a *Response*. This mediational model emerged from the behaviourist *S-R* model which conveniently discarded the O-part as unsuitable for research because it could not be observed directly. However, since the cognitive revolution (Newell & Simon, 1956), the study of processes contained in the black box has been reinstated along with the method of systematic introspection which measures objectively what is internally perceived subjectively. For example, Wundt's (1874) studies on "just noticeable differences" in sensory input revealed that a candle light can just be seen in a clear dark night on a distance of 30m or that sweetness can just be tasted if one teaspoon of sugar is mixed with two gallons of water. This studious introspection bears some resemblance to awareness meditation as a tool to view inside the mind and to scrutinize the objects of the mind, a procedure disseminated by the Buddha some 2600 years ago. The seeds of a Buddhist Psychology can be traced in the Buddha's discourses.

The concatenating confluence of CBT and Buddhist Psychology comes dramatically to the fore in the "street sequence" (*vithi*) described in the *Abhidhamma* (the third of three Theravada canonical works containing an abstraction of the *Nikayas*, the discourses of the Buddha). The following edited illustration, derived from the *Jataka* stories, might be helpful to clarify this point:

Once, in a forest, a hare heard a hullabaloo. Believing it to herald the end of the world, he began to run. Thinking the same, others joined him: the deer also thought so and joined the flight and one species after the other started running until all animals were in a frantic sprint that would eventually have lead to their demise. When the Buddha saw them in panic, he asked them: "why?" "Because the world ends", they said. The Buddha: "That can't be true... let's find out why you think so." Questioning them in succession, he finally arrived at the hare that started the run: "where and what were you doing when you thought 'it's the end of the world'?" The hare: "I was sleeping under a mango tree"... the Buddha: "you probably heard a mango fall... startling you (the impinging *Stimulus*), you thought it's the end of the world (the *Organism*'s invalid/irrational belief), you took fright (the emotional *Response*) and ran (the behavioural *Response*)... let's go back to that tree... to falsify"... Thus, the Buddha saved the animal kingdom.

As can be interpreted from this vignette, the Buddhist model of the mind is similar to the CBT model of the psyche. The *Abhidhamma* describes the mind as a flow of discrete mind-moments (*cittas*) each one of which is said to last for "1/64th of a finger snap"; in other words, the mind is momentary and is changing in an incredible pace. Nevertheless comparable to the psyche in an *S-O-R* model a certain consistency and steadiness can be distinguished in a mind sequence or emotional episode (cf. *Honeyball Sutta*). Apparently, as demonstrated by Nobel laureate Ruhterford in 1910, the silent reality of atoms and cells is that all of them are 99% empty space. Thirty billion nerve-cells and one million billion neuronal connections flicker in our brain when we think. According to Greer of the National Science Foundation < www.hvacprofitboosters.com > we have for about 1000 thoughts per hour, which is about 16000 thoughts a day or perhaps even more; 85% of these thoughts are negative and ripe for semantic correction.

A discernable episode starts by (1) *bodily contact* (*rupa-sparsa*) with a particular *Stimulus* attended to and which is the mere sensory perception of an object arising in awareness (sight, sound, smell, taste, touch, and "*dharmas*", mind objects). Contact is the "pure" sensory perception one is aware of which includes the external perceptions of the five known sense organs plus the brain's internal perceptions, i.e. the images, conceptions, memories, and dreams of the "mind's eye", which appear in consciousness and are described in the first chapter as a social constructional metaphor. Immediately ensuing contact, (2) *feeling* (*vedana*) enters the field of attention which hedonically checks the contact as being relatively pleasant, painful, or neutral evoking a consequential direction. Next to feeling, (3) *conceiving* (*samjna*) occurs in the *Organism*, an ongoing interpretation of the contact and feeling experience against the backdrop of a vast pool of stored data in memory. Does it fit into the network of available information? Is it recognizable? How does it connect to previous experiences? Can it be labelled? Thus, the experience is classified-categorized, stored in memory, and becomes the next building block to an intelligible world. After conceiving, (4) *conation* (*samskara*) surfaces as a *Response* to the *Stimulus'* contact and feeling, to the *Organism's* conceiving to play a part as will, affect, or emotion which motivates one to approach or avoid the object, or to be indifferent. One is not always aware of volition which can be instinctive, intuitive, and subconscious or unconscious but is always hungry and on the lookout for satisfaction. As the process unfolds, (5) *awareness (vijnana)*, reflection and mind-making of the experience takes place (*manisakara*), which is an active attentive evaluating of the entire episode whereby not only attention/concentration but also discriminative awareness play the role of figuring out whether long-term goals – to end emotional suffering (Duhkha) – will be attained. This is a skilful/insightful reflective scrutinizing to be done in a sane, sound, and sensible way with reason and savvy (*yoniso-manisakara*), thus developing wisdom (*panna*) and wholesomeness (*kusala*).

In more detail the *Abhidhamma* describes the sequence following 17 steps of infinitesimal mind-moments (*cittas*) as follows:

> There is a *Stimulus* (e.g. a mango falling): 1 baseline consciousness (e.g. deep sleep) ~ 2 vibrating~input (a sound) ~ 3 interruption (waking up) ~ 4 adverting (on the Sense doors) ~ 5 perception (e.g. eye consciousness) ~ 6 receiving awareness/noting-attending ~ 7 investigating awareness to fit into stored memories ~ 8 determining awareness of the interpreting *Organism* ~ steps 9~10~11~12~13~14~15, which are moments of post-perceptual impulse awareness, a reflecting on feeling/thought processes, previous karmic (un)wholesome experiences, and wilful choice to intentionally act or not act, resulting in an affective/behavioural-interactional output or *Response* ~ 16~17, and which is finally, for the unawakened, followed by a subliminal storage and retention of an I-me-mine/self experience of identity leading to the illusion of separateness from others and a rebirth of craving.[1]

This epistemological sequence remarkably corresponds with the ladder of abstraction that begins with the lower levels of perception and description, and shifts to the higher levels of interpretation and evaluation (Korzybski, 1933), and which likewise contemplates the rationality of one's reflections. Moreover, its emphasis conforms to a social constructionist view that we are all inseparably interconnected or in Gergenian terms: the self is the common intersection of multiple relationships. This view is appealing from a Buddhist Psychology perspective as this endorses Dependent Origination (*pratityasamutpada*), the Buddha's causality hypothesis. Ironically, it replicates Skinner's black-box, although on very different grounds and with quite different implications. A social constructivist "new" Buddhist Psychology proposes a relational conception of mental life. Any psychological interior consists of theoretical presumptions one brings to bear. Not embedded in relationships all being would perish.

---

1. Nota Bene: 6~7~8 refer to apperception that is post-perceptual and pre-conceptual; 9-17 refer to the awareness that may eradicate unwholesome *cittas* to attain Nirvana – the extinction of emotional arousal. Interestingly, the term extinction is used in the same way in both CBT and the Dharma.

The karmic sequence of an emotional episode

The structures of the CBT emotional episode and the street sequence of mind-moments show inevitable correspondence. The Buddhist sequence also emphasizes cognition and behaviour by highlighting intentional motivation and behavioural action, two essential components in the definition of Karma as (meaningful) intentional (inter)action. The CBT sequential centrepiece is the *S-O-R* paradigm, used in Beck's Cognitive Therapy, and is here translated into the ABC format of Ellis' REBT and into Lazarus' BASIC-I.D. modalities of multimodal assessment. REBT's A stands for the Activating event (or *Stimulus*), which can be external or internal, the B stands for Beliefs (*Organism*), which can be irrational or rational, and the C stands for Consequence (*Response*), which can be emotional and behavioural. The BASIC-I.D. is an acronym for the modalities of Behaviour (action, doing), Affect (emotion, feeling), Sensation (perception, feeling), Imagery (visualization, thinking), Cognition (conception, thinking), Interpersonal relations (interaction, doing), and neurogenetic Drives, biological motivators like the need for water, food, sex, clothing, shelter, and medication, the origin of basic intentions. Interestingly, a survey of 800 counselling and clinical psychologists, members of the American Psychology Association (Smith, 1982) – a more recent one is not available – ranked Ellis, Lazarus, and Beck respectively as the second, fifth and seventh most influential therapists at the time the survey was taken.

Interestingly, the concept of intentional activity was recently discovered in the literature of Positive Psychology and happiness (Lyubomirsky, 2008), without being aware of the Buddhist definition of Karma. In the Buddhist lore happiness is a relevant aim considered to be a fluid experience amidst adversities and an epiphenomenon in the pursuit of meaning while practicing the Dharma. Research (e.g., Lyubomirsky, Sheldon, & Schkade, 2005) suggests that sustainable happiness is determined by three factors: a genetic set-point (50%), circumstantial factors (10%), and intentional activity (40%), a window of opportunity to be happy which from a social constructionist's view is necessarily within relationship. Human beings are equipped by an idiosyncratic genetic set-point for happiness comparable with a set-point for weight or length which is hardly modifiable. People with high set-points will find it easier to be happy, while people with low set-points will have to work harder to achieve and maintain happiness under similar conditions. Long term overall circumstances include correlational "demographics" which happen to us like age, health, education, money, country, religion, or marital status. While these factors matter, they only determine a small percentage to happiness. Due to human hedonic adaptation, it is a misguided hope that they will impact long-lasting happiness. Rapidly accustomed to sensory or physiologic changes, they deliver short-lived boosts of happiness. Happy people do not just sit around being happy. They make things happen and this activity spins off a by-product which is happiness over and above the genetic set range and life circumstances.

Table 1. The CBT and Buddhist Centrepieces of an Emotional Episode (S-O-R/ABC /BASIC-I.D.) in Parallel with the Buddha's Karma Sequence

CBT/REBT Model (S-O-R/ABC)	BASIC-I.D. Multimodal & *Trimodal* Assessment	The Buddha's Karma Sequence
Stimulus (Activating event) Discriminative Generalized	Sensation (*feeling*)	Awareness via 6 Senses, felt: + / 0 / - (*vedana*/perception)
Organism Cognitive (Beliefs) Somatic	Imagery (*thinking*) Cognition (*thinking*)	Ignorance: Illusion (self) / Delusion (god) (*samjna*: conception/intention)
Response (Consequences) Emotional Behavioural	Affect (*feeling*) Behaviour (*doing*)	Craving: Greed-Grasping, Hate-Clinging (*samskara*: conation/motivation/action)
Contingency Reinforcement Punishment	Interactions (*doing*) Drives/Biology	Body/Speech/Mind: to be mindfully aware (*vijnana*/consciousness)

How the *S-O-R*/ABC and BASIC-I.D. models and the Buddha's Karma sequence parallel each other, is depicted in Table 1. The Karma sequence starts with the felt sensory perception through one of the six sense doors, immediately registered as relatively positive, neutral, or negative. These qualifications are on the input level of Sensory feeling and the Activating event sparked by the *Stimulus* the quality of which can be discriminatively new or habitually generalized. On the subsequent level, processing in ignorance will likely result in the illusion of self, the delusion of god(s), as well as in unwholesome intentions, thoughts-Cognitions/Images, irrational beliefs within the *Organism*. These intentions guide motivation by intensifying affect and emotions into detrimental behaviour, *Responses* like greed-grasping and hatred-clinging. All of this takes place in awareness emanating from Body/Speech/Mind in an interpersonal context and karmic activity might increase or decrease depending on contingent and other forms of conditioned learning, for instance by reinforcement. Sequential emotional episodes are part of a chain preceded and followed by other episodes and may form cycles that are either vicious or virtual.

Various passages in the Buddhist scriptures corroborate this analysis. One of the appropriate quotes transparently linking the Karma sequence and CBT stems from the *Dhammapada* (the Buddha's sayings in 423 verses), a booklet belonging to the gems of the world literature. There, we read (in Byrom's [2001] translation) the opening verses:

> We are what we *think*. All that we are arises with our *thoughts*. With our *thoughts* we make the world. *Speak* or *act* with an impure mind, and trouble will follow you as the wheel follows the ox that draws the cart. We are what we *think*. All that we are, arises with our *thoughts*. With our *thoughts* we make the world. *Speak* or *act* with a pure mind, and happiness will follow you as your shadow, unshakable... "Look how he abused me and hurt me, how he threw me down and robbed me." Live with such *thoughts* and you live in *hate*. "Look how he abused me and hurt me, how he threw me

down and robbed me." Abandon such *thoughts* and live in *love*. In this world *hate* never yet dispelled *hate*, only *love* dispels *hate*. This is the law, ancient and inexhaustible... However many holy words you read, however many you *speak*, what good will they do you, if you do not *act* upon them?

As the italicized words indicate, the Buddha subtly unveiled the major modalities of thinking, doing, and feeling. Another illustration of the Buddha's alleged cognitive-behavioural stance was found in the following (also from the *Dhammapada*):

> By oneself [unwholesomeness] is done, by oneself one suffers, by oneself evil is left undone, by oneself one is purified, purity and impurity depend on oneself, no one can purify another (Humphreys, 1987, p.93).

A cognitive behavioural position is not restricted to analysing the psychological problem but is also and foremost concerned about modifying feeling-action-thought by cognitive insights and performance-based interventions. An example how the Buddha proficiently applied a cognitive behavioural intervention by assigning homework is in the following vignette (*Dhammapada* 287):

> Kisa Gotami mourned the death of her two years son bitten by a snake. Not accepting the fact, she was in a prolonged grief. Desperately she went to the Buddha. "How can my son be cured?" The Buddha replied: "There is only one way to help you and your child. Look for a black mustard seed that must come from a house where no one ever died and which should be given to you by someone who has no deceased relatives." Kisa Gotami left with her dead boy. Seeking from one house to the next, she could nowhere find such seed. Finally, she realised what the assignment was about, buried her son, and was cured.

Emotional disturbance lies at the heart of the karmic sequence of morbid emotional episodes and are based on the root poisons of relational harmony: greed and hatred. Whereas greed encompasses grief-sadness (of parting) and panic-fear (losing somebody), hatred encompasses anger (blaming others) and depression (blaming self).

The Buddha: the first psychologist ever?

Psychology as a science emerged out of religion and philosophy and was boosted by Descartes' artificial dualistic split of mind-body in the 17th century. Although the word psychology was first used by Goclenius in 1590, the science formally started in 1879 when Wundt opened the first psychological laboratory in Leipzig, Germany. There is an interesting analogy with the present status of the Dharma. Broadly, the Dharma is regarded as a religion and a metaphysical or ethical philosophy, and at best as a philosophical psychology. Like in the days prior to Wundt's lab, many psychologists are nowadays transforming the Dharma into a contemporary psychology. This transformation is made possible by *Upayakaushalya*, the Buddhist skilful means that allow the Dharma to adjust itself to changing mentalities across times and cultures.

The subject of self is at the heart of psychology and the Buddha dealt with self or rather not-self at length. Unlike the proliferation of self psychologies in the West, the Buddha's psychology is the only not-self psychology to date which is a view that starkly resembles a social constructivist relational view of self. Not-self could well form the foundation for a unified science of psychology, similar to what has been established in the exact sciences, where one finds only one science of physics, of chemistry, and of biology. Whether not-self will turn out to be *the* unifier in psychology remains to be seen. In his synoptic teaching on the "Three Empirical Marks of Existence", the Buddha observed that there is Duhkha, trouble that emanates from the world's impermanence and imperfection, particularly when craving, grasping, and clinging give rise to the illusion of a permanent existence of I-me-mine/self or soul and to the delusional wishful thought of a perfect god. His advice is to let go erroneous views and to dis-identify from false identifications to a non-existing self, like e.g. to a name. One would need to see through the emptiness of a provisional self on an I.D.-card to get the awakening aha experience of ultimate not-self and Relational Interbeing. To maintain a provisional self – also called an empirical, conventional, or householder's self – is functional for daily life. The Buddha dismissed the existence of an ultimate self, because:

(1) I-me-mine/self cannot – in an impermanent world – ever be the exact same in the next moment of the universe's flux

(2) I-me-mine/self cannot be something else but an reified, abstract, and airy concept that does not tangibly exists, and

(3) I-me-mine/self can be studied *as if* it is an atomistic entity, but it cannot exist in solipsism: to act means to *inter*act.

Awakening to not-self does not mean becoming an aimless, vegetating organism, a selfless being without any desires whatsoever. It means to live a life full of affect – Kazantzakis' "full catastrophe of living" – while simultaneously being deeply aware that the non-enduring self of daily life is ultimately empty. Therapists are obliged not to confuse clients with distorted self-images or self-concepts by immediately zeroing in on not-self, nor should they awaken clients to emptiness against their will. By no means to be sneezed at is some comfort as in the following *Jataka* story:

Once, the Buddha spent a rainy night in a tavern. The inn-keeper was an opponent of the Dhamma. To test the Buddha he gave him a room with a leaking roof and when the Buddha asked for another room, the keeper sarcastically asked: "How can a little bit of water disturb someone who has conquered all suffering?" The Buddha smiled and countered: "Indeed, a little water means nothing for someone who has conquered suffering, but if I want to sleep I don't want to swim."

Another Buddhist road to arrive at self's emptiness is Nagarjuna's (2nd century) Sunyata, the "emptiness of all that is not enduring" which is everything conceivable.

In CBT Ellis (1976) abolishes most of the self. Clients suffering from self-blaming and self-damning propensities communicate global self-ratings characterized by overgeneralized self-appraisals. They are taught to deflate the ego and spin-off healthy self-talk that sounds as follows (Lazarus, 1997, p.69):

> Instead of viewing myself as possessing a unitary "self" that amounts to my *total being*, it is important to tune into a plurality of "selves" across numerous situations. Thus, "I am useless!" is a self-statement that implies zero value in all areas of life - useless as a sibling, a son or daughter, spouse, parent, friend, acquaintance, colleague, movie-goer, tennis-player, oyster-eater, TV-viewer, music-lover, plus innumerable other roles that constitute my "self"...

In place of the widespread proclivity to place one's entire being on the line, this simple exercise can often counterbalance such an unfortunate tendency. A client who had extreme anticipatory anxiety over a speech he was to deliver was addressed as follows:

> ...Instead of saying "I am giving a speech", think of your "self" not as one big "I" but as a whole complex of "iiiiiiiiiii's". Each little "i" corresponds to some facet of your being. So instead of saying "I am giving a speech", consider the fact that you are not on trial. It's not the total you. Think instead: "i am giving a speech".

Ego-deflating tactics like these are only one little step away from penetrating the empty self. However, the two psychologies systematically pursue complementary but different goals. While aiming at removing "neurotic" suffering by emotional disturbance, CBT remains within the framework of the provisional self. Buddhist Psychology aims at liberation from "existential" suffering in a process that moves beyond the circumference of provisional self into the realm of the empty not-self.

Another pointer indicating that the Buddha was a practitioner of psychology and that his Dharma can be interpreted as a transformational healing approach through dialogue, is the illness metaphor implied in the *4-Ennobling Realities*: (1) there is existential suffering due to death, birth, illness, and aging (to be understood: assessment), (2) this is due to ignorance on Dependent Origination of Relational Interbeing (to be abandoned: cause), (3) there is a way out by harmonizing relationships (to be realized: prognosis), and (4) this way comprises the *8-Fold Balanced Practice* of collaborative practice (to be cultivated: therapy), i.e.: balanced view-understanding, intention-thought, speech-communication, action-behaviour, living-habitude, effort-commitment, attention-concentration, and awareness-introspection. As the illness to be cured is a psychological *dis*-ease and the cure is not the prescription of medication but the instruction of meditation next to the assignments to meaningfully think/intend and act/behave differently (Kwee & Holdstock, 1996), it is safe to bet that the Buddha's acumen to teach how to overcome the *3-Poisons* of greed, hatred, and ignorance – is that of a clinician who through conversation adjusts his approach to the unique individual as a psycho-physiological entity. His wholistic view of Body/Speech/Mind is like a 21st century mental health professional endorsing the World Health Organization's view of the human being as a Bio-Psycho-Social system (Engel, 1977). The Buddhist literature is clear about his prime interest to cease Duhkha by the art of interpersonal skilful responses to the human predicament and Karma, a down-to-earth craftsman's approach, comparable to that of a horse or elephant trainer. He was focussed on sensing-feeling-thinking-doing-relating and what is effective to alleviate karmic anguish, to stop "faring ill", and to boost contentment by "faring well" by upholding wholesome intention and action.

Therefore, one might ask whether the Buddha was perhaps a psychologist *avant la lettre*? The *Sallatha Sutta* points at the Buddha's psychological insight on the effect of mental training by meditation. If hit by an arrow, the untrained mind touched by bodily pain grieves and laments, while the skilled meditator will not be distraught. The untrained mind experiences two kinds of pain: a bodily pain and a mental pain. He feels pains as if hit by two arrows, but the meditator, if touched by a bodily pain, grieves and laments not. He feels only bodily pain, not mental pain, as if hit by just one, not by a second arrow. In another narrative (*Cula-Malunkyovada Sutta*) on a man shot by a poison arrow (of greed, hate, and ignorance), it is made quite clear that the Dharma is an action oriented psychology, not a navel-staring philosophy. The man would die if, instead of treating him immediately, one first quizzes the archer's name, caste, appearance, and home, the arrow's type, and the bow and bowstring that were used.

Karma and the "Skandhas"

Although the term Karma has been adopted in vernacular English and in many other languages without being translated, this appropriation did not help to fully grasp its Buddhist psychological meaning. In Brahmanism the term Karma carries a religious meaning where it is believed to be a spiritual law of retributive justice that works like a bank account stretching across reincarnated lifetimes wherein meritorious deeds are rewarded, unmeritorious deeds punished. Also allocating Karma a central place, the Buddha attributed a secular/non-metaphysical meaning to the concept as an emotional episode of meaningful intentional action and event-specific related consequences adhering to Dependent Origination applied on feeling-action-thought and Relational Interbeing. The most radical aspect of the Buddha's causality view lies in his "this/that conditionality": (1) when this is, that is; (2) from the arising of this comes the arising of that; (3) when this isn't, that isn't; and (4) from the cessation of this comes the cessation of that. This causality comprises interplay of a linear principle and a synchronic principle which combined form a non-linear pattern. The linear principle takes 2 and 4 and the non-linear is 1 and 3. When the two principles combine, a given event is influenced by (relational) input from the past and (relational) input from the present. Interaction makes their consequences complex (*Mahakammavibhanga Sutta*).

The Buddha depicted an emotional episode of Dependent Origination as the interplay of *12 interlinked co-dependent factors* of a single karmic sequence of personal experience. This *originates* at birth (*1 jati*), decays as it proceeds, and *ceases*-dies eventually (*2 jaramarana*); an emotional episode arises due to ignorance (*3 avidya*), which produces a psychological state of some detrimental intentional activity like e.g. negative Speech (*4 samskara*), awareness of which dawns in consciousness (*5 vijnana*), which only exists in conjunction with Mind-Body (*6 nama-rupa*), which are the condition for the six senses (*7 sadayatana*), which through sense contact (*8 phasa*) with attended stimuli evoke feelings (*9 vedana*) of greed or hatred, which might be craved for (*10 tanha*) and grasped or clung onto (*11 upadana*), which works like fuel perpetuating the fire of passion and become (*12 bhava*) a (re)birth of the next emotional episode eventually resulting in being stuck in Duhkha. Thus, Karma is not a mystifying "what goes around comes around" formula, neither does it allude to a fate or destiny arrangement of reincarnation – a Himalayan atavism – but to *active choice according to corresponding intention grounded in relational meaning* in a dynamic homeostatic process. Feeling-action-thought interdependently originating and ceasing have the potential to develop toward entropy (decay and chaos), like in depression, or toward negentropy (growth and order), like in joy. Karmic trouble arises when ignorance on the emptiness of self leads to greed-grasping and hatred-clinging. It is therefore of the utmost importance to elucidate self's emptiness and analyse the interpersonal meaning of grasping and clinging. Grasping and clinging are, like most daily experiences, habitual behavioural patterns learned in interaction and seemingly happening automatically. Bad habits form the bulk of regrettable Karma and regret is usually the starting point for reflection, contemplation, and meditation.

Table 2. Buddhist Scholars' Different Interpretations of the Skandhas

AUTHOR	RUPA	VEDANA	SAMJNA	SAMSKARA	VIJNANA
Bernard-Thierry	corporeality	*sensation*	*representation*	formation	knowledge
Edgerton	physical form	feeling sensation	*notion/idea conception*	predispositions	practical knowledge
Guenther	expressive form	feeling	sensation	motivation	discrimination psych process mentalism
Inagaki	matter/form	*perception*	*conception*	*volition*	*Cs*
Kalupahana	material form	feeling	perception	dispositions	*Cs*
Monier-Williams	bodily forms	sensation	perception	aggregate of formations	Cs/thought faculty
Nyanatiloka	corporeality	feeling	perception	mental formations	*Cs*
Rahula	matter	*sensation*	perception	mental formations	conscience knowledge
C. Rhys-Davids	*seen-thing/ body*	feeling	perception	*activities planning*	mind/ survivor
Soothill	form, sensuous quality	reception feeling *sensation*	*thought/Cs/* perception	action mental activity	cognition
D.T. Suzuki	material existence	*perception sensation*	mental perception ideas	*volition & related activities*	*Cs* of mind
Gethin	form	feeling	recogniton	volitional for-ces/formations	self-*Cs*
Takakusu	form	*perception*	*ideas conception*	*volition*	*Cs*/mind

Habits come about by interplay of the Skandhas. The Buddha used the analogy of the lute (*Sigalovada Sutta*), whose elusive music (the self's Gestalt) is comprises the combination of strings, box, and bow which are full of momentary experience but empty of eternal sound, i.e. of substantial self. On its own, each of the constituents lacks a sound. The whole is more than the sum of its parts. Elsewhere, in a famous 2nd century metaphor Bhikshu Nagasena taught king Milinda that the mind's constituents, the Skandhas, are like the parts of a chariot. Mind deconstructed in its modalities disintegrates like a decomposed body like a chariot that is nothing but a temporary assemblage of components. Notably, Pirsig's *Zen and the Art of Motorcycle Maintenance* (1974) deals with the same issue: where does inherent existence, eternal soul or substantial self, reside if the bike is torn apart? The self exists only as a mind construction that artificially freezes the flux of BASIC-I.D. processes. Neither an *S-O-R* paradigm, nor a Skandhas' view contends a self, a soul or a ghost in the machine. The Skandhas, also known as the Skandhas of clinging, are: body (*rupa*) and mind (*nama*), i.e., perceiving (*vedana*), conceiving (*samjna*), conating (*samskara*), and consciousness-awareness (*vijnana*), the sequential factors of an emotional episode. From a New Buddhist Psychology perspective, the BASIC-I.D. modalities reflect the meaning of Skandhas most adequately. Buddhist scholars have offered various different, often contradictory, translations, inferences, and meanings for the Skandhas as in Table 2 (cf. Gethin, 1998). The italicized terms correspond with a multimodal view of the Skandhas.

Karma's candle flames and domino pieces

In order to see the congruence of Karma, the BASIC-I.D., and the Skandhas in Dependent Origination, two classical analogies to explicate Karma are presented next: the *candle flame analogy* on craving fires to be extinguished by de-conditioning and the *domino analogy* which refers to the Karma cycle of conditionality comprising the above 12 item series. Habitual patterns form the bulk of regretful actions whose intentionality one is not aware of; remorse is the point at which sorrow and reflection might begin. Habits come about through interplay of the co-depending BASIC-I.D. modalities which reflect the topography and structure of a provisional state, called self (or personality) which at bottom is viewed as an intersection of relationships. Taking place in relative awareness, depending on the wilfully paid consecutive concentration to what is attended, daily experiencing is often habitual. Habitual responses happen automatically as described in the principles of classical, operant, and vicarious learning (Kwee & Lazarus, 1986).

Viewed from a social constructivist perspective these learning principles are metaphors which together constitute a coherent narrative for change. Change takes place in collaborative conversation, a practice characterized by scepticism (about immutable knowledge and "*the* truth"), particularism (nobody is the same), interactionism (intelligibility emerges through co-action), and connectivism (we cannot but be interlinked and exist in Dependent Origination). A habit as an inadequate reaction to a *Stimulus* situation requires a new adequate Response to be figured out by the *Organism*. Whether what was emitted is adequate and wholesome is an evaluation on the cognitive/affective level. Affect inheres in relational meaning and can be any inner short-lived or long-term feeling varying from moods, preferences, stances, attitudes, dispositions, to strong emotive experiences with a positive, negative, or neutral quality. An inadequate *Response* is connected to some emotional disturbed or unhappy feeling, candle flames to be extinguished, and is often the beginning of a voluntary paying attention and minutely focussing on concentration and awareness to the modalities involved for the sake of change. These might be experienced as succeeding in a SICAB firing order: Sensation-Imagery-Cognition-Affect-Behaviour.

A comprehensive way to explicate Karma is through the Skandhas: the body enables the psyche to experience firing orders like a SICAB sequence. Experiencing may take place within or without awareness, depending on the purposeful attention-concentration paid to the object of choice. Regrettable responses are usually connected to some emotional disturbance or unhappy feeling and the beginning of focussing. The SICAB firing order corresponds to the Karma sequence which is discerned in the introduction and systematically worked out in the below steps of Dependent Origination:

(1) Mind-Body Skandha (*nama-rupa*): A momentary *Stimulus* configuration contacts (*sparsa*) and impinges on the *Organism*, i.e. the somatic radar screen of the sense organs which detects and wilfully attends in awareness amidst streaming consciousness a momentary stimulus configuration of external and/or internal *dharmas*: the smallest mind objects/units of experience.

(2) Perceiving Skandha (*vedana*): Sensation – After wilfully attending, there is perception and apperception, a post-perceptual but pre-conceptual tiny moment of *dharma* perception, impacted by memory and recognition and weighing in on Affect; the *Organism* experiences a sensory-affective feeling immediately rated as relatively positive, negative or neutral.

(3) Conceiving Skandha (*samjna*): Imagery/Cognition – The *Stimulus*, i.e. the *dharma*, becomes a representation through visualization and conceptualization, dualistically classified as black/white, good/bad, right/wrong, etc., against the backdrop of memory fits-misfits, further fabricated and proliferated as beliefs, attitudes, judgments, and values by the *Organism*.

(4) Conating Skandha (*samskara*): Affect/Behaviour – Subsequently, having appraised, the *Organism* emits an emotive *Response* that motivates a volitional or intentional act of Karma, a karmic *Response* which is automatic and habitual or planned and prepared through self-talk and more often than not expressed in a context of Interpersonal relationships through speech.

(5) Consciousness Skandha (*vijnana*): One can only be aware of *dharmas* in the space of consciousness as an *S-O-R*/SICAB/Skandhas sequence wherein usually the formation of I-me-mine/self illusions and egotistic god delusions takes place automatically and the attack of others as self defence is sanctioned; meditation is a measure to bypass a resort to a self.

One can learn to become aware of the (re)birth – origination-arising-peaking-subsiding-ceasing – of emotional episodes, i.e. of joy, sadness, fear, or anger, of the interplay and firing order of the modalities, and discover that craving leads to grasping and clinging onto illusory certainties, and eventually produces illusions. These illusions can be unveiled by being mindfully aware of the sense-perception of the *dharmas* which can be designated as social construc-tions, notably *"perceivables"* – i.e., *visibles, hearables, smellables, tasteables* and *touchables* – and *"knowables"*, i.e. images, concepts as well as memories and dreams. Meditation accru-ing virtue and wisdom is a means to de-condition or unlearn and extinguish karmic agony like candle flames. Extinction that bypasses I-me-mine/self is called Nirvana.

The domino metaphor of Karma delineates Dependent Origination more extensively than the previous metaphor by explicating the interplay of 12 interlinked steps that are connected like domi-no pieces (Conze, 1980). Laid out earlier in the previous paragraph, it is here detailed as a cycle which is a this-worldly and here-now *S-O-R* interpretation of a 12 steps' process in three phases of awareness: an initial phase, a middle phase, and a final phase, like in the following example:

(A) An initial multi-causal phase, implicated by a past history of ignorance and intentional formations (steps 1/2):

Step 1. Conveys that the interlinked model is about karmic greed, hatred, and particularly ignorance; this model concurs with an *S-O-R*/CBT paradigm.

Step 2. Out of ignorance regrettable Karma arises in sense perception, e.g. a fight.

(B1) A middle or present phase, comprising awareness of Body/Speech/Mind, the six senses, contact, and feeling as the present result (steps 3/4/5/6/7):

Step 3. Out of this, negative thoughts about the fight might arise in awareness

Step 4. Out of the thought, Body/Speech/Mind Karma arises, e.g. more anger

Step 5. Out of a Body/Speech/Mind as condition sense organ perceiving arises

Step 6. Out of perceiving, sense contact arises, e.g. seeing John as the enemy

Step 7. Out of contact, feeling experience arises, e.g. blind, by an arrow of rage

(B2) A middle or present phase, comprising awareness of craving, grasping, clinging, and becoming as the present "multi-causation" (steps 8/9/10):

Step 8. Out of feeling, craving thoughts arise, e.g. I must beat him to death

Step 9. Out of craving, grasping greed to winning self and clinging hate to kill

Step 10. Out of hate, more aggressive Karma is conceived to become materialized

(C) A final phase with future consequences, i.e. birth, aging, and death with sorrow and lamentation as the outcome (steps 11-12):

Step 11. S-O-R cycling: the origination, conception, and (re)birth of a new cycle

Step 12. S-O-R cycling: Karma cycles age, die, reappear or dissolve in Nirvana

The metaphors of aging, death, and rebirth have made many credulous Buddhists believe that this traditional 12 steps exposition is about reincarnation, the soul, and Transcendental Truth, rather than about a meditative scrutiny from mind-moment-to-mind-moment of the Buddha's Dependent Origination.

Nirvana, a shorthand for extinction of emotional arousal, is not a place to go literally after death or a state of being out-of-orbit, but an unmoved state of silence, a cessation phase of an emotional episode and the opposite of being moved or emotional. Nirvana is a state which belongs to the human realm of experience. Temporary Nirvana is attained if an anxiety disorder is extinguished for instance by CBT's exposure treatment or when depression is dispelled by cognitive change. Nirvana and Duhkha states alternate in daily life as the consequential outcome of Karma. Samsara, cyclical recurrent states of Duhkha, is pictured by ambiguous metaphors feeding metaphysical ideas of transmigration and reincarnation which are irrational in a secular teaching of not-self. Rather than endorsing the idea of rebirths of emotional episodes, these metaphors opened the back door for the import of other-worldly speculations. Instead of archaic qualifiers, a contemporary psychology of emotions is here advocated.

The heart of "Karma": affect and emotion

Karma delineates the Buddha's postulate of Dependent Origination as an interactive psychology of feeling-action-thought, modalities co-dependently originating-arising-peaking-subsiding-and-ceasing in a relational context. These are, metaphorically, systemic processes with the potential to develop unwholesomeness (entropy, decay, and chaos) or wholesomeness (negentropy, growth, and order). Morbid Karma originates when ignorance in the emptiness of self evolves into greed-grasping and hatred-clinging. The root poisons of greed and hatred – incorporating the negatively experienced emotions of sadness, anxiety, anger, and depression – require abatement. The positively experienced emotions of love (kindness and compassion) and joy as well as of silence, Nirvana, and emptiness via the extinction of emotional flames call for cultivation. In the Buddhist lore the *Brahmaviharas* (a metaphor for where the divine feelings dwell) to be accrued by the social meditations of loving kindness, empathic compassion, shared joy, and meditative equanimity need to be immeasurably amplified to secure wholesome Karma. Outcome research on loving-kindness meditation showed that this practice produces increases over time in daily positive experiences leading to increases in personal resources like increased mindfulness, purpose in life, social support, and decreased illness symptoms. These increments predict increased life satisfaction and reduced depressive symptoms (e.g., Frederickson, Cohn, Coffey, Pek, & Finkel, 2008; Hutcherson, Seppala, & Gross, 2008).

From a social constructivist perspective emotions are viewed as relational performatives and appropriated expressions within a particular cultural context. In order to understand this view, we need to abandon the traditional emotional concepts as discrete indexes of the mind or the cortex which try to differentiate properties in search of essence (in Buddhist terminology: inherent existence) and reconstruct the individualist conception of emotions as embodied actions in complex patterns of relational interchange scenarios. Thus, from a social constructivist perspective the terms affect/emotion inhere in a relational meaning overall; this is conform to the Buddhist Dependent Origination. Thus, I grieve about someone's death, I fear to be fired by the boss, I am angry at my kid, I feel sad about her rejection, I felt joy meeting him, I love her, I was silently thinking of my deceased mother, etc. Affect may denote *secondary affective feelings* interpreted as emotions mixed – in addition to being interpersonally related – with thinking, sensing, and/or doing. Thus one may not only silently think about one's mother but one might also silently sense her or visit her grave. The term "basic emotions" is reserved to denote *primary affective feelings*, hypothesized elemental but elusive experiences to be used as a compass in collaborative practice. There is no consensus as to the number of basic emotions due to the high abstraction level of basic and the lack of the meaning and criteria for basic (Scherer, 2005). Based on clinical experience with more than 2000 clients, I submit the following list of eight elementary categories. Already occurring in interaction with a parent from birth on and thus viewed as basic are *Anxiety, Anger, Sadness, Joy,* and *Love*, and to complete the list, *Depression* and *Silence/Nirvana* are added as special instances of primary affect. During the journey from the cradle to the grave interpersonal relationships can be thus painful that a depressed state may emerge. Reprocessing relations, for instance by mindfulness meditation, one might quench emotional flames toward Nirvana (extinction).

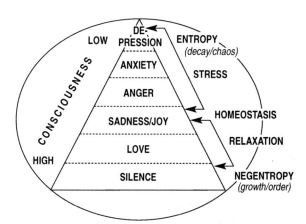

Figure 1. The Varieties of Primary Affect (Basic Emotions)

Designed to serve clinical assessment on an atomistic and elemental level of abstraction, Figure 1 depicts a metaphor of basic emotions as layers of an onion which can be peeled consecutively. Thus, one may find from the outer to the inner: Depression, Anxiety, Anger, Sadness, Joy, Love, Silence, and Nirvana. The first group of four are karmic unwholesome, to be decreased; the second group of four is karmic wholesome, to be increased. While one might experience several of these emotions at one time in various degrees, there is a dynamic homeostasis balancing in-between the stressful-chaotic (entropy) experiences of low awareness and the relaxed-orderly (negentropy) experiences of high awareness. In the pristine Buddhist languages, Pali and Sanskrit, as well as in other eastern languages of the Dharma, there is no word for psychology and emotion. For instance, in Mandarin the term for psychology is Xin Li Xue, meaning the science of the heart, a metaphoric denotation to guide a balanced way of life. This concurs with the Buddhist view of the mind "located" in the heart rather than in the head as in Cartesian thought. The heart, affect/emotions, and the mind are evidently indispensable to unravel the "who, what, where, when, and how" to end suffering. Between the state of emotions gone awry (Depression) and non-emotion (Silence/Nirvana) all possible variants of emotional experience from suffering (Duhkha) to happiness (Sukha) have a place in the spectrum.

From a Buddhist perspective Depression is not merely a negative experience. The Buddha awakened during a state of despair. Depression can be considered positive, if viewed as an obstacle to be turned into a path that may mark the beginning of a meditative way of life, a learning experience leading to self-reflection and awakening to emptiness and interconnection. Depression is enriching if conducive to become "sadder but wiser". Depressive clients erroneously attribute failures to themselves and successes to external factors. Their sombreness is fed by a negative view of themselves, others, and the future (Beck, 1976). Sometimes, the urge to commit suicide prevails. Such death wishes differentiate Depression from Love. Heralded as the most important experience in life, *magna res est amor*, Love is the most sought after emotion in all cultures designating the *raison d'être* of life (Sternberg & Barnes, 1988). It is not a discrete state that lends itself easily to experimental investigation. There are two variants of Love: infatuation (passionate) and compassion (dispassionate). Featured by altruism, compassion figures prominently in the Buddhist value system next to kindness and joy. Enlightened compassion is endorsed which is a down-to-earth practice of empathizing with the suffering of others and is to be applied sensibly, like in what I have called the oxygen mask principle. In case of emergency in the air, use the mask yourself first before applying it to your kids to secure the best survival chances for all.

The above taxonomy can be more fully understood by scrutinizing the functional relationships of emotions to Karma, intentional thought, and behavioural action *vis à vis* a goal with an inevitable interpersonal impact. Inhering in will, volition, or conation (*samskara*), Affect motivates purposeful action aiming a target. Karma becomes transparent in terms of intended goals of action by peeling each emotion, layer by layer, until Nirvana is unveiled. Thus, in Depression – the end result of chronic and massive emotional repression – no goals are worthwhile to pursue: one feels intensely dejected, down, disordered, confused, demoralised, and hopeless. However, even depression harbours a potential to reassess things. In Anxiety the attainment of an intended goal is threatened; fear can be functional or dysfunctional. In the latter case it might take the form of a disorder. For example, claustrophobia, the irrational fear of confinement, might be the result of locked-up Anger or Sadness. In Anger the striving for an intended goal is blocked and frustrated. Its burning heat usually goes along with lowered levels of awareness and a loss of control. If chronically repressed, psychosomatic illness, e.g. hypertension, might be the end result. The relieving expression of Anger depends on culture and various rationales. From a Buddhist stance it is wisely transformed into compassionate assertiveness; to throw garbage on somebody usually leads to escalation. In Sadness there is a loss of an attained or intended goal; sadness has a healing effect if expressed in crying. Sadness and Joy are like two sides of a coin, both are melting experiences. Joy conveys a relevant progression to or attainment of an intended goal. In Love an intended goal of attachment and merger is met; this usually requires total acceptance and surrender. In Silence there is minimal intention, no goal. Silence is fulfilling and profound because it is energizing and the door to Nirvana, emptiness, and a Buddhahood of social service from a deep understanding of interconnectedness of Relational Interbeing, the true nature of humankind.

The varieties of primary affect (basic emotions)

Karma Transformation endorses the hedonic rating of feelings as painful, pleasurable, or neutral and backs people's striving for happiness and avoiding unhappiness. However, happiness is a multifaceted phenomenon characterized (1) by not being a goal in itself but an epiphenomenon of people's working at creating a meaningful life and (2) by not being an absolute condition but a fortunate incidence amidst life's inescapable adversities, called "chaironic happiness" < www.meaning.ca >. On the level of secondary affect, there are numerous words on mixtures of affective compositions, like melodies created from a basic set of musical notes, analogous to the BASIC-I.D. Another metaphor points at the rainbow that appears if white light (Silence) is bent by a prism resulting in six basic colours: red (Love), orange (Fear), yellow (Joy), green (Anger), blue (Sadness), and violet (Depression) with uncountable hues in-between. The affective lexicon consists of for about 4000 English words, each of which represents a secondary affect and can be subsumed under a basic emotion. For clinical assessment a semantic analysis can be made as illustrated in Table 2, a taxonomy depicting a small sample of these relationships describing and impacting words.

Table 2. Basic Emotions and the Semantic Varieties of Secondary Affect

Depression	Anxiety	Anger	Sadness	Joy	Love	Silence	Nirvana
blue	worried	annoyed	pity	amused	tenderness	relaxed	
dejected	apprehended	contempt	sorrow	glad	fondness	trustful	
dysphoric	anguish	hostility	distress	happy	intimacy	contented	
downhearted	fear	animosity	grief	humour	compassion	grateful	
despondent	fright	fury	affliction	delight	infatuated	safe	
low spirits	horror	rage	agony	euphoric	eroticised	serene	
melancholic	terror	hate	mourning	manic	kindness	satisfied	
dysthymic	panic	resenting	hurt	content	affection	peaceful	
etc...	etc...	etc...	etc...	etc...	etc...	etc...	

The implication of classifying thus is not to be accurate but to facilitate negotiating through "reflexive deliberation" on the karmic problem. Enigmatically, naming the particular affect within a cultural scenario might evaporate the "magic spell" and terminate an emotional hijack like in the fairy tale of Rumpelstiltskin. The exercise is linked to mindfulness meditation (Kwee, 1996, 1998, 2009, 2010ab).

In terms of modalities, an Affect is secondary if, in the context of Interpersonal issues, it is "contaminated" by Behaviour, Sensation, Imagery, and/or Cognition. There are 14 lists of basic emotions creating a Babel of tongues on this topic (e.g., Ortony, Clore, & Collins, 1988), the most relevant are proposed by Plutchik (1994), Izard (1972), Frijda (1987), and Ekman (1996) (Davidson, Scherer, & Goldsmith, 2003). Plutchik listed Anger, Joy, Fear, Sadness, *Surprise, Disgust, Anticipation,* and *Acceptance*; Izard listed Anger, Joy, Fear, *Surprise, Disgust, Contempt, Distress, Shame, Guilt,* and *Interest*; Frijda listed Anger, Joy, Fear, *Surprise, Contempt, Distress, Shame, Aversion, Desire,* and *Pride*; and Ekman listed Anger, Enjoyment, Fear, Sadness, *Surprise, Disgust,* and *Contempt*. In an atomistic analysis of modalities, the italicized feelings are considered secondary: *Surprise* may vary from Cognition about an unanticipated event to a sudden activation of a neural reflex (Lazarus, 1991). *Disgust* impresses as a Sensory experience. *Anticipation* comprises Imagery and Cognition, beliefs that cannot even be classified as an emotion. *Acceptance* is considered to be an attitude with predominantly Cognitive, Behavioural, and Interpersonal features. *Contempt* inheres in Cognition with the quality of anger and defensive fear. *Distress* is the a-specific term for the Sensory feeling of being tensed or upset. *Shame* is a variant of fear with Imagery, Cognitive, Interpersonal, and Sensory aspects. *Guilt* largely consists of Cognitions, Interpersonal values, and a social fear. *Interest* is conative and motivational rather than emotive, thus foremost Cognitive (intentional and volitional) as well as Sensory (perceptual and attentional). *Aversion* (Latin: *aversio,* turning away) has a Behavioural emphasis due to a Sensory-based dislike, *Desire* refers to the future and consequently contains Images/Cognitions of hope, and *Pride* connotes enjoyment based on Interpersonal comparison and a standing on a pedestal at a Cognitive/Imagery level (Johnson-Laird & Oatley, 1992).

The rationale of discerning primary and secondary feelings is to enable practitioners of Karma Transformation to pragmatically find and match appropriate interventions. Thus Acceptance, Anticipation, Contempt, Desire, and Guilt call for Cognitive/Imagery interventions, Disgust, Distress, Interest, and Surprise call for Sensory interventions, Shame and Pride call for Interpersonal interventions, and Aversion call for Behavioural interventions. If, for instance, Anticipation is considered to be primary, Cognitive and Imagery material would be lost for scrutiny. Another example is Guilt. Despite the vernacular of guilt feelings, Guilt comprises fear provoking Cognitions and Imagery of self-blame. If Guilt is not recognised as secondary, "cognitive restructuring" would not be considered the treatment of choice. Comparably, Distress (Sensory) is apt for "relaxation exercises", Shame (Interpersonal) for "assertion training", and Aversion (Behaviour) for "systematic exposure". A strategic stance to intervene in Karma Transformation is not solely based on the SICAB sequence of the Skandhas in the candle flames' analogy. This "Buddhist" firing order, which corresponds with the *S-O-R*/CBT working model and appeals for heuristic reasons, happens to concur with Cannon-Bard's firing order: I perceive a bear (S), I appraise danger (I/C), I feel fear (A), I tremble and run (B). However, other firing orders are possible like James-Lange's firing order (SICBA): I perceive a bear (S), I appraise danger (I/C), I tremble and run (B) and I feel fear (A). Darwin-Plutchik point at a SBAC/I firing order: I perceive a bear (S), I tremble and run (B), I feel fear (A), and I appraise danger (C/I) (cf. Scherer, 2005). Many other firing orders can be experienced: BASIC-I.D. transmutations equal the faculty of seven letters (7!), thus 5040 firing orders are theoretically possible. The postulate of Dependent Origination did not freeze any firing order and in fact the *Sammaditthi Sutta* and *Mahahatthipadopama Sutta* contend that "if this arises that arises, if this ceases, that ceases", leaving any variant open. Moreover, the Buddha also stated many times that one who sees this interdependent arising and ceasing sees the Dharma.

In conclusion

Whether a social constructivist Buddhist Psychology might turn out to be a fruitful contribution in expediting the cessation of Duhkha, the noble aim of the Buddha, remains to be seen. This requires commitment and hard work, the reason why Karma Transformation is not particularly suitable for the faint-hearted who would benefit more from the "do's and don'ts" of ethics (*Sigalovada Sutta*), and from the metaphysics of heaven. However, for those who wish to decide for themselves and use their capacity to think, pick, and choose rather than to follow commandments, Karma Transformation of collaborative practice and dialogue might be advisable to create bright futures.

The present this-worldly view of Karma endorses the writings of Dahlke (1865-1928), a pioneer of a non-metaphysical interpretation of Karma, the Skandhas, and *dharmas* < www.buddhistisches-haus.de >. Buddhist and contemporary psychology, having overlapping concerns and being different in several respects, might learn from each other. Karma Transformation is a multiphase approach in line with the *4-Ennobling Realities* and with the *8-Fold Balanced Practice* to lift emotional hurdles through educating toward awakening, if necessary preceded by CBT. Whereas CBT aims to cure, Karma Transformation's prime concern is to attain Buddhahood by developing Arahantship (someone who has eradicated inner enemies and lives in emptiness and interconnectedness). To get "enlightened" is not an end in itself, but only a means to awaken and a beginning to understand how emotional suffering due to the "slings and arrows" of existential *mis*-fortune can be extinguished. This depends on proficiency to gain insight and to see the light what Karma is about, a long way to go which often needs professional guidance. The "karmavadin", while taking care of people's Karma might be called upon to attend impediments of emotional disturbance. Growth-hampering hurdles necessitate help by a professional who is proficient in both disciplines or else a referral to a mental health expert is indicated in order to eventually pursue wholesome Karma. Wholesome Karma is free from ignorant craving, greedy grasping, and hateful clinging. Unwholesome Karma – noticeable in feelings of craving, thoughts of grasping, and behaviours of clinging – is shackling. Wholesomeness is attained when ignorance is replaced by wisdom and savvy, and when virtues resolve greed and dissolve hatred.

Although meaningful intentions form the seed for future performance, like in a court of justice, only manifest action and observable deeds, not mere planning and intending, are held accountable and capable to extinguish agony. Being mindfully attentive-concentrative and vigilantly aware-introspective on Karma's working might prevent unwholesome Karma to occur and increase the frequency of wholesome Karma. The crux is to keep Karma serenely unafflicted by choosing not to become attached to greedy or hateful feeling-action-thought. By meditating conditioned habitual patterns, one might experience each instance, from mind-moment-to-mind-moment, fresh and anew, and while exploring life's events *du jour* one might move into unchartered territories, awaken, and find – through harmonious relationships – peace inside. The empty interconnectedness of not-self is a this-worldly evidence of liberation as a benefit of un-craving/un-grasping/un-clinging called Nirvana, the extinction of conditioned emotional flames in the empty goal getter, which can be temporary or long-standing. Not-self is a state of being wherein one is completely at ease and content to serve the community at large.

Chapter 21

Karma Functional Analysis, Strategic Interventions, And Mindfulness Meditation

Maurits G.T. Kwee & Marja K. Kwee-Taams

Introduction

Psychology could develop as a scientific discipline by adopting the 17th century Cartesian view that separates Body/Mind enabling the rationalization of the psyche: "my thought" is the foundation for "my existence". This places the individual mind in the centre of the study that aims to decipher the vagaries of human conduct. But is the inquiry into individual minds feasible and sufficient to understand meaningful action? Is the experimental method borrowed from the exact sciences the royal road to reveal psychological causal relationships? Are psychological processes causally related to environmental antecedents and behavioural consequences? Can persons as objects "out there" be accurately described by a subject "in here"? Or does each of us perhaps speak from intelligibilities of a particular cultural background, personal histories, textual and linguistic forestructures within which we direct and interpret our observations?

What "is" real and true about human functioning seems to be an epiphenomenon of the particular communities' belief about what is real and true (Gergen, 2001). It is extremely difficult to go beyond the shared social construction of one's own tradition to understand alien intelligibilities such as *an-atman* (not-self) or the Buddha's 6th sense. Comprehending individual mind seems to depend on one's participation in the linguistics of a particular theory. Indeed, findings of empirical research can verify or falsify hypotheses, but only within the confines of one's pet theory and thus, mostly the evidence does not impact those who do not subscribe to the theory. Psychological theories are not accurate mirrors of the world as language is not a "child of the mind" but rather a cultural process which derives meaning, descriptions, and explanations from ongoing interactions. In keeping with the meta-psychology of Social Construction we therefore submit that reality or truth does not mirror actual events but rather mirrors people's engagement within a Wittgensteinian language game. The Buddhist language game corroborates Wittgenstein's adage "Wovon man nicht sprechen kann, darüber muss man schweigen". From an empty conceptualization of the real and the truth, any cultural interpretation (social construction) of the Dharma is possible and allowed. This includes inferring the Dharma as a *Stimulus-Organism-Response* psychology with a cognitive behavioural language game.

This connects to a growing interest amongst scientists-practitioners – health care clinicians, corporate coaches, and academic teachers – in the Dharma (Buddhist teachings) as a cognitive behavioural approach to guide peoples' functioning (e.g., Kabat-Zinn, 2005; Wallace & Shapiro, 2006; Sugamura, Haruki, & Koshikawa, 2007; Kelly, 2008; Whitfield, 2006;

Christopher, 2003; Kwee & Ellis, 1998; Docket, Dudley-Grant, & Bankart, 2003; Germer, Siegel, & Fulton, 2005; Kwee, Gergen, & Koshikawa, 2006; Didonna, 2009; Shapiro & Carlson, 2009). Advanced adepts are aware that the Dharma is basically not a religious belief system or a metaphysical ideology even though it can be moulded into these categories (e.g. *Samannaphala Sutta*). Not surprisingly, the Dharma is viewed by many non-Buddhists and Buddhists as a religion rather than as a non-theistic soteriology. However, the Buddha did not endorse a theistic eternalism, nor did he embrace an atheistic nihilism. Instead, he proposed a "Middle Way" by meditation in action – a this-worldly transformational psychology – to end "existential suffering", i.e. daily relational-emotional problems of living (Duhkha).

The Dharma's quintessential ingredient is the practice of meditation. Meditation is a day-to-day application which grounds the foundation of a down-to-earth art of living to cease inescapable Duhkha. According to the scriptures, the Buddha aims at liberation from the pervasive imperfection of life which leads to the agony and the "un-satisfactoriness" – discontentment, distress, or disarray – which is inherent in unavoidable propensity of life to decay. From birth onwards, and despite of human beings' longing for (unattainable) perfection, the human predicament is aging, illness, and death due to the impermanence of the universe. Sooner or later the vicissitudes of life reveal "existential neurosis", a *dis-ease* arising from unwholesome choices which have been prompted by greed ("musts") and/or hatred ("musts-not") out of ignorance about the mind's propensity to project illusions of self and delusions of god(s). Not dealt with adequately, Duhkha may cycle viciously into emotional disturbance like clinical depressions or anxiety disorders. The Dharma might be described as an effort to counter ignorance by learning to understand the psyche and its concomitant behaviours and to act accordingly. Meditation practice is embedded in a process of verifying or falsifying, for oneself, the Buddha's *4-Ennobling Realities*: (1) suffering is immanent in life and embedded in interpersonal emotions, (2) suffering arises from causes due to unsatisfactory or disharmonious relationships, (3) these relational causes can be stopped by loving kindness, empathic compassion, and shared joy, and (4) this solution lies in the painstaking training of the *8-Fold Balanced Practice,* an inter/intrapersonal method to eradicate greed, hatred, and ignorance by changing one's view/understanding, intention/thought, speech/self-talk, action/behaviour, living/habitude, effort/commitment, attention/concentration, and awareness/introspection.

As admonished down the ages, it is quintessentially important to watch over these four realities by minding Karma – intentional/meaningful (cognitive) action/interaction (behaviour) – and particularly by observing how feelings (sensation and emotion) come about. To deal with "existential neurosis", we call for Karma Transformation, a process which (1) scrutinizes the functionality of psychological modalities in originating and perpetuating Karma and by developing an idiosyncratic treatment plan, (2) guides the selection of cognitive and behavioural interventions using a hands-on functional-analytic scheme, and (3) is able to allocate specific meditation exercises within the framework of a roadmap designed for clinical/coaching purposes. Karma Transformation asks:

(1) Which factors are functional in contributing to Karma's Dependent Origination (also non-independent, interdependent, or co-dependent origination, arising, peaking, subsiding, and ceasing of feeling-doing-thinking/relating)?

(2) Which remedies can be applied to alleviate psychological suffering, i.e. which psychological interventions and meditations for which idiosyncratic emotional disturbance can be implemented in collaborative practice?

These questions lead us to design a tentative roadmap and routes to find out what is wholesome (*kusala*) and to suggest remedies for what is unwholesome (*akusala*). This boils down to a self-quest to feel-think-(inter)act differently.

Functional analysis of the "Skandhas" and karmic cycling

The Cartesian view of psychology as a function of underlying mechanisms in the mind, such as the atomistic modalities of Behaviour-Affect-Sensation-Imagery-Cognition could create a misguided vision of individuals as self-contained entities living in isolation instead of a more promising vision of human lives as interconnected with one another from the cradle to the grave. A social constructionist psychology implies that all which one used to define as private or separated from others is envisioned as pervasively relational and inseparable from communal activity. Psychological processes are constituted within relationships because our lives are embedded in languages (lexical, body, and so on) existing long before we do and which will continue to be there long after we perish. Our thinking and beliefs do not precede language but speech and self-talk is the thinking or the belief itself, both of which are collaboratively created through "languaging". The same applies to feeling and doing. Thus, attitudes are considered not as determinants of affect and action but as a stance in a dialogue; and emotions are by themselves interpersonal performances or scenarios "prescribed" within one's culture. By the same token, memory depends on a social process of what is considered by the community as tolerable or intolerable and the self is viewed as a social construction through various relationships. What is considered as science or rationality is only accepted when the community accepts its definitions and language game. Having understood this and being continuously aware that Mind/Body is a wholistic mechanism without underlying determinants, there is no objection to provisionally use an elementalistic/dualistic vocabulary of the mind.

Cartesian dualism enables the mind to become an object of study, by splitting it from the body and considering it as though it is a separate entity. Such a split is nowhere to be found in the Buddhist perspective which subscribes to a wholistic view while pragmatically endorsing the primacy of the tangible body. Thus, in the Buddhist view mind is embodied in the heart, radiating throughout the whole body rather than located in the head. Having considered heart as the seat of mind, the unity of Body/Mind is bridged in the Buddhist lore by interpersonal and intrapersonal Speech, a social/linguistic dimension (which can be verbal and non-verbal) entwined in a Body/Speech/Mind system. The Buddha's Body/Speech/Mind is a paradigm which parallels a kindred wholistic view of the human being as a discernable but inseparable tri-partition known as the Bio-Psycho-Social system (Engel, 1977). Hence, we seem to be witnessing a merger of two paradigms applicable in medicine and psychology. Our experience in the past two decades as clinicians shows that there is a two-way street between western psychology and Buddhist Psychology: the two approaches are not incompatible and begin to concatenate and confluence (e.g., Kwee, 1990; Kwee & Holdstock, 1996; Haruki & Kaku, 2000; Kwee & Taams, 2003, 2006; Kwee, Gergen, & Koshikawa, 2006).

Both psychologies deal with feeling-thinking-(inter)acting as the stuff to mould in order to change for the better. Feelings (Sensation/Affect), we contend, are a function of thought (Cognition/Imagery), action (Behaviour/Interaction), and body/genetic Drives (Kwee & Lazarus, 1987; Kwee & Ellis, 1997). These modalities, represented by the acronym BASIC-I.D., are consistent with what Buddhists call Skandhas (see previous chapter). Comprising Body/Mind, consciousness-awareness, perceiving (S), conceiving (I/C), and conating (A/B/I.), these modalities/Skandhas form the building blocks of Karma. Karma's definition as intentional/meaningful (inter)action opens the possibility of presenting a cognitive behavioural interpretation which reflects the functional relationships between cause (thought/feeling or meaningful intention) and effect (behavioural interaction).

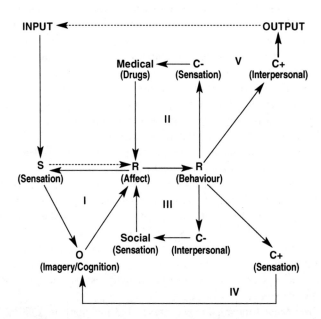

Figure 1. Blueprint of Karma Functional Analysis in S-O-R and BASIC-I.D. terms depicting 5 hypothetical karmic cycles; gyrations perpetuate either the virtuous processes of affective order (emptiness, silence, love, joy) or the vicious processes of affective disorder (sadness, anger, anxiety, depression), processes which occur between the environmental input and the behavioural output of the person (C+: positive Consequences; C–: negative Consequences)

A functional analysis of karmic emotional episodes is elaborated in a multisequential template which follows an "input-output" *Stimulus-Organism-Response (S-O-R)* schematic structure of five major karmic cycles. This blueprint is an assessment tool and an intervention plan, a guide for the therapist/coach and the client during the process of implementing change in collaborative practice. Figure 1 depicts how habits of feeling (S/A), thinking (I/C), and doing (B/I.) are perpetuated via spiralling cycles circling around Affect along notable sequential orders. This is a macro-analytic theoretical reconstruction of the functional co-dependent inter-relations between modalities within hypothetical cycles.

The cycles picture and expand the putative vicissitudes of the *Sallatha Sutta*'s educational narrative about a man with an untrained mind, who, hit by a poison arrow, experiences two kinds of pain: a bodily pain and a psychological pain, as if he had been hit by two arrows instead of just one. What happened to him psychologically and how does this narrative apply to all of us? Shot by poison arrows daily, we can start any moment to feel bad, mad, or sad, and tumble into a morbid spiralling process. "Karma Functional Analysis" discerns the highway of this process, comprising five vicious cycles, which adhere to the Buddha's "this-that conditionality". This conditionality refers to a linear function ("when this is/isn't, that is/isn't") and a synchronous function ("from the arising/ceasing of this, comes the arising/ceasing of that"), implying that past and present influences are interacting in complex patterns (*Mahakammavibhanga Sutta*). The following illustrates each cycle:

> The *1ˢᵗ cycle* starts with a *Stimulus* (an "arrow" penetrating a Sensory organ), subsequently the *Organism* responds (by Images of doom-gloom, Cognitions of despair, and anticipation of catastrophe), evoking a *Response* (Affect of fear-panic, anger-rage, or sadness-depression), e.g. the hateful intention to retaliate (Behaviour), and meanwhile complaining on what happened (Interpersonal); feedback activates a new event causing more Affective misery, rounding up the first "cognitive mediation" cycle which follows a SICABI.-sequence.

> The *2ⁿᵈ cycle* follows a BSD.A firing order, reflecting a spiral of "long-term intrinsic loss". As a result of the dysfunctional aggression (Behaviour), the person harbours chronic tensions (Sensation), a negative consequence which eventually transforms into chronic pains or causes psychosomatic illness necessitating medication (Drugs) and extending the emotional disturbance (Affect).

> The *3ʳᵈ cycle* follows a BI.SA firing order, reflecting a spiral of "long-term extrinsic loss". As a result of the aggression (Behaviour), the person evokes adverse social reactions (Interpersonal), a negative consequence, leading to drift in social isolation and eventually – having lost contact with work and family – in a state of sensory deprivation (Sensation), which aggravates disturbed Affect.

> The *4ᵗʰ cycle* (BSI/CA firing order) represents "short-term intrinsic gain" (negative reinforcement, a positive consequence by the alleviation of a negative condition like tension). Initially, the aggression (Behaviour) leads to tension reduction (Sensation), but in the long run this short-term relief does not solve any of the problems. Thoughts of doom-gloom (Imagery) and of guilt-remorse (Cognition) accumulate, increasing the emotional disturbance (Affect).

> The *5ᵗʰ cycle* (BI.SA firing order) represents "short-term extrinsic gain" (positive reinforcement, a positive consequence like a reward). Initially, the

aggression (Behaviour) seems advantageous, but in the long run it turns out to be rampant and disastrous (Interpersonal). One may gain social attention by manipulative ploys or be excused from responsibilities through face-saving tactics, but in the end these reactions will likely backfire and generalize into even more stressful events (Sensations) escalating disturbed Affect to the person's detriment.

This blueprint is presented as a ready to use hands-on template in Appendix 1, a form to be completed for a client. The template is a roadmap or treatment plan which the clinician/coach completes in reflexive negotiation with the client. It provides strategic clues where and when to intervene in order to curb the vicious cycles, to break up the spiralling, and to find the inflexion point leading to virtuous change.

Disrupting karmic vicious cycles: CBT/REBT interventions

The notion of Karma is closely related to Dependent Origination (*pratityasammutpada*), the Buddha's hypothesis of multi-causality "if this happens, that happened", which lies at the very heart of the Dharma and includes circularity wherein cause is effect and effect is cause. Karma Transformation quizzes the whereabouts of the *3-Poisons* – hatred, greed, and ignorance. Which antecedent and consequent factors play a role in karmic formation and which factors make Karma perpetuate, subside, and cease? In a universe of impermanence and in a mental space of *dharmas* (smallest units of experience) events take place in a flux of concurrent-momentary flashes of experience. Snapshots can only provisionally capture putative firing orders. It should be noted that after the Buddha the functional relationships between *dharmas* – ranging from loosely connected correlation to hard-wired connections – were scrutinized in the last book of the third canonical tome of the Theravada (*Abhidhamma*) which deals with 24 functional relationships (*patthanas*), "interactive conditions and relations" of *dharmas'* Dependent Origination.

In spite of available psychological knowledge, not only does the causality "how psychological experience comes about" remain hypothetical but also the why of an intervention's effectiveness cannot be exactly pinpointed. In order to intervene meaningfully, one needs to know the client's psychology by collecting data through an intake procedure and by scrutinizing the client's emotional/interpersonal life history. This includes the client's emotional development in the context of family, education, and work. A simple BASIC-I.D. profile can be sketched in order to know one's proclivities, whether s/he is a thinking, doing, or feeling type of person, by rating these questions on a 0-10 scale: How much of a doer am I? (B); How deeply emotional am I? (A); How much am I tuned into my senses? (S); How vividly do I visualize/think in pictures? (I); How analytic of a thinker or planner am I? (C); How much engaged am I in social activities? (I.); and, How often am I ill (times a year)? (D.). Scores can be displayed on a histogram. It requires reflexive negotiation to agree on a position and to choose interventions.

Interventions for each cycle are preferably evidence-based. Thus: *the 1ˢᵗ cycle of cognitive mediation* might be tackled by cognitive behavioural interventions (e.g. those included in Rational Emotive Behavior Therapy [REBT]). The *2ⁿᵈ cycle of distress* might require stress inoculation, relaxation training, Samatha/tranquilizing meditation, or medication (e.g. antidepressants).[1] The *3rd cycle of deprivation* might require relationship activation and motivation, like social skills training, assertiveness training, or communication training. The *4th cycle of intrinsic gain* refers to short-run sensory satisfaction, a maintaining factor requiring insight which can be acquired through Vipassana meditation. And the *5th cycle of extrinsic gain* refers to short term relational satisfaction, a maintaining factor requiring family therapy, marital therapy, or divorce counselling. While these strategies suggest a general approach for disrupting each of these cycles, there exist various other interventions proven useful for targeting psychological problems with some technical precision. At bottom, in working with people, techniques need to be applied with clinical acumen, proficient skills, and unique artistry. This call for a technical eclecticism (Lazarus, 1997): no matter where a technique has originated or who spawned it, as long as there is evidence for its clinical effectiveness its use is warranted. As clarified in the previous chapter the *S-O-R* model is congruent with the epistemology of Buddhist Psychology which aims at insight, at disruption of unwholesome Karma, and at enhancement of wholesome Karma. There is a plethora of terms for "unlearning": General Semantics *dis-identifies* from cognitive maps, Behaviour Therapy *de-conditions* habits, REBT *de-"musturbates"* musts, Cognitive Therapy *distances* and *de-automatizes* dysfunctional thoughts, Dialectical Behavior Therapy *de-creases* extremes, and Acceptance and Commitment Therapy *de-fuses* negativity. Although they all belong to the grand family of CBT, the innovators' underlying theories may be at odds with one another. However, it is not necessary to endorse a theory which prompts an effective technique in order to successfully utilize it.

Karma Transformation advocates not-self and emptiness by dis-solving, dis-owning, un-clinging, un-grasping, un-craving, and de-constructing the sense of I-me-mine/self. A Buddhist Psychology supporting the *S-O-R* model uses cognitive behavioural interventions. The most frequently applied and effective techniques are listed in Appendix 2 (from Lazarus, 1989). These are not a random mélange or a ragtag collection, but are the therapist's toolkit for strategically implementing a rational treatment plan. Karma Transformation and CBT show considerable overlap. Firstly, the Buddha serves as a model for a "humane being" and Buddhist meditations are subsumed under Meditation. Various meditations are described below.

A strategic intervention plan is based on a deductive assessment formulating the "Karma Functional macro-Analysis" as above. It subsequently formulates the "Karma Functional micro-Analysis" which is limited to the first cycle. While macro-analysis adheres to circular causality, micro-analysis follows a linear causality format embedded within the circularity. A micro-analysis suffices in most cases; macro-analysis is indicated for complex cases to get a complete picture of the client. The former is equivalent to the ABC centrepiece of REBT proposing that it is not the Activating event (A) which emotionally upsets us (Consequence, C), but our own irrational Beliefs (B) about A. The micro-analytic scheme is not only an assessment tool but also a working tool for cognitive modification as well. The ABC corresponds with an *S-O-R* structure and provides a framework for applying REBT techniques as listed below.

---

1.   In a pilot study (n=19) Bitner, Hilman, Victor, and Walsh (2003) found that antidepressants (so-called Selective Serotonine Reuptake Inhibitors) not only reduced levels of major depression but also facilitate the practice of Vipassana meditation in experienced meditators who suffered from clinical disorders.

Cognitive techniques (to tackle Imagery and Cognition): 1. Active disputing of "musts" and other irrational beliefs; 2. Using rational coping statements; 3. Summing up dysfunctional behaviours' disadvantages; 4. Modelling; 5. Distracting (e.g. biofeedback, relaxation, yoga, meditation); 6. Changing cognitions by homework (e.g. forms, books, cassettes); 7. Reframing by seeing the bright side of "awfulness"; 8. Correcting semantics (like black-or-white thinking, arbitrary inferences, overgeneralizations, absolutisms, etc.).

Emotive techniques (to tackle Affect and Sensation): 9. Shame attacking exercises (including judicious use of profane language); 10. Rational-emotive imagery; 11. Forceful coping statements; 12. Forceful self-dialogues (disputing irrational beliefs on tape); 13. Use of humor (e.g. rational humorous songs); 14. Use of group processes for experiential and emotive-evocative exercises; 15. Interpersonal and family processes; 16. Role play processes; 17. Reverse role playing; 18. Other emotive techniques like strong encouragement, forceful disputing, self-disclosure, analogies/metaphors, unconditional acceptance, etc.

Behavioural techniques (referring to Behaviour and Interrelations): 19. In vivo desensitisation; 20. Implosive desensitisation; 21. Remaining in awful situations; 22. Response prevention, 23. Penalizing (as well as rewarding and using other reinforcements), 24. Medication; 25. Social skills training to enhance assertiveness, communication, relationships, or sexuality. (See for a detailed description of these techniques: Kwee & Ellis, 1997).

REBT techniques overlap up to 80% with CBT techniques. Allocating them to specific problems is a heuristic exercise of artistry rather than a strict procedure.

Reality is a perceptual construction which includes cognitive representation, memory/feeling, and projection/visualization. Edelman's (1987) experiments revealed that perception precedes electrical correlates of thinking by 100-200ms: seeing is 20% retinal and 80% brain activity. This is in line with the Buddha's awakening experience leading to the *4-Ennobling Realities*, particularly his perception of the cohesive web of conditionality (*idappaccayata*) which corresponds with the ABC: "when this is, that is; this occurring, that occurs; when this is not, that is not; this ceasing, that ceases." (*Ariyapariyesana Sutta*, on the ennobling quest). In REBT terms: C (feeling) is a function of B (thinking) and A (perceiving), while A and B are a function of C. A, B, and C are interdependent and predicated upon each other; they originate and cease in Dependent Origination. The ABC is also depicted in the *Loka Sutta*:

> Dependent on the eye and forms, eye-consciousness arises; this meeting of three is contact; with contact as condition there is feeling; what one feels that one perceives; what one perceives that one thinks about; what one thinks about that one mentally proliferates.

In the "ABC Karma sequence" proliferation takes place just as it does in the metaphor of the archer targeting the swordsman who was successfully intercepting poison arrows due to unbroken mindfulness until he was distracted and fatally hit. As in the *Vinaya Sutta*, it is not the distraction (A) that killed the swordsman (C) but his own interrupted mindfulness (B). This metaphor implies that we are all constantly being fired upon by poison arrows and that we cannot prevent this. However, we are able and capable to wilfully modify Karma by intending and acting in such a way that we intercept irrational thinking. Due to the speed of thinking, it seems that we only have the choice to cut off "automatic" thought and that we do not have the freedom to prevent it from occurring.

This brings up the subject of "free will" which is from a Buddhist stance an illusion (otherwise the human predicament of suffering would not exist). This proposition is corroborated experimentally (Libet, 1985): preparatory brain activity occurs hundreds of milliseconds prior to the choice to move. This finding was reinforced by brain imaging methods (Soon, Brass, Heinze, & Haynes, 2008). Subjects had their brains scanned while they decided to press a button with an index finger. "Free" decisions are determined by brain activity ahead of time up to 10 seconds before entering awareness. This delay likely reflects a network of cortical control areas that begin to prepare an upcoming decision long before it enters consciousness. Unconscious brain determinants of free decisions suggests a "free won't", rather than a "free will", reason why we usually work on our ABC's after the fact. Whether this "free won't" could later on be transformed into a new habit of a "free will" remains an open question.

CBT/REBT's rational and the Buddhist valid cognitions

In a Nobel Prize awarded study, Kahneman (2003) presented a psychology of rational judgment and choice. He argued that humans rarely make rational decisions because perceptual processes run fast, in parallel, automatically, effortlessly, and associatively, but learn slowly, as reasoning runs slowly, serially, controlled, effortful, rule-governed, and flexible. Unfortunately, the human perceptual apparatus is structurally weak, leading us to see the world – by intuition – through a pair of illusory glasses, quite often the basis of automatically made irrational decisions. Such mistakes are difficult to control because we tend to be carried away by illusions (called Maya in the Buddhist lore).

Amazingly, the Buddha, in the *Vitakkasanthana Sutta,* talked about such automatisms and proposed rational tactics to "therapeutically" modify them:

> (1) Whenever an unwanted thought intrudes awareness, replace this in full awareness by switching to an opposite incompatible thought and by supplanting a wholesome thought instead (e.g., compassion vs. hate or generosity vs. greed).

> (2) If that fails, closely examine the harmful, perilous, and negative long term effects of the unwanted thought: suffering. Redirect and divert attention by averting and distracting activities. Contemplate its many ugly consequences.

(3) If that fails, ignore/forget the thought, engage in distracting activities or focus concentration on something wholesome/healing and do not pay attention to the unwanted thought e.g. by having a walk or doing some other physical activity.

(4) If that fails, take a breather and question its arising. Scrutinize the unwanted thought, its formation, causes, or antecedents, like e.g. anger, fear, or sadness. Investigate its function, and reflect how to remove or stop its putative cause.

(5) If that fails, resist, dominate, and control the unwanted thought by forceful effort: "seize it, restrain it, control it and crush it". Be firm, harsh, and radical, e.g. by clenching the teeth. Thus, one part of the mind controls the other.

Because this practical program seems to refer to thoughts that are "sticky" (intrusive, unwanted, and persistent), the Buddha presumably dealt with obsessions. In the *Sabbasava Sutta* he discussed an overall strategy to abandon afflicting thoughts (*asavas*). In essence, afflictions will not be resolved by magic but by wise reflection. This premise leads to a checking within the deliberate collaborative dialogue for the presence of antidotes by attending appropriately to these questions as regards past and current proclivities and capacities (Premasiri, 2006):

(1) Is there insight that unwholesome thoughts, e.g. on self, actually precede mental misery and that one is fully responsible for feeling-thinking-doing?

(2) Is there self-control of thought impulses in reaction to perception and wise moderation in responding to attraction and repulsion?

(3) Is there rational attention paid to fulfilling basic needs in order to safeguard against illness or is one inclined to indulge in harmful habits like overeating?

(4) Is there a build-up of endurance for tolerating harsh environmental conditions, physical stress or social pressure, to free the person from mental worries?

(5/6) Is there recognition and wise avoidance of intoxicating places and friends, and proactive dropping of them before they can pollute?

(7) Is there cultivation of "awakening factors", i.e. being mindful, investigative, persistent, enthusiastic, serene, focussed, and balanced?

In the 4th century, the Yogacara-Vijnavada school espoused an epistemology that concurs explicitly with the ABC (Anacker, 2005): afflictions are not caused in the world-out-there, but by our own invalid (illusory/delusional) perceptions and thoughts about the world, the other, and the "self". It was Dharmakirti (7th century), the last original Buddhist thinker before the Dharma demised on the Indian subcontinent (1193), who discerned the difference between valid (*prama*) versus invalid (*aprama*) perception and thought (Scheepers, 1994). His discernment is congruent with REBT's rational versus irrational concepts/images. While meditation emphasizes the cleansing of invalid perception and thought, REBT aims at *changing* thoughts' content by disputing irrational beliefs and modifying behaviours which impact emotion.

In REBT cognitions are considered irrational – and invalid for that matter – if they (1) do not correspond with known facts and logics, (2) do not lead to self-chosen wholesome emotive and behavioural goals, and (3) do not advance interpersonal harmony. Therapeutically, it is insufficient to only point at irrational thinking, it is also absolutely necessary to formulate rational alternatives. For instance, a client is depressed when thinking: "He must love me or else I am a worthless human being." Applying the rational criteria, this helpful alternative was constructed in collaborative practice:

> Thinking that way, I won't reach my goal – to feel contentment. There is no evidence that he must love me, nor is there any proof that my worth depends on being loved by him. If he loves another woman, he must not love me, which feels sad but is no reason to detest myself as a human being. My worth of "self" can't be judged, because there is no accurate way to rate it. My mere existence warrants my worth unconditionally. Thus, I'll feel OK and avoid unnecessary conflicts with myself and with him.

By applying the ABC format and adding rational Disputation (D) targeting emotional-behavioural Effects (E), and formulating wholesome and rational thoughts – one acquires an irrationality dissolving relativism leading to contentment amidst adversity. We have to be courageous ("noble"), like the Buddha, not to flee from inevitable Duhkha. The Arahant attains awakening by defeating his inner enemies: the self-chosen detrimental Karma transparent in the ABCDE scheme of rational self-analysis.

There is another instance where Karma Transformation concurs with REBT. The common ground is Korzybski's "General Semantics" (Kwee, 1982) whose axiom is to be aware that language (Speech) is a map, not the territory. Words verbalise the "silent level", the atomic processes of objects and events, along the ladder of abstraction discerning three levels of abstraction: facts/descriptions, interpretations/assumptions, and evaluations/beliefs. As words refer to a range from the concrete to the abstract and from the specific to the general, abstractions can easily confound and truncate our maps of the world resulting in "un"-sane views and emotional disturbance. To be mindful about our Speech we must awaken and see that we mostly react to our own constructed semantic meanings rather than to the pure perception on the silent level. "Unsanity" arises when we take wrong steps on the abstraction ladder. Erroneous semantics include: dead level abstracting (e.g., fear of fear, angry at anger, sad about sadness, etc.), selective abstracting, arbitrary inferring, misattributing, inexact labeling, dichotomous reasoning, over-generalizing, magnifying, minimizing, catastrophising, personifying, and reifying I-me-mine/self-soul and other concepts. These categories are subject to semantic correction. This boils down to awareness of the "is of identity" and understanding of the unwholesomeness, invalidity, irrationality, or dysfunctionality of the verb to be. Thus aware, it is clear that there is no static self to identify with: I consists of many "iiiiiiiiiii's". Rather than saying "I am bad", it is better to say "I behaved badly yesterday". This corresponds with the Buddhist dis-identifying adage: "this is not me, not mine, not myself". The I is not identifiable with a behaviour, thought, or feeling, but is basically empty.

With regard to self, REBT abolishes most of the ego, but does not totally eradicate the self. Thoughts on self violate the *3-Empirical Marks of Existence*:

(1) Because the universe is continuously in a state of flux, the nature of things, including I-me-mine/self, is empty (without essence or inherent existence);

(2) I-me-mine/self is not only an abstraction, i.e. an insubstantial reification, it is also impermanent, thus empty, and nothing but a heap of modalities; and

(3) Craving/grasping/clinging for perfection and non-existing substantial permanence result in Duhkha, an existential agony of emotional/physical *dis-ease*.

Carrying the Buddha's metaphor of Duhkha as inescapable *dis-ease* a step further, the analogy of Duhkha as a self-inflicted "auto-immune" *dis-ease* comes to the fore because emotional agony is in principle inflicted by oneself. If Duhkha is inferred as suffering from the unsatisfactoriness of existence itself, Duhkha can be accurately called "existential neurosis". This run-of-the-mill existential suffering that is "hopeless but not serious" is clearly depicted in Woody Allen's *Deconstructing Harry*. Duhkha is a term defying translation. No doubt, Duhkha is inextricably entwined in life's impermanence and imperfection. Life's flow is troubled like the wheel of a chariot which does not roll smoothly and is somehow stuck due to the stress of life. The stress of Duhkha starts right after birth and becomes manifest and clear in our dealings with decay, disease, and death. First used by Selye in the 1930s, the term stress seems adequate to denote Duhkha if it is conceptualized as the burden bearing on an individual due to situational and emotional changes which evoke non-specific Body/Speech/Mind adaptive reactions. An enduring state of distress might transform *dis-ease* into disease, physical illness due to a long-term exposure to stress-hormones like adrenaline and cortisol. Duhkha as stress has the potential to exacerbate not only psychological disorders like depression, panic/phobia, or Post Traumatic Stress Disorder, but psychosomatic anomalies like high or low blood pressure, heart failure, psychogenic pain, skin irritation, and gastro-intestinal ills as well. Although the Dharma was not meant to cure psychological disorders, the stress definition of Duhkha opens the door to probing whether stress reducing meditation might perhaps ameliorate these types of disorders; psoriasis is a case in point (e.g., Kabat-Zinn, 2003a).

Curbing karmic vicious cycles: Buddhist meditations

Mindfulness meditation is an overarching process constituting both the general and central factor for clearing the mind to practice the *12-Meditations* which the Buddha offered humanity as a gift of compassion. As a central factor the *Mahasatipatthana Sutta* and the *Satipatthana Sutta* refer to the four frames of reference of mindfulness: (1) the body, (2) the body's "behaviours" (i.e. feelings: sensations and emotions), (3) the mind, and (4) the mind's "behaviours" (i.e.

thoughts: visualizations and conceptions). Thus, the first half dozen of the meditations refers to mindfulness of the body and bodily feelings, while the second half dozen refers to mindfulness of the mind and "brainy" thoughts. Inseparably belonging to the Buddha's soteriological system to cease Duhkha, these exercises have the following themes:

(1) *Breathing:* Can we be mindful of how the air of abdominal breathing passes the nostrils and use the breath as an anchor to concentrate, absorb, and contemplate towards clarity and contentment?

(2) *Behaviours:* Can we be mindful of the four dignities (sitting, walking, standing, lying) and all other varieties of body motor conduct, like looking, drinking, chewing, savouring, or silencing?

(3) *Repulsiveness:* Can we be mindful of the body as a bag with two openings and full of grain, wheat, rice, beans, seeds, etc. enveloped by the skin, and made of 32 parts like hair, nails, teeth, flesh, nerves, bones, etc.?

(4) *Elements:* Can we be mindful of the corpse of a cow cut into pieces by a butcher's knife and of the body's elements earth, water, fire, and wind, which awareness is conducive to dis-identify the body from I-me-mine/self?

(5) *Decomposing:* Can we be mindful of a dead body over one to three days, how it is blue, swollen, festering, thrown in the charnel ground, eaten by crows, hawks, vultures, dogs, jackals, worms and reduced to bones and dust?

(6) *Feelings:* Can we be mindful of feelings, noticing whether they are skin deep or heartfelt, how does craving originate/cease; and without grasping/clinging, rate the feeling by questioning: was it pleasant, painful, or neither?

(7) *Hindrances:* Can we be mindful of a sense pleasure, ill-will, sloth/torpor, agitation/worry, and doubt/worry; watch these moods and gently remain aware of impermanence, and query: what valuable teaching is contained in the obstacle?

(8) *Skandhas:* Can we be mindful of Body/Speech/Mind (*Rupa/Nama*), *vedana* (Sensation), *sanna* (Imagery/Cognition), *samkhara* (Affect/Behaviour) in present awareness (*vinnana*) and ask ourselves: is there any self identification?

(9) *Sense-bases:* Can we be mindful thusly: does contact between the organs (eye, ear, nose, tongue, skin, brain) and corresponding external objects (sight, sound, odour, taste, touch, thoughts) sense as pleasant, painful, or neutral?

(10) *Awakening factors:* Can we be mindful and cultivate skilful observation, investigation, persistence, enthusiasm, serenity, focus, and equanimity in order to un-grasp and un-cling, and remain un-craving?

(11) *4-Ennobling Realities* (experiences, data, facts, inquiries, examinations, quests, hypotheses, postulates, or propositions): Being mindful, can we experience Duhkha, know that there is a cause for Duhkha, have confidence that there is a way out of Duhkha, and start to see which way that is?

(12) *8-Fold Balanced Practice:* Being mindful, we question: are our "view-understanding, intention-thought, speech-communication, action-behaviour, living-habitude, effort-commitment, attention-concentration, awareness-introspection" in balance?

There are many more meditations.[2] Well-known are the contemplations on loving-kindness, empathic compassion, and joy/happiness. Because the Dharma is a *modus vivendi*, our whole lives are preferably spent in a meditative way. Formal meditation exercises can be done on all precious experiences in daily life, like e.g. laughing, smiling, singing, drinking, or eating. Embedded in the *8-Fold Balanced Practice*, mindfulness is a scaffold for a meditative *modus vivendi* comprising a balancing of attention-concentration and awareness-introspection. Mindfulness can be process (the practice) or outcome (awareness) and operates in the sensory modality. It is an inward concentration of attention (changeable foreground presence) and awareness (changeable backdrop presence) illuminating consciousness (unchangeable backdrop presence) and enabling introspecting the Dependent Origination of experience. The first step is to tame the restless mind through the practice of Jhana/Dhyana using breathing as an anchor to sharpen concentration in four stages: 1st Jhana (one-pointedness/pleasure/joy), 2nd Jhana (one-pointedness/joy/happiness), 3rd Jhana (one-pointedness/contentment), and 4th Jhana (one-pointedness/equanimity-stillness). One-pointed concentration is a run-up to accessing mindfulness and to awakening in emptiness. Table 2 depicts a quadrant of mindfulness, encompassing: Samatha meditation leading to Samadhi (stabilization) and Vipassana meditation leading to Sunyata (not-self/emptiness) (cf. Table 2 of Ch.1).

Mindfulness starts with cultivating Samatha which is a state of composure characterized by self-control, calm, serenity, balance, undisturbed tranquillity and equanimity of Body/Mind anchored in a bottom up practice in relaxed concentration and bare attention by neutrally observing perceptual stimuli. Practice gradually shifts this state of quiescence into Samadhi, a receptive and non-suppressing stability or flowing absorption resting in an advanced gentle concentration upon occurring *dharmas* (indices of inner stimuli: "perceivables", "knowables", and their concomitants) in the full present and with clear comprehension. This results in the extinction of emotional arousal (Nirvana), a momentary state which may become an enduring trait. Having thus tamed afflicted affect, one evolves into Vipassana, a Mind/Body top-down practice to cleanse the doors of perception enabling perceiving in a special way, i.e. to see "things as they *become*": in

---

2. Formal meditation is mostly practiced in a sitting position with the back held upright, not slouched forward. Research findings suggest that holding the back straight strengthens confidence in the emitted thoughts whether negative or positive (Brinol, Petty, & Wagner, 2009) and that this posture boosts positive mood, while a doubtful posture invites or worsens a dejected mood (Haruki, Homma, Umezawa, & Masaoka, 2001).

Dependent Origination. This insight comes about by remembering to be attentive and vigilantly watchful regarding the un/wholesomeness of Karma. While alert in unclouded luminosity, clearly discerning/comprehending (*sampajanna*) and constantly heedful (*appamada*), one wisely introspects Karma and gradually shifts into the awakening insight of an *empty not-self*, also called luminous "suchness" or vast zeroness (Sunyata). Thus telescoping inner galaxies and encountering *dharmas* in inner spaces, insight dawns that *dharmas* are empty on the ultimate level and socially constructed on the provisional level. Speech, thought, and self-dialogue – to be mindful of – arise in all squares except of square 4. The process from square 1 to 4 is a track of *social deconstruction*. Point zero of emptiness is not a goal in itself. A blank mind is a resetting point and a scaffold for jumpstarting the collaborative practice of *social re-construction* by embodying kindness, compassion, and joy toward what we already are: Relational Interbeing.

Table 2.- Quadrant of Mindfulness Meditation ©

MINDFULNESS *remember* to awaken in the context of the *4-Ennobling Realities & 8-Fold Balanced Practice*[3]	Bare attention: perception of *dharmas* via the 6 senses (knowledge by description); *sati, in attentiveness*	Choiceless awareness: 6th sense *dharmas'* apperception (wisdom by acquaintance); *sampajanna, in luminosity*
Relaxed/gentle/focused concentration on object or process *(by jhana/dhyana)*	1.SAMATHA (Body/Mind) Composure/ tranquility/ equanimity: *Quiescence*	2.SAMADHI (Body/Mind) Receptive absorption/flow-stabilization: *Nirvana*
Vigilant introspection of un/wholesome Karma *(by appamada/watchfulness)*	3.VIPASSANA (Mind/Body) Insight in the "causality" of *Dependent Origination*	4.SUNYATA (Mind/Body) *Not-self/Emptiness Reset-point:* (0)

Despite the fact that a quadrant suggests strict categories, there is overlap. The cultivation of Samatha and Vipassana and the experience of Samadhi and Sunyata are not mutually exclusive phenomena but may occur partly simultaneously. During the initial stages, Samatha and Samadhi work like a *metonym*: "there is no way to mindfulness, mindfulness is the way". This

---

3. Zen's connection with the Samurai (i.e. killing and be killed) is a historical datum and continued into WWII (Victoria, 2006). "If you march, march; if you shoot, shoot; the only thing, don't wobble; awakening manifests itself thusly"; such slogans were used when Zennists were blackmailed to collaborate with the warmongering rulers of their time. Without the *8-Fold Balanced Practice*, Zen (meditation and mindfulness) can be misused deforming the Dharma. Try to steal from a shop while not wanting to be caught; eyes will grow on the back of the skull. Mindfulness is indeed just a human quality, that's old news (Shapiro & Carlson, 2009). So, why mindfulness needs to be torn apart from the *4-Ennobling Realities* (mumbo jumbo?), by silencing and substituting them by the Hippocratic Oath (Kabat-Zinn, 2009a), while psychologists and microbiologists are not MD's, and, at the same time, flirting with a "universal dharma" (not the small d) is mind boggling. Patients and clients too are well able to desecrate mindfulness by turning MBSR into for instance "mindfulness-based sniping and raping", to say it ironically.

is realizing that we are not going anywhere for we are "already there" and therefore nothing needs to be done: "the grass will grow out of itself". Containing means and goals, mindfulness implies that there are no aims to strive for, except for perceiving sensory experience by an effortless effort of a beginner's mind (Zen's *shoshinsha*) with no aim and no gain (Zen's *mushotoku*).[4] However, in the advanced stages, Vipassana and Sunyata are purposeful indeed as they aim to further wise reflection on Karma's vicissitudes (*yoniso manasikara*). In the *Sabbasava* it is advised to implement mindfulness "rightly" (methodically and skillfully) by heedfully introspecting the un/wholesomeness of Karma to gain illuminating insight. Furthermore, note that "choiceless awareness" implies that there is no prejudice, sympathy, or antipathy for what appears in the spaces of Body/Speech/Mind while apperceiving *dharmas*. Apperception is a pre-conceptual perception which excludes pre-conceived ideas which are by definition conceptual and judgmental.

On the frenzy of "Mindfulness-Based" approaches

Mindfulness has become a hot topic amongst health care workers and corporate coaches who refer their work to studies done on mindfulness-based interventions < www.umassmed.edu/cfm/mbsr > (e.g., Shapiro & Carlson, 2009). "Mindfulness-Based Stress Reduction" (MBSR), an 8-week outpatient intensive course, comprises body scan visualization, Hatha Yoga, sitting, walking, CD-guided homework, and self-monitored practice (Kabat-Zinn, 2003a). Mindfulness-based practices have sparked a marketing frenzy amongst adherents who have developed "Mindfulness-Based Cognitive Therapy", "Mindfulness-Based Relapse Prevention", and "Mindfulness-Based Eating Awareness Training", to mention a few programs. "Mindfulness-Based Cognitive Therapy" was efficacious in preventing relapse into depression for up to 60 weeks for those who have suffered three or more depressive episodes (Segal, Williams, & Teasdale, 2002; Ma & Teasdale, 2004; Kenny & Williams, 2007) and could reduce the use of anti-depressant maintenance medication (Kuyken, Byford, Taylor, Watkins, Holden, et al., 2008). Shown to be more effective than waiting-list or "treatment as usual" control groups in heterogeneous samples, MBSR meets the American Psychological Association's "probably efficacious" designation (Baer, 2003; Grossman, Niemann, Schmidt, & Walach, 2004; Shigaki, Glass, & Schopp, 2006) and the UK's National Institute for Clinical Excellence approval for its use in the National Health Service. Studies of what might be its mechanisms of action have mushroomed since mindfulness is surmised to be a common factor in psychotherapy < http://marc.ucla.edu >. Despite promising results, suggesting the intervention is beneficial for psychological and physical symptoms, the jury is still out. In a review

---

4.   To indulge in a Zen metaphor (*mizu no kokoro*), the protagonist develops a mind like water which is a state of mind that flows, reflects, and adapts. Flowing to the lowest point like water the natural state of the mind is never to get clogged or stuck by any thought or feeling. Water does not react, it responds appropriately, adequately, and effectively. A centred mind is just like a pond that returns to a state of a reflecting mirror after a pebble is tossed in. In total readiness and never losing control the mind's natural proclivity is to return to inner calm and flexibility after disturbance. Like water, the nature of the mind is not to be rigid and will always take the shape of any container. It requires rigorous training to keep a total awakening (*shonen shozoku*).

of 15 controlled studies, Toneatto and Nguyen (2007) found that MBSR does not have a reliable effect on clinical symptoms of anxiety and depression. It seems that the state of the art of mindfulness-based procedures is statistically "efficacious" rather than clinically "effective".

Nonetheless, and even though its definition is subject of continuous debate, mindfulness is embraced as an important ingredient in clinical treatment. Kabat-Zinn's (2003b, p.145) working definition is "the awareness that emerges through paying attention on purpose, in the present moment, and non-judgmentally to the unfolding of experience, moment to moment." A more detailed definition includes: (1) non-judging; (2) non-striving; (3) acceptance; (4) patience; (5) trust; (6) openness; and (7) letting go (Kabat-Zinn, 1990). In another instance (Kabat-Zinn, 2003b), mindful attention includes a stance of (8) compassion, (9) interest, (10) friendliness, and (11) open-heartedness toward the experience observed regardless of its quality. Later on (12) non-reactivity and (13) intentionality were added (Kabat-Zinn (2005). "Intentionality" refers to the development of mindfulness which can be either deliberate or effortless. Others added: gentleness, generosity, empathy, gratitude, loving kindness (Shapiro, Schwartz & Bonner, 1998), self-regulation, values clarification, cognitive, emotional, behavioural flexibility, and exposure (Shapiro, Carlson, Astin & Freedman, 2006). Defining mindfulness as intentional, open, and non-judgmental attending, they infer "intentional" as "on purpose", a personal view why one practices (e.g. to reduce hypertension), and believe that "re-perceiving" is the meta-mechanism of change. There is no consensus about what exactly constitutes either mindfulness or intention in the mindfulness-based approaches.

A consensus panel proposed a two-component definition: "the self-regulation of attention so that it is maintained on immediate experience, thereby allowing for increased recognition of mental events in the present moment"... and "adopting a particular orientation toward one's experiences in the present moment, an orientation that is characterized by curiosity, openness, and acceptance" (Bishop, Lau, Shapiro, Carlson, Anderson, et al., 2004, p.232). While acknowledging "intention" as the investigative effort to observe thoughts and feelings, the consensus emphasizes acceptance. According to Siegel, Germer, & Olendzki (2008), non-judgment, compassion, and acceptance are clinical expansions of the original meaning of *sati*: attention, awareness, and remembering. Therapists embrace the acceptance component as one needs first to be aware of the problem to be able change it. A synthetic study of existing questionnaires (Baer, Smith, Hopkins, Krietemeyer, & Toney, 2006) revealed the psychometric potential for assessing five factors of mindfulness: (1) non-reactivity to experience, (2) observing inner experience, (3) acting with awareness, (4) describing with words, and (5) non-judgmental about experience. Whether mindfulness is a state or trait, process or outcome, cure or care will remain the subject of study going forward. Meanwhile, we may conclude that the term "intention" as used by the authors mentioned above does not reflect the meaning of intention of the Dharma as karmic wilful/meaningful activity toward Buddhist values of un/wholesomeness. It seems that there is skittishness to embrace Buddhist values due to perceiving the Dharma as a religion and therefore privileging "universal values" instead. By declaring (the pristine Buddhist) intention to be a direction rather than a destination (emptiness), Karma (nowhere mentioned) is blurred and the Dharma torn apart (e.g., Shapiro & Carlson, 2009, p.9).

In light of this review, we submit that mindfulness as conceived and dispensed in health care is floating adrift not only from the pristine method from which it has been wrest, but also from its avowed purpose as it is sadly missing its crucial Dharma basics.

Mindfulness in the mindfulness-based and kindred approaches like Dialectical Behavior Therapy (DBT, M. Linehan) and Acceptance and Commitment Therapy (ACT, S. Hayes), which include mindfulness in their treatment package, advertently exclude the Dharma. We therefore urgently ask: can mindfulness actually be invoked without subscribing to the Dharma? Traditionally, mindfulness is not a goal in itself but a tool. It has an inextricable function in the Buddha's project to liberate humanity from Duhkha. This is a larger aim than "simply" alleviating patients' suffering. Although in MBSR it is emphasized that mindfulness is not a quick fix, the Buddhist psychological underpinning is in effect conspicuously absent. This leaves the practitioner with a procedure de-contextualized from Dharma theory essential to guide its practice. The tactics behind the stripping of mindfulness from its roots is to not burden clients with Buddhism and to not repel mainstream professionals, a successful strategy.

The mindfulness professional is not obliged to study Buddhist Psychology (e.g., Grepmair, Mitterlehner, & Nickel, 2008). Furthermore, Kabat-Zinn (2003b) is categorical in stating that:

> [Dharma] is at its core truly universal, not exclusively Buddhist... *a coherent phenomenological description of the nature of mind, emotion, and suffering and its potential release...* mindfulness... being about attention, is also of necessity universal. There is nothing particularly Buddhist about it (italics added, p.145)... It is an inherent human capacity... received its most explicit and systematic articulation and development within the Buddhist tradition... although its essence lies at the heart of other ancient and contemporary... teachings as well (p.146)... [MBSR] needed to be free of the Buddhist origins... the objective was not to teach Buddhism... but to... experiment with... novel... methods... At the same time, the program needed to remain faithful... to the universal dharma dimension alluded to, which... lies at the very core of... mindfulness. The task... is to translate the meditative challenges and context into... the lives of the participants, yet without denaturing the dharma dimension... This requires... understanding of that dimension... through... personal engagement... meditation retreats at Buddhist centers or... professional training programs in MBSR (p.149).

We are left with the bewildering impression that the Dharma is diluted to some "universal lawfulness". Buddhist Psychology is given credit through a half-hearted gesture. In fact, in a following article Davidson and Kabat-Zinn (2004, pp.150-152) totally dismissed Buddhist Psychology by stating that mindfulness, defined as moment-to-moment nonjudgmental awareness, "does not include Buddhist psychology"; it is an isomorphic translation "for greater awareness, self-knowledge, equanimity, and self-compassion"... practiced "across all activities of daily living" aimed at "the cultivation of insight and understanding of self and self-in-relationship"... "the cultivation of openhearted presence (has) nothing particularly Buddhist." Revisiting these issues once more, Kabat-Zinn (2009, pp.xxviii-xxix) obfuscates the above by contriving that his use of the mindfulness concept is also:

[A]n umbrella term that subsumes... the Eightfold Noble Path, and... the dharma itself... We never limit our use of mindfulness to its most narrow technical sense... I offered an *operational* definition... [which] leaves the full dimensionality and impact of mindfulness... implicit and available for ongoing inquiry... [T]he word *mindfulness* does double-duty as a comprehensive but tacit umbrella term that included other essential aspects of dharma, [the choice] was made as a potential skilful means to facilitate introducing what Nyanaponika Thera referred to as *the heart of Buddhist meditation* into the mainstream of medicine... and the wider society in a wholly universal rather than Buddhist formulation and vocabulary... [His] inclusive and non-dual formulation offered both validation and permission to trust and act on my own direct experience of the meditation practice and the dharma... even if... it was glossing over... Buddhist psychology... that I felt could be differentiated and clarified later, once...

To give this justification the benefit of the doubt, one needs to believe that Kabat-Zinn never dismissed Buddhist Psychology. If this *post hoc* rationalization is acceptable, disgruntled psychologists with a Buddhist background, who expressed their worry about MBSR and other "Buddhist Lite" approaches, cannot but feel relieved.[5] Without any doubt Kabat-Zinn has earned credit for drawing scholarly attention to mindfulness.

Wrapping up

This present overview of Buddhist Psychology brings in several new viewpoints at different levels of abstraction. First of all, our clinical practice that we call Karma Transformation embraces the meta-psychological perspective of Social Construction as expounded by Gergen (2009) which views everything conceivable as embedded in language and thus interpersonally created. We are all engaged in meaning making through our conversations and dialogues; meaning is not a given but a communal act of discourse and negotiation. It is therefore relevant to participate in collaborative action and reflexive deliberation, and to be aware of the relational origin and impact of our activity. We endorse Korzybski's "to be is to be related", Gergen's "I am linked therefore I am", and add: "to act means to interact" and "to be implies to inter-be". This implies that in therapy and coaching it behooves us to look for the conjoint meeting points which will enhance the participants' motivation to work on a set task of meaning-making and conducting, in togetherness. Espousing a social constructivist position is not per se in disagreement with existing models of psychology; no model is ruled out. Particular models are viewed as voices of particular communities of psychologists standing behind a shared language game. Thus, psychoanalysts use a jargon to communicate with each other which is different from the jargon used by cognitive-behaviour therapists. A social construc-

---

5.   For instance at the 2nd Asian CBT conference, Bangkok, 2008.

tionist stance recognizes that psychology is a multi-vocal endeavour and does not a priori consider one model superior to the other. A model of the mind is at best a narrative or a metaphor of the real or the truth only valid in particular local communities. Although one model can be more influential than the other, no model is preferred as being universal. Our model of choice is the S-O-R model which concurs in a way with the Buddhist model of the mind. While Social Construction provides Buddhist Psychology with a meta-theoretical and interpersonal perspective for meaning and action, the next levels of abstraction refer to the toolkit of Karma Transformation which is on the level of macro-analysis, when assessment and strategy of change are concerned, and on the level of micro-analysis, when the minute to minute application of change techniques are concerned.

On the macro-analytic level it is meaningful to assess the client's status, done here with the help of a blueprint structure called "Karma Functional Analysis" comprising a template of five cycles which provides clues for how to disrupt and curb each of these cycles by developing and using a negotiated strategic action plan opening vistas on what to emphasize in case all five cycles apply to the presenting client. Most clients do not need an elaborate macro-analysis. A cognitive behavioural approach like REBT which offers various techniques including raising awareness might suffice. It should, however, be noted that the primary aim and interest of Karma Transformation is awakening into Dependent Origination implying an understanding of selflessness and interconnectedness. This practice might include therapy and *12-Meditations* to acquire a Buddhist *modus vivendi*. The core practice of meditation is mindfulness.

Although Buddhist scholars are not unanimous on how to define mindfulness, they are unanimous about its inextricable concatenation with the Dharma. This is in sharp contrast with the western view contended by MBSR practitioners who consider mindfulness as a universal human capacity. Although not incorrect, the advantages of mindfulness can be used for other aims than awakening, including, for instance, deepening religious beliefs in one's god. However, as the Dharma is a non-theistic system mindfulness is from a Buddhist point of view a double-edged sword implying the consequence that practitioners also need to incorporate Buddhist teachings. To only use mindfulness chopped from its longstanding tradition impresses as an act of expropriation or pilfering, or a bit of both. A Dharma-embedded wholistic mindfulness repudiates the reduction of mindfulness to the status of a pill. We submit that the use of mindfulness is advisably accompanied by Buddhist Psychology. This is not to make Buddhists out of clients but to be completely honest and, pertinenty, to not be evasive about the Buddhist origins of mindfulness.

Appendix 1: Blueprint of Karma Functional Analysis
Cycle I: SI/CA: cognitive mediation model with interpersonal impact
Cycle II: BSD.A: intrinsic negative consequences or long term primary loss
Cycle III: BI.SA: extrinsic negative consequences or long term secondary loss
Cycle IV: BSI/CA: intrinsic positive consequences or short term primary gain
Cycle V: BI.SA: extrinsic positive consequences or short term secondary gain

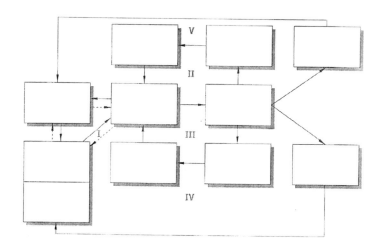

Appendix 2: A Compendium of CBT Evidence-Based Techniques ©

 1 Anger expression
 2 Anti-future shock imagery
 3 Anxiety management training
 4 Associated imagery
 5 Aversive imagery
 6 Behavioural rehearsal
 7 Bibliotherapy
 8 Biofeedback
 9 Communication training
10 Contingency contracting
11 Correcting misconceptions
12 Ellis' ABCDE disputation paradigm
13 Feeling identification
14 Focusing
15 Friendship training
16 Goal-rehearsal or coping imagery
17 Graded sexual approaches
18 Grief therapy
19 Hypnosis
20 Meditation

21 Modelling
22 Non-reinforcement
23 Paradoxical strategies
24 Positive imagery
25 Positive reinforcement
26 Problem-solving
27 Recording & self-monitoring
28 Relaxation/Autogenic training
29 Self-instruction training
30 Sensate focus training
31 Social skills & assertiveness training
32 Stimulus control
33 Systematic exposure
34 The empty chair
35 The step-up technique
36 Threshold training
37 Time limited intercommunications
38 Time projection, forward or backward
39 Thought blocking
40 Tracking

Chapter 22

Meditating Selflessly

James H. Austin

The doctrines which best repay critical examination are those which for the longest period have remained unquestioned.

— Alfred North Whitehead (1861-1947)

Introduction

Even the one-cell amoeba distinguishes between itself and its local environment. Neurobiology reflects this fundamental Self/other distinction. Our brains are hard-wired to pay very close attention to events down in front of us. How else could we wield a hammer to strike just the head of the nail, not those fingers of our other hand? This is a "top-down" form of voluntary attentive processing. It differs from the way our gaze turns up automatically to identify which bird we've just heard call in the sky above.

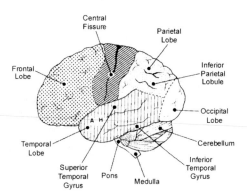

Figure 1: Simplified version showing major anatomical landmarks on the left side of the brain.

At the viewer's left is the convex surface of the *frontal* lobe. Just behind it is the primary motor cortex, then the central fissure, followed by the primary somatosensory cortex. Within the *parietal* lobe, the smaller portion at the top is the superior parietal lobule. The intraparietal sulcus is the boundary separating it from the cortex of the larger inferior parietal lobule beneath. The *occipital* lobe is at the far right. The long *temporal* lobe extends from it. The letters A and H refer to the much deeper locations of the amagydala and hippocampus, both located in the innermost (medial) portions of the temporal lobe. Below the cerebral hemisphere is the *cerebellum* and the *brainstem*. The spinal cord descends from the medulla.

What guides our hammer down toward this nail head? Visual information from the lower visual fields that first spreads through the upper part of the occipital lobe (see Figure 1). These visual messages then speed on up through the *parietal* lobe and forward into our frontal regions. The functions of these networks are action-oriented. Their metrics help us execute commands related to events taking place *close to our central physical axis of Self*. They play a tangible role that is practical, *ego*centric, and Self-relational.

Very different pathways look up when we process distant information. When information from the sky enters these upper fields of vision, it spreads first through the *lower* occipital lobe. These messages then relay *down* through the *temporal lobe* and into the *lower* frontal region. The visual functions along this lower route help us both to identify objects "out there," farther away, and to interpret what these objects might *mean*. Another term for these *other*-relational functions is *allo*-centric. It comes from the Greek, *allo* meaning other.

Figure 2 illustrates the differences. Note how the upper course of the more *dorsal ego-centric* pathway (**E**) first arches up through the *parietal* lobe. This parietal pathway is designed to answer a specific personal question: "*Where* is it *in relation to me*?" How can this upward trajectory into our somatosensory and association cortex satisfy our immediate needs to manipulate tangible things? It takes advantage of two parietal assets: our sensations of *touch* and *proprioception*. The reader is encouraged to consult the brief glossary at the end of this chapter for the meaning of proprioception and of other technical terms.

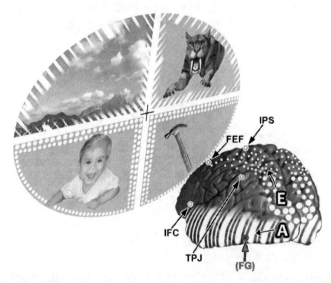

Figure 2: Major Differences in the efficiencies of attentive processing.

---

1. Self is being capitalized throughout simply to suggest that its operations can create many large problems.

This view contrasts our dorsal egocentric, top-down networks with those other networks representing our ventral allocentric, bottom-up pathways. The observer's vantage point is located at a position behind the left hemisphere. The brain is shown gazing up and off to the left into quadrants of scenery, where (imaginary) items are not shown to scale. Starting at the top, the two major dorsal modules for "top-down" visual attention are the intraparietal sulcus (IPS) and the frontal eye field (FEF). They serve as the immediate sharp-pointed vanguards for our subsequent sensory processing and goal-oriented executive behavior. Running through each module, in turn, is the overlapping upward trajectory of the upper parietal → frontal egocentric **(E)** system. It is shown as an arc composed of white circles. Why do rows of similar white circles also surround the *lower* visual quadrants containing the baby (at left) and the hammer (at right)? Because this dorsal attention system attends more efficiently to the way we carefully handle such important items *close* to our body when they are located down in the corresponding *lower* parts of our visual fields. In contrast, our two other modules for cortical attention reside lower down. They are the temporo-parietal junction (TPJ) and the inferior frontal cortex (IFC). We activate them – *chiefly on the right side of the brain* – during involuntary "bottom-up" attention. The lower bands of diagonal white lines suggest that the attentive functions of the lower modules in this ventral attention system serve as the vanguard for the nearby allocentric processing **(A)** networks in our temporal and lower frontal lobes. Why are similar diagonal white lines also shown surrounding the *upper* visual quadrants? Up here, the purpose is to suggest things that a *ventral* temporal ? frontal system could detect most efficiently when it stays globally on the alert. Automatically, it remains poised to identify other items when their more distant stimuli enter the *upper* parts of the visual (and auditory) field. Note the survival advantage in quickly detecting the rustling noises of a potential predator and in identifying it as a sabertooth tiger while it still remains a *relatively long* distance away from one's body. The FG in parenthesis points toward the left fusiform gyrus, hidden on the undersurface of the temporal lobe, where its V4 nerve cells help generate complex visual associations.

Note the different implications in the route taken by the lower cortical networks. Those in the *ventral, allocentric* pathway (A) first pursue a downward course before they then stream on through the temporal lobe. Our pattern-recognition functions emerge along this lower pathway. Their refined associations answer a different question, "*What* is this?" They depend on different special senses – those of *vision* and *hearing*. What we see and hear helps us discriminate among the many other stimuli that enter from distant objects. Often located far beyond our reach, these objects are not yet tangible.

While such dorsal/ventral differences in functional anatomy are elementary, their consequences prove crucial in daily life. They determine how efficiently we deploy attention. Can we insert our house key into its slot on a dark night? Can we glance up in time to realize that the traffic light suddenly switched from yellow to red? Moreover, when we meditate, their two underlying physiologies help decide: will we always keep training our pathways in ways that are *Self*-referential? Or will we allow the field of consciousness to open out in ways that may ultimately become more selfless and *other*-referential?

Two complementary categories of meditation

A standard way to begin seated meditation is first to look down and then to engage in more effortful attempts to: (a) sustain visual attention while focusing on one spot, and (b) still stay focused on the in and out movements linked to one's breathing or on a part of one's body. These examples suggest how *concentrative* meditation tends to begin. We remain the central agency. Our task is to "pay attention" during each of these deliberate, intentional kinds of top-down attentive processing. Any such *voluntary* approach is inherently Self-referential. Moreover, each time we willfully intensify and sharpen our focusing, it means that we must exclude all other items while concentrating on only one small area (see Table 1).

Table I. The Attentive Art of Meditation

CONCENTRATIVE MEDITATION	RECEPTIVE MEDITATION
A more effortful, sustained attention, focused and exclusive	A more effortless, sustained attention, unfocused and inclusive
A more deliberate, one-pointed awareness.	A more open, universal, bare attention.
It requires *voluntary* top-down processing	It expresses *involuntary* modes of bottom-up processing
More *Self*-referential	More *other*-referential
May evolve into absorptions	May shift into intuitive, insightful modes
Choosing to "pay attention"	A bare, choiceless awarenesss

Receptive modes of meditation are more nuanced. Why are they so difficult to appreciate? In part, because their underlying physiologies begin as *less* narrowly focused, involve much *less* effort, and tap into subconscious resources of which we are not aware. Receptive techniques then open up increasingly into more universal kinds of bare awareness. They express, *involuntarily*, our varieties of bottom-up attentive processing.[2] They are inherently inclusive, and *other*-referential. Moreover, the global extent of their intuitive reach evolves at such a glacial pace that its subtleties are difficult to recognize.

Let it be clear at the outset: the individual assets and liabilities of the two styles of meditation are as complementary as Yin and Yang. Concentrative techniques are absolutely fundamental for strengthening one's capacities to focus attentively and to sustain an undistractible clarity of vivid perception. Subsequently, as you intensify concentrative meditative techniques, some may evolve into the superficial absorptions.

Receptive meditative techniques engage subtler potentials to shift into intuitive and insightful modes of consciousness. Much later, and unpredictably, they may open into the rare, transformative, moments of selfless-insight wisdom.

---

2. The order of the two words, attentive processing, serves as a reminder that *attention comes first*. Each sharp salient point of attention impales its target, helping to mobilize and focus our subsequent processing. Moreover, pre-attentive functions also facilitate pre-cognitive processing, many milliseconds before recurrent processes can begin to perceive events consciously.

The selfless states of insight-wisdom: a working hypothesis

In Zen, these later potentially transformative states are termed *kensho* or *satori*. They are more advanced "happenings" of an extraordinary kind. Rigorous Zen criteria insist that they not be confused with the ordinary "quickenings," the brief "epiphanies," or the shallow states of absorption. Some advanced states seem to evolve spontaneously. Others occur in immediate response to a triggering stimulus. When? Only at those crucial moments when every last vestige of the psychic and physical Self vanishes (Austin, 1998, 2000, 2006). These advanced states appear to represent a basic shift in consciousness at very deep subcortical levels. What kind of a shift? Only a shift with a dual capacity can:

- channel attention and perception into *all-out allocentric processing*
- *delete egocentric processing simultaneously* (Austin, 2008, pp.211-230)

In this regard, consider what kinds of training are implied in the opening-up styles of receptive meditation. True, their techniques build upon the foundations of those focusing skills acquired during concentrative meditation (Table 1). Yet, their general approach is to *let go*, in order to enlist *global attentive capacities*. Letting go allows the brain to *open up to intuit meanings in that other world, out there*. The scenery in Figure 2 keeps emphasizing that this more distant environment tends usually to lie beyond the immediate grasp of the physical Self. One also needs to let go of the psychic Self with its intrusive, emotional layers of the *I-Me-Mine* before this allocentric dimension of consciousness can enter.

How do the words in these last two sentences translate into functional anatomy? Beyond the grasp of the physical Self means beyond our conventional occipital ? parietal ? frontal pathways that are so inherently Self-centered. Beyond the reach of the psychic Self? This means beyond the huge investments we've made since infancy in our personal fictions of Self. For decades, we've been representing our overconditioned hopes and fears in countless journal entries. These Self-referential narratives are represented chiefly in certain *medial* frontal-parietal regions, ones not yet discussed. Note that such medial cortical circuits will be buried deep, *between* our two hemispheres. Figure 2 shows the outside of the brain, not these medial Self-centered networks.

Therefore, we'll have to search even deeper to answer the following questions:

- How could all these medial Self attachments drop off, so that their veils of Self no longer conceal other-centered processing?
- If such Self-centered dysfunctions were to stop, how would this free flow of allocentric processing enter experience?

The thalamic gateway to states of experience beyond those constraints imposed by our physical and psychic Self

Some answers to these questions begin down deep in the normal brain. Here, in the thalamus, is a two-tier system of major nuclei. These dorsal and ventral nuclei of the thalamus are the gateways to crucial interactions with their respective dorsal and ventral partners in the cortex above (Austin,

2009², 2010, pp.79-121). It turns out that the nuclei in our dorsal level are organized ego-centrical-ly. What makes their integrative role so Self-centered? Because these nuclei in the upper tier include:

- *The dorsal pulvinar*, the largest nucleus in the whole thalamus. It serves a perceptual role as our major association nucleus. In milliseconds, the pulvinar assigns salience appropriately to countless messages on their way to and from the cortical mosaic in the back of our brain. It has a smaller ally in these silent, Self representational functions,

- *The lateral posterior nucleus*. This nucleus interacts with the most dorsal part of the parietal cortex, our superior parietal lobule. This superior lobule serves as the chief cortical anchor of our somatosensory associations. These thalamo-cortical interactions help create our ongoing *physical* sense of Self. Farther forward in the dorsal thalamus lie:

- *The three limbic nuclei* (lateral dorsal, medial dorsal, and anterior). These limbic nuclei are constantly preoccupied by the polarized messages that relate to our emotions and instinctual drives. Having received these charged resonances from the limbic system, the mission of these limbic nuclei is to conduct a dialogue with particular parts of the cortex. It will not come as a surprise to find that their cortical partners then become *over*stimulated. Indeed, even at rest, these parts of the cortex remain hyperactive, as shown in PET scans and functional MRI scans. Nor is it too surprising to discover that these are the same large *medial* parts of the frontal and parietal cortex referred to in the previous section, the particular regions designed to maintain our pervasive sense of Self. Moreover, these "hot spots" at rest also include the angular gyrus on the outside of the parietal convexity (with which the dorsal pulvinar also shares an intimate dialogue.)

In brief, within the constraints of our present discussion, the *ventral* pulvinar can be said to serve allocentric perceptual functions. Notably, many of its refined visual properties begin with the way it interacts with the *fusiform gyrus* on the undersurface of the temporal lobe (FG in Figure 2). Its pathways for attentive processing continue their other-referential course farther on through the rest of the temporal lobe. (On these pages, the reader will also be spared the intricate – but crucial – inhibitory activities of the reticular nucleus of the thalamus and of its two allied nuclei. Suffice it to note that their powerful inhibitory functions can enable the brain to *selectively* inhibit these five *dorsal* nuclei of the thalamus. The immediate result is to deactivate their Self-centered dorsal networks, *yet still spare the allocentric functions* that flow into conscious experience through the remaining *ventral* pathways.

---

3. Color plate 4 helps to appreciate these intimate interactions between particular parts of the thalamus and the corresponding regions of the cortex.

Can the results of such thalamic inhibitory processes be seen to occur during meditation? The frontice piece (Austin, 1998) is a full color PET scan. It suggests that meditation can indeed cause such observable changes. The relaxed subject had been meditating for two hours, had let go of thoughts, and was paying bare attention to the movements of abdominal breathing. Differences in the degree of red color in the PET scan revealed the asymmetries of metabolic activity that had developed in his brain. Which differences were consistent with a more bottom-up mode of allocentric attentive processing? (1) The relatively greater degrees of activity over the lateral cortex on the right side; (2) The apparent reductions of activity in both the right and left medial prefrontal regions; and (3) The reduction of activity in the right thalamus. Interested readers are referred to Austin (2008, 2009, 2010) for further details.

The earlier sections described how this allocentric path, streaming through the lower occipital → temporal → frontal regions, processes visual stimuli most efficiently when they enter the *upper* visual fields. These stimuli will be arriving from altitudes *above* our horizontal position of gaze (Figure 2). Our visual receptivities attend especially to these superior visual fields in order to identify and evaluate *more distant items*, not those nearby items down inside that personal envelope of space which surrounds our axis of Self. Moreover, it will be in the lower modules of our *right cerebral hemisphere* (those on the opposite side from the TPJ and IFC shown in Figure 2) that we chiefly represent such pre-attentive and attentive capacities. This right side can respond quickly to visual stimuli entering *both* sides of these superior visual fields, aided by its extensive networking capacities with its partner and by its overlappings with other-centered functions nearby.

Do these findings influence how we practice meditation? Yes, they translate into a vast volume of space. This immensity can open up and be accessed for thought-free receptive meditative practices. Consider the options: This huge volume could encompass not only that visual space in front of us, including space just above our forehead. Its sophisticated auditory counterpart stays attuned to an even vaster sphere of sonar-tuned space. Within this more immense volume, we localize and identify faint external sounds, even when these weak auditory stimuli enter from sites far *behind* our ears. We decode visual and auditory stimuli in milliseconds, long before we attach left-sided word thoughts to them in the form of labels.

Zen eyes; Zen ears

In Japan, Shodo Harada-Roshi serves as the highly-regarded abbot of Shogenji in Okayama. Internationally, he is also the visiting abbot of the One Drop Zen association. With regard to the distinctions being drawn throughout this chapter, he explains why our special senses of audition and vision are so crucial in Zen meditation: "The senses, particularly sight and hearing, provide the most basic link between the outside world and the activities of the mind. Unless we learn to integrate each such sensory input with our zazen, our training will be of little practical use." (Shodo Harada-Roshi, 2000, p.56)[4]

---

4. The chapter on zazen (pp. 49 to 67) is recommended, both for its general description, and for its explanations of how the path of concentrative meditation can evolve through stages into the one-pointedness of meditative absorption.

Nanrei Kobori-Roshi (1918-1992) introduced me to Zen training in Kyoto. During his first set of instructions, Kobori-Roshi hinted at the immense volume of enveloping space when he said, "Breathe all the universe in; let it all slide back out." (Austin, 1998, p.65) As later described by Milton Moon (1994, p.33 and p.36), he began his initial instructions during a week-long training period by saying: "At first, I do not want you to focus on things close to you, but on something preferably a little distance away – perhaps on the other side of the room in which you sit." Then, on the last day, he addressed his trainees' basic Self/other distinction in the following manner. He invited them to imagine a sound, one that "can be behind your forehead, or at the back of your head, or close to your left temple, or left ear, or your right temple, or right ear... What we are doing is nothing more than learning to train both our other-awareness and our self-awareness." [sic]

The late contemporary Zen master, Sheng-Yen, advocated a meditative practice called "silent illumination." (Sheng-yen, 2001, pp.139-158) It exemplifies the simplified practice of first "letting go" of one's preoccupations and of becoming goal-less, while in a setting that encourages mental silence. This condition gradually evolves – *by itself* – into an enhanced degree of awareness that becomes "extremely direct, keen and penetrating." Along the way, any personal thoughts of Self will tend to drop off, together with prior barriers that had separated the Self from the environment.

Sheng-yen includes several metaphoric descriptions of the resulting advanced experience that had originated with Hongchi Zengjue (1091-1157). One image by this Sung dynasty master was that of a cool, crisp Autumn sky, "so high and clear that one can see the birds gliding gently high up in the blue." Another was the moon of Autumn shining so clearly in the sky that "everything in the land is illuminated by its cool and gentle light."

These are not descriptions by a person who kept looking down every time he meditated. They point to a style of no-thought meditation (Ch: *wu-shin*) that is no longer subjected to the discursive antics of the "monkey mind." In its earlier phases, such an objective mental field becomes more open to receive – without judgment – whatever might enter from the environment. In its later phases, brief states of illuminating insight can supervene spontaneously. Silent illumination techniques offer a sharp contrast with concentrative techniques that can invoke the agencies of one's physical or psychic Self to focus on willful tasks that have deliberate goals in mind.

Advanced Tibetan meditative techniques of "sky gazing"

When the more adept Tibetan meditators approach their practice of "sky gazing," they gradually learn how to cultivate a stable form of receptive, intensified "open presence" awareness. Great subtleties abound in this complex practice. (Lutz, Dunne, & Davidson, 2008[5]) The adept meditators choose to direct their open eyes slightly upward – toward empty, cloudless space – while still trying to maintain an empty mind that remains open to realize the unity of space and awareness. In the Dzogchen tradition, the term *rigpa* refers to a particular "knowing" of uncon-

---

5. This chapter notes that it is a delicate matter, even for an adept, to enter into the voluntary and discursive cultivation of such advanced refinements of open receptivity.

structed space at this deepest experiental level. A state devoid of all concepts, it is regarded as exemplifying the "unity of emptiness and cognizance." (Urgen, 1995[6])

Semantic problems: spaciousness; monitoring

At this point, it becomes crucial to distinguish between different conditions that relate to the spectrum of visual performance. The first usage of the word "spaciousness" refers to something that is Self-created willfully within one's own imagination. A second usage refers to much more advanced levels and degrees of spaciousness. "Quickenings" and states of this second kind supervene more or less spontaneously. At such moments, one might experience being liberated within an ambient, boundless expanse, lacking all sense that a physical Self exists back in the center. Years pass before meditators discover how to reconcile the paradoxes that are inherent in trying to become "task-less" in order to proceed on the long path toward greater degrees of psychic selflessness. (Austin, 1998, pp.495-499)

Meanwhile, as a covert mental condition, the term "spaciousness" is sometimes also interpreted as a particular brief opening – a "gap" in ongoing experience. It is during these few milliseconds that enough "letting go" occurs, so that visual perspectives can change. One example given is the perceptual change enabling us to switch from one set of the lines of an artificial 2-D "cube" to the other version. (Arpaia & Rapgay, pp.88-109[7]) Several techniques are cited for arriving at such "openings" that could be used to cultivate various kinds and degrees of spaciousness. Some begin with the deliberate attempt to revisualize an actual episode drawn from the past, during which one had beheld a vast, open space.

In English, the word "monitoring" tends to mean some active supervisory agency. Monitoring functions are not neutral. They're set up not simply to observe but to warn or admonish. Their operations then discriminate actively based on the particular kinds of top-down intelligent decisions that one had already made.

Why can so common a usage of this word cause confusion? Because it doesn't yet acknowledge the fact that evolution (having designed intelligently on our behalf) long ago endowed different circuits down in our brainstem and subcortical networks with the hard-wired skills to administer major *bottom*-up forms of discrimination. These covert, reflexive functions remain on-line down in our collicular $\rightarrow$ pulvinar $\rightarrow$ amygdala pathways. Unfortunately, they can become overconditioned.

One premise of selfless meditation is straightforward: liberate lower networks from such unfruitful, dysfunctional limbic and other top-down subjectivities. Freed from their negative

---

6. The implicit non-duality of this state corresponds with the states of kensho-satori in Zen. In sky practice, the eyes are directed upward toward empty, cloudless space, realizing a unity of space and awareness, while in the presence of an open, empty mind (pp. 63-64.) It is essential to appreciate that one might employ a technique of sky gazing either in the sense of gazing in "real time" up into the actual sky, or while exercising and engaging one's imagination in a vivid virtual "re-visualization."
7. While you are looking at the intersecting lines that form a 2-dimensional "cube" on paper, a shift into such a gap happens when you disengage from this first act of apparently seeing it in "3-dimensions" and then see its other partner instead.

intrusions, our avenues of inherent pre-conscious discernment can open wider, allowing us to respond more objectively, affirmatively, and compassionately within the world as *"it really is"*.

Stimuli occurring in natural outdoor settings that trigger extraordinary states of consciousness (e.g. kensho-satori)

Receptive meditation is a generic term. Its practices are not limited to sitting quietly on a cushion indoors. Receptive techniques incorporate a wide variety of practices that openly engage us in mindful attentive behaviors during each and every aspect of our daily life. Earth Day, in mid-April, reminds us to go outdoors and inhale the wonders of the natural world as it reawakens. Studies show that our normal physiological response is to grow calm when we gaze up toward trees that have spreading canopies, especially when they wear the bright green colors of Springtime (Lohr, 2007). In China and Japan, moon-gazing meditative retreats tend to be held on the crisp nights in early October when one gazes up into a clear sky to see the full moon.

Suppose you happen to be a bird watcher, automatically deploying a variety of flexible top-down and bottom-up attentional skills. "Birders" stay openly receptive, alert to glimpse or to hear their quarry in distant field or forest, ready to adjust the focus on their binoculars to get a sharper image of this bird. Meditators can literally "raise their sights" above the horizon by adopting the wide range of more spacious, actual "sky-watching" practices that they engage in naturally whenever they are out of doors. Several brief examples involving Zen meditators illustrate the kinds of "lucid waking" events that might sometimes occur. While their descriptions draw on contemporary sources, they confirm similar observations recorded during many centuries. Over time, as "awakening" and "enlightenment" have entered the vernacular, they often tend to be used as synonyms.

- It was when this Zen meditator happened to look up – into a bit of distant, open sky – that the state of kensho began. (Austin, 1998, 536-539)

- A different Zen meditator recently described an impressive state of consciousness. This episode started with an almost quasi-physical projection: "I looked up at the sky, and that experience was exactly like looking at a mirror… It was a physical sensation, as if the sky had my eyes and could see me staring up at it." (Austin, 2006, p.345)

- The sound of a bird call outside his window served as the auditory stimulus for a third Zen meditator. It triggered an extraordinary emotionless state of "emptiness" and "Oneness" (Austin, 2006, pp.354-355). Incidentally, in the Rinzai Zen tradition, it was when Master Ikkyu (1394-1481) heard the unexpected sound of a crow's "caw," as the bird flew overhead at night, that he was suddenly enlightened.

Earlier examples of visual or auditory events that served as triggering stimuli

The legends about Siddhartha's awakening afford another intriguing example. After he had been meditating all night under the Bodhi tree, the legends also say that he became enlightened when he gazed up before daybreak to glimpse the bright morning "star" *in the sky above the horizon.* This was the culmination of his six-year quest for awakening, the pivotal moment when his transformation began into the kind of humane being they would call a Buddha, One who is Awakened (Austin, 2006, p.621). To ancient astronomers, this bright celestial object was the planet Venus, then low in the Eastern sky. It was the same wandering "star" known to the Greeks as "the bringer of dawn."

A polychrome statue in the Seattle Asian Art Museum dates back to the late thirteenth to fourteenth century in China. Significantly, it is entitled "Monk at the Moment of Enlightenment." This statue clearly depicts a Buddhist monk looking up and into his *left* upper field of vision (Austin, 2009, p.116[8]; Mamassian & Goutcher, 2001).

At the University of Florida, researchers led by Heilman have recently reported further evidence that our two cerebral hemispheres normally show different physiological biases. These biases influence the ways each side of our brain attends and behaves when its motor performances are tested (Drago, Foster, Webster, et al., 2007). How does the normal right hemisphere manifest its biased sensitivities? In ways relevant to the present allocentric theme. Its physiological biases enable this right hemisphere to attend and perform with greater efficiency when its visual targets: (a) are located in the *left upper visual field*, and (b) are increasingly *farther away* from the subject's reaching hand. Moreover, normal subjects reveal such biases not only when researchers insist that they perform specified tasks. They occur *spontaneously* when the subjects are free to deploy pegs anywhere they wish, at random into multiple holes on a two foot square board. How do the subjects insert the pegs when they become free to do so? In directions that tend to lead upward and off toward the left.

A sentence might be cited from the Old Testament as an ancient Judeo-Christian hint of some basic physiological orientations towards stimuli that enter the upper level of our visual fields. Psalm 121 says "I will lift up mine eyes unto the hills from whence cometh my help." A more recent phrasing makes a similar point in an explicit manner (Ricard, 2006, p.195[9]). The words originate in Shabkar (1781-1851), an enlightened sage in the Tibetan tradition.

> I raised my head, looking up,
> And saw the cloudless sky.
> I thought of absolute space, free from limits,
> …Then experienced a freedom
> Without center, without end.

---

8. Normal persons show a curious, innate physiological bias. This visual bias leads us to assume that an external object is subtly illuminated by a diffuse source of light. This illumination seems to originate not only from above our head, but also to arise from a position off to our left by some 26 degrees or so.

9. "Liberation" can be interpreted, in this instance, as the emancipation from all the bonds imposed by the psychic Self (not from only the physical Self, as occurs during the absorptions). When the more advanced "freedom without center, without end" arrives acutely during states of kensho/satori, its complete psychic release (moksha) conveys a novel impression of uncluttered "mental spaciousness." Later, in an authentic sage like Shabkar, one might anticipate that a similar kind of ongoing mental freedom could be a quality manifested among those several trait changes associated with the exceptional "Stage of Ongoing Enlightened Traits" (as discussed in Austin, 1998, pp.637-641.)

Higher ceilings can exert a positive influence

People perceive the space outside their bodies in ways that go on to reshape the nature of their subsequent mental processing. Meyers-Levy and Zhu (2007)[10] studied the way 164 Rice college students responded to either a high- or a low-ceiling room. Higher ceilings were associated: (a) with thoughts related to freedom; (b) with greater degrees of abstract ideation, and (c) with greater abilities to recall items that were previously seen during conditions of free recall (as opposed to memories recalled only after prior cues were given).

Optional positions of gaze: up or down

During a later meditative retreat, Kobori-Roshi might start with the standard instruction to look down at something on the floor a few feet away in front. At first looking slowly and softly, and then "really, *really*" sustaining that focus on something "outside yourself." (Moon, 1994, pp.82-83; the italics are in the original) The next instruction was to let the eyelids close halfway, and then "shift your concentration to a point just above your eyes, between your eyebrows." Such a procedure was not intended to require effort. It remained "very simple: all you are doing is shifting your 'presence of mind,' your 'awareness' or your 'focusing,' from *outside* to *inside*." ... "Then let this relaxed awareness sink down very slowly inside yourself, bringing your awareness back up between your eyebrows, then letting it sink down again." These alternations between soft focusing and intense focusing, between outside and inside, exemplify the use of a *flexible* approach, encouraging trainees to remain open to experiment.

Even though a normal person's upper fields of vision will then be blocked by the overhanging upper eyelids, such an upward gazing position of the eyes underneath is well illustrated in a contemporary statue of Bodhidharma. (Zen traditions regard Bodhidharma, who lived during the 6th century, as the first Zen patriarch in China.) The artist carved this 12 inch wooden statue with great skill. He also placed the black pupils in a noteworthy position. The result depicts the monk's eyes as directed upward, at an angle of 45 degrees. Up there, both eyes are deviated slightly to the left while being held in the parallel position (of conjugate gaze).[11]

Moving away from the Self; the effects of bowing and prostrating

Buddhist practices are also embodied in the active tasks of bowing and prostrating. It turns out that similar intentional motor commands to move one's head favor the mental shift into an allocentric frame of reference (Austin, 2006, pp.201-203). Unfortunately, current neuroimaging

---

10. The 13 pages are not numbered in the version of August 2007 that is published electronically.
11. The interested reader can view this statue, carved in the late 20th century, at picasa.google.com by searching for "Bodhidharma Looking Up." It is also in the author's possession. By convention, the artist also depicts Bodhidharma as lacking his upper and lower eyelids. This enables the white sclera to be seen to an unusual degree around the pupils.

techniques are not able to measure such major changes in the position of one's head and body. However, certain nerve cells in the brain are highly sensitive to the direction in which the head is pointing. These nerve cells are represented both in the limbic system and in two of the three limbic nuclei of the thalamus. (The anterior and lateral dorsal nuclei, just discussed in the previous section) (Austin, 2006, 172-174).

It is plausible to consider that, when we pay mindful attention to our acts of bowing and prostration, we also set in motion a sequence of deactivations that serve to diminish the sense of Self at different physiological levels.

Commentary

The foregoing examples are cited to stimulate further discussion. The point is to suggest that a wider range of supplementary meditative techniques is available and simply to raise the possibility that some might be useful empirically. None are esoteric. They orient one toward normal basic sensitivities and modes of attentive processing to which the human brain is already attuned.

Meditative traditions have already left us a legacy of confusing techniques. Most of them involve tasks that require some degree of *top-down* attentiveness. These have obvious highly practical applications. Indeed, every day, they serve to direct our physical body and our personal goals toward the many useful activities that we conduct relatively close to our own bodies. Accordingly, they also involve our being intrusively Self-centered at one or another level.

On the other hand, trade-offs are implicit in all techniques. Once one attains sufficient skill at applying the techniques of concentrative meditation, it can also prove useful to learn how to *let go* into bottom-up modes of attentiveness and open receptivity. Other-centered styles of processing can become increasingly useful at later stages along the maturing meditative path. By enhancing intuitive modes of awareness and reshaping attitudes, they can help orient behaviors toward more compassionate, externally oriented styles of living. Experimenting with allocentric approaches that open up alternative avenues for seeing and hearing can help one dissolve habitual Self-centered attachments. In this regard, Harada-Roshi advises us to "always work creatively and inventively on how to let go of ourselves... we have to let go and see the world exactly as it is." (Shodo Harada-Roshi, 2000, p.133)

Still, by way of re-emphasizing how important are the basic skills of top-down attention, it is noteworthy that the "pop-out" functions we generally attribute to bottom-up attentive processing (Austin, 1998, pp.278-281) can be further enhanced by using spatial priming cues that also serve to activate the frontal eye field in the upper parts of the left frontal region (O'Shea, Muggleton, Cowey, et al., 2007). This same report includes explanations for how a long-term program of meditation could gradually train one's various powers of attention.

It is counterproductive to add top-heavy multitasking programs that only burden meditators' left hemispheres with more monkey-minded word thoughts. The Zen approach to "no-thought" styles of silent meditation allows the brain to gradually calm the excessive auditory language functions that would otherwise constantly agitate one's *left* temporal → frontal networks. One result of this quieting could be greater opportunities for *right-sided* allocentric intuitive functions to take the initiative (Austin, 2009, pp.150-152).

This working hypothesis finds preliminary support in a study of ten patients with aphasia (Etcoff, Ekman, Magee, & Frank, 2000). Chronic, *left-sided* brain damage had impaired their abilities to comprehend speech. While watching videotapes of faces showing expressions that yielded emotional clues, their task was to discern who was lying. These ten patients were significantly better than were their matched controls who were either normal (n=10) or who had sustained right-sided damage (n=10).

In conclusion, a *dual*, flexible program of attention training would seem to be optimal. Its complementary attributes could enable one's brain not only to let go of its old Self-referential habits, but also to open up into allocentric modes of consciousness that are potentially more creative.

In the interim, whatever might be the practical and heuristic usefulness of such propositions, it seems appropriate to close with a comment made back in the 9th century. Then, old Master Huang-po reminded us that a "full understanding can come to you only through an inexpressible mystery."

Glossary

amygdala	a key nucleus in the limbic system responsible for the primal resonances of our instinctual fears.
angular gyrus	the most posterior part of the inferior parietal lobule.
collicular	referring to the superior and inferior colliculi of the upper brain stem. These generate our reflex responses to visual and auditory stimuli.
convexity	the curved outer surface of the brain.
cortex	the outer layer of the brain, rich in nerve cells.
dorsaloriginally	referring to the back, rather than in the belly. In the brain, dorsal often refers to the uppermost.
functional MRI	functional magnetic resonance imaging (fMRI): a neuroimaging technique that shows momentary local changes in blood oxygenation; these changes help to generate images that provide an indirect index of how active the brain is locally.
lateral	on the outside surface of.
limbic system	a consortium of interacting structures that help generate our emotions, motivations, memories, and instinctual drives. This system includes the amygdala, hippocampus, hypothalamus, septal nuclei and cingulate gyrus. It contributes to the assets and liabilities of our psychic Self.
medial	on the inside surface, closer to the midline.
PET scans	positron emission tomography. A neuro-imaging technique that shows how metabolic activity differs in various regions of the brain.
proprioception	he subtle sensations entering from our muscles, joints, and tendons that contribute to our subliminal sense of a physical Self.
reticular nucleus	the "cap" surrounding the thalamus that inhibits thalamo ↔ cortical transmissions.
thalamus	that major cluster of nuclei deep in the center of the brain. All of our sensations (except for smell) pass through the thalamus on their way up to the cortex.
ventral	originally referring to the belly rather than the back. In the brain, ventral often refers to the lowermost.
visual fields	the area in which one pays attention to visual stimuli entering from the outside world (see Figure 2).
V4 nerve cells	nerve cells that perform higher level discriminations in the visual association cortex.

Closing Chapter

Chapter 23

Relational Buddhism: On "Interhumane Multibeing" And Buddhist Social Action

Maurits G.T. Kwee

Introduction

This chapter starts with the historical developments of "Humanistic Buddhism" and "Engaged Buddhism", and shifts into the basic tenets of "Relational Buddhism". Developed in the latter part of the past century and *en vogue* today, a socially engaged Dharma serves the laudable aim of helping suffering communities and societies. Although this social engagement has lead to more political involvement and action, it has not, per se, brought about a revolutionary perspective for the Dharma at the level of content in search for "Truth". At the practical level an antidote against inaction and indifference, the social meditations of the *Brahmaviharas* – kindness, compassion, joy, and equanimity – have always been an intrinsic part of the pan-Buddhist culture of soteriology. Amalgamating Buddhist Psychology and Social Construction, Relational Buddhism views individual functioning emerging out of relationship. Viewing the relational preceding the personal appears particularly promising in understanding the self/not-self binary and self-other dualism as "Interhumane Multibeing". The hope is that this transcending development will regenerate the Dharma's "non-foundational" teaching of emptiness as a practice of communal construction of reality by continuing to apply collaborative methods from a rich source of transformational activity lodged in variegated Buddhist cultural traditions to create a future of togetherness.

Background of Humanistic Buddhism

From the latter part of the past century up until today, much attention has been drawn by the currents of Humanistic Buddhism (HB) and Engaged Buddhism (EB). The terms "humanistic" and "engaged" reflect separable though also overlapping concepts that refer to a social movement from within Buddhist circles. Because of the "movement" connotation, the term Buddh-*ism* as a pan-Buddhist philosophy that guides this current is warranted. Guruge (2005) pointed at the reformative quality of the movement. Another trail that connects the engaged and humanistic aspects in Buddhism is "Action Dharma" which places modern social action next to the past ways of knowledge, ritual, and devotion (Queen, Prebish, & Keown, 2003). Despite the general acceptance of Buddhism by the public at large and in academia (Kotler, 1996), the question arises whether these manifestations of the Dharma are relatively meaningless labels or reflect something new for daily practice? Do they have the power to rejuvenate the Dharma and make it apt for the 21st century? Or is social Buddhist activism nothing but an imitation of Christian protest movements? How do HB and EB relate to Relational Buddhism, Buddhist Psychology, and Social Construction?

As explained by Hsing Yun (born 1927) of the Fo Guang Shang order, HB is neither a new teaching nor a new form of the Dharma, but the teaching of the Buddha that emphasizes social engagement based on the wisdom of kindness, compassion, joy, and equanimity (the social meditations). For Hsin Yun (BLIA Newsletter, 5/1998), the Buddha's message is: (1) Karma. We reap what we sow: our own actions determine our own destinies. There is no god that manipulates our lives. When we act positively, we plant a positive seed. When we act negatively, we plant a negative seed. (2) Dependent Origination. Nothing in this world exists independently of causes and conditions. We exist in a web of (social) inter-relatedness in becoming as well as in ceasing. Extremes are to be avoided in favour of a Middle Way. (3) Equality (democracy). The idea that superior or inferior beings exist is erroneous: no one is on a pedestal. Aliveness makes us all equal. The Buddha and other humans only differ in the state of being: we are not yet awakened. (4) Abolishing the notion of self. The duality of self and others is a factor of ego to which we are attached. Whenever able to see the interrelatedness of being, all existence on this globe reveals itself in non-dual distinction. The basic stance is not to flee the world and this stance goes back to the Buddha's teaching to understand and deal with events with an awakened mind.

Belonging to the Lin-chi (Japanese: Rinzai) lineage, in fact as its 48th patriarch, Hsing Yun also points at Hui-neng (638-713, 6th Chan patriarch), who stated that the Dharma is to be found in this world of our senses, not in another world: leaving this world to look for the Dharma is as futile as searching for the rabbit's horn < http://experts.about.com/e/h/hs/Hsing_Yun.htm >. Hsing Yun's direct inspiration stems from the actual contact with and reading of the work of Tai Xu (1889-1947). Rather than the passivity of reclusion, the latter emphasized activity in society and disseminated his then new ideas in a periodical *Humanity Magazine* that he edited. The Buddhist Pure Land (bliss and happiness) is not some escape after this lifetime, but a mind state to open up to right now. The widely travelled Tai Xu was in Europe and the USA before WWII, and propagated what he called EB. He targeted a revival of Buddhist practices from the Tang Dynasty (618-907) which was the golden age of Chan. In that era, the Buddhist community contributed greatly to the society at large by, for instance, banking and offering zero interest loans to the have-nots and providing shelter for the homeless. He and his people did not work solely on their own salvation; they also helped to redeem all living beings by being actively involved in communal life. After the demise of the Tang Dynasty, Buddhists were suppressed; their leaders mostly retreated in monasteries.

This emphasis on the improvement of society counters the prevailing misunderstanding that the Dharma is an escapist's abandonment of society's needs. After all, the Buddha practiced, awakened, shared his insights, and hence is a man of this world. HB highlights six essentials:

> (1) Humaneness. The Buddha was a "humane" being with a family who had an awakened "this-worldly" orientation. He is neither a prophet, nor a divine being or a god, but a model for humanity to acquire wisdom through the practice of kindness, compassion, and joy in mindful awareness.

(2) Daily living. The Buddha provided guidelines on how one advisably should mindfully live one's life. His instructions include walking, standing, sitting, lying, sleeping, eating, dressing, working, relating, and how to conduct one's life in the private and social realms to realize one's "true nature".

(3) Altruism. As interdependent beings, we do not exist in isolation and are obliged to serve those who suffer. (NB: Altruism implies enlightened self-interest: helping oneself first to be able to give more to others, like a mother wearing an oxygen mask before helping her child in an airplane calamity.)

(4) Joyfulness. Joy is an antidote and relief of existential suffering. The cessation of suffering from dissatisfaction due to life's imperfection and impermanence is a quintessential Buddhist value. The laughing Buddha is a symbolic representation of this quality that ideally immerses humanity in the future.

(5) Timeliness. The emphasis is to work on a "pure land" in the "herenow" by examining current social issues and advocating peaceful/non-violent solutions based on loving kindness. This implies a commitment to caring for sentient beings and the environment and being involved in any kind of social action.

(6) Universality. The potential to cultivate wisdom and awaken (See Things As They Are/Become) is a human potential, regardless of status, race, or gender. In line with the Buddha's spirit to save all beings, the intention is to reach out to all peoples of the world in a progressive and practical mode.

Few will disagree with the above tenets. They go back to a 2600 year history of pristine origin and that exude a Chan/Zen spirit with a "Pure Land" heavenly flavour.

HB as an engaged practice in service of the communities symbolizes the aims of Buddhism as a whole. Thus, it might serve as a unifying headline to redefine the Dharma for the benefit of contemporary humanity (Kimball, 2000; Santucci, 2000). Chinese people are the majority of present day Buddhists, but unfortunately most of them have a mistaken idea of the Dharma from a HB point of view. They unfortunately render an image of the Dharma as a religion that worships the Buddha, deities, and ghosts, devotionally ask favours from demigods and pray for a better rebirth of the dead. Frequently confused with primitive folk beliefs, it is criticized as superstition. Such criticism is fuelled by many Buddhists themselves, who seek an early rebirth in a pure Buddha-land in the beyond as their priority in life, thus infusing in the general public a false idea of their practice as a vain, passive, and escapist faith. However, HB's essential characteristic of being engaged, Tai Xu's "pure land on earth", emphasizes the practice of ethics, morals, and awakening. This implies taking responsibility for one's multiple roles in interaction with others, as a child, parent, teacher, student, employer, employee, husband, wife, or friend. The advice is to uphold ten virtues rooted in five precepts: not to kill, steal, misconduct, lie, or use toxic drugs. Right awakening is the practice of the *4-Ennobling Realities*: There is suffering due to dissatisfaction in (interpersonal) life, there is a cause for this misery due to karmic meaningful/intentional (inter)action, there is a way out of psychological suffering, and this is the *8-Fold Balanced Practice* improving relationship: balanced view, intention, speech, action, livelihood, effort, mindfulness, and attention. A pure land is attained by liberating oneself toward Nirvana, a condition wherein ignorance and negative emotional states are extinguished by the practice of the social meditations.

Hsing Yun is the living example of engaged Buddhist practice. In the 1950s he established a cultural centre, Fo Guang Cultural Enterprise Co., Ltd., which publishes books, audio and visual aids. In the 1960s he founded the Fo Guang Shan Buddhist Order with headquarters in Taiwan. Over 150 temple branches in thirty countries have been established, the largest of which are situated in California, Australia, and South Africa. Emphasizing education and service, the Order maintains universities, colleges, libraries, art galleries, free mobile clinics, as well as a children's' and a retirement home, a high school, and a TV station. Under the venerable Hsin Yung more than 1000 disciples were tonsured, among them a large number of females. He organized conferences to bring together the various Buddhist schools and is a prolific writer whose over one hundred books in Chinese have been translated into other languages. Living by his adage that community transcends the individual and by so doing fulfilling the individual in the most complete way possible, he encourages people to unite the local and global communities into a world of equality, joy, and peacefulness. With over a million members, the Order's lay organization, "Buddha's Light International Association" is active worldwide. Fo Guang Shan has developed in almost 40 years into an influential movement that propagates an HB attitude toward capitalism, democracy, women's rights, and other contemporary issues, such as filial piety, abortion, capital punishment, and so forth.

The term "humanistic" has also been used in western psychology since the 1950s. Psychologists concerned with advancing a wholistic vision then founded an association dedicated to focusing on uniquely human issues, such as self-actualization, love, and creativity in order to learn to understand what it means to be human. It became the "third force" in psychology after behaviourism and psychoanalysis (Bugental, 1964). Human beings cannot be reduced to components, possess uniquely human context – a consciousness that includes an awareness of oneself in the context of other people – have choices and responsibilities, and are intentional. Human beings seek meaning, value, and creativity. A leading proponent, Maslow (1908-1970), discerned human needs in five stages topped by "self-actualization", an ideal state beyond "subject" and "object" which is connected to the Buddhist notions of "selflessness", "true self", and "Nirvana". Congruent with HB, humanistic psychology is also oriented toward social issues like the holocaust and global peace, reducing of violence and promoting social justice. The tenets of HB lack the understanding of what "relational humanism" (Gergen, 1997) which is a social account of human agency in the context of Social Constructionism (SC). The social constructional view is the broad perspective from which this chapter is written.

Thich Nhat Hanh's Engaged Buddhism

It seems evident that a socially and politically engaged Dharma is inherent in the teaching itself, particularly in the practice of interdependence/non-selfness, compassion/kindness, and generosity/helpfulness. Nevertheless, there appears to be a tacit controversy about the origin of the term EB. While the HB group would proclaim Tai Xu as the one who has coined the EB concept, others would point at Thich Nhat Hanh (Thay), who used the concept in the sixties (Thich, 1967). As Tai Xu died in 1947, it is likely that EB is his legacy, although Thay, who was a social activist during the Vietnam War, contributed significantly in moving the Buddhist ideal from a limited individualistic, internal work of meditation to one of social engagement. In the 1980s the broad label Socially Engaged Buddhism emerged. Comprised of various individuals from diverse backgrounds and inspired by Buddhist values, more or less synchronously appearing movements act, motivated by the aim to lessen the world's suffering by engaging in social/secular realities, instead of focusing on transcendent/spiritual truths and renouncing society's socio-cultural, political and economic structures. Engagement may take different forms, like voting, lobbying, and protesting, activities that challenge and change institutionalized perpetuation of suffering through oppression. A Dharma that is socially engaged encompasses all domains of life, private and public, and includes ecological concerns < http://jbe.gold.ac.uk/7/yarnall001.html >.

As Thay (1993) explained EB is just and nothing but the Dharma called by another name. The Dharma is intrinsically engaged. If it is not engaged, it is not the Dharma. When one practices the Dharma based on its precepts, in the family or in the community, it is EB. In fact, the rationale is to emphasize the social meditations. EB gained momentum through the work of Buddhist activists like Thay (peacemaking, Vietnam), Buddhadasa Bhikkhu and Sulak Sivaraksa (social justice, Thailand), A.T. Ariyaratne (Sarvodaya Shramadana movement, Sri Lanka), Daisaku Ikeda (Soka Gakkai movement, Japan), Dr. B.R. Ambedkar (the late Dalit leader, India), Aung San Suu Kyi (Nobel Prize laureate and human rights leader, Myanmar), and many Buddhist women throughout Asia. These adherents have campaigned for social and economic responsibility in various areas of community life, risked their lives, and attracted millions of new adherents. Leading proponents of this emerging current can be found in Northern and Southern schools, the exoteric and esoteric traditions, and in Asia and the West. Among the movements in the West are the Order of Interbeing (Thay), the Free Tibet Movement (Dalai Lama) and the Peacemaker Order (Bernie Glassman). A social and engaged Buddhism removes ignorance not only by reading ancient scriptures, but also by working on peace and with the underdog, the destitute and downtrodden, like prisoners, HIV infected and dying people. Thus, there is no place for apathy. Liberation comes from helping to liberate others, which is consonant with the defining element of the Bodhisattva ideal. The Buddha's Dependent Origination and reciprocal conditioning cannot but force one to also step out of the meditation hall and to do something to change the *faux pas* in the world, and to thus liberate each other in the world of "Interbeing".

Kotler's (1996) reflects the state of the art at the end of the past century in an anthology that presents a comprehensive retrospective of 60 socially engaged writings on humanity's everyday concerns by prominent voices. Morgan (2005) points at Upaya or *upayakausalya* (*fang-pien* in Mandarin and *hoben* in Japanese): a socially engaged Dharma inheres in the Buddhist skilful methodology to deal with social circumstances. This methodology makes it possible to adequately translate the Dharma into a way of life, philosophy, metaphysics, or religion. Two western pigeon holes of the Dharma are: social activism and scientific psychology. To meet the needs of changing circumstances any Upaya is sanctioned if only the underlying motivation is to compassionately save fellow human beings (Pye, 1978). The contention that the Dharma is intrinsically engaged is but one voice in the choir. Morgan discerns overlapping but distinctive other hymn sheets that contain melodies varying: from – some social activists just happen to be Buddhists, social engagement is a western/Christian colonizing of the Dharma, a socially engaged Dharma is a new Buddhist vehicle for the West – to: the Buddha taught a soteriology, not social activism. Obviously there is no necessity to be a Buddhist in order to be socially active. Most social engagement is demonstrated by political left-wingers. The point is that socialist Christians began to see activism as a religious practice and that this attitudinal shift most probably pressed the new Buddhists in the West, who are inspired by socialism, to emphasize their engagement. However, to view a socially engaged Dharma as a "new yana", the next vehicle post-Theravada and post-Mahayana, presents a position that endorses a political colour for the Dharma.

On the level of content, a socially active Dharma by itself does not seem to warrant the predicate of a new vehicle. An emphasis on social engagement does not resolve for instance the issue that the philosophical, metaphysical, and religious Upayas of the past seem to have outlived their usefulness for disseminating a practical teaching of non-selfness and non-theism in a postmodern era. To proclaim the Dharma as a religion uses western vocabularies, idioms, and linguistics that mould and keep on moulding a way of life (*Magga*), founded on psychological principles, into something that was not intended (as the Buddha never claimed to be a god or a prophet). After all, by bashing the Brahmins, the Buddha in fact bashed (poly)theism in all its guises. Unfortunately, the Upayas of Mahayana and Vajrayana, full of metaphysics and cosmology (although both are founded on emptiness) did themselves invite distorted views. Thus, up until today we may frequently read the mistaken opinion that the Dharma is an "other-worldly religious tradition", a sound that is understandable in a metaphysical/cosmological context.

The question whether the Dharma is authentically a socially active tradition or not is less important than to practice the genuine feelings of kindness, compassion, and joy in meditative balance towards sentient beings in daily life. However, this belongs to the field of social psychology rather than to the field of religion and theology, and requires a relational view of life based on the basic observation that the relational precedes and supersedes the personal and which questions the autonomous. Little is known in the West about the Dharma's social dimension (Rahula, 1988), but its influence on societies in Buddhist dominated areas and countries are unmistakable (Victoria, 2006). According to Yarnall (2000), there is a group of adherents emphasizing the continuity with Buddhism's traditional past that made no split between awakening and being social. To be a meditator implies being this-worldly socially aware (especially of institutionalized greed [e.g., CEO's grabbing culture] and hatred [e.g., war and terrorism] due to ignorance, i.e. people as independent agencies). These "traditionalists" can be juxtaposed to the "modernists", who emphasize a discontinuity with the past by believing in the absolute value of reason, objectivity, scientific truth, order, prediction, experimentation, and control. Since its inception socio-political teachings and practices have been there, even if only latent. These came to the fore when the Dharma encountered western ways of modern living, particularly socialism. A modern engaged Dharma contains essential features of traditional teachings, but also essential differences. It is therefore viewed as a quite new form of the Dharma. Is it really as new as it appears?

Traditionalist authors functioning in the West like the 14th Dalai Lama, Khemadhammo, Kato Shonin, Rahula, Sivaraksa, and Thay stem(med) from Buddhist cultures. A few stem originally from western cultures (e.g., Stephen Batchelor, Lyn Fine, Bernard Glassman, Paula

Green, Patricia Hunt-Perry, Joanna Macy, and Robert Thurman). In the case of modernists, only a few of them come from historically Buddhist cultures. Predominantly, modernists originate from western cultures (e.g., Robert Aitken, Cynthia Eller, Nelson Foster, Richard Gombrich, Ken Jones, Joseph Kitagawa, Kenneth Kraft, Christopher Queen, Sangharakshita [English-born], Gary Snyder, Judith Simmer-Brown, and Max Weber). The traditionalists criticize the modernists of not understanding the spirit of the Dharma and for missing the Buddhist social essence of which the social meditations are a case in point. On the other hand, modernists accuse traditionalists of reconstructing history. They assert that Theravada in particular has been only indirectly and moderately interested in socio-political issues. It must be admitted that the Buddhist social activism of the past decades has little direct allegiance to the meditative and devotional tradition of the Dharma. Buddhist scholars traditionally emphasized philosophy rather than sociology and social psychology. Whether social engagement (and for that matter social activism) is really something new or has always been an intrinsic (but untapped) source is for the reader to conclude.

A New Buddhist Psychology: a Neoyana?

Traditionality/pre-modernity, modernity, and post-modernity co-exist and complement each other. The postmodernist world-view is located on the cutting edge of a developing Dharma by challenging the modernist values of reason, objectivity, science, order, prediction, experimentation, and control, and holding these values as untenable; postmodernists seek for more promising avenues. While postmodernism is a highly general term, SC may be inferred as a specific outcome. Since the late 20th century, it seems that the modernist Buddhists seem to be overhauled by postmodern Buddhist psychologists (e.g., Kwee, Gergen, & Koshikawa, 2006) who are active in translating and integrating western and Buddhist Psychology into a merger of East/West practices that aim to transform emotional suffering of individuals and organizations into nirvanic contentment through the relational paradigm of SC.

While HB and EB exclusively reflect the socialist side of the Dharma, a full picture of the Dharma comprises attending the full catastrophe of Body/Speech/Mind. The wholistic functioning of these discernible but inseparable modalities can be operationalized in social-clinical-neuro-psychological terms. The Dharma as a psychology that combines Buddhist and western, particularly relational, insights – a "new" Buddhist Psychology – appears to be a promising candidate for an innovative, full-fledged, western Dharma manifestation that might even include a Dharma of socialism. Discussion about whether HB and EB were or were not part of the Dharma since its inception, however important, seems futile, since social action is always relevant to those millions of people who suffer from a lack of food, water, and shelter, and require assistance. The postmodern Zeitgeist does not dismiss or exclude but includes modernist ideas and actions to eradicate the suffering and misery of communities in societies at large (De Silva, 2002). Social action had always been an intrinsic part of the Dharma as evidenced by its ultimate awakened practice of the social meditations. *From its beginnings in the iron-age up to the present day, the Dharma has gone through many cultural transformations while keeping its pan-Buddhist tenets.* By emphasizing the Buddha's Body/Speech/Mind wholistic model as a paradigm, also conceptualized as Bio-Psycho-Social, a socially engaged Buddhism can be subsumed as a part of this large context. We are Body conceived in sexual interaction, we are Speech from the cradle to the grave in social interaction, and we are Mind.

Is mind self-contained behind the eye-balls under the skin or is mind located in-between inter-acting people?

The 3ʳᵈ century Mahayana teaching on the turnings of the wheel (*dharmachakra*) reflects a dialectics in the Dharma's history (Powers, 1995). The *Sandhinirmocana Sutra* elu-cidate Upaya as a skilful way of education that adapts the form aspects of the Dharma to spe-cific individuals and audiences, each with their specific capacities and levels of understanding in specific time periods, as each group requires specific teachings in a particular time. The scriptures reveal that:

> (1) The 1ˢᵗ turning: the Buddha's pristine teachings (5/6ᵗʰ century BCE) as in the Nikayas and in its later abstraction the *Abhidhamma* (worked on until the 5ᵗʰ century), deal with a provisional reality that hides a pervasive empti-ness of ultimate reality. It is a Middle Way of the personal *not*-self which dissolves all conceptual dualities by proclaiming them to be "neither this, nor that".

> (2) The 2ⁿᵈ turning: the philosophical teachings of Nagarjuna (Madhyamaka, 2ⁿᵈ century) view the self's emptiness as insufficient. This wisdom of ultimate emptiness of all phenomena (*non*-self) through a com-plete emptiness of emptiness, at the cost of the advantages of the positive, settles the substantial remnants left unattended in the negation of the previ-ous turning (a *via negativa*).

> (3) The 3ʳᵈ turning (a *via positiva*): the teachings of Asanga and Vasubandhu (Yogacara, 4ᵗʰ century) regard non-self's emptiness as "somethingness" and eradicate this problem by dissolving the "last" of binaries, the subject-object binary by meditating non-dual awareness, unveiling a mirror-like "suchness" without intruding thoughts, and bringing the social meditations into action.

The Dharma may guide coaches and therapists to abolish the self and acquire a helicopter view by penetrating the old Buddhist Psychology of the *Abhidhamma*, Nagarjuna's empti-ness, Asanga-Vasubandhu's non-duality, and Fa-tsang's universal interpenetration (7ᵗʰ centu-ry). The latter corresponds surprisingly with SC (Gergen, 2009), a postmodern metapsychol-ogy contending that reality is derived from and only found within communal agreement (beyond community there is silence). While Asanga's teachings (*Cittamatra*) developed into an ontological, cosmological, and devotional practice that was eventually absorbed into the Sino-Japanese and Himalayan cultures, Vasubandhu's epistemology-psychology (*Vijnavada*) remained relatively undeveloped. Picking up Vasubandhu's thread, the time seems ripe to regenerate the Dharma as an applied psychology and transcultural practice. As Mahayana doctrines outlive their usefulness, a new era that deserves the predicate "Neoyana" appears on the horizon. In order to modulate action its emphasis lies in correlating brain effects of meditation through sophisticated devices, in applying meditation in clinical settings, and in the metapsychology of SC.

Ironically, the Dharma preceded the essence of postmodern culture that prioritizes inter-dependence and interconnectedness as well as deconstruction and emptiness to the detriment of the existence of eternal Truths. The Dharma is characterized by inescapable parallels with these and other postmodern insights, such as that the self is not an independent entity, but an empty abstraction of a relational interpenetrating matrix. Recently, a New Buddhist Psychology (NBP) had been proposed (Kwee & Taams, 2006) which has the potential to fathom, accommodate, and underpin most of the practice-research-theory of Theravada and Mahayana/Vajrayana, and the teachings of Nagarjuna and Vasubandhu. NBP is a synthesis of western mainstream psychologists longing for the wisdom of the Dharma. From a NBP perspective Buddhist realities may be viewed through the lens of SC which prime locus of understanding is not within the self-contained individual's psyche but in psychological processes in-between relationships of reciprocal interaction. Mind is not self-contained in-between the ears but arises in Dependent Origination amongst people. Viewed from a SC perspective, pan-Buddhist central themes, like Dependent Origination, Karma, Nirvana, self/not-self, emptiness, non-duality, awakening, consciousness, and mindful awareness, may be explained from a relational perspective. This implies a paradigm shift into a methodical practice which comprises an all-encompassing convergence of western and Buddhist Psychology, as well as a confluence of traditionalist/modernist and postmodernist Buddhist practices. A veritable new vehicle – a Neoyana – appears on the horizon. At this juncture in history, a worldwide current founded on social-clinical-neuro-psychological insights and research is infusing the Dharma. We nourish high hopes that this will soon be recognized as a 4th turning of the wheel, a turning that replaces religious and metaphysical stories with narratives and metaphors derived from psychology. Thus, Neoyana may landmark the Dharma as a "social constructional evidence-based psychology" with all its ramifications.

What does a SC input entail? Abandoning the subject-object dualism, a turn is made to reconceptualise the subjective experience in the framework of SC which leans heavily on Gergen's work (Gergen, 1997, 2009). SC is pivotal in reasserting that experiences in all varieties are integers of relational processes: the personal is because of the interpersonal and not the other way around. Individuality emerges out of relationship. The binary individual-social is dealt with by recasting the artificial qualifications of the individual as a separate agency that is independent from social processes. The attribution of meaning to experience is generated and regenerated in dialogues of collaborative practice. Experience is not akin to a subjective mirror-in-here which reflects an objective reality-out-there. Mind is not confined within the individual's subjective experience but is an impermanent process between interacting individuals from which the experience derives its meaning. These individual actors are viewed as relational integers which gain meaning through the enacted relational process. Experience is a variety of relational action which is in form not unlike all other actions, i.e. it can be indexed but cannot stand on its own. This relational view of experience as grounded in dialogical engagement is congruent with the Buddhist view of "relational mind" arising in Dependent Origination.

Experience is a phenomenon of Dependent Origination *par excellence*, embedded and interwoven in relationship(s) as part of oneness in being with somebody else, actually or imaginary. Conscious experience is a form of relational action and individual subjectivity is a mark of relatedness and Dependent Origination. Can there be happiness outside of the communal culture one is a part of and from which shared idea of what happiness means one escapes? This meaning is generated in Dependent Origination through the particular culture and its tradition of dialogue, and becomes intelligible through collaborative practice of interdependence.

Whether an experience is real, happy, or sad is shaped historically and immersed in the tradition and culture one lives by. Thus, what is experienced, perceived, or felt in awareness is an extension of relationship and relatedness which speaks through me. The interpersonal context generates a "forestructure" which inheres in relational processes which make the subjective comprehensible for others rather than separate from the communal. My subjective experience is not an isolated phenomenon but a relational process of duplicating and replicating of each other. In a sense I am you, you are me, and we are each other. Our subjective experiences are born and reborn of each other through our dialogues. To be comprehensible action cannot be anything else than a social construction which cannot be generated in interpersonal independence. Disavowing the subject-object unity as a foundation for experiencing, subjectivity, thus inferred, lifts the self-other duality.

Interpersonal relatedness and Dependent Origination of mind do not warrant the end of differentiation or human conflict. Because we owe all that we value to relationship, all that we find psychologically painful can be transformed through relationship. The key is "transformative dialogue" which is a conversational exchange that dissolves the barriers of conflicting meanings.

More on Social Construction

Buddhists' deifying worship and metaphysics impress as cultural atavisms that hijack the Dharma in a religious trap. This imprisonment is reinforced by using 19th century colonial terms like "enlightenment" for *bodhi*. NBP aims to liberate the Dharma from these wrenching shackles and proposes appropriate and adequate semantics for a way of practice toward awakening by sparking four paradigm shifts. Although paradigm shifts have not brought us any closer to reality (Kuhn, 1962) the present shifts might help to render practices to make life more bearable in the social orbit. They are: (1) a *re-generation* of the Dharma by discerning the Theravada-Mahayana scriptures and Buddhist meditations as a social constructivist psychological practice rather than as a devotional practice of prayer; (2) a *re-visioning* of "empirical" by expanding the categories of human beings' *sensorium* with a 6th sense, here called the mind's eye, the brain's capacity to be aware of awareness of *dharmas* in non-duality; (3) a *re-conceptualization* of what one observes in the mind's eye: everything one perceives/labels externally or conceives/visualizes internally is a social construction; and (4) a *re-definition* of *dharmas* – the smallest unit of experience – as social constructions by considering them as "real" only if agreed upon by the community involved (thus corroborating pervasive emptiness/non-self); this thesis is elaborated below. These shift are the result of a love affair between NBP and SC which is embodied in the writings of Kenneth J. Gergen, who might be considered as a postmodern innovator of the Dharma (e.g., Gergen & Hosking, 2006). The Buddhist social meditations concur with Gergen's (1999) adage: "I am linked, therefore I am." As we cannot escape the social predicament of the culture we live in, all that we systematically conceive is a polyvocal narrative, including hard-wired science. Without eternal truths everything is empty; what remains is this: kindness, compassion, and aha/hahaha.

If human beings are "biochemical-sensing-moving-thinking-emoting-relational-constructions", they usually function at the pre-rational (child-like), irrational (foolish), and rational (scientific) levels, but seldom at the post-rational (wisdom) level. This latter layer enables to understand Interbeing as Thay calls it conform the *Diamond Sutra* or "Relational Being" as Gergen calls it. Thrown from birth onwards into a social web, we cannot be self-contained. There is nothing that we can conceive of that is not injected with interpersonal meaning. To be is to be related and to act is to interact. Even private worlds are encapsulated in inextricable relational networks. Although we often take our being embedded within bonds for granted, interrelatedness is here to stay from the cradle to the grave. This concurs with a Buddhist metavision which views reality as a joint venture in a networked world, depicted as "Indra's jewel net" (*Avatamsaka Sutra*; Cleary, 1993), a matrix which at each juncture gems/mirrors/beings that reflect and interpenetrate each other *ad infinitum*. No gem exists on its own. Each jewel reflects and is reflected in all the others, thus creating an image of multiple/polyphonic co-action. In such a vision, reality is always provisional, linguistically co-constructed by a group and negotiated in a dance of meanings. In the same vein reality – even if unveiled by science – is intersubjective, relative, time-and-culture-bound. Reality is conceived as narratives to be replaced by more appealing constructions, going forward. Actually, this is happening with the Dharma in its present transition from a religion into a contemporary psychology.

In order to deal effectively with emotions affecting ourselves and others, the social constructionist practice of appreciating and accepting our fellow human beings (but not necessarily always their actions) is based on the insight on Relational Being – that overlaps Interbeing – and is helpful. Such a positive attitude toward life is based in the premise that whatever we do, think, or feel has an interpersonal meaning. This is mostly taken for granted. However, when we are deeply aware of it, we might be able to see that our "real" self consists of relational rather than self elements. A quintessential Buddhist insight is that there is no self. If we nevertheless insist on having a self, the only feasible construction of a self is a "relational" self. Provisionally, it is functional to have a name, but can we identify ourselves with a name? Obviously, we are not our names, neither are we our bodies, nor are we our minds, or our personalities. It is an illusion to conclude that these social constructions based on impermanence are eternal realities. The only reality we have seems to be the present moment in the flux of time, which process-nature requires us to state that whatever we say something is so or so, it is not. As Thay pointed out, individuality and interrelatedness can be metaphorically depicted as being comparable to the leaves hanging on the branches of a tree that exists due to the non-leaves and non-tree elements, like the sun, the earth, and the rain.

Dependent Origination in the relational orbit necessitates an in-depth understanding of the social-interpersonal and of co-action that gives birth to meaning which cannot be a solipsistic invention of a single individual. What generates a sense of meaning that is intelligible is a linguistic coordination within relationship through dialogue. Communal coordination and dialogue create intelligibility and in this linguistic process meaning itself is an epiphenomenon. A special eye is necessary to see our being enmeshed in relationships through the language that we use. Our motivation – all that we want, wish, desire, care, seek, search, or strive for – is not some inner possession but a relational integer that is intertwined in interpersonal patterns, the actual or imaginary presence of someone. An in-depth understanding of SC views the relational as being implicitly but always already present in all our actions. There is no escape from the condition of relatedness; there is always someone in our actions. Although in the "old stream" scholarly traditions, like e.g. in humanistic or positive psychology, one considers the person as an independent agent, SC questions the validity of the "independent agency" viewing this as inextricable from relational engagement: the individual is an actor in a continuing process of interpersonal dependence. From this perspective every individual action is embedded in a network of relationships of which one is part. Rather than determined by a god or by her/himself in independent origination, this view makes the voluntarism versus determinism duality redundant and god as an explanatory factor and a heavenly originator, who pulls the strings of social action, superfluous.

Who then is responsible? If a private individual is held solely responsible for the action, s/he would be positioned as an agent who takes a superior stance toward mortal others, the evil and the good. Rather than relying on judgment of some human agency, SC submits that action, including moral decisions, is the outcome of engaged mutual relationships in social networks. Instead of owning responsibility, the impact of others is recognized by making the inextricability of relational engagement transparent. Thus, responsibility is relational responsibility, blame is relational blame, and praise is relational praise. This happens to be the essence of the Buddha's Dependent Origination. The hope is that such a relational mentality will promote the necessary social action toward a society and culture of solidarity. Let us uncover our own share in the worldwide cultures of greed and hatred which brought about a financial crisis and a society plagued by xenophobic angst in order to create a *humane* society and communal well-being. The traffic jam is not created by others, we are the traffic jam. Because we are the society a *humane* society is only possible if based on *humane* relationship which is only possible and viable through an in-depth understanding of what Gergen has called "Multibeing" (a variety of Relational Being and Interbeing): the individual subject as the common intersection of multiple voices based on a multiplicity of relationships-potentials, differences-contradictions, and agreements-harmonies. I submit that the Buddhist spirit can be comprehensively summarized in the "Interhumane Multibeing" that reflects our relational multiplicity in Dependent Origination.

Morality offers another overlap of SC and Buddhist Psychology. The *humane* society cannot but rest on a community of members who take moral responsibility based on ethics guided by the intelligibilities of a cultural tradition. Without a private self, ethics is a relational morality which is "non-foundational" and based on co-action. One's actions are meaningless in themselves. They become meaningful through collaborative actions and become collaborative as they are supplemented by other people. Intelligibility emerges not from individual actors but through co-action. In Buddhist terms: ethics is at bottom "empty" and needs to be socially constructed again and again within the traditional culture of interdependence one lives by. Without collaborative practice one man's meat is another man's poison. Going beyond absolutism and relativism, the collaborative practice of conversation is superior in process and outcome of humaneness as compared to taking up arms. Gergen (2009) invites his readers to re-distribute concerns of conflict, wrong-doing, and blame to the source from which they arise – the network of relational responsibility – through infinite moral deliberation. Relational Being (Interbeing) is a challenge of conversation on antagonistic moralities which range from tolerant to rigid. To achieve collaborative relationship the conversation needs to focus on "2nd order morality" which refers to the relationship itself. The "1st order morality" refers to the shared "good" of coherent groups like families or friendships. There may be differing relationships creating moral tensions, e.g. having an extramarital affair. More importantly, when each group proclaims its own good opposing views will spark conflict between "us" versus "them" (e.g. liberals vs. fundamentalists). This requires a "2nd order morality" that works on the process of relationship itself by bringing struggling groups together. Honouring the process of relationship, one works toward generating innovative practices to reduce the language of conflict and at creating new meaning and shared values through dialogue. Such a meaning-making practice of relational ethics will hopefully lead to a morality that joins rather than separates people.

To bring about a contemporary Buddhist Psychology from a SC perspective is a Herculean task. A major stumbling block is the lack of communication between psychologists and Buddhist scholars. They do not speak each other's language and do not know, nor understand each other's discipline. Psychologists often have a limited view of the Dharma that they mostly see as an exotic religion to be mistrusted. Buddhist adherents insist that their own *Abhidhamma* psychology is as valid as ever, because it has survived the ravages of time, and is as good as mainstream psychology. Dharma teachers have only rudimentary knowledge and a minimal understanding of psychology as a science. Despite these and other hurdles the attraction for each other is unmistakable. A promising approach to enable convergence of the two disciplines is seemingly provided by psychologists whose background is Buddhist or by buddhologists who are well-versed in mainstream psychology. These are combinations requiring "Relational Interbeing in action"; e.g. exemplified by this anthology.[1]

Concluding remarks

Buddhists might get stuck with outdated paradigms for interpersonal practices which have been experienced down the centuries as salubrious. Shackled by closed systems of a predominantly introverted tradition, it seems to be difficult to innovate and regenerate the Dharma from within. Western inspired innovations like HB and EB impress as being the add-ons of social-political action rather than as a basic transformation of Buddhist wisdom teachings, still as yet dominated by philosophical/metaphysical and religious overtones. Social action is a valuable modernist endeavour and a very much needed practice to benefit humankind, particularly the many people in need of the bare supplies for everyday life. A *socialistic Dharma* explores Buddhist stances to issues, such as in education and socializing of the youth, eradicating crime and poverty, securing lasting peace, human rights, and our habitat (Guruge, 2005). But does it offer guidelines to the Buddhist moral stance as a teaching of non-foundational emptiness on issues of bioethics like abortion, euthanasia, suicide, or genetic engineering? However laudable and revolutionizing a socialistic Buddhism might be, does it possess the potential to adapt the Dharma for the postmodern era?

The last transformation of the Dharma on the content level was by 4th century Yogacara scholars. Since then only cultural variations have been developed which are characterized by a merger with local cultures such as with Bon shamanism in Tibetan Vajrayana, with Taoism-Confucianism in Chan, and with Shinto Samurai ideology in Zen. As an anti-dogmatic/liberal school of thought, the Dharma is a living educational system that legitimizes its taking dif-

---

1.   Relational Being, Interbeing, or Relational Interbeing as it already exists in the Far East has a shadow side, for instance as manifested in a "collective" conscience. This suggests that what the family, group, community, or nation thinks is sanctioned to be followed blindly, without critical scrutiny. Thus, mavericks swimming against the stream by following their "own" conscience, like refusing to join the army during WWII, are a rare breed of people in such societies. Reinforcing imitative conduct, traditional eastern cultures seem to hamper originality and creativity.

ferent shapes and appearances depending on the particular time, place, and people in history. Such Upaya necessitates a dialectical process to adjust to changing circumstances, which – due to the open discursive nature of the Dharma – implies a listening to each other's multiple voices. In this traditionally poly-discursive spirit the Dharma has been exchanging ideas with myths dispelling psychologies for roughly a century (e.g., Kwee & Holdstock, 1996). The interaction of the Dharma and psychology has resulted in various endeavours in the past century to regenerate Buddhist Psychology and has now become a movement that is gaining momentum. As a social constructive endeavour, NBP will likely help to reinvent the Dharma as a contemporary psychology. This can only be done from the ground up and from within. This is in line with the meaning of *yana* as vehicle and with the Buddhist idea that its *raison d'être* is to be a provisional means and not an end in itself. Moving beyond Theravada and Mahayana and going forward from there, a call is made here for a transcultural Neoyana: an applied, evidence-based, and integrated psychology of the Buddha grounded in narratives and metaphors of social-clinical-neuro-psychology which discards illusions, delusions, metaphysics, and religious beliefs, and which involves SC as an innovative way to understand the Dharma. A NBP that serves as the 3rd great vehicle and the 4th turning of the wheel in the history of the Dharma would pertinently include social action arising from non-self and Interbeing. Although views differ and there may be different strokes for different folks, meditating remains functional in fostering resilience and growth for roughly 100 generations since the Buddha. Eventually, these shifts reveal the Dharma as postmodern co-constructing practices of "transcultural interhumane multibeings in Dependent Origination". If the social meditations are not fully practiced, NBP would be about-ism, mere talk, and opium for the intellectuals.

Let me conclude by noting that I have consequently avoided the cloudy term "spiritual" throughout this entire book. It is correct to infer that the spiritual has been replaced by the terms interpersonal and relational; for the poetic activist "the social is spiritual enough" and that being pro-social is already so immensely difficult to implement that there is no compelling need to go other-worldly. A 10-fold comprehensive summary adumbrates how Buddhist Psychology and SC embrace each other:

> (1) Buddhist Psychology does not discard psychobiology, but sketches the contours of the human being as Body/Speech/Mind: Speech and "Relational Interbeing" are neither within body, nor within mind, but in dialogical encounters (discover the mind as not in-between the ears but in-between people).

> (2) Focusing on interactions, the dualities inner-outer/I-other/you-me collapse and crumble in emptiness, inviting a socially constructed "relational self" that necessarily repudiates the individual self under the skin as an independent agency (how can persons be empty of the pure private?).

> (3) If the individual is not an isolated independent being but a manifestation of relationships, Relational Interbeing necessitates the emptiness of solitary selves: even private thoughts cannot be solipsistic, they emerge from a history of language, long lasting relations and time-honoured values

(4) Because of unobstructed mutual identity penetration, individuals are interrelated in Dependent Origination (the Buddha's causality hypothesis): can a change in one individual generate and result in a relative change in all interconnections?

(5) In the context of interdependency, even the private realm is encapsulated in an inextricable relational network: looking outside in the social orbit, we see projections of our inner worlds and looking inside in the private space (like in meditation), we see the social everywhere

(6) Although we are dancing alone in the room the social dimension is still omnipresent and because we are intricately interrelated, it is safe to conclude that even the private is a social construction and that we are all subsumed under a sublime meta-order of the relational and the interpersonal

(7) Life is socially entwined/intertwined, there is no other way; existing in a social web and since conception is a social construction, it is impossible to be self-contained even in the absence of the other (anything conceivable is injected by inter-personal meaning and even if we take our being embedded in bonds for granted, interrelatedness is ubiquitous and pervasive)

(8) For Relational Interbeing and local realities to become, community members move together like in a dance as both are defined by what the group believes they are, in other words: reality is not solipsistic but something provisional, linguistically co-constructed by people and negotiated in a dance of meanings

(9) Even if unveiled by science, data remain a communal construction: the "game of science and reason" is inextricably space-time-and-culture bound conceived by scientists as a value narrative rather than as a final map of the Truth, thus to be continuously replaced by new constructions going forward

(10) Thus, we discard Transcendental Truths; if reality, facts, and even social construction itself are made in relational contexts as cultural-historical interpersonal narratives, this may be unsettling and necessitates a joint venture of caring relationships to create new vistas and practices of togetherness

I call this love affair between Buddhist Psychology and SC: Relational Buddhism (or Relational Dharma). The use of the term Buddh-*ism* is justified here because the relational dimension refers to all aspects of the pan-Buddhist teachings. This views Transcendental Truths and the self of Body/Speech/Mind as ultimately empty (non-foundational), but recognizes variegating truths and realities as provisional-constructional practices of Interbeing (a social group congealed by common language). Its aim is the making of a Buddha through meditating toward mindful emptiness, enlightened self-interest, and illuminating other-interest. The way is to first become a humane multibeing by transforming fear into creativity and compassion, anger into concern and kindness, sadness into joy and even-mindedness, and practice happiness through the social meditations based on insights of Relational Interbeing.

References

Ainslie, G. (2001). *Breakdown of will.* Cambridge: Cambridge University Press.

Albee, G.W. (1982). Preventing psychopathology and promoting human potential.*American Psychologist, 37,* 1043-1050.

Alexander, F. (1931). Buddhist training as an artificial catatonia. *Psychoanalytic Review, 18,* 129-45.

Allen, C. (2003). *The search for the Buddha.* New York: Carroll & Grof.

Almaas, A.H. (2004). *The inner journey home.* Boston: Shambhala.

Alston, W.P. (1967). Emotion and feeling. In P. Edwards (Ed.), *The encyclopedia of philosophy* (Vol. 2). New York: Collier Macmillan.

American Psychiatric Association (2000). *Diagnostic and Statistical Manual of mental disorders (DSM-IV-TR).* Washington, DC: Author.

Anacker, S. (2005). *Seven works of Vasubandhu: The Buddhist psychological doctor.* New Delhi: Motilal Banarsidass.

Analayo (2003). *Satipatthana: The direct path to realization.* Kandy, Sri Lanka: Buddhist Publication Society.

Anderson, D., & Smith, H. (Eds).(1913-1948). *Suttanipata.* London: Pali Text Society.

Andresen, J. (2000). Meditation meets behavioural medicine. *Journal of Consciousness Studies, 7,* 17-73.

Aronson, H.B. (2004). *Buddhist practice on western ground.* Boston: Shambhala.

Arpaia, J., & Rapgay, L. (2008). *Real meditation in minutes a day.* Boston, MA: Wisdom Publications.

Astin, J.A. (1997). Stress reduction through mindfulness meditation. *Psychotherapy & Psychosomatics, 66,* 97-106.

Atkinson. J. (1957). Motivational determinants of risk-taking behaviour. *Psychological Review, 64,* 359-372.

Austin, J. (1998). *Zen and the brain: Toward an understanding of meditation and consciousness.* Cambridge, MA: MIT Press.

Austin, J. (2000). Consciousness evolves when the Self dissolves. *Journal of Consciousness Studies, 7,* 209-230.

Austin, J. (2006). *Zen-brain reflections.* Cambridge, MA: MIT Press.

Austin, J. (2008). Selfless insight-wisdom: A thalamic gateway. In Sounds True (Eds.), *Measuring the immeasurable: The scientific basis of spirituality* (pp.211-230). Louisville, CO: Sounds True, Inc.

Austin, J. (2009). *Selfless insight: Zen and the meditative transformations of consciousness.* Cambridge, MA: MIT Press.

Austin, J. (2010) The thalamic gateway: How the meditative training of attention evolves toward selfless states of consciousness. In B. Bruya (Ed.) *Effortless attention: A new perspective in the cognitive science of attention and action* (pp.79-121). Cambridge, MA: MIT Press.

Averill, J.R. (1980). Emotion and anxiety: Sociocultural, biological and psychological determinants. In A. Rorty (Ed.), *Explaining emotions* (pp.37-72). Berkeley, CA: University of California Press.

Baer, R.A. (2003). Mindfulness training as a clinical intervention: A conceptual and empirical review. *Clinical Psychology: Science & Practice, 10,* 125-143.

Baer, R.A., Smith, G.T., & Allen, K.B. (2004). Assessment of mindfulness by self-report: The Kentucky Inventory of Mindfulness Skills. *Assessment, 11*, 1-16.

Baer, R. A., Hopkins, J., Krietemeyer, J., Smith, G. T., & Toney, L. (2006). Using self report assessment methods to explore facets of mindfulness. *Assessment, 13*, 27-45.

Baker, T.B., Piper, M.E., McCarthy, D.E., Majeskie, M.R., & Fiore, M.C. (2004). Addiction motivation reformulated: An affective processing model of negative reinforcement. *Psychological Review, 111*, 33-51.

Bandura, A. (2001). Social cognitive theory: An agentive perspective. *Annual Review of Psychology, 52*, 1-26.

Bankart, C.P. (1997). *Talking cures: A history of western & eastern psychotherapies.* Pacific Grove, CA: Brooks/Cole.

Bankart, C.P., Koshikawa, F., Nedate, K., & Haruki, Y. (1992). When West meets East: Contributions of eastern traditions to the future of psychotherapy. *Psychotherapy, 29*, 141-149.

Baumeister, R.R., & Vohs, K.D. (Eds.).(2004). *Handbook of self-regulation: Research, theory, and applications.* New York: Guilford.

Bechert, H. (Ed.). (1995). *When did the Buddha live? The controversy on the dating of the historical Buddha.* New Delhi: Sri Satguru Publications.

Beck, A.T. (1976). *Cognitive therapy and the emotional disorders.* New York: International Universities Press.

Benson, H. (1975). *The relaxation response.* New York: Morrow.

Bien, T., & Bien, B. (2002). *Mindful recovery: A spiritual path to healing from addiction.* New York: Willey.

Bitner, R., Hillman, L., Victor, B., & Walsh, R. (2003). Subjective effects of antidepressants: A pilot study of the varieties of antidepressant-induced experiences in meditators. *Journal of Nervous & Mental Disease, 11*, 660-667.

Bishop, S.R. (2002). What do we really know about mindfulness-based stress reduction? *Psychosomatic Medicine, 64*, 71-84.

Bishop, S.R., Lau, M., Shapiro, S., Carlson, L., Anderson, N. D., et al. (2004). Mindfulness: A proposed operational definition. *Clinical Psychology: Science & Practice, 11*, 230-241.

Blackburn, S. (1998). *Ruling passions.* New York: Oxford University Press.

Blazer, D.G., Hughes, D., George, L.K., Swartz, M., & Boyer, R. (1991). Generalized Anxiety Disorder. In L.N. Robins & D.A. Regier (Eds.), *Psychiatric disorders in America* (pp.180-203). New York: Free Press.

Bloch, S., & Singh, B.S. (2004). *Understanding troubled minds.* Melbourne University Press.

Bodhi, B. (Ed.) (1993). *A comprehensive manual of Abhidhamma.* Kandy, Sri Lanka: Buddhist Publication Society.

Bodhi, B. (2000). *The Connected Discourses of the Buddha: A new translation of the Samyutta Nikaya.* Boston, MA: Wisdom Publications.

Bodhi, B. (2002). *Connected discourses of the Buddha* (Vols. I & II). Boston, MA: Wisdom Publications.

Bodhi, B. (2006). The nature of mindfulness and its role in Buddhist meditation. A correspondence between Alan Wallace and Bhikkhu Bodhi. Unpublished.

Boorstein, S. (1997). *Clinical studies in transpersonal psychotherapy.* Albany, NY: State University of New York Press.

Borkovec, T.D., Ray, W.J., & Stober, J. (1998). Worry: A cognitive phenomenon intimately linked to affective. physiological, and interpersonal behavioral processes. *Cognitive Therapy & Research, 22*, 561-576.

Borkovec, T.D., Robinson, E., Pruzinsky, T., & DePree, J.A. (1983). Preliminary exploration of worry: Some characteristics and processes. *Behaviour Research & Therapy, 21,* 9-16.

Brazier, D. (1995). *Zen therapy.* New York: Wiley.

Breslin, F.C., Zack, M., & McMain, S. (2002). An information-processing analysis of mindfulness: Implications for relapse prevention in the treatment of substance abuse. *Clinical Psychology: Science & Practice, 9,* 275-299.

Brinol, P., Petty, R.E., & Wagner, B. (2009). Body posture effects on self-evaluation: a self-validation approach. *European Journal of Social Psychology, 39,* 1053-1064.

Brown, K.W., & Ryan, R.M. (2003). The benefits of being present: Mindfulness and its role in psychological well-being. *Journal of Personality & Social Psychology, 84,* 822-848.

Brown, K.W., & Ryan, R.M. (2004). Perils and promise in defining and measuring mindfulness: Observations from experience. *Clinical Psychology: Science & Practice, 11,* 242-248.

Buddhadasa, B. (1992). *Paticcasamuppada: Practical dependent origination.* Nonthaburi, Thailand: Vuddhidhamma Fund.

Bugental, J.F.T. (1964). The third force in psychology. *Journal of Humanistic Psychology, 4,* 9-25.

Bühler, K.E. (2005). The effect of Autogenic Training on feeling and mood of outpatients in psychotherapy. *Schweizer Archiv für Neurologie und Psychiatrie, 156,* 247- 256.

Buswell, R.E. (Ed.).(2003). *Encyclopedia of Buddhism.* New York: Macmillan.

Butler, A.C., Chapman, J.E., Forman, E.M., & Beck, A.T. (2006). The empirical status of cognitive-behavioral therapy: A review of meta-analyses. *Clinical Psychology Review, 26,* 17-31.

Byrom, T. (Transl.).(2001). *The Dhammapada. New* York: Bell Tower.

Caldwell, C. (1996). *Getting our bodies back.* Boston, MA: Shambala.

Caplan, G. (1964). *Principles of preventive psychiatry.* New York: Basic Books.

Carey, B. (2008). Lotus Therapy. *New York Times* (online).

Carlson, L.E., Speca, M., Patel, K.D., & Goodey, E. (2003). Mindfulness-based stress reduction in relation to quality of life, mood, symptoms of stress, and immune parameters in breast and prostate cancer outpatients. *Psychosomatic Medicine, 65,* 571-581.

Carlson, L.E., Speca, M., Faris, P., & Patel, K.D. (2007). One year pre-post intervention follow-up of psychological, immune, endocrine and blood pressure outcomes of mindfulness-based stress reduction in breast and prostate cancer outpatients. *Brain, Behavior & Immunity, 21,* 1038-1049.

Carlson, L.E., Ursuliak, Z., Goodey, E.A.M., & Speca, M. (2001). The effects of a mindfulness meditation based stress reduction program on mood, & symptoms of stress in cancer outpatients: Six month follow-up. *Support Care in Cancer, 9, 112-123.*

Carrithers, M. (1983). *The Buddha.* Oxford: Oxford University Press.

Carson, J.W., Carson, K.M., Gil, K.M., & Baucom, D.H. (2004). Mindfulness-based relationship enhancement. *Behavior Therapy, 35,* 471-494.

Carus, P. (1904). *The gospel of the Buddha* (4th ed.). Chicago: The Open Court Publishing.

Cassel, R.N. (1995). Assessing the harmony of one's feelings in relation to culture embraced by use of biofeedback (where today is tomorrow in health care). *Education, 116,* 251-259.

Chambless, D.L., & Gillis, M.M. (1993). Cognitive Therapy for anxiety disorders. *Journal of Consulting & Clinical Psychology, 61,* 248-260.

Chandavimala, R. (1994). *Vancaka dharma hascittopakle adharma.* Boralesgamuwa, Sri Lanka: Prabuddha Publishers (originally published in 1952).

Chödron, P. (2001). *The places that scare you: A guide to fearlessness in difficult times.* Boston, MA: Shambhala.

Christopher, M.S. (2003). Albert Ellis and the Buddha: Rational soul mates? A comparison of Rational Emotive Behavior Therapy and Zen Buddhism. *Mental Health, Religion & Culture, 6,* 283-293.

Clark, D. A. (2005).(Ed.). *Intrusive thoughts in clinical disorders.* New York: Guilford.

Claxton, G. (1992). *The heart of Buddhism.* London: Aquarian Press.

Claxton, G. (2000). *Hare brain, tortoise brain.* New York: Harper-Collins.

Cleary, T. (1993). *The flower ornament scripture.* Boston, MA: Shambala.

Coleman, J. (1983). *Wolfgang Luthe's cathartic Autogenic methods: A practice manual for Autogenic therapists.* London: BAFATT.

Conze, E. (1980). *A short history of Buddhism.* Oxford, UK: One World.

Cortright, B. (1997). *Psychotherapy and spirit.* Albany, NY: State University of New York Press.

Cowings, P.S. (1997). *Autogenic feedback training exercise: Methods and system.* U.S. Patent #5,964,939. USPTO Full Text and Image Database 1997. Available at < www.uspto.gov/patft/index.html >.

Craske, M.G., & Hazlett-Stevens (2002). Facilitating symptom reduction and behavior change in GAD: The issue of control. *Clinical Psychology: Science & Practice, 9,* 69-75.

Crick, F. (1994). *The astonishing hypothesis: The scientific search for the soul.* London: Methuen.

Crits-Christoph, P., Gibbons, M.B.C., & Crits-Christoph, K. (2004). Supportive expressive psychodynamic therapy. In R.G. Heimberg, C.L. Turk, & D.S. Mennin (Eds.), *Generalized Anxiety Disorder: Advances in research and practice* (pp.320-350). New York: Guilford.

Csikszentmihalyi, M. (1990). *Flow: The psychology of optimal experience.* New York: Harper & Row.

Dalgleish, T., & Watts, F.M. (1990). Biases of attention and memory in disorders of and depression. *Clinical Psychology Review, 10,* 589-604.

Damasio, A. (1994). *Descartes' error.* New York: Putnam.

Das, S. (1997). *Awakening the Buddha within.* New York: Broadway Books.

Davidson, R.J., & Kabat-Zinn, J. (2004). Response to J.C. Smith. *Psychosomatic Medicine, 66,* 148-152.

Davidson, R.J., Scherer, K.R., & Goldsmith, H. (Eds.).(2003). *Handbook of the affective sciences.* New York: Oxford University Press.

Davidson, R.J., Kabat-Zinn, J., Schumacher, J., Rosenkranz, M., Muller, D., et al. (2003). Alteration in brain and immune function produced by mindfulness meditation. *Psychosomatic Medicine, 65,* 564-570.

Davis, B. (1993). *An Introduction to the philosophy of religion* (2nd ed.). Oxford: Oxford University Press.

Davis, M. (1997). Neurobiology of fear responses: The role of the amygdala. *Journal of Neuropsychiatry & Clinical Neuroscience, 9,* 382-402.

Dawkins, R. (1976). *The selfish gene.* Oxford: Oxford University Press.

DeCharms, C. (1997). *Two views of mind: Abhidhamma and brain.* Ithaca, NY: Snow Lion.

De la Vallée Poussin, L., & Thomas, E. J. (Eds.).(1916-1917). *Mahaniddesa* (2 vols.). London: Pali Text Society.

De Maria, E.P., & Mikulas, W.L. (1991). Women's awareness of their menstrual cycles. *Journal of Psychology & Human Sexuality, 4,* 71-82.

De Silva, M.W.P. (1973). *Buddhist and Freudian psychology.* Colombo: Lake House Publications.

De Silva, M.W.P. (1978/1992a). *Buddhist and Freudian psychology* (2nd/3rd eds.). Singapore: National University of Singapore Press.

De Silva, M.W.P. (1992b). *Twin peaks: Compassion and insight.* Singapore: Buddhist Research Society.

De Silva, M.W.P. (1995). Theoretical perspectives on emotions in Early Buddhism. In R. Ames & J. Marks (Eds.), *Emotions in Asian thought.* Albany, NY: The State University of New York Press.

De Silva, M.W.P. (2002). *Buddhism, ethics and society.* Clayton: Monash Asia Institute.

De Silva, M.W.P. (2005). *An introduction to Buddhist psychology* (4th ed.). London: Palgrave-Macmillan

De Silva, P. (1984a). Buddhism and behaviour modification. *Behaviour Research & Therapy, 22,* 661-678.

De Silva, P. (1984b). The Buddhist attitude to alcholism. In G. Edwards, A. Arif, & J. Jaffe (Eds.), *Drug use and misuse: Cultural perspectives* (pp.33-41). London: Croom Helm.

De Silva, P. (1985). Early Buddhist and modern behavioral strategies for the control of unwanted intrusive cognitions. *Psychological Record, 35,* 437-443.

De Silva, P. (1986). Buddhism and behaviour change: Implications for therapy. In G. Claxton (Ed.), *Beyond therapy.* London: Wisdom Publications.

De Silva, P. (1990). Meditation and beyond: Buddhism and psychotherapy. In M.G.T. Kwee (Ed.), *Psychotherapy, meditation & health: A cognitive-behavioural perspective* (pp.165-182). London: East-West.

De Silva P. (1996). Buddhist psychology: Theory and therapy. In M.G.T. Kwee & T.L. Holdstock (Eds.), *Western & Buddhist psychology: Clinical perspectives* (pp.125-147). Delft, Netherlands: Eburon.

De Silva, P. (2001). A psychological analysis of the Vittakkasanthana Sutta. *Buddhist Studies Review, 18,* 65-72.

De Silva, P. (2003). Obstacles to insight: Some reflections on an aspect of Buddhist psychology. *Constructivism in the Human Sciences, 8,* 173-180.

De Silva, P., & Samarasinghe, D. (1998). Behaviour therapy in Sri Lanka. In T.P.S. Oei (Ed.), *Behaviour therapy and cognitive behaviour therapy in Asia* (pp.141-147). Glebe, NSW: Edumedia.

DelMonte, M.M. (1985). Meditation and anxiety reduction: A literature review. *Clinical Psychology Review, 5,* 91-102.

De Vibe, M. (2006). Mindfulness and health intervention. In M.G.T. Kwee, K.J. Gergen, & F. Koshikawa (Eds.), *Horizons in Buddhist Psychology: Practice, research & theory* (pp.197-208). Chagrin Falls. OH: Taos Institute Publications.

Didonna, F. (Ed.).(2009). *Clinical handbook of mindfulness.* New York: Springer.

Docket, K.H., Dudley-Grant, G.R., & Bankart, C.P. (2003). *Psychology and Buddhism: From individual to global community.* New York: Kluwer.

Drago, V., Foster, P., Webster, D., et al. (2007). Lateral and vertical attentional biases in normal individuals. *International Journal of Neuroscience, 117,* 1415-1424.

Dugas, M.J., Gagnon, F., & Ladouceur, R, (1998). Generalized Anxiety Disorder: A preliminary test of a conceptual model. *Behaviour Research & Therapy, 36,* 215-226.

Dunn, B.R., Hartigan, J.A., & Mikulas, W.L. (1999). Concentration and mindfulness meditation: Unique forms of consciousness? *Applied Psychophysiology & Biofeedback, 24,* 147-165.

Dutt, N. (1945). *Early monastic Buddhism* (Vol. II). Calcutta: Calcutta Oriental Press.

Easterbrook, J.A. (1959). The effects of emotion on cue utilization and the organization of behavior. *Psychological Review, 66,* 183-201.

Ekman, P. (2003). *Emotions revealed: Recognizing faces and feelings to improve communication and emotional life.* London: Times Books.

Ekman, P., & Friesen, W. V. (1975). *Unmasking the face: A guide to recognizin emotions from facial clues.* Englewood Cliffs, NJ: Prentice-Hall.

Ekman, P., Davidson, R., Ricard, M., & Wallace, A. (2005). Buddhist and psychological perspectives on emotions and well-being. *Current Directions in Psychological Science, 14,* 59-63.

Ellis, A. (1976). RET abolishes most of the human ego. *Psychotherapy, 13,* 343-348.

Elster, J. (1999). *Strong feelings: Emotion, addiction, and human behaviour.* Cambridge, MA: MIT Press.

Engel, G.L. (1977). The need for a new medical model: A challenge for biomedicine. *Science, 196,* 129-135.

Engler, J. (1984). Therapeutic aims in psychotherapy and meditation: Developmental stages in the representation of the self. *Journal of Transpersonal Psychology, 16,* 25-61,

Engler, J. (2003). Being somebody and being nobody: A re-examination of the understanding of self in psychoanalysis and Buddhism. In J.D. Safran (Ed.), *Psychoanalysis and Buddhism* (pp.35-79). Boston, MA: Wisdom Publications.

Epstein, M.D. (1984). On the neglect of evenly suspended attention. *Journal of Transpersonal Psychology, 16,* 193-205.

Epstein, M.D. (1996). *Thoughts without a thinker: Psychotherapy from a Buddhist perspective.* New York: Basic Books.

Fairbairn, W.R.D. (1952). *An object-relations theory of the personality.* New York: Basic Books.

Farnè, M., & Gnugnoli, D. (2002). Effects of autogenic training on emotional distress symptoms. *Stress Medicine, 16,* 259-261.

Farnè, M., & Jimenez-Muñoz, N. (2002). Personality changes induced by autogenic training practice. *Stress Medicine, 16,* 263-268.

Feer, L. (Ed.).(1884-1904). *Samyutta Nikaya* (6 vols.). London: Pali Text Society.

Flanagan, O. (2003). The colour of happiness. *New Scientist, 178,* 44.

Fleischman, P.R. (1999). *Karma and chaos: New and collected essays on Vipassana meditation.* Onalaska, WA: Paryatti.

Fleischman, P.R. (2004). *Cultivating inner peace* (2nd ed.). Onalaska, WA: Pariyatti.

Fontana, D. (1987). Self-assertion and self-negation in Buddhist psychology. *Journal of Humanistic Psychology, 27,* 175-195.

Foucher, A. (1964). *The life of the Buddha*. Connecticut, NE: Wesleyan University Press.

Fredrickson, B.L., Cohn, M.A., Coffey, K.A., Pek, J., & Finkel, S.M. (2008). Open hearts build lives: Positive emotions, induced through loving-kindness meditation, build consequential personal resources. *Journal of Personality & Social Psychology, 95*, 1045-1062.

Freeston, M.H., Dugas, M.J., & Ladouceur, R. (1996). Thoughts, images, worry, and anxiety. *Cognitive Therapy & Research, 20,* 265-273.

Freeston, M.H., Ladouceur, R., Thibodeau, N., & Gagnon, F. (1991). Cognitive intrusions in a non-clinical population. I. Response style, subjective experience, and appraisal. *Behaviour Research & Therapy, 29*, 589-597.

Frijda, N. (1987). *The emotions*. New York: Cambridge University Press.

Fromm-Reichmann, F. (1955). Psychiatric aspects of anxiety. In C.M. Thompson, M. Mazer, & E. Witenberg (Eds.), *An outline of psychoanalysis* (pp.113-133). New York: Modern Library.

Gardner, F.L., & Moore, Z.E. (2004). A mindfulness-acceptance-commitment-based approach to athletic performance enhancement: Theoretical considerations. *Behavior Therapy 35*, 707-723

Gastaldo, G., & Ottobre, M. (1994). *Il Training Autogeno in quattro stadi: L'appuntamento con se stessi*. Roma, Italy: Armando.

Gergen, K.J. (1996) Social psychology as social construction: The emerging vision. In C. McGarty & A. Haslam (Eds), *The message of social psychology: Perspectives on mind in society*. Oxford: Blackwell

Gergen, K.J. (1997). Social theory in context: Relational humanism. In J. Greenwood (Ed.), The mark of the social (pp.213-230). New York: Rowman & Littlefield.

Gergen, K.J. (1999). *An invitation to Social Construction*. London: Sage.

Gergen, K.J. (2000). *The Saturated self: Dilemmas of identity in contemporary life*. New York: Basic Books.

Gergen, K.J. (2001). Psychological science in a postmodern context. *The American Psychologist, 56,* 803-813.

Gergen, K.J. (2009). *Relational Being: Beyond the individual and community*. Oxford: Oxford University Press.

Gergen, K.J. (2009a). An invitation to Social Construction (2nd ed.). London: Sage.

Gergen, K.J., & Gergen, M. (2004). *Social Construction: Entering the dialogue*. Chagrin Falls: Taos Institute Publications.

Gergen, K.J., & Hosking, D.M. (2006). If you meet Social Construction along the road: A dialogue with Buddhism. In M.G.T. Kwee, K.J. Gergen, & F. Koshikawa (Eds.), *Horizons in Buddhist Psychology: Practice, research & theory* (pp.299-314). Chagrin Falls, OH: Taos Institute Publications.

Germer, C. K., Siegel, R.D., & Fulton, P. R. (Eds.).(2005). *Mindfulness and psychotherapy*. New York: Guilford.

Gethin, R. (1998). *The foundations of Buddhism*. Oxford, UK: Oxford University Press.

Gilbert, P., & Procter, S. (2006). Compassionate mind training for people with high shame and self-criticism: Overview and pilot study of a group therapy approach. *Clinical Psychology & Psychotherapy, 13*, 353–379.

Giommi, F. (2006). Mindfulness and its challenge to cognitive-behavioral practice. In M.G.T. Kwee, K.J. Gergen, & F. Koshikawa (Eds.), *Horizons in Buddhist Psychology: Practice, research & theory* (pp.209-224). Chagrin Falls. OH: Taos Institute Publications.

Glasser, W. (1976). *Positive addiction.* New York: Harper & Row.

Gleick, J. (1988). *Chaos: Making a new science.* New York: Pantheon.

Goenka, S.N. (2004). *Fifty years of Dhamma service.* Igatpuri, India: Vipassana Research Institute.

Goldie, P. (2002). *The emotions.* Oxford: Oxford University Press.

Goldbeck, L., & Schmid, K. (2003). Effectiveness of autogenic relaxation training on children and adolescents with behavioral and emotional problems. *Journal of the American Academy of Child and Adolescent Psychiatry, 42,* 1046-1054.

Goldstein, J. (1993). *Insight meditation.* Boston: Shambhala.

Goleman, D. (1988). *The meditative mind.* Los Angeles: Tarcher.

Goleman, D. (Ed).(2003). *Destructive emotions.* New York: Bantam Dell.

Goleman, D. (1997). *Emotional intelligence.* New York: Bantam Books.

Gombrich, R.F. (1988). *Theravada Buddhism.* London: Routledge & Kegan Paul.

Gombrich, R.F. (1996). *How Buddhism began.* London: Athlone Press.

Gould, R.A., Safren, S.A., O'Neill Washington, D., & Otto, M.W. (2004). A meta analytic review of cognitive behavioral treatments. In R.G. Heimberg, C.L.Turk, & D.S. Mennin (Eds.), *Generalized Anxiety Disorder: Advances in research and practice* (pp.248-264). New York: Guilford.

Govinda, L.A. (1969). *Foundations of Tibetan mysticism.* York Beach, ME: Red Wheel.

Griffith, J.P. (1985). *On being mindless: Buddhist meditation and the mind-body problem.* La Salle, IL: Open Court.

Grepmair, L., Mitterlehner, F., & Nickel, M. (2008). Promotion of mindfulness in psychotherapists in training. *Psychiatry Research, 158,* 265.

Grossman, P., Niemann, L., Schmidt, S., & Walach, H. (2004). Mindfulness-based stress reduction and health benefits: A meta-analysis. *Journal of Psychosomatic Research, 57,* 35-43.

Grossman, P. (2008). On measuring mindfulness in psychosomatic and psychological research. *Journal of Psychosomatic Research, 64,* 405-408.

Groves P., & Farmer R. (1994). Buddhism and addictions. Addiction Research, 2, 183-194.

Gunaratana, H. (1993). *Mindfulness in plain English.* Boston, MA: Wisdom Publications.

Gunaratna, V.F. (1968). *The significance of the Four Noble Truths.* Kandy, Sri Lanka: Buddhist Publication Society.

Guruge, A.W.P. (Ed.).(1965). *Return to righteousness: A collection of speeches, essays and lectures of the Anagarika Dharmapala.* Colombo, Ceylon: The Government Press.

Guruge, A.W.P (1999). *What in brief is Buddhism?* Monterey Park, CA: Mitram Books.

Guruge, A.W.P. (2005*). Buddhist answers to current issues: Studies in socially engaged humanistic Buddhism.* Bloomington, IN: House Publications.

Guttmann, G. (2002). *Conversation with Dr. Heinrich Wallnöfer, Vienna, Austria.* Unpublished video recording, transl. from the German by Tamara Callea.

Gyatso, T. (Dalai Lama) & Beck, A.T. (2006). Himalaya Buddhism meets Cognitive Therapy: The Dalai Lama and Aaron T. Beck in dialogue, narrated by Marja Kwee-Taams and Maurits G.T. Kwee. In M.G.T. Kwee, K.J. Gergen, & F. Koshikawa (Eds.), *Horizons in Buddhist Psychology: Practice, research & theory* (pp.27-48). Chagrin Falls. OH: Taos Institute Publications.

Hanson, N.R. (1958). *Patterns of discovery.* Cambridge: Cambridge University Press.

Hanson, R. (2009). *Buddha's brain: The practical neuroscience of happiness, love, and wisdom.* Oakland, CA: New Harbinger.

Hardy, E. (Ed.).(1902). *Nettippakarana*. London: Pali Text Society.

Hart, W. (Ed).(1987). *The art of living: Vipassana meditation as taught by S.N. Goenka*. San Fransisco: Harper & Row.

Haruki, Y., & Kaku, K.T. (Eds.).(2000). *Meditation as health promotion: A lifestyle modification approach*. Delft, Netherlands: Eburon.

Haruki, Y., Homma, I., Umezawa, A., & Masaoka, Y. (2001). *Respiration and emotion*. Tokyo: Springer-Verlag.

Harvey, P. (1997). Psychological aspects of Theravada Buddhist meditation training: Cultivating an I-less self. In K.L. Dhammajoti, A. Tilakaratne, & K. Abhayawansa (Eds.), *Recent researches in Buddhist studies: Essays in honour of Professor Y. Karunadasa*. Colombo, Sri Lanka: Y. Karunadasa Felicitation Committee.

Harvey, P. (2000). *An introduction to Buddhist ethics*. Cambridge: Cambridge University Press.

Hayes, A.M., & Feldman, G. (2004). Clarifying the construct of mindfulness in the context of emotion regulation and the process of change in therapy. *Clinical Psychology: Science & Practice, 11*, 255-262.

Hayes, S. C., & Smith, S. (2005). *Get out of your mind and into your life: The new acceptance and commitment therapy*. Oakland, CA: New Harbinger.

Hayes, S.C., Follette, V.M., & Linehan, M.M. (Eds.).(2004). *Mindfulness and acceptance*. New York: Guilford.

Hayes, S.C., Strosahl, K., & Wilson, K.G. (1999). *Acceptance and commitment therapy*. New York: Guilford.

Hayward, L.R.C. (1965). Reduction in stress reactivity by Autogenic Training. In W. Luthe (Ed.), *Autogenic Training: Correlationes psychosomaticae* (pp.98-110). New York: Grune & Stratton.

Hetherington, I. (2003). *Realizing change: Vipassana meditation in action*. Seattle: Vipassana Research Publications.

Higgins, E.T. (1987). Self-discrepancy: A theory relating self and affect. *Psychological Review, 94*, 319-340.

Hobson, J.A., & Pace-Schott E.F. (2002). The cognitive neuroscience of sleep: Neuronal systems, consciousness and learning, *Nature Reviews Neuroscience, 3*, 679-693.

Horney, K. (1950). *Neurosis and human growth: The struggle towards self-realization*. New York: Norton.

Horowitz, M.J. (2002). Self and relational observation. *Journal of Psychotherapy Integration, 12*, 115-127.

Hsing Yun (1998). *How I practice Humanistic Buddhism*. Taipei, Taiwan: IBTS.

Humphreys, C. (1987). *The wisdom of Buddhism*. London: Curzon.

Hutcherson, C.A., Seppala, J.M., & Gross, J.J. (2008). Loving-kindness meditation increases social connectedness. *Emotion, 8*, 720-724.

Huynh, T.V., Gotay, C., Layi, G., & Garrard, S. (2007). Mindfulness meditation and its medical and non-medical applications. *Hawaii Medical Journal, 66*, 328-330.

Ingram, R.E. (1990). Self-focused attention in clinical disorders: Review and a conceptual model. *Psychological Bulletin, 107*, 156-176.

Izard, C.E. (1972). *The face of emotion*. New York: Appleton-Century-Crofts.

Izard, C.E. (1993). Four systems for emotion activation: Cognitive and non-cognitive processes. *Psychological Review, 100*, 68-90.

Jack, B.N., W. Heller, P.A. Palmieri, & G.A. Miller (1997). Contrasting patterns of brain activity in anxious apprehension and anxious arousal. *Psychophysiology, 36,* 628-637.

Jackson, P. (1995). *Sacred hoops: Spiritual lessons of a hardwood warrior.* New York: Hyperion.

James, W. (1890). *Principles of psychology.* New York: Holt.

Jing Yin. (2002). *The Vinaya in India and China: Spirit and transformation.* Unpublished Ph.D.-thesis submitted at the School of Oriental and African Studies, University of London.

Johnson-Laird, P.N., & Oatley, K. (1992). Basic emotions, rationality, and folk theory. In N.L. Stein & K. Oatley (Eds.), *Basic emotions.* Hove, UK: Erlbaum.

Jung, C.G. (1969). *Psychology and religion: West and East* (Vol. 11) (2nd ed.). Princeton: Princeton University Press.

Kabat-Zinn, J. (1982). An outpatient program in behavioral medicine for chronic pain patients based on the practice of mindfulness meditation: Theoretical considerations and preliminary results. *General Hospital Psychiatry, 4,* 33-47.

Kabat-Zinn, J. (1990). *Full catastrophe living: Using the wisdom of your body and mind to face stress, pain, and illness.* New York: Delacourt Press.

Kabat-Zinn, J. (1994). *Wherever you go, there you are: Mindfulness meditation in everyday life.* New York: Hyperion.

Kabat-Zinn, J. (2000). Indra's net at work: The mainstreaming of Dharma practice in society. In G. Watson, S. Batchelor, & G. Claxton (Eds.), *The psychology of awakening: Buddhism, science, and our day-to-day lives* (pp.225-249). York Beach, ME: Samuel Weiser.

Kabat-Zinn, J. (2003a). Mindfulness-Based Stress Reduction (MBSR). In M.G.T. Kwee & M.K. Taams (Eds.), Special issue: A tribute to Yutaka Haruki. *Constructivism in the Human Sciences, 2,* 73-106.

Kabat-Zinn, J. (2003b). Mindfulness-based interventions in context: Past, present and future. *Clinical Psychology: Science & Practice, 10,* 144-156.

Kabat-Zinn, J. (2005). Coming to our senses. New York: Hyperion.

Kabat-Zinn, J. (2009). Foreword. In F. Didonna (Ed.), *Clinical handbook of mindfulness* (pp. xxv-xxxiii). New York: Springer.

Kabat-Zinn, J. (2009a). Foreword. In S.L. Shapiro & L. Carlson (Eds.), *The art and science of mindfulness* (pp. ix-xii). Washington, DC: American Psychological Association.

Kabat-Zinn, J., Lipworth, L., & Burney, R. (1985). The clinical use of mindfulness meditation for the self-regulation of chronic pain. *Journal of Behavioral Medicine, 8,* 163-190.

Kabat-Zinn, J., Lipworth, L., Burney, R., & Sellers, W. (1987). Four-year follow-up of a meditation program for the self-regulation of chronic pain: Treatment outcome and compliance. *Journal of Clinical Pain, 2,* 159-173.

Kabat-Zinn, J., Massion, A.O., Kristeller, J., Peterson, L.G., Fletcher, K.E., et al. (1992). Effectiveness of a meditation-based stress reduction program in the treatment of anxiety disorders. *America Journal of Psychiatry, 149,* 936-943.

Kabat-Zinn, J., Wheeler, E., Light, T., Skillings, Z., Scharf, M.J., et al. (1998). Influence of a mindfulness-based stress reduction intervention on rates of skin clearing in patients with moderate to severe psoriasis undergoing phototherapy (UVB) and photochemotherapy (PUVA). *Psychosomatic Medicine, 50,* 625-289.

Kagan, J. (1998). *Three seductive ideas.* Cambridge, MA: Harvard University Press.

Kahneman, D. (2003). A Perspective on judgement and choice: Mapping bounded rationality. *American Psychologist, 58,* 697-720.

Kalupahana, D.J. (1987). *The principles of Buddhist psychology.* Albany, NY: State University of New York Press.

Kalupahana, D.J. (1995). *Ethics in Early Buddhism.* Honolulu: University of Hawaii Press.

Kalupahana, D.J., & Kalupahana, I. (1982). *The way of Siddhartha,* Boulder, CO: Shambhala.

Kanji, N., White, A., & Ernst, E. (2004). Autogenic Training reduces anxiety after coronary angioplasty: A randomised clinical trial. *American Heart Journal, 147,* 10, K1-K4.

Kanji. N., White, A., & Ernst, E. (2006). Autogenic Training to reduce anxiety in nursing students: Randomized controlled trial. *Journal of Advanced Nursing, 53,* 729-735.

Katz, N. (1982). *Buddhist images of human perfection.* New Delhi: Motilal Banarsidas.

Kelly, B.D. (2008). Buddhist psychology, psychotherapy and the brain: A critical introduction. *Transcultural Psychiatry, 45,* 5-30.

Kennett, J. (2001). *Agency and responsibility.* Oxford: Oxford University Press.

Kenny, M.A., & Williams, J.M.G. (2007). Treatment-resistant depressed patients show a good response to mindfulness-based cognitive therapy. *Behaviour Research & Therapy, 45,* 617-625.

Keown, D. (2005). Buddhism: Morality without ethics. In G. Piyadassi, L. Perera, & R. Wijetunge (Eds.), *Buddhism in the West.* London: World Buddhist Foundation.
Kermani, K. (1990). *Autogenic Training: The effective holistic way to better health.* London: Souvenier Press.

Khema, A. (1997). *Who is my self?* Somerville, MA: Wisdom Publications.

Kimball, R.L. (2000). Humanistic Buddhism as conceived and interpreted by grand master Hsing Yun of Fo Guang Shan. *Hsi Lai Journal of Humanistic Buddhism, 1,* 1-52.

Kircher, T., Teutsch, E., Wormstall, H., Buchkremer, G., & Thimm, E. (2004). Effects of Autogenic Training in elderly patients. *Zeitschrift für Gerontologie und Geriatrie, 35,* 157-165.

Klein, M. (1975). *Envy and gratitude and other words 1946-1963.* New York: Delacorte.

Koster, E.H.W., Verschuere, B., Geert, C., & Houwer, J.D. (2004). Selective attention to threat in the dot probe paradigm: Differentiating vigilance and difficulty to disengage. *Behaviour Research & Therapy, 42,* 1183-1192.

Kotler, A. (Ed.).(1996). *Engaged Buddhist reader: Ten years of engaged Buddhist publishing.* Berkeley, CA: Parallax Press.

Korzybski, A. (1933). *Science and sanity.* Lakeville, Connecticut: Institute of General Semantics

Koshikawa, F. & Ishii, Y. (2006). Zen Buddhism and psychology: Some experimental findings. In M.G.T. Kwee, K.J. Gergen, & F. Koshikawa (Eds.), *Horizons in Buddhist Psychology: Practice, research & theory* (pp.175-184). Chagrin Falls, OH: Taos Institute Publications.

Krampen, G. (1999). Long-term evaluation of the effectiveness of additional autogenic training in the psychotherapy of depressive disorders. *European Psychologist, 4,* 11-18.

Kristeller, J.L., & Hallett, C.B. (1999). An exploratory study of a meditation-based intervention for binge eating disorder. *Journal of Health Psychology, 4,* 357-363.

Kristeller, J., & Jones, J. (2006). A middle way: Meditation in the treatment of compulsive eating. In M.G.T. Kwee, K.J. Gergen, & F. Koshikawa (Eds.), *Horizons in Buddhist Psychology: Practice, research & theory* (pp.85-100). Chagrin Falls, OH: Taos Institute Publications.

Kuhn, T. (1962). *The structure of scientific revolutions*. Chicago: University of Chicago Press.

Kurak, M. (2003). The relevance of the Buddhist theory of dependent co-origination to cognitive science. *Brain and Mind, 4*, 341-351.

Kuyken, W., Byford, S., Taylor, R.S., Watkins, E., Holden, E., et al. (2008). Mindfulness-Based Cognitive Therapy to prevent relapse in recurrent depression. *Journal of Consulting & Clinical Psychology, 76*, 966–978.

Kwee, M.G.T. (1982). Psychotherapy and the practice of general semantics. *Methodology & Science, 15*, 236-256.

Kwee, M.G.T. (1990). *Psychotherapy, meditation & health: A cognitive-behavioural perspective*. London: East-West.

Kwee, M.G.T. (1996). A multimodal systems view on psyche, affect and the basic emotions. In M.G.T. Kwee & T.L. Holdstock (Eds.).(1996), *Western and Buddhist Psychology: Clinical perspectives* (pp.221-268). Delft, Netherlands: Eburon.

Kwee, M.G.T. (1998). On consciousness and awareness of the BASICI.D. In M.M. DelMonte & Y. Haruki (Eds.).(1998), *The embodiment of mind* (pp.21-42). Delft, Netherlands: Eburon.

Kwee, M.G.T. (2009). A cognitive-behavioural approach to Karma Modification. In T.P.S. Oei & C.S. Tang (Eds.).(2009), *Current research & practices on cognitive behaviour therapy in Asia* (pp.89-111). Brisbane, Australia: CBT Unit Toowong Private Hospital.

Kwee, M.G.T. (2010a). Relational Buddhism: A psychological quest for meaning and sustainable happiness. In P.T.P. Wong (Ed.). *The human quest for meaning* (2nd ed.). London: Psychology Press.

Kwee, M.G.T. (2010b). Buddhist Psychology. In N.P. Azari (Ed.), *Encyclopedia of sciences and religions*. Heidelberg: Springer.

Kwee, M.G.T., & Ellis, A. (1997). Can Multimodal and Rational Emotive Behavior Therapy be reconciled? *Journal of Rational-Emotive & Cognitive-Behavior Therapy, 15*, 95-133.

Kwee, M.G.T., & Ellis, A. (1998). The interface between Rational Emotive Behavior Therapy (REBT) and Zen. *Journal of Rational-Emotive & Cognitive-Behavior Therapy, 16*, 5-44.

Kwee, M.G.T., & Holdstock, T.L. (Eds.).(1996). *Western and Buddhist psychology: Clinical perspectives*. Delft, Netherlands: Eburon.

Kwee, M.G.T., & Lazarus, A.A. (1986). Multimodal therapy: The cognitive behavioural tradition and beyond. In W. Dryden & W.L. Golden (Eds.), *Cognitive-behavioural approaches to psychotherapy* (pp.320-355). London: Harper & Row.

Kwee, M.G.T., & Taams, M.K. (Eds.).(2003). Special issue: A tribute to Yutaka Haruki. *Constructivism in the Human Sciences, 2*, 73-106.

Kwee, M.G.T., & Taams, M.K. (2005). Neozen. In M.G.T. Kwee (Ed.).(2005), *Buddhist Psychology: A transcultural bridge to innovation and reproduction*.
< www.inst.at/trans/16Nr/09_2/kwee_taams16.htm >

Kwee, M.G.T., & Taams, M.K. (2006a). A New Buddhist Psychology: Moving beyond Theravada and Mahayana. In M.G.T. Kwee, K.J. Gergen, & F. Koshikawa (Eds.), *Horizons in Buddhist Psychology: Practice, research & theory* (pp.435-478). Chagrin Falls, OH: Taos Institute Publications.

Kwee, M.G.T., & Taams, M.K. (2006b). Buddhist Psychology and Positive Psychology. In A. Delle Fave (Ed.), *Dimensions of well-being: Research and intervention* (pp.565-582). Milano, Italy: Franco Angeli.

Kwee, M.G.T., Gergen, K.J., & Koshikawa, F. (Eds.).(2006). *Horizons in Buddhist Psychology: Practice, research & theory.* Chagrin Falls, OH: Taos Institute Publications.

Ladner, L. (2004). *The lost art of compassion: Discovering the practice of happiness in the meeting of Buddhism and psychology.* New York: Harper Collins.

Lamotte, E. (1988, French original 1958). *History of Indian Buddhism from the origins to the Saka era.* Louvain-la-Neuve: Université Catholique de Louvain Institut Orientaliste.

Lancaster, B.L. (1997). On the stages of perception: Toward a synthesis of cognitive neuroscience and the Buddhist Abhidhamma tradition. *Journal of Consciousness Studies, 4,* 122-142.

Lazar, S. W., Kerr, C. E., Wasserman, R. H., Gray, J. R., Greve, D. N., et al. (2005). Meditation experience is associated with increased cortical thickness. *Neuroreport, 16,* 1893-1897.

Lazarus, A.A. (1985). Setting the record straight. *American Psychologist, 40,* 1418-1419.

Lazarus, A.A. (1989). *The practice of Multimodal Therapy.* Baltimore: Johns Hopkins University Press.

Lazarus, A.A. (1997). *Brief but comprehensive psychotherapy: The multimodal way.* New York: Springer.

Lazarus, R.S. (1991). Progress on a cognitive-motivational-relational theory of emotion. *American Psychologist, 46,* 1019-1024.

LeDoux, J. E. (1996). *The emotional brain.* New York: Simon & Schuster.

Leahy, R.L. (2004). Cognitive Behavioral Therapy. In R.G. Heimberg, C.L.Turk, & D.S. Mennin (Eds.), *Generalized Anxiety Disorder: Advances in research and practice* (pp.143-163). New York: Guilford.

Levine, M. (2000). *The positive psychology of Buddhism and yoga.* Mahwah, NJ: Erlbaum.

Levis, .D.J. (1989). The case for a return to two-factor theory of avoidance: The failure of non-fear interpretations. In S.B. Klein & R.R. Mowrer (Eds.), *Contemporary learning theories* (pp.227-278). Hillsdale, NJ: Erlbaum.

Libet, B. (1985). Unconscious cerebral initiative and the role of conscious will in voluntary action. *Behavioral & Brain Sciences, 8,* 529-566.

Libet, B. (2004). *Mind-time.* Cambridge, MA: Harvard University Press.

Linehan, M. M. (1993). *Skills Training manual for treating borderline personality disorder.* New York: Guilford.

Lodro, G.G. (1992). *Walking through walls: A presentation of Tibetan meditation.* New York: Snow Lion Publications.

Lohr, V. (2007). Benefits of nature: What we are learning about why people respond to nature. *Journal of Physiological Anthropology, 26,* 83-85.

Lusthaus, D. (2002). *Buddhist phenomenology: A philosophical investigation of Yogacara Buddhism and the Cheng Wei Shih Lun.* London: RoutledgeCurzon.

Luthe, W. (1983). *Lectures in Autogenic methods, delivered to the British Association for Autogenic Training and Therapy*. London: Unpublished Audiotape.

Lutz, A., Dunne, J.D., & Davidson, R.J. (2007). Meditation and the neuroscience of consciousness: An introduction (pp.499-555). In P.D. Zelazo, M. Moscovitch, & E. Thompson (Eds.), *Cambridge handbook of consciousness*. New York: Cambridge University Press.

Lyubomirsky, S. (2008). *The how of happiness: A scientific approach to getting the life you want*. New York: Penguin.

Lyubomirsky, S., King, L. A., & Diener, E. (2005). The benefits of frequent positive affect: Does happiness lead to success? *Psychological Bulletin, 131*, 803-855.

Lyubomirsky, S., Sheldon, K. M., & Schkade, D. (2005). Pursuing happiness: The architecture of sustainable change. *Review of General Psychology, 9*, 111-131.

Ma, H.S.W., & Teasdale, J.D. (2004). Mindfulness-Based Cognitive Therapy for depression: Replication and exploration of differential relapse-prevention effects. *Journal of Consulting & Clinical Psychology, 72*, 31-40.

Macy J. (1991). *Mutual causality in Buddhism and general systems theory*. Albany, NY: State University of New York Press.

Magid, B. (2005). *Ordinary mind* (2nd ed.). Boston, MA: Wisdom Publications.

Mahasi Sayadaw (1978). *The progress of insight*. Kandy, Sri Lanka: Buddhist Publication Society.

Mahasi Sayadaw (1980). *Practical insight meditation*. Kandy, Sri Lanka: Buddhist Publication Society.

Malach, R., Harel, M., Chalamish, Y., & Fish. L. (2006). *Perception without perceiver.* < www.weizman.ac.il >

Mamassian, P., & Goutcher, R. (2001). Prior knowledge on the illumination position. *Cognition, 81*, B1-B9.

Margolis, J. (1989). *Text without referents: Reconciling science and narrative*. New York: Blackwell.

Marks, J., & Ames R. T. (1995). *Emotions in Asian thought*. Albany, NY: The State University of New York Press.

Marlatt, G.A. (2002). Buddhist philosophy and the treatment of addictive behaviour. *Cognitive & Behavioural Practice, 9*, 44-50.

Marlatt, G.A., & Chawla, N. (2007). Meditation and alcohol use. *Southern Medical Journal, 100*, 451-453.

Marlatt, G.A., & Kristeller, J. (1999). Mindfulness and meditation. In W.R. Miller (Ed.), *Integrating spirituality in treatment: Resources for practitioners* (pp.67-84). Washington, DC: American Psychological Association Books.

Martin, I., & Levey, A.B. (1978). Evaluative conditioning. *Advances in Behavioural Research & Theory, 1*, 57-102.

Martin, J. R. (1997). Mindfulness: A proposed common factor. *Journal of Psychotherapy Integration, 7*, 291-312.

Martin, M.W. (2007). *Everyday morality*. Belmont, CA: Thompson Wadsworth.

Martin, M., Williams, R.M., & Clark, D .M. (1991). *Behavior Research & Therapy, 29*, 147-160.

Maslow, A. H. (1968). *Toward a psychology of being*. New York: Van Nostrand.

Matthews, A., & Mackintosh, B. (1998). A cognitive model of selective processing in anxiety. *Cognitive Therapy & Research, 22*, 539-560.

Mathews, B. (1983). *Craving and salvation: A study of Buddhist soteriology*. Waterloo, Ontario: Wilfred Laurier University Press.

Maul, G., & Maul, T. (1983). *Beyond limit*. Glenview, IL: Scott Foresman.

May, R. (1967). *Psychology and the human dilemma*. New York: Van Nostrand.

McGuigan, F.J., & Lehrer, P.M. (2007). Progressive Relaxation: Origins, principles, and clinical applications. In P.M. Lehrer, R.L. Woolfolk, & W. E. Sime (Eds.), *Principles and practice of stress management* (3rd ed.) (pp.88-124). New York: Guilford.

Meichenbaum, D. (1985). *Stress inoculation training*. New York: Pergamon.

Mele, A.R. (1996). Addiction and self-control. *Behaviour & Philosophy, 24*, 99-117.

Mennin, D.S., Heimberg, R.G., & Turk, C.L. (2004). Clinical presentation and Diagnostic Features. In R.G. Heimberg, C.L.Turk, & D.S. Mennin (Eds.), *Generalized Anxiety Disorder: Advances in research and practice* (pp.3-28). New York: Guilford.

Metzner, R. (1996). The Buddhist six-worlds model of consciousness and reality. *Journal of Transpersonal Psychology, 28*, 155-166.

Meyers-Levy, J., & Zhu R. (2007). The influence of ceiling height: the effect of priming on the type of processing that people use. *Journal of Consumer Research, 34*.

Mikulas, W.L. (1978a). *Behavior modification*. New York: Harper & Row.

Mikulas, W. L. (1978b). Four Noble Truths of Buddhism related to Behavior Therapy. *Psychological Record, 28*, 59-67.

Mikulas, W.L. (1981). Buddhism and Behavior Modification. *Psychological Record, 31*, 331-342.

Mikulas, W.L. (1983). Thailand and Behavior Modification. *Journal of Behavior Therapy & Experimental Psychiatry, 14*, 93-97.

Mikulas, W.L. (1986). Self-control: Essence and development. *Psychological Record, 36*, 297-308.

Mikulas, W.L. (1987). *The way beyond: An overview of spiritual practices*. Wheaton, IL: Theosophical Publishing Housing.

Mikulas, W.L. (1990). Mindfulness, self-control, and personal growth. In M.G.T. Kwee (Ed.), *Psychotherapy, meditation & health: A cognitive-behavioural perspective* (pp.151-164). London. East-West Publications.

Mikulas, W.L. (2000). Behaviors of the mind, meditation, and health. In Y. Haruki & K.T. Kaku (Eds.), *Meditation as health promotion* (pp.32-49). Delft, Netherlands: Eburon.

Mikulas, W.L. (2002). *The integrative helper: Convergence of eastern and western traditions*. Pacific Grove, CA: Wadsworth.

Mikulas, W.L. (2004a). Not-doing. *Constructivism in the Human Sciences, 9*, 113-120.

Mikulas, W.L. (2004b). Working with the clinging mind. In M. Blows, S. Srinivasan, J. Blows, P. Bankart, M. DelMonte, & Y. Haruki (Eds.), *The relevance of the wisdom traditions in contemporary society: The challenge to psychology* (pp.189-194). Delft, Netherlands: Eburon.

Mikulas, W.L. (2007). Buddhism and western psychology: Fundamentals of integration. *Journal of Consciousness Studies, 14*, 4-49.

Miller, G.A., Galanter, E.H., & Pribram, K.N. (1960). *Plans and the structure of behavior*. New York: Holt, Rinehart & Winston.

Miller, J.J., Fletcher, K., & Kabat-Zinn, J. (1995). Three-year follow-up and clinical implications of a mindfulness meditation-based stress reduction intervention in the treatment of anxiety disorders. *General Hospital Psychiatry, 17*, 192-200.

Molino, A. (Ed.).(1993). *The couch and the tree*. New York: North Point Press.

Molina, S., Borkovec, T.D., Peasley, C., & Person, D. (1998). Content analysis of worrisome streams of consciousness in anxious and dysphoric participants. *Cognitive Therapy & Research, 22,* 109-123.

Moon, M. (1994). *The living road.* Newtown NSW, Australia: Millennium,

Moray, N. (1969). *Attention.* New York: Academic Press.

Morgan, P. (2005). Skilful means and socially engaged Buddhism in the transplantation of Buddhism to the West. In G. Piyadassi, L. Perera, & R. Wijetunge (Eds.), *Buddhism in the West* (pp.71-88). London: World Buddhist Foundation.

Morris, R. & E. Hardy, E. (Ed.).(1922-1938). *Anguttara Nikaya* (5 vols). London: Pali Text Society.

Moses, E. B., & Barlow, D. H. (2006). A new unified treatment approach for emotional disorders based on emotion science. *Current Directions in Psychological Science, 15,* 146-150.

Murphy, M., & Donovan, S. (1997). *The physical and psychological effects of meditation* (2nd ed.). Sausalito, CA: Institute of Noetic Sciences.

Myint, A. (2007). *Theravada treatment and psychotherapy.* Western Australia: Murdoch University, Ph.D. Thesis.

Nanamoli, B. (1956). *The path of purification.* Colombo, Ceylon: A. Semage.

Nanamoli, B. (Transl.).(1975). *The path of purification (Vissuddhimagga) by Buddhaghosa.* Kandy, Sri Lanka: Buddhist Publication Society.

Nanamoli, B (1992). *The life of the Buddha.* Onalaska, WA: Pariyatti.

Nanamoli, B.,& Bodhi, B. (1995/2001). *Middle length sayings of the Buddha* (2nd ed.). Boston, MA: Wisdom Publications.

Nanavira, T. (1987). *The tragic, the comic and the personal.* Kandy, Sri Lanka: Buddhist Publication Society.

Naruse, G. (1965). Autogenic Training in Japan. In W. Luthe (Ed.), *Autogenic Training: Correlationes psychosomaticae* (pp.290-292). New York: Grune & Stratton.

Naylor, R., & Marshall, J. (2007). Autogenic Training: A key component in holistic medical practice. *Journal of Holistic Healthcare, 4,* 14-19.

Neimeyer, R.A. (1995). An invitation to constructivist psychotherapies. In R.A. Neimeyer (Ed.), *Constructivism in psychotherapy* (pp.1-8). Washington, DC: American Psychological Association.

Neu, J. (1977). *Emotion, thought, and therapy.* Berkeley, CA: University of California Press.

Newell, A., & Simon, H.A. (1956). The logic theory machine: A complex information processing system. *IRE Transactions on Information Theory, IT-2,* 61-79.

Newell, A., & Simon, H.A. (1972). *Human problem solving.* Englewood Cliffs, NJ: Prentice-Hall.

Newman, M.G., Castonguagy, L.G., & Borkovec, T.D. (1999). New dimensions in the treatment of Generalized Anxiety Disorder: Interpersonal focus and emotional deepening. Paper presented at the *Annual Meeting of the Society for the Exploration of Psychotherapy Integration,* Miami, FL.

Newman, M.G., Castonguay, L.G., Borkovec, T.D., & Molnar, C. (2004). Integrative therapy for Generalized Anxiety Disorder. In R.G. Heimberg, C.L. Turk, & D.S. Mennin (Eds.), *Generalized Anxiety Disorder: Advances in research and practice* (pp.320-350). New York: Guilford.

Nicholson, P.T. (2002a). The soma code, Parts I-III: Luminous visions in the Rig Veda; soma's birth, purification, and transmutation into Indra; Visions, myths, and drugs. *Electronic Journal of Vedic Studies, 8*, 31-92.

Nicholson, P.T. (2002b). Meditation, slow wave sleep and ecstatic seizures: The etiology of kundalini visions. *Subtle Energies & Energy Medicine, 12*, 183-240.

Nicholson, P.T. (2004). Theoretical-empirical studies of meditation: Does a sleep rhythm hypothesis explain the data? *Subtle Energies & Energy Medicine, 13*, 109-130.

Norman, H.C. (Ed.).(1906-1914). *Dhammapadatthakatha* (4 vols.). London: Pali Text Society.

Nussbaum, M. (2001). *Upheavels of thought: The intelligence of emotions.* Cambridge: Cambridge University of Press.

Nyanaponika, T. (1983). *Contemplation of feelings.* Kandy, Sri Lanka Buddhist Publication Society.

Nyanaponika, T., & Bodhi, B. (Transl.).(1999). *Numerical discourses of the Buddha.* Kandy, Sri Lanka: Buddhist Publication Society.

Oldenberg, H. (Ed.).(1879-1889). *Vinaya Pitaka* (4 vols.). London: Pali Text Society.

Onda, A. (1965). Autogenic Training and Zen. In W. Luthe (Ed.), *Autogenic Training: Correlationes psychosomaticae* (pp.251-257). New York: Grune & Stratton.

Ornstein, R.E. (1986). *The psychology of consciousness* (rev. ed.). New York: Viking Penguin.

Orsillo, S.M., Roemer, L., & Barlow, D.H. (2003). Integrating acceptance and mindfulness into existing cognitive-behavioral treatment for GAD: A case study. *Cognitive & Behavioral Practice, 10*, 223-230.

Ortony, A., Clore, G.L., & Collins, A. (1988). *The cognitive structure of emotions.* New York: Cambridge University Press.

Ospina, M.B., Bond, T.K., & Karkaneh, M. (2007). *Meditation practices for health: State of the research. Evidence report/technology assessment no.155* (Prepared by the University of Alberta evidence-based practice center). Rockville, MD: E010.

Ott, M.J., Norris, R.L., & Bauer-Wu, S.M. (2006). Mindfulness meditation for oncology patients: A discussion and critical review. *Integrative Cancer Therapy, 5*, 98-108.

Pabongka, R. (1997). *Liberation in the palm of your hand.* Boston, MA: Wisdom Publications.

Pandita, S.U. (1992*). In this very life.* Boston, MA: Wisdom Publications.

Peele, S. (1998). *The meaning of addiction.* San Fransico: Jossey-Bass.

Pert, C. (1997). *The molecules of emotion.* New York: Scribner.

Pirsig, R.M. (1974). *Zen and the art of motorcycle maintenance: An inquiry into values.* New York: Bantam Books.

Plutchik, R. (1994). *The psychology and biology of emotion.* New York: Harper Collins.

Powers, J. (Transl.).(1994). *Wisdom of Buddha: The Sandhinirmocana Sutra.* Berkeley Dharma Publishing.

Pradhan, E.K. (2007). Effect of Mindfulness-Based Stress Reduction in rheumatoid arthritis patients. *Arthritis & Rheumatism, 57*, 1134-1142.

Premasiri, P.D. (2006). *Studies in Buddhist philosophy and religion.* Sri Lanka: University of Peradeniya.

Psychodynamic Diagnostic Manual (2006). Silver Springs, MD: Alliance of Psychoanalytical Organizations.

Pye, M. (1978). *Skilful means.* London: Duckworth.

Queen, C., Prebish, C., & Keown, D. (Eds.).(2003). *Action Dharma: New studies in Engaged Buddhism*. London: RoutledgeCurzon.

Rabten, G. (1992). *The mind and its functions* (transl. by S. Batchelor, 2nd ed.). Mont Pelerin, Switzerland: Editions Rabten Choeling.

Rahula, W. (1967). *What the Buddha taught*. London: Gordon Fraser.

Rahula, W. (1974). Gotama Buddha. In *Encyclopaedia Britannica* (on line).

Rahula, W. (1990). *What the Buddha taught*. New York: Grove Press.

Rahula, W. (1988). The social teachings of the Buddha. In F. Eppsteiner (Ed.), *The path of compassion: Writings on socially engaged Buddhism* (pp.103-110). Berkeley, CA: Parallax Press.

Ranty, Y. (2007). The evolution of Schultz's Autogenic Training in France. *European Journal of Autogenic & Bionomic Studies, 1*, 55-69.

Rapgay, L., & Bystritsky, A. (2008). Introduction to classical mindfulness: Its clinical application. *NYAS Special Issue on Mind Body Medicine & Optimal Health*. New York: Academy of Sciences.

Rausch, S. M, Gramling, S. E., & Auerbach, S. M. (2006) Effects of a single session of large-group meditation and progressive muscle relaxation training on stress reduction, reactivity, and recovery. *International Journal of Stress Management, 13*, 273-290.

Reat, N.R. (1994). *Buddhism: A history*. Berkeley, CA: Asian Humanities Press.

Reibel, D.K., Greeson, J.M., Brainard, G.C., & Rosenzweiz, S. (2001). Mindfulness-based stress reduction and health-related quality of life in a heterogeneous patient hospital. *General Hospital Psychiatry, 23*, 183-192.

Rhys Davids, C.A.F. (1900). *A Buddhist manual of psychological ethics* (transl. of the *Dhammasangani*). London: Royal Asiatic Society.

Rhys Davids, C.A.F. (1914). *Buddhist psychology*. London: G. Bell & Sons.

Rhys Davids, C.A.F. (Ed.).(1920-1921, reprint 1975). *The Visuddhimagga* (2 vols.). London: Pali Text Society.

Rhys Davids, T.W. (1881). *The Hibbert lectures on Indian Buddhism*. London: Williams & Norgate.

Rhys Davids, T.W., & Carpenter, J.L. (Eds.).(1890-1911). *Digha Nikaya* (3 vols). London: Pali Text Society.

Rhys Davids, T.W., & Stede, W. (Eds.).(1921-1925). *Pali-English dictionary*. London: Pali Text Society.

Rhys Davids, T.W., Carpenter, J. E., & Stede, W. (Eds).(1886-1932). *Sumangalavilasini* (3 vols.). London: Pali Text Society.

Ricard, R. (2006). *Tibet: An inner journey*. New York: Thames & Hudson.

Ridley, M. (1996). *The origin of virtue: Human instincts and the evolution of cooperation*. New York: Penguin.

Robinson, F.P., Mathews, H.L., & Witek-Janusek, L. (2003). Psycho-endocrine-immune response to mindfulness-based stress reduction in individuals infected with the human immunodeficiency virus: A quasi experimental study. *Journal of Alternative & Complementary Medicine, 9*, 683-694.

Roemer, L., & Orsillo, S.M. (2002). Expanding our conceptualization of and treatment for generalized anxiety disorder: Integrating mindfulness/acceptance-based approaches with existing cognitive-behavioral models. *Clinical Psychology: Science & Practice, 9*, 54-68.

Roemer, L., Orsillo, S.M., & Barlow, D.H.B. (2003). Generalized Anxiety Disorder. In D.H. Barlow (Ed.), *Anxiety and its disorders: The nature and treatment of anxiety and panic* (2nd ed.) (pp.477-515). New York: Guilford.

Rogers, C.R. (1961). *On becoming a person.* Boston: Houghton Mifflin.

Rorty, A.O. (1998). Political sources of emotions: Greed and anger. *Midwest Studies in Philosophy, 22,* 21-33.

Rosen, H. (1996). Meaning-making narratives: Foundations for constructivist and social constructionist psychotherapies. In H. Rosen (Ed.), *Constructing realities: Meaning-making perspectives for psychotherapists* (pp.3-51). San Francisco: Jossey-Bass.

Rosenzweig, S. (2003). Mindfulness-Based Stress Reduction lowers psychological distress in medical students. *Teaching & Learning in Medicine, 15,* 88-92.

Rosenzweig, S., Reibel, D., Greeson, J., Brainard, G., & Hojat, M. (2003). Mindfulness-Based Stress Reduction lowers psychological distress in medical students. *Teaching & Learning in Medicine, 15,* 88-92.

Rosenzweig, S., Reibel, D., Greeson, J., Edman, J., Jasser, S., et al. (2007). Mindfulness-Based Stress Reduction is associated with improved glycemic control in type 2 diabetes mellitus: A pilot study. *Alternative Therapies in Health & Medicine, 13,* 36-38.

Rubin, J.D. (1996). *Psychotherapy and Buddhism.* New York: Plenum.

Ruden, R. (2000). *The craving brain.* New York: Harper Collins.

Rychlak, J.F. (2000). A psychotherapist's lessons from the philosophy of science. *American Psychologist, 55,* 1126-1132.

Safran, J.D. (Ed.).(2003). *Psychoanalysis and Buddhism.* Boston, MA: Wisdom Publications.

Sakairi, Y. (2000) Psychotherapy and 'do' in Japanese culture: Self-cultivation through tackling a set task. In W. Weidong, Y. Sasaki, & Y. Haruki (Eds.).(2000). *Bodywork and psychotherapy in the East* (pp.205-212). Delft, Netherlands: Eburon.

Salmon, P. G., Santorelli, S. F., & Kabat-Zinn, J. (1998). Intervention elements promoting adherence to mindfulness-based stress reduction programs in the clinical behavioral medicine setting. In E.B.S.S.A. Shumaker, J.K. Ockene, & W.L. Bee (Eds.), *Handbook of health behavior change* (pp.239-268). New York: Springer.

Salzberg, S. (1997). *Loving kindness.* Boston, MA: Shambhala.

Santucci, J. (2000). Humanistic Buddhism in Tibetan tradition. *Hsi Lai Journal of Humanistic Buddhism, 1,* 129-138.

Schaler, J.A. (1998). *Drugs.* Amherst, NY: Prometheus Books.

Schultz, J. H. (1956). *Das Autogene Training, konzentrative Selbstentspannung: Versuch einer klinisch-praktischen Darstellung* (9th ed.). Stuttgart: Georg Thieme Verlag.

Scheepers, A. (1994). *A survey of Buddhist thought.* Amsterdam: Olive Press.

Scherer, K. (2005). What are emotions and how can they be measured? *Social Science Information, 44,* 695-729.

Schumann, H.W. (1989). *The historical Buddha.* London: Arkana Books.

Segal, S.R. (2005). Mindfulness and self-development in psychotherapy. *Journal of Transpersonal Psychology, 37,* 143-163.

Segal, Z.V., Williams, J.M.G., & Teasdale, J.D. (2002). *Mindfulness-Based Cognitive Therapy for depression: A new approach to preventing relapse.* New York: Guilford.

Shapiro, D. (1982). Overview: Clinical and psychological comparison of meditation and other self-control strategies. *American Journal of Psychiatry, 139,* 267-274.

Shapiro, S.L., & Carlson, L.E. (2009). *The art and science of mindfulness: Integrating mindfulness into psychology and the helping professions.* Washington DC: American Psychological Association.

Shapiro, S.L., & Walsh, R. (2003). An analysis of recent meditation research and suggestions for future directions. *Humanistic Psychologist, 31,* 86-114.

Shapiro, S.L., Schwartz, G.E., & Bonner, G. (1998). Effects of mindfulness-based stress reduction on medical and premedical students. *Journal of Behavioral Medicine, 21,* 581-599.

Shapiro, S.L., Carlson, L.E. Astin, J.A., & Freedman, B. (2006). Mechanisms of mindfulness. *Journal of Psychology, 62,* 373-386.

Sheng-yen (2001). *Hoofprint of the ox: Principles of the Chan Buddhist path as taught by a modern Chinese master.* New York: Oxford University Press.

Sherwood, P. (2005). Grief and loss work in Buddhist psychotherapy, *PACAWNews, 33,* 4-5.

Shodo Harada-Roshi (2000). *The path to Bodhidharma.* Boston, MA: Tuttle.

Shigaki, C. L., Glass, B., & Schopp, L. (2006). Mindfulness-based stress reduction in medical settings. *Journal of Clinical Psychology in Medical Settings,* 13, 209-216.

Siegel, D.J. (2007). *The mindful brain: Reflection and attunement in the cultivation of well-being.* New York: Norton..

Siegel, R.D., Germer, C.K., & Olendzki, A. (2008). Mindfulness: What is it? Where does it come from? In F. Didonna (Ed.), *Clinical handbook of mindfulness* (pp.17-36). New York: Springer.

Smith, A. (1959). *The theory of the moral sentiments.* Princeton: Princeton University Press.

Smith, A. (2004). Clinical uses of mindfulness training for older people. *Behavioural & Cognitive Psychotherapy, 32,* 423-420.

Smith, D. (1982). Trends in counseling and psychotherapy. *American Psychologist, 37,* 802-809.

Smith, J.C. (2004). Alterations in brain and immune function produced by mindfulness meditation: Three caveats. *Psychosomatic Medicine, 66,* 148-152.

Smith, J.E., Richardson, J., Hoffman. C, & Pilkington, K. (2005). Mindfulness-based stress reduction as supportive therapy in cancer care: A systematic review. *Journal of Advanced Nursing, 52,* 315-327.

Smith, V.A. (1958). *The Oxford history of India,* Oxford: Clarendon Press.

Sole-Leris, A. (1986). *Tranquillity and insight.* London: Rider.

Solomon, R.C. (Ed.).(2004). *Thinking about feeling.* Oxford: Oxford University Press

Soon, C.S., Brass, M., Heinze, H.J., & Haynes, J.D. (2008). Unconscious determinants of free decisions in the human brain. *Nature Neuroscience,* 11, 543-545.

Speca, M., Carlson, L.E., Goodey, E., & Angen, M. (2000). A randomized, wait-list controlled clinical trial: The effect of a mindfulness meditation-based stress reduction program on mood and symptoms of stress in cancer outpatients. *Psychosomatic Medicine, 62,* 613-622.

Stein, K.F., & Markus, H.R. (1996). The role of the self in behavioral change. *Journal of Psychotherapy Integration, 4,* 317-353.

Sternberg, R.J., & Barnes, M.L. (Eds.).(1988). *The psychology of love.* New Haven: Yale University Press.

Stickgold, R. (2002). Inclusive versus exclusive approaches to sleep and dream research. *Behavior & Brain Science, 32,* 1011.

Stocker, M. (1996). *Valuing emotions.* Cambridge: Cambridge University Press.

Stocker, M. (1979). Desiring the bad: An essay in moral psychology. *Journal of Philosophy,* *76,* 738-753.

Sugamura, G., Haruki, Y., & Koshikawa, F. (2007). Building more solid bridges between Buddhism and western psychology. *American Psychologist, 62,* 1080-1081.

Sujato, B. (2003). *A history of mindfulness: How insight worsted tranquillity in the Satipatthana Sutta.* Taipei, Taiwan: The Corporate Body of the Buddha Educational Foundation

Suler, J.R. (1993). *Contemporary psychoanalysis and eastern thought.* Albany, NY: State University of New York Press.

Sullivan, H.S. (1953). *The interpersonal theory of psychiatry.* New York: Norton.

Sumangala Thera, S. (Ed.).(19194). *The Dhammapada.* London: Pali Text Society.

Sutherland, G., Andersen, M.B., & Morris, T. (2005). Relaxation and health-relate d quality of life in multiple sclerosis: The example of Autogenic Training. *Journal of Behavioral Medicine, 28,* 249-256.

Swaris, N. (1997). *Magga: The Buddha's way to human liberation: A socio-historical approach.* Ph.D. Dissertation, University of Utrecht, Netherlands.

Tagore, R. (1961). *The religion of man.* Boston, MA: Beacon Press.

Teasdale, J.D. (2000). Mindfulness-Based Cognitive Therapy in the prevention of relapse and recurrence in major depression. In Y. Haruki & K.T. Kaku (Eds.), *Meditation as health promotion: A lifestyle modification approach* (pp.3-18). Delft, Netherlands: Eburon.

Teasdale, J.D., Segal, Z.V., & Williams, J.M.G. (2003). Mindfulness training and problem formulation. *Clinical Psychology: Science & Practice, 10,* 157-160.

Teasdale, J.D., Moore, R.G., Hayhurst, H., Pope, M., Williams, S., & Segal, Z.V. (2002). Metacognitive awareness and prevention of relapse in depression: Empirical evidence. *Journal of Consulting & Clinical Psychology, 70,* 275-287.

Teasdale, J.D., Segal, Z.V., Williams, J.M.G., Ridgeway, V.A., Soulsby, J.M., & Lau, M. A. (2000). Prevention of relapse/recurrence in major depression by mindfulness-based cognitive therapy. *Journal of Consulting & Clinical Psychology, 68,* 615-623.

Tejaniya, S.U. (2008). *Don't look down on the defilement, they will laugh at you.* Rangoon, Burma: Shwe Oo Min Dhamma Sukha.

Thanissaro, B. (Transl.).(1998). *Lonaphala Sutta, the salt crystal. Anguttara Nikaya III 99.* London: Pali Text Society.

Thanissaro, B. (Transl.).(2000). *Mahasatipatthana Sutta, the great frames of reference (Digha Nikya 22).*

Thanissaro, B. (2002). *The agenda of mindfulness.* Transcription of the author's file.

Thera, N. (1973). *The heart of Buddhist meditation.* New York: Samuel Weiser.

Thich, N.H. (1967). *The lotus in the sea of fire.* London: SCM Press.

Thich, N.H. (1993). *Love in action: Writings on nonviolent social change.* Berkeley, CA: Parallax Press.

Thich, N.H. (1998). *Interbeing: Fourteen guidelines for engaged Buddhism.* Berkeley, CA: Parallax Press.

Thich, N. H. (1999). *The miracle of mindfulness.* Boston, MA: Beacon Press.

Tilakaratne, A. (1993). *Nirvana and ineffability: A study of the Buddhist theory of language and reality.* Colombo, Sri Lanka: Postgraduate Institute of Pali and Buddhist Studies.

Toneatto, T., & Nguyen, L. (2007). Does mindfulness meditation improve anxiety and mood symptoms? A review of the controlled research. *Canadian Journal of Psychiatry, 52*, 260-266.

Treckner, V. (Ed.).(1886). *Milindapanha*. London: Pali Text Society.

Trenkner, V., & R. Chalmers, R. (Eds.).(1888-1902, republished 1948-1951). *Majjhimanikaya* (3 vols.). London: Pali Text Society.

Twemlow, S.W. (2001). Training psychotherapists in attributes of 'mind' from Zen and psychoanalytic perspectives. *American Journal of Psychotherapy, 55*, 1-39.

Urgen, T. (1995). *Rainbow painting*. Hong Kong: Rangjung Yeshe Publications.

Ustun, T.B., & Sartorius, N. (Eds.).(1995). *Mental illness in general health care: An international study*. Chichester, UK: Wiley.

Varela, F.J., Thompson, E., & Rosch, E. (1991). *The embodied mind*. Cambridge, MA: MIT Press.

Varela, F., Lachaux, J-P., Rodriguez, E., & Martinerie, J. (2001). The brainweb: Phase synchronization and large-scale integration. *National Review of Neuroscience, 2*, 229-239.

Vasumitra (1925). Origin and doctrine of early Indian Buddhist schools (transl. of the Huanchwang version of Vasumitra's treatise). *Asia Major, 2*.

Victoria, B. (2006). *Zen at war* (2nd ed.). Lanham, MD: Rowman & Littlefield.

Von Hinüber, O. (1996). *Handbook of Pali literature*. Berlin: Walter de Gruyter.

Wallace, B.A., & Shapiro, S.L. (2006). Mental balance and well-being: Building bridges between Buddhism and western psychology. *American Psychologist, 61*, 690-701.

Walsh, R.N., & Vaughan, F. (Eds.).(1993). *Paths beyond ego*. Los Angeles: Tarcher.

Walshe, M. (1987). *Thus have I heard: The long discourses of the Buddha*. London: Wisdom Publications.

Watts, F.N. (1996). Are science and religion in conflict? *The Psychologist, 9*, 15-18.

Weidong, W., Sasaki, Y., & Haruki, Y. (Eds.).(2000). *Bodywork and psychotherapy in the East*. Delft, Netherlands: Eburon.

Wells, A. (1995). Meta-cognition and worry: A cognitive model of Generalized Anxiety Disorder. *Behavioral & Cognitive Psychotherapy, 23*, 301-320.

Wells, A. (2002). GAD, meta-cognition and mindfulness: an information processing analysis. *Clinical Psychology: Science & Practice, 9*, 95-100.

West, M.A. (Ed.).(1987). *The psychology of meditation*. Oxford: Clarendon Press.

Whitfield, H.J. (2006). Towards case-specific applications of mindfulness-based cognitive-behavioural therapies: A mindfulness-based rational emotive behaviour therapy. *Counselling Psychology Quarterly, 2*, 205-217.

Wilber, K. (2000). *Integral psychology*. Boston: Shambhala.

Wilhelm, R. (1962). *The secret of the golden flower: A Chinese book of life*. New York: Harcourt, Brace & World.

Williams, J.M.G. (2000). Mindfulness-Based Cognitive Therapy reduces overgeneral autobiographical memory in formerly depressed patients. *Journal of Abnormal Psychology, 109*, 150-155.

Williams, J.M.G., Teasdale, J., Segal, Z., & Kabat-Zinn, J. (2007). *The mindful way through depression: Freeing yourself from chronic unhappiness*. New York: Guilford.

Witkiewitz, K.A., & Marlatt, G. A. (2007). *Therapist's guide to evidence-based relapse prevention*. Burlington, MA: Academic Press.

Witkiewitz, K., Marlatt, G.A., & Walker, D.D. (2005). Mindfulness-based relapse prevention for alcohol use disorders: The meditative tortoise wins the race. *Journal of Cognitive Psychotherapy, 19*, 221-228.

Wittgenstein, L. (1953). *Philosophical investigations*. New York: Macmillan.

Wolpe, J. (1973). *The practice of Behavior Therapy*. New York: Pergamon.

Woods, J.H., Horner, I.B., & Kosambi, D. (Eds.).(1922). *Papanasudani* (5 vols.). London: Pali Text Society.

Woolfolk, R.L. (1975). Psychological correlates of meditation: A review. *Archives of General Psychiatry, 32*, 1326-1373.

Wright, S., Courtney, U., & Crowther, D. (2002). A quantitative and qualitative pilot study of the perceived benefits of Autogenic Training for a group of people with cancer. *European Journal of Cancer Care, 11*, 122-130.

Wundt, W. (1874). *Grundzüge der physiologischen Psychologie*. Leipzig: Engelmann.

Yalom, I. D. (1980). *Existential psychotherapy*. New York: Basic Books.

Zsombok, T., Juhasz, G., Budavari, A., Vitrai, J., & Bagdy, G. (2004). Effect of Autogenic Training on drug consumption in patients with primary headache: An 8-month follow-up study. *Headache: The Journal of Head & Face Pain, 43*, 2

Suttas and sutras can all be googled and found in various English translations

(e.g. log on for suttas to < www.buddhanet.net > from where one may find < www.metta.lk
> or < www.accesstoinsight.org > and for sutras to < www4.bayarea.net >.)

Abbreviations referring to the Buddhist original sources:

A or AN: Anguttara Nikaya – The numerical discourses.
D or DN: Digha Nikaya – The long discourses.
K or KN: Khuddaka Nikaya – The division of short books that includes the Suttanipata (Sn),
    the Dhammapada (Dhp) and the Jataka stories.
M or MN: Majjhima Nikaya – The middle-length discourses
S or SN: Samyutta Nikaya – The grouped discourses

Contributors

James H. AUSTIN is an Emeritus Professor of Neurology at the University of Colorado Health Sciences Center. His first sabbatical was sent at the All-India Institute of Medical Sciences in New Delhi. During the second sabbatical at Kyoto University Medical School in 1974, he began Zen meditative training with Kobori-Roshi, an English-speaking Rinzai Zen master. His early research was in clinical neurology, neuropathology, and neurochemistry. As a Zen practitioner, he has since become keenly interested in the ways that neuroscience research can help clarify the meditative transformations of consciousness. His MIT Press books include *Selfless Insight* (2009), *Zen-Brain Reflections* (2006), *Zen and the Brain* (1998), and *Chase, Chance, and Creativity* (2003). Mail: 4510 Revere Court, Columbia, MO, 65203, USA.

M.W. Padmasiri DE SILVA, Emeritus Professor and Head of the Philosophy and Psychology Department, University of Peradeniya, Sri Lanka, is currently Research Fellow at Monash University, Victoria, Australia. He earned his M.A. and Ph.D. (in Comparative Philosophy) from the University of Hawai'i. Having obtained an Advanced Diploma in Buddhist Psychotherapy, Sophia College, Australia, he is a member of the Counsellors' And Psychotherapists' Association of Victoria. He held visiting positions at the University of Pittsburgh, USA, the National University of Singapore, and the University of Waikato, New Zealand. Among his publications are *Introduction to Buddhist Psychology, Buddhist & Freudian Psychology, Environmental Philosophy & Ethics in Buddhism*, and *Explorers of Inner Space*. Email: pdesilva@alphalink.com.au

Padmal DE SILVA was an Emeritus Senior Lecturer in Psychology at the Institute of Psychiatry, King's College, University of London, and consultant clinical psychologist at the South London and Maudsley National Health Service Trust, in the U.K. His clinical and research interests include anxiety disorders, eating disorders, couple problems and Buddhist Psychology. He co-authored *Obsessive-compulsive Disorders: the Facts* and co-edited *Obsessive-compulsive Disorders: Theory, Research and Treatment*. He has authored many articles and chapters on Early Buddhist teachings and Cognitive-Behaviour Therapy.

GUANG Xing received his Ph.D. from School of Oriental and African Studies. He is currently an assistant professor of Buddhist Studies at the University of Hong Kong and the Tung Lin Kok Yuen Canada Foundation visiting professor in Buddhism and Contemporary Society at the University of British Columbia , Canada. His publications include *The Concept of the Buddha: Its Evolution from Early Buddhism to the Trikaya Theory* (2005, Routledge) and he is currently working on the issue of filial piety in Chinese Buddhism, a topic about which he already published several papers. Email: guangxingsu@gmail.com

Paul R. FLEISCHMAN is a psychiatrist. He is the 1993 recipient of the American Psychiatric Association Oskar Pfister Award which acknowledges his outstanding contributions to the field of psychiatry and religion. A Phi Beta Kappa graduate of the University of Chicago and a member of the Alpha Omega Alpha medical honours society, he received his M.D. from the Albert Einstein College of Medicine and was trained in psychiatry at Yale University. He is the author of *The Healing Spirit, Spiritual Aspects of Psychiatric Practice, Karma and Chaos, The Buddha Taught Nonviolence, Not Pacifism*, and *Cultivating Inner Peace*. His recent focus has been on poetry. Email: paulandsusanf@yahoo.com

David J. KALUPAHANA is Emeritus Professor of Philosophy at the University of Hawai'i, Manoa, USA. He has published more than 20 books and 100 chapters and articles in peer reviewed journals, is an Editorial Board member of *Philosophy East and West* and *History and Philosophy of Logic*, and serves as a Consultant Editor for the *Encyclopaedia of Buddhism* and *Encyclopaedia of Philosophy* (Supplementary Volume). Professor Kalupahana had several international visiting appointments, fellowships and grants and delivered numerous invited lectures at universities all over the world, among others at Harvard and at Waseda University, Tokyo. He is multilingual, is fluent in Sinhala, is competent in Pali, Sanskrit, and Prakrit (Asokan and North Western) and has a working knowledge of Chinese and Tibetan. Email: kalu@hawaii.edu

Tilak KARIYAWASAM graduated (B.A., First Class Hons) from Sri Jayewawawardanepure University, Sri Lanka, in 1967, and was appointed as a lecturer to the same University in 1969. He was engaged in postgraduate research work at the University of Lancaster, U.K. (1970-1973) where he obtained his Ph.D. (1973) and was subsequently appointed to the University of Kelaniya (1975), where he functioned as Head of the Department of Pali and Buddhist Studies (1988-1997) and later as Director of the Postgraduate Institute of Pali and Buddhist (1998-2003). He currently serves as a Senior Chair of Buddhist Studies. Professor Kariyawasam has authored many articles, supervised a large number of local and foreign post-graduate research students, and co-edited *Therapadana Sangaha*, a directory about leading monks of Sri Lanka. Email: tilak.kariyawasam@gmail.com

Yakupitiyage KARUNADASA obtained his B.A. Hons from the University of Ceylon, Peradeniya and his Ph.D. from the University of London, U.K. He is a Professor Emeritus of the University of Kelaniya, Sri Lanka, and the former Director of its Postgraduate Institute of Pali and Buddhist Studies. At present he is a Visiting Professor of the Centre of Buddhist Studies of the University of Hong Kong. He has held the Numata Chair during which he served as Distinguished Visiting Professor of Buddhist Studies at the University of Calgary. He also held the Bukyo Dendo Kyokai Professorship in Buddhist Studies at the School of Oriental and African Studies of the University of London. Email: karunadasa@hotmail.com

Maurits G.T. Kwee, PhD (Em. Hon. Prof.), Clinical Psychologist and Taos Institute Associate, is currently involved in supervising PhD-canditates of Tilburg University, Netherlands. A psychotherapist over three decades and co-founder of the *Trans-cultural Society for Clinical Meditation*, Japan, he is now president of the *Institute for Buddhist Psychology and Relational Buddhism*, France. Among his publications are more than hundred articles and chapters in professional journals and books, and more than a dozen books. His latest, a joint-work, is *New Horizons in Buddhist Psychology: Relational Buddhism for Collaborative Practitioners* (Taos Institute Publications, 2010). Dr. Kwee conducts 2-day master classes on the Borobudur Mahayana teachings (six books carved in stone) which include the transmission of twelve pristine Buddhist meditations in the framework of postmodern social construction. Languages: Nederlands, English, Deutsch, Français, Bahasa Indonesia (W: http://taos.publishpath.com/maurits-gt-kwee-phd1 & E: mauritskwee@gmail.com).

Marja K. KWEE-TAAMS graduated at the University of Leiden, The Netherlands. She is a Registered Clinical Psychologist and a cognitive-behaviour therapist in private practice. She is an executive board member of the Transcultural Society for Clinical Meditation and president of a foundation that supports and educates patients with anxiety and depressive disorders in the Netherlands. She served as a member of a national multidisciplinary task force that formulates evidence-based clinical practice guidelines for anxiety and depressive disorders for professionals as well as for patients. As a student of Buddhist meditations for more than 25 years, she co-edited Festschrift for Yutaka Haruki (a Special Issue on Clinical Buddhist Meditation) in *Constructivism in the Human Sciences* (2003). Email: marjataams@gmail.com

William L. MIKULAS received his psychology degrees from the University of Michigan and then went to the University of West Florida, where he is a professor of psychology. In addition to traditional courses, such as "Learning and Behavior Modification", he also teaches courses in Buddhist Psychology and Conjunctive Psychology, the latter being an integration of world psychologies as found in health systems and wisdom traditions. Recent research with students has focused on "behaviors of the mind" as described in this chapter. Dr. Mikulas has authored several books and many articles on these topics and has travelled, lived and worked in many places in the world, including as a visiting professor in Ireland and Thailand. Email: wmikulas@uwf.edu

Aung MYINT, earned his Ph.D. at Murdoch University, Perth, Australia. He is a senior clinical psychologist at the "Department of Corrective Services" of the government of Western Australia and is a meditation teacher of the Buddhist Society of Western Australia in Perth. He has been a practising clinical psychologist in the treatment of offending behaviours and addictions for over thirty-three years. As a meditation teacher, a past convenor, and supervisor of clinical psychology courses, he advocates the translation of Buddhist Psychology to evidence-based psychotherapy. While arguing for scientific research on Tripartite Mindfulness Practice, he challenges mislabelling of attention control training per se as mindfulness psychotherapy. Email: bomyint@hotmail.com

Ruth T. NAYLOR is an Autogenic Therapist practising in Surrey and Hampshire Borders in England. Ruth earned her M.Sc. in General Experimental Psychology at Tufts University (1976) and was then awarded a US Public Health Service Fellowship for MBA (Hons) study in Health Care Management at Boston University (1979). Ruth spent many years working in mental health planning and in private sector marketing, public relations, and organization development in the USA, the UK and South Africa. More recently, Ruth earned an AA (Hons) degree in Studio Arts and then a Diploma in Autogenic Training. She is currently enrolled in Ph.D. studies in Applied Mental Health Psychology at Canterbury Christ Church University, Canterbury, England, and sits on the Research Committee of the British Autogenic Society. Email: ruth@ruthnaylor.com

Pahalawattage D. PREMASIRI is an Emeritus Professor of Pali and Buddhist Studies at the University of Peradeniya, Sri Lanka. He obtained a B.A. degree in Pali in 1963 from the University of Peradeniya, a B.A. degree in Philosophy from Cambridge University, UK in 1967, and a Ph.D. degree in Comparative Philosophy from the University of Hawai'i, Manoa, USA, in 1980. He was conferred the degree of Master of Arts from Cambridge University, England, in 1971. His publications are mainly in the area of Buddhist Ethics and Buddhist Philosophy. He has served as a Visiting Professor in a number of universities and educational institutes in the USA, Norway, Singapore, and Malaysia. Email: ppremasiri@hotmail.com

Lobsang RAPGAY is a Clinical and Health Psychologist and a member of the Research Faculty, Department of Psychiatry, University of California, Los Angeles (UCLA) School of Medicine, USA, and the Director of UCLA's Clinical Research Program on Classical Mindfulness-Based Integrative Cognitive-Behavior Therapy (CBT) for Anxiety Disorders. He is also a Research Associate, Department of Psychiatry, Massachusetts General Hospital, Harvard Medical School. Formerly the Director of the UCLA Behavioral Medicine Clinic and Program for six years, he is currently Principal Investigator on three feasibility studies on Classical Mindfulness as an intervention for Obsessive-Compulsive Disorders, Generalized Anxiety Disorders (GAD), and Mixed Anxiety-Depressive Disorders. He has published in peer reviewed journals and is currently writing a book on Classical Mindfulness-Based Integrative CBT for GAD. Dr. Rapgay was trained as a Tibetan Bhikshu for 20 years. Email: LRapgay@mednet.ucla.edu

SIK Hin Hung is a Buddhist monk ordained in the Mahayana tradition. His main interest lies in making the teachings of Buddhism more accessible to everyone. He is one of the Founding Fellows of the Centre of Buddhist Studies at The University of Hong Kong where he also teaches. Ven. Sik provides counselling and spiritual guidance to the staff of the Hong Kong Hospital Authority and the needy. He has published many books and articles on Buddhism, psychotherapy and personal growth. The motto of the Awareness Spiritual Growth Centre he founded is "Be mindful of your heart!" His current research projects include: "Orientation to Life Enhancement Project" designed for high school students and Dharma Therapy. Email: hinhung@hkucc.hku.hk

Soorakkulame PEMARATHANA was an Assistant Lecturer at the Department of Pali and Buddhist Studies, University of Peradeniya, Sri Lanka, and is presently acting abbot of the Pittsburgh Buddhist Center, USA, while in a track to complete a Ph.D. thesis. He holds a Bachelor's degree in Buddhist Studies from University of Peradeniya and a Master's degree in Philosophy from the National University of Singapore. His research interest is focused on Buddhist techniques in Positive Psychology and Cognitive-Behaviour Therapy (CBT). His chapter was rewarded the Yutaka Haruki Award for upcoming Buddhist psychology scholars at the 2nd Asian CBT conference, 2008, in Bangkok. Ordained in the Theravada tradition of Sri Lanka, he has been a practicing Buddhist Bhikkhu, for more than 10 years. He personally practices the Buddhist methods of personality development (bhavana) and provides consultation services to local communities. Email: spemaratana@yahoo.com

Asanga TILAKARATNE graduated from Peradeniya University, Sri Lanka, where he specialized in Buddhist Philosophy and offered Pali and Sanskrit as subsidiary subjects. He studied Philosophy at the University of Hawai'i at Manoa, USA, where he earned his Masters in Western Philosophy and Doctorate in Comparative Philosophy. He was a Professor at the Postgraduate Institute of Pali and Buddhist Studies of the University of Kelaniya, and is currently a Professor of Buddhist Studies at the University of Colombo. He has published extensively in Sinhala and English, on Buddhist philosophy/epistemology/logic, philosophy of language, philosophy of religion, practical ethics and contemporary social-political issues. Email: tasanga@yahoo.com

Paul J.C.L. VAN DER VELDE studied Indian languages at the Universities of Leiden (classical Tamil) and Utrecht (Sanskrit, Hindi, Pali), The Netherlands, where he earned his Ph.D. (1993) in medieval Hindi and Hinduism. He taught Hinduism, Hindi, and the History of India at the Institute of Oriental Studies and Indology of Utrecht University and presently sits on the Faculty of Religious Studies at Radboud University Nijmegen, where he now is full Professor on Hinduism and Buddhism. He recently finished a study on the *Saundaranand*, a Sanskrit biography on Nanda, half brother of the Buddha. Presently he works on the concepts of Navayana (new vehicle), Upaya (skilled action) and the biography in Buddhism. He also guides cultural tours in India, Sri Lanka, Bhutan, Tibet, Nepal, China, Mongolia, Japan, Korea, Vietnam, Laos, Cambodja, Thailand, Myanmar, and Indonesia. Email: p.vdvelde@rs.ru.nl

YAO Zhi Hua received his Ph.D. from Boston University. He is currently Associate Professor at the Department of Philosophy, The Chinese University of Hong Kong, and specializes in Buddhist Philosophy and Philosophy of Religion. His publications include *The Buddhist Theory of Self-Cognition,* 2005 (New York: Routledge). Email: zyao@cuhk.edu.hk

Lightning Source UK Ltd.
Milton Keynes UK
UKOW052233271112

202852UK00016B/953/P